OPERATIONS MANAGEMENT

THEORY AND PROBLEMS

McGRAW-HILL SERIES IN MANAGEMENT

Fred Luthans and **Keith Davis**, Consulting Editors

THIRD EDITION

OPERATIONS MANAGEMENT

THEORY AND PROBLEMS

JOSEPH G. MONKS

Gonzaga University

McGRAW-HILL BOOK COMPANY

New York   St. Louis   San Francisco   Auckland   Bogotá
Hamburg   Johannesburg   London   Madrid   Mexico
Milan   Montreal   New Delhi   Panama   Paris
São Paulo   Singapore   Sydney   Tokyo   Toronto

OPERATIONS MANAGEMENT
THEORY AND PROBLEMS

1 2 3 4 5 6 7 8 9 0 D O C D O C 8 9 4 3 2 1 0 9 8 7

ISBN 0-07-042727-5

This book was set in Caledonia by Better Graphics.
The editors were Kathleen L. Loy, Jo Satloff, and Larry Goldberg;
the production supervisor was Leroy A. Young;
the designer was Joan E. O'Connor.
The drawings were done by Fine Line Illustrations, Inc.
R. R. Donnelley & Sons Company was printer and binder.

Library of Congress Cataloging-in-Publication Data

Monks, Joseph G.
Operations management.

(McGraw-Hill series in management)
Includes bibliographies and index.
1. Production management.   I. Titles.   II. Series.
TS155.M67   1987   658.5   86-21091
ISBN 0-07-042727-5

ABOUT THE AUTHOR

Joseph G. Monks is a professor of operations management at Gonzaga University in Spokane, Washington. He has undergraduate degrees in mechanical and industrial engineering, and a Ph.D. in business. He also holds professional certification in Production and Inventory Management (CPIM) and is a registered engineer (PE).

Dr. Monks held positions with Westinghouse, General Electric, and the U.S. Government prior to doing his graduate work at the University of Washington. He taught at Oregon State University and in Europe before joining Gonzaga University, where he holds an endowed chair in management. He was a senior Fulbright lecturer in Europe in 1985.

Although his major interests are in teaching and research, Dr. Monks does a limited amount of consulting and conference activities. These have given him an opportunity to compare production operations in the U.S. with those in Asia and Europe.

To Angelica

CONTENTS

PART THREE   MAINTAINING EFFECTIVE OPERATIONS   531

APPENDIXES   687

PREFACE

Production operations run the U.S. economy, from the steel factories of Pittsburgh and Chicago to the hospitals, airlines, and government agencies that deliver services to every state. Every industry faces the common problems of "operating," such as forecasting demand, managing employees, scheduling work, and controlling quality levels. And the pressures of international competition have made it imperative that today's managers solve these problems creatively and efficiently. This applies to the financial, accounting, and marketing managers who interact with operation employees, as well as to those who are engaged directly in production operations.

This book is intended for a first course in production or operations management at the undergraduate or graduate level. Its aim is to provide students with an understanding of the theory underlying operations management and enable them to contribute to improved operating decisions. Statements of theory are intentionally basic, concise, and even simple. Because I am convinced that applications and skill-building exercises are the key to learning important concepts, there are well over 200 examples and solved problems plus an ample supply of problems to solve. A special effort has been made to illustrate problem solutions in a clear and logical way.

Operations management courses have gradually incorporated an increasing amount of quantitative methodology because quantitative techniques improve management decision making. Years in the classroom, however, have convinced me that students frequently "forget" some of their statistics and mathematical algorithms. So the necessary concepts are reviewed briefly as we progress. Any significant diversions into quantitative methodologies are relegated to solved problems at the end of the chapter or marked as optional materials. This allows instructors to adjust to the level of quantitative and problem solving emphasis they deem is most appropriate. In addition, some problems, marked with a computer logo, lend themselves to computer solution (although they can also be solved by hand calculation). A few other problems, marked with an asterisk (*), offer a challenge slightly beyond the basic expectations of the chapter. Answers to all odd-numbered problems are given in Appendix B.

This third edition of the text incorporates even more service industry applications than the second edition. It also extends the priority/capacity organizational concepts to encompass the entire text, giving the text an exceptionally strong and unifying thread throughout. Significantly more emphasis is placed on analysis of manufacturing and service operations (see Chapter 13) and upon the strategy underlying operations (see Chapter 16). And, of course, the latest in automated systems, bar codes, MRP II, CAD/CAM, quality circles, group technology, robotics, JIT, Kanban, flexible systems, cellular systems, and other advances are incorporated throughout.

I've enjoyed working on this third edition of the text and have tried to make it interesting as well as informative. I think both students and instructors will find the addition of self quizzes at the end of each chapter helpful. The answers are in Appendix A. Students that can handle those quizzes in stride should have a good head start at examination time.

The study guide that was initiated with the second edition is also being revised and will include more opportunity to work through the materials covered in the chapter, but in a step-by-step fashion. It also includes specific learning objectives, key terms, true/false questions (with answers), and some cases and other exercises. If your bookstore does not carry the study guide, you can ask them to order a copy for you.

I wish to thank all the individuals and organizations who helped in one way or another to produce this book—and the help came from far and wide. Paul Coughlin at University College Cork (Ireland) gave me some valuable insights into service industry management. Shen Lin Chang of the Taiwan Institute of Technology (Taipei) helped with some queuing materials. I'm also appreciative of discussions with Virgilio Machado at the New University of Lisbon (Portugal), Minoru Saito at the Nittu Research Center (Tokyo), and through frequent correspondence, Kang Duk Su of the Chejn National University (Korea), and for help on some of the computer work from Augustin Navarro of Caracas, Venezuela. And considerable inspiration for the Chapter 16 materials came from my good (Dutch) friend, Arnold Schoffelmeer.

Here at Gonzaga, I'd like to express appreciation for the continued support from my dean, Dr. Clarence Barnes, and his able assistant Terry Coombes, who helped by managing my teaching schedule and arranging secretarial help. My thanks also to Dr. Erwin Graue for the many luncheon conversations we have shared concerning productivity problems. Special thanks goes to Sr. Phyllis Tauffen, S.N.J., for adding some final touches to the manuscript, and to Vivian Watson for handling the word processing chores with expertise, and to Kathy Morrison.

I am particularly indebted to my reviewers for an outstanding job and some extremely useful comments. These were Herbert Blake, California State University-Sacramento; Richard H. Deane, Georgia State University; Douglas Elvers, University of North Carolina; Matthew J. Liberatore, Villanova University; Fred Luthans, University of Nebraska; James Pope, Old Dominion University; Mildred Golden Pryor, E-Systems; Roger Schoenfeldt, Murray State University; Michael Umble, Baylor University; and George Yorke, Texas Southern University.

Finally, the book would not have taken shape without the very capable assistance of my editors and others at McGraw-Hill, including Jo Satloff, Kathy Loy, Joan O'Connor, and Leroy Young.

Joseph G. Monks

OPERATIONS MANAGEMENT
THEORY AND PROBLEMS

PART ONE
DESIGN OF THE PRODUCTION SYSTEM

PREVIEW: SYSTEM DESIGN AND PLANNING ACTIVITIES

Productive systems transform input resources into higher-valued outputs. The inputs are typically classified as human, material, and capital. Outputs range from assembled products like automobiles to all manner of services, such as medical and educational services.

In this section we study system design and planning activities for producing goods and services. Figure I-1 illustrates two simplified production systems. Both have many of the same managerial problems and opportunities. But services usually give the consumer an immediate benefit, whereas goods store the benefits until the consumer is

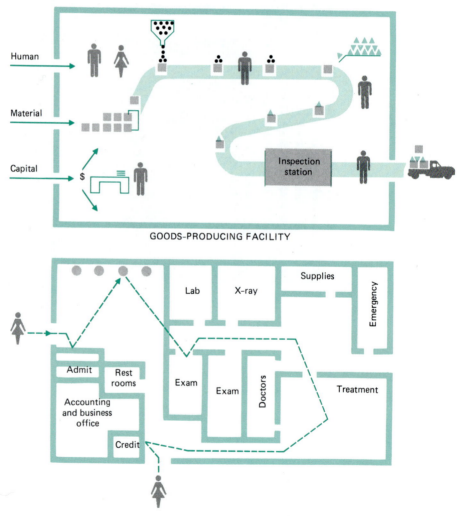

GOODS-PRODUCING FACILITY

SERVICES-PRODUCING FACILITY

FIGURE I-1   Goods- and Services-Producing Facilities

ready to use them. Thus services are less "inventory"-oriented. Nevertheless, both types of systems use human, material, and capital resources to develop higher-valued outputs.

Our study of system design and planning activities will encompass the following topics.

OPERATIONS AND PRODUCTIVITY CONCEPTS (Chapter 1)

We begin with some historical background and a definition of operations management. Chapter 1 identifies some productivity concerns and contains some fundamentals on the role of management.

OPERATIONS DECISION MAKING (Chapter 2)

Decision concepts are studied next because decision making is one of the prime functions of a manager. Potential managers can sharpen their decision-making skills by using systematic procedures and employing proven analytical techniques. This chapter outlines a framework for decision making and reviews some methodology that is especially appropriate for the management of operations.

SYSTEMS DESIGN, CAPACITY, AND INVESTMENT (Chapter 3)

Manufacturing activities store value in the goods they produce. Their production systems differ in function and in capacity from those of service activities, whose outputs are usually consumed as they are produced. Chapter 3 notes these differences and delves into capacity considerations. Capacity costs money and commits an organization to long-run costs—a burden that Chapter 3 addresses by including ways of making the best use of available capital.

FACILITY LOCATION AND LAYOUT (Chapter 4)

Facility location and layout is an early and significant concern because it usually entails a large investment of capital. Facility decisions require careful analysis of both economic and environmental effects. This chapter offers some guidelines for making location decisions and describes alternative ways of laying out facilities for the production of goods and services.

PRODUCTS AND PROCESSES (Chapter 5)

Chapter 5 describes how goods and services are developed and produced, with special attention to service delivery systems. It includes consideration of an appropriate product mix, as well as some methods for analyzing and evaluating various production processes.

JOB DESIGN AND WORK MEASUREMENT (Chapter 6)

Human resources are the most intrinsically valuable assets of any organization. Being both physically and psychologically sensitive, people require special consideration. They cannot be treated like machines, even though their (variable-paced) activities must often be interfaced with the work of (fixed-pace) machines. This chapter offers some principles for managing the human resources of an organization and describes some techniques for developing standards of performance for workers.

As you take up each topic in Part I, read the chapter through quickly to grasp the organization and major ideas. Don't try to pick up every detail at this stage. Save the intensive study for a second reading, wherein you spend enough time to gain a thorough understanding of the content, including examples and solved problems. You'll find that most theory sections and examples bring out only a few key methodological points. So after you have waded through a section or an example, take an extra moment to get the full benefit from your study. Crystallize the main idea in your mind or identify that critical step in a problem which really turned on the light of a solution. Then jot that down. The few moments you spend *abstracting key concepts* can be as valuable as many hours of reading and working out problems.

CHAPTER 1
OPERATIONS AND PRODUCTIVITY CONCEPTS

INTRODUCTION

"How's business?" Ask any group of managers or economists that question, and you're likely to get very diverse answers. Some feel our economy is in a deplorable state, with industries "on the verge of collapse" [9]. Others are quite enthusiastic and look for impressive productivity gains in the future [11,18]. You could quickly conclude that American industry faces both some serious *problems* and some challenging *opportunities*.

PROBLEMS AND OPPORTUNITIES

Problems   Some dramatic changes are taking place in the U.S. economy. Basic industries that have characterized our country in the past, such as textiles, steel, and auto production, are losing their competitiveness. Robert Reich has equated this slump with industry's inflexibility [16]:

> The central problem of America's economic future is that the nation is not moving quickly enough out of high-volume, standardized production. The extraordinary success of the half-century of the management era has left the United States a legacy of economic inflexibility. Thus our institutional heritage now imperils our future.

In the future, lower employment in manufacturing industries will probably be accompanied by greater consumption of imported goods. Foreign car manufacturers, who already enjoy about 30 percent of the U.S. market, are expected to have 40 percent of the market within a few years [8]. Our TVs and other consumer electronics are already largely imported. And it appears that the multibillion-dollar computer chip industry, which blossomed in California's "Silicon Valley," is being "lost" to overseas competition [15]. "Even worse," says one analyst, "some of that market dominance has been won through higher quality as well as lower prices" [14].

Opportunities   But all is not doom and gloom in the boardrooms of corporate America. In the words of the chief economist for TRW, Inc., "The outlook is reasonably bright for U.S. manufacturing" [18]. Some firms are in fact moving aggressively to reduce costs, upgrade quality, and improve the work environment of their personnel.

Countless firms are benefiting from computerized processes, robotics, and better managerial techniques such as MRP and JIT inventory systems (which we will take up later in the text). For example, although steel production is down over 25 percent in the last decade, today's steel is of better quality and is produced with about 50 percent fewer workers [18]. Firms in the textile industry are investing heavily in computer controls and new "air-jet" looms that deliver two to three times as much cloth as conventional looms. General Motors is experimenting with the use of artificial intelligence systems to help design cars and develop factory production schedules. Ford Motor Company is even attempting to "change its culture" by schooling its managers to use more teamwork and participative methods [6].

Of perhaps equal (or greater) significance is the fact that the United States is shifting from a manufacturing economy to a *service-based economy*. Service industries already employ about three-quarters of the nation's workers in activities ranging from transportation and communications to medical and financial services. And although service productivity is usually assumed to be lower than in manufacturing, employment in services is diverse and frequently more stable. In addition, facility-based services, such as postal and transportation services, lend themselves to the benefits of automation.

WHAT IS THE ROLE OF PRODUCTION OPERATIONS?

American industry is in a challenging period of change, and we'll want to explore that further. But before getting into the heart of this first chapter, let's first take a moment to step back and see where production operations fit into the "big picture" of a nation's activities. Then we'll identify the objectives of our study in this book and direct the focus to this chapter.

Purpose of Production Activities Our earth has two important ingredients for production: people and natural resources. As social beings, we tend to group ourselves into communities or cultures which have political, economic, and religious characteristics. Our cultural environment, in turn, determines how we will use our limited supply of natural resources. As depicted in Fig. 1-1, the objective of using environmental resources is to gain benefits that continue to raise the standard of living of members of our society. These production activities thus add value to society.

More specifically, production is a major element of the technology and economics component of our culture shown in Fig. 1-1. Production systems *deliver the goods, services, and information* that allow modern societies to function. They feed, house, transport, and maintain the 5 billion people who inhabit our planet. In addition to their direct value, work activities also *give people a sense of purpose* and an opportunity for self-development and socialization.

Why Study Operations Management? Yes, it may be required—but for good reason. Production operations lie at the heart of business activity. They use human and material resources to create the products that either make an organization healthy and competitive, or cause it to fail.

The term "operations management" evolved from factory-oriented terms like "manufacturing management" and "production operations," but its present meaning has been broadened to embrace service industries and nonprofit activities as well. The underlying theory of operations management is common to both goods and services production. Forecasting, scheduling, quality control, and other managerial activities have much in common from one type of operation to the next. Thus most of the theory you are about to study is as applicable to the management of hospital or airline operations as it is to the manufacture of automobiles.

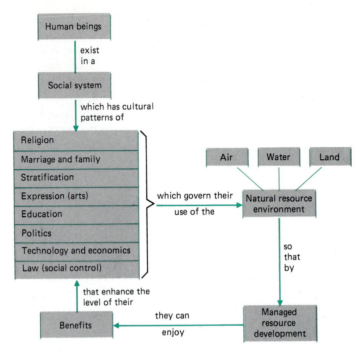

FIGURE 1-1   Our Use of Resources

Understanding the role of operations, as well as its multifaceted interface with financial, marketing, personnel, engineering, and other functions, is essential for anyone assuming major responsibilities in an organization. Moreover, production operations are one of the most strategically vital areas of managerial concern. That is to say, the success or failure of a business can be assessed by measuring specifics such as inventory levels, production schedules, and quality assurance programs.

Studying this book should help you (1) gain a comprehensive understanding of the operations management function, and (2) develop a theoretical framework for analyzing the types of decision problems faced by operations managers. But theory without practice is empty, so we shall be careful to work on the corresponding skill of application with frequent illustrations and example problems. Problems are like miniature cases. They will help build your confidence in facing future managerial decisions.

Our interest lies primarily with the strategy, analysis, and methodology you may want to use in a given situation—not necessarily with grinding out the numbers of a solution. That can often be done on a computer. And you will find computer-oriented problems at the end of many chapters. But you must be alert to the conceptual and qualitative dimensions of a problem as well as its quantitative aspects. So as you go through the chapters, you will also (perhaps unwittingly) be developing your ability to conceptualize the problems in the field of operations management.

This Chapter After a brief look at some historical background, operations management is defined and explained in terms of a schematic model. Then we focus upon the meaning of productivity and the influence of the social and economic environment upon productive operations. The chapter ends with a classification of the types of decisions that confront today's operations managers.

This chapter establishes the structure for the theory and applications that follow. With close attention to the terms and definitions, you will be well prepared to apply them in later chapters of the text. For example, once you understand the concept of control, it is a short step to extend it to inventory control, quality control, and cost control.

HISTORICAL DEVELOPMENT

Figure 1-2 depicts some of the key individuals and events that contributed to the development of production operations in the United States over the past 250 years. The four major stages of development are the (1) handicraft era, (2) indus-

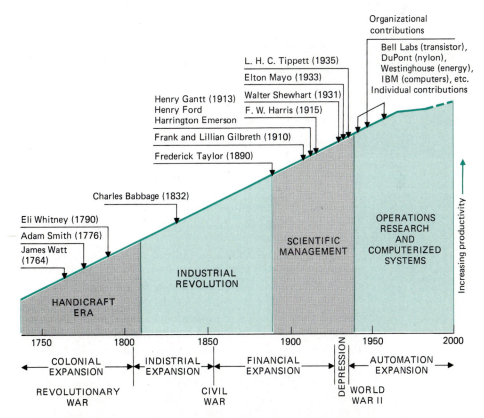

FIGURE 1-2 Key Individuals and Events in the Development of Production Systems

trial revolution, (3) scientific management era, and (4) operations research and computerized systems era.

HANDICRAFT ERA

Some of the earliest business ventures in America were colonies begun by the settlers who were sponsored by European businesses in the early 1600s. But most of those endeavors were economic disasters, largely because the American pioneers were less skilled and more independent than the craftsmen of Europe. Production of goods remained at a handicraft level until the industrial revolution took hold in the early 1800s.

As colonization continued, merchants developed trade which depended on England for imports. But the colonists objected to paying high taxes to England. By 1776, the efforts at trade reform became political reform. Three noteworthy events occurred within the span of a few years:

1 James Watt's steam engine (1764) advanced the use of mechanical power to increase productivity.
2 The Revolutionary War (1776) and resulting U.S. Constitution (1789) encouraged capital investment and trade by protecting private property and contract rights.
3 Adam Smith's *Wealth of Nations* (1776) publicized the advantages of the division of labor; these included skill development, time savings, and the use of specialized machines.

INDUSTRIAL REVOLUTION

In the early 1800s the factory system began to develop, spurred on by Henry Slator's use of water and steam power in textile mills in New England, and by Eli Whitney's concept of "interchangeable parts." Growth of the factory system was rapid; there was no well-established craft system to supplant, and unskilled labor was available. Specialization of jobs and division of labor began to take place. Charles Babbage promoted an economic analysis of work and pay on the basis of skill requirements.

Starting about 1830, the railroad expansion to the west generated new demands for steel and industrial products. The railroads also placed heavy demands on capital, which businesses began to procure by selling shares of stock to "outsiders." This hastened the separation of ownership from management and marked the beginning of professional management.

By the mid-1800s, many northern industrialists had strong business ties to the south. They did not want a civil war, but gave President Lincoln their support when dissolution of the Union looked inevitable. As it turned out, the Civil War encouraged the industrial growth of the north. Amendments to the Constitution passed as a result of the war and (ultimately) made business firms "persons" in the eyes of the law. This gave firms more constitutional rights, and some firms expanded into large financial empires. Congress finally had to enact antitrust laws (1890 and 1914) to curb their monopolistic practices. Nevertheless, the nation grew in productive capacity, and the shift toward work-force urbanization continued at a rapid pace.

SCIENTIFIC MANAGEMENT ERA

By the early 1900s the factory system was well established. Thomas Edison's first electric generating station was opened in New York City in 1882, and the nation soon had over 2,000 power stations supplying electricity to factories and mills. Frederick Taylor was a dissatisfied worker in one of those mills in Philadelphia. He had begun work as a laborer with the Midvale Steel Company in the late 1800s. Advancing through the ranks to foreman, master mechanic, and chief engineer, he came to know, and deplore, the "boondoggling," loafing, and general inefficiencies that existed in his company.

Taylor refused to accept such practices. Fortunately, he was advanced to a position where he could experiment with some ideas for improvement. Believing that a scientific approach to management could improve labor efficiency, he proposed the actions outlined in Fig. 1-3. Taylor's philosophy became widely known through his consulting work; his testimony before a congressional committee; and his book, *Principles of Scientific Management*, published in 1915. His "shop system," which included attention to training and instruction, specifications, standards (by stopwatch studies), and incentive pay systems, brought him the title "Father of Scientific Management."

Taylor's colleagues and followers helped the young nation become a powerful mass producer of industrial goods. Frank and Lillian Gilbreth developed motion economy studies, Henry Gantt instituted a charting system for scheduling production, and Henry Ford inaugurated assembly-line mass production for automobiles. Others, like F. W. Harris (economic order quantity model) and Walter Shewhart (statistical quality control), made analytical contributions. Elton Mayo directed attention to behavioral factors, and L. H. C. Tippett contributed to work-sampling activities.

---

1 Collect data on each element of work and develop *standardized procedures* for workers.
2 Scientifically select, train, and *develop workers* instead of letting them train themselves.
3 Strive for a *spirit of cooperation* between management and the workers so that high production at good pay is fostered.
4 *Divide the work* between management and labor so that each group does the work for which it is best suited.

FIGURE 1-3   Taylor's Philosophy of Scientific Management

By the late 1920s, the United States had become so production-oriented that many firms overproduced. Prices fell, and a depression ensued. President Franklin Roosevelt championed the National Labor Relations Act, which fostered collective bargaining and helped get the country back on its feet. This revived industrial capacity came just in time for the United States to help bring World War II to a close.

OPERATIONS RESEARCH AND COMPUTERIZED SYSTEMS ERA

Operations Research   Operations research involves using quantitative techniques in a systematic way to arrive at solutions to problems. During World War II, careful analysis was needed of battle problems and risk situations, such as those encountered in transporting troops across submarine-infested waters. Researchers used mathematical equations to simulate and analyze the effects of various warfare decision strategies. These techniques of competitive analysis were later applied to problems in the business world.

As computers became available in the 1950s, the power of operations research (OR) was multiplied. The speed and capacity of computers made them ideal for applying OR methods, such as linear programming and simulation, to complex business problems. But at first some of the scheduling and production control problems seemed even too complex for the computers. Unlike the well-documented accounting systems, good production control systems were not already available to automate.

By the late 1960s some new (but simple) concepts of independent demand, time phasing, and material and capacity requirements planning (MRP and CRP) were introduced by Joseph Orlicky, Oliver Wight, and others. These new approaches took advantage of the speed and memory capacity of computers and enabled planners to control production in a way that could never have been done manually because of the tremendous number of calculations involved. The 1970s and 1980s witnessed continued development of MRP II systems and integration of just-in-time (JIT) inventory concepts plus selected Japanese developments (for example, quality circles, Kanban), which will be discussed in later chapters.

Today, the manufacturing sector of our economy is undergoing nothing short of an electronic revolution. It began with *microprocessors*, which are the "chips," or processing elements, used in computers. Manufacturers are installing microprocessors and computers in virtually all types of material handling and processing equipment. The movement now is toward more fully automated factories and service systems.

Computers   Computerized scanners can readily identify products by reading the *bar codes* printed on them. *Automated storage and retrieval systems* can receive, store, select, and retrieve information without any human intervention. *Computer-guided vehicles* can deliver materials to where they're needed, when they're needed. Individual *computer-controlled machines* can follow programmed instructions, control their own operations, and respond to directions and requests for information from larger (mainframe) computers. Some machines even inspect their own output—and reject it if it doesn't meet the machine's preset standards! And, in some operations, computers respond to spoken commands. (Fortunately, not many have the capability of talking back—yet.)

In offices, computers are equally valuable, if not more so. We're all familiar with their data processing and problem-solving functions. But Boeing, Chrysler, and other companies employ computers for everything from product design (CAD/CAM) and purchasing to marketing and public relations. General Electric offers customers factory-modeling software that allows them to simulate a new factory design on a computer screen before their plant is constructed. Computers now manage the energy loads in buildings, adjust window shades, and turn lights on automatically when a person enters an office.

Robots Robots are now doing much of the monotonous, dirty, and possibly dangerous work that can be done by machines. In factories, they perform assembly, painting, welding, and other repetitive tasks.

The simplest industrial robots are mechanical arms or fingers that are powered to follow a fixed pattern of instructions. Robots that are equipped with microprocessors (or a computer) are "smart": they can react to individualized and online information. For example, instructions may call for a change in color of the next unit to be painted. A smart robot can receive the instructions, select materials, and proceed with the task on its own—and at high speed. An increasing number of firms are using robots to deliver customized products at volumes that were previously available only under "hard-wired" mass-production automation. Their use helps temper the inflexibility of U.S. industry, a problem mentioned in the opening of this chapter.

THE TREND: INFORMATION AND NONMANUFACTURING SYSTEMS

An increasingly significant trend in the U.S. economy is the gradual shift of productive effort from manufacturing (industrial) to service (and information-based) products mentioned earlier. As we become more affluent, our demand for communication and information-based products is gradually restructuring our society. Traditional ways of doing things (for example, delivering mail) are being replaced by more efficient methods (electronic mail). By the year 2000, about 80 percent of our work force will likely be engaged in nonmanufacturing activities. Computers will, of course, play a major role in this transition too, along with fiber optics, microwaves, lasers, and other communication technologies.

Services Whereas manufacturing produces tangible goods that can be numbered, stored, and consumed at a later date, services are intangible performances. In fact, intangibility is the most universally cited distinction between goods and services [19]. Some service systems do handle tangible goods (warehousing,

- Intangible product
- Quality of output can be highly variable
- Production and consumption occur simultaneously
- No inventory is accumulated

FIGURE 1-4   Characteristics of Most Service Systems

distribution, auto repair), but they also involve an intangible element (the storage, handling, and actual repair work).

Figure 1-4 summarizes four of the most commonly recognized characteristics of services [19]. In addition to *intangibility*, services possess a potential for high *variability in the quality* of output. Machines produce steadily, but people's work may differ from one day to the next and from one customer to the next. Third, production and consumption occur *simultaneously*. Customers are participants in the service delivery system, and they receive the value as the service is produced. Finally, services cannot be inventoried. This quality, of course, gives rise to numerous capacity and scheduling problems.

Some services (entertainment, travel agencies, stockbrokerage, legal counsel) depend largely on the performance of people, while others (phone companies, utilities) rely more heavily on equipment or facilities. The people–equipment mix is important because people provide a more variable service than machines. Machines are more predictable and measurable. But people can also learn better ways of doing jobs, whereas most machines cannot.[1]

Of perhaps more significance to managers, however, is that manufacturing systems deal largely with planning, scheduling, and controlling *materials*. With services, the production control efforts concentrate upon the flow of *customers*.

OPERATIONS MANAGEMENT

Having reviewed the history of industrial operations, we now turn to the meaning of the term "management" and define "operations management" in a precise way. Over the years, several approaches have been developed to explain what management is all about. Four of the most widely accepted approaches to management are summarized in Fig. 1-5.

MANAGEMENT

The *functional* (traditional) approach stems from the work of classical theorists who regard management as a universal, or common, process. *Behaviorists* focus

---

[1] Using the concepts of artificial intelligence, however, machines can "learn" to improve their output and make changes to see that the improvement takes place.

- **Functional**   Managers plan, organize, direct, and control the activities of an organization.
- **Behavioral**   Managers lead the activities of an organization by working through other people to get things done.
- **Contingency**   Managers survive and function most effectively by adapting to the environmental demands on the organization.
- **Decision-making**   Managers make decisions that guide operating systems toward organizational goals.

FIGURE 1-5   Approaches to Management

on human relations and emphasize interpersonal relationships, communication, and organizational behavior. The *contingency* approach holds that different situations call for different managerial functions, behavioral skills, and quantitative capabilities. Finally, the *decision-making* approach stresses the use of data and scientific methodology to make decisions that relate to both functions and people. In this context, managers are primarily decision makers. They use quantitative techniques and systems analysis to help reach decisions, so modeling and computers are important tools of their profession. Each approach to management offers some valid insight, so we shall draw from them all. However, for purposes of this text, we will define management rather simply.

Management is the process of developing decisions and taking actions to direct the activities of people within organizations toward common objectives.

The objectives of organizations differ, but studies suggest that most organizations have multiple goals that include (1) the welfare of employees, (2) service to customers, (3) returns to owners, and (4) responsibility to society. Managers usually try to accomplish organizational objectives by formulating policies, operating plans, procedures, and rules. In Fig. 1-6, an upside-down pyramid illustrates how broad-based objectives (for example, good customer service) are eventually operationalized via specific rules (maintaining a reserve stock of 50 units). It also shows how an organization's database forms a foundation for decision making at all levels. Note that managerial values influence policies and plans by filtering down through the organizational structure, often in a subtle way. Values even influence the database, and factual data can modify values.

OPERATIONS MANAGEMENT DEFINITION

Operations managers may be found working under titles such as vice president of operations, general manager, or production manager. Having considered management in general, let us now define operations management.

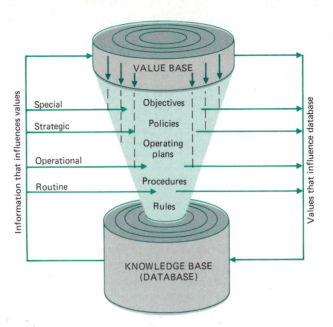

FiGURE 1-6   Knowledge and Value Bases for Decision Systems

Operations management is the process whereby resources, flowing within a defined system, are combined and transformed in a controlled manner to add value in accordance with policies communicated by management.

As illustrated in Fig. 1-7, operations managers have the prime responsibility for processing inputs into outputs. They must bring the inputs together under a production plan that effectively uses the materials, capacity, and knowledge available in the production facility. Given a demand on the system, work must be scheduled and controlled to produce the goods and/or services required. Meanwhile, control must be exercised over such parameters as costs, quality, and inventory levels. In addition the facility itself must be maintained.

Our definition of operations management contains some key terms which merit further consideration: (1) resources, (2) systems, and (3) transformation and value-adding activities.

RESOURCES

Resources are the human, material, and capital inputs to the production process. Human resources are often the key asset of an organization. In the United States, we are gradually moving human work to a higher level, leaving physical tasks that can be done by machines for the machines. As production technology advances, a larger proportion of the human input is in planning and controlling activities. By

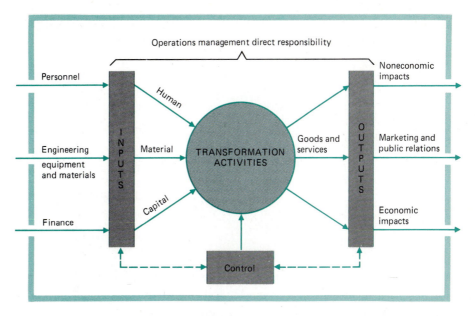

FIGURE 1-7   Schematic Model of a Production System

using the intellectual capabilities of people rather than limiting them to mindless tasks, managers can multiply the value of their employees' input by many times. But people must still interface with machines. Integrating the human and machine systems in a way that yields worker satisfaction along with increased productivity is one of the greatest challenges of job design.

Material resources are the physical facilities and materials such as plant equipment, inventories, and supplies. These often are the major assets of an organization (in an accounting sense). Capital in the form of stock, bonds, and/or taxes and contributions is also a vital asset. Capital is a store of value which is used to regulate the flow of other resources.

SYSTEMS

Systems are arrangements of components designed to achieve objectives according to plans. Our cultural environment includes numerous economic and social systems. For example, we have a monetary system that facilitates the exchange of goods and a transportation system that can move those goods quickly and efficiently to any part of the country. Business and government organizations are subsystems of larger social systems. The business systems, in turn, contain subsystems, such as personnel, engineering, finance, and operations, which all function for the good of the organization.

Figure 1-8 is an organizational chart that depicts some subsystems of an organization. Within the operations subsystem, for example, are both line and staff functions. A line (chain) of command exists from the president through the

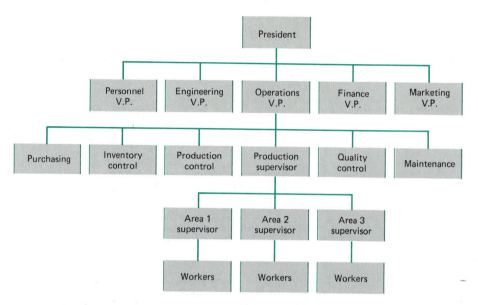

FIGURE 1-8   Line and Staff Organization for Production

operations manager and production supervisors to the workers. Personnel in purchasing and quality control are components of the operations subsystem; but they function in a staff or advisory capacity to the production and area supervisors.

A *systems approach to operations management* recognizes the hierarchical nature of subsystems but places strong emphasis on the integrative nature of management responsibilities. If subsystem goals are pursued independently, *suboptimization* may result. For example, unless the production and marketing groups cooperate closely, the firm may be increasing production of one product while vigorously promoting a different one. A consistent and integrative approach will lead to *optimization* of overall system goals.

The *systems approach to specific problems* requires that the problem first be identified and "bound," or isolated, from the maze of less relevant data that constitute the environment. In other words, the problem is abstracted from the overall (macro) environment. Then it can be broken down into manageable (micro) parts and analyzed, and solutions proposed. But to assess the impact of proposed changes on the whole system, the components must again be restructured or synthesized (macro). Analysts sometimes refer to this as the *macro-micro-macro* cycle or the *analysis-synthesis* approach. The advantages of doing this analysis on paper or by computer before actually making any changes are probably obvious. If the solution appears to solve the problem in a satisfactory way, changes can be made to the real (physical) system in an orderly and more predictable manner.

Design and Control   The ability of any system to achieve its objectives depends on (1) its design and (2) its control.

Systems design is a predetermined arrangement of components. It establishes the relationships that must exist between inputs, transformation activities, and outputs in order to achieve the system objectives. The more structured the design is, the less planning and decision making will be involved in the operation of the system. Similarly, a highly structured design, although suitable for high-volume production of standardized products, is usually less adaptable to change. This lessens the firm's ability to compete with broader product lines, at smaller volumes, or on shorter notice from the customer. However, improved scheduling techniques, along with the microprocessors and robotics, can help adapt systems to meet changing demands.

Systems control consists of all actions necessary to ensure that activities conform to preconceived plans or goals. Control involves four essential elements:

1 *Measurement* by an accurate sensory device
2 *Feedback* of information in a timely manner
3 *Comparison with standards* such as time and cost standards
4 *Corrective action* by someone with the authority and ability to correct

A *closed-loop* control system can automatically function on the basis of data from within its own system. Some computer-controlled machines function on this principle. They measure their own output variability and automatically make adjustments for normal wear on their own tools. Most large-scale systems, however, are open-loop systems. *Open-loop* control systems are influenced by "outside" information. They do not have sufficient internal feedback with automatic control to maintain desired standards. Any system that interfaces with the environment is open to the extent that it receives stimuli from outside its own system. For example, spaceships that depend on navigational information from computers on earth are operating (at least partially) as open systems.

TRANSFORMATION AND VALUE-ADDING ACTIVITIES

The objective of combining resources under controlled conditions is to transform them into goods and services having a higher value than the original inputs. The transformation process usually applies some form of technology (mechanical, chemical, medical, electronic, and so forth) to the inputs. The effectiveness of production factors in the transformation process is commonly referred to as productivity.

Productivity is an index expressed as the ratio of the value of the output per worker-hour to the cost of the inputs.

$$\text{Productivity index} = \frac{\text{value of output}}{\text{cost of inputs}} \qquad (1\text{-}1)$$

For example, suppose the value of services generated by a group of computer operators in a day is $2,000, and their total operational costs are $1,200. The ratio of value produced to costs incurred is $2,000/$1,200, or 1.67. A firm's overall ratio must be greater than 1, or it is losing money. This concept of value added differs from the notion of engineering efficiency, which maintains that energy losses within any physical system prohibit the ratio of output to input from being greater than 1.

Note that the numerator of the ratio, or *value of the output,* is established largely by consumers in the marketplace. Some outputs, such as customer satisfaction and environmental impacts, are unique and difficult to value. But as a large volume of output enters a competitive market, prices (or related costs) typically emerge as indicators of value. On the other hand, the denominator, or *cost of inputs,* is dictated largely by what the organization must pay its suppliers. Operations managers are caught in the middle, doing what they can to improve the efficiency of the transformation activities and better the ratio. This is a critical responsibility, so much attention has been given to the factors affecting productivity.

FACTORS AFFECTING PRODUCTIVITY

The United States still has a total productive capacity unmatched by any other industrialized nation. Its resource base, population size, and technological expertise all contribute to this leadership role. In addition, the United States has abundant energy, highly trained workers, and a relatively large amount of investment in automated production equipment. The U.S. *rate of growth* in productivity, however, now lags behind that in other industrialized nations such as Japan, West Germany, France, and Canada. As depicted in Fig. 1-9, after increasing at an annual rate of about 3 percent until the mid-1960s, our rate of increase in productivity dropped to about 2 percent until 1973. Then it averaged less than 1 percent for the next 10 years. Now it is fluctuating with economic recession and recovery, but it is not solidly strong. Whereas the average Japanese manufacturing workers produced only 27 percent as much as his American counterpart in 1960, by 1974 the gap had lessened to 67 percent—and output is now approaching

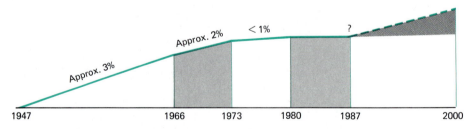

FIGURE 1-9 Productivity Trend in the United States (*Source:* Modified from [3].)

equality [1]. Some economists report that manufacturing output per worker-hour in Germany and France already exceeds that of the United States [17: 48].

Economists cite a variety of reasons for changes in productivity. Some of the principal factors influencing the drop in the U.S. productivity rate are:

- Capital/labor ratio
- Scarcity of some resources
- Work-force changes
- Innovation and technology
- Regulatory effects
- Bargaining power
- Managerial factors
- Quality of work life

The *capital/labor ratio* is a measure of whether enough investment is being made in plant, machinery, and tools to make effective use of labor hours. Many of the factories (and much of the equipment) in the United States are over 20 years old. The aging infrastructure is indicative of a hesitancy on the part of management to invest for the long term and/or the diversion of funds to less productive but financially attractive ventures. European and Japanese business people recognize this short-term financial orientation as a failing of American managers [8].

A *scarcity of some resources*, such as energy, water, and a number of metals, has already created some productivity problems. For example, as a result of increased energy costs, aluminum plants that once had favorable cost-volume relationships are no longer economical to operate. Emphasis is now shifting toward the use of renewable resources, such as the production of fuel from agricultural or waste products.

Work-force changes include a steady shift away from blue-collar occupations. High-technology production demands a higher level of educational preparation in mathematics and sciences. But the level of education and retraining for new jobs has not been sufficient to maintain full employment. U.S. firms have devoted fewer resources to worker training than countries like West Germany and Japan, partially because U.S. workers are more mobile and less committed to long-term employment with the same company. The shift to service occupations is also seen by some as a depressant of productivity statistics. Productivity in the service sector is thought to be lower than in goods production, and some services offer little opportunity for the economies of automation.

Innovation and technology have been major causes of increased productivity in the past, with some estimates claiming that technology accounted for roughly half the growth in productivity between 1948 and 1966 [16]. But investment in research and development (R&D) as a percentage of the gross national product, declined from the 1970s to the 1980s. In addition, much of the nation's research effort has been channeled to defense-related products. Also, foreign competitors sometimes "copy" and market similar products before the R&D investment can be recovered.

Regulatory effects have imposed substantial constraints on some firms. One journal reported that, "regulation was the fastest growing industry of the 1970s," pointing out that a productive society cannot afford regulations that do more harm than good [4]. Pollution, health, and safety requirements are estimated to have reduced productivity growth rates by about one-fourth in the decade following 1968. On the other hand, some of the earlier "productivity gains" were made at the cost of environmental quality, and the costs of cleaning up the environment will continue for many years to come.

The *bargaining power* of organized labor to command wage increases in excess of output increases has had a detrimental effect on productivity. Even though union membership in the United States has dropped from about 30 percent of the work force in the 1950s to less than 20 percent today, collective bargaining agreements impact many of the traditional industries that are currently struggling for survival (for example, steel, textiles, autos). The requirement to pay artificially high wages to some unionized workers limits a firm's ability to hire more workers, and this ultimately contributes to the unemployment of others. This effect is illustrated by the number of applications for some high-paying longshoreman and marine clerk jobs in Los Angeles and Long Beach, California in 1984. About 40,000 people applied for the 350 unionized jobs. The union president estimated another 10,000 would have applied but the Maritime Association ran out of forms [5].

Managerial factors are the ways an organization benefits from the unique planning and managerial skills, or business acumen, of its managers. Managers often command high salaries as a result of their education, training, and experience. In turn, they are expected to make decisions, take action, and direct activities in a professional way. This means being innovative and willing to take risks for the long-run viability of the organization. Weak planning, poor organization, or lax controls can be difficult to detect. But they can have a more detrimental effect on productivity than highly publicized salaries or unwarranted stock options that executives command.

Quality of work life is a term that describes the organizational culture, and the extent to which it motivates and satisfies employees. Numerous firms such as Hewlett-Packard, IBM, Intel, General Motors, and Westinghouse have undertaken projects to substantially enhance the physical (and/or mental) health of their workers by improving their work environment. For example, IBM provides recreational facilities for their employees, and Ceneral Motors offers counseling services. Many firms utilize participative activities designed to foster the loyalty, teamwork, and commitment of employees to the organization.

INTERNATIONAL DIMENSIONS OF PRODUCTIVITY

About three-fourths of all goods produced in the United States now compete with foreign-made goods [16]. Many of these products are being produced in developing nations that desperately need income and employment. Their factories are relatively new and labor costs are substantially lower than in the United States. High-volume machinery that produces standardized products can be installed almost anywhere. Hong Kong, Korea, Singapore, Taiwan, Malaysia, the Philippines, and India are producing clothing, shoes, toys, and electronics; Brazil, Spain, and Mexico are producing automobiles, televisions, and more electronics.

How can steel and electronic companies in the United States compete with foreign-made products? Companies often cry for import quotas in their own industry (while opposing them in general). But tariffs restrict free trade among nations and isolate noncompetitive products from the free market. They force the public to subsidize less efficient operations by creating artificially high prices. Such forced consumption undermines the economic stability of a country. Tariffs may temporarily preserve wages or profits in a given industry, but they only prolong and intensify the economic adjustment that must inevitably follow.

Industrialized nations are developing two strategies to remain competitive: (1) moving on to new and more advanced products, and (2) employing better and more automated production techniques.

New Products As brought out earlier, the high-volume products that once constituted our industrial base (steel, textiles, automobiles) are no longer secure. Nations such as Japan, France, and West Germany are already shifting their industrial base toward products and processes that make better use of their research capabilities and skilled workers. Their future lies in microelectronics, precision manufactured castings, specialty steels, custom fabrics, fiber optics, lasers, and technology-driven products that require sophisticated skills to produce.

Trend Toward More Flexible Systems The production runs of these higher-valued specialty items and custom-designed products are often much shorter than for traditional mass-produced goods. But the nonproductive time (downtime) required to set up equipment for producing different options, new models, and new products is very costly. So production facilities must be designed with the utmost flexibility to accommodate changeovers in rapid fashion. This is where computers, microprocessors, and robotics come into play. Because new technology demands new skills, firms must be willing to give workers the training they need to solve the nonroutine problems associated with these more complex systems.

The quotation at the beginning of this chapter suggests that American managers are not moving rapidly enough away from high-volume mass production into specialized products and flexible systems. Professor Robert Reich of Harvard, who made the observation, points out that the problem may lie in "paper entrepreneurialism" [16]. By this he means the shrewd financial, legal, and tax maneuvers that have been used to give the appearance of profitable operations while producing "nothing of tangible value." He suggests that "creative accounting mergers" and "earnings management" have replaced product investment and process modernization. For example, RCA yielded development of the videocassette to the Japanese because it claimed to lack the $200 million needed for the new project. Nevertheless, that same year RCA spent $1.2 billion on a "lackluster finance company" and the tax advantages that went with the acquisition. Similarly, U.S. Steel scrapped plans for a new steel plant but began building a cash reserve to buy Marathon Oil Company. This relentless drive to generate paper profits, says Reich, has come at the cost of long-term growth. He feels that the current diversion of resources away from the tough job of production will only make the catch-up effort more difficult for the United States in the future.

German executives appear to understand the need for a strong technological focus and the dangers of hierarchical bureaucracies and paper profits [1]. Over 50 percent of Germany's large manufacturing firms are managed by Ph.D's with technical backgrounds (as opposed to financial or legal ones). Karlheinz Kaske, chief executive of Siemens AG, the giant German electrical company, has said, "One of my biggest challenges is to fend off bureaucracy and paralysis." His company is shifting its emphasis from turbines, power plants, and telephone exchanges to microelectronics. They are moving decisively to speed up research time and hasten bringing products to market. The German firm of Trumpf G.m.b.H manufactures machine tools. Half the sales volume of the firm comes from tools designed within the past three years. German firms also have a strong tendency to focus on longer-term benefits as opposed to quarterly earnings and dividends. One executive of the Trumpf company, who used to work for ITT, recalls that in ITT there was pressure to keep short-term earnings rising. But at Trumpf, he "can look three or four years ahead" [1].

In recent years, the managerial techniques and productivity methods in Japanese firms have attracted worldwide attention. A careful examination of Japanese companies reveals some interesting contrasts with American firms, as

- **Corporate objectives** Employees and customers are given priority over shareholders. Honesty in business is important.
- **Time horizon** Long-run viability is more important than short-term profits.
- **Production systems** Automated systems with extensive use of microprocessors and robotics. Quality is paramount, and things happen on schedule.
- **Employment relations** Long-term employment of loyal workers. Unions cooperate to benefit total firm. Politeness and harmony are emphasized.
- **Materials** Resources are limited. Space is used efficiently and inventories are kept to a bare minimum.
- **Financing** More use is made of debt capital and less of equity capital.
- **Training** Employees are thoroughly trained and rotated to learn a variety of skills. There is less emphasis on job description.
- **Worker participation** Employees are directly involved in productivity improvements via suggestions, quality circles, and consultation with supervisors.

FIGURE 1-10 Characteristics of Japanese Firms

summarized in Fig. 1-10. Most American managers have recognized a productivity problem, and many have embarked on programs, to combat it in their own organizations [12,13]. Corning Glass has developed new glass furnaces, Ford has implemented extensive quality inspections, Westinghouse has developed their own productivity center, and Burger King has computerized their order processing. Xerox has even described its product *as* productivity, noting that it is "in the business of making the offices of the world more productive." Technology and innovative management have both played a significant role in these efforts to improve our nation's productivity. The question is, "Are we moving in the right direction and rapidly enough to safely preserve our future?"

David Kearns, president of Xerox, thinks that American industry *is* moving in the right direction *and at a good pace.* In a lecture at Rochester Institute of Technology he cited a "renewal of productivity" and a "rededication to product quality." He sees an extraordinary change taking place that is giving American industry a new vitality and a new sense of confidence [10].

THE ENVIRONMENT OF OPERATIONS

One of the most encompassing influences on productivity is the environment in which organizations operate. Anyone driving through a smog-filled city or living within the reaches of a smelter or paper mill can readily attest to the fact that firms produce more than they market. Years ago, the social and ecological by-products of production activities were unwittingly accepted as inevitable. Communities had no voice in the location or closure of facilities. Streams became polluted, smog filled the air, and bottles cluttered the highways. To some extent, our productivity gains were achieved at the expense of our environment. Today, American managers are assuming an increasing responsibility for the multitude of impacts their organizations have on society.

The social impact of an organization is a reflection of the values held by top management. Yet, one's value system cannot be purchased or acquired in a quick and easy manner. It evolves from the religious and cultural norms of society; from childhood training, education, and reflection on the purpose of life and the value of one's self and of others. The preferred values of the majority of our society reflect purpose, integrity, and a respect for the life and humanity of others.

It would be preferable to permit managers to act in response to their individual respect for others (and for society in general), but the irresponsible action of some has necessitated the passing of numerous laws that apply to all. Thus we find almost every facet of our economic and social environment regulated and controlled by laws designed to protect "the general public." Antitrust statutes, for example, guard against monopolies while a plethora of environmental and hiring regulations as well as safety rules define how companies are allowed to interact with their environment. Figure 1-11 illustrates some of these laws' impacts on firms.

The "costs of compliance" with bureaucratic regulations are now recognized

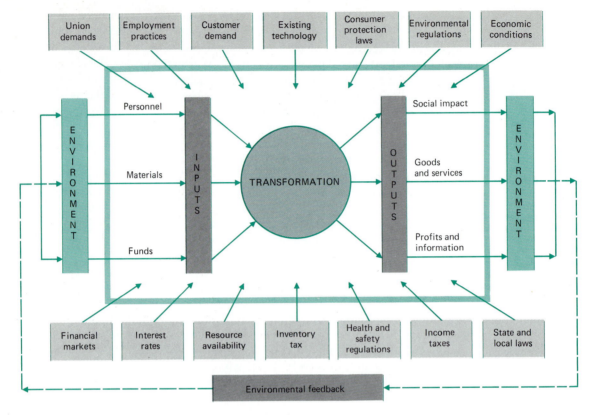

FIGURE 1-11   Environmental Impacts on the Organization

as a major contributor to our declining rate of productivity. In some cases they are driving small entrepreneurs out of business, or are forcing mergers and takeovers. Such costs could be reduced if managers accepted more individual and social responsibility. But that may be a problem. The development of responsible managers represents one of the greatest challenges we face in the future. According to Warren Bennis, "finding men with the right technical capability will not be nearly as difficult as finding men with the right set of values and attitudes" [3].

PRODUCTION SYSTEM DECISIONS: A LOOK AHEAD

Thus far we have discussed the historical context of operations, the definition of operations management, and the environment in which operations managers work. This last section of the chapter suggests a useful framework for understanding operations and relates our definition of operations management to the topics we will be studying.

A MANAGERIAL PHILOSOPHY: PRIORITY AND CAPACITY

During the past decade, the American Production and Inventory Control Society (APICS) has been one of the fastest growing professional societies in the world. APICS emphasizes professional education for operations, and it conducts a nationally accredited certification program (CPIM) with examinations in five areas. Much of the theory underlying the examinations is incorporated in the chapters of this text. This is not because the text is designed to prepare students for the APICS certification examinations—our scope is broader than that—but because the examinations encompass a solid core of theory and applications relevant to operations.

Imbedded in the chapters that follow is an emphasis on two very powerful concepts that have evolved from APICS literature over the past few years. Although the terms *priority* and *capacity* have been in use for a long time, APICS literature has brought increased meaning to them. And we will continue to build on that base in this text. Figure 1-12 introduces the two concepts.

Priority, in a broad sense, is an ordering of goals or activities in accordance with an individual's or organization's system of values. More specifically, priority refers to the ranking or importance of something—often materials. The measure of importance stems primarily from society, in other words, what customers want. Customer demands are, in turn, translated into purchase and production orders that must then be guided through operations until the desired good or service is produced. So customer orders have "priorities."

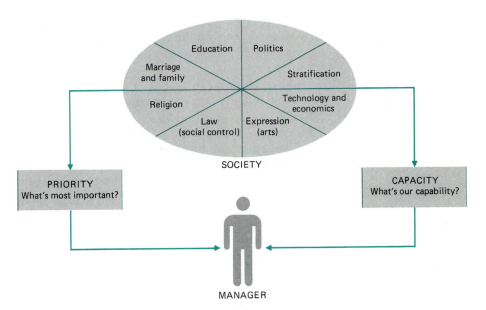

FIGURE 1-12   A Managerial Philosophy: Priority and Capacity

Capacity is a measure of an organization's ability to accomplish its prioritized goals, or, more simply, the ability to produce. In a production facility, this "ability" usually translates into having enough human and equipment capability and time to do the job.

Although priority and capacity are simple concepts, they play a key role in the managerial philosophy that underlies the organization of this text. You will find them cropping up frequently in the chapters that follow—from the principles of job design to scheduling activities and quality control. Look for them to surface in sketches and flowcharts too. For consistency, we will show priority factors on the left and capacity considerations on the right.

Why do we put such emphasis on these two concepts? Because priorities and capacities are the key ingredients in a successful strategy for managing operations. These concepts provide us with a simple, yet comprehensive, framework for evaluating each of the topics we study. They force us to begin with the big picture of "what is really important to the organization?" and then to follow through with queries like "are the resources available to accomplish that?" This, of course, is what managers are paid to do—help chart the objectives of the organization and make best use of the resources to accomplish them.

LOOKING AHEAD

As you will recall, our initial definition of operations management was translated into a schematic model (Fig. 1-7), and in the last section we added a number of environmental impacts (Fig. 1-11). Figure 1-13 extends the model by relating it more specifically to the topics we will be studying in the text.

Part I is concerned with the design of a production system. After reviewing some decision-making methodology (Chapter 2), we take up system design, capacity, and capital investment decisions (Chapter 3), and then go on to consider facility location and layout (Chapter 4). We then turn our attention to the products being produced and production processes used (Chapter 5). The last chapter in this section discusses the job design and human resources necessary to do the work (Chapter 6).

Part II contains topics traditionally known as production and inventory control (P&IC). First, the demand must be forecast (Chapter 7), and that forecast translated into a plan and schedule for production (Chapter 8). Materials must be acquired (Chapter 9), and inventory levels carefully controlled to be sure they are appropriate (Chapter 10). In manufacturing firms, this means tracking all the material components that go into finished products, and ensuring there is enough capacity to accomplish the planned work (Chapter 11). Chapter 12 finishes this section by following through with the actual production and control activities.

Part III is concerned with maintaining effective operations. This entails analyzing ongoing operations and properly managing any major projects (Chapter 13). Controlling quality (Chapter 14) and maintaining the facilities in good operating condition (Chapter 15) are two of the most essential considerations here. We finish with a look to the future (Chapter 16).

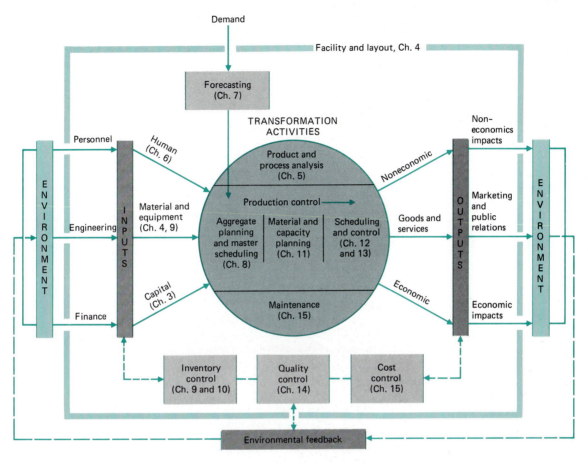

FIGURE 1-13 Physical and Information Flows in a Production System

SUMMARY

Production activities use resources to make products that enhance our standard of living. Modern operations management has developed from the industrial revolution, the scientific management era, and more recent advances in operations research and computers. More information and nonmanufacturing (service) systems are taking the place of traditional goods production.

Operations management is concerned with combining resources to add value and accomplish goals. Operations decisions are influenced both by values of the decision makers and by the information (database) available in the organization.

The historical 3 percent annual increase in productivity in the United States appears to have ground to a halt. Most industrialized nations are growing at a faster rate than the United States. Among the many explanations are reduced investment stemming from a short-range perspective, a hesitancy to innovate with more flexible production systems, excessive regulatory and collective bargaining effects, and an inadequate quality of work life. Improvements are under way on many fronts.

Priority and capacity concepts will be emphasized throughout the book. The three parts of the text concern (I) design of the production system, (II) production and inventory control, and (III) maintaining effective operations.

QUESTIONS

1-1   Explain how production activities fit into the cultural patterns of a society, that is, where they belong and what they accomplish.

1-2   Manufacturing usually takes place in factories. Does the term "operations management" also apply to nonmanufacturing activities? If so, why?

1-3   What events around 1776 were instrumental in the development of our industrial system?

1-4   Which aspect, or principle, of Taylor's philosophy of scientific management corresponds most closely with some firms' efforts to improve the quality of work life today?

1-5   Who is the individual most closely identified with each of the following contributions? (a) interchangeable parts, (b) motion economy, (c) scheduling charts, (d) statistical quality control, and (e) work sampling?

1-6   Is the trend in the U.S. economy toward more heavy manufacturing or less? Explain.

1-7   What are some salient characteristics of most service systems?

1-8   Identify four different approaches to management, and then define what you mean by the term "management."

1-9   How can a manager's values influence the operations of an organization?

1-10   Define operations management.

1-11   Distinguish between systems design and systems control.

1-12   Explain the concept of productivity.

1-13   Describe and justify (explain) the trend in productivity growth in the United States in recent years.

1-14   How have managerial factors influenced U.S. productivity in recent years?

1-15   In what ways do Japanese firms encourage workers to improve their productivity?

REFERENCES

[1]   Anders, George: "German Bosses Stress Consensus Decisions, Technical Know-How," *The Wall Street Journal*, Sept. 25, 1984, p. 1.

[2]   "Behind the Productivity Slowdown," *Business in Brief*, The Chase Manhattan Bank, September/October 1979.

[3]   Bennis, Warren: "Organizations of the Future," *Personnel Administration*, September/October 1967.

[4]   Fisher, John W.: "A More Productive Society to Benefit All," *Enterprise: The Journal of Executive Action*, National Association of Manufacturers, February 1980, pp. 2–5.

[5]   "40,000 Still Competing for 350 High-Pay Jobs," *Spokane Daily Chronicle*, Spokane, WA, Sept. 24, 1984.

[6] Guiles, Melinda G., and Paul Ingrassia, "Ford's Leaders Push Radical Shift in Culture as Competition Grows," *The Wall Street Journal*, Dec. 3, 1985, p. 1.

[7] Hayes, Robert H., and William J. Abernathy: "Productivity: Management Has Tools to Help Its Own Cause," *Spokesman Review*, Spokane, WA, Sept. 14, 1980.

[8] Ingrassia, Paul, and Doran P. Levin, "Auto Industry Faces Era of Plant Closings Due to Overcapacity," *The Wall Street Journal*, Feb. 14, 1986, p. 1.

[9] Karatsu, Hajime, "The Deindustrialization of America: A Tragedy for the World," *KKC Brief*, Japan Institute for Social and Economic Affairs, October 1985, pp. 1–9.

[10] Kearns, David T.: "Product Quality and Productivity," William D. Gasser Distinguished Lecture, Rochester Institute of Technology, Rochester, NY, 1984.

[11] McNamee, Mike, "Americans: More Productive," *USA Today*, Dec. 27, 1984.

[12] Main, Jeremy: "Westinghouse's Cultural Revolution," *Fortune*, June 15, 1981, pp. 74–93.

[13] Meadows, Edward: "How Three Companies Increased Their Productivity," *Fortune*, Mar. 10, 1980, pp. 92–101.

[14] Meyers, Henry F.: "U.S. Productivity Gains Still Fall Short," *The Wall Street Journal*, Feb. 10, 1986, p. 1.

[15] Miller, Michael W.: "Precipitous Decline of Memory-Chip Firm Shakes the Industry," *The Wall Street Journal*, Jan. 17, 1986, p. 1.

[16] Reich, Robert B.: "The Next American Frontier," *The Atlantic Monthly*, March 1983, pp. 43–58.

[17] Thurow, Lester C.: *The Zero-Sum Solution*, Simon and Schuster, New York, 1985.

[18] Winter, Ralph E.: "U.S. Manufacturing? It's Still Alive and Well," *The Wall Street Journal*, Dec. 23, 1985, p. 1.

[19] Zeithaml, Valarie, A. Parasuraman, and Leonard L. Berry: "Problems and Strategies in Services Marketing," *Journal of Marketing*, vol. 49 (Spring 1985), pp. 33–46.

SELF QUIZ: CHAPTER 1

Part I True/False [1 point each = 6]

1 _____ Production activities are a major component of the cultural characteristic of "Expression."

2 _____ One of the ideas proposed by Frederick Taylor was to strive for a spirit of cooperation between management and workers.

3 _____ Operations management is defined as the process of developing decisions and taking actions to direct the activities of people within organizations toward common objectives.

4 _____ About one-quarter of the U.S. work force is engaged in nonmanufacturing activities where the principles of operations management do not apply.

5 _____ One of the more successful characteristics of Japanese firms stems from their emphasis on short-term profits.

6 _____ In production control terminology, priority often refers to materials and capacity to time availability.

Part II Multiple Choice [3 points each = 9. Circle the correct answer.]

1 Which of the following is *not* a characteristic of most service systems?

(a) Product is tangible.
(b) Quality of output can be highly variable.
(c) Production and consumption occur simultaneously.
(d) No finished goods inventory is accumulated.
(e) Mark this answer if all the above are service system characteristics.

2 According to Professor Reich, why has the growth rate of productivity declined in the United States?

(a) Collective bargaining contracts
(b) Paper entrepreneurialism
(c) Environmental regulations
(d) Younger work force
(e) None of the above

3 How does the author explain the proliferation of regulations and controls over business in the United States, that is, why are there so many and why are they necessary?

(a) Irresponsible managers
(b) Satisfaction of special interests
(c) Creation of order
(d) Democracy in action
(e) None of the above

CHAPTER 2
OPERATIONS DECISION MAKING

INTRODUCTION

Sony Corporation management faced a critical decision in the early development of the compact disk player [2]. The potential for using a laser to obtain both sounds and pictures from a plastic disk had seemed tremendous. But after 4 years of effort Sony still didn't have a videodisk system that could record as well as play back prerecorded disks. It was not easy to communicate to and from a plastic disk by laser in accuracies of less than a thousandth of an inch.

Then the Dutch electronics company that had first developed the technology offered Sony the chance to help popularize its new 4½-inch audiodisk. This was at the time when Zenith dropped its disk research (too risky), and RCA was absorbing a $500 million loss. After careful evaluation, Sony management decided the risk was worth the potential rewards and added 30 audio engineers. Five years later, the disk players were on the market. But they were still too big and expensive ($800 or more) to satisfy Sony.

Then Mr. Kozo Ohsone, who had guided development of the Sony Walkman cassette player, took charge of the project. Mr. Ohsone insisted the compact disk player be no larger than the small block of wood (about 5 in × 5 in × 1½ in) he placed in front of his engineers. According to *The Wall Street Journal* [2]:

> His next decision reflected another Japanese strength: manufacturing. He brought in some of his production engineers to help with the design. The disk players would be so small that researchers needed to know at each step whether their tightly packed circuitry could be mass-produced by robots.

Within two years, the Sony mini-compact disk was on the market at one-twentieth the size of the original players. Its cost was only about $300, partially because it used fewer materials and was assembled by robots. Within 2 years, the Sony compact disk dominated the market, and Sony forged on into new projects, including an erasable disk.

Sony's success with the compact disk player as well as with the Walkman and pocket-sized (2-inch Watchman) TVs attests to their strength in two key areas. They have (1) a highly perfected decision-making process, and (2) the technical ability (and tenacity) to carry out good decisions until they pay off in the market.

Thousands of business decisions are made every day—and not all will "make or break" the organization. But each one adds a measure of success (or failure) to the operations. For example, DuPont Company managers must decide which of several potential products to develop. An electronics manufacturer must decide whether to invest in a new process or to stay with a "proven" one that is producing defective chips at a rate of 1 in 3. An airline company bargaining team must decide whether to propose a new contract or risk a strike. A purchasing agent for NASA must decide whether to order more spare parts or to take a chance that there are enough on hand.

Does the ability to make good decisions come "naturally," or can it be learned? This chapter examines management as a science and the characteristics of decisions. The framework for making decisions presented here should prove useful as you move into more responsible positions in the business world. We also illustrate the use of economic and statistical models and end with some insight into the use of decision trees.

MANAGEMENT AS A SCIENCE

Management scientists hold that education, scientific training, and experience can improve a person's ability to make decisions. The idea of management as a science is founded on its similarity to other sciences as expressed in Fig. 2-1. *First*, the principles and methodology of management (for example, organization theory, span of control) form an organized or codified body of knowledge. *Second*, real-world data are available for analysis. The business world is essentially a laboratory for the management scientist. *Third*, an objective and systematic analysis of the data can often be made. *Finally*, another experimenter (decision maker) could use the same data and arrive at consistent results.

The association of management with the scientific method involves drawing objective conclusions from facts. Facts come from the analysis of data, which must be gathered, compiled, and digested into meaningful (quantifiable) form, such as graphs and summary statistics. Computers are especially helpful in these tasks because they can easily store data and assist us with the more sophisticated mathematical and statistical analyses.

But not all variables are quantifiable, so decision makers must still use some value-based judgments in a decision process. This doesn't necessarily brand the decision process as nonscientific, or the results as unpredictable. Many business decisions are based on facts that do not carry value-laden implications. In other cases, existing legal or environmental controls may accurately reflect individual or organizational ethics. Further, many organizations have codes of ethics which they follow in a consistent manner. But personal value systems do influence some decisions.

CHARACTERISTICS OF DECISIONS

Operations decisions range from simple judgments to complex analyses—which can also involve judgment. Judgments typically incorporate basic knowledge, experience, and what we often refer to as "common sense." They enable us to

- Organized principles of knowledge
- Use of empirical data
- Systematic analysis of data
- Repeatable results

FIGURE 2-1   The Scientific Method in Management

blend objective and subjective data to arrive at a choice. Fortunately the human brain is capable of selecting and integrating relevant information into a meaningful decision. Quantitative methods of analysis add to the objectivity of such decisions.

The appropriateness of a given type of analysis depends on (1) the significance of the decision, (2) the time and cost limitations, and (3) the degree of complexity of the decision.

Significant or *long-lasting decisions* deserve more consideration than trivial or routine ones. For example, decisions to produce untested medical products, or proceed with offshore drilling for oil, can have strongly secondary effects on society and the environment. Similarly, a long-range decision such as a plant investment may deserve more thorough analysis than a short-term decision to stock an inventory item for Christmas.

Time availability and the *cost of analysis* also influence the amount of analysis. During a recent General Motors contract negotiation, a very complex proposal was presented just a few days before the existing contract expired. There was inadequate time to study the complete financial ramifications of the proposal. But it was accepted and a strike was averted. In cases like this, decision makers must utilize whatever database and staff assistance are readily available, and ballpark estimates may have to suffice.

The *decision complexity* increases when (a) many variables are involved, (b) the variables are highly interdependent or sequentially related, and (c) the data describing the variables are incomplete or uncertain. For example, new factory location decisions are complex because they involve economic, social, and environmental concerns. In addition, once a firm is committed to a site, the technology employed and the amount of automation will affect costs for many years to come.

Business decision makers have always had to work with incomplete and uncertain data. Figure 2-2 depicts the information environment of decisions. In some situations a decision maker has (or is assumed to have) complete information about the decision variables; at the other extreme, no information is available. Operations management decisions are made all along this continuum.

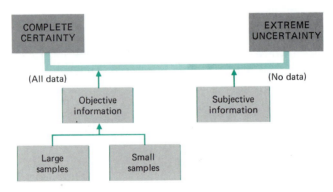

FIGURE 2-2   Information Continuum

Complete certainty in decision making requires data on all elements in the population. If such data are not available, large samples lend more certainty than do small ones. Beyond this, subjective information is likely to be better than no data at all.

FRAMEWORK FOR DECISION MAKING

An analytical and scientific framework for decisions implies several systematic steps, as summarized in Fig. 2-3. Not all managers follow this formal process—nor do all decisions necessitate it. Regardless of the situation, experience and good judgment are always important ingredients in decision making.

Defining the problem entails identifying the relevant variables and the cause, rather than symptoms, of the problem. For example, the problem may be low productivity in an office. Those variables that have a significant effect on productivity (for example, amount of training) should be included as parameters of the problem. Careful definition of the problem is crucial; even a brilliant solution to the wrong problem doesn't help much. Finding the root cause of a problem may take some questioning and detective work. If a problem is defined too narrowly, relevant variables may be omitted. If too broadly, so many tangential aspects may be included that it is difficult to sort out the complex relationships.

Establishing the decision criteria is important because the criteria reflect the goals and purpose of the work efforts. For many years, profits served as a convenient and accepted goal for many free-enterprise organizations, perhaps because early models of organization behavior were based largely on economic theory. Today, research shows that organizations typically have multiple goals, such as employee welfare, high productivity, stability, market share, growth, industrial leadership, and other social objectives.

Formulation of a model lies at the heart of the scientific decision-making process. Models describe the essence of a problem or relationship by abstracting relevant variables from the real-world situation. Their purpose is not to duplicate reality in all respects, for models that do this reveal nothing new. Instead, we use models to simplify or approximate reality, so the underlying relationships can be

---

1 Define the problem and its parameters (relevant variables).
2 Establish the decision criteria (objectives).
3 Formulate a model relating the parameters to the criteria.
4 Generate alternatives by varying the values of the parameters.
5 Evaluate the alternatives and select the alternative that best satisfies the criteria.
6 Implement the decision and monitor the results.

FIGURE 2-3   Framework for Decisions

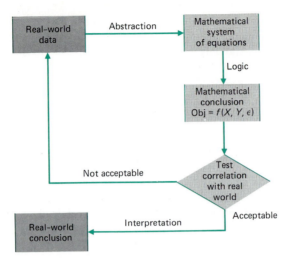

FIGURE 2-4   Mathematical Models

expressed in testable form and studied in isolation. Some of the more useful types of models are:

- Verbal (words and descriptions)
- Physical (modified scale)
- Schematic (diagrams and charts)
- Mathematical (equations and numbers)

Modeling a decision situation usually requires both formulating a model and collecting the relevant data to use in the model. Management scientists typically find that mathematical and statistical models are most useful for understanding complex business problems. Mathematical models are more abstract than pictorial or scale models, and they can incorporate factors that cannot readily be visualized. And with the aid of computers and simulation techniques, these quantitative models are also quite flexible. For example, it is much easier to change an equation on a computer than it is to change the physical structure of a new product, such as an automobile.

Figure 2-4 shows the mathematical modeling process in the form of a schematic model. This abstraction must begin and end with the real world. Its validity is judged by how well it reflects what it models. A good forecasting model, for example, is one that accurately predicts real-world demand. We will discuss some techniques for evaluating the validity of models in later chapters. Let us illustrate a mathematical model with an example.

EXAMPLE 2-1 | Chicago Computer Company uses a simple linear model to project next period's production requirements in situations where "on-hand" and "in-process" inventory is less than current demand.

$$P_{t+1} = D_t - (I + I_{t+1})$$

where P_{t+1} = units of production (P) required next period ($t + 1$)
D_t = estimated current period demand in units (an unknown and uncontrollable variable)
I = present inventory level (units)
I_{t+1} = in-process inventory (units)

The current period demand is estimated at 421 units plus or minus 5 percent. The present inventory level is 30 units, and in-process inventory is 280 units. Use the model above to develop an interval estimate of next period's production requirements.

SOLUTION

The model is defined, so we can assign the appropriate data values to the variables. Thus $I = 30$ and $I_{t+1} = 280$. But D_t can take on values in a range of from 5 percent below to 5 percent above the point estimate of 421. Using these two values as endpoints will give us the "interval estimate" requested.

For the *minimum* estimate:

Let $D_t = 421 - .05(421) = 400$ units

Then $P_{t+1} = D_t - (I + I_{t+1}) = 400 - (30 + 280) = 90$ units

For the *maximum* estimate:

Let $D_t = 421 + .05(421) = 442$ units

Then $P_{t+1} = D_t - (I + I_{t+1}) = 442 - (30 + 280) = 132$ units

Using this model, next period's production requirements are estimated to lie in the interval from 90 to 132 units.

The example above used mathematical equations to model the production situation. Mathematical models offer decision makers a number of advantages. First, they necessitate a good understanding of the problem. (In the example, the problem was to develop an interval estimate of next period's production.) And they require a recognition of all the relevant varibles. (The variables that affect production were identified as the estimated current demand, on-hand inventory level, and in-process inventory. Models also help decision makers to understand the relationship, costs, and tradeoffs that exist among the variables. (In the example, the *volume* relationship was of concern. It was expressed as an equation.) Finally, mathematical models permit analysts to manipulate the variables and test alternative courses of action. This is the next step in the decision process.

Alternatives are generated by varying the values of the parameters. Mathematical and statistical models are particularly suitable for generating alternatives because they are so easily modified. The model builder can "experiment" with a model by substituting different values for controllable and uncontrollable variables. In the example above, the estimated current demand of 421 units was an uncontrollable variable. Different estimates of current demand could be used in the model to see how next period's production would be affected.

Evaluation of the alternatives is relatively objective in an analytical decision process because the criteria for evaluating the alternatives have already been precisely defined. The best alternative is the one that most closely satisfies the criteria. Some models, such as linear programming, are inherently of an optimizing nature. They automatically seek out a maximizing or minimizing solution. Other models are more suitable for use in situations that are so complex, uncertain, or subjective that optimal solutions cannot be guaranteed. In these cases, various heuristic and statistical techniques can be used to suggest the best course of action.

Implementation and monitoring are not strictly part of the decision process, but they are essential for completing the managerial action, so we include them here. The best course of action or solution to a problem determined via the use of a model is just that—a solution to a model! The true test of the decision process comes when the theoretical solution is implemented in the business world. But implementation is not automatic. Other managers usually have to be convinced of the merits of the solution; otherwise nothing will happen. So the decision-making process needs implementation and follow-up procedures to ensure that appropriate action is taken. This includes an analysis and evaluation of the solution plus any recommendations for changes or adjustments.

DECISION METHODOLOGY

The kind and amount of information available help determine which analytical methods are most appropriate for modeling a given decision situation. Figure 2-5 shows some useful quantitative techniques classified according to the degree of certainty that exists with respect to the decision variables and possible outcomes. In many cases, more than one approach (methodology) may be suitable for a given problem. The degree of certainty is classified as (a) complete certainty, (b) risk and uncertainty, and (c) extreme uncertainty.

COMPLETE CERTAINTY METHODS

Under complete certainty conditions, all relevant information about the decision variables and outcomes is known (or assumed to be known). This does not necessarily imply that decision making is easy, for the problem may be ill-defined, the decision criteria may be unclear, or there may be too many variables to handle

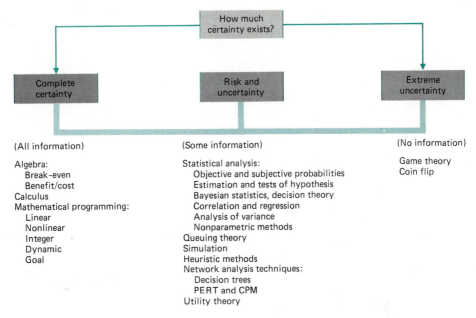

FIGURE 2-5   Quantitative Methods Available to Operations Managers

economically, even though the model is theoretically feasible. For many of these situations, however, the following methods are useful:

- *Algebra.*   This basic mathematical logic is useful in both certainty and uncertainty analysis. Given valid assumptions, algebra provides a deterministic solution in situations such as break-even analysis and benefit-cost analysis.
- *Calculus.*   This branch of mathematics provides a useful tool for determining optimal values (limits) where functions, such as inventory costs, are to be maximized or minimized.
- *Mathematical programming.*   Programming techniques have found extensive applications in making product-mix decisions, minimizing transportation costs, planning and scheduling production, and numerous other areas.

RISK AND UNCERTAINTY METHODS

In risk and uncertainty situations, information about the decision variables or the outcomes is usually probabilistic. Objective data (from large samples) lend more certainty than subjective data. These approaches might be useful:

- *Statistical analysis.*   The use of probability and probability distributions is increasing. Classical estimation and testing techniques as well as Bayesian methods have also proved valuable. Some of the numerous applications include the setting of labor standards, forecasting, inventory and production control, and quality control.

- *Queuing theory.* The analysis of queues in terms of waiting-line length and mean waiting time is particularly useful in analyzing service systems, maintenance activities, and shop floor control activities.
- *Simulation.* Simulations duplicate the essence of an activity or system without actually achieving reality. Computer simulations are valuable tools for the analysis of investment outcomes, production processes, scheduling, and maintenance activities.
- *Heuristic methods.* Heuristic methods involve sets of rules which, though perhaps not optimal, do facilitate solutions of scheduling, layout, and distribution problems when applied in a consistent manner.
- *Network analysis techniques.* Network approaches include decision trees, CPM, and PERT methods. They are particularly helpful in identifying alternative courses of action and controlling research, investment, and a multitude of project activities.
- *Utility theory.* Utility or preference theory allows decision makers to incorporate their own experience and values into a relatively formalized decision structure.

EXTREME UNCERTAINTY

Under extreme uncertainty, no information is available to assess the likelihood of alternative outcomes. A manager's strategy might be:

- *Game theory.* Game theory helps decision makers to choose courses of action when there is absolutely no information about what conditions will prevail.
- *Coin flip.* In spite of the "unscientific" nature of flipping a coin, random measures such as this are sometimes used in situations where the decision makers are wholly indifferent.

In recent years, there has been significant growth in the use of mathematical and statistical techniques (for example, in forecasting, inventory control, and quality control). On the other hand, only very limited use is made of some techniques, such as game theory. In general, large firms tend to use formal quantitative methods more frequently than smaller firms.

DECISION SUPPORT SYSTEMS

Computers first "earned" their way into business as machines for processing accounting data. As their speed and capacity were improved, they became the centralized database of organizations. Today, the processing speed and memory capacity of personal computers far exceeds those of the mainframes of yesterday.

And as the price dropped, the number of computers in use skyrocketed. Along with decentralizing computer operations, this increased availability has also prompted an exponential growth in the number of software packages designed to incorporate operating data and model ongoing operations.

Decision support systems (DSS) are computer-based systems designed to aid decision makers at any stage of the decision process—especially in the development of alternatives and evaluation of possible courses of action. Their purpose is to provide the information and analytical support that enables managers to better control and guide the decision process. Emphasis is not on delivering a specific answer or solution, but on supplying useful information (rather than "all" information) and appropriate quantitative models that support the manager's inherent skills. DSS are thus a logical extension of the managerial decision processes, just as robots are a step in the automation of physical assembly activities. We can expect their development to continue as managers learn better how to apply the data processing and modeling capabilities of computers to the analysis of ill-structured and value-based decision situations.

We now consider three types of models that illustrate some of the quantitative methods outlined above. Break-even analysis is an economic model describing cost-price-volume relationships. It is usually a complete certainty type of model because we usually *assume* costs and revenue are known quantities. Then we illustrate how to deal with risk and uncertainty by a statistical probability model and by a decision tree model.

ECONOMIC MODELS[1]

In this section we will consider break-even analysis and a companion measure, contribution, which has many of the same advantages and limitations as break-even analysis.

BREAK-EVEN ANALYSIS

Break-even analysis is based on the fundamental model of economic theory which states that profits arise from the excess of total revenues (TR) over total costs (TC). Recognizing that total costs are composed of both fixed costs (FC) and total variable costs (TVC), we can express the profit function as follows:

$$\text{Profit} = \text{TR} - \text{TC}$$
$$= \text{TR} - (\text{FC} + \text{TVC}) \qquad (2\text{-}1)$$

---

[1] The analysis of break-even type problems is often taught in accounting or financial courses, so some instructors may choose not to assign this material or to designate it as optional.

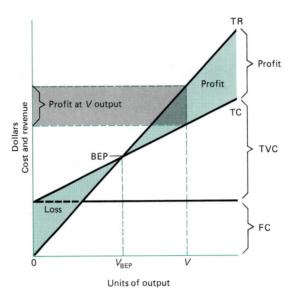

FIGURE 2-6   Break-even Chart

Major cost categories often include direct labor, direct material, and over-head (or indirect production expenses). The direct labor and direct material, plus some other items such as factory supplies, are usually classified as variable costs because they typically change with the volume of production. Supervision, taxes, office salaries, and building depreciation are of a more fixed or semivariable nature. Fixed costs are essentially constant over a given range of output but admittedly do change over the long run as plant expansions are made, taxes change, and the like. Depreciation and insurance are examples of fixed costs.

A break-even chart is a convenient means of graphically describing the relationship between costs and revenues for different volumes of output. Figure 2-6 depicts this relationship over a range of volume where total revenue increases linearly with each unit sold, and total cost reflects both an unavoidable fixed cost plus a per unit variable cost. The break-even point (BEP) is that volume of output where the fixed and variable costs are covered, but no profit exists. Thus at the BEP, the total revenues equal the total costs (TR = TC). Recognizing that revenues reflect the price, P, charged per item times the volume, V, sold, we can restate the TR = TC expression as follows:

$$P(V) = FC + VC(V) \qquad (2\text{-}2)$$

And the expression for the break-even volume is as follows:

$$V_{BEP} = \frac{FC}{P - VC} \qquad (2\text{-}3)$$

EXAMPLE 2-2

A producer of small printers has the production information shown. What is the break-even point?

SOLUTION

The solution involves identifying the relevant variables and expressing them in the economic relationship of the break-even model, as shown by the equation at the bottom of the illustration.

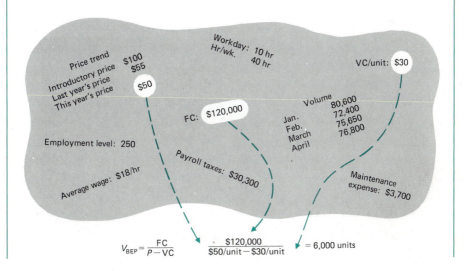

Price trend
Introductory price $100
Last year's price $55
This year's price $50

Workday: 10 hr
Hr/wk. 40 hr

VC/unit: $30

Employment level: 250

FC: $120,000

Volume
Jan. 80,600
Feb. 72,400
March 75,650
April 76,800

Average wage: $18/hr

Payroll taxes: $30,300

Maintenance expense: $3,700

$$V_{BEP} = \frac{FC}{P-VC} \qquad \frac{\$120{,}000}{\$50/unit - \$30/unit} = 6{,}000 \text{ units}$$

Break-even analysis is simple and easy to visualize, and it condenses decision information into a form that is readily understandable by almost anyone. Also, it is concerned with a vital aspect of the free enterprise of organizations: profitability. However, it is a technique based wholly on economic factors. It assumes that one has complete knowledge about all the economic parameters, for the price, cost, and demand data must be either known for certain or assumed. Viewed in this perspective, it is an algebraic technique that resides on the complete certainty end of the spectrum described in Fig. 2-5.[2] Furthermore, the relationship between these variables is assumed to follow a simple linear function which may be acceptable over short ranges but often is really not satisfactory for long-range decisions. Extrapolation to high outputs involves an increasing amount of risk, for the model fails to account for any effects of decreasing returns to scale as facilities become overloaded or markets become saturated.

In theory, fixed costs do not fluctuate with levels of activity, while variable costs do change directly. In practice, it is not always easy to classify all costs as fixed or variable; some costs appear to be semivariable. However, break-even analysis lends itself readily to this more realistic situation by using the total costs at two known volumes to estimate variable costs.(See Solved Prob. 5.)

---

[2] Break-even analysis can, however, be extended to conditions of uncertainty.

CONTRIBUTION

Contribution is a measure of economic value that tells how much the sale of one unit of product will contribute to cover fixed costs, with the remainder going to profits. The per-unit contribution C of a product is determined by subtracting the variable cost per unit, VC, from the price P.

$$C = P - VC \qquad (2\text{-}4)$$

Note that the per-unit contribution of Eq. (2-4) is exactly what is in the denominator of the break-even quantity expression [Eq. (2-3)]. The BEP occurs when the contribution per unit times the number of units sold just equals the total fixed costs.

EXAMPLE 2-3

Stylecut Shops, Inc. operates eight haircut shops in California on a 250-days-per-year, 8-hours-per-day basis. They charge $9 for a haircut. One shop has annual fixed costs of $84,000 and variable costs estimated at $2 per customer. (a) What is the contribution per customer? (b) How many customers per hour must the shop average in order to break even?

SOLUTION

(a) $C = P - VC = \$9 - \$2 = \$7$ per customer

(b) $V_{BEP} = \dfrac{FC}{P - VC} = \dfrac{FC}{C} = \dfrac{\$84,000/yr}{\$7/customer} = 12,000$ customers/yr

This is equivalent to

$$\frac{12,000 \text{ customers/yr}}{(250 \text{ days/yr}) (8 \text{ hr/day})} = 6 \text{ customers/hr}$$

When the contribution of a product is divided by its price, the result is called a contribution ratio, CR. Contribution ratios are useful for comparing the profitability of several products within a product line. The products that contribute the most can be emphasized. Of course, a product line as a whole should have sufficient contribution to cover all its fixed costs, but individual products in a line often cover differing shares of the total fixed costs.

Figure 2-7 depicts the contribution difference one might expect to find between a capital-intensive industry and a labor-intensive industry. To some extent, it also reflects the difference between goods-producing and services-producing industries. When fixed costs are a large portion of total costs, as shown in Fig. 2-7a, small changes in volume or prices can result in significant changes in profits. So managerial efforts aimed at increasing volume or raising prices are likely to be most effective in improving profits.

Many service industries are labor-intensive, as indicated by the low-contribu-

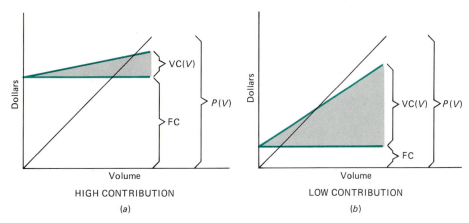

FIGURE 2-7   Difference between High and Low Contribution

tion sketch in Fig. 2-7*b*. In this situation, a reduction in variable costs may be more effective in generating profits (or trimming losses) than changes in the total volume or in per-unit prices.

STATISTICAL MODELS[3]

Most business decisions are made with only limited (or incomplete) information. For example, performance standards for many workers are usually based on studies of only a few. And the quality level of large shipments is typically estimated from small samples of the products.

No statistical techniques can substitute for having accurate, up-to-date, and unbiased data for decisions. But statistical theory can help control the error associated with the *amount* of data used in the decision process. In general, the larger the database, the less the risk of error from making a wrong decision. The tradeoff is, of course, the cost. Although having more data is desirable, the significance of the decision may not justify the cost of additional data.

In this section we review some probability concepts that will be especially useful as you work through the text. First we review the definition of probability and the rules for applying probabilities. Applications of basic probability concepts permeate the text because of the need to make so many decisions on the basis of limited information. Then we distinguish between discrete and continuous probability distributions. An understanding of probability and sampling distributions will be necessary for making correct choices in areas such as work sampling, inventory, quality control, and maintenance. But regardless of the technique employed, one should always apply good judgment to see if the answer is reasonable.

---

[3] This section constitutes a brief review of basic statistical concepts used in chapters that follow. Some instructors may choose not to assign this material or to designate it as optional.

FIGURE 2-8 Probability Rules

Complement:

$$P(A) = 1 - P(\overline{A}) \tag{2-5}$$

Multiplication:

$$P(A \text{ and } B) = P(A)P(B|A) \tag{2-6}$$
$$= P(A)P(B) \quad \text{(if independent)}$$

Addition:

$$P(A \text{ or } B) = P(A) + P(B) - P(A \text{ and } B) \tag{2-7}$$
$$= P(A) + P(B) \quad \text{(if mutually exclusive)}$$

Bayes' rule:

$$P(A|B) = \frac{P(A \text{ and } B)}{P(B)} = \frac{P(A)P(B|A)}{P(A)P(B|A) + P(\overline{A})P(B|\overline{A})} \tag{2-8}$$

PROBABILITY RULES

Probability is the most basic measure of uncertainty, for it attaches a quantitative value to the occurrence of an event. The first probabilities considered by classical statisticians were those that could be computed prior to an event, or *a priori*, such as in the role of a die. Most operations management applications today involve either *empirical* probabilities (based on observed frequency data) or *subjective* probabilities (based on personal experience or judgment).

In all the above cases, the probability rules of Fig. 2-8 hold. Recall that events are *independent* if the occurrence of one in no way affects any other one. *Mutually exclusive* events automatically preclude each other, such as classifying an item as good or defective. A simple example will illustrate the application of these probability rules to a production situation.

EXAMPLE 2-4

Three molding machines (X, Y, and Z) are used to produce 600 computer terminal keys which are rushed (without inspection) to a customer. The number of good (G) and defective ($\overline{G}$) keys from each machine are as shown.

	Machine X	Machine Y	Machine Z	Row Total
Good (G)	45	225	270	540
Not Good ($\overline{G}$)	5	25	30	60
Total	50	250	300	600

When the customer receives the keys, they are randomly selected for installation in CRTs. What is the probability that a key selected (a) is defective, (b) was produced by machine Z and is good, (c) was either produced by machine Z or is good?

SOLUTION

Given the data we can estimate the empirical probabilities as follows:

$$P(G) = \frac{\text{number of good}}{\text{total number keys}} = \frac{540}{600} = .900$$

$$P(Z) = \frac{\text{number from Z}}{\text{total number keys}} = \frac{300}{600} = .500$$

$P(G|Z)$, which is read "Good, given it is from Z," is found as follows:

$$P(G|Z) = \frac{\text{number from Z that are good}}{\text{total number from Z}} = \frac{270}{300} = .90$$

Now, using the rules of probability we have:

(a) $P(\overline{G}) = 1 - P(G) = 1 - .90 = .10$

(b) $P(Z \text{ and } G) = P(Z)P(G|Z) = (.50)(.90) = .45$

(c) $P(Z \text{ or } G) = P(Z) + P(G) - P(Z \text{ and } G)$

$$= .50 + .90 - .45 = .95$$

Careful examination of Example 2-4 will reveal that the probability of selecting a good key is independent of the machine from which the key was made. Thus, the $P(G)$ does not depend on whether the key is from machine X, Y, or Z:

$$P(G) = P(G|X) = P(G|Y) = P(G|Z)$$

$$= \frac{540}{600} \quad = \frac{225}{250} \quad = \frac{45}{50}$$

$$= .90 \quad = .90 \quad = .90$$

DISCRETE AND CONTINUOUS DISTRIBUTIONS

The "good" versus "defective" classification of the computer terminal key data is an example of a dichotomous classification of discrete data. As suggested by Fig. 2-9, we have used the empirical frequency data to form a discrete probability distribution. Had we been interested in a measurable characteristic of the keys, such as the depth of the numeral indentations, we would have been working with a continuous random variable. For example, suppose the depths vary from .010

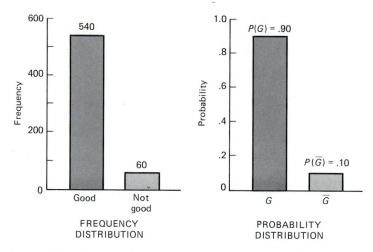

FIGURE 2-9   Discrete Distribution of Computer Terminal Key Quality

inch to .050 inch. They could be illustrated as a continuous distribution as shown in Fig. 2-10.

The distinction between discrete and continuous distributions is important in work sampling, quality control, and elsewhere because of the need to identify the underlying probability distribution. The correct identification of the distribution affects sample sizes and the risk of drawing incorrect conclusions about the quality of the populations.

Figure 2-11 summarizes the major differences in the inference process when using discrete versus continuous data, where π and μ are the population proportion and mean, respectively, and σ is the population standard deviation. The

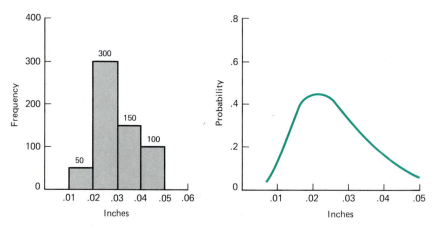

FIGURE 2-10   Continuous Distribution of Depth Measurements

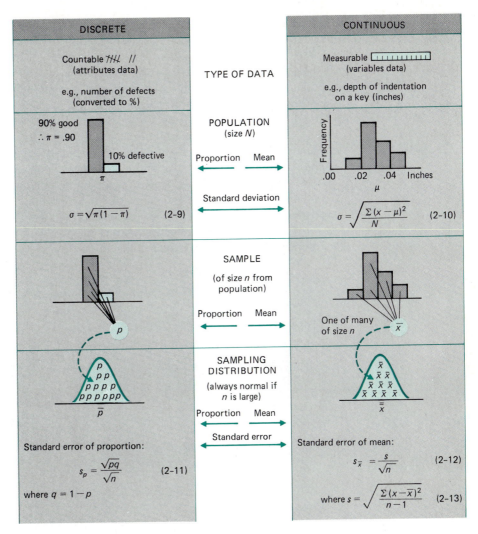

FIGURE 2-11 Inference Using Discrete versus Continuous Distributions

figure traces the data from a population to a sample and on to a theoretical sampling distribution. Underlying the concept of a sampling distribution is, of course, the *central limit theorem*. It states that for sufficiently large samples, the distributions of both sample proportions and sample means tend to follow a normal (smooth, bell-shaped) pattern.

Sampling distributions are theoretical distributions of *all* the sample proportions (p) of a given sample size, or of *all* the sample means ($\bar{x}$) of a given size. Although we may never obtain *all* possible p's or $\bar{x}$'s, the distributions are very useful. Our primary use will be with the estimated standard errors (s_p and $s_{\bar{x}}$).

They provide a measure of how much the sample p's and $\bar{x}$'s can reasonably be expected to differ from population values of π and μ. As we shall see later on in the text, these estimates of s_p and $s_{\bar{x}}$ enable us to make better estimates of sample sizes needed for work standards and quality control charts. The application of these statistical concepts is illustrated below with one example involving discrete data and another involving continuous data.

EXAMPLE 2-5
(Discrete data)

Valley Savings and Loan is considering the purchase of an automatic banking machine if the tellers are idle more than 15 percent of the time. In a random sample of 200 observations of a bank teller, the teller was idle 36 times.
(a) Use these data to make a point estimate of the percentage of idle time.
(b) Compute the estimated standard error of proportion.
(c) If the true (population) proportions of idle time were $\pi = 15$ percent, what would be the likelihood of getting samples which suggest that the proportion of idle time is more than 15 percent?

SOLUTION

(a) Sample proportion $= p = \dfrac{36 \text{ idle observations}}{200 \text{ total observations}} = .18 = 18\%$

(b) Standard error $= s_p = \sqrt{\dfrac{pq}{n}}$

where $q = 1 - p = 1 - .18 = .82$

$n = 200$

$$\therefore s_p = \sqrt{\dfrac{(.18)(.82)}{200}} = .027 = 2.7\%$$

(c) Because the distribution of sample proportions is normal and symmetrical, 50 percent of the area lies above 15 percent.

$\therefore P(p > 15\%) = .50$

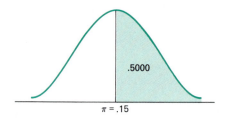

.5000

$\pi = .15$

There is a 50 percent chance of getting a sample of $> 15\%$ idle time.

EXAMPLE 2-6
(Continuous
data)

The Mountainview Bank operations manager is concerned about how long it takes her tellers to service customers. In one study of a teller who was busy for 3.5 hours, the teller served 121 customers. Data on the individual service times revealed a standard deviation of .22 minutes. (a) Estimate the average service time per customer. (b) Compute the standard error of the mean and explain its meaning. (c) Assume the service times are normally distributed. What percent of the customers require two minutes or longer for their service?

SOLUTION

Let x equal the time to service a customer. Then $\Sigma x = 3.5$ hr $= 210$ min.

(a) $\bar{x} = \dfrac{\Sigma x}{n} = \dfrac{210}{121} = 1.74$ min/customer

(b) $s_{\bar{x}} = \dfrac{s}{\sqrt{n}} = \dfrac{.22}{\sqrt{121}} = .02$ min

This is the estimated standard deviation of the *theoretical* distribution of means from all possible samples of 121 customers served by this teller. It would be of use if we wished to make some inference or statement of confidence using sample *means*.

(c) Assuming the *individual* service time distribution is normal, the 2.00-min point is 1.18 standard deviations (Z units) away from the mean time of 1.74 min.

From

$$Z = \frac{x - \bar{x}}{s}$$

(2-14)

We have $Z = \dfrac{2.00 - 1.74}{.22} = 1.18$

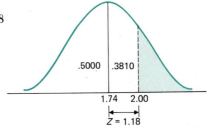

From Appendix C, the probability associated with $Z = 1.18$ is .3810, so the area under the normal curve above 2.00 min is .5000 − .3810 = .1190, or about 12 percent. See Solved Probs. 7 and 8 for a more detailed review of the use of the normal distribution.

DECISION TREES

Decision trees incorporate several of the concepts discussed earlier in the chapter. They can deal with economic variables, are mathematical (as well as schematic) in nature, and use probabilities to determine expected value amounts. We first review the concept of expected value.

Expected Value You may recall that mathematical expectation is the sum (Σ) of the products obtained by multiplying each possible event's value X by the probability P with which it occurs. In symbols, the expected value of X, $E(X)$, is

$$E(X) = X_1P_1 + X_2P_2 + \cdots + X_nP_n = \Sigma[X \cdot P(X)] \qquad (2\text{-}15)$$

Thus the expected value of the number of dots on the roll of one six-sided die is $1(\frac{1}{6}) + 2(\frac{1}{6}) + \cdots + 6(\frac{1}{6}) = 3.5$. When X represents monetary units, we designate the $E(X)$ as the expected monetary value, EMV. So if each dot represented a \$1 gain, the EMV would be \$3.50. To maximize an expected value choice one would select the action (or branch of a decision tree) that yields the highest EMV (which is sometimes designated EMV*).

Structure Decision trees are schematic diagrams that show the alternative outcomes and interdependence of choices in a multiphase, or sequential decision process. The treelike diagram is constructed from left to right, using square boxes for controllable (decision) points and circles for uncontrollable (chance) events. Each branch leads to a payoff that is stated in monetary (or utility) terms on the right.

   Decision trees are analyzed backward (from right to left) by multiplying the payoffs by their respective probabilities (which are assigned to each chance event). The highest expected value then identifies the best course of action and is entered at the preceding decision point. It then becomes the payoff value for the next higher-order expectation, as the analysis is continued back to the trunk of the tree. Computer models are available to handle the calculations on complex decision trees.

EXAMPLE 2-7 | A glass factory specializing in crystal is developing a substantial backlog, and the firm's management is considering three courses of action: (a) arrange for subcontracting, (b) begin overtime production, and (c) construct new facilities. The correct choice depends largely on future demand, which may be low, medium, or high. By consensus, management ranks the respective probabilities as .10, .50, and .40. A cost analysis reveals the effect on profits that is shown in the following table.

| | Profit ($000) if demand is | | |
Courses of Action	Low (P = .10)	Medium (P = .50)	High (P = .40)
A = Arrange subcontracting	10	50	50
B = Begin overtime	−20	60	100
C = Construct facilities	−150	20	200

Show this decision situation schematically in the form of a decision tree.

SOLUTION

As shown in Fig. 2-12, the controllable (choice) decision variables are A, B, and C, and the uncontrollable variable is demand. We begin on the left by showing the decision choices first, followed by the chance alternatives of demand. The payoff values under each alternative are shown at the right, with associated probabilities below each value. The expected value of each

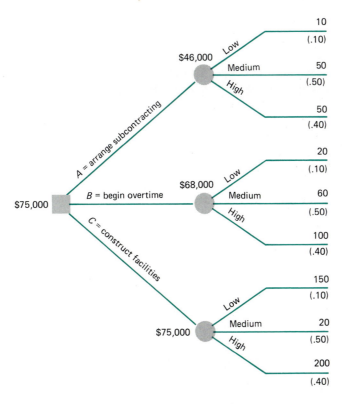

FIGURE 2-12   Decision Tree

branch is then computed by summing the profit times probability for each. For example, for A:

$$E(A) = 10(.10) + 50(.50) + 50(.40) = \$46,000$$

These values (such as $46,000) are entered at the nodes, and the choice at the preceding node is dictated by the highest respective values. In this example our choice to construct new facilities (C), with an expected value of $75,000, has a higher expected value than that of the other two alternatives.

Advantages of a decision tree approach include helping us structure decisions in an objective way, forcing an explicit identification of alternatives, and fostering a clear distinction between controllable and uncontrollable variables. The method also permits us to incorporate uncertainty in a systematic, objective way. But monetary and probability values must still be estimated. Also, the expected value approach may not be the best for a given situation, so it should not be accepted automatically.

SUMMARY

The classification of management as a science rests on an organized body of management knowledge, the use of empirical data, a systematic analysis of the data, and the repeatable nature of results. Many decisions, however, still involve judgment and value considerations.

The level of analysis applied to business decisions depends on how significant they are and the time/cost limitations that exist. In addition, problems that involve numerous variables and uncertain information make decision making more complex. Steps in the analytical framework for decisions include (1) defining the problem, (2) establishing the decision criteria, (3) formulating a model, (4) generating alternatives, (5) evaluating and selecting the best alternative, and (6) implementing and monitoring the results.

Three quantitative methods included here for analyzing decisions are economic break-even models, statistical models, and decision trees. Break-even models identify the volume where revenues just cover the fixed plus variable costs. Contribution, the difference between price and variable cost, is a companion measure of economic value.

Statistical models frequently use standard rules of probability and probability distributions. Discrete distributions arise from populations with countable items, whereas continuous distributions stem from measurable quantities. Both yield (theoretically) normally distributed sampling distributions. Later we will use the standard errors from these distributions, s_p and $s_{\bar{x}}$, for establishing sample sizes and control limits for production processes.

Decision trees are schematic models that depict sequential decision situations. They force the decision maker to identify alternatives and distinguish between choice and chance events. They also permit us to incorporate uncertainty by assigning probability values to the chance outcomes. Then the best course of action is theoretically the one with the highest expected monetary value. However, other considerations (for example, amount of assets) may warrant pursuing a different course of action.

SOLVED PROBLEMS

FRAMEWORK FOR DECISIONS

1 Mike Collins is the operations manager of Supermarket Suppliers, Inc., which runs a large old warehouse that services 80 delivery trucks. He must decide how many loading docks to include in a new warehouse. He decided that they should plan on enough capacity to handle average demand plus about 25 percent extra for growth.

To help make his decision, Mike collects some data on the current dock usage and simulates the unloading and loading activities on the company computer. The simulation generates values ranging from 7 to 14 docks. However, 12 loading docks handle average demand, and Mike tells the design engineer to plan for 15. Two weeks later Mike calls the design engineer to make sure everything is working out satisfactorily.

List the sequential steps in the decision process and the corresponding activity from the situation described.

Solution

Decision Process Step	*Corresponding Activity in Situation*
1 Define the problem and its parameters.	1 Problem is to determine number of loading docks required. Parameters are demand and load-unload time.
2 Establish decision criteria	2 Criterion is capacity to meet average demand plus 25 percent.
3 Construct a model.	3 Model is a simulation model on computer.
4 Generate alternatives.	4 Alternatives range from 7 to 14 docks.
5 Evaluate and choose best alternative.	5 Best alternative is to plan for 15 docks (12 plus 25 percent).
6 Implement and monitor solution.	6 Tell design engineer and follow up 2 weeks later.

ECONOMIC MODELS

2 If fixed costs are $20,000 and variable costs are estimated at 50 percent of the unit selling price of $80, what is the BEP?

Solution

$$V_{\text{BEP}} = \frac{FC}{P - VC} = \frac{\$20{,}000}{\$80/\text{unit} - \$40/\text{unit}} = 500 \text{ units}$$

3 Process X has fixed costs of $40,000 per year and variable costs of $9 per unit, whereas process Y has fixed costs of $16,000 per year and variable costs of $24 per unit. At what production quantity Q are the total costs of X and Y equal?

Solution

Set total costs equal:

$$TC_X = TC_Y$$

$$FC_X + VC_X\ (V) = FC_Y + VC_Y\ (V)$$

$$\$40,000 + \$9V = \$16,000 + \$24V$$

$$\$15V = \$24,000$$

$$V = 1,600 \text{ units}$$

4 A firm has annual fixed costs of $3.2 million and variable costs of $7 per unit. It is considering an additional investment of $800,000, which will increase the fixed costs by $150,000 per year and will increase the contribution by $2 per unit. No change is anticipated in the sales volume or the sales price of $15 per unit. What is the break-even quantity if the new investment is made?

Solution

The $2 increase in C will decrease VC to $7 − $2 = $5 per unit. The addition to FC makes them $3.2 million + $150,000 = $3,350,000.

$$V_{BEP} = \frac{FC}{P - VC} = \frac{\$3,350,000}{\$15/\text{unit} - \$5/\text{unit}} = 335,000 \text{ units}$$

5 A producer of calculator watches sells his product through a credit card firm at $30 each. The production costs at volumes of 10,000 and 25,000 units are as follows:

	10,000 units	25,000 units
Labor	$ 60,000	$100,000
Materials	120,000	200,000
Overhead (FC + VC)	90,000	110,000
Selling and administration	50,000	60,000
Depreciation and other FC	80,000	80,000
Total	$400,000	$550,000

Use the data to prepare a break-even chart and determine the BEP.

Solution

Note that the slope (that is, change in Y/change in X) of the total-cost line is the variable cost per unit:

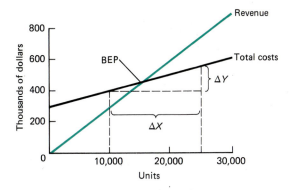

$$VC = \frac{\text{change in } Y}{\text{change in } X} = \frac{\Delta Y}{\Delta X} = \frac{\$550{,}000 - \$400{,}000}{25{,}000 - 10{,}000} = \$10/\text{unit}$$

By subtracting 10,000 units of variable cost from the total cost at 10,000 units, we can evaluate the implied fixed cost as follows:

$$FC = \text{total cost @ } 10{,}000 \text{ vol} - (10{,}000 \text{ units})(\text{variable cost/unit})$$

$$= \$400{,}000 - (\$10/\text{unit})(10{,}000 \text{ units})$$

$$= \$400{,}000 - \$100{,}000 = \$300{,}000$$

$$\therefore V_{BEP} = \frac{FC}{P - VC} = \frac{\$300{,}000}{(\$30 - \$10)/\text{unit}} = 15{,}000 \text{ units}$$

STATISTICAL MODELS

6 *Bayes' rule.* Let θ represent the probability of defective wiring and A represent an accidental fire. In a large old factory, spot checks have established that $P(\theta) = .20$. Given that a plant has defective wiring, the probability of a fire occurring at some time during the year is .7 (that is, $P(A|\theta) = .7$); and if the wiring is not defective, the chance of a fire is reduced to .1 (that is, $P(A|\overline{\theta}) = .1$). A recent fire burned one employee severely and caused $90,000 damage. Although evidence is destroyed, the operations manager has been asked by an insurance company to estimate the likelihood that the fire was caused by defective wiring.

Solution

$$P(\theta) = .2 \quad \text{thus} \quad P(\overline{\theta}) = 1 - .2 = .8$$

$$P(A|\theta) = .7 \quad \text{thus} \quad P(\overline{A}|\theta) = 1 - .7 = .3$$

$$P(A|\overline{\theta}) = .1 \quad \text{thus} \quad P(\overline{A}|\overline{\theta}) = 1 - .1 = .9$$

We wish to find the probability of defective wiring θ given the occurrence of the recent fire A. Using Bayes' rule we have:

$$P(\theta|A) = \frac{P(\theta)P(A|\theta)}{P(\theta)P(A|\theta) + P(\bar{\theta})P(A|\bar{\theta})} = \frac{(.2)(.7)}{(.2)(.7) + (.8)(.1)} = .64 \text{ or } 64 \text{ percent chance}$$

7 *Discrete data.* Use Example 2-5 data: $n = 200$, $\pi = .15$, $p = .18$. If the population proportion is $\pi = .15$, what is the probability of getting a random sample of $p = .18$ or more?

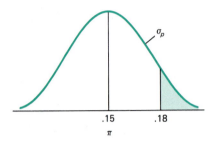

.15   .18
π

Solution

This requires use of the normal distribution tables.

First, we must determine the value of the standard error as computed from the (assumed) true value of π. Because we know π, we can compute σ_p instead of its estimate, s_p.

$$\sigma_p = \sqrt{\frac{\pi(1 - \pi)}{n}} = \sqrt{\frac{(.15)(.85)}{200}}$$

$$= .025 = 2.5\%$$

Second, we determine how many standard normal deviates, Z, the sample statistic $(p = .18)$ is from the population parameter $(\pi = .15)$. We do this by dividing the difference $(p - \pi)$ by the amount of one standard error (σ_p).

$$Z = \frac{p - \pi}{\sigma_p} = \frac{.18 - .15}{.025} = 1.19$$

Third, we look up this value of Z in the normal distribution table to find the area between the mean and Z = 1.19. From Appendix C, the area is .3830.

Fourth, because we seek the probability above .18, we subtract the value of .3830 from .5000, which is one-half the area of the distribution.

$$P(p > .18) = .5000 - .3830 = .1170$$

Conclusion: The chance of getting a random sample of $p = .18$ or more is nearly 12 percent.

8 *Continuous data.* Ten samples of the time to perform two successive activities on a television assembly line were taken. The frequency distribution for station B is as shown. For station B find (a) $\bar{x}$, (b) s, and (c) $s_{\bar{x}}$. (d) Suppose that a larger sample (say 30

or more) revealed that the time distribution for station A has a mean of $\bar{x} = 4.3$ minutes and a standard deviation of $s = .1$ minute. If A's and B's activities are both normally distributed, will B be able to keep pace with A? Assume that no storage ahead of B is permitted.

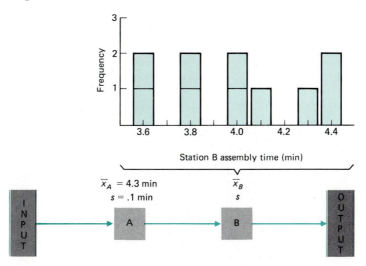

Station B assembly time (min)

$\bar{x}_A = 4.3$ min
$s = .1$ min

$\bar{x}_B$
s

Solution

(a) $\bar{x} = \dfrac{\Sigma X}{n} = \dfrac{3.6 + 3.6 + 3.8 + 3.8 + 4.0 + 4.0 + 4.1 + 4.3 + 4.4 + 4.4}{10} = 4.0$

(b) $s = \sqrt{\dfrac{\Sigma(X - \bar{x})^2}{n - 1}} = \sqrt{\dfrac{(3.6 - 4)^2 + (3.6 - 4)^2 + \cdots + (4.4 - 4)^2}{10 - 1}} = .3$ min

(c) $s_{\bar{x}} = \dfrac{s}{\sqrt{n}} = \dfrac{.3}{\sqrt{10}} = .095$

(d) On the average, station B completes the task faster than station A (4.0 minutes versus 4.3 minutes), so it would appear that B could easily keep pace with A.

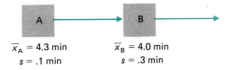

$\bar{x}_A = 4.3$ min
$s = .1$ min

$\bar{x}_B = 4.0$ min
$s = .3$ min

However, B has considerably more deviation, as evidenced by a comparison of the standard deviations (.1 minute for A versus .3 minute for B). As shown by the sketch below, 50 percent of A's work will be completed in less than 4.3 minutes. Station B will be unable to keep pace with all this because 15.87 percent of its work will exceed 4.3 minutes.

Note: The 4.3 minutes is 1 standard deviation (Z unit) away from B's mean of 4.0 on the normal distribution as measured by the following expression:

$$Z = \frac{X - \bar{x}}{s}$$

$$= \frac{4.3 - 4.0}{.3} = 1.00$$

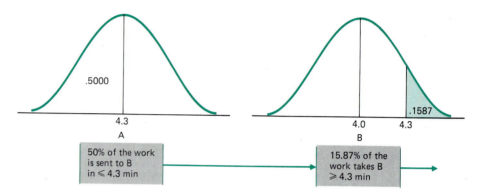

From Appendix C, the probability associated with Z = 1.00 is .3413, so the probability above 4.3 minutes is .5000 − .3413 = .1587, or 15.87 percent.

DECISION TREES

9   A manufacturer of small power tools is faced with foreign competition, which necessitates that she either modify (automate) her existing product or abandon it and market a new product. Regardless of which course of action she follows, she will have the opportunity to drop or raise prices if she experiences a low initial demand.

Payoff and probability values associated with the alternative courses of action are shown in Fig. 2-13. Analyze the decision tree and determine which course of action should be chosen to maximize the expected monetary value. (Assume monetary amounts are present-value profits.)

Solution
Analyze the tree from right to left by calculating the expected values for all possible courses of action and choosing the branch with the highest expected value. Begin with the top (modify product) branch.

At chance event 2

Drop price branch: $E(X) = \$20,000\,(.2) + \$150,000\,(.8) = \$124,000$
Raise price branch: $E(X) = \$40,000\,(.9) + \$200,000\,(.1) = \$56,000$

Therefore, choose to drop price and use $124,000 as the value of this branch at decision 2. *Note*: The $124,000 is an expected monetary value (EMV) and can be entered near the square box under decision 2. Place slash marks through the other (nonusable) alternative.

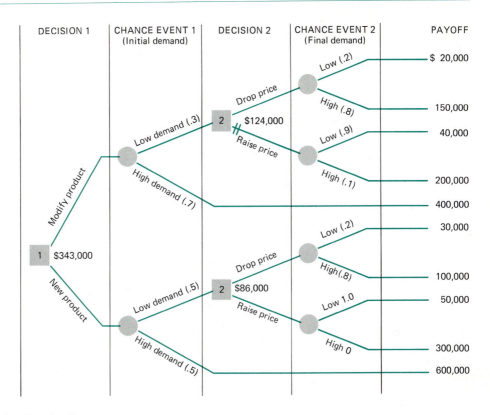

FIGURE 2-13   Decision Tree

At chance event 1

If low demand:	$124,000 (.3) =	$ 37,200
If high demand:	400,000 (.7) =	280,000
	E(X) =	$317,200

Therefore, use $317,200 as value of this branch at decision 1. Similarly, for the bottom (new product) branch, the values are $86,000 at decision 2 and $343,000 at decision 1. The new product branch thus has a higher expected value and is selected as the best course of action under the expected value criteria.

QUESTIONS

2-1   What support exists for the claim that management is a science?

2-2   Does the existence of values negate the validity of the decision-making process? Why or why not?

2-3   How do the characteristics of the decision situation affect the choice of a technique to use in decision analysis?

2-4   What factors contribute most to the complexity of a decision situation?

2-5   Select a business decision situation, and work through the analytical framework for decisions as given in the chapter. Write out each step and the corresponding element in your example.

2-6 What is a model, and how does it relate to the scientific decision-making system?

2-7 Would you always prefer decision making under complete certainty to decision making using sample or subjective information? Illustrate your answer with an example.

2-8 What assumptions underlie the basic break-even point analysis (under certainty)?

2-9 In what type of industry would you expect to find a relatively high versus low contribution?

2-10 Distinguish between a priori, empirical, and subjective probabilities.

2-11 What is the difference between discrete and continuous distributions?

2-12 Why is an understanding of the use of the normal probability distribution so important for operations analysis? Is it because all production activities follow a normal pattern?

2-13 What is the difference between the standard error of proportion and the standard error of the mean?

2-14 Does the expected monetary value criterion (EMV*) always provide the decision maker with the best course of action? Explain.

2-15 What kinds of decision situations are particularly well suited to analysis by the use of decision trees?

PROBLEMS[4]

1 The owners of a professional hockey team have leased a 30,000-seat stadium for six games for a fixed cost of $840,000. They expect variable costs to run $2 per spectator and tickets will sell for an average of $12 each. How many tickets, on average, must be sold per game for the owners to just break even?

2 A copier company plans to produce 30,000 copiers next year. They will sell for $700 each. The fixed costs of operation are $5 million and total variable costs are $6 million. What is the break-even point?

3 An audiodisk player sells for $350 and has a variable cost of $85.
(a) Find the contribution.
(b) Find the contribution ratio.

4 Taiwan Shoe Company produces 12,000 pairs of running shoes per month. Annual fixed costs are $420,000 and the contribution from each pair is 60 percent of their $10 per-unit selling price. Find the break-even volume.

5 Hibernia Airlines offers customers a vacation plan for $520. The airline estimates that the fixed costs associated with this plan are $720,000 and at a volume of 3,000 passengers, total variable costs would be $480,000 and profits should be $360,000.
(a) Find the break-even volume.
(b) If fixed costs remained constant, how many additional passengers (beyond break-even) would be required to increase profits to $500,000?

6 Florida Packing Company packages orange juice in 16-ounce cans which they sell to

[4] Problems marked ⌨ can be done *either* by hand calculation or by a microcomputer software program. In this chapter, however, none of the problems is so long as to necessitate the use of a computer.

grocery distribution warehouses for $24 per case. The packing company has fixed costs of $162,000 and variable costs of $15 per case. The plant has a capacity of 50,000 cases per season.

(a) Find the contribution.

(b) How many cases must be sold to break even?

(c) What is the profit, or loss, if the plant operates at full capacity for the season?

7 Given the break-even chart of Fig. 2-14,

(a) For a 300-unit output, what are the appropriate FC, TVC, and profit?

(b) What is the BEP?

(c) How would you explain the step increase in the TC line?

8 Shosmere Electronics has the capacity to produce 30,000 networking devices per year at a plant in Holland. Their variable costs are $12 per unit. They are currently operating at 80 percent of plant capacity, which generates a revenue of $720,000 per year. At current volume, the fixed costs are $360,000.

(a) What is the current annual profit or loss?

(b) What is the break-even quantity?

(c) What would be the firm's profit if they could operate at 95 percent of capacity?

9 Product X sells for $100 each and Y sells for $120 each. Product X has fixed costs of $20,000 per year and variable costs of $12 per unit, whereas product Y has fixed costs of $8,000 and variable costs of $40 per unit. At what production rate (volume) are the profits from both products equal?

10 Great Falls Export Company has 30 employees and handles 1500 loads per year of grain from a North Dakota warehouse. The firm has fixed costs of $70,000 per year and variable costs of $170 per load. The operations manager is considering installing an $80,000 automated material handling system that will increase fixed costs by $20,000 per year. It will also increase the per unit contribution of each load by $20. The firm operates 250 days per year, and they receive an average of $300 revenue for each load passed through the warehouse.

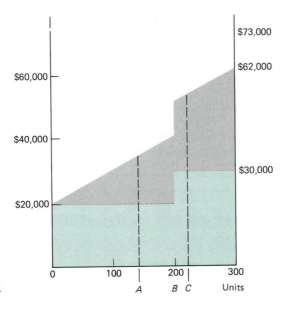

FIGURE 2-14

(a) What is the current annual profit (or loss)?

(b) What is the new BEP volume if the investment is made?

11 Data for a break-even analysis revealed that total costs at volumes of 600 and 800 units were $80,000 and $96,000, respectively. Revenue is $144 per unit. Based upon this information, what are (a) the variable costs per unit, and (b) the fixed costs?

12 Precast Pools, Inc. sells their product for $3,000 each. At a volume of 20 units, their labor, materials, overhead, and other costs total $60,000, and at a volume of 40 units, the total is $80,000.

(a) What is your best estimate of the variable cost per unit?

(b) Estimate the fixed costs.

(c) At what volume does the firm break even?

(d) Estimate the profit at a volume of 60 units.

13 Two assembly robots (X and Y), each working at the same rate, together produce 400 environmental filters per day. During a recent day, 40 filters were defective. Given that a filter is defective, there is a .40 probability it was produced by robot X (that is, $P(X|D) = .40$). What is the probability that a filter selected at random is:

(a) Defective?

(b) Produced by robot Y?

(c) Defective *and* produced by robot X?

(d) Defective *or* produced by robot X?

14 Boone Avenue Bottling Company has three soft drink bottling lines that have not been filling bottles accurately. A study of one order of 800 filled bottles revealed the following:

	Number of Bottles Filled by Machine			
	X	Y	Z	Total
Correctly filled	270	138	302	710
Incorrectly filled	30	12	48	90
Total	300	150	350	800

(a) Suppose a bottle is selected randomly from the shipment. What is the probability it was either produced by machine Z or is correctly filled?

(b) Is the probability of selecting a correctly filled bottle independent of the bottling machine that filled it?

15 An inventory control worker at a defense contractor's factory has received some unmarked arm support brackets for the left and right front doors of a military vehicle and cannot easily tell them apart. Neither can he distinguish the type of mounting (that is, A, B, or C). With this shipment, there are actually 500 brackets (total) on hand, in quantities as follows:

	Type A	Type B	Type C
Right front brackets	264	0	36
Left front brackets	152	45	3

The inventory clerk receives an urgent call for a right front bracket, type A, randomly selects a bracket from the bin that contains them all, and rushes it to the shop.

(a) What is the probability that he sends the correct bracket?

(b) Suppose the clerk could identify the type of mounting but not whether it was for a right or left door. What would be the probability of a correct choice in this case?

16   A Ridgeview City transit study of 37 observations of peak load on a certain bus route has shown that the load is normally distributed with a mean demand of 114 passengers and $\Sigma(X - \bar{x})^2 = 2,304$. If the transit operations office plans to supply two buses, each with a 62-person capacity, what percentage of the potential passengers will not be accommodated by this city service?

17   Arkansas Snack Company produces dried meats for marketing in supermarkets. A production inspector in the plant has obtained a random sample of 64 packages of a large shipment bound for Memphis. The true (but unknown) average weight of packages in the shipment is 3.20 ounces, but the sample mean shows only 3.16 ounces, and $s = .16$ ounce.

(a) Is this data discrete or continuous?

(b) What is the value of the standard error of the mean?

(c) Knowing that the true average weight is 3.20 ounces, what is the probability of obtaining a sample mean of ≤ 3.16 ounces in a random sample of 64?

18   The McDonnell Bank and Trust Company operations officer is concerned that her tellers may be idle about 20 percent of the time. She made a study to find out if her hypothesis was correct. In a random sample of 385 observations, tellers were idle 85 times. If the true proportion of idle time was 20 percent, what is the likelihood she would get a sample of $p = .22$ or more?

19   A Transcontinent Airlines baggage clerk was interested in estimating the baggage weight their customers take on flights from Boston to Phoenix. She selected 10 passengers at random and recorded the following weights.

Customer No.	1	2	3	4	5	6	7	8	9	10
Baggage, lb	29	38	18	40	43	35	22	34	44	39

Find (a) $\bar{x}$, (b) s, and (c) $s_{\bar{x}}$

20   National Cereal Mills is considering research into a dog food product that expands when it is microwaved prior to serving. The chances of success are estimated to be 75 percent. If successful, the firm would improve profits by $4 million. If unsuccessful, the result would be a $6 million loss. Should the firm forgo the research and stay with their traditional product line, their profit would depend on how their competition advertises. If competitive advertising is down, profits would be $6 million; if the same, they would be $2 million; and if up, −$2 million. The respective probabilities are down = .2, same = .4, and up = .4.

(a) Draw a decision tree of this situation.

(b) Compute the expected monetary value (EMVs) and identify the best action on an EMV basis.

21   Long-range planners of Mountain Electric Co. have forecast the need to add 200 megawatts of power to their system in year 5. They must decide between a solar plant that will cost about $150 million and a coal-fired plant that will cost 20 percent less. Both plants would have a 20-year life. Construction of a solar plant would require

public approval, but management feels there is a good probability (.9) of obtaining this. If the plant is not approved, the utility will still have incurred an engineering fee of 5 percent of the estimated cost in the second year and will have to purchase the necessary power from another utility at a cost of $12 million a year.

If power demand is heavy and the solar plant can operate at base load, operating costs (not including depreciation) are estimated at $4 million a year. However, planners feel that there is a 40 percent chance the plant will have to operate at cycle load, which will increase operating costs by 10 percent.

Should the firm decide on a coal-fired plant, operating costs are expected to be $5 million a year, unless additional costs for pollution control prove inevitable. Unsatisfactory air filters could cost the utility an additional $10 million in the third year after the plant comes on-line. Management feels that there is a 50:50 chance this will occur and requests some guidance in making the choice between a solar or coal-fired plant. Use a decision tree along with accompanying financial data to help identify the appropriate decision, based on an expected value criterion. (Do not convert to present value figures for this exercise.)

REFERENCES

[1] Brown, Carl, Joseph G. Monks, and James R. Park, *Decision Making in Water Resource Allocation*, Lexington Books, Lexington, MA, 1973.
[2] Browning, E. S.: "Japanese Triumph: Sony's Perseverance Helped It Win Market For Mini-CD Players," *The Wall Street Journal*, Feb. 27, 1986, p. 1.

SELF QUIZ: CHAPTER 2

Part I True/False [1 point each = 6]

1 _____ One justification (basis) for viewing management as a science is that empirical data is used in the decision process.
2 _____ Managers who make decisions consistent with their own value systems cannot be following a scientific framework.
3 _____ Models should not necessarily try to duplicate all aspects of reality.
4 _____ In the decision-making process, alternatives are generated by varying the values of the parameters.
5 _____ When a product that sells for $600 has a contribution that is 70 percent of its selling price, its variable cost is $180.
6 _____ If a firm bidding on two contracts estimates their chance on A as .60 and on B as .25, then their chance of either A or B is .85.

Part II Problems [3 point each = 9. Calculate and select your answer.]

1 Last year a maufacturer produced 15,000 audiodisk players which sold for $300 each. At that volume, the fixed costs were $1.52 million and total variable costs were $2.10 million. What was the break-even quantity?
   (a) 4,000
   (b) 7,800
   (c) 8,400
   (d) 9,500
   (e) None of the above

2 An appliance assembly line moves electric clothes dryers through a motor installation area at the rate of 1 every 2 minutes. The average time required to install a motor is 1.77 minutes with a standard deviation of .14 minutes. If installation times are normally distributed and no storage is allowed, what percent of the motor installations would not be completed on time?
   (a) 1 percent
   (b) 5 percent
   (c) 8 percent
   (d) 12 percent
   (e) None of the above

3 A productivity study offered two alternatives for improvement: (1) purchase a new machine that would improve profits by $80,000, or (2) initiate a training program that would, if highly successful, ($p = .6$), result in a $110,000 improvement, and if moderately successful, ($p = .3$) result in a $60,000 improvement. If unsuccessful, the program would result in a $40,000 loss. Using decision tree and expected value concepts, the expected value of the optimal course of action is:
   (a) $44,000
   (b) $80,000
   (c) $84,000
   (d) $110,000
   (e) None of the above

CHAPTER 3
SYSTEMS DESIGN, CAPACITY, AND INVESTMENT

71-80

INTRODUCTION

Before products can "flow" into a market, someone must design and invest in the facilities and organization to produce them. This chapter concerns the planning and financing of systems needed to produce goods and services. Subsequent chapters deal with the location and layout of facilities (Chapter 4), the products produced and processes used (Chapter 5), and the management of the work force (Chapter 6).

In this chapter, we address the size, timing, and capital investment questions posed in Fig. 3-1. The schematic tree diagram shows three alternative plant sizes, along with some options and associated costs for bringing additional capacity online. For example, if a medium-sized plant is chosen, it can either be brought fully online in year 3 or phased in partly during year 2 and partly during year 3. The size and timing decisions do, of course, have a significant effect on capital requirements.

After pointing out some differences between manufacturing and service system capacities, we examine the relationship of design and system capacity to actual output. This examination includes an example of how to estimate the amount of equipment needed to deliver the planned production. Then we take up some approaches to long-term and short-term capacity planning. Finally, we review some methods that managers use to help decide which personnel or equipment investments make the best use of the firm's capital funds. These techniques are payback, present value, equivalent annual cost, and rate of return.

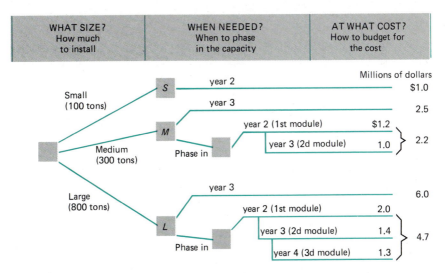

FIGURE 3-1   Some Major Considerations in a Capacity Decision

MANUFACTURING AND SERVICE SYSTEMS

Manufacturing and service systems are arrangements of facilities, equipment, and people designed to produce goods and services under controlled conditions.

Manufacturing systems often produce standardized products in large volumes. The plant and machinery have a finite capacity and constitute *fixed* costs that must be borne by the products produced. *Variable* costs are added as labor is employed to combine or process the raw materials and other components. The physical product is thus a store of the value added during the production process. Because actual costs can be measured, the value of the outputs relative to the cost of inputs (that is, productivity) can be determined with some precision.

Service systems present more uncertainty with respect to both capacity and costs. Services are often produced and consumed in the presence of the customer, and there is little or no opportunity to store value, as in a finished goods inventory. As a result, the capacity of hospitals, restaurants, and many other services must be sufficiently flexible (or consciously managed) to accommodate a highly variable demand. In addition, many services (such as legal and medical) involve professional or intellectual judgments that are not easily standardized. This makes it more difficult to accumulate costs and measure the productivity of services.

Nevertheless, both manufacturing and service systems must be designed with capacity limitations in mind. And both must provide a satisfactory return on the invested capital (or benefit for each tax dollar spent in the case of public services). Otherwise the organization will not remain economically viable.

DESIGN AND SYSTEMS CAPACITY

Production systems design involves planning for the inputs, transformation activities, and outputs of a production operation. Design decisions are far-reaching because (1) they often entail a significant investment of funds, and (2) they establish cost and productivity patterns that continue far into the future. So they affect both fixed and variable costs.

DESIGN CAPACITY

Preliminary estimates of capacity typically come from long-range forecasts that may project demands as much as 5 or 10 years into the future. Long-range projections help ensure that the demand is not just temporary, and they also allow enough lead time for construction of major facilities.

The *design capacity* of a facility is the planned (engineered) rate of output of goods or services under normal, or full-scale, operating conditions. For example, a mill may be designed to accept 300 tons per day of lead-zinc ore, or a new university may need enough classrooms and staff to accommodate 6,000 students.

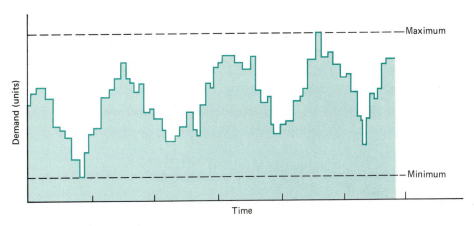

FIGURE 3-2   Demand-Capacity Relationships

The uncertainty of future demand is one of the most perplexing problems facing new-facility planners. Steel companies are uncertain of the demand for steel from automobile manufacturers, universities are uncertain of the future enrollments, and hospital administrators hope everyone doesn't become ill at the same time. Although some trends in demand may be evident, seasonal and cyclical factors often generate swings in demand, and random events cause unexpected fluctuations. As a result, demand over time may appear as depicted in Fig. 3-2.

Organizations do not necessarily plan for enough capacity to satisfy all their immediate demand. If an airline maintained enough regular capacity to meet its holiday peak demands, its airplanes (capital equipment) and personnel would not be utilized very effectively during the remainder of the year. On the other hand, although a design for minimum demand would result in high utilization of facilities (and no fluctuations in employment), inadequate capacity might also result in inferior service and dissatisfied or lost customers. The design capacity should reflect management's strategy for meeting demand. Very often, the best approach is to plan for some in-between level of capacity, that is, a happy medium. Expected value techniques can be useful here.

EXAMPLE 3-1

Freddie's Fast Foods has enjoyed considerable success by using call-box ordering stations and multilane service channels. Freddie's can serve 32 cars per hour in one lane of its drive-thrus. Now they are planning for a new drive-thru facility in Sacramento. Market research data suggests it may have the peak hourly demands estimated below.

	Number of Cars per Hour				
	0 < 40	*40 < 80*	*80 < 120*	*120 < 160*	*160 < 200*
Probability (% Chance)	.10	.35	.40	.13	.02
Cumulative Probability	.10	.45	.85	.98	1.00

The operations manager is considering two alternatives for deciding how much capacity to install. What capacity is required to (a) meet 85 percent of the estimated *peak* hourly demands, and (b) accommodate 110 percent of the estimated *average* demand plus a 25 percent allowance for growth?

SOLUTION

(a) From the cumulative probability row, 85 percent of the estimated demands is less than 120 cars. Therefore:

$$\text{Number of lanes} = \frac{\text{total capacity}}{\text{lane capacity}} = \frac{120 \text{ cars/hr}}{32 \text{ cars/hr-lane}} = 3.75, \text{ say 4 lanes}$$

(b) For average demand we can use $E(X) = \Sigma[XP(X)]$, where the X value is represented by the midpoint of each class interval:

$$E(X) = 20(.10) + 60(.35) + 100(.40) + 140(.15) + 180(.02) = 88 \text{ cars}$$

$$\text{Base-level capacity} = 110\%(88) = 97 \text{ cars/hr}$$

Add for 25 percent allowance:

$$97 + .25(97) = 121 \text{ cars/hr}$$

$$\text{Number of lanes} = \frac{\text{total capacity}}{\text{lane capacity}} = \frac{121 \text{ cars/hr}}{32 \text{ cars/hr-lane}} = 3.8, \text{ say 4 lanes}$$

It appears that having four service lanes will satisfy both criteria.

SYSTEM CAPACITY

System capacity is the maximum output of a specific product or product mix that the system of workers and machines is capable of producing as an integrated whole. It is typically less than or equal to the design capacity of the individual components because the system may be limited by the product mix, quality specifications, or the current balance of equipment and labor. The actual output may be even less, for it is affected by short-range factors such as actual demand, equipment breakdowns, and personnel absences or productivity. For example, output at General Motors ultramodern Hamtramck (Michigan) assembly plant was only 30 to 35 cars per hour for the first several months of operation—much less than the 60 per hour design capacity [2]. Problems stemmed from coordinating the sophisticated machinery and automatic guided vehicles. (The plant has 260 robots for welding, assembling, and painting cars, and the software that controlled them wasn't properly debugged. So at times the robots even spray painted each other instead of the cars.)

Figure 3-3 illustrates the relationships among design capacity, system capac-

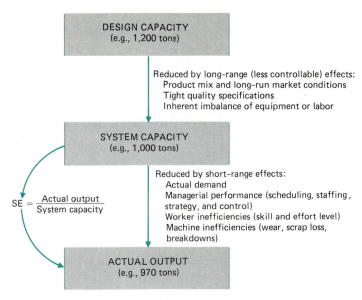

FIGURE 3-3   Relationship between Capacities and Output

ity, and actual output. Note that the ratio of the actual measured output of goods or services to the system capacity is referred to as the *system efficiency* (SE).

$$\text{SE} = \frac{\text{actual output}}{\text{system capacity}} \tag{3-1}$$

EXAMPLE 3-2   A chemical processor has been making a white plastic compound for dishwear on a continuous basis by processing it through a series of four tanks (for mixing, heating, molding, and cooling) at a rate of 50 gallons of chemical per minute. The firm now plans to produce different colored plastic compounds on the same equipment. However, the individual capacities of the tanks will then be limited because of the time needed for cleanout, different temperature requirements, and other factors. If the individual capacities (in gal/min) and actual output for new operations are as shown below, what is (a) the system capacity and (b) the system efficiency?

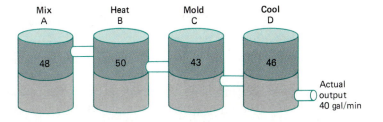

SOLUTION

(a) System capacity = capacity of most limited component in the line
$$= 43 \text{ gal/min}$$

(b) System efficiency SE $= \dfrac{\text{actual output}}{\text{system capacity}} = \dfrac{40}{43} = 93\%$

The next section uses the relationships expressed in Fig. 3-3 to illustrate how the capacity requirements for specific plant equipment can be calculated.

DETERMINATION OF EQUIPMENT REQUIREMENTS

When the actual output requirements from a system are known, the amount or size of equipment required to deliver that output can be determined by "working backward" to allow for normal system inefficiencies. Capacity limitations are often stated in terms of equipment efficiencies or an amount of scrap loss. For example, if the ordinary scrap loss is 3 percent, then the system efficiency is only 97 percent. And the required system capacity can be determined by dividing .97 into the actual output required. Dividing this system capacity by the individual machine capacity yields the number of machines required.

EXAMPLE 3-3

A metals processing firm wishes to install enough automatic molders to produce 250,000 good castings per year. The molding operation takes 1.5 minutes per casting, but its output is typically about 3 percent defective. How many molders will be required if each one is available for 2,000 hours (of capacity) per year?

SOLUTION

$$\text{Required system capacity} = \frac{\text{actual (good) output}}{\text{SE}}$$

$$= \frac{250,000}{.97} = 257,732 \text{ units/yr}$$

$$= \frac{257,732 \text{ units/yr}}{2,000 \text{ hr/yr}} = 129 \text{ units/hr}$$

$$\text{Individual machine capacity} = \frac{60 \text{ min/hr}}{1.5 \text{ machine min/unit}} = 40 \text{ units/machine hr}$$

$$\text{Number of machines required} = \frac{129 \text{ units/hr}}{40 \text{ units/machine hr}} = 3.2 \text{ machines}$$

The firm should probably plan for the installation of four machines. However, with careful scheduling, off-shift maintenance, or a small amount of overtime, it might be able to handle the small overload and get by with three machines.

CAPACITY PLANNING

Capacity was defined earlier as a measure of the ability to produce, or serve, that is, having enough worker or equipment *time* to do the job. More informally, capacity is often referred to as a rate of output (for example, number of customers per hour, gallons per minute, labor hours per week, or units per day). A less acceptable measure is in monetary terms (such as $40,000 per week) because price changes do not necessarily reflect volume changes. However, dollar volumes are frequently the best (aggregate) measure of capacity for firms producing a wide range of products.

Regardless of the measure, capacity expresses some bounds on the organization's ability to produce. And although we tend to focus on the "maximum" capacities, remember that minimum operating levels are equally important because volumes below the break-even point are not sufficient to cover the fixed and variable costs of operation.

Capacity planning is concerned with defining the long- and short-term capacity needs of the organization and determining how those needs will be satisfied. Figure 3-4 depicts this interaction in a conceptual sense. Notice that capacity decisions must merge consumer demands (from the market) with the human, material, and financial resources of the organization.

LONG-TERM CAPACITY STRATEGIES

Top management decisions to develop new product lines, expand existing facilities, and construct or phase out production plants can have a significant impact on capacity. They also take a long time to implement—often more than a year. *Long-term capacity planning* is concerned with accommodating major changes that affect the *overall level* of output in the longer term. Assessing the market environ-

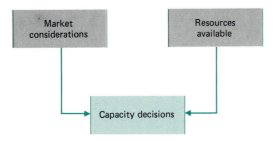

FIGURE 3-4   Inputs to Capacity Decisions

ment and implementing long-term capacity plans in an orderly and effective way are major (strategic) responsibilities of management.

Multiple Products   Firms typically produce more than one type of product in the same facilities. By doing so they increase the opportunities for profit and diminish the risks from failure of one of the products. Having more than one product also enables capacity planners to do a better job. This is because most products pass through a "life cycle" wherein demand is slow at first, rises (perhaps rapidly) to maturity, and then gradually tapers off. By scheduling the introduction of new products while other products are in the growth and maturity stages, planners can maintain a higher overall utilization of their capacity.

Phasing In Capacity   Firms in some high-technology industries face a unique capacity-planning problem. The pace of new developments forces them to get products onto the market very quickly, before they become obsolete. In some cases, the time required to construct a factory may be longer than the "technological window" or time frame within which their production decisions must be implemented. Some firms convert old warehouses or rent available space. Established firms like Hewlett-Packard sometimes commit funds and people to facilities over a 3- or 5-year time span into the future, without even knowing specifically what products will be produced in those plants. Then they phase in portions of the capacity on a modular (or partial) basis as new products become available. This can be an effective way of capitalizing on technological breakthroughs without tying up an excessive amount of capital at an early stage.

Phasing in new technology can be risky, however, as suggested above. At one of Ford's "factories of the future" the computer-controlled machinery was so sophisticated that workers couldn't operate it properly, even after they had months of training. The plant's body-assembly area manager observed that "it's just part of installing significant automation. The mistake we made is putting in all these technologies at once" [2]. A General Motors plant also experienced significant capacity reduction when phasing in some vision-equipped robots that were being used to install windshields. The robots were pushing too hard while putting in the glass (Crash!) because their vision system lacked the proper depth perception [2].

Phasing Out Capacity   As mines, mills, and outdated manufacturing facilities face growing competitive pressures, communities can also be faced with disruptive layoffs and plant closings. For example, analysts predict that 10 to 20 percent of the existing U.S. and Canadian car-assembly plants will be closed during the next few years.

> And every assembly plant that closes during the next five years will take with it factories that make components ranging from seats to bumpers to pistons—a disappearing act that would cost thousands of people their jobs [1].

In the past, capacity planners have concerned themselves primarily with having the equipment installed and trained personnel ready to start up plants when they were scheduled to go online. Today, as firms face more intense domestic and international competition, planners must also know how to *phase out* operations that are no longer competitive. And some plant closure decisions come rather suddenly, especially in high-tech industries.

The impacts of plant closures are not limited to the fixed costs of the plant and equipment involved. Skilled and unskilled employees are made "redundant," and whole communities may suffer unexpectedly high social and economic costs. An increasing number of firms are accepting (or being forced to accept) the social responsibility of phasing out major operations in a "humanistic" way. This may mean retraining workers for other jobs, offering to move them to different locations, or compensating the local community in other ways. In some cases, companies even assist employees to assume ownership of the plant if the takeover has prospects of success, either because the new owners will accept lower wage costs or productivity improvements can be made which were previously unacceptable to the local unions.

SHORT-TERM CAPACITY STRATEGIES

In the shorter-term planning horizon, capacity concerns involve the fluctuations in demand caused by seasonal and economic factors. *Short-term capacity planning* is concerned with responding to relatively immediate (explained and unexplained) *variations* in demand. Manufacturing and service-oriented firms adjust to the ups and downs of demand in many different ways.

Manufacturing firms with sufficient equipment capacity may use overtime or a second or third shift to meet a temporarily strong demand. Or they may route the work to alternate processes or subcontract it to other firms. Many firms simply accumulate inventories during seasons of slack demand. We shall do some economic analysis of these alternatives in a later chapter.

Service industries tend to rely more heavily on work scheduling and strategies aimed at shifting demand to suit their capacity. Restaurants and hospitals frequently use *flexible work hours*, *part-time employees*, and *overtime work scheduling* to meet peaks in demand. Professional services such as medical and dental offices use an *appointment system* to smooth out demand. Some capital-intensive services such as subway systems and airlines accomplish the same thing by adopting a *fixed service schedule*. This arrangement forces the customers to adapt to the system's capacity. Other services, such as appliance repair services, simply use *queues* and delay the delivery of the service until they can produce it with their regular work force. Of course, numerous combinations of these and other strategies are in use.

Having discussed the amount of capacity needed and the phasing in (or out) of that capacity, we conclude now with some techniques for making the best economic choice from among alternative investments in capacity. The investment evaluation methods we take up now are, nevertheless, quite general. They will be used for other economic analysis in the remainder of the text as well.

CAPITAL BUDGETING AND ANALYSIS[1]

Capital is a resource of funds owned or used by an organization. When funds are proposed for a new facility or equipment, the proposal is usually reviewed by a budget committee and given a technical, market, and financial evaluation. If the proposal is feasible, the capital requirements are planned for in the organization's capital budget.

A *capital budget* is a financial plan that shows the expected *sources* and *uses* of funds for some designated time period into the future. External sources of funds are capital stock (equity) and loans (debt) or taxes (for nonprofit organizations). The major internal source is retained earnings from profits generated in the past.

The proposed uses of funds typically exceed the available sources, so a careful evaluation of alternative uses is necessary. In this evaluation, both the *timing* and *quantity* of cash flows are important. Cash is not a static resource: funds have an earning power over time, that is, a sum today is worth more than the same sum at some point in the future. The money could be invested or loaned out at an interest rate that would generate an even greater sum in the future. This earning capacity, therefore, has to be taken into account in choosing among various investment alternatives.

INTEREST AND PRESENT-VALUE CONCEPTS

Interest is, of course, the cost of money or the rental rate for funds. Interest rates are determined by the availability of capital funds in the economy, the alternative opportunities investors enjoy to use those funds, and the risk of loss the lenders must take. Funds used in very safe investments involve little risk of loss and can usually be obtained at a moderate cost. Funds used in more speculative ventures typically offer a greater potential earning power, but the borrower must compensate the lender for the greater risk of loss by paying a higher rate of interest. Thus the risk, along with economic conditions in general, helps establish a basic interest rate.

If you were to invest $1,000 at 12 percent interest for 1 year, you would have earned ($1,000)(12%/yr)(1 yr) or $120 interest by the end of the first year. Your new total would be $1,120. During the second year, the 12 percent interest on the larger total would yield $134.40 interest as a result of *compounding*, or interest gained on the earlier interest. If i represents the interest rate, P the present value,

---

[1] Capital budgeting and investment evaluation techniques are often taught in financial management courses, so some instructors may choose not to assign this material or to designate it as optional. For reference, see [3].

and F the future sum after n years, we can express the future sum F of any present value P as:

$$F = P(1 + i)^n \tag{3-2}$$

Substituting into this equation, you could readily confirm the value of F as ($\$1,000$) $(1 + .12)^2$, or $\$1,254.40$.

Equation 3-2 can easily be modified to solve for the present value P of the future sum F, *discounted* (reduced in value back to the present) at an interest rate i for n periods:

$$P = \frac{F}{(1 + i)^n} \tag{3-3}$$

The above expression can be restated in a convenient form:

$$P = F\frac{1}{(1 + i)^n} = F(\text{factor}) = F(\text{PV}_{sp})^{n\ \text{yr}}_{i\%} \tag{3-4}$$

where PV_{sp} is a certain factor for the present value of single payments made in n years if the interest rate is i percent. This PV_{sp} factor, when multiplied by the amount of the future payment, F, will yield a discounted present value amount, P. Appendix F contains PV_{sp} factors for payments of $\$1$ over a commonly used range of interest rate (i) and period (n) values. Many calculators are programmed to produce these factors directly, once the i and n values are specified.

EXAMPLE 3-4

What is the present value of the salvage on a piece of construction equipment if the salvage price 10 years from now is $\$9,000$ and if the cost of funds is 12 percent?

SOLUTION

$$P = F(\text{PV}_{sp})^{10\ \text{yr}}_{12\%}$$

$$= \$9,000(.322)$$

$$= \$2,898$$

On many occasions one must determine the present value or future sum of a series of equal payments made over n years when they are discounted or compounded at an interest rate i. These *equal sums paid* or *received regularly* are *annuities* and are designated as R or A. Appendix G contains present value factors for annuities (PV_a) of $\$1$. Thus, the present value of annuities can be determined in a manner similar to that used for single payments, except that the factor differs.

$$P = A(\text{PV}_a)^{n\ \text{yr}}_{i\%} \tag{3-5}$$

EXAMPLE 3-5

Find the present value of $100 paid at the end of each of 4 years, when the interest rate is 14 percent.

SOLUTION

$$P = A(PV_a)^{n\ \text{yr}}_{i\%}$$

$$= \$100(PV_a)^{4\ \text{yr}}_{14\%}$$

$$= \$100(2.914) = \$291.40$$

This means that the sum of $291.40 now is equivalent to annual payments of $100 at the end of each of 4 years if the interest rate is 14 percent. That is, if $291.40 were placed in a bank at 14 percent interest, sums of $100 could be withdrawn at the end of each of 4 years. With the fourth-year withdrawal of $100, the balance would be exactly zero.

Because interest is the price paid for the use of funds, the cost of funds to an organization will vary as the interest rate varies. In the United States, the prime interest rate, which is the "favorable" rate charged by lending institutions to large borrowers, has fluctuated from around 6 percent to over 20 percent during the past several years. With a high interest rate, future incomes (or expenses) of cash have a lower present value than when interest rates are lower. Thus the relative economic advantage of one project over another may very well change as the interest rate changes.

DEPRECIATION, TAXES, AND INFLATION

Depreciation and Taxes   When an investment is made in plant or equipment, cash is paid out at the time of purchase. However, the assets will be used to generate revenues over many years. *Depreciation* is an accounting procedure for reducing the value of an asset by gradually charging it off as an *expense* against the income it produces over its useful life. No cash actually flows out of the organization when this accounting entry is made. But the depreciation expense does reduce the reported profits and therefore affects the amount of taxes paid.

$$\text{Tax} = (\text{tax rate})(\text{income} - \text{expense}) \tag{3-6}$$

Although the total amount of depreciation write-off is ultimately the same, a faster (accelerated) write-off in early years reduces taxes in those early years and releases cash that can be invested in other projects. In this sense, depreciation is sometimes referred to as a *tax shield*.

The methods available to firms for depreciating production equipment can be classified as (a) use methods and (b) time methods. *Use methods* are typically based on the number of service hours expected from an asset. For example, if a machine cost $200,000 and was expected to produce 400,000 units, the depreciation rate would be $.50 per unit. Most tangible property is depreciated on a *time* basis, and the *time method* is strongly influenced by the tax liability involved. Probably the simplest approach is straight-line depreciation, where the value of the asset decreases at a constant rate over its life.

$$\text{Straight-line depreciation} = \frac{\text{investment} - \text{salvage}}{\text{life}} = \frac{I - S}{n} \qquad (3\text{-}7)$$

EXAMPLE 3-6

An investment of $60,000 in new equipment is expected to have a salvage value of $8,000 after a useful life of 5 years. What is the straight-line depreciation?

SOLUTION

$$\text{Depreciation} = \frac{I - S}{n} = \frac{\$60,000 - \$8,000}{5 \text{ yr}} = \$10,400/\text{yr}$$

For purposes of calculating taxable income, firms in the United States must compute depreciation on their plant and equipment in accordance with the applicable Internal Revenue Code. The principal methods used in the past include straight-line, double declining balance, and sum-of-the-years'-digits depreciation. For most tangible depreciable property placed in use after 1980, the capital cost was recovered according to the Accelerated Cost Recovery System (ACRS) specified by the Internal Revenue Code. Under that code, property is assigned a 3-, 5-, 10-, or 15-year recovery period and depreciated on an accelerated basis. However, legislative changes to the tax laws make it imperative that the currently approved methods be checked prior to making final tax calculations.

Fortunately, from a decision-making standpoint, the economic value or useful service life of an asset is more important than an arbitrary book value determined by a tax code. And straightforward estimates of depreciation are often satisfactory for making comparisons among investment alternatives.

Inflation Inflation makes future (expense and income) cash flows worth less in terms of today's dollars. This means that investments in plant capacity and inventories made today will tend to appreciate in value and be worth more in the inflated dollars of the future. It also means that inflated cash inflows in the future may not be sufficient to offset a cash outlay for an asset made today.

Inflation thus has the effect of reducing the future values of cash inflows beyond whatever discount rate the firm is using. For example, suppose a firm invests $100,000 cash today in expectation of a 20 percent per year return on an investment over the next several years. If 8 percent of the return is due to inflation, their effective rate is only 12 percent. On the other hand, if a firm borrows money to construct a plant today but pays its loan off with inflated dollars in the future, then the effective cost of the plant is reduced. Many investments require some cash down and future payments on the borrowed portion. In this situation, some inflation effect will be realized.

CAPITAL INVESTMENT EVALUATION TECHNIQUES

Capital resources always have alternative uses. A quantitative evaluation of the economic gains and/or losses of different alternatives can help decision makers select the use which most closely conforms with the organization's objectives.

Because operations activities have time, rate, and magnitude dimensions, a decision criterion which focuses on one aspect of investment to the exclusion of others may be inadequate—or even misleading. Thus, for two alternatives requiring different investment amounts, we might favor a project that offers a 35 percent rate of return over one offering 30 percent—until we found that the total magnitude of return on the first is $6,000, but $50,000 on the second. Similarly, a project that pays for itself in 3 years is not necessarily better than one that returns its cost in 4 years if the latter continues yielding a return over many more years in the future.

There are several criteria that are widely used to evaluate capital investments in production operations activities. While each method has its advantages and shortcomings, some are more appropriate than others in given situations. Many organizations have found that more than one technique of analysis is necessary to ensure that all dimensions of the decision alternatives are considered.

PAYBACK

Payback (payoff) tells the number of years for an investment to pay for itself.

$$\text{Payback} = \frac{\text{investment} - \text{salvage}}{\text{operating advantage/yr}} = \frac{I - S}{\text{OA/yr}} \tag{3-8}$$

The operating advantage (OA) reflects the improvement in cash flows from increased income or decreased expenses or both, as illustrated in Fig. 3-5. Note that it does not yet have depreciation expenses deducted from it. On the contrary, payback measures how quickly the savings will recoup the investment. In effect the denominator is a net cash flow figure resulting from increased earnings but no depreciation expense.

In its simplest form, payback does not consider salvage values or taxes. However, they can be included in the analysis by reducing the investment I by the value of any salvage S and subtracting any tax amounts from the operating advantage.

EXAMPLE 3-7 | National Insurance Company is considering the purchase of an information-processing system that will cost $27,000, last for 6 years, and have a guaran-

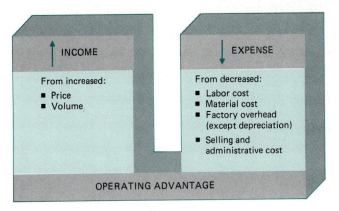

FIGURE 3-5   Components of Operating Advantage

teed $3,000 salvage value. It will generate savings of $11,000 per year (before depreciation) but necessitates that $3,000 of the savings be paid in taxes. If management insists on a 4-year, after-tax payback period, does this investment qualify?

SOLUTION

$$\text{Payback} = \frac{I - S}{OA/yr - tax} = \frac{\$27,000 - \$3,000}{(\$11,000 - \$3,000)/yr} = 3.0 \text{ yr}$$

The investment does meet the management criteria.

Payback is simple and quick to calculate, easy to understand, and a useful measure of the time required to return an original investment. However, it does not consider the economic life of the investment, the total return on investment, or the time value of money.

PRESENT VALUE

Present value tells the worth of future income or expense flows in terms of present dollars. These cash flows are typically the investment value, the maintenance and operating costs, and the income flows. The initial investment is usually already in present-value terms, so there is no need to consider its depreciation and interest changes. Operating expenses, however, do involve cash outlays in the future and must be discounted (reduced) to present values.

Present-value cost = PV investment + PV other costs − PV salvage

$$PV_{cost} = I(PV_{sp}) + \Sigma OC(PV_{sp}) - S(PV_{sp}) \tag{3-9}$$

Apics Aluminum is considering an investment of $20,000 in an environmental monitoring system that will have a salvage value of $6,000 after an economic life of 5 years. Maintenance and operating costs are $4,000 the first year and increase by $200 per year thereafter. The firm's cost of capital is 12 percent. What is the present-value cost of this investment?

SOLUTION

$$\text{Present-value cost} = \text{PV investment} + \text{PV other costs} - \text{PV salvage}$$

$$\text{PV investment} = I(PV_{sp})^{0\ yr}_{12\%} = \$20,000(1.00) = \$20,000$$

$$\text{PV other costs} = \Sigma\ OC(PV_{sp})^{n\ yr}_{12\%}$$

yr 1	($4,000)(.893) =	$3,572
yr 2	($4,200)(.797) =	3,347
yr 3	($4,400)(.712) =	3,133
yr 4	($4,600)(.636) =	2,926
yr 5	($4,800)(.567) =	2,722
		$15,700

$$ \underline{15,700}$$
$$\text{Total} \quad \$35,700$$

$$\text{Less: PV salvage} = -S(PV_{sp})^{5\ yr}_{12\%}$$

$$= -\$6,000(.567) = -3,402$$
$$\text{PV cost} \quad \$32,298$$

Present value considers the total return, includes time-value considerations, easily handles fluctuations in costs or revenues, and includes the effect of taxes, if applicable. However, it does not consider the rate of return or time for an investment to be paid off, and it assumes that cash inflows can be reinvested at the cost of capital. It is one of the most widely used techniques.

EQUIVALENT ANNUAL COST

Equivalent annual cost is a time-adjusted method of calculating an equal annual cost over the life of an investment. It permits nonuniform costs to be apportioned equally over the life of the investment, as depicted in Fig. 3-6. Thus it is especially useful for comparing projects with different economic lives because it offers comparable per-year figures.

The equivalent annual-cost method discounts and compounds cost amounts at a specified interest rate in such a way as to convert them all into annuity amounts.

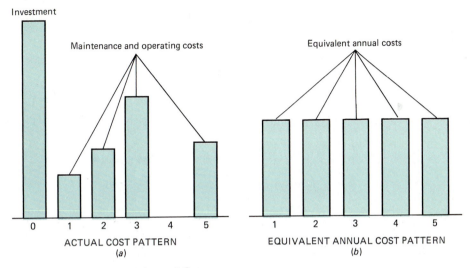

FIGURE 3-6   Actual versus Equivalent Annual Costs

It includes three components: (1) capital recovery and return on the investment, less any salvage, (2) interest on the salvage, and (3) other annual maintenance and operating costs.

$$\left\{\begin{array}{l}\text{Equivalent} \\ \text{annual cost}\end{array}\right\} = \left\{\begin{array}{l}\text{Capital recovery} \\ \text{and return}\end{array}\right\} + \left\{\begin{array}{l}\text{Interest} \\ \text{on salvage}\end{array}\right\} + \left\{\begin{array}{l}\text{Other} \\ \text{costs}\end{array}\right\}$$

$$\text{EAC} = (\text{CR\&R}) + i(\text{S}) + \text{OC} \qquad\qquad (3\text{-}10)$$

Apportioning the present-value investment amount into an annuity is the reverse of converting an annuity into a present value, so we use $(1/\text{PV}_a)$, which is known as the capital recovery factor (CRF). Thus the CR&R is (investment − salvage) $(1/\text{PV}_a)$.

EXAMPLE 3-9   Apics Aluminum (of Example 3-8) has received a bid for an environmental monitoring system from a second supplier. This second proposal would cost $24,000 and have an estimated salvage value of $5,000 after an estimated useful life of 7 years. Maintenance and operating costs are expected to be $4,000 per year.

(a) What is the equivalent annual cost of this investment? Use the firm's 12 percent cost of capital.

(b) Compare this proposal with the one in Example 3-8.

SOLUTION

(a) The equivalent annual cost consists of:

Capital recovery and return:

$$\text{CR\&R*} = (\text{investment} - \text{salvage}) \frac{1}{\text{PV}_a}$$

$$= (I - S) \frac{1}{(\text{PV}_a)7\,\text{yr}_{12\%}}$$

$$= (\$24{,}000 - \$5{,}000) \frac{1}{4.564} = \qquad \$4{,}163/\text{yr}$$

Interest on salvage: $(i)S = (.12)(5{,}000) =$ ⟶ 600/yr

Other: $OC = \text{maintenance and operation} =$ ⟶ $\dfrac{4{,}000/\text{yr}}{\$8{,}763/\text{yr}}$

(b) This proposal costs $4,000 more initially and has a salvage value that is $1,000 less, but the equipment lasts 2 years longer and costs about $400 to $500 less per year to operate. It is difficult to decide which proposal is less costly on the basis of these individual variables, especially with the different lifetimes. However, we can compare the two on an equal basis by converting the first proposal into an equivalent annual cost by multiplying its present value cost by the appropriate CRF for 5 years and 12 percent.

Proposal I Equivalent annual cost = $\text{PV [CRF]} = \text{PV} \dfrac{1}{(\text{PV}_a)5\,\text{yr}_{12\%}}$

$$= \$32{,}298 \frac{1}{3.605} = \$8{,}959/\text{yr}$$

Proposal II Equivalent annual cost = ⟶ $8,763/yr

Difference Proposal II advantage = ⟶ $196/yr

Thus proposal II costs will average about $200 per year less after the discounting and compounding at 12 percent is taken into consideration.

The equivalent annual cost has many of the same advantages as present value, for it is readily convertable into a present-value amount (and vice versa). It is especially useful for comparing projects of different lifetimes, but it does not consider the total cost as a lump sum or income aspects of a project.

INTERNAL RATE OF RETURN

The *internal rate of return* (IRR) is the discount rate which equates an investment cost with its projected earnings. It involves a time-adjusted method in that it

* Alternatively, CR&R $= (I - S)(\text{CRF}) = (\$19{,}000)(.219) = \$4{,}163$.

equates the discounted present-value earnings with the discounted present-value cost. In concept it is similar to the simple rate of return. Whereas simple rate of return is the ratio or percentage of total profit to total investment, the internal rate of return is the same ratio except that profit and investment values are converted to present-value terms.

As depicted in Fig. 3-7, the calculation technique is an attempt to determine at what interest rate, i, the cash inflow equals the cash outflow from an investment I over n years.

$$\text{IRR} = i \text{ rate, where PV (cash outflow)} = \text{PV (cash inflow)} \qquad (3\text{-}11)$$

If the annual cash inflows are equal annuities A and there is no salvage value, the IRR can easily be determined by using the PV_a table:

$$PV_a = \frac{\text{initial investment}}{\text{annuity cash flow}} = \frac{I}{A} \qquad (3\text{-}12)$$

EXAMPLE 3-10

A baggage-handling device will cost \$18,000 but will generate savings (positive cash flow) of \$4,000 per year for 8 years (no salvage). Find the IRR.

SOLUTION

The PV_a ratio associated with this return is:

$$PV_a = \frac{I}{A} = \frac{\$18{,}000}{\$\ 4{,}000} = 4.50$$

Referring to the PV table for the row $n = 8$ years, we find the PV_a factor is 4.639 for $i = 14$ percent and 4.487 for $i = 15$ percent. The IRR is thus very close to 15 percent.

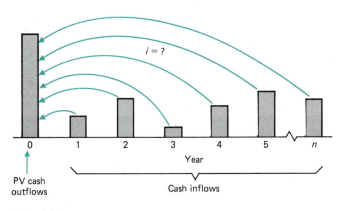

FIGURE 3-7   Rate of Return

For nonuniform cash flows, as depicted in Fig. 3-7, the IRR is more difficult to calculate because a different PV_{sp} factor must be used for each year's cash flow. The calculation technique thus involves trial and error, starting first at some arbitrarily selected i rate. If on first try the present value of future earnings (inflow) is less than the present value of the investment (outflow), the true IRR must be lower than that initially tried. With a lower i rate, the present value of a series of earnings will be more—and vice versa.

EXAMPLE 3-11

A proposed machine costing $20,000 is expected to generate cash inflows of $4,000 in year 1, $6,000 in year 2, $10,000 in year 3, and a salvage value of $10,000 in year 4. Find the IRR.

SOLUTION

Try several i rates (for example, 10 percent, 15 percent, and others) until the PV of cash inflow is approximately equal to the PV of cash outflow ($20,000), as shown in Fig. 3-8.

FIGURE 3-8   Finding the IRR by Trial and Error

		10 Percent		15 Percent		16 Percent	
Year	Cash Flow	PV_{sp} Factor	PV Amount	PV_{sp} Factor	PV Amount	PV_{sp} Factor	PV Amount
1	4,000	.909	$ 3,636	.870	$ 3,480	.862	$ 3,448
2	6,000	.826	4,956	.756	4,536	.743	4,458
3	10,000	.751	7,510	.658	6,580	.641	6,410
4	10,000	.683	6,830	.572	5,720	.552	5,520
			$22,932		$20,316		$19,836

The IRR appears to be a little closer to 16 percent than to 15 percent, but in view of the many uncertainties that accompany such calculations, either value (or perhaps 15½ percent) would be a reasonable estimate.

The internal rate of return technique considers the time of cash flows and discounts them accordingly. It also defines a rate at which profits are earned and which can be compared with similar rates from other projects, and provides a useful measure to compare against the cost of capital. (If a rate of return does not equal or exceed the cost of capital, the firm has a losing venture.) Disadvantages are that it does not consider the total magnitude of the project, it requires estimates of return as well as costs, and it assumes that the returns are (or can be) reinvested at the same internal rate of return once they are received.

SUMMARY

Capacity is a measure of the ability to produce, or serve. But the design capacity, systems capacity, and actual output may be different. System capacity is limited by the most restrictive component in the production line, and it may be affected by such factors as the product mix, quality specifications, and equipment balance. The system efficiency is the ratio of actual output to system capacity.

Manufacturing systems store value in a physical product that can be inventoried. Thus the fluctuations in demand can be absorbed by the inventory of finished products, making capacity management easier. Having many products in various stages of their life cycles enables planners to utilize their capacity even more efficiently. *Services* are consumed as they are produced, which makes capacity planning more difficult. Service systems frequently rely on work scheduling and strategies for shifting demand to off-peak time periods.

A significant amount of *capital* is frequently needed to acquire capacity. Because capital itself costs money to use (that is, interest) and because there are many alternative uses for the capital, investments should be carefully evaluated to ensure that the best choices are made.

Payback is a measure of how long it takes for an investment to pay for itself. Its extensive use is probably attributable to its simplicity. *Present value* is more sophisticated in that it considers the time value of money. Net present value is the net result of all future incomes and outflows of cash if they are discounted to a given point in time. *Internal rate of return* is similar in that it incorporates the compounding effect of interest over time. However, instead of yielding a net monetary advantage (as does present value), the internal rate of return represents an interest rate that equates the investment costs with future income resulting from the investment. It is really just another way of looking at the same advantage; we view it as a monetary amount under present value and as a compounding percentage under rate of return.

Equivalent annual cost and present-value cost are even more similar because both are monetary amounts. The *equivalent annual cost* simply represents the amount of an annuity that is equivalent to the present-value amount. It is sometimes advantageous to compare alternatives on an annual cost basis, and equivalent annual cost is ideal for this. Many organizations use more than one evaluation technique so as not to overlook any critical aspects of the investment.

SOLVED PROBLEMS

DESIGN AND SYSTEM CAPACITY

1   A plastics firm has four work centers (A, B, C, and D) in series with individual capacities (units per day) and actual output as shown.
    (a) What is the system capacity?
    (b) What is the system efficiency?

A		B		C		D		
450	—	390	—	360	—	400	→	actual output = 306/day

Solution

(a) System capacity = capacity of most limited component in the line

$$= 360 \text{ units/day}$$

(b) System efficiency = SE = $\dfrac{\text{actual output}}{\text{system capacity}} = \dfrac{306}{360} = 85\%$

2   A forest ranger in charge of constructing a new campground has been instructed to provide enough campsites to accommodate 10 percent more than the average summer weekend demand at the nearby Fall Creek site. The ranger obtains the following estimate from an employee who patrols the Fall Creek area. For what capacity should the ranger design the new campground?

Campsite Demand	0–10	10–20	20–50	50–80	80–100
Percentage of Time	5	30	50	10	5

Solution

The employee has provided the ranger with a distribution which has unequal class sizes and overlapping class limits—that is, we do not know into which class the 20, the 50, and the 80 fall. Nevertheless, if this is the best information available, we should use it.

Midpoint X	P(X)	XP(X)
5	.05	.25
15	.30	4.50
35	.50	17.50
65	.10	6.50
90	.05	4.50
		33.25

$$E(D) = \Sigma[XP(X)] = 33.25 \text{ campsites}$$
$$\text{Add } 10\% \quad \underline{3.32} \text{ campsites}$$
$$\text{Design capacity} \quad 36.57 \text{ campsites}$$

$$\text{Best estimate} = 37 \text{ campsites}$$

DETERMINATION OF EQUIPMENT REQUIREMENTS

3   Rocket Propulsion Company is considering the expansion of a solid-propellant manufacturing process by adding more 1-ton-capacity curing furnaces. Each batch (1 ton) of propellant must undergo 30 minutes of furnace time, including load and unload operations. However, the furnace is used only 80 percent of the time due to power restrictions in other parts of the system. The required output for the new layout is to be 16 tons per shift (8 hours). Plant (system) efficiency is estimated at 50 percent of system capacity.

(a) Determine the number of furnaces required.
(b) Estimate the percentage of time the furnaces will be idle.

Solution

(a) Required system capacity $= \dfrac{\text{actual output}}{\text{SE}} = \dfrac{16 \text{ tons/shift}}{.50} = 32 \text{ tons/shift}$

$= \dfrac{32 \text{ tons/shift}}{(.8)(8 \text{ hr/shift})} = 5 \text{ tons/hr}$

Individual furnace capacity $= \dfrac{1 \text{ ton}}{.5 \text{ hr}} = 2 \text{ tons/hr per furnace}$

Number of furnaces required $= \dfrac{5 \text{ tons/hr}}{2 \text{ tons/hr per furnace}} = 2.5 \text{ furnaces (say 3)}$

(b) Percentage of idle time:

Total hours available per shift = 3 furnaces @ 8 hours = 24 furnace hours
Total hours of actual use per shift = 16 tons(.5 hr/ton) =   8 furnace hours
Idle time = 16 hours

Percentage of idle time $= \dfrac{16 \text{ hours idle}}{24 \text{ hours total}} = 67\% \text{ idle time}$

4   A film developing agency must determine how many photo-enlarger cubicles are required to maintain an output of 200 good prints per hour. The set up and exposure time can theoretically be done in 2 minutes per print, but operators are on the average only 90 percent efficient and, in addition, 5 percent of the prints must be scrapped and redone. Also, the cubicles can be utilized for enlarging only 70 percent of the time.
(a) What is the required system capacity in prints per hour?
(b) What average output per hour can be expected from each cubicle, taking its use factor and efficiency into account?
(c) How many enlarger cubicles are required?

Solution

(a) Required system capacity $= \dfrac{\text{good output}}{\text{SE}} = \dfrac{200}{.95} = 210.5 \text{ prints/hr}$

(b) Output/hr = (unit capacity)(utilization %)(efficiency)

where unit capacity $= \dfrac{60 \text{ min/hr}}{2 \text{ min/print}} = 30 \text{ prints/hr}$

Output/hr = (30 prints/hr)(.70)(.90) = 18.9 prints/hr

(c) Number of cubicles $= \dfrac{210.5 \text{ prints/hr required}}{18.9 \text{ prints/hr } - \text{ cubicle}}$

$= 11.14 \text{ cubicles (use either 11 or 12)}$

INTEREST AND PRESENT VALUE CONCEPTS

5   Let $n = 12$ years and $i = 15$ percent.
(a) Find the discounted present value of a future sum of $20,000.
(b) Find the discounted present value of an annuity of $5,000 per year.

Solution

(a) $P = F(PV_{sp})_{15\%}^{12\ yr} = \$20,000(.187) = \$3,740$

(b) $P = A(PV_a)_{15\%}^{12\ yr} = \$5,000(5.421) = \$27,105$

6 Operating costs for a machine are estimated at \$500 per year for 10 years plus an additional \$1,000 for overhaul at the end of the fifth year. Assuming a 10 percent cost of capital, convert the maintenance and operating (M&O) cost of the machine into a total present-value amount.

Solution

We can depict the problem on the accompanying time-cost diagram.

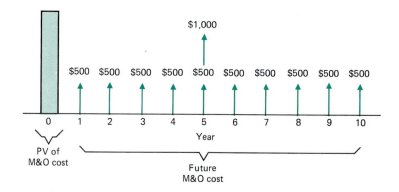

$$\text{PV of M\&O cost} = \text{PV annual operating costs} + \text{PV maintenance cost}$$

$$= \$500(PV_a)_{10\%}^{10\ yr} + \$1,000\ (PV_{sp})_{10\%}^{5\ yr}$$

$$= \$500(6.145) + \$1,000(.621)$$

$$= \$3,072 + \$621 = \$3,693$$

CAPITAL INVESTMENT EVALUATION TECHNIQUES: PAYBACK

7 A \$40,000 extrusion machine is expected to be obsolete after 10 years, with no salvage value. During its lifetime, it should generate an \$8,000-per-year operating advantage, of which \$3,000 must be paid in taxes. What is the payoff period?

Solution

$$\text{Payoff} = \frac{I - S}{\text{OA/yr}} = \frac{\$40,000 - 0}{\$8,000 - \$3,000} = 8 \text{ yr}$$

8 A proposed new \$16,400 automatic machine will have operating costs of \$.30 per unit produced, whereas the existing machine costs are \$.70 per unit. The existing machine has a market value of \$8,700 now and has another 5 years of life. It would cost \$500 to remove the existing machine and install the new one. If the firm requires a 3-year payout period, how many units must be produced annually to justify the new machine? Disregard taxes.

Solution

$$\text{Payout} = \frac{\text{investment}}{\text{OA/yr}}$$

where   Payout = 3 yr

$$\Delta \text{ Investment} = \$16,400 - \$8,700 = \$7,700$$

Add installation cost: $\underline{\quad 500}$

Total $\overline{\$8,200}$

$$\text{OA/unit} = \$.70 - \$.30 = \$.40/\text{unit}$$
$$\text{OA (total)} = \$.40 \; (N \text{ units/yr})$$

Therefore, $3 \text{ yr} = \dfrac{\$8,200}{\$.40(N)}$

$$\therefore N = \frac{\$8,200}{\$1.20/\text{unit}} = 6,833 \text{ units/yr}$$

CAPITAL INVESTMENT EVALUATION TECHNIQUES: PRESENT VALUE

9   Computer Services, Inc., offers maintenance services at $1,000 per year for 5 years plus an additional $2,000 at the end of the third year for overhaul. If a firm contracts for 5 years of services, what is the net present value cost to the firm? The firm estimates its capital cost at 14 percent and has sales of $3.5 million per year.

Solution

The sales data are not relevant to computing the present-value cost.

Present-value cost = PV other costs

$$= \text{PV (maintenance cost)} + \text{PV (overhaul cost)}$$

$$= \$1,000(PV_a)^{5 \text{ yr}}_{14\%} + \$2,000(PV_{sp})^{3 \text{ yr}}_{14\%}$$

$$= \$1,000(3.433) + \$2,000(.675)$$

$$= \$3,433 + \$1,350 = \$4,783$$

10   An instrument transformer manufacturer in Long Island is considering the purchase of an ultrasonic welding machine to replace an existing manually operated machine. The existing machine cost $12,000 two years ago and has been depreciated down to a $10,000 book value, using a 12-year life and no salvage. However, the market value of the machine is only about $4,000 now. The ultrasonic welder would improve product quality enough to boost revenue from an existing $80,000 per year to $100,000 per year. It would cost $44,000 and have a 10-year life. Any salvage value on it would be consumed in the removal expense. An advantage of the ultrasonic machine is that by reducing annual labor costs, it would cut operating expenses from $8,000 to $3,000 annually. The manufacturer is in a 30 percent tax bracket and estimates the firm's cost of capital at 12 percent. Use present-value analysis to determine whether the manufacturer should purchase the ultrasonic welder.

Solution

Determine the after-tax profit under each alternative, and select the most favorable one. It will be most convenient to do calculations on an annual basis and then convert to present value.

Existing Machine

Revenue	$80,000
Less:	
Operating costs	8,000
Depreciation	1,000
Income subject to tax	$71,000
Income tax (@ 30%)	$21,300

Cash inflow = revenue − operating costs − taxes
$$\$80,000 - \$8,000 - \$21,300 = \$50,700/\text{yr}$$

Present value of cash inflow (after tax) $= A(PV_a)_{12\%}^{10\ yr} = \$50,700(5.65)$
$$= \$286,455$$

Net PV gain after taxes = PV (cash inflow) − PV(I)
$$= \$286,455 - \$4,000 = \$282,455$$

New Ultrasonic Machine

Revenue	$100,000
Less:	
Operating costs	3,000
Depreciation	4,400
Income subject to tax	$ 92,600
Income tax (@ 30%)	$ 27,780

Cash inflow = $100,000 − $3,000 − $27,780 = $69,220

Present value of cash inflow after taxes = $69,220(5.65) = $391,093

Net PV gain after taxes = $391,093 − $44,000 = $347,093

Note that the after-tax net PV gain from the ultrasonic machine installation exceeds the existing arrangement by $64,638, and thus the new machine should be installed. Note also that the relevant investment cost of the existing machine is the market value, *not the book value*. There is no relevant advantage to be gained from writing off some of the existing machine as a loss, since this write-off should take place whether the new machine is purchased or not. The write-off advantage is not relevant to the decision problem.

CAPITAL INVESTMENT EVALUATION TECHNIQUES: EQUIVALENT ANNUAL COST

11 Alaska Construction Company is purchasing a portable generator from Lyon Electric for $5,026 and hopes to finance the purchase from a private loan at 8 percent interest. The contract stipulates that Lyon Electric will pay the construction company $1,000 for the used machine after 10 years. What is the equivalent annual purchase cost to Alaska Construction Company?

Solution

$$\text{CR\&R} = (I - S)\frac{1}{(PV_a)^{10 \text{ yr}}_{8\%}}$$

$$= (\$5,026 - \$1,000)\frac{1}{6.71} = \$600/\text{yr}$$

$$(i)S = (.08)(\$1,000) = \qquad 80/\text{yr}$$

Other costs: none considered $\qquad \underline{00/\text{yr}}$

Total $\quad \$680/\text{yr}$

12 Porter & Fisher Ltd. plans to sign a 3-year lease for automobiles for its production supervisors at a seafood plant in Norway. The company can obtain car A for $2,000 plus $.15 per mile or car B for $1,200 plus $.30 per mile. If funds cost 18 percent, how many miles must be driven before the use of car A is justified? Use the equivalent annual-cost method.

Solution

$$\text{CR\&R} = (I - S)\frac{1}{(PV_a)^{3 \text{ yr}}_{18\%}}$$

Car A	Car B
CR&R: $(\$2,000)\dfrac{1}{2.174} = \$920/\text{yr}$	$(\$1,200)\dfrac{1}{2.174} = \$552/\text{yr}$
Interest on salvage: no salvage	no salvage
Mileage charges: $\$.15N$	$\$.30N$
Total: $\$920 + \$.15N$	$\$552 + \$.30N$

Setting the total costs for car A equal to the total costs for car B:

$$\text{TC}_A = \text{TC}_B$$

$$\$920 + \$.15N = \$552 + .30N$$

$$\$.15N = \$368$$

$$N = 2,453 \text{ miles}$$

CAPITAL INVESTMENT EVALUATION TECHNIQUES: INTERNAL RATE OF RETURN

13 An investment of $5,650 is expected to yield an operating advantage (before depreciation and taxes) of $4,000 at the end of the first year, $2,000 at the end of the second year, and $1,000 at the end of the third. What is the time-adjusted rate of return?

Solution
Try various discount rates until the PV (income) = $5,650.

Try 14 percent: 1st-year earnings $= F(PV_{sp})^{1 \text{ yr}}_{14\%} = \$4,000(.877) = \$3,508$

2d-year earnings $= F(PV_{sp})^{2 \text{ yr}}_{14\%} = 2,000(.769) = 1,538$

3d-year earnings $= F(PV_{sp})^{3 \text{ yr}}_{14\%} = 1,000(.675) = \underline{\quad 675}$

$\$5,721$

Since PV(income) > PV(I), try a higher rate.

Try 16 percent:

$$
\begin{aligned}
\text{1st-year} &= \$4,000(.862) = \$3,448 \\
\text{2d-year} &= 2,000(.743) = 1,486 \\
\text{3d-year} &= 1,000(.641) = \underline{641} \\
& \$5,575
\end{aligned}
$$

Since PV (income) < PV(I), try a lower rate. Note that the 16 percent rate yields a PV (income) figure $75 below the investment amount, whereas the 14 percent yields a figure $71 above. Thus the correct value should be about midway between, or 15 percent.

Try 15 percent:

$$
\begin{aligned}
\text{1st-year} &= \$4,000(.870) = \$3,480 \\
\text{2d-year} &= 2,000(.756) = 1,512 \\
\text{3d-year} &= 1,000(.641) = \underline{658} \\
& \$5,650
\end{aligned}
$$

The before-tax IRR is 15 percent.

QUESTIONS

3-1   What is meant by "phasing in" capacity?

3-2   Why must some services be more "flexible" toward meeting demand than manufacturing activities?

3-3   Distinguish between design capacity and system capacity.

3-4   Which do you feel is more of a challenge to management, phasing in capacity or phasing out capacity? Why?

3-5   How might the following organizations adjust to the daily (or weekly) fluctuation in demand?
   (a) Airline   (b) Transformer manufacturer
   (c) Restaurant   (d) Dentist

3-6   What is a capital budget?

3-7   Suppose you were responsible for choosing between two capital investments, one of which was estimated to yield a 30 percent internal rate of return. What other information would you want before you make your decision?

3-8   Distinguish between the following: (a) PV_{sp}, (b) PV_a, (c) CRF

3-9   Distinguish between interest rate i as used in present-value calculations and as determined in the internal rate of return calculation.

3-10   Compare the equivalent annual cost method of evaluation with the present value cost. Which would you prefer and why?

3-11   Prepare a brief, concise table listing the traditional methods of capital investment evaluation along with two major advantages and disadvantages of each.

3-12   When projected cash earnings were discounted to determine the rate of return on a proposed $20,000 investment, the present value, using a 12 percent discount rate, was found to be $19,072. Is the correct figure greater or less than 12 percent? Why?

PROBLEMS

DESIGN AND SYSTEMS CAPACITY

1 A manufacturer of television watches uses three TR87 electronic chips in each TV watch produced. Demand estimates for the number of TV watches that could be sold next year are shown.

Demand X	20,000	40,000	50,000
P(X)	.30	.50	.20

(a) Assuming the firm decides to produce on an expected-value basis, how many TR87 chips should they plan to produce for next year's sales?

(b) What capacity is required to meet 150 percent of expected demand?

2 The individual component capacities (in units per day) for an assembly line that consists of five activities are as shown in the accompanying diagram.

(a) What is the system capacity?

(b) What is the efficiency of the system?

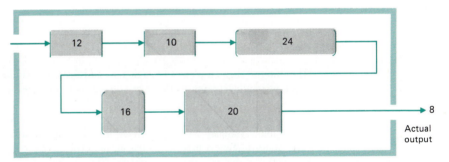

Actual output

3 An automatic drive-in teller at American National Bank has the capacity of handling 2,000 entries per regular banking day (according to the firm that sold it to the bank). However, because of limitations imposed by automobile access, the teller is available only 60 percent of the time. It is actually being used for about 800 entries per day. What is the system efficiency?

DETERMINATION OF EQUIPMENT REQUIREMENTS

4 Bloomsday Outfitters produces T-shirts for road races. They need to acquire some new stamping machines to produce 30,000 good T-shirts per month. Their plant operates 200 hours per month, but the new machines will be used for T-shirts only 60 percent of the time and the output usually includes 5 percent that are "seconds" and unusable. The stamping operation takes 1 minute per T-shirt, and the stamping machines are expected to have 90 percent efficiency when considering adjustments, changeover of patterns, and unavoidable downtime. How many stamping machines are required?

5 An aerospace manufacturer must acquire some molding machines capable of producing 160,000 *good* parts per year. They will be installed in a production line that normally produces 20 percent rejects because of the tight aerospace specifications.

(a) What is the required systems capacity?

(b) Assume that it takes 90 seconds to mold each part and the plant operates 2,000 hours per year. If the molding machines are used only 50 percent of the time and are 90 percent efficient, what actual (usable) molding machine output per hour would be achieved?

(c) How many molding machines would be required?

INTEREST AND PRESENT-VALUE CONCEPTS

6 Find the value of the following:

(a) PV of $15,000 received 8 years from now, if discounted at 12 percent.

(b) PV of an annuity of $5,000 per year if the payments are made at the end of each of 20 years. Use a discount rate of 16 percent.

(c) Future value (in 6 years) of a sum of $20,000 deposited today in a savings account that pays 8 percent interest compounded annually.

7 Convalescent Hills, Inc. has borrowed $120,000 from First National Bank for 4 years at 15 percent interest per year. How much must the company repay at the end of 4 years?

8 National Sales Company has an opportunity to sign a contract whereby it can lease a new car from a rental agency for $3,000 per year for 6 years. What is the present value cost, using a 12 percent discount factor?

PAYBACK

9 Hamburger Heaven plans to install a second drive-up window at a cost of $54,000. If the new window increases the firm's operating advantage by $20,000 per year (before depreciation and taxes), what is the payback?

10 A $30,000 machine will last 10 years, have no salvage, and generate a $5,000-per-year operating advantage, $1,000 of which must be paid in taxes. Find the payoff period.

11 The Majestic Tape Corporation has an opportunity to replace a machine with a new $10,000 unit that is expected to last for 10 years (no salvage) and save the firm $4,000 per year in labor and material costs. If taxes (at a 50 percent rate) are taken into account in the calculation, what is the payback period? *Hint*: Taxes must be paid on savings less any expenses. Depreciation is an expense that should be deducted from the before-tax operating advantage of $4,000 per year.

PRESENT VALUE

12 New equipment for a television station will cost $82,000 and is expected to have a $10,000 salvage value at the end of an 8-year useful life. The operation and upkeep costs are expected to run about $5,000 per year. Using 12 percent interest, what is the present-value cost of owning and operating the new equipment for the 8 years?

13 A logging company supervisor is evaluating the use of a new logging skidder which has an initial cost of $120,000. The supervisor expects that the skidder will last 10 years and have a salvage value equal to 15 percent of the original purchase price. Annual operating and maintenance costs are estimated at $17,000. Using a 6 percent interest rate, find the net present value cost of this logging equipment investment.

14 Superior Cement Company is considering purchasing a mixer and has two alternatives. Mixer X has a net present value cost of $125,000 (all costs considered). Mixer Y has an

initial cost of $94,000 and an expected salvage value of $8,000. The annual labor cost for Y is $16,000, and taxes, insurance, and other costs are estimated at 10 percent of the initial cost. Both mixers would have the same 4-year life under the heavy use expected. If Superior Cement uses a 12 percent interest rate and straight-line depreciation, how would the net present value cost of mixer Y compare with that of mixer X?

EQUIVALENT ANNUAL COST

15 A foreman at Vermont Paper Company has suggested a design modification on the roll-goods packaging machine which could save up to $8,000 in scrap over a year. Engineering estimates that the modification would cost $11,000 to install and would require extra servicing costs of about $50 a month. The modification would be removed when the original equipment is replaced in 8 more years, and it would have an estimated $1,000 salvage value at that time. Find the equivalent annual cost of this modification. Use a 10 percent cost of capital.

16 A large bakery in Philadelphia is considering two alternatives for adding new machinery as shown below:

	Plan 1	Plan 2
New machinery cost	$28,000	$22,000
Installation cost	3,500	3,000
Annual savings expected (in operating costs)	10,500	9,000

The new machinery is expected to be suitable for 8 years of operation, with no salvage value.

(a) If the bakery has a 14 percent cost of capital, what is the equivalent annual cost (or savings) for each plan?

(b) Which plan should be adopted?

INTERNAL RATE OF RETURN

17 What is the IRR on an investment of $9,000 in digitizing equipment that is expected to generate a savings of $3,000 per year for each of the next 5 years (no salvage value)?

18 A food products producer is considering buying some new conveyor belts at a cost of $23,040. Engineering estimates that the new belts will yield an operating advantage of $15,000 at the end of the first year and $3,000 at the end of each of the next 5 years. What is the before-tax internal rate of return?

19 A supervisor for Crescent City Gas Company has proposed that the company authorize $40,000 for an online computer unit in the customer services center. A study has indicated that the installation will generate an operating advantage of $11,225 per year (before deducting depreciation), of which $2,020 per year will be lost in taxes. What is the company's after-tax rate of return on this investment? Assume that there is an 8-year life and zero salvage value.

MISCELLANEOUS PROBLEMS

20   A subcontractor for a new automotive plant in Tennessee wishes to install enough robots to assemble 188,000 control panels per year. The assembly operation takes 6 minutes per panel, but the output from the robots is typically about 4 percent defective. How many robots are required if each one is available for 4,000 hours of capacity per year?

21   Zag Engineering Corporation is evaluating two electronic analyzers capable of doing the same job. Their cost of capital is 14 percent.

	Machine A	Machine B
Installation cost	$80,000	$60,000
Economic life	6 years	4 years
Maintenance and operations cost/yr	$8,000	$6,000
Salvage value (estimated)	$10,000	$7,000

(a) What is the present-value cost of machine A?
(b) Compute the equivalent annual cost of machine B.
(c) Which machine is the most economical on a cost-per-year basis? Assume no obsolescence or change in design, prices, etc., and explain the logic of your answer.

22   Forest Paper Company is considering the purchase of a $10,000 paper-box press which would be used for 3 years and sold for $1,000 in salvage value. Operating costs are $400 per year, and maintenance costs are $500 the first year and increase by $500 each year thereafter. Production volume is 1,000 units per year, and the firm operates on a 3-shifts-per-day basis. It uses straight-line depreciation, is in a 40 percent tax bracket, and estimates its cost of capital at 10 percent.

(a) Determine the present-value cost of owning and using the machine before tax is considered.
(b) Determine what effect taxes have on the present-value cost.
(c) Assume that the maintenance costs remain constant at $1,000 per year and that all sales and administrative costs are included in the operating costs of $400 per year. If the firm achieves a paper-box sales revenue of $12,000 per year from the press, what is the after-tax payoff period?

REFERENCES

[1]   Ingrassia, Paul, and Duron P. Levin, "Auto Industry Faces Era of Plant Closings Due to Overcapacity," *The Wall Street Journal*, Feb. 14, 1986, p. 1.
[2]   Nag, Amal: "Auto Makers Discover 'Factory of the Future' is Headache Just Now," *The Wall Street Journal*, May 13, 1986, p. 1.
[3]   Weston, J. Fred, and Eugene F. Brigham: *Essentials of Managerial Finance*, 7th ed., Holt, Rinehart, & Winston, New York, 1985.

SELF QUIZ: CHAPTER 3

Part I True/False [1 point each = 6]

1 _____ The diversification of a firm's product mix could make its system capacity less than its original design capacity.

2 _____ Manufacturing and service systems typically employ the same strategies for managing short-term capacities.

3 _____ The risks of underutilization of capacity increase proportionally as firms produce more product lines in the same plant facilities.

4 _____ Firms should not plan for (and commit funds to) new plant capacity without knowing specifically what products will be produced in those plants.

5 _____ The operating advantage (OA) is equal to the increased income minus any labor, material, and depreciation expenses for the period.

6 _____ When the IRR is computed by trial and error, the present value of a series of cash flows decreases as the interest rate being used is increased.

Part II Problems [3 points each = 9. Calculate and select your answer.]

1 An operations consultant for an automatic car wash wishes to plan for enough capacity to handle 60 cars per hour. Each car will have a wash time of 3 minutes, but there is to be a 20 percent allowance for setup time, delays, and payment transactions. How many car wash stalls should be installed?
(a) 3
(b) 4
(c) 5
(d) 6
(e) None of the above

2 Management at a corn processing plant is considering adding a $90,000 conveyor belt that engineers estimate will last 10 years and generate savings (over the current material handling system) of $20,000 per year. Assuming no salvage, what is the approximate internal rate of return expected on the conveyor?
(a) 10%
(b) 12%
(c) 18%
(d) 45%
(e) None of the above

3 An investment of $39,000 in construction equipment is expected to have a salvage value of $11,000 after an estimated useful life of 8 years. If maintenance and operating costs are $7,000 per year, what is the equivalent annual cost? (The firm's cost of capital is 15 percent.)
(a) $14,890
(b) $15,690
(c) $15,740
(d) $24,240
(e) None of the above

CHAPTER 4

FACILITY LOCATION AND LAYOUT

105-115
117-121
122-130
132-136
139-147

INTRODUCTION

Location decisions are crucial because they commit organizations to long-lasting financial, employment, and distribution patterns. As such, they deserve the careful attention of finance, personnel, marketing, and other managers, as well as that of the operations managers who "run" the facilities.

But locational decisions need not always be "cast in concrete." Relocation opportunities arise as firms alter their product lines, as labor and material requirements change, or as market conditions change. So management should always be alert to the advantages of expanding or closing existing facilities, or of developing new ones. Facility location is not a static decision that can be made and forgotten.

Facility layout choices follow the location decisions. They influence the type of equipment (and level of technology) employed, the flow of work and design of jobs, inventory levels, and other operating characteristics of the firm. Layouts can be changed more easily than locations, however, so they represent more of a continuing concern. In addition, they fall more directly within the responsibility of operations managers because they deal with the physical arrangement of productive facilities.

We begin this chapter with a broad approach to location decisions that encompasses facilities for both goods and services. Then we review some methods for evaluating the economic advantages of different locations. These include locational break-even analysis and transportation linear programming. This review is followed by an explanation of a method of incorporating qualitative factors into such an analysis.

The second part of the chapter focuses on the layout of facilities within a goods- or services-producing system. Our objective here is to understand the characteristics underlying different types of layouts so that the layout can be an effective element of managerial strategy. The basic types of layout are described, along with some techniques for analyzing potential layouts. These include materials-handling cost minimization in process layouts and line balancing in product-line layouts. When you finish the chapter, you should have a good understanding of the managerial concerns underlying location and layout decisions.

LOCATION PLANNING FOR GOODS AND SERVICES

No method of analysis assures a firm that it has selected an optimal location. But for most firms, there are many potentially "satisfactory" locations. On the other hand, some locations would be exceptionally poor. Unexpected problems can arise from a multitude of issues: zoning regulations, water supply, waste disposal, labor supply, transportation costs, tax laws, community acceptance, and more. So in location analysis, avoiding a disastrous location may be more important than trying to find an "ideal" location. One of the best ways of finding a good location (and avoiding a poor one) is to *follow a systematic decision process*.

1 Define the location *objectives* and associated constraints.
2 Identify the relevant decision *criteria*.
  (a) Quantitative (e.g., economic).
  (b) Qualitative (i.e., less tangible).
3 Relate the objectives to the criteria using appropriate *models* (e.g., economic cost models, break-even analysis, linear programming, qualitative factor analysis).
4 Do field research to generate relevant data and use the models to *evaluate the alternative* locations.
5 *Select* the location that best satisfies the criteria.

FIGURE 4-1   Steps in a Facility Location Decision Process

THE LOCATION DECISION PROCESS

Figure 4-1 presents a generalized procedure for making a location decision. There are many others, of course, and the actual approach varies with the size and scope of operations. But this approach is consistent with the framework for decisions discussed in Chapter 2.

Location Objective Location decisions must typically compromise the multiple objectives of owners, employees, suppliers, customers, and any others impacted by the organization. In general, firms seek "profitable" locations that also provide a suitable, or even attractive, environment for their employees. For example Hewlett-Packard and Tektronix assign special importance to having a quality, campuslike environment for their employees.

Constraints should also be recognized. Firms like Kennecott Copper Company and Exxon Oil Company may be restricted by the source of their raw material inputs. The high cost of land and equipment impose financial constraints on some firms, while markets and consumers constrain the location of others. Thus we find limited choice in the locations of fire stations, elementary schools, and transit systems.

Relevant Decision Criteria Organizations choose locations for both economic and noneconomic reasons. To remain viable they must give high priority to economic measures, such as labor and material costs. In addition, less quantitative factors, such as the environmental impact of the facility upon the community and the suitability of the community for the employees, warrant consideration [1].

Facility location is a complex issue which cannot usually be solved on the basis of a single criterion. The important point is that the relevant criteria should be objectively delineated in advance of the modeling and data collection phases so that a sound data-based decision can be reached.

Use of Locational Models   Models are convenient means for abstracting relevant variables and relating them to an objective. Break-even analysis and linear programming are particularly helpful in evaluating the economic variables of location. Qualitative factor analysis is a useful tool for incorporating the less tangible elements into a location decision.

Although we encourage the modeling of the locational decision process in a systematic and quantitative manner, we must recognize that a totally objective analysis of this complex decision is usually impossible. Because the intangibles are so difficult to quantify, we must also rely on the judgments of responsible managers to augment our model solutions. Judgmental refinements are a way of incorporating individual expertise and institutional values into the locational decision process [4:466].

Data and Alternatives   Large organizations can collect much of their own primary data. Some of this data is a by-product of environmental impact studies which require that organizations clearly project the long-range effects of a new facility on the proposed location.

Both large and small firms can benefit from the abundance of secondary data available from federal and state governments, from local industrial development agencies, and from private publications. For example, *Duns Review* publishes a *Business Site/Construction Planner*; it gives firms information on "the desirability of one location over another" [14:16].

One method of systematically evaluating alternatives is to first evaluate those factors that can be quantified and then consider the less tangible items. Very often, economic costs are the primary quantifying medium. If a location is economically infeasible, further analysis may not be justified. If the economics are satisfactory, other (perhaps even more important) considerations, such as community attitude and environmental impact, can be assessed.

Selection of the Site   A careful analysis of the locational decision should lead to the selection of a site that both meets the objectives of the organization itself and also provides benefits to the new community as well.

INFLUENCE OF OPERATIONS: GOODS VERSUS SERVICES

Although the world seems to offer an infinite number of potential locations, practical considerations reduce them to a manageable few. And as the location problem becomes more fully defined, the constraints associated with a specific organization reduce the options even more. One of the more influential determinants of location is the extent to which the operation being located is more *goods* (and materials) or *services* (and information) oriented.

Goods are usually standardized products that can be produced, stored, and transported to customers for use at a later date. Companies that produce and process bulky resources tend to be oriented to the source of their materials. Thus

Weyerhaeuser's paper mills and Interstate Potato Packers (makers of frozen french fries) are located close to their sources of supply. Other plants that produce bulky products (for example, auto assembly plants) may be more heavily influenced by their market locations. Companies that depend on uniquely skilled labor may be drawn to a labor pool. This magnetism is illustrated by the hundreds of electronics firms in "Silicon Valley," California, and around Boston.

Services are produced and consumed simultaneously. Unless they are produced in the presence of consumers, most services convey no value. Thus medical and transportation services, for example, are highly dependent on the location of their consumers.

Although services are consumer-oriented, many of them still enjoy considerable flexibility of location. Figure 4-2 illustrates the range of flexibility for some goods facilities and some service facilities. The increasing flexibility for goods manufacturers stems largely from processing activities that bring the refined or finished product closer to the consumer. For services, the life support need (medical, fire, police) is the strongest constraint. Flexibility increases as the proliferation and competitive nature of the service increase. Services that are more strongly people-based, such as restaurants and motels, also tend to be more flexible than equipment-based services that utilize expensive technology (for example, medical services and communication services).

LOCATIONAL DECISION VARIABLES

Location decisions involve so many variables that it is difficult to ensure that they will all receive the proper attention. One method that some firms use to guard against overlooking a critical item is a systematized review, or the use of a standardized checklist. Figure 4-3 presents a schematic model that provides a framework for identifying and analyzing the relevant locational variables. It calls for paying systematic attention to the inputs and outputs while at the same time recognizing that the level of decision typically progresses from national and

FIGURE 4-2   Locational Flexibility of Facilities Producing Goods and Services

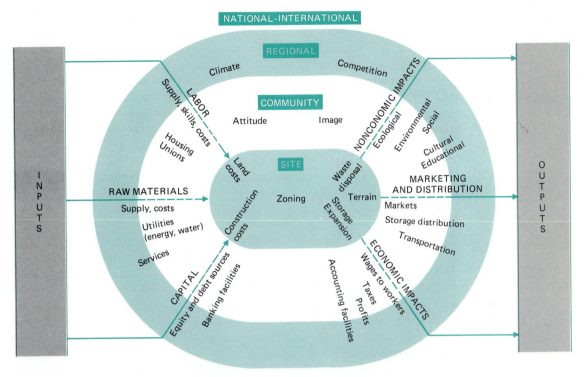

FIGURE 4-3 A Model of Facility Location Factors

regional (macro) considerations to community considerations to specific site (micro) considerations. The final choices are often narrowed down to an evaluation of three or four different community-site combinations.

Labor Although checklists are helpful, they do not reveal the relationships between the variables. For example, the differences in labor costs often account for the major differences in operating costs at different locations. However, the labor costs alone may not reflect true differences in production costs because the productivity of labor also varies from one location to another. Productivity, in turn, is related to the degree of industrialization, the climate, the skill level of the work force in the community, and so on. But comparative productivity figures for different locations in the country are not readily available. This means that plant location analysts must use some subjective judgment when comparing labor cost figures.

The difficulties of relocating existing employees are another aspect of the location problem. According to the Employee Relocation Council in Washington, D.C., about 500,000 employees are transferred each year [13:1]. Relocation is a traumatic event, one that is resisted by many, especially if it does not involve a promotion.

Relocation can also be costly. Aside from the interruption of activities and the physical transfer of equipment and inventories, firms are finding it necessary to provide monetary incentives to encourage employees to move. In an effort to relocate 900 workers from New York to Columbus, Ohio, the American Electric Power Company offered $5,000 interest-free home and auto loans, gifts, counseling, and free moves back to New York if workers were not satisfied with Columbus. For the 50 to 60 percent of the employees who accepted the relocation, the company estimated the relocation costs to be over $20,000 per employee [13:1].

Materials Raw *material supplies* are a major concern for manufacturing firms. The logistics of regional and community transportation add another dimension of uncertainty.

Having adequate *utilities* is also an increasingly significant concern. Pressures on limited water, fuel, and power supplies are great and will continue to mount during the latter years of the twentieth century. Some large users of electricity (for example, aluminum producers) have already been forced to curtail operations or shut down plants because of a shortage (or high cost) of, power in some regions.

Although plant location concerns of the past have focused on the absolute costs of *electric power*, the more relevant concerns of the future may relate to the probabilities of shortage. It takes from 5 to 10 years to design and construct a new power plant, so power shortages could be a reality if utilities are constrained from building needed plants.

Water supply promises to be an equally perplexing problem for numerous regions of the United States. What was once plentiful is now becoming scarce. Demand for water continues to mount, while the water tables in many regions of the country continue to drop. In addition many of the natural supplies are becoming polluted. Impending shortages and pollution could bring escalating costs, rationing, and some curtailment of business activity. Water is already more expensive than gasoline in some parts of the world.

Fuel costs affect not only the firm's variable costs of operations but also its ability to attract skilled personnel from nearby communities. As fuel prices increase, commuters may place heavier demands on mass transit systems. The availability of such systems will then become more critical for firms employing large numbers of workers at new locations.

Site Considerations Industrial site locations tend to be influenced more by the inputs and processing technology, whereas service facility locations are influenced more by the outputs and proximity to the market. Industrial parks ease some of the zoning, water, waste disposal, and other considerations for some firms. Others, such as paper mills and food processing plants, airline terminals, and television stations, have their own unique requirements. Public service buildings and service industries in general require that more consideration be given to customer access.

The need for continued attention to future sites is exemplified by the following statement from Tektronix, Inc., a multinational producer of sophisticated electronic test equipment. Explaining the recent purchase of three sites (totaling 450 acres), the firm's annual report states [12:9]:

> *Growing with the communities.* As our search for property goes on, our future neighbors often wonder why we're buying more land than we need. Here's what we tell them: Tektronix wants to stay in this part of the country; and good industrial sites are getting harder to come by. Our intent is neither land speculation nor (in most cases) immediate industrial development. It is merely to ensure that we will have room to grow. As to building sites, the time to prepare for tomorrow is not tomorrow.
>
> Tek's policy is to grow *with* each community rather than impose growth on it; to be part of what they see as their future; to participate, if possible, in their formal long-term planning; and to provide lasting employment there as we have in other communities where we have made our home.
>
> Also, with energy growing shorter, it doesn't seem smart for people to have to travel ever farther to work. Dispersing our operations will help by moving the jobs to the people. It also lets us attract more first-rate employees.

Environmental Considerations   Environmental impacts have now become one of the most complex aspects of facility location. But environmental concerns are not limited to ecological impacts that would violate the Clean Air Act or the Clean Water Act. The broad range of effects is illustrated in Fig. 4-4, which shows the table of contents for a study describing the impact of a new Hewlett-Packard facility on a small community.

The project involved adding 5,000 or more employees to a city of approximately 35,000 people. The direct employment was expected to generate secondary employment effects estimated on the basis of a multiplier of 2.5 for employment and 2.8 for income [7:50]. Needless to say, such significant changes cannot help but affect the existing way of life. A small-town atmosphere was about to give way to the complexities of city life. The important point, however, is that the firm's management undertook a conscientious study to discover the impacts well in advance, held open meetings with the residents to discuss potential problems and solutions to them, and recognized their corporate responsibility to manage the impact as smoothly and successfully as possible.

FOREIGN LOCATIONS

Foreign locations offer some strong advantages to a firm, many of which stem from the cost benefits of producing goods closer to their markets. But there are numerous pitfalls, so each location deserves a thorough analysis. This systematic review should examine the political, social, and economic aspects of the potential location.

POLITICAL ASPECTS

One of the first concerns should be the stability of the country and its attitude toward outside investment. Some areas, such as Western Europe and Asia, have

FIGURE 4-4 Table of Contents from an Environmental Impact Study [7]

List of Tables		i
List of Figures		v
Section 1	Introduction	1
Section 2	Background	2
Section 3	Socioeconomic systems	6
	Plant development costs and timing	6
	Plant employment	16
	Plant payroll	37
	Local interindustry relations and spin-offs	40
	Projected secondary employment/payrolls	42
	Estimated population changes	51
	Estimated housing requirements	58
	Plant tax payments	62
	Local service charges	70
	Oregon state taxes	70
Section 4	Traffic and related environmental considerations	76
	Home to work traffic patterns	76
	Environmental effects of traffic	82
	Other air emission considerations	84
	Service vehicles	85
	Other transportation requirements	85
	Mass transit	86
Section 5	Urban systems impact	87
	Water supply	91
	Waste treatment	93
	Solid waste	99
	Fire protection	99
Section 6	Unavoidable adverse effects and suggested mitigating measures	103
	Site improvement considerations	103
	Air quality considerations	103
	Traffic considerations	104
Section 7	Project alternatives	105
	Alternate sites	105
	Alternate development densities	105
	No project	106

welcomed foreign investment. In others, copper mines, chemical plants, and oil refineries have been expropriated (taken over) by the foreign government as a result of political maneuvers. Some countries, such as India, Mexico, and Brazil, essentially dictate what a foreign plant will produce by virtue of their tax laws and local "sourcing" requirements. *Sourcing* requires that firms producing a given product must also obtain or produce a specified percentage of the components for that product within the host country. Other regulations relate to limitations on the use of outside capital and outside employees and the actual transfer of earnings out of the country. Many third-world countries feel pressured to limit imports because they already have a dangerously high external debt.

SOCIAL ASPECTS

Any proposal for operations in another culture deserves careful study. Language and cultural differences can present operating, control, and even policy problems. Units of measure differ (for example, metric versus English). Operating and maintenance instructions must be translated, and local employment customs must be observed. The accepted "pace" of business varies, from the fast pace in the streets of Hong Kong to the slow style of Spain and some Mediterranean countries. For example, whereas a business contract might be efficiently handled in a 1-day meeting in Germany, the same contract may require more time in Italy, where custom dictates that a more social relationship be established before business is transacted.

ECONOMIC ASPECTS

The advantages of "cheap foreign labor" are not necessarily sufficient reasons for establishing plants in other countries. Some industrialized countries have wage rates that are equal to or greater than those in the United States. Many also have higher social costs for medical care, welfare, and governmental operations. In third-world countries where labor rates are substantially lower, the productivity of workers typically lags behind that of workers in industrialized nations. This difference is not because the workers are inferior or do not work as hard, but because of the lower level of capital equipment and technology used. As a result, the production output per worker-hour is typically lower.

Although we tend to feel that highly mechanized and automated production equipment is most desirable, this is not always true in foreign locations. Governments of some countries see advanced technology as a cause of their perplexing problems of massive unemployment. Sometimes an intermediate level of technology using second-hand and labor-intensive equipment is more suitable to both the company and the community in a developing country.

JOINT VENTURES: "IF YOU CAN'T BEAT 'EM—JOIN 'EM!"

In 1972, imported car sales accounted for less than 15 percent of the U.S. retail passenger car market. By 1984, this market chunk had risen to 23 percent and estimates are that Japanese car sales alone will constitute 40 percent of the U.S. car market in 1990 [6]. As many as 25 percent of these may be built in U.S. plants.

Ever since the initial Honda plant was built in Ohio in 1982, the "big three" (General Motors, Ford, and Chrysler) have faced stiff competition from U.S.-produced Honda, Toyota, Mazda, and Nissan vehicles. These Japanese plants *in the United States* enjoy substantial labor cost advantages over their U.S. competitors because they employ fewer workers in Japanese-style teams and have no retiree work force to support. Mazda's overall labor cost rate per employee is estimated to be $6 per hour less than Ford's [6].

Competition in price, quality, and productivity in general has prompted many American firms to undertake joint ventures with foreign firms. Ford Motor Company now owns 25 percent of Mazda, Chrysler and Mitsubishi Motors are in a joint venture in Japan, and General Motors and Toyota are jointly operating a plant in Fremont, California. (The General Motors-Toyota plant received a number of union concessions in exchange for job security agreements.) Although ownership is scheduled to revert to Toyota after 8 years, in the meantime the joint venture is giving General Motors managers a unique opportunity to learn first-hand about Japanese management techniques.

Joint ventures are also under way in the electrical, metals, chemical, and other industries. They are proving to be an effective means of gaining the advantages (and expertise) of foreign operations while at the same time sharing the risk with firms that are already established in a foreign environment.

SPACE FACTORIES

Perhaps the ultimate foreign location is a factory in space. McDonnell Douglas and Minnesota Mining and Manufacturing have already experimented with trial production on space shuttles, and Fairchild Industries hopes to have a production platform in space by 1990. NASA is also planning an $8 billion manned space station to be under construction by 1992.

Space factories will take advantage of the very low gravity environment, where particles can be separated and purified much more efficiently than on earth. Because of this, the first commercial users of space facilities will probably be electronic and pharmaceutical firms producing crystals, enzymes, and anti-cancer substances. A Cambridge, Massachusetts, consulting company projects that annual revenues from pharmaceutical production in space could reach $27 billion by the year 2000 [5].

RESPONSIBILITY IN INTERNATIONAL OPERATIONS

A final topic we cannot overlook here is managerial responsibility. In the past, some foreign governments have resisted the entry of outside firms because those firms have exploited both their host country's natural resources and its human resources.

Foreign countries are justifiably concerned about having multinational firms siphon off their limited resources while leaving their own poverty-stricken citizens no better off than when the firms first came in. United Fruit Company's exploitation of Guatemala is a vivid example of managerial irresponsibility. The story of how U.S. business interests undermined and then toppled Guatemala's legitimate government (which had sought to limit that exploitation) is well documented [10].

Responsible management has an obligation to look beyond their company's economic role to its total social impact on the other culture. If the impact is significant, their social responsibility to the local community and the country is also significant. Business responsibility does not stop at international boundaries. The Soviet nuclear accident (at Chernobyl in 1986) that spread radioactivity around the world was a vivid reminder of this.

Foreign locations do offer some unique advantages—especially when the firms are selling their products to foreign markets. And these locations provide a means of giving better, faster service to foreign customers. However, the costs of overlooking a crucial handicap appear to far outweigh the benefits of hurriedly capitalizing on a location that makes an attractive first impression. When all factors are considered, the firm must act in a responsible, thoroughly businesslike manner in both its domestic and foreign operations.

ECONOMIC ANALYSIS

The economic objective of location analysis is to find locations that will maximize revenues and minimize costs. Nonprofit and public service organizations usually work from limited budgets; their economic pressure is to minimize costs, or possibly balance the costs with the budget.

The extent to which revenues and costs influence the location decision depends on the type of product. Service industries tend to concentrate their analysis on the revenue-generating aspects of the alternative locations. This is because the production and consumption of services are so intimately linked to the market. Goods-producing industries concentrate upon cost minimization because the costs are stored (accumulated) in the product, and it can be shipped and marketed wherever they choose. In economic terms, the best location for them is the one that allows for the lowest total production and distribution costs.

The alternative revenues from various locations can often best be analyzed on a probabilistic or expected value basis, as we have done in Chapter 2. In the next two sections we will look at techniques for identifying locations with (1) the lowest total production cost and (2) the lowest distribution costs. The transportation linear programming model that will be used in discussing distribution costs is capable of minimizing both production and distribution costs if they can be stated in linear form.

LOCATIONAL BREAK-EVEN ANALYSIS

In comparing several potential locations on an economic basis, the only revenues and costs that need to be considered are the ones that vary from one location to another. If revenue per unit is the same regardless of where the good is produced (which is often the case), the total revenues can be eliminated from consideration. An economic comparison can be made by identifying the fixed and variable costs and graphing them for each location. This method is sometimes referred to as *locational break-even analysis*. The graphic approach has an advantage over a tabular approach in that one can easily identify the ranges over which a location is preferable.

The methodology for locational break-even analysis may be summarized as follows (assuming that there are equal revenues from all locations):

1 Determine all relevant costs that vary with the locations.
2 Categorize the costs for each location into annual fixed costs (FC) and variable per-unit costs (VC).
3 Plot the total costs associated with each location on a single chart of annual cost versus annual volume.
4 Select the location with the lowest total annual cost (TC) at the expected production volume (V).

If revenues per unit vary from one location to another, revenues must also be included, and the comparisons should be made on the basis of profits (that is, TR − TC) at each location rather than simply on the basis of total annual cost at each location.

EXAMPLE 4-1

Potential locations A, D, and T have the cost structures shown for producing a product expected to sell for $90. Find the most economical location for an expected volume of 1,850 units per year.

Site	Fixed Cost/Year	Variable Cost/Unit
A = Austin	$20,000	$50
D = Durham	40,000	30
T = Tulsa	80,000	10

SOLUTION
For each site, plot the fixed costs (costs at zero volume) and total costs (fixed costs + total variable costs) at the expected volume of output.

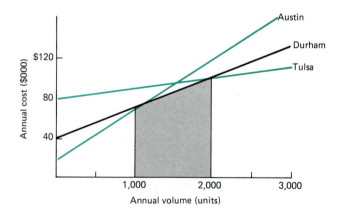

$$TC = FC + VC(V)$$

Site A's TC = \$20,000 + \$50(1,850) = \$112,500

Site D's TC = \$40,000 + \$30(1,850) = \$ 95,500

Site T's TC = \$80,000 + \$10(1,850) = \$ 98,500

The graph shows that the most economical location for a volume of 1,850 units is Durham. Expected profit here = TR − TC = (\$90/unit) (1,850 units) − \$95,500 = \$71,000/per year. Note that for volumes less than 1,000 units, Austin would be preferred. For volumes greater than 2,000 units, Tulsa would be preferred.

Locational break-even analysis is a means of comparing all relevant costs for several alternative locations and selecting a plant location that will minimize costs for a given volume. It is desirable that the "relevant costs" include transportation and/or distribution costs if they vary from one location to another, which is usually the case. When transportation costs are especially significant or when the same product can be produced at more than one plant and/or transported to more than one distribution point, a detailed analysis of transportation costs is warranted.

COST MINIMIZATION USING TRANSPORTATION LINEAR PROGRAMMING

Assume that the managers of a national baking company feel that they can justify another new plant to produce the company's standard line of breads and bakery goods. They wish to give specific consideration to transportation costs, because they have a relatively bulky, low-unit-value product to distribute. Before reaching their final plant location decision they will want to anticipate how the addition of another plant will affect their existing production-distribution patterns. Which plants will ultimately be used to produce what quantities? And to which distribution warehouses should the various quantities be shipped?

If the location problem can be formulated (modeled) as one of minimizing some given cost, such as transportation expense, the methods of transportation (or distribution) linear programming are useful techniques for minimizing the cost function subject to supply and demand constraints.

The transportation method of linear programming is widely used for minimizing transportation costs and is indeed useful in numerous other minimization or maximization situations, such as minimizing unit production costs, minimizing materials handling costs, and maximizing revenues available from various alternative locations.

This method of linear programming is a variation of the standard linear programming approach we will utilize later in the text. All linear programming models are mathematical techniques for maximizing or minimizing some objective function subject to constraints. In the transportation format, the objective is usually to minimize the total transportation costs while meeting the demands of the various distribution points without exceeding the individual capacities of the supply locations.

Supply locations (factories)	Demand locations: Chicago	Denver	Nashville	
Boston	$5.00	$6.00	$5.50	2,000
Seattle	$7.00	$4.00	$7.00	6,000
Miami	$5.00	$7.00	$3.00	5,000
New location				4,000
	6,000	5,000	6,000	17,000

FIGURE 4-5 Distribution Linear Programming Matrix

The demand requirements and supply availabilities (demand-supply constraints) are typically formulated in a rectangular arrangement (matrix), with the transported amounts (cell loadings) being governed by the cost or profit for the particular demand-supply route.

Figure 4-5 presents a demand-supply matrix arranged for a transportation linear programming solution which we will use for illustration purposes. Demand stems from Chicago (6,000), Denver (5,000), and Nashville (6,000), for a total of 17,000 units. Supply locations are Boston, Seattle, and Miami, plus a new location under consideration. Costs in the upper corner of each cell are the transportation costs between the supply and demand points. They come from purchasing and logistics data and quotes from transportation firms. Thus the cost for transporting each unit from Boston to Chicago is estimated at $5.

Note that the total supply and demand quantities are balanced (at 17,000). If they were unequal, a "dummy" supply plant or absorption location would be created either to produce the additional needed supply or to absorb the excess supply:

If demand > supply: Create a dummy supply, and assign a zero transportation cost to it so that excess demand is satisfied.

If supply > demand: Create a dummy demand, and assign a zero transportation cost to it so that excess supply is absorbed.

The matrix in Fig. 4-5 has equal supply and demand, so no dummy columns or rows would be required for it. However, some research would be necessary to determine the best transportation methods and costs for shipment from the proposed locations to Chicago, Denver, and Nashville. Then separate solutions would have to be worked out using each of the proposed new locations.

The "solution" to a transportation linear programming problem results in entries into the cells that will allocate supply to meet demand at the lowest total cost. Several methods of obtaining initial and final (optimal) solutions have been developed, including Vogel's approximation method (for initial solutions) and the modified distribution (MODI) method (for final solutions). Simple problems can be done by hand, but most realistic problems are solved by computer, and programs to solve them are readily available for personal computers as well as mainframe computers.

Although we shall not present a solution technique here, the Solved Problem section at the end of the chapter illustrates the use of the northwest-corner method to obtain an initial (feasible—but not necessarily optimal) solution and the stepping-stone method for converting the initial solution into a final (optimal) solution. The northwest-corner and stepping-stone methods are not usually the most expedient to follow when the problem is complex, but they have intuitive value and quickly convey the basic methodology. Making initial allocations on the basis of minimum costs also makes a good deal of intuitive sense, and a solved problem illustrates this as well.

Our purpose here is to demonstrate the formulation and interpretation of transportation problems as applied to plant location problems. Exercises at the end of the chapter will enable you to practice this formulation and hand calculation of these problems, or you may go on to solve the problems on a computer if you like. The example below utilizes data from Fig. 4-5 and illustrates how easy it is to incorporate different production costs as well as distribution costs into the analysis.

EXAMPLE 4-2

Plastic Cabinet Supply Company (PCS) is a wholly owned subsidiary of an international firm which has major interests in the housing industry. PCS has cabinet plants located in Boston, Seattle, and Miami. The plants produce prefabricated housing components, which are delivered to other company assembly plants in Chicago, Denver, and Nashville. Demand has grown to the point where PCS can justify the construction of another plant. The immediate problem is determining a location that will minimize production and transportation costs to the existing assembly plants. In order to be close to raw material supplies and to service other potential markets, the alternative plant locations have been narrowed down to Omaha and Phoenix. The demand, supply, and cost data for the existing locations are as shown in Fig. 4-5. The data for the Omaha and Phoenix locations are as follows:

Location	Production capacity	Production cost/unit	Transportation cost to assembly plant in		
			Chicago	Denver	Nashville
Omaha	4,000	$6.90	$4.00	$3.00	$5.00
Phoenix	4,000	$6.20	$6.00	$4.50	$5.00

Which of the two plant locations (Omaha or Phoenix) is more desirable from an economic standpoint?

SOLUTION

We must now generate two independent solutions. Then we can compute the transportation costs and add production costs for each location and determine which location has the lowest costs. By allocating via the northwest corner (initially) and making adjustments by means of the stepping-stone method, we would arrive at the following matrices:

Solution using Omaha data

Demand locations

Supply locations	Chicago	Denver	Nashville	
Boston	$5.00 **2,000**	$6.00	$5.50	2,000
Seattle	$7.00	$4.00 **5,000**	$7.00 **1,000**	6,000
Miami	$5.00	$7.00	$3.00 **5,000**	5,000
Omaha	$4.00 **4,000**	$3.00	$5.00	4,000
	6,000	5,000	6,000	17,000

Transportation costs:

2,000 units, Boston to Chicago, at $5	$10,000
5,000 units, Seattle to Denver, at $4	20,000
1,000 units, Seattle to Nashville, at $7	7,000
5,000 units, Miami to Nashville, at $3	15,000
4,000 units, Omaha to Chicago, at $4	16,000
	$68,000

Add production costs:

4,000 units (from Omaha) at $6.90/unit	$27,600
Total relevant costs	$95,600

Solution using Phoenix data

Demand locations

Supply locations	Chicago	Denver	Nashville	
Boston	$5.00 **2,000**	$6.00	$5.50	2,000
Seattle	$7.00 **1,000**	$4.00 **5,000**	$7.00	6,000
Miami	$5.00	$7.00	$3.00 **5,000**	5,000
Phoenix	$6.00 **3,000**	$4.50	$5.00 **1,000**	4,000
	6,000	5,000	6,000	17,000

Transportation costs:

2,000 units, Boston to Chicago, at $5	$10,000
1,000 units, Seattle to Chicago, at $7	7,000
5,000 units, Seattle to Denver, at $4	20,000
5,000 units, Miami to Nashville, at $3	15,000
3,000 units, Phoenix to Chicago, at $6	18,000
1,000 units, Phoenix to Nashville, at $5	5,000
	$75,000

Add production costs:

4,000 units (from Phoenix) at $6.20/unit	$24,800
Total relevant costs	$99,800

Conclusion: The Omaha location has lower costs per month.

If production costs were different at all the supply locations, and if the entire capacity were not utilized, it would be most expedient to simply add the costs to each cell in the matrix. Then the matrix solution would result in an optimal production *and* distribution arrangement, and the production costs would not have to be added on separately as we did above.

Plant sites are expected to serve the company for several years, during which time transportation costs will change. To explore the sensitivity of the solution to changing costs, it may be desirable to forecast cost changes (as far as possible) and recheck the solution to ensure that the best long-range—as well as short-range—result is obtained. As the price of transportation fuels escalates, the benefits of making these types of studies become ever more apparent. The transportation method of linear programming offers much potential to the astute manager.

QUALITATIVE FACTOR ANALYSIS

We noted earlier that if economic criteria were not sufficiently influential and the net result of numerous other criteria was unclear, a system of weighting the criteria might be useful in making a plant location decision. This approach is referred to as *qualitative factor analysis*. It is another means of allowing the decision maker to inject values into a decision-making structure in a relatively formalized manner, and is described in the following procedure. Note, however, that it assumes a good deal of knowledge about each site, so it is not useful in all situations.

1 *Develop a list of relevant factors* (use a checklist).
2 *Assign a weight to each factor* to indicate its relative importance (weights may total 1.00).
3 *Assign a common scale to each factor* (0–100 points), and *designate any minimum*.
4 *Score each potential location* according to the designated scale, and *multiply the scores* by the weights.
5 *Total the points* for each location, and *choose the location* with the maximum points.

EXAMPLE 4-3

National Glass Company is evaluating four locations for a new plant and has weighted the relevant factors as shown below. Scores have been assigned with higher values indicative of preferred conditions. Using these scores, develop a qualitative factor comparison for the four locations.

SOLUTION

Relevant Factor	Assigned Weight	Atlanta		Baltimore		Chicago		Denver	
		Score	Weighted Score	Score	Weighted Score	Score	Weighted Score	Score	Weighted Score
Production cost	.33	50	16.50	40	13.20	35	11.35	30	9.90
Raw material supply	.25	70	17.50	80	20.00	75	18.75	80	20.00
Labor availability	.20	55	11.00	70	14.00	60	12.00	45	9.00
Cost of living	.05	80	4.00	70	3.50	40	2.00	50	2.50
Environment	.02	60	1.20	60	1.20	60	1.20	90	1.80
Markets	.15	80	12.00	90	13.50	85	12.75	50	7.50
Total location score	1.00		62.60		65.40		58.25		50.70

Weighted scores are computed by multiplying the score times the assigned weight (for example, $50 \times .33 = 16.50$) and summing those products. Based on this data, Baltimore is the preferred location.

FACILITY LAYOUT

Layout decisions are concerned with the arrangement of production, support, customer service, and other facilities used in operations. The flow patterns for future work activities affect the efficiency of handling materials, the utilization of capital equipment, inventory storage levels, the number and productivity of workers, and even behavioral characteristics such as group communications and employee morale.

DETERMINANTS OF LAYOUT

Although our introduction to layouts comes in the context of new locations, any significant change in operations may warrant a review (and possibly a revision) of an existing layout. The type of layout is generally determined by the following:

- *Type of product.* This concerns whether the product is a good or a service, the product design and quality standards, and whether the product is produced for stock or for order.
- *Type of production process.* This relates to the technology used, the type of materials handled, and/or the means of providing the service.
- *Volume of production.* Volume affects the present facility design and capacity utilization, plus provisions for expansion or change.

TYPES OF LAYOUT

Although it is convenient to classify layouts into two or three basic types, in reality there is a continuum of different types of layouts which can be combined in a variety of ways. Classified on the basis of the volume of identical products, these layouts range from fixed position facilities assembled to produce just one product (e.g., to construct a building), to continuous-flow facilities that produce millions of identical units (such as gallons of gasoline) [11:155].

Figure 4-6 presents an overview of some of the principal types of layouts and singles out the fixed position layout as being somewhat unique. The arrows extending from the job shop to continuous flow layouts suggest that these and the batch and line processing layouts can be adapted to a wide range of product, process, and volume differences. Furthermore, it is not uncommon for organizations to use more than one type of layout within a given facility.

TYPE OF LAYOUT	TYPE OF PRODUCT	TYPE OF PROCESS	VOLUME OF PRODUCTION
FIXED POSITION (e.g., building a factory, managing a marathon)	Customized (influenced by location)	Individual projects (unique or tailored specifications)	Very low (possibly only one)
JOB SHOP (e.g., machine shop, hospital)	Customized	Flexible process	Relatively low (short runs)
	Many different products	Materials and labor requirements less certain	More work-in-process inventory
	Compete via features and service	Labor is higher percentage of total costs	Planning horizon is relatively short
BATCH PROCESSING (e.g., winery, airline)			
LINE PROCESSING (e.g., auto assembly, plant, cafeteria)	Compete via distribution and price	Labor is lower percentage of total costs	Planning horizon is relatively long
	Fewer new products	Material and labor requirements more certain	More finished goods inventory
CONTINUOUS FLOW (e.g., oil refinery, electric utility)	More standardized	Standardized process	Relatively high (long runs)

FIGURE 4-6   Characteristics of Different Types of Layouts

Space does not permit us to discuss each type of layout in detail, but we will illustrate the commonly encountered fixed position, job shop, and line processing types below. Note, however, that two examples are provided for each type of layout in Fig. 4-6. The first is that of a goods-producing facility and the second that of a services-oriented facility. Much of the theory underlying effective layouts applies equally to goods and services. However, in goods manufacturing, our major concerns lie with the efficiency of the flow of physical materials, whereas with services our concerns are more often with the flow or satisfaction of customers.

Fixed Position Layouts   Fixed position layouts are perhaps the simplest type of layout. They are arrangements whereby labor and materials are brought to the location where the work is done. Managerial skills, workers, subcontractors, and materials are all brought to a job site. Custom design, building, and construction projects are often done on this basis. Examples include homebuilding, shipbuilding, dam construction, and relay station construction.

Figure 4-7 illustrates the fixed position type of layout, which often arises out of the necessity of having to complete a project in place. It has the advantage of minimizing the handling costs of the end product. It enables managers to take advantage of the more goal-oriented planning and control techniques that apply to project-type activities. However, the costs of attracting skilled personnel to the job site may be high, support facilities are sometimes limited, and expensive equipment may not be as fully utilized as with other types of layouts.

Job Shop Layouts   Job shop layouts are arrangements that group the people and equipment performing similar functions. They are sometimes referred to as *pro-*

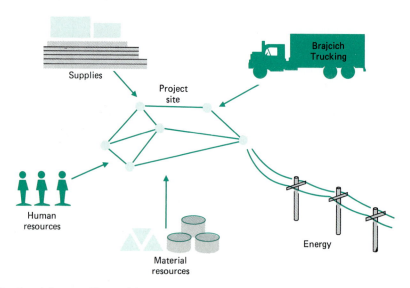

FIGURE 4-7   Fixed Position (Project) Layout

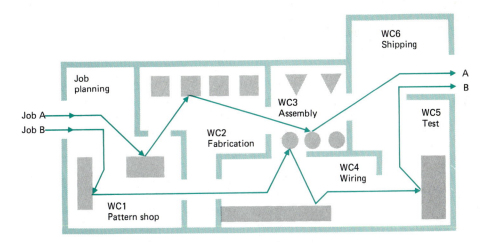

FIGURE 4-8   Job Shop Layout for Sign Production

cess layouts or functional layouts because specific functions, such as inspection, painting, or x-raying, are performed in one location for various products. Machine shops, hospitals, and carnivals have these layout characteristics.

Figure 4-8 illustrates a job shop layout for a firm producing made-to-order advertising signs. The work flow in this custom shop is intermittent and is guided by individual shop orders according to the specific nature of the work to be performed.

Job shop layouts tend to rely heavily on the planning and professional skills of people. They have the advantages of (1) being flexible to do custom work, (2) promoting job satisfaction by offering employees diverse and challenging tasks, and (3) limiting investment in highly specialized, high-volume equipment. Disadvantages are the higher costs of (1) materials handling, (2) skilled labor (coupled with a lower productivity because of the uniqueness of each job), and (3) more complex production control. Because the work flow is intermittent, each job must be individually routed through the system and scheduled at the various work centers (WCs). All special drawings, tools, and equipment setups must be individually arranged for, and the status of each job must be monitored.

Batch Processing Layouts   Job shops that process large orders of identical units as a group through the same production sequence are employing principles of batch processing. Batch processing layouts enable producers to achieve some economies of scale by performing the same activities on conveniently managed volumes (or batches) of product. Batch processing is used for a wide range of goods and services from cheese and furniture production to classrooms and theaters.

Line Processing Layouts   Line processing layouts are arrangements of people and equipment according to the sequence of operations that are performed on the product or for the customer. Line layouts are sometimes called *product line* (or *assembly line*) *layouts* because they lend themselves to the use of straight-line conveyors and automated equipment, which minimizes the amount of manual material handling. Automobile assembly plants, food processing plants, and cafeterias are examples of line layouts. In some service facilities such as cafeterias, the customer, rather than a physical product, moves down the line.

Figure 4-9 illustrates a line processing layout with one main assembly line, two feeder lines, and twelve work stations. This facility is designed to produce large volumes of a single item (or relatively few items) on specialized fixed-path equipment and has a continuous work flow.

Line layouts capitalize on the commonality of operations. They offer the advantages of (1) lower material-handling costs, (2) simplified tasks that can be done with low-cost, unskilled labor, (3) reduced amounts of work-in-process inventory, and (4) much simplified production control activities. All units are routed along the same fixed path, and scheduling consists primarily of establishing a production rate. Work is dispatched to the shop and monitored more easily by controlling the rates of flow of materials and subassemblies to the line and the shipment of items off the line.

Disadvantages of line layouts are their (1) inflexibility, (2) job design characteristics (which can be very monotonous), (3) high fixed costs of investment in specialized equipment, and (4) heavy interdependence of all operations. A breakdown in one machine or an uncompleted task at one work station can idle much of the equipment and reduce or halt the total production output. The proper balancing of the capacities of workers and work stations is a major consideration, and we shall direct our attention to it shortly.

Continuous Flow Layouts Continuous flow layouts are frequently oriented around a technological process, such as the production of chemicals or electricity.

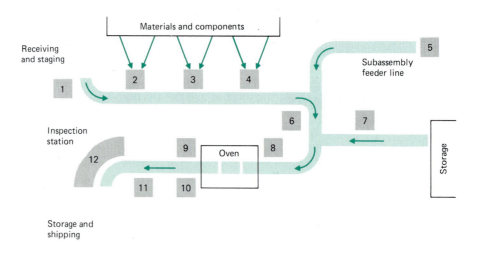

FIGURE 4-9 Line Layout for Electronic Toy Manufacturing

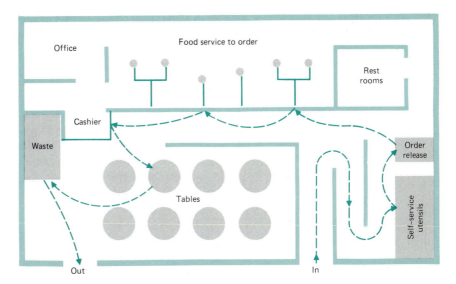

FIGURE 4-10   Fast-Food Service Facility

The processing facilities (which may represent a substantial capital investment), are often highly automated and designed to operate as one integral unit. Plant layout here is largely an engineering design function, and there is little flexibility for change except via a design modification to the plant.

Comparison of Layouts for Goods and Services   Layouts do not usually conform to the classifications described above in all respects. For example, behind the picturesque, smooth-running automobile assembly lines lie job and batch processing shops producing the needed components and subassemblies. And some of these production activities are highly automated whereas others are not.

Service systems also blend characteristics of job shop, batch, and line processing layouts. At one end of the spectrum, hospitals make full use of the *job shop* characteristics. Patients (instead of materials) are uniquely routed to different "work centers" for *customized* x-rays, EKGs, blood tests, surgery, and so forth. Like machine shops, many service facilities also rely on queues to regulate the flow of customers. However, empty hospital beds, idle firefighters, and unfilled airline seats represent the costs of idle capacity, much as idle machines do in a manufacturing plant.

But as the services offered become more standardized, characteristics of continuous flow emerge. Customers entering movie theaters and subway systems are "batch processed" in similar ways by personnel and equipment geared to a limited variety of outputs.

Figure 4-10 incorporates some characteristics of both job shop and *line processing*. In this fast-food service facility, customers select from a limited menu so their food is provided "to order." Still, the customers themselves move down the "service line." Individual flows stop at the tables, where a larger in-process storage-consumption area must be provided, just as for in-process inventories in batch or line layouts.

Line processing and *continuous flow* service systems also capitalize on the same economies of scale (high volume and low processing costs) as manufacturing systems. And as the service becomes highly standardized, the "tailored" nature of the service (or the marketing strategy) shifts to choices concerning the time and quantity of service desired. The use of electricity, phone service, stock quotations, computer banking, and so forth illustrate this shift. An increasing number of these continuous flow-type services are information- and/or communications-oriented. So the "layout strategies" here focus on better ways of making the service available wherever and whenever the customer wants it.

COMPUTER-GUIDED FLOWS: FLEXIBLE AND CELLULAR SYSTEMS

Facility layouts are influenced by the level of automation and cost of manufacturing equipment. Many numerically controlled (NC) machines and industrial robots perform simple tasks such as drilling holes or welding joints. They can be used independently, or moved to where they are needed. However, as the number of tasks performed by automated machinery increases, the machines can become quite large (and expensive). In these situations, the equipment design and configuration significantly influence the layout and product flow. Two of the more advanced systems gaining acceptance in U.S. firms today are flexible and cellular manufacturing systems.

Flexible Manufacturing Systems (FMS)
Flexible manufacturing systems are production systems that include a supervisory computer, plus automated machine tools and automated materials-handling equipment. The tools and handling equipment can follow the computer's instructions to produce hundreds of different parts in whatever order is specified. Items are loaded, processed, assembled, and inspected without being transported to different processing centers throughout the plant.

By producing exactly what is needed, companies with FMSs can keep their inventories very low (goods arrive "just in time" to support other needs) and minimize their work-in-process costs. The FMSs also reduce labor costs and improve productivity; a plastics firm in Ohio realized a productivity rate two to three times above that in a shop dependent on human operators [15]. Finally, FMSs help ensure a consistently high level of product quality; the system will automatically reject any defective parts.

FMS installations can cost between $5 million and $20 million. Large manufacturers, such as Caterpillar Tractor Company, General Electric, and McDonnell Douglas can realize the benefits of these systems, but most companies cannot afford such sums "for one machine." As a result, there are fewer than 100 full-fledged FMSs operating in the United States today [15].

Cellular Manufacturing Cellular manufacturing is a building-block step toward FMS. *Manufacturing cells* are smaller groups of machines that are arranged according to a similarity in the operations performed. For example, the steps in a sequence might be: (1) cut, (2) weld, (3) mill, and (4) drill. Items are thus grouped according to either a commonality in their design or in their manufacturing that would enable the equipment to capitalize on the similar processing activities (that is, group technology). Many automotive components, appliance parts, and defense products are now produced in manufacturing cells.

Manufacturing cells also enable a firm to operate with less work-in-process inventory. Cells are typically connected with materials-handling equipment so that these costs are reduced. Also, they can be expanded toward a FMS by adding a supervisory computer and more machines as investment funds become justified.

ANALYSIS AND SELECTION OF LAYOUTS

Facility layouts must integrate numerous factors, such as work-center locations, offices, computer facilities, toolrooms, storage space, and washrooms. Two of the major criteria for selecting and designing a layout are (1) materials-handling cost and (2) worker effectiveness.

Materials-handling cost has often been considered the most important criterion of a layout. Costs are minimized by using belts and conveyors to automate product flows (as much as is practical) and keeping the flow distances as short as possible. Sequential processing activities are usually located in adjacent areas. In service systems such as subways, customers are frequently the "material" that moves through the system. So the customer service time becomes a relevant variable.

Worker effectiveness is an increasingly important criterion in facilities today. Good layouts provide workers with a "satisfying" job and permit them to work effectively at the highest skill level for which they are being paid. This applies just as much to an office layout (where an engineer might spend unnecessary time delivering memos) as it does to a factory layout (where a machinist might have to walk long distances for tools). Good communications systems and well-placed supporting activity locations are critical to the success of any facility.

The major layout concerns differ along the continuum from job shop layouts to continuous flow layouts (see Fig. 4-6). The job shop and line processing layouts exemplify the difference:

- *Job shop layouts* attempt to minimize materials-handling costs by arranging departmental sizes and locations according to the volume and flow rate of the products.
- *Line processing layouts* attempt to maximize worker effectiveness by grouping

sequential work activities into work stations that yield a high utilization of labor and equipment with a minimum of idle time.

MINIMIZING COSTS IN JOB SHOP LAYOUTS

Materials-handling costs in job shop layouts can be divided into (1) the load and unload costs and (2) the transportation costs. The load-unload costs are a function of the frequency of trips (and the capacity of equipment—which should be considered when evaluating the investment in materials-handling equipment). The analysis of transportation costs rests largely on the amount of material moved and the distance it is moved. Hence it is often referred to as *load-distance analysis* [3:628].

Most forms of load-distance analysis try to reduce the transportation costs of in-process work by reducing the flows of material to nonadjacent (or noncontiguous) work centers. The objective is to locate the work centers with high interaction near each other. In office systems, transportation costs refer to the time required for employees to move themselves to necessary locations for interaction with others.

Simple Graphic Approaches In the following example, a travel chart and a simple graphic approach are used to establish a facility layout. The travel chart shows the *number of moves* made between departments and identifies the most active departments. The solution methodology is a trial-and-error process which attempts to minimize nonadjacent flows by centrally locating the active departments. The work centers are depicted as circles in the solution. Connecting lines represent the loads transported during a given time, such as 50 units per month. Departments next to each other or diagonally across from each other are regarded as adjacent.

| EXAMPLE 4-4 | Mohawk Valley Furniture has purchased a plant with six production areas as shown in the facility outline below. The firm proposes to locate six departments (A, B, C, D, E, F) which have the number of moves per day between departments as shown in the accompanying travel chart. |

1	2	3
4	5	6

Facility Outline Locations

From	Number of moves to					
	A	B	C	D	E	F
A	—	7	—	—	—	5
B	—	—	—	4	10	—
C	—	7	—	—	2	—
D	—	—	8	—	—	—
E	4	—	—	—	—	3
F	—	6	—	—	10	—

Travel Chart

Develop a layout of the six departments which minimizes the nonadjacent flows.

SOLUTION
First, determine which departments have the most frequent links with other departments. This can be done by totaling the *number of entries* in each row and column. Thus, A has two row entries (B and F) and one column entry, for a total of 3 links.

Department	A	B	C	D	E	F
Number of links	3	5	3	2	5	4

Second, try to locate the most active departments in central positions. Thus, we place departments B and E in locations 2 and 5.
Third, use trial and error to locate the other departments so that nonadjacent flows will be minimized.

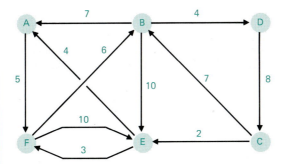

Fourth, if all nonadjacent flows are eliminated, the solution is complete (as in the accompanying figure). If nonadjacent flows still exist, try to minimize the *number of units* flowing to nonadjacent areas as weighted by the distance away.

Load-Distance Analysis A refinement in minimizing layout transportation costs is to evaluate alternative layouts on the basis of the sum of actual distance (feet) times load (units) for each alternative. A variation of this is to compute the materials-handling cost directly by multiplying the number of loads by the materials-handling cost per load. The layout with the lowest (load) × (distance) total, or (load) × (cost) total, is the best choice. In Prob. 12, distance values (in feet) are assigned to the facility outline of Example 4-4 and you are asked to calculate the load-distance total for the layout arrived at in that example. In a realistic situation, it would then be compared with alternative arrangements to select the "best" one, that is, the one with the lowest Σ (load) (distance). Remember, however, that

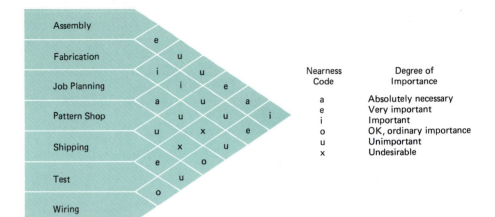

FIGURE 4-11   Nearness Codes for Process Layout of Fig. 4-8.

these are limited criteria, and other considerations might very well take precedence.

Systematic Layout Planning   A systematic approach to incorporating other considerations into the layout has been promoted by Richard Muther [8]. His method utilizes a half-matrix to display ratings of the relative importance of locating one department close to another. The importance ratings are indicated by code letters (a, e, i, o, u, x) in the matrix; the ratings range from absolutely necessary (a) to undesirable (x). A reason code (usually a number) can also be assigned. For example, reason 1 might be use of common personnel; 2, noise isolation; and 3, safety purposes.

Figure 4-11 illustrates the systematic layout planning (SLP) approach as applied to the sign production layout of Fig. 4-8.

Several *computerized approaches* are available for developing and analyzing process layouts. The analytical (software) packages are primarily heuristic, step-by-step (iterative) methods. The ALDEP (automated layout design programs) and CORELAP (computerized relationship layout planning) programs attempt to maximize a nearness rating within the facility dimension constraints. The CRAFT (computerized relative allocation of facilities technique) program attempts to minimize materials-handling costs by calculating costs, exchanging departments, and calculating more costs until a good solution is obtained. None of the methods guarantees optimality.

LINE BALANCING IN ASSEMBLY LINE LAYOUTS

Line layouts are appropriate for high-volume activities where moving conveyors bring the work units to the worker and then carry them along to the next station.

Similar operations, which are repeated on each unit, may take anywhere from a fraction of a second up to perhaps half an hour per item. For example, we would find that a cannery line for processing corn on the cob requires a very short inspection and culling time per cob, whereas a line for upholstered furniture may require 20 or 30 minutes per sofa.

Line balancing is the apportionment of sequential work activities into work stations in order to gain a high utilization of labor and equipment and therefore minimize idle time. Compatible work activities are combined into approximately equal time groupings that do not violate the order (or precedence) in which they must be done. The length of work time, or operating time, that a component is available at each work station is the *cycle time* (CT).

$$CT = \frac{\text{available time/period}}{\text{output units required/period}} = \frac{AT}{\text{output}} \qquad (4\text{-}1)$$

From Eq. (4-1) we can see that CT is also the time interval at which completed products leave the production line (once it is operating at full capacity). If the time required at any station exceeds that which is available to one worker, additional workers may have to be added to the station. The theoretical or ideal number of workers needed on the assembly line is the product of the actual worker time it takes to complete one unit and the number of output units required, divided by the available time.

$$\begin{aligned} \text{Theoretical minimum} \atop \text{number of workers} &= \frac{(\text{worker time/unit})\,(\text{output units/period})}{\text{available time/period}} \\ &= \Sigma t \left(\frac{\text{output units/period}}{\text{available time/period}} \right) = \frac{\Sigma t}{CT} \qquad (4\text{-}2) \end{aligned}$$

where Σt is the sum of the actual worker time required to complete one unit.

EXAMPLE 4-5

The precedence diagram for assembly activities A through G is shown below, with the element time requirements shown in minutes. The line operates 7 hours per day, and an output of 600 units per day is desired. Compute (a) the cycle time, and (b) the theoretical minimum number of workers.

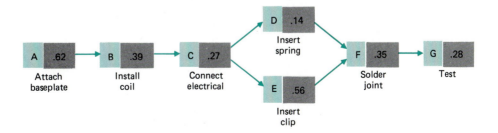

SOLUTION

(a) $\text{CT} = \dfrac{\text{available time/period}}{\text{output units reqd/period}}$

$= \dfrac{(7 \text{ hr/day}) \ (60 \text{ min/hr})}{600 \text{ units/day}} = \dfrac{420}{600} = .70 \text{ min/unit}$

(b) Theoretical minimum $= \dfrac{\Sigma t}{\text{CT}}$

where $\Sigma t = .62 + .39 + .27 + .14 + .56 + .35 + .28 = 2.61$

Theoretical minimum $= \dfrac{2.61}{.70} = 3.73 \text{ workers}$

(*Note*: This is theoretical—not actual.)

The procedure for analyzing line balancing problems involves (1) determining the number of stations and time available at each station, (2) grouping the individual tasks into amounts of work at each station, and (3) evaluating the efficiency of the grouping. When the available work time at any station exceeds that which can be done by one worker, additional workers (or robots) must be added at that station. The key to efficient balancing is to group activities in such a way that the work times at a work station are at or slightly under the cycle time (or a multiple of the cycle time if more than one worker is required).

An efficient balance will minimize the amount of idle time. The balance efficiency (Eff_B) can be computed in either of two ways:

$$\text{Eff}_B = \frac{\text{output of task times}}{\text{input of station times}} = \frac{\Sigma t}{(\text{CT})n} \qquad (4\text{-}3)$$

$$\text{Eff}_B = \frac{\text{theoretical minimum number of workers}}{\text{actual number of workers}} \qquad (4\text{-}4)$$

where CT is the cycle time per station and n is the number of stations. The grouping of tasks is done heuristically with the aid of a precedence diagram. Designate work zones on the precedence diagram and move appropriate activities into preceding zones (that is, to the left) until the cycle time is as fully used as possible.

EXAMPLE 4-6

Using the data and precedence diagram from Example 4-5, (a) group the assembly-line tasks into an appropriate number of work stations, and (b) compute the balance efficiency. (*Note*: CT = .70 minute and $\Sigma t = 2.61$ minutes.)

SOLUTION

(a) The CT of .70 means that .70 minute is available at each work station. Activity A consumes .62 of the .70 minute available at the first station, but the next downstream activity (B) is too large to combine with A. Activities B and C can be combined, however, for they total only .66 minute. Similarly, D and E and F and G can be combined as shown:

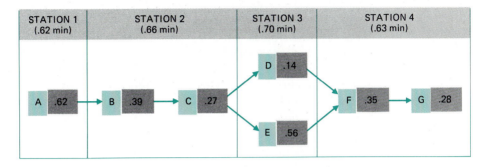

| STATION 1 (.62 min) | STATION 2 (.66 min) | STATION 3 (.70 min) | STATION 4 (.63 min) |

(b) $\text{Eff}_B = \dfrac{\Sigma t}{(CT)n} = \dfrac{2.61}{(.70)\,(4)} = 93\%$

Also $\text{Eff}_B = \dfrac{\text{theoretical minimum number of workers}}{\text{actual number of workers}} = \dfrac{3.73}{4} = 93\%$

Computerized routines are available for testing the multitude of potential work-station configurations that exist for realistic large-scale, line balancing problems. Although they utilize heuristic decision rules, they can rapidly converge on a reasonably good balance. One commonly used heuristic is to move down the network diagram, selecting first those tasks that have the longest activity times, but that still fit within the cycle time available at the work station, while meeting precedence requirements.

In the preceding examples, the output and activity times specified the production-line output and determined the number of work stations. If, instead of output, the number of work stations n is specified, production-line output can be used to define a target cycle time, CT_t:

$$CT_t = \frac{\Sigma t}{n} \qquad (4\text{-}5)$$

where Σt is the summation of activity times. The target cycle time then represents the minimum average time necessary at a work station and must be greater than or equal to the longest activity time.

SUMMARY

The location and layout of a facility involve far-reaching decisions which affect an organization's success. There is no optimizing theory for location, but following a systematic decision process will help ensure that crucial factors are not overlooked. One approach is to first establish *economic feasibility* and then follow with a *qualitative analysis* of the less tangible factors. Foreign locations warrant extra attention.

Locational break-even analysis is a method of considering relevant fixed and variable costs. It provides a graphic aid which illustrates the sensitivity of a given site to a change in volume. If transportation costs are particularly relevant, transportation linear programming methods are useful for locating sites in a manner that will minimize costs.

Facility layout depends largely on (1) the type of product, (2) type of process, and (3) volume of production. The continuum of types of layout ranges from fixed position layouts to job shop, batch processing, line processing, and continuous flow. *Job shop* layouts have equipment grouped according to the function it performs and handle small, customized volumes. *Batch processing* layouts are designed to accommodate larger volumes but still perform the production activities in a step-by-step fashion. *Line processing* layouts typically have conveyors and/or automated processing equipment sequenced to produce large quantities of similar products. *Continuous flow* layouts are designed around a technological process to operate as one integral unit. Service facilities can exhibit characteristics of many different types of layout, but it is usually the recipients of the service (customers) that move rather than goods being produced.

In analyzing layouts, attention has been directed mostly toward minimizing the materials-handling costs of job shop layouts and achieving efficient line balances of line layouts. But good layouts should also provide workers with a satisfying job design.

Several graphic, tabular load-distance, and computerized methods (for example, CRAFT) have been developed to help design layouts that minimize materials-handling costs. All are heuristic approaches that can provide good, but not necessarily optimal, solutions. For line layouts, the balance efficiency is a standard of comparison for judging one layout against another.

SOLVED PROBLEMS

LOCATION PLANNING FOR GOODS AND SERVICES

1 Briefly describe a logical approach to locating a new facility.

Solution
   (a) Follow a systematic decision procedure involving (1) objectives, (2) criteria, (3) a model, (4) alternatives, and (5) selection.
   (b) Evaluate relevant factors in a systematic manner. For example, use an

$$\text{Input} \longrightarrow \text{Processing} \longrightarrow \text{Output}$$

format with sequential attention to national, regional, community, and site considerations.
(c) Determine the economic feasibility first, then follow up with consideration of less
tangible factors.

ECONOMIC ANALYSIS

2 A manufacturer of farm equipment is considering three locations (A, B, and C) for a new
plant. Cost studies show that fixed costs per year at the sites are $240,000, $270,000,
and $252,000, respectively, whereas variable costs are $100 per unit, $90 per unit, and
$95 per unit, respectively. If the plant is designed to have an effective system capacity of
2,500 units per year and is expected to operate at 80 percent efficiency, what is the most
economic location, on the basis of actual output?

Solution

$$\text{Actual output} = (\text{system efficiency}) \ (\text{system capacity})$$

$$= (.80) \ (2,500) = 2,000 \text{ units/yr}$$

$$\text{Cost/site} = \text{FC} + \text{VC} \ (V)$$

$$A = \$240,000 + \$100(2,000) = \$440,000$$

$$B = 270,000 + 90(2,000) = 450,000$$

$$C = 252,000 + 95(2,000) = 442,000$$

The most economical location is A. Note that the actual output is specified, and a
locational break-even chart is not necessary for the solution.

3 A firm is considering four alternative locations for a new plant. It has attempted to study
all costs at the various locations and finds that the production costs of the following items
vary from one location to another. The firm will finance the new plant from bonds
bearing 10 percent interest.

	A	B	C	D
Labor (per unit)	.75	1.10	.80	.90
Plant construction cost (million $)	4.60	3.90	4.0	4.80
Materials and equipment* (per unit)	.43	.60	.40	.55
Electricity (per year)	30,000	26,000	30,000	28,000
Water (per year)	7,000	6,000	7,000	7,000
Transportation (per unit)	.02	.10	.10	.05
Taxes (per year)	33,000	28,000	63,000	35,000

* This cost includes a projected depreciation expense, but no interest cost.

Determine the most suitable location (economically) for output volumes in the range of
50,000 to 130,000 units per year.

Solution

Costs	A	B	C	D
Fixed costs (per yr):				
10% of investment	$460,000	$390,000	$400,000	$480,000
Electricity	30,000	26,000	30,000	28,000
Water	7,000	6,000	7,000	7,000
Taxes	33,000	28,000	63,000	35,000
Total	$530,000	$450,000	$500,000	$550,000
Variable costs (per unit):				
Labor	$.75	$1.10	$.80	$.90
Materials and equipment	.43	.60	.40	.55
Transportation	.02	.10	.10	.05
Total	$1.20	$1.80	$1.30	$1.50
Total costs	$530,000 + $1.20/unit	$450,000 + $1.80/unit	$500,000 + $1.30/unit	$550,000 + $1.50/unit

The points for a plant location break-even analysis chart are as follows. At zero units of output, use fixed-cost values. At 100,000 units of output,

$$A = \$530,000 + 100,000(\$1.20) = \$650,000$$

$$B = \$450,000 + 100,000(\$1.80) = \$630,000$$

$$C = \$500,000 + 100,000(\$1.30) = \$630,000$$

$$D = \$550,000 + 100,000(\$1.50) = \$700,000$$

See the graph of these linear functions in Fig. 4-12. For minimum cost, use site B for a volume of 50,000 to 100,000 units; use site C for a volume of 100,000 to 130,000 units.

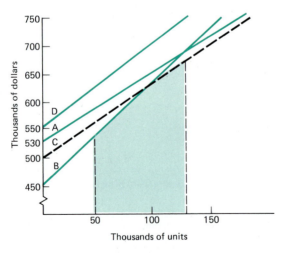

FIGURE 4-12 Plant Location Break-Even Chart

4   Using the data from Solved Prob. 3 assume that the market research department of the firm has estimated the market volume for the product per year over the next 10 years. For volumes (in thousands) of 50, 75, 100, and 200 units, the probabilities are .4, .2, .1, .3, respectively. What is the most suitable location on the basis of an expected value criterion?

Solution

Select site C.

Volume X	Probability P(X)	Expected value XP(X)
50,000	.40	20,000
75,000	.20	15,000
100,000	.10	10,000
200,000	.30	60,000
	Expected demand	105,000

* 5   *Transportation linear programming (Optional)*[1]   The Milltex Company has production plants in Albany, Bend, and Corvallis, all of which manufacture similar paneling for the housing market. The products are currently distributed through plants in Seattle and Portland. The company is considering adding another distribution plant in San Francisco and has developed these transportation costs in dollars per unit:

Production Plants	Cost to ship to distribution plant in:		
	Seattle	Portland	San Francisco
Albany	$10	$14	$ 8
Bend	12	10	12
Corvallis	8	12	10

The production capabilities at the Albany, Bend, and Corvallis plants are 20, 30, and 40 unit loads per week, respectively. Management feels that a San Francisco plant could absorb 20 units per week, with Seattle and Portland claiming 40 and 30 units per week, respectively. Determine the optimal distribution arrangement and cost if the San Francisco site is selected.

Solution

We will use the northwest-corner method for the initial allocation and the stepping-stone method for the final solution. This requires that the data be arranged in a matrix. Figure 4-13 shows supply on the horizontal rows, demand on the columns, and unit transportation costs ($) in the small boxes in the matrix.

The initial allocation via the northwest (NW)-corner method is made as follows.

(a) Assign as many units as possible to the NW-corner cell A1 from the total available in row A. Given the 20-unit available supply in row A and the 40-unit demand in column 1, the maximum number of units that can be assigned to cell A1 is 20.

[1] The solution of transportation linear programming problems is often taught in management science courses, so some instructors may choose not to cover this technique or to designate it as optional.

FIGURE 4-13   Initial Solution to Transportation Linear Programming Matrix

This is shown as (20), indicating an initial allocation.

(b) Assign additional units of supply from row B (or additional rows) until the demand in column 1 is satisfied. This requires 20 additional units in cell B1 and leaves 10 units of B's unassigned.

(c) Assign remaining units in the subject row to the next column, continuing as above until its demand requirements are satisfied. This means the 10 units left in B are assigned to cell B2. Because this does not satisfy demand in column 2, an additional 20 units are allocated from row C.

(d) Continue down from the NW corner until the whole supply has been allocated to demand. The initial assignment is completed by assigning the 20 units remaining in row C to cell C3.

(e) Check allocations to verify that all supply and demand conditions are satisfied. Since all row and column totals agree, the initial assignment is correct. Also, the number of entries is five, which satisfies the $R + C - 1$ requirement (discussed below) for $3 + 3 - 1 = 5$.

The initial solution is, perhaps obviously, not an optimal (or least-cost) allocation scheme. The transportation cost for this arrangement is:

20 units	A to Seattle @ $10/unit =	$200
20 units	B to Seattle @ $12/unit =	240
10 units	B to Portland @ $10/unit =	100
20 units	C to Portland @ $12/unit =	240
20 units	C to San Francisco @ $10/unit =	200
		Total $980

An optimal solution can be obtained by following a stepping-stone approach, which requires calculation of the net monetary gain or loss that can be obtained by shifting an allocation from one supply source to another. The important rule to keep in mind is that every increase (or decrease) in supply at one location must be accompanied by a decrease (or increase) in supply at another. The same holds true for demand. Thus there must be two changes in every row or column that is changed—one change increasing the quantity and one change decreasing it. This is easily done by evaluating reallocations in a closed-path sequence with only right-angle turns permitted and only on occupied cells. Of course, a cell must have an initial entry before it can be reduced in favor of another, but *empty (or filled) cells may be skipped over to get to a corner cell.* To be sure that all reallocation possibilities are considered, it is best to proceed systematically, evaluating each empty cell. When any changes are made, cells vacated earlier must be rechecked.

Only unused transportation paths (vacant cells) need to be evaluated, and there is only one available pattern of moves to evaluate each vacant cell. This is because moves are restricted to occupied cells. Every time a vacant cell is filled, *one* previously occupied cell must become vacant. The initial (and continuing) number of entries is always maintained at $R + C - 1$, that is, number of rows plus number of columns minus 1. When a move happens to cause fewer entries (for example, when two cells become vacant at the same time but only one is filled), a "zero" entry must be retained in one of the cells to avoid what is termed a "degeneracy" situation. The zero entry should be assigned to an independent cell, that is, to one that cannot be reached by a closed path involving only filled cells. The cell with the zero entry is then considered to be an occupied and potentially usable cell.

The criterion for making a reallocation is simply the desired effect on costs. The net loss or gain is determined by listing the unit costs associated with each cell (which is used as a corner in the evaluation path) and then summing over the path to find the net effect. Signs alternate from + to − depending upon whether shipments are being added or reduced at a given point. A negative sign on the net result indicates that a cost reduction can be made by making the change. The total savings are, of course, limited to the least number of units available for reallocation at any negative cell on the path.

Evaluate cell A2:
Path   A2 to B2 to B1 to A1 (designated as I in Fig. 4-14)
Cost $+14 - 10 + 12 - 10 = +6$ (cost increase)
∴ Make no change.

Evaluate cell C1:
Path   C1 to B1 to B2 to C2 (designated as II in Fig. 4-14)
Cost $+8 - 12 + 10 - 12 = -6$ (cost savings)
∴ This is a potential change. Evaluate remaining empty cells to see if other changes are more profitable.

Evaluate cell A3:
Path   A3 to C3 to C2 to B2 to B1 to A3 (not shown in Fig. 4-14)
Cost $+8 - 10 + 12 - 10 + 12 - 10 = +2$ (cost increase)

Evaluate cell B3:
Path   B3 to C3 to C2 to B3 (not shown in Fig. 4-14)
Cost $+12 - 10 + 12 - 10 = +4$ (cost increase)

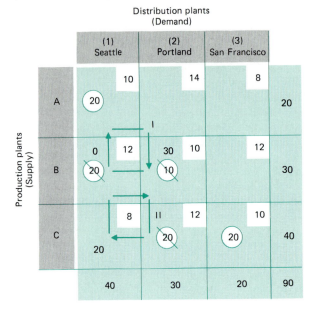

FIGURE 4-14   Revision of Matrix

Cell C1 presents the best (only) opportunity for improvement. For each unit from C reallocated to Seattle and from B reallocated to Portland, a $6 savings results. Change the maximum number available in the loop (20) for a net savings of ($6)(20) = $120. (The maximum number will always be the smallest number in the cells where shipments are being reduced, that is, cells with negative coefficients.) The crossed circles and arrows on loop II of Fig. 4-14 show that transformations have been made. Note that cells B1 and C2 have both become vacant (a degenerate situation), so a zero has been assigned to one of the vacant cells (B1) to maintain the $R + C - 1$ requirement of 5. Since a reallocation was made, the empty cells are again evaluated for further improvement:

Cell A2:   A2–B2–B1–A1 = +6 (no change)

Cell C2:   C2–C1–B1–B2 = +6 (no change)

Cell A3:   A3–C3–C1–A1 = −4 (a possibility)

Cell B3:   B3–C3–C1–B1 = −2 (a possibility)

Cell A3 has the greatest potential for improvement. (Note that the loop evaluating cell B3 has zero units available for transfer from cell B1, so no reallocation could take place without first locating another route to B3. This would be done by relocating the zero.[2] However, in this example cell A3 offers the best improvement, so we capitalize

_____

[2] If a cell evaluation reveals an improvement potential in a given cell but no units are available because of a zero entry in the path to that cell, the zero (zero units) should be transported to the vacant cell just as any other units would be shipped. Then the matrix should be reevaluated. Improvements may still be possible until the zero entries are relocated to where evaluations of all vacant cells are ≥ 0.

Distribution plants
(Demand)

		(1) Seattle	(2) Portland	(3) San Francisco	
	A	10	14	8	20
			20		
	B	12	10	12	30
		0	30		
	C	8	12	10	40
		40		0	
		40	30	20	90

Production plants (Supply)

FIGURE 4-15   Optimal Solution

upon the opportunity to load cell A3.) A reallocation of 20 units to cell A3 results in the matrix shown in Fig. 4-15. Note that a zero has again been retained in one of the vacated cells (C3) to satisfy the $R + C - 1$ constraint.

Further evaluation of the cells reveals that no additional savings can be achieved. The optimal solution is as shown in Fig. 4-15. The transportation cost for this arrangement is:

40 units from C to Seattle @ $8/unit	$320
30 units from B to Portland @ $10/unit	300
20 units from A to San Francisco @ $8/unit	160
Total	$780

Net savings over the initial allocation: $980 - $780 = $200/week.

ANALYSIS AND SELECTION OF LAYOUTS

6   *Load-distance analysis*   A facility that will be used to produce a single product has three departments (A, B, C) that must be housed in the configuration shown on the right below. Two trial-and-error layouts are shown on the left.

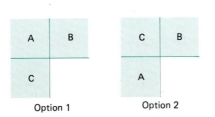

Option 1   Option 2

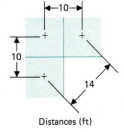

Distances (ft)

The interdepartmental workload flows and travel distances between work centers are given below. Evaluate the two layouts on a load-distance basis and identify the preferred layout. Assume that the cost to transport this product is $1 per load-foot.

Interdepartmental
Workload per Week

To / From	A	B	C
A	—	30	25
B	20	—	40
C	15	50	—

Solution

No. Loads per Week (Both Directions)	Option 1 (load)(distance)	Option 2 (load)(distance)
A to B and B to A = 30 + 20 = 50	(50)(10) = 500	(50)(14) = 700
A to C and C to A = 25 + 15 = 40	(40)(10) = 400	(40)(10) = 400
B to C and C to B = 40 + 50 = 90	(90)(14) = 1,260	(90)(10) = 900
	Total 2,160	2,000

At $1 per load-foot, option 2 would be preferred at a total cost of $2,000. However, 3 factorial (!) or $3 \cdot 2 \cdot 1 = 6$, options are possible, and a different arrangement may be less costly.

7 Suppose the activities shown in Example 4-5 are to be grouped into a three-station assembly line.
(a) Find the new target cycle time.
(b) Which grouping of activities results in the largest output per hour?
(c) What output will result from a 7-hour day?

Solution

$$CT_t = \frac{\Sigma t}{n} = \frac{2.61 \text{ min}}{3 \text{ stations}} = .87 \text{ min/station}$$

The largest output will result from the smallest CT. Three possible groupings (trials) are as follows—although none are within 10 percent of the target.

Trial	Station 1	Station 2	Station 3	CT
1	.62	.39 + .27 = .66	.14 + .56 + .35 + .28 = 1.33	1.33
2	.62	.39 + .27 + .14 = .80	.56 + .35 + .28 = 1.19	1.19
3	.62 + .39 = 1.01	.27 + .56 = .83	.14 + .35 + .28 = .77	1.01

The third grouping is best. Using the 1.01 CT, we have:

$$\text{Output} = \frac{(7 \text{ hr/day})(60 \text{ min/hr})}{1.01 \text{ min/unit}} = 416 \text{ units/day}$$

8 A Los Angeles producer of electronic equipment needs to add a component subassembly operation that can produce 80 units during a regular 8-hour shift. The operations have been designed for three activities with times as shown below:

Operation	Activity	Standard Time (min)
A	Mechanical assembly	12
B	Electric wiring	16
C	Test	3

(a) How many work stations (in parallel) will be required for each activity?

(b) Assuming that the workers at each station cannot be used for other activities in the plant, what is the appropriate percentage of idle time for this subassembly operation?

Solution

(a) With 480 minutes per day available to each activity, the output capacities per single work station would be as shown in the accompanying diagram.

	A	B	C
Capacities per station	$\frac{480}{12} = 40/day \rightarrow$	$\frac{480}{16} = 30/day \rightarrow$	$\frac{480}{3} = 160/day \rightarrow$
Capacities required	80/day	80/day	80/day
Number of stations	$\frac{80}{40} = 2$	$\frac{80}{30} = 2.7$	$\frac{80}{160} = 0.5$
Rounded to min number	2 stations	3 stations	1 station

(b) Idle time can be determined by comparing the total time available with the standard time.

Time Available (at 480 min/day)	Standard Time (min)
A: 2 stations = 960	A: 80 units at 12 min = 960
B: 3 stations = 1,440	B: 80 units at 16 min = 1,280
C: 1 station = 480	C: 80 units at 3 min = 240
2,880	2,480

$$\text{Percent idle time} = \frac{\text{total available} - \text{standard}}{\text{total available}} = \frac{2,880 - 2,480}{2,880} = 14\%$$

9 An electric appliance assembly area is as shown in the accompanying figure, with potential work stations A through F. The tasks that must be done, along with their respective times, are indicated in the precedence diagram.

The machine scan is automatic and can come anytime after task 2. The manufacturer desires an output of 367 units per 8-hour day and stops the line for a 20-minute break in the middle of the morning and the afternoon.

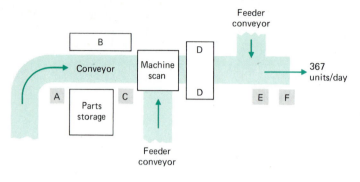

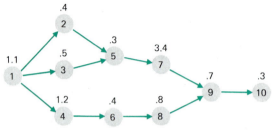

(a) Group the assembly line tasks into appropriate work stations.
(b) Compute the balance efficiency.

Solution

(a) The precedence diagram is given, complete with task times. We first compute the cycle time:

$$CT = \frac{AT}{output}$$

where   AT = 480 min/day − 40 min/day = 440 min/day
output = 367 units/day

$$CT = \frac{440}{367} = 1.20 \text{ min/unit}$$

This means that each worker can be scheduled for up to 1.2 minutes of work at a work station. If any station requires more than 1.2 minutes of work, additional workers will be needed at that station.

Next, we group the tasks into amounts of work that can be done at a work station. For reference, we can number the precedence diagram columns. Column 1 time at 1.1 minutes almost fully consumes a work station time (1.2 minutes), and there are no .1 minute downstream tasks that can be moved up, so column 1 is filled.

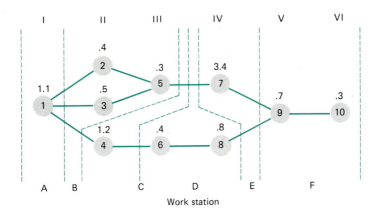

Task 4 in column 2 requires the full 1.2 minutes available, but tasks 2 and 3 add up to only .9 minute, and there appears to be sufficient time to bring task 5 into the same work station zone. We proceed in this manner, marking off zones with dotted lines, until our ultimate grouping is as shown in the following table. Note that task 7 requires 3.4 minutes of work. Because the nearest ($\geq$) multiple of cycle time is 3.6 (i.e., 3 × 1.2), this station will require three workers. The addition of two extra workers makes the *equivalent* number of work stations (or number of workers) eight rather than six; so we will use that for our calculations.

Work Station	A	B	C	D	E	F	
Tasks	1	2, 3, 5	4	6, 8	7	9, 10	
Actual time (min)	1.1	1.2	1.2	1.2	3.4	1.0	$\Sigma t = 9.1$

(b) $$\text{Eff}_B = \frac{\Sigma t}{(CT)n} = \frac{9.1}{1.2(8)} = 94.8\%$$

QUESTIONS

4-1   What (five) steps are suggested for making location decisions?

4-2   Four different organizations are considering your hometown as a potential plant location: (1) a medical research center, (2) a soft-drink producer, (3) a steel mill, (4) a uranium-mining firm. Select one of the four, and systematically evaluate the relevant locational factors.

4-3   You are given the assignment of developing an economic evaluation of four potential plant sites. The analysis is to be applicable to a relatively wide range of volumes. It is to be presented to the board of directors in summary form for their consideration. Describe how you would develop and present the data.

4-4   In what respect is the location of goods-producing facilities more flexible than that of services-producing facilities?

4-5   How do international location considerations differ from domestic location considerations? (You may answer by briefly identifying some problem areas that are unique to international locations.)

4-6 An equipment supplier has collected the following data on possible plant locations. Costs are in dollars per year.

	Site A	Site B	Site C
Rent and utilities	$ 10,000	$ 12,000	$ 15,000
Taxes	2,000	1,500	1,000
Labor	95,000	80,000	90,000
Materials	130,000	132,000	127,000
	$237,000	$225,500	$233,000
Community services	Good	Poor	Average
Community attitude	Indifferent	Indifferent	Favorable

If you were responsible for making the decision on the basis of the information given, which site would you select, and why?

4-7 Describe briefly how transportation linear programming can be used to help analyze location problems.

4-8 What three factors are especially significant in determining the type of layout?

4-9 Distinguish among the following types of layout: (a) fixed position, (b) job shop, (c) line processing.

4-10 Select a service system of your choice and describe its type of layout. What is the major difference between that layout and one designed to produce tangible goods?

4-11 How do the major layout concerns vary between job shop and line processing layouts?

4-12 How does the systematic layout planning approach differ from the basic load-distance analysis?

PROBLEMS

1 Powerpac Equipment Company is evaluating three cities for a new plant designed to produce lawn mowers which will sell for $170 each. The economic portion of a plant location study shows the following cost and market data.

Cost data	City A	City B	City C
Fixed costs/yr	$300,000	$200,000	$150,000
Variable costs/unit	30	45	65

Market data	
Volume X	P(X)
4,500	.10
5,500	.30
6,500	.60

(a) On the basis of maximizing an economic expected value, graph the plant location cost curves using appropriate scales.

(b) Which city should be selected on the basis of the given volume estimate? (Use your graph.)

(c) What is the break-even volume for the city selected?

2   The Hadley Steel Tank Company has conducted a cost study of three potential locations for a new plant. The company plans to construct the plant, sell it to an investment firm, and lease it back. Estimated costs are shown in the following table.

	Birmingham	Detroit	Savannah
Plant rental (per year)	$90,000	$100,000	$160,000
Tank materials (per unit)	7,900	7,500	7,000
Utilities (annual cost)	24,000	28,000	30,000
Labor cost per tank	1,700	2,200	2,400
Taxes (per yr)	12,000	12,000	15,000
Transportation (per unit)	1,400	800	600

Management's best-researched estimate of the market is as follows:

No. of Tanks/Yr	Percentage Chance
500	.20
800	.50
1,000	.30

On the basis of the number of tanks expected to be sold, which plant location is best from an economic standpoint? (Graphing the solution is optional.)

3   Western Agricultural Products Company has chemical fertilizer plants in Pomona, Red Bluff, and Sacramento with capacities (tons/week) of 350, 500, and 280, respectively. The physical distribution manager wishes to determine which shipping arrangement would be best for meeting demands of 400 tons per week in each of two locations (Boulder and Claremont), with the remainder going to Kent. The transportation cost (dollars) associated with shipping unit loads of a fertilizer is as shown below:

From \ To	Boulder	Claremont	Kent
Pomona	5	2	7
Red Bluff	11	5	3
Sacramento	10	8	5

Set up a transportation matrix that could be solved by transportation linear programming methods to determine the optimal allocation of supply to meet demand.

4   Use transportation linear programming to determine the optimal distribution arrangement for Prob. 3.
(a) What is the optimal shipping arrangement?
(b) What is the weekly shipping cost?

5   A large copper producer has refineries in Magna, Utah; Yuma, Arizona; and Grants, New Mexico—all of which receive ore from mines identified as MX-1, MX-2, MX-3, and MX-4, located in the Four Corners area. The mine supply and mill capacities (units/day) and shipping cost ($/unit load) data are shown.

| | Refineries | | | |
	Magna	Yuma	Grants	Supply
MX-1	3	5	5	400
MX-2	5	7	8	500
MX-3	2	9	5	200
MX-4	10	7	3	700
Capacity	500	500	800	1,800 units/day

The vice president of operations has requested that you analyze the transportation costs and determine an optimal distribution.

6   Suppose that in Prob. 5, MX-4 is closed because of low-grade ore and MX-5, which has the same capacity (700 units/day), is opened. It has shipping costs to Magna, Yuma, and Grants of $4, $8, and $12, respectively. What is the optimal distribution now?

7   Suppose that in Prob. 5, the variable production costs ($/unit load) for mines MX-1, MX-2, MX-3, and MX-4 are $2, $1, $3, and $1, respectively. What is the optimal distribution, taking production as well as distribution costs into account?

8   A firm producing automobile components has the following production capacities (units/month), assembly requirements, and transportation costs ($).

| Production plant | Assembly location | | | |
	Memphis	Newark	San Jose	Capacity
Atlanta	5	7	10	160
Boston	11	6	12	240
Chicago	7	8	10	200
*				200
Requirement	220	280	300	800

The asterisk in the box under "Chicago" indicates a new plant with a capacity of 200 units/month. It is to be located in either Dallas or Denver.

	Fixed Costs/Mo	Variable Costs/Unit	Cost to Ship to		
			Memphis	Newark	San Jose
Denver	$6,000	$5.70	$6	$8	$ 6
Dallas	5,100	5.50	5	9	11

From a cost standpoint, which is the better site for the fourth plant, Denver or Dallas? Structure your answer in such a way as to show the total relevant costs under each alternative.

9 Coombes Container Company is considering three potential locations for a new aluminum can plant, and management has assigned the scores shown below to the relevant factors on a 0 to 100 basis (100 is best).

Score of Relevant Factor for Plant Location

	Hong Kong	Manila	Honolulu
Material supply	50	90	80
Labor cost	90	80	40
Regulations	100	60	30
Distribution	30	80	70

The relevant factors have been assigned the following weights: material supply = .3, labor cost = .3, regulations = .2, distribution = .2. Using a qualitative factor-rating analysis, which location is preferred?

10 The Miltex Company, which has distribution plants in Syracuse and Philadelphia, is considering adding a third assembly and distribution plant in either Athens, Baltimore, or Chapel Hill. The company has collected the economic and noneconomic data shown below.

Factor	Athens	Baltimore	Chapel Hill
Transportation cost/week	$ 780	$ 640	$ 560
Labor cost/week	$1,200	$1,020	$1,180
Selected criteria scores (based on a scale of 0–100 points):			
Finishing material supply	35	85	70
Maintenance facilities	60	25	30
Community attitude	50	85	70

Company management has preestablished weights for various factors, ranging from 0 to 1.0. They include a standard of .2 for each $10 per week of economic advantage. Other weights that are applicable are .3 on finishing material supply, .1 on maintenance facilities, and .4 on community attitudes. Maintenance also has a minimum acceptable score of 30. Develop a qualitative factor comparison for the three locations.

11 A small facility for producing leather and wool sportswear is to be housed in a structure that has the configuration shown below on the left. Two alternative layouts of the four

departments are also shown. These layouts are to handle the following workloads per week.

From \ To	A	B	C	D
A	—	30	20	—
B	10	—	20	—
C	50	5	—	40
D	—	20	10	—

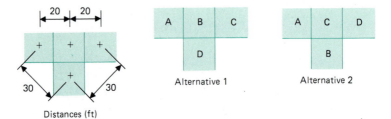

Distances (ft)

Alternative 1

Alternative 2

Assuming that the cost to transport the product is $.10 per load-foot, evaluate the two layouts and identify the least-cost layout.

12 The distances between the centers of the departments described in Example 4-4 are as shown.

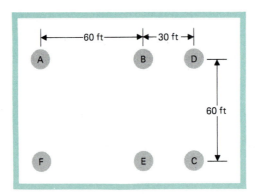

(a) Using daily totals, compute the (load)(distance) for the arrangement offered as a solution.
(b) Suppose the cost to move a load is $.025 per foot. Compute the materials-handling cost per day.
(c) Use trial and error to develop a better (less costly) layout, and diagram it. Approximately how much of a saving per day and per (250-workday) year results from your layout?

13 Six work centers (WCs) are to be located in the facility shown below in a layout that satisfies the following:

WC1 must adjoin WC4 and must also adjoin WC5.
WC5 must adjoin WC6.
WC2 and WC5 must be separated.

(a) Using only the nearness codes a, o, and x, state these requirements in terms of a Muther grid. Assume unspecified relationships are all of ordinary importance.
(b) Develop one acceptable arrangement on a trial-and-error basis.

14 Given the Muther grid requirements shown below for a facility with six work centers (WCs), arrange the WCs into a three-row by two-column grid that satisfies the nearness criteria shown.

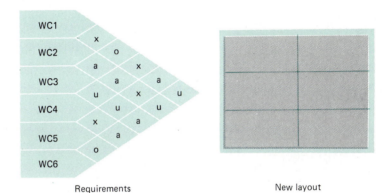

Requirements   New layout

15 A line balancing problem involves 10 work stations having a Σ times = 24.0 minutes (where the shortest is 2.1 minutes and the longest is 3.0 minutes). Assuming only one worker is located at each station, and using the longest time as the cycle time, what would be the balance efficiency?

16 A line balancing analysis resulted in a precedence grouping as shown below. Find the balance efficiency, assuming the longest actual time is the cycle time.

Work Center	Activity Numbers	Actual Time (min)
A	1, 2	1.2
B	3, 5, 6	1.4
C	4, 7	.9
D	8, 10, 11	1.3
E	9	1.5

17 A furniture-manufacturing activity requires the times shown in the diagram to perform five tasks in an assembly line. Operations are to be scheduled for producing six units per hour, and each employee can contribute 48 minutes per hour of productive work.
(a) What is the cycle time in minutes per unit?

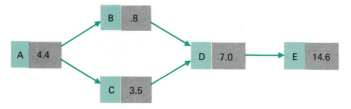

(b) What is the theoretical minimum number of personnel?

(c) Combine the tasks into the most efficient grouping of work stations. What is the resulting efficiency of balance?

18 A computer manufacturing line operates 7 hours and 45 minutes each day at a rate sufficient to produce 1,395 personal computers per day. The line has six work stations (A . . . F) with total work times as shown below in seconds.

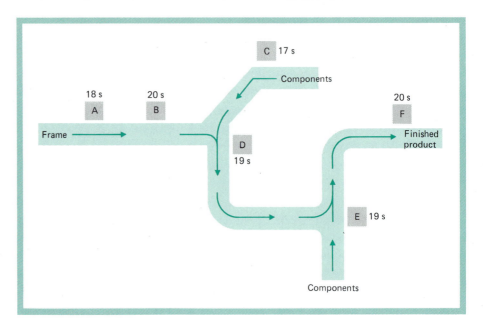

(a) What is the cycle time?

(b) What is the balance efficiency?

19 A toy manufacturer produces dollhouses on a product line geared to an output of one per minute. The assembly precedence relationships and activity times (in minutes) are as shown.

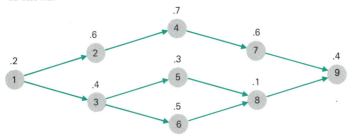

(a) Group the activities into the most efficient arrangement.

(b) What is the balance efficiency (Eff_B)?

20 Robotic Controls Corporation uses a robotic-controlled flexible production system to assemble the robots it sells. Five robots are available and must complete the tasks specified in the table.

Task	Time (sec)	Preceding Task(s)
A	10	None
B	24	None
C	17	A
D	49	A
E	12	C
F	14	C
G	27	B
H	9	E
I	20	F, G
J	23	D, H, I
K	36	I
L	18	J, K

(a) Draw a precedence diagram.

(b) What is the theoretical minimum (target) cycle time if all five robots are fully utilized in a five-station assembly line?

(c) Group the tasks into the most efficient five-station assembly line.

(d) What is the cycle time?

(e) What is the balance efficiency?

REFERENCES

[1] Buffa, Elwood S.: *Modern Production/Operations Management*, 7th ed., Wiley, New York, 1984.

[2] Francis, R., and J. White: *Facility Layout and Location: An Analytical Approach*, Prentice-Hall, Englewood Cliffs, NJ, 1974.

[3] Gaither, Norman: *Production and Operations Management*, 2d ed., Dryden Press, Hinsdale, IL, 1984.

[4] Hendrick, Thomas E., and Franklin G. Moore: *Production/Operations Management*, 9th ed., Richard D. Irwin, Homewood, IL, 1985.

[5] Koenig, Richard, "U.S. Is Looking for New Ways to Spur Space Manufacturing," *The Wall Street Journal*, Nov. 16, 1984, p. 35.

[6] Miller, Edward, "Japan Pursues Auto Market," in *The Spokesman Review & Spokane Chronicle*, Spokane, WA, Oct. 13, 1985, p. B3.

[7] Moreland, Unruh, Smith, and Parametrix, Inc.: *An Assessment of the Impact of the Proposed Hewlett-Packard Facility on the City of Corvallis*, Eugene, OR, September 1974.

[8] Muther, Richard, and K. McPherson: "Four Approaches to Computerized Layout," *Industrial Engineering*, February 1970.

[9] Reed, Rudell: *Plant Location, Layout, and Maintenance*, Richard D. Irwin, Homewood, IL, 1967.

[10] Schlesinger, Stephen, and Stephen Kinzer: *Bitter Fruit: The Untold Story of the American Coup in Guatemala*, Doubleday, London, 1982.

[11] Schmenner, Roger W.: *Production/Operations Management*, 2d ed., Science Research Associates, Palo Alto, CA, 1984.

[12] Tektronix, Inc.: Annual Report, Beaverton, OR, 1980.

[13] "What Does It Take to Get 600 Workers to Relocate in Ohio? American Electric Layouts $20,000 Each in Benefits: Loans to Driving Lessons," *The Wall Street Journal*, July 15, 1980.

[14] "What Management Needs to Know before Picking a Plant Site," *Duns Review*, October 1979, pp. 14–19.

[15] Winter, Ralph E.: "Computer-Guided Tools Are Catching On," *The Wall Street Journal*, Feb. 28, 1986, p. 6.

SELF QUIZ: CHAPTER 4

POINTS: 15

Part I True/False [1 point each = 6]

1 _____ There is no general method of analysis that assures a firm it has selected an optimal location.

2 _____ The productivity of workers in third-world countries typically lags behind that of workers in the United States.

3 _____ Qualitative factor analysis is a method of evaluating a potential location without applying quantitative values to the decision criteria.

4 _____ The three determinants of the type of layout are type of product, type of process, and volume of production.

5 _____ An appliance manufacturing plant where products are made on assembly lines would be classified as a job shop type of layout.

6 _____ The major layout concern for a line processing layout is to minimize materials-handling costs by selecting layouts with the smallest (load) (distance) totals.

Part II Problems [3 points each = 9. Calculate and select your answer.]

1 Potential locations A, B, and C have the cost structure shown. For which yearly volume of production would location B be most economical?

(a) 0– 500 units
(b) ≤ 600 units
(c) 500–1,000 units
(d) 600–1,000 units
(e) ≥1,000 units

Site	Fixed Cost/Yr	Variable Cost/Unit
A	$10,000	$70
B	30,000	30
C	40,000	20

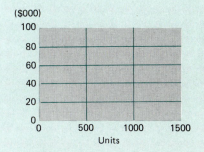

2 A transportation linear programming problem was solved to yield the transportation (only) costs shown in the matrix. If production costs of $10 per unit (at all locations) are included, the total costs associated with this solution are:

(a) $ 700
(b) 1,500
(c) 2,200
(d) 8,000
(e) None of the above

Distribution Center

Plant	X	Y	Z	Dummy	
A	10	14 __20__	8	0	20
B	12	10 __30__	12	0	30
C	8 __30__	12	10	0 __10__	40
	30	30	20	10	90

3 A computer assembly line has the precedence relationships and work station time requirements shown. Output is to be 400 units during a 440-minute work day. Determine the required cycle time and group the activities into the most efficient balance.

The balance efficiency is:

(a) 86 percent
(b) 95 percent
(c) 96 percent
(d) 98 percent
(e) None of the above

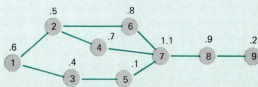

CHAPTER 5
PRODUCTS AND PROCESSES

154-170
175-188

INTRODUCTION

How are new products created for the market? Synthetic "natural" gas is now flowing in commercial pipelines for the first time. New electronic talking toys are appearing almost weekly. "Scent strips" didn't exist a short time ago. Now they are widely used in magazines to advertise perfumes and lotions. The 3M Company even has one that contains some 50 million tiny fragrance capsules on one square inch of paper [5]. Before long you may be studying out of "books" that have a computer screen on the back inside cover—so you'll simply flip to it to look up table values, solve your homework problems, or even store your class notes.

New services are also entering the market at a rapid clip. General Electric's electronic mail service now permits subscribers to send and receive their mail through their computers instead of physically handling millions of sheets of paper. Over 25,000 new franchises are opening up yearly. (McDonald's is opening new restaurants at the rate of 1 every 17 hours [8]. Banks are branching out into brokerage businesses and supermarkets are offering savings accounts. New product innovation is truly the essence of competition for many U.S. companies.

Products are the goods and services produced, and *processes* are the facilities, skills, and technologies used to produce them. The two go together—products require processes and processes limit what products can be produced.

In today's competitive environment, both products and processes are critical elements of an organization's operating strategy. Successful products must reflect a creative and intimate knowledge of the *market* environment. And the processes used to produce or deliver them must make effective use of the firm's resources and available levels of *technology*. The person challenged to respond to the market demands by making best use of the firm's capabilities is the operations manager.

We begin this chapter by identifying the sources of new-product ideas and tracing their flow through the feasibility study into product design. Then we will consider ways to choose what mix of products to produce. Next we turn to an analysis of the production process. The chapter concludes with some recommendations for analyzing ongoing processes to improve their overall effectiveness.

PRODUCT AND PROCESS OVERVIEW

The path from an idea to a finished product is by no means fixed. It depends upon the nature of the firm, the product, and numerous other factors. Figure 5-1 illustrates one of many possible routes through the product and process design stages. In general, the environmental (priority) influences are shown on the left and the organizational (capacity) capabilities on the right. The major steps include new-product development, a feasibility study, the product and process design stages, and the implementation stage. But before examining selected aspects of this process, we should note some differences in planning for goods versus planning for services.

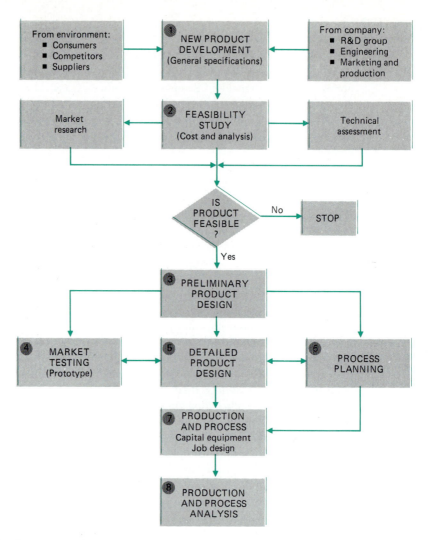

FIGURE 5-1   Product and Process Design and Analysis

PLANNING FOR GOODS AND SERVICES

Firms actively search out new-product ideas from both external and internal sources. Externally, customers and competitors are major contributors of ideas. Customer surveys and warranty correspondence sometimes suggest product changes and improvements. Assessment of competitive products is another common source of ideas. Unscrupulous firms even engage in "industrial espionage" to steal ideas before they are marketed. This has prompted the more innovative firms to establish tight security over their new-product development activities. Large firms often retain patent attorneys to secure patents on their new inventions and process legal claims against companies infringing on them.

Other firms take different approaches, such as that of ISC Systems Corporation, an electronics company producing bank teller machines [4].

> ISC does not hold any patents or licenses. Management believes that patents and licenses are of lesser significance than the innovative software skills, technological engineering and service experience, and marketing ability of its personnel.

GOODS VERSUS SERVICES

New-product planning for goods and services must allow for such differences between the two types of products as those listed in Fig. 5-2.

Goods Planning for goods tends to be formalized because product design, processing activities, and quality standards can be specified in detail. In addition, the manufacturing environment, because it is separated from the consumer, can be more tightly controlled.

Services Service activities are distinguished by (1) the absence of a physical product, (2) the dependence upon trained personnel, and (3) a close linkage with the market environment. These characteristics have tended to make the development of services more flexible than the planning for goods.

In the past, detailed specifications of services were often neglected, resulting in nonstandard and inconsistent levels of performance. Today, performance specifications are more common. We have standards for sorting mail, cooking hamburgers, responding to fires, and even making beds. The quality of these and other services rests heavily upon the capability and training of the "servers." In contrast, with goods production, quality standards can be designed into the production process.

Finally, the close proximity of services to the changing marketplace means that service providers must have the flexibility to adapt to individual needs.

Goods	Services
▪ *Tangible* (physical) product	▪ *Less tangible* product
▪ Value stored *in product*	▪ Value conveyed *as used*
▪ Produced in *industrial environment* (away from customers)	▪ Produced in *market* environment (with customer)
▪ Often *standardized*	▪ Often *customized*
▪ Quality inherent in *good* (a function of materials)	▪ Quality inherent in *process* (a function of personnel)

FIGURE 5-2 Differences in Planning for Goods versus Services

Medical and insurance products are custom-designed on the spot for the consumer. Architectural and advertising services rely strongly on customer suggestions. Many services, from cafeterias to college degree programs, even give the customer a significant role in designing his or her own product.

SERVICE DELIVERY SYSTEMS

Services consist of social processes that involve a physical or informational interaction between a provider and a client. Customers enter service systems with the expectation of receiving some self-satisfying benefit such as transportation, food, advice, knowledge, or medical care. They expect to emerge from the process feeling better off [6:18].

But directing and controlling social interactions is a difficult task—often more complex than managing physical processes. Intangible psychological or emotional benefits are not easily delineated, conveyed, or measured. This means that planning effective service delivery systems can be more difficult than planning manufacturing systems.

The interaction of clients and employees really lies at the heart of most service systems. As illustrated in Fig. 5-3, the inputs to a service delivery system, like inputs to a goods-producing system, are (1) the market priorities and (2) the organizational capacities. But service delivery systems integrate consumers more fully as active participants in the production system itself.

With customers participating in the service activities, the distinction between production and marketing functions is less definite for services than for goods. Production employees carry a marketing responsibility as they interact directly with customers. The knowledge they gain from this interaction then becomes the

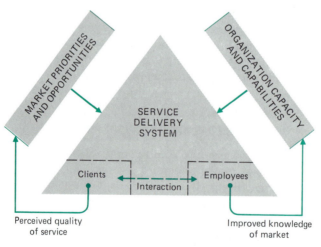

FIGURE 5-3   Client as Participant in Service Delivery System

basis for improvements and training efforts that enhance the organization's service capability.

Customer perceptions of the service delivery system are also vital to marketing efforts designed to retain existing customers and attract new ones. Services such as recreation and legal counseling, being intangible products, cannot be physically purchased and demonstrated in the same manner as a good, such as a refrigerator. Instead, the providers of services must rely upon customers' perceptions of quality. This forces service organizations to integrate their marketing strategy more fully into the service delivery system.

RESEARCH AND DEVELOPMENT

Research and development (R&D) activities are a major internal source of new-product ideas. *Research* is a consciously directed investigation to find new knowledge. It is the forerunner of an increasing number of products and processes—from the first nylon fiber to the latest discoveries in fiber optics that may someday eliminate the need for light sockets and bulbs.

As technology advances, new breakthroughs become ever more difficult to achieve, for they depend increasingly upon the knowledge base of the past. That is why today—more than ever before—research is a team effort, bringing many disciplines together on a single project. And it is expensive, sometimes commanding up to 5 or 6 percent of total company sales revenue. The U.S. government spends approximately $30 to $40 billion per year on R&D, and private companies spend from $50 to $60 billion per year.

Types of Research   *Basic research* seeks knowledge for knowledge's sake, without regard for any marketable use of discoveries. Universities and foundations conduct a considerable amount of basic research, though in balance far more effort is put into applied research. *Applied research* is directed toward solving specific problems as well as developing certain products or processes. Firms in high-technology industries are heavily dependent upon applied research. In many cases a large percentage of their current sales (perhaps up to 80 or 90 percent) is from products that did not exist a few years earlier.

Development includes the simulated (or pilot plant) production of new products plus the test marketing of prototype products. These efforts often consume the bulk of R&D funds.

Challenges in R&D Management   Research, by definition, has an uncertain outcome and much of it must be written off as a loss. Sometimes the impracticability of a project is not discovered until the developmental stage.

Research activities can also be difficult to manage because of unexpected problems and unavoidable delays. Time and cost estimates are often understated, even when slippage is allowed for. That is one reason why project scheduling and control techniques, such as PERT (to be described in a later chapter), are so important to government and defense contractors like the Boeing Company.

PRODUCT DESIGN

Product design is the structuring of component parts or activities so that as a unit they can provide a specified value, such as a 1,000-hour-life guarantee on a lightbulb. Typically an engineering function, design entails preparing detailed drawings or specifications that give dimensions, weights, colors, and other physical characteristics. In service industries, *product specification* describes what services employees will provide for their clients. The specification may include an environmental requirement, such as a no-smoking section, or a procedure for service delivery, such as the steps for admitting a patient to a hospital.

Standardization Design, production, and marketing costs are reduced by standardizing and simplifying the product. *Standardization* involves producing items to a commonly accepted standard to assure the interchangeability and/or the quality level of the product. The use of a limited number of uniform parts reduces the sizes and number of items to be purchased, cuts inventory storage and handling costs, and enables firms to work with larger (and more economical) quantities of fewer items. Standardization makes both mass production and maintenance much easier. However, standardization limits the options available to consumers.

Modular designs also facilitate production and maintenance. Modules are common components grouped into interchangeable subassemblies. They can range in size from microelectronic components to pieces of prefabricated houses.

Value Analysis and Simplification Once developed, many products undergo *value engineering* or *value analysis*. This is an attempt to see if any materials or components can be substituted or redesigned in such a way as to continue to perform the desired function, but at a lower cost. After prototype units are designed and produced, the products are further analyzed and tested to see how well the quality, performance, and costs conform to the design objectives. *Simplification* may take place to reduce unnecessary variety in the product line by decreasing the number and variety of products produced. For example, IBM simplified their Selectric typewriter offerings by reducing the number of color choices from 36 to 1 (ivory).

CAD/CAM CAD/CAM activities reflect the trend toward a fully automated manufacturing facility, which may ultimately link product design and manufacturing activities with material and capacity planning, scheduling, materials handling, and finished inventory control. The potential for such an integrated factory rests upon the use of computers and a carefully designed database. In the common database, each element (for example, a part number) is listed only once, but the relevant characteristics of the elements (size, composition, number in stock) are available online to many functional users such as production, engineering, and marketing personnel.

Computer-aided design (CAD) is the use of computerized work stations, complete with database and computer graphics, to rapidly develop and analyze a product's design. The designer can input specifications, then use computerized programs to create a three-dimensional geometric model of the product. That image can be rotated on the screen for a display from different angles of the product's characteristics and appearance even before it is manufactured. In addition, these programs allow designers to determine costs and test such variables as stress, tolerances, product reliability, and serviceability.

Computer-aided manufacturing (CAM) follows CAD. It is the extensive use of computers to accomplish and control production operations. Materials requirements and fabrication sequences must first be specified in detail. Computers are then used in conjunction with numerically controlled (NC) machines and process controllers to automate the manufacturing process as much as is practical.

Computerized NC machines convert CAD specifications into precise machine commands that will produce a given part. In addition, groups of NC machines can be linked in a hierarchical network that makes use of production, scheduling, downtime, quality, and other information that can improve productivity. This linkage, of course, is highly dependent upon having a common database. The use of laser markers, machine-readable bar codes, and even voice-monitoring systems is contributing to the success of these systems.

Group technology (GT) is a method of grouping similar parts or products into families to facilitate both design and manufacturing activities. This grouping minimizes the differences due to individual designs and routings, in favor of standardized processes. By reducing setup and changeover times, GT concepts help firms produce customized products at medium to high volumes.

Very highly automated computer-controlled systems can operate essentially on their own. Some executives even speak of turning off the lights at the end of the day shift and going home—leaving the factory to run automatically during the night shift (in the dark!). Robots then do much of the work, making such diverse products as appliances (for General Electric), printers (for IBM), and automobile parts (for General Motors).

PRODUCT LIFE CYCLES

Most products pass through the common stages of introduction, growth, maturity, and decline, as depicted in Fig. 5-4. Sales often begin slowly as the market for the new product is developed. With customer acceptance and design improvements, the product's sales grow rapidly and its use becomes more widespread. As the market becomes saturated, sales may stabilize for a time (perhaps even for many years). Eventually, the product is modified or superseded by a new product, and demand subsides.

Not all products follow the same pattern, and the demand for some goods doesn't seem to decline at all (such as for paper clips). But a knowledge of the product life cycle curve helps planners to forecast demand and to maintain a viable mix of products in the firm's product line.

Multiproducts A firm's mix of products directly affects its return on investment. Products in an introductory stage often have low (or no) profits because of the high

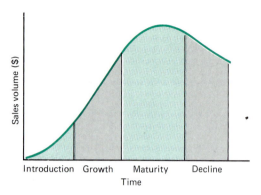

FIGURE 5-4 Typical Good/Service Life Cycle

start-up costs of new production processes and market penetration efforts. As on-the-job learning takes place, operations become more efficient. With increased volume, profits tend to climb until competition, rising costs, or a decline in usage narrows the profit margins.

Most production processes are adjustable within product lines, and firms often produce several products from the same production system. Figure 5-5 identifies some benefits of multiproduct systems.

PRODUCT SELECTION CONSIDERATIONS

Product selection decisions are influenced by (1) the firm's resource and technology base, (2) the market environment, and (3) the firm's motivation to use its capabilities to meet the needs of the marketplace. Motivation is often economic, but it can also be social, political, religious, or other, especially where services are involved. Figure 5-6 depicts some of the factors involved and suggests that successful organizations match their resource capabilities against market demands to produce at an economic or social advantage.

LINEAR PROGRAMMING FOR PRODUCT-MIX DECISIONS

Within the product-line groupings, decisions must be made to select which process to use or which mix of products to produce in view of cost, capacity, and other constraints. Product-mix decisions typically involve major marketing concerns. But where marketing or other considerations are not overriding criteria, linear programming methods are useful techniques for assisting in the product-mix decisions. Such a situation may arise, for example, when the firm has a current market for whatever quantities of two or more products it can produce. The selection of the least costly mix of raw materials or processes to use from among several available is a more localized example of the same type of mix decision.

- High utilization of facilities and personnel
- Better customer service via broader product line
- Diversified risk of loss due to product failure
- Opportunity to manage life cycle of products

FIGURE 5-5   Advantages of Multiproduct Systems

Linear programming is a quantitative method of analysis that has found extensive application within business systems. It has been applied to capital budgeting problems, line balancing, product-mix determination, and numerous other operating situations. One of the earliest and most extensive uses has been in planning and scheduling. It is convenient to introduce graphic and simplex linear programming here, for we shall be making reference to it throughout the remainder of the text.

Linear programming, as we saw earlier with respect to distribution problems, is a technique for maximizing or minimizing an objective function subject to constraints. While it is the final solution that we seek, we must go through the mechanics of a solution to arrive at our goal. The graphic method is perhaps most enlightening, but for more complicated problems the simplex method is useful. Most large problems are solved by computer, however, so a basic understanding of the methodology, along with knowledge of how to set up a problem and interpret the results, is perhaps the most essential.

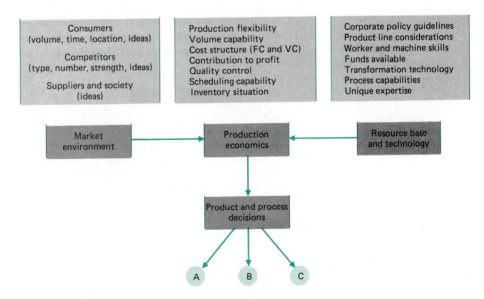

FIGURE 5-6   Factors Relevant to Product Selection Decisions

GRAPHIC METHOD OF SOLVING LINEAR PROGRAMMING PROBLEMS

The graphic method of solution is satisfactory for problems involving two decision variables and consists of the following five steps:

1 Formulate the problem in terms of a linear objective function and linear constraints.
2 Set up a graph with one decision variable on each axis, and plot the constraints. They define the feasible region.
3 Determine the slope of the objective function, and indicate the slope in the feasible region on the graph.
4 Move the objective function in an optimizing direction until it is constrained.
5 Read off the solution values of the decision variables from the respective axes.

EXAMPLE 5-1

A chemical firm produces automobile cleaner X and polisher Y and realizes $10 profit on each batch of X and $30 on Y. Both products require processing through the same machines, A and B, but X requires 4 hours in A and 8 in B, whereas Y requires 6 hours in A and 4 in B. During the forthcoming week machines A and B have 12 and 16 hours of available capacity, respectively. Assuming that demand exists for both products, how many batches of each should be produced to realize the optimal profit Z?

SOLUTION
1 *Objective function*

$$\text{Max } Z = \$10X + \$30Y$$

Constraints

A: $4X + 6Y \leqslant 12$

B: $8X + 4Y \leqslant 16$

2 *Graph*
The variables are X and Y. The constraints are plotted as equalities.

A: If $X = 0$, $Y = 2$

If $Y = 0$, $X = 3$

B: If $X = 0$, $Y = 4$

If $Y = 0$, $X = 2$

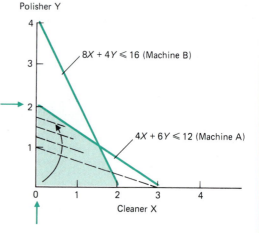

FIGURE 5-7 Graphic Linear Programming Solution

Note that the graph (Fig. 5-7) establishes a feasible region bounded by the explicit capacity constraints of A and B and the implicit constraints that production of $X \geq 0$ and production of $Y \geq 0$.

3 *Slope of objective function*

$$Z = 10X + 30Y$$

The standard slope-intercept form of a linear equation is

$$Y = mX + b \tag{5-1}$$

where m is the slope of the line (that is, change in Y per unit change in X) and b is the Y intercept.

Expressing our objective in this form, we have:

$$30Y = -10X + Z$$
$$Y = -\frac{1}{3}X + \frac{Z}{30}$$

Slope $= -\frac{1}{3}$, that is, a line decreasing one unit in Y for every three positive units of X. This is plotted at any convenient spot within the feasible region (shown dotted). The dotted line from $Y = 1$ to $X = 3$ illustrates this.

4 *Move objective function to optimize.* The slope of the objective function is moved away from the origin until restrained by the furthermost intersection of constraint A and the implicit constraint $X \geq 0$. The solution will always be at a corner in the feasible region.

5 *Read solution values.* The arrows point to the solution, which is determined by the X and Y coordinates at the corner. In this example $X = 0$ and $Y = 2$, so the firm should produce no cleaner and two batches of polisher for a profit of:

$$Z = \$10(0) + \$30(2) = \$60$$

As can be seen from the graph, the constraint imposed by machine B (that is, that $8X + 4Y \leq 16$) has no effect, for it is the 12 hours of machine A (denoted by $4X + 6Y \leq 12$) that are constraining production of the more profitable polisher. The graph also reveals that profit would continue to increase if more hours could be made available on machine A up to the point of doubling output (to $X = 0$ and $Y = 4$). At this point the time available from machine B would become constraining.

The linear programming example described above assumed that demand was assured and that profit contribution, processing time, and available machine time were known with certainty. In many cases there is enough certainty so that decisions can realistically be made with the aid of linear programming. Problem 2 in the Solved Problems section is a problem with two decision variables and three constraint equations. The solution exists at the intersection of two explicit constraints, and additional comments are made with respect to the sensitivity of the solution to changes in the constraints.

SIMPLEX METHOD OF SOLVING LINEAR PROGRAMMING PROBLEMS

Realistic linear programming problems often have several decision variables and dozens of constraint equations. Such problems cannot be solved graphically, and algorithms, such as the simplex procedure, are used—usually in conjunction with a computer. The *simplex method* is an iterative procedure which progressively approaches and ultimately reaches an optimal solution. In this section the simplex formulation of the problem described in Example 5-1 will be illustrated, and the simplex solution will be interpreted. Those who are unfamiliar with the computational routine or want to review it may refer to Solved Prob. 5 at the end of the chapter. Alternatively, computerized linear programming (LP) packages may be used.

Initial Solution   The simplex method begins with a statement of the objective function and constraint equations. Computerized LP routines will automatically arrange these inputs, but for manual solutions we must construct our own simplex table. This necessitates that the constraints be stated as equalities rather than as inequalities. In maximization problems we accomplish this by adding a *slack variable* (S) to each constraint. The slack represents an unused amount, or the difference between what *is* being used and the limit of what *could be* used. For example, by adding slack variables to the inequality constraints of Example 5-1, we get new equations as follows.

Constraint	Inequality	Equation with Slack
Machine A hr	$4X + 6Y \leq 12$	$4X + 6Y + S_A = 12$
Machine B hr	$8X + 4Y \leq 16$	$8X + 4Y + S_B = 16$

The machine A constraint now says 4 hours times the number of units of X produced plus 6 hours times the number of units of Y produced plus slack hours = 12 hours. Thus, if 1 unit of X and 1 unit of Y are produced, we have 2 hours of slack time, S, on machine A, since $4(1) + 6(1) + 2 = 12$. If no X or Y is produced, we "produce" all slack, and $S_A = 12$.

The simplex method always begins with a feasible solution wherein only slack is produced. This corresponds to the origin of the graphic solution, where both X and Y equal zero.

Each simplex table is a solution that (graphically) corresponds to a corner of the feasible region. We begin with a (poor, but feasible) solution that corresponds to the origin, where only slack is produced (that is, zero profit). Thus the slack variables (for example, S_1 and S_2) are "in solution," and the other decision variables (X and Y) are not in solution (that is, have values of zero). Figure 5-8 illustrates the initial simplex format.

EXAMPLE 5-2

Arrange the objective and constraint equations from Example 5-1 into an initial simplex table.

Objective function

$$\text{Max } Z = \$10X + \$30Y$$

Constraints

Machine A hr: $\qquad\qquad 4X + 6Y \leqslant 12$

Machine B hr: $\qquad\qquad 8X + 4Y \leqslant 16$

SOLUTION

FIGURE 5-8   Simplex Format

C →↓		10	30	0	0	
	Variables in Solution	Decision Variables				Solution Values (RHS)
		X	Y	S_A	S_B	
0	S_A	4	6	1	0	12
0	S_B	8	4	0	1	16
	Z	0	0	0	0	0
	C − Z	10	30	0	0	0

Figure 5-8 illustrates a simplex format. Elements of the table are described below.

The *central portion* of the simplex table consists of the coefficients of the constraint equations from:

$$4X + 6Y + 1S_A + 0S_B = 12$$
$$8X + 4Y + 0S_A + 1S_B = 16$$

Note that a one (1) has been assigned to the slack variable associated with its own constraint and a zero to the other slack variable.

The "variables in solution" column tells what variables are in solution (in this case, only slack), and the "solution values" column gives the amount in solution. The numbers come from the right-hand side (RHS) of the constraint equations (in this case, 12 hours of slack for machine A and 16 hours of slack for machine B).

The C in the upper left corner is both a row heading and a column heading. It specifies the amount of contribution to the objective function from each unit of the variables it refers to. Thus, each unit of X (cleaner) contributes $10 to profits, and each unit of Y (polisher) contributes $30 to profits, but the slack time from machines A and B yields $0 contribution for both S_A and S_B.

The Z row in the table shows the opportunity cost, or the amount of contribution that must be given up to introduce (or produce) one unit (or one more unit) of the variable in each column. It is computed for each column by multiplying the elements of the column by the contribution in the C column and then adding. For example, the Z value for column X is $(4 \times 0) + (8 \times 0) = 0$. This means that to introduce one unit of X (cleaner) into solution, we must give up 4 hours of slack time on machine A at a cost of $0 and 8 hours of slack time on machine B, also at a cost of $0. The Z value for the RHS column represents the total contribution from variables currently in solution. Because this (initial) solution is to "produce" 12 hours of slack on machine A (at $0 contribution) and 16 hours of slack on machine B (at $0 contribution), our total profit from this initial solution is zero. The Z row in the initial solution always has zeros, but it changes as the solution progresses.

The values in the bottom $(C - Z)$ row represent the *net contribution* from introducing one unit of the column variable into solution. In the initial table, they are simply the coefficients of the objective function followed by zeros for the slack variable columns. Thus, we would increase the value of the objective function by a full $10 for each unit of X produced and by $30 for each unit of Y because nothing but worthless slack must be given up to introduce X or Y at this stage. Producing more slack would obviously not improve profits.

Computational Methodology The solution methodology for maximization problems involves selecting a pivot column and row and revising the table values until all quantities in the bottom row are less than or equal to zero. Solved Prob. 5 illustrates the computational procedure.

Optimal Solution Referring back to Fig. 5-8, note the configuration of 1s and 0s in the two rows directly below the slack variable symbols. They form what is called an *identity matrix*. It is a square array of numbers with 1s on the diagonal and 0s elsewhere. A problem with three constraints would have three rows consisting of 1 0 0 and 0 1 0 and 0 0 1.

In a simplex table, a decision variable column that has a (positive) 1 with zeros elsewhere in that column identifies a variable in solution. In our initial table the 1 and 0 below the slack variables indicated that both S_A and S_B were in solution (that is, being produced). The value, or amount, of the variable in solution is given in the RHS column. (The RHS values for variables not in solution are automatically equal to zero.) Thus our initial table had 12 hours of machine A slack time and 16 hours of machine B slack time in solution, and no cleaner or polisher was produced (that is, neither X nor Y was in the initial solution, so $X = 0$ and $Y = 0$).

Example 5-3 presents and interprets the optimal solution to the problem posed in Example 5-1. Figure 5-9 illustrates the simplex solution. The graphic solution is repeated to aid in understanding the corresponding elements of the simplex solution.

EXAMPLE 5-3

Present and interpret the optimal solution to the cleaner-polisher problem in Example 5-1.

SOLUTION

The solution shown here is optimal because all values in the $C - Z$ row are less than or equal to zero.

FIGURE 5-9   Simplex Solution

$C \rightarrow$		10	30	0	0	
$\downarrow$		*Decision Variables*				*Solution Values*
	Variables in Solution	X	Y	S_A	S_B	*(RHS)*
30	Y	⅔	1	⅙	0	2
0	S_B	¹⁶⁄₃	0	−⅔	1	8
	Z	20	30	5	0	60
	$C - Z$	−10	0	−5	0	*(Profit)*

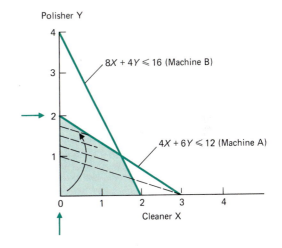

Variables in solution

Two columns have 1s and 0s.

Y is in solution with a RHS value of 2.

S_B is in the solution with a RHS value of 8.

The value of $Y = 2$ can be read from the RHS column in the table (and agrees with the graph).

Recall that each unit requires 4 hours of machine B time, so 2 units of Y use 8 hours of the 16 hours available. This leaves 8 hours of machine B slack, as indicated by the RHS value of 8 for S_B, which is also in solution.

Value of the objective function
   Z = $60 profit, as shown in the RHS column. This comes from producing two units of Y at $30 each plus eight units of slack at $0.

Values in the C − Z row

The figures in the bottom row of the final table $(-10, 0, -5, 0)$ reveal the following:

(a) (-10) To produce one can of X (cleaner) would reduce profits by $10 because it would take machine A time away from the production of Y.

  Note: The $10 amount is explained by the X column. Introducing one unit of "out variable" X would:

	X	
Y	⅔	← reduce Y by ⅔ unit @ $30/unit = $20 reduction
S_B	1⅔	← reduce S_B by 1⅔ units @ $0/unit = $0 reduction
Z	20	← for a total amount of $20 − $0 = $20 cost
C − Z	−10	← which is partially offset by $10 profit from each unit of X

The result is a net (loss) contribution of $C - Z = \$10 - \$20 = -\$10$.

(b) (0) The first zero indicates that Y is in solution (being produced).

(c) $(-5$ and $0)$ These two values are referred to as *shadow prices. Shadow prices go with constraints* and show the amount of change in the objective function that would result from each unit of change in the constraint. Thus they show the net effect of increasing (or decreasing) the slack or idle time of machines A and B by one unit.

(d) (-5) Since machine A is fully utilized, to take 1 hour out of production and "acquire" 1 hour of idle time would reduce profit by $5. (Profit from Y is $30 for each 6 hours of work on A, that is, a rate of $5 per hour.) Conversely, if another hour could be made available, say by shifting a current job from A, the time on A could be profitably utilized at a profit rate of $5 per hour.

(e) (0) The zero corresponding to the constraint of machine B signifies that machine B already has slack time (see the graphic solution). Increasing B's available time (or decreasing it) by one unit would have no effect on profits.

SENSITIVITY ANALYSIS

A glance at the graphic solution shows that if the time availability for machine A were increased, the profits would increase (at $5 per additional hour) until they were ultimately constrained by machine B. Sensitivity analysis is concerned with the determination of ranges over which the shadow prices hold. For ≤ constraints, the range can be determined by dividing the RHS value by the negative of the values in the columns with shadow prices. The smallest positive quotient then tells how much the constraint can be changed until another constraint takes over.

For example, from Fig. 5-9, the only active (explicit) constraint is machine A hours. The sensitivity ratios for this constraint are as follows:

For Y:

$$\frac{RHS}{-S_A} = \frac{2}{-\frac{1}{6}} = -12$$

For S_B:

$$\frac{RHS}{-S_A} = \frac{8}{\frac{2}{3}} = \frac{24}{2} = 12$$

The smallest positive ratio is the 12 associated with S_B. This tells us that constraint A may be relaxed by 12 hours (to 24 hours) before the machine B constraint begins to limit the solution.

A glance at the graphic solution shows that as constraint A is relaxed (that is, as more hours are added), the machine B constraint takes effect at $Y = 4$. At that point, the profit would be $Z = \$10X + \$30Y = \$10(0) + \$30(4) = \$120$. Also, at $Y = 4$, both machines would be fully utilized.

MINIMIZATION AND OTHER FORMS OF CONSTRAINTS

The simplex procedure can also be used to solve cost minimization problems which have objective functions of the form Min $Z = AX_1 + BX_2 + \cdots + MX_n$. Constraints in minimization problems are often of a $\geq$ type rather than the $\leq$ type we just encountered. In these types of constraints we must subtract a "surplus" variable (instead of adding a slack variable). To handle both = and $\geq$ types of constraints, artificial variables are also used (in addition to the S variables). The artificial variables serve only to state the equations in a form suitable for the simplex table and have no other meaning. Thus they are typically assigned very large negative values $(-M)$, which will quickly drive them out of solution. References at the end of the chapter provide additional information on minimization problems, as well as on shadow prices, duality, degeneracy, and other conceptual foundations of linear programming [1].

PROCESS PLANNING AND SELECTION

The production process is what actually transforms the resources and expertise of an organization into higher-valued goods and services. As illustrated in Fig. 5-10, it merges inputs from the market environment and the firm's own technological base into an economically efficient productive activity. The processes that add value range from mechanical, assembly, electrical, and chemical processes (largely for goods) to educational and informational processes (for services).

INTERMITTENT AND CONTINUOUS PRODUCTION SYSTEMS

The production process is strongly influenced by the *type of work flow* and the *design of the work center* [9]. Work flow may utilize any combination of the layouts described earlier (Chapter 4), which may be generally classified into either intermittent or continuous processing activities.

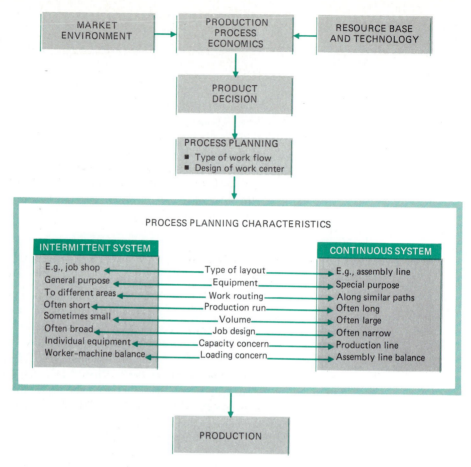

FIGURE 5-10   Process Planning Considerations in Intermittent and Continuous Systems

Intermittent systems are used to produce small quantities (or batches) of many different items on relatively general-purpose equipment. Most manufacturing is done in batches, and some services (such as movies and subways) are handled in batches. Processing equipment and personnel are located according to function, and products flow through the facilities on irregular paths. Work orders are frequently individually routed, scheduled, and controlled on a job or shop *order-control* system. The goods or services are often customized or *made to order*.

Continuous systems are used to produce large volumes of a single item (or relatively few items) on specialized equipment following a fixed path. Items follow a similar production sequence, which can be anything from a pipeline (for oil) to an assembly line (for computers). Routing and scheduling focus on *flow controls* that govern the rate of flow of raw materials and finished products. High-volume, line-assembled products are often of standardized design and *made for stock*. Continous flow systems for services tend to be equipment-oriented (such as phone services and utilities) or equipment-dependent (ski lifts).

FLEXIBLE AND ROBOTIC SYSTEMS

Flexible production systems are a computer-enhanced form of continuous system and are used to produce large volumes of customized products on highly automated equipment that is individually responsive to logic commands. They rely heavily on microprocessors to store, manipulate, and transmit information for production activities. By using computer-aided manufacturing (CAM) systems, firms are able to combine the benefits of intermittent layouts with the speed advantages of continuous layouts.

Robots are computerized manipulators that can perform a variety of tasks in response to programmed commands or sensory input (for example, from vision, sound, or touch systems). The simplest robots do manual manipulations or fixed-sequence activities. More intelligent robots have microprocessors that can store, manipulate, and react to information concerning materials, times, locations, and manufacturing activities.

Robots are a vital element in most flexible production systems because they can handle information and do physical work. The quality of work done by robots is typically more consistent than the quality of work done by humans, and the uniformity of the work allows savings on the amount of material used.

Traditional "hard automation" is designed to accomplish specific tasks that produce identical outputs. Robots are more flexible; they can perform a variety of functions. Programmable robots can be reprogrammed simply by changing their software, or instructions. "Smart" robots can even respond (almost instantaneously) to online needs. They can (with a camera-sensitive lens) locate parts on a moving conveyor, retrieve, assemble, inspect, sort, and relocate those parts as necessary. Some robots can even recognize voice commands and respond to questions by way of a speech synthesizer.

Firms like Ford and General Motors employ robots in such diverse tasks as materials-handling, welding, painting, assembly, inspection, and testing activities. A robot's cost ($50,000 to $150,000) can often be recovered in 2 to 3 years. Savings stem from higher machine utilization, improved quality, and reduced space requirements, plus reductions in material and labor costs. Labor savings are often dramatic. For example, with robots, 100 robots may do the work of 500, or output may be doubled without any increase in the number of workers. Moreover, robots do not require collective bargaining agreements, and there are no retirement costs to fund.

Robots do replace workers, however, so employees' concerns over the consequences of widespread use of robots are legitimate. Nevertheless, industries that do not automate with robots may face decline or collapse. Thus one challenge to industry is to consciously direct human efforts away from tasks that can be done by machines toward more people-oriented functions. This is, in fact, taking place in the United States as our economy moves toward service-producing activities. A second challenge is to retrain some of the work force for new and upgraded positions in programming, control, and maintenance of high-technology equipment.

PROCESS PLANNING AIDS: CHARTS, GRAPHS, AND COMPUTATIONS

We saw earlier (Fig. 5-6) that product decisions are influenced by the market environment, the firm's resource base, and the production process economics. *Process planning* is concerned with designing and implementing a work system that will produce the desired good or service in the required quantities. But fims must continually adapt to product and volume changes, so process planning is really an ongoing activity. This section reviews a few of the charts and graphs that have proven to be especially useful to process planners as they continually redesign, update, and evaluate their production processes.

ASSEMBLY AND PROCESS CHARTS

Assembly charts, operations charts, and flow process charts are valuable aids for planning and managing the various transformation processes.

Assembly charts show the material requirements and assembly sequence of components that make up a mechanical assembly. Operations are symbolized by circles and inspections by squares, as illustrated in Fig. 5-11.

Operations process charts are similar to assembly charts, except that they include specifications for the component parts as well as operating and inspection times. Thus they provide more complete instructions on how to produce an item. Most firms that produce custom products in a jobshop layout summarize the operations and process routing information for a given item on a route sheet. The *route sheet* specifies precisely how to produce an item by identifying the equipment and tools to use, the operations and sequence to follow, and the machine setup and run-time estimates.

Flow process charts are similar to operations process charts, except that the nonproductive activities of storage (∇), delay (D), and transport ($\Diamond$) are also included. Figure 5-12 shows a flow process chart. It is designed to facilitate analysis by asking why each activity is done and whether it can be improved by eliminating a task, combining tasks, changing the sequence of tasks, or simplifying tasks. These aids make flow process charts very useful for the analysis of process efficiency.

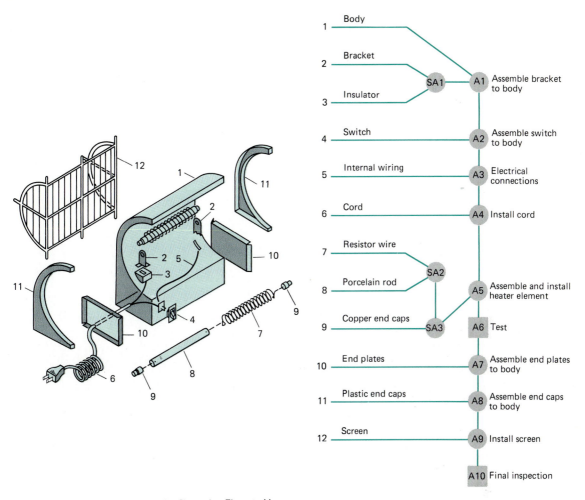

FIGURE 5-11   Assembly Chart for Electric Heater

WORKER-MACHINE AND ACTIVITY CHARTS

Worker-machine charts are graphic devices for modeling the simultaneous activities of a worker and the equipment he or she operates. They help identify idle time and costs of both workers and machines. Process planners can then analyze alternative worker-machine combinations and determine the most efficient arrangement.

Worker-machine charts show the time required to complete tasks that make up a work cycle. A *cycle* is the length of time required to progress through one complete combination of work activities. Many worker-machine activities are

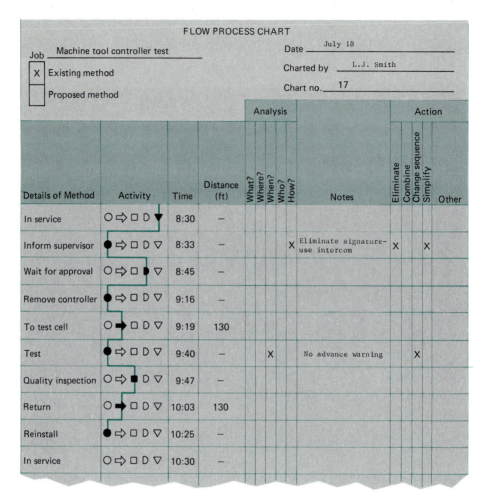

FIGURE 5-12   Flow Process Chart

characterized by a load-run-unload sequence. The chart must be continued long enough past the start-up time to reach an equilibrium cycle time.

EXAMPLE 5-4 | An operator at Goodtire Rubber Company is expected to take 2 minutes to load and 1 minute to unload a molding machine. There are several machines of this type, all doing the same thing, and the automatic run time on each is 4 minutes. Respective costs are $8 per hour for the operator and $20 per hour for each machine.

(a) Construct a worker-machine chart for the most efficient one-worker, two-machine situation.

(b) What is the cycle time?

(c) What is the worker's idle time per cycle?
(d) What is the total idle time per cycle for both machines?
(e) What is the total cost per hour?
(f) What is the total cost per cycle?
(g) What is the idle time cost per hour?

SOLUTION

(a) If the operator begins by loading machine 1, the cycle does not reach an efficient steady state until the ninth minute, as shown in Fig. 5-13.

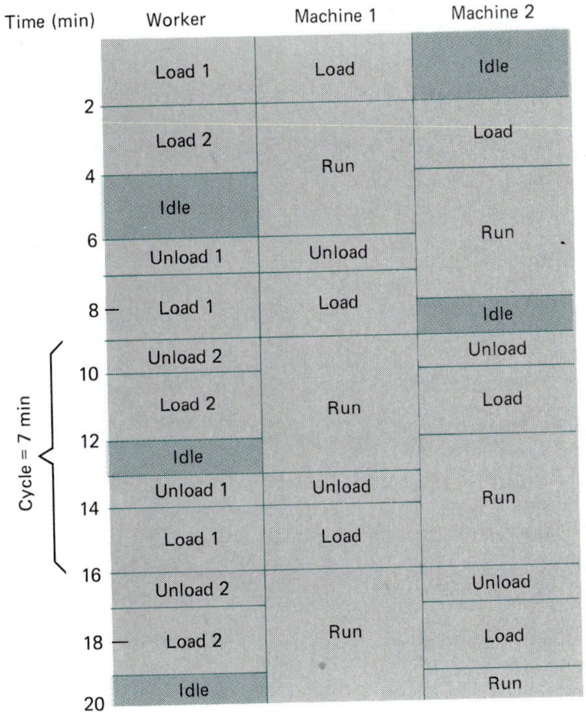

FIGURE 5-13   Worker-Machine Chart

(b) CT = 7 min
(c) The worker is idle 1 minute per cycle.
(d) The machines are not idle (at steady-state operation).
(e) Cost = worker cost + 2 (cost for each machine) = $8 + 2($20) = $48/hr
      = $48 per 60 min.

(f) Cost/cycle $= \dfrac{\$48}{60 \text{ min}}\left(\dfrac{7 \text{ min}}{\text{cycle}}\right) = \$5.60/\text{cycle}$

(g) Idle time cost/hr $= \dfrac{1 \text{ min}}{\text{cycle}}\left(\dfrac{60 \text{ min/hr}}{7 \text{ min/cycle}}\right)\left(\dfrac{\$8}{60 \text{ min}}\right) = \$1.14/\text{hr}$

The operation and control of complex or mobile equipment often restricts process activities to a one-worker-per-machine operation. Much construction and materials-handling equipment falls into this category. These activities can be portrayed in an *activity chart*, which is similar to a worker-machine chart, except that all components represent machines (or workers).

EQUIPMENT SELECTION (MACHINE BREAKPOINTS)

Many process planning decisions relate to equipment capacities required to produce a specified level of output. When the processing costs of alternative ways of doing a job can be broken down into their fixed and variable cost components, the most economical alternative is the one with the lowest costs at the expected volume. A graph of the respective costs will show the machine breakpoints.

EXAMPLE 5-5

Some brackets for a circuit breaker can be machined on any of three machines. The costs are as shown.

	Machine A	Machine B	Machine C
Fixed cost (setup)	$10	$30	$60
Variable cost/unit	.30	.20	.10

What machines should be used for production volumes up to 400 units?

SOLUTION
At 400 units, the total costs are:

$TC_A = \$10 + 400(\$.30) = \$130$

$TC_B = \$30 + 400(\$.20) = \$110$

$TC_C = \$60 + 400(\$.10) = \$100$

For:

$0 < 200$ units, use A

200–300 units, use B

> 300 units, use C

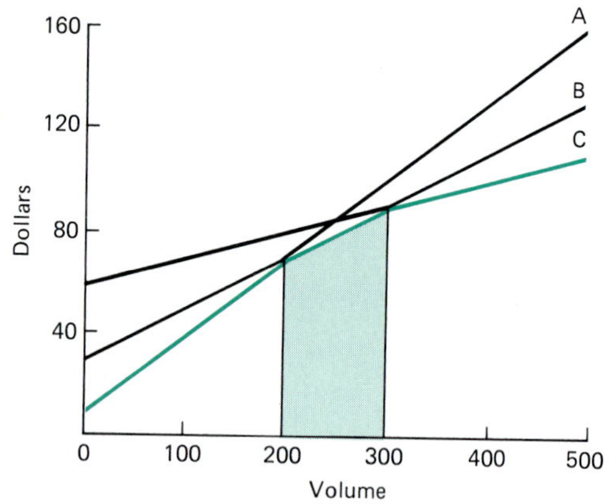

FIGURE 5-14   Machine Breakpoints

In addition to equipment and process selection decisions, the process planning stage often generates make versus buy decisions. Many components or subassemblies of a firm's product can be either bought or produced, and these decisions must be carefully analyzed as they arise during the process planning activities.

The loading problems of intermittent layouts relate more to individual worker-machine balance, whereas with line layouts they relate to the overall balance of the whole assembly line. The individual worker-machine charts were described earlier in this chapter and the assembly line balancing techniques in Chapter 4. The next section discusses some simulation techniques which are useful for modeling production processes so that the appropriate numbers of machines and personnel can be assigned to operations.

SIMULATING OPERATIONS

Suppose it takes workers at a conveyor belt exactly 25 seconds to attach a switch to a television set, and the workers have 30 seconds available. They should be able to complete all installations satisfactorily. However, if their time requirements vary from 24 to 32 seconds, depending upon parts availability or tolerances of the switch, then they will not be able to complete every unit. Allowing enough time (such as 32 seconds) for them to finish the installation *every* time may result in excessive idle time, whereas providing them with some lesser amount (such as 30 seconds) will mean that some units will pass by without being completed. The "correct" time allowance depends upon the workers' time requirements as well as other objectives of the job design, such as job satisfaction.

Economically, the designer would probably like to decrease the idle time of workers to the point where the idle-time cost is just offset by the costs that would be incurred by allowing incomplete sets to leave the work station. Statistical and empirical data on the workers' performance time are useful to the job designer in establishing the necessary time availability for activities at each work station.

Assume that there are two work stations, A and B, in a line, followed by a rigidly paced activity, C, as shown in Fig. 5-15. Operators A and B may have average performance times that are relatively close to each other, but their output

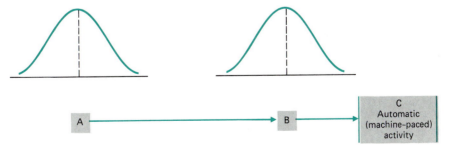

FIGURE 5-15   Work Stations on Paced Assembly Line

rates are still likely to fluctuate because of the inherent variability of human operators. If B must deliver units to C at a specified rate, then either B's mean production rate must exceed the set rate of C or an in-process inventory must be maintained. The production rate of B is in turn affected by that of A, and a similar requirement would hold for their interface.

EXAMPLE 5-6

The time taken by worker A to perform an airplane assembly operation is normally distributed, with mean = 2.8 minutes and standard deviation = .1 minute. If this worker feeds a machine that accepts units only at 3.0-minute intervals (and no inventory buildup is permissible), what percentge of the time will the worker be unable to feed the machine on time?

SOLUTION

Since the distribution of times is normal, the number of standard deviations is

$$Z = \frac{X - \mu}{\sigma} = \frac{3.0 - 2.8}{0.1} = 2.0$$

∴ Using the table of areas under the normal curve:

$$P(X > 3.0) = .5000 - .4772 = .0228$$

$$\cong 2\% \text{ of the time}$$

Mean time of ⟶ (Operator)   (Machine)
2.8 min   3.0 min

Example 5-6 involved only one activity whose time distribution was known to be normal. More complex problems may involve either (1) two or more statistical distributions (perhaps in sequence), or (2) a pattern of activities that does not follow a known statistical distribution. Analysts sometimes construct simulation models of these types of problems and use a trial-and-error approach to arrive at a reasonable solution.

> **Simulation** is a means of modeling the essence of an activity or system so that experiments can be conducted to evaluate the system's behavior or response over time.

Simulations may be done manually or physically, but most business problems are modeled on computers. It is not an optimizing technique (like linear programming) but it does offer a number of advantages, which are listed in Fig. 5-16.

We end this chapter with a brief explanation of how simulated values might be derived to model and study production processes using a computer. Numerous

- Applies to problems that are too complex for mathematical solution
- Helps one to understand the total (complex) system
- Avoids risk or disruptive experimentation on actual system
- Compresses time to reveal long-range effects
- Costs less than real-world experimentation

FIGURE 5-16   Advantages of Using Simulation

simulation languages (such as GPSS and SIMSCRIPT) are available for modeling large-scale problems, so we shall limit our discussion to a brief explanation of how to use the known statistical distributions as well as the empirical data simulations mentioned above. Finally, we review an interesting application.

SIMULATIONS USING KNOWN STATISTICAL DISTRIBUTIONS

If the time required to perform a work activity has a known statistical distribution, then simulated time values of that activity can be obtained by using random numbers that reflect the characteristics of that distribution. To illustrate, Appendix J contains normally distributed random numbers. The numbers represent plus and minus Z scores from a normal distribution having a mean of zero and standard deviation of 1. To stimulate a normal distribution having a mean μ and standard deviation σ, simply begin at any point in the table and take numbers consecutively. Each random number (Z score) from the table is then "adjusted" to the particular distribution by multiplying it by σ and adding it to the value of the mean μ.

Normal Distribution:

$$\text{Simulated value} = \mu + \sigma\,(RN_Z) \qquad (5\text{-}2)$$

where μ = mean of the distribution being simulated
σ = standard deviation of the distribution
RN_Z = random number (as a Z score) from table of normally distributed numbers (Appendix J)

EXAMPLE 5-7   A patient-care service in a hospital has normally distributed times with a mean of 15.0 minutes and a standard deviation of 2.0 minutes. Use a table of normally distributed random numbers to simulate four values of the times required to perform this service.

SOLUTION

For ease in identification, we shall use numbers from column 1 of Appendix J. Using Eq. (5-2) we have:

RN_Z	$\mu + \sigma (RN_Z)$	= Simulated Value (min)
.34	$15 + 2(.34)$	= 15.68
−1.09	$15 + 2(−1.09)$	= 12.82
−1.87	$15 + 2(−1.87)$	= 11.26
1.57	$15 + 2(1.57)$	= 18.14

The four values generated in the example above would be insufficient for a realistic study, but a computer would probably generate hundreds or thousands of such values). The values might then be used to study the personnel requirements for this patient-care activity in conjunction with other activities under study.

When activity times are known to follow other distribution patterns, then other statistical distributions can be used. For uniformly distributed times, the table of uniform random numbers (Appendix I) is used and the simulated values are obtained by means of Eq. (5-3).

Uniform Distribution:

$$\text{Simulated value} = a + (b - a)(RN_\%) \qquad (5\text{-}3)$$

where
- a = minimum value
- b = maximum value
- $RN_\%$ = random number (as a percentage) from table of uniformly distributed random numbers (Appendix I)

SIMULATIONS USING EMPIRICAL DATA

Many production activities have uncertain demands, variable work times, or other factors that cannot be defined mathematically or by a known statistical distribution. In such cases, if empirical (or experimental) data are available, the activity can also be simulated—although this is a little more difficult.

The available data are first described as a cumulative probability distribution that duplicates (as closely as possible) the variability pattern in the system under study. Then random numbers are used to obtain simulated values from the data. These simulations, which use a (stochastic) random sampling process to obtain simulated values from the probability distributions under study, are sometimes referred to as *Monte Carlo methods.*

1 Collect actual (empirical) data on the distribution of assembly times (or estimate them from a pilot activity).
2 Develop a probability and cumulative probability distribution.
3 Assign an interval of random numbers to each class of the distribution. (Optionally, the cumulative distribution may be plotted, showing relative frequency on the vertical axis.)
4 Using random numbers, derive simulated assembly times.
5 Interpret the results (for example, determine the proportion of actual times that exceed some specified time or the effect of one work station on the next).

FIGURE 5-17   Steps in Empirical Simulation of Assembly Activity

The steps to simulate an assembly activity using empirical data are summarized in Fig. 5-17. Computers are commonly used for simulation and could, of course, produce hundreds or thousands of simulated times in a few seconds. However, simplified examples (using hand calculations) are included in the Solved Problems section of this chapter to illustrate the methodology involved. Solved Problem 9 illustrates the strictly algebraic method, whereas Solved Problem 10 uses a graphic plot of the cumulative distribution referenced in step 3 of Fig. 5-16 [2].

SIMULATION APPLICATION: BRITISH LEYLAND

A large-scale simulation was done of a new conveyor network system at a British Leyland automobile plant in England [7]. The computerized system carries autobodies from two robotic lines through 72 conveyor stops to four manual finishing lines.

The entire conveyor system was modeled on computer. Then production loads were imposed to check the logic and timing of travel between all the different conveyor stops. The simulation revealed assembly line flow problems by showing animated graphics of where breakdowns, jams, and problems were occurring. British Leyland was able to try out different solutions to the problems before the equipment was installed—instead of waiting to correct the problems on a real-life trial-and-error basis. The simulation helped them ensure that the costly automation equipment would run smoothly when installed, resulting in an estimated savings of $120,000 per week.

SUMMARY

Products are the goods and services that are produced, and *processes* are the skills and equipment used to produce them. Planning for goods can be more straightforward than planning for services. Services rely upon clients as participants in the service delivery system, and the social processes of service systems can be more difficult to control.

New-product ideas come from the market environment and from internal sources. High-technology firms are often heavily dependent upon applied research for these ideas. Three aspects of product feasibility are carefully assessed before a new product is taken on: (1) the technical capability of the firm to produce the product, (2) the product's marketability, and (3) its economics. If the product is feasible and consistent with the organization's orientation, it goes through preliminary and detailed design stages. As details are firmed up, market testing is done, and the production process is planned. Highly automated systems may make use of robotics, CAD/CAM, and group technology techniques.

Knowing about the life cycle of products helps planners maintain a balanced and profitable product line. *Linear programming* can be effective in selecting from among product and process alternatives when cost and demand functions are known. In linear programming, we maximize or minimize a linear objective function subject to linear constraints. The graphic method is only suitable for handling two decision variables, but the simplex method can handle many variables and constraints. The simplex table is systematically revised until an optimal solution is reached. Complex problems require the use of a computer.

Process planning aids include several types of charts: assembly, operations process, flow process, worker-machine, and activity. In addition, economic techniques are useful, such as machine breakpoint analysis for equipment selection.

Computer simulation is a technique for modeling production processes so that appropriate numbers of machines and personnel can be assigned to operations. Simulations useful for analyzing operations include both those based on known statistical distributions and those using empirical data only.

SOLVED PROBLEMS

LINEAR PROGRAMMING FOR PRODUCT-MIX DECISIONS[1]

1 What is the slope of the objective function Max $Z = 15X + 45Y$?

Solution
The slope form is $Y = mX + b$ where $m = $ slope
Rearranging,

$$45Y = -15X + Z$$

$$Y = -\frac{15X}{45} + \frac{Z}{45}$$

Slope is $-15/45$ or $-1/3$.

[1] The solution of simplex linear programming problems is often taught in management science courses, so some instructors may choose not to assign this material or to designate it as optional. Alternatively, numerous computer programs are available for solving linear programming problems.

2 An electronic-goods manufacturer has distributors who will accept shipments of either transistor radios or electronic calculators to stock for Christmas inventory. Whereas the radios contribute $10 per unit and the calculators $15 per unit to profits, both products use some of the same components. Each radio requires 4 diodes and 4 resistors, while each calculator requires 10 diodes and 2 resistors. The radios take 12.0 minutes and the calculators take 9.6 minutes of time on the company's electronic testing machine, and the production manager estimates that 160 hours of test time are available. The firm has 8,000 diodes and 3,000 resistors in inventory. What product or mix of products should be selected to obtain the highest profit?

Solution

The decision variables are radios, R, and calculators, C, and we must determine how many of each should be produced to maximize profit, Z.

(1) *Objective function*

$$\text{Max } Z = \$10R + \$15C$$

Constraints

Diodes (8,000 available): Radios require 4 each, and calculators require 10 each.

$$\therefore 4R + 10C \leq 8,000$$

Resistors (3,000 available): Radios require 4 each, and calculators require 2 each.

$$\therefore 4R + 2C \leq 3,000$$

Testing (9,600 minutes available): Radios require 12.0 minutes, and calculators require 9.6 minutes.

$$\therefore 12.0R + 9.6C \leq 9,600$$

(2) *Graph of variables and constraints*

Plotting this as an equality, we have:
   If $R = 0$, then $C = 800$
   If $C = 0$, then $R = 2,000$

Resistors: $4R + 2C \leq 3,000$

   If $R = 0$, then $C = 1,500$
   If $C = 0$, then $R = 750$

Testing: $12.0R + 9.6C \leq 9,600$

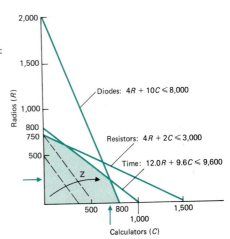

Note: The resulting graph establishes a feasible region bounded by the time, diode, and resistor constraints and the implicit constraints that $R \geqslant 0$ and $C \geqslant 0$.

(3) *Slope of objective function.* We can express our objective function in slope-intercept form, where the Y axis corresponds to R and the X axis to C.

$$Z = 10R + 15C$$

or $$10R = -15C + Z$$

$$\therefore R = -\frac{15}{10}C + \frac{Z}{10} = -\frac{3}{2}C + \frac{Z}{10}$$

$\therefore$ Slope $= -\frac{3}{2}$, which means that for every 3-unit decrease in Y there is a 2-unit increase in X. This slope is plotted as a dotted line in the graph by marking off 3 units (negative) in R for each 2 units (positive) in C.

(4) *Move objective function to optimize.* The slope of the objective function (iso-objective line) is moved away from the origin until constrained. In this case the binding constraints are the diode inventory supply and testing machine time availability.

(5) *Read solution values.* The arrows point to the approximate R and C coordinates of the constraining intersection.

$$\text{Number of radios} \cong 240$$

$$\text{Number of calculators} = 700$$

Note that the simultaneous solution of the two binding constraint equations would lend more accuracy to the answer:

$$(4R + 10C = 8,000) \times (-3) = -12R - 30C = -24,000$$
$$\text{Add:} \quad \underline{12R + 9.6C = \quad 9,600}$$
$$-20.4C = -14,400$$
$$C = 705 \text{ calculators}$$

Substituting to solve for R:

$$4R + 10(705) = 8,000$$

$$\therefore R = \frac{8,000 - 7,050}{4} = 237 \text{ radios}$$

Comment: We had two decision variables (that is, products) to choose from and established a profit function, Z, and constraints and optimized the function by moving it away from the origin. The graph of this example showed that the resistor supply was not constraining, so only two constraints (diodes and test time) were binding. Similarly, there were two decision variables in the solution, that is, we ended up producing both radios and calculators. The number of variables in solution will always equal the number of explicit constraints that are binding.

The graphic linear programming solution gives an indication of the sensitivity of the solution to changes in the constraints. If, for example, additional diodes could be purchased from an outside supplier with no increase in cost, profit would be maximized by extending the iso-objective line to the next corner and producing 1,000 calculators and no radios. In this case we would have one explicit constraint (time) binding and only one decision variable (calculators) in the final solution.

3 The Simplex Calculator Company makes a profit of $5 on each model X and $20 on each model Y. Each calculator requires the following time (in minutes) on the cleaning and testing machines.

	X Requirements	Y Requirements	Time Available
Cleaning	2	4	10
Testing	6	3	12

(a) State the objective function and constraints.
(b) Arrange the equations in a simplex format.

Solution

(a) *Objective function*   Max $Z = 5X + 20Y$

Constraints:

Cleaning $2X + 4Y \leq 10$

Testing $6X + 3Y \leq 12$

(b)

C →		5	20	0	0	
↓		Decision Variables				Solution Values
	Variables in Solution	X	Y	S_1	S_2	(RHS)
0	S_1	2	4	1	0	10
0	S_2	6	3	0	1	12
	Z	0	0	0	0	0
	C − Z	5	20	0	0	

4 The initial matrix of a maximization linear programming problem was as shown where the decision variables are designated A, B, etc.

C →		4	8	6	0	0	0	
↓	Variables in Solution							RHS
		5	9	0	1	0	0	36
		0	8	5	0	1	0	24
		2	0	5	0	0	1	7
		0	0	0	0	0	0	0
		4	8	6	0	0	0	

(a) State the original constraint equations.
(b) How many decision variables are there?
(c) State the objective function.

Solution

(a) $5A + 9B \leq 36$, $8B + 5C \leq 24$, and $2A + 5C \leq 7$
(b) Three
(c) Max $Z = 4A + 8B + 6C$

5 *The simplex method* The following problem utilizes the simplex procedure described below.

Simplex Procedure

1 *Set up initial simplex table.* Formulate the objective function and constraints, and enter the decision variables, variables in solution, solution (RHS) values, C (contribution from the variable), Z (cost of introducing the variable), and C − Z (net contribution of the variable).

2 *Select the pivot column.* It is the column with the largest positive number in the bottom (C − Z) row. It becomes the new variable in solution.

3 *Select the pivot row.* It is the row with the smallest ratio of RHS value divided by pivot column value. Use only positive numbers. This identifies the variable leaving the solution.

4 *Circle the pivot.* It is at the intersection of the pivot row and pivot column.

5 *Convert the pivot into a 1.* Do this by dividing each value in the pivot row by the pivot value. Enter this new row in a new table.

6 *Generate other rows for the next table with zeros in the pivot column.* This is done by multiplying the new row (from step 5) by the negative of the element in the pivot column that is to be converted and adding the result to the old row. Enter the revised row in the new table, and continue this procedure for each row in the center section of the table.

7 *Test for optimality.* Compute the values of Z and C − Z. Z values for each column are Σ(column elements)(C). If all C − Z values are ≤ 0, the solution is optimal. Read the values for the variables in solution from the RHS column and the value of the objective function from row Z in the RHS column. If the solution is not optimal, return to step 2.

Use the simplex method to solve the following problem presented in Example 5-2:

$$\text{Max } Z = \$10X + \$30Y$$

subject to:

$$4X + 6Y \leq 12$$

$$8X + 4Y \leq 16$$

Solution

(1) The objective and constraints are as follows:

$$\text{Max } Z = \$10X + \$30Y$$

$$4X + 6Y + 1S_1 + 0S_2 = 12$$

$$8X + 4Y + 0S_1 + 1S_2 = 16$$

The *simplex matrix* is similar to that in Fig. 5-8.

C →		10	30	0	0		
↓		Decision Variables				Solution Values	
	Variables in Solution	X	Y	S_1	S_2	(RHS)	
0	S_1	4	(6)	1	0	12	¹²⁄₆ = 2 (minimum)
0	S_2	8	4	0	1	16	¹⁶⁄₄ = 4
	Z	0	0	0	0	0	
	C − Z	10	30	0	0		

(2) The *pivot column* has the largest positive number (30) in the bottom row.
(3) The *pivot row* has the smallest ratio:

$$\frac{12}{6} = 2 \quad \text{and} \quad \frac{16}{4} = 4$$

Therefore row 1 is the pivot row.
(4) The pivot is *circled*.
(5) Divide each value in the pivot row by the pivot (6), and enter the values in a new table.

	X	Y	S_1	S_2	RHS
Y	⅔	1	⅙	0	2

(6) Generate other rows for the next table such that all elements in the pivot column equal zero.

We begin with the S_2 row, which has a 4 in the Y column. Multiply the new row (from step 5 above) by the negative of the value we wish to convert (−4), and add it to the old S_2 row:

Multiply the new row by −4

	X	Y	S_1	S_2	RHS
	−4(⅔)	−4(1)	−4(⅙)	−4(0)	−4(2)

to get result	$-\frac{8}{3}$	-4	$-\frac{2}{3}$	0	-8
Add to old row	8	4	0	1	16
to get new row	$\frac{16}{3}$	0	$-\frac{2}{3}$	1	8

And enter into new table:

$C \rightarrow$ $\downarrow$ Sol.		10 X	30 Y	0 S_1	0 S_1	RHS
30	Y	$\frac{2}{3}$	1	$\frac{1}{6}$	0	2
0	S_2	$\frac{16}{3}$	0	$-\frac{2}{3}$	1	8
	Z					

If there were more rows to convert, we would repeat this step for the next row. Since there are no more, we go on to compute Z and $C - Z$.

(7) Values in the Z row are Σ(column elements)(C). For example:

for X:	$Z = (\frac{2}{3})(30) + (\frac{16}{3})(0) = 20$
for Y:	$Z = 1(30) + 0(0) = 30$
for S_1:	$Z = \frac{1}{6}(30) - \frac{2}{3}(0) = 5$
for S_2:	$Z = 0(30) + 1(0) = 0$
for RHS:	$2(30) + 8(0) = 60$

After entering these and the $C - Z$ values in the next matrix we have:

$C \rightarrow$ $\downarrow$	Variables in Solution	Decision Variables				Solution Values (RHS)
		10	30	0	0	
		X	Y	S_1	S_2	
30	Y	$\frac{2}{3}$	1	$\frac{1}{6}$	0	2
0	S_2	$\frac{16}{3}$	0	$-\frac{2}{3}$	1	8
	Z	20	30	5	0	60
	$C - Z$	-10	0	-5	0	

Repeat steps 2 through 7 until all values in the bottom row are ≤ 0. Since all values are ≤ 0, the optimal solution is already reached. Variables in solution are identified by columns in the central portion of the table that have one entry of 1 and remaining values of zero. The solution values are given in the right-hand column.

	X	Y	S_1	S_2	RHS
	—	1	—	0	2
	—	0	—	1	8
Z	—	—	—	—	60

$$\therefore X = \text{not in solution}$$

$$Y = 2 \text{ units}$$

$$Z = \$60$$

Note that the slack variable associated with constraint 2 also has a 1 and zeros, which signifies that we have slack in solution and that the constraint is not binding. Thus we have only one (nonslack) decision variable in the solution (Y) and one binding constraint (number 1). This agrees with the fundamental theory of linear programming, which states that the number of (nonslack) decision variables in solution always equals the number of constraints that are binding.

This solution is the same as that given for Examples 5-1, 5-2, and 5-3, so you may want to review those examples for further interpretation of the output.

6 A commercial fertilizer manufacturer produces three grades, W, X, and Y, which net the firm $40, $50, and $60 in profits per ton, respectively. The products require the labor and materials per batch that are shown in the accompanying table.

	W	X	Y	Total Available
Labor hours	4	4	5	80 hr
Raw material A (lb)	200	300	300	6,000 lb
Raw material B (lb)	600	400	500	5,000 lb

(a) Set up the initial simplex table.
(b) Use a computer program (or hand calculations) to find the mix of products that would yield maximum profits. Indicate what variables are in the final solution and the optimal profit value.

Solution
(a) *Objective function*

$$\text{Max } Z = 40W + 50X + 60Y$$

Constraints
Labor: $4W + 4X + 5Y \leq 80$
Material A: $200W + 300X + 300Y \leq 6,000$
Material B: $600W + 400X + 500Y \leq 5,000$

Using the simplex method, the initial table would be as follows:

$C \rightarrow$ $\downarrow$		40	50	60	0	0	0	
	Variables in Solution	Decision Variables						Solution Values (RHS)
		W	X	Y	S_1	S_2	S_3	
0	S_1	4	4	5	1	0	0	80
0	S_2	200	300	300	0	1	0	6,000
0	S_3	600	400	(500)	0	0	1	5,000
	Z	0	0	0	0	0	0	0
	C − Z	40	50	60	0	0	0	

(b) Using any standard linear programming software package, one could enter the objective function and constraint equations given above. The second matrix (if included in the output) would call for production of 10 units of Y (only) for a profit coefficient of $600. However, a positive 2 in the bottom row under the X variable column would indicate that for every unit of X introduced the objective function would increase by $2. The final solution calls for 12.5 units of X, which raises the profit an additional $25 to a total of $625, as shown in the final matrix below.

$C \rightarrow$ $\downarrow$		40	50	60	0	0	0	
	Variables in Solution	Decision Variables						Solution Values (RHS)
		W	X	Y	S_1	S_2	S_3	
0	S_1	−2	0	0	1	0	−$\frac{1}{100}$	30
0	S_2	−250	0	−75	0	1	−$\frac{9}{20}$	2,250
50	X	$\frac{3}{2}$	1	$\frac{5}{4}$	0	0	$\frac{1}{400}$	$25\frac{1}{2}$
	Z	75	50	$125\frac{1}{2}$	0	0	$\frac{1}{8}$	625
	C − Z	−35	0	−$\frac{5}{2}$	0	0	−$\frac{1}{8}$	

WORKER-MACHINE CHARTS

7 The accompanying portion of an activity chart is for an automatic-loader mining operation. The loader, in the mine, requires 8 minutes to load a skip car. There are three skips, and they take 9 minutes to travel loaded to the ore dump, 2 minutes to dump, and 7 minutes to return empty. The operating cost of each skip is $200 per hour, and the automatic-loader cost (including worker and machine) is estimated at $350 per hour.

(a) What is the length of the cycle?

(b) What is the idle-time cost per hour?

Time scale	Skip 1		Skip 2		Skip 3		Loader	
	Element	T	Element	T	Element	T	Element	T
	Load	8	Return	7	Travel	9	Load 1	8
					Dump	2		
10	Travel	9	Load	8	Return	7	Load 2	8
	Dump	2	Travel	9	Load	8	Load 3	8
20	Return	7						
			Dump	2			Idle	2
30	Load	8	Return	7	Travel	9	Load 1	8
					Dump	2		

Solution

(a) *Cycle length*: The system is in a similar state at times 8 and 34.

$$\therefore \text{Cycle length} = 34 - 8 = 26 \text{ min}$$

(b) *Idle-time cost*: The loader is idle 2 minutes per cycle = $2/26$ = $1/13$ of each hour.

$$\therefore \text{Cost/hr} = 1/13(\$350) = \$26.92/\text{hr}$$

SIMULATING OPERATIONS

8 *Uniform distribution*   The diameters of trees arriving at a lumber mill vary uniformly from 2 feet to 3 feet. The time required to saw a 2-foot log is 5 seconds and to saw a 3-foot log is 8 seconds; within that range it varies directly with the diameter. Simulate the time required to saw five logs selected at random in the 2- to 3-foot range.

Solution

$$\text{Simulated value} = a + (b - a)(\text{RN}_\%)$$

where a = 5 seconds, b = 8 seconds, and $b - a$ = 3 seconds. $\text{RN}_\%$ will be taken from the first five values of three-digit numbers from column 2 of the Random Number Table (Appendix I).

RN	$a + (b - a)(RN_\%) = $ Simulated Value (sec)	
435	5 + 3(.435)	= 6.31
143	5 + 3(.143)	= 5.43
362	5 + 3(.362)	= 6.09
620	5 + 3(.620)	= 6.86
573	5 + 3(.573)	= 6.72

9 *Using empirical data* A process planner is working on plans for producing a new detergent. She wishes to simulate a raw material demand in order to plan for adequate materials-handling and storage facilities. On the basis of usage for a similar product introduced previously, she has developed a frequency distribution of demand in tons per day for a 2-month period. Use this data (shown below) to simulate the raw material usage requirements for 7 periods (days).

Demand, X (tons/day)	10	11	12	13	14	15	
Frequency (days)	6	18	15	12	6	3	Total = 60

Solution

The steps below correspond to those in Fig. 5-17.

(1) Data are given in frequencies.

(2) To formulate a probability distribution, divide each frequency by the total (60); for example, 6 ÷ 60 = .10, and 18 ÷ 60 = .30. Then formulate a cumulative probability distribution by successively summing the probability values.

Demand (tons/day)	Frequency (days)	Probability P(X)	Cumulative Probability
10	6	.10	.10
11	18	.30	(.10 + .30) = .40
12	15	.25	.65
13	12	.20	.85
14	6	.10	.95
15	3	.05	1.00
	60	1.00	

(3) Next, assign random-number intervals so that the number of values available to each class corresponds with the probability. Using 100 two-digit numbers (00–99), we assign 10 percent (00–09) to the first class, 30 percent (10–39) to the second class, and so on.

Demand (tons/day)	Probability P(X)	Corresponding Random Numbers
10	.10	00–09
11 ←	—.30 ←	10–39 ←
12	.25	40–64
13	.20	64–84
14	.10	85–94
15	.05	95–99
	1.00	RN = 27

(4) We obtain random numbers (RN) from column 1 of Appendix I (for convenience), so the first seven numbers are:

$$27 \qquad 13 \qquad 80 \qquad 10 \qquad 54 \qquad 60 \qquad 49$$

The first RN, 27, falls into the second class of the distribution and corresponds to a demand of 11 tons per day.

Random Number	27	13	80	10	54	60	49
Simulated Demand	11	11	13	11	12	12	12

(5) This extremely small simulation yields a mean of $\overline{X} = 11.7$ tons and a standard deviation of $s = .76$ tons. The expected value from the empirical probability distribution is $E(X) = \Sigma[XP(X)] = 12.05$ tons, suggesting that the small sample size of only 7 periods has resulted in some error. A much larger sample should be simulated before the simulation results are used for making decisions.

Note that the width of the random number "target" in each class corresponds *exactly* to the relative frequency of the class. This helps to ensure that the simulated results have the same type of distribution as the original data. This is more apparent in the graphic method where the vertical distances on the graph correspond to the relative frequencies of the respective classes.

10 Empirical data collected on the time required to weld a transformer bracket were recorded to the nearest ¼ minute, as shown in the accompanying table.

Weld Time (min)	Number of Observations
< .25	0
.25 < .75	24
.75 < 1.25	42
1.25 < 1.75	72
1.75 < 2.25	38
2.25 < 2.75	14
2.75 < 3.25	10

(a) Formulate a cumulative distribution in percentage terms.
(b) Graph the frequency and cumulative distributions.
(c) A simulation is to be conducted using random numbers. What simulated weld times (to the nearest .25 minute) would result from the random numbers 25, 90, and 59?
(d) What proportion of the times exceed 2.0 minutes?

Solution

(a) Cumulative distributions are usually formulated on a scale where the cumulative percentage is "more than" or "less than" a corresponding X axis amount. We shall use a "less than" percentage and so will need to identify the upper-class boundaries (UCB) as the Y coordinates for the cumulative distribution.

Weld Time (min)	Frequency in Numbers	Upper-Class Boundary (UCB)	Cumulative Number of Times < UCB	Cumulative Percentage of Time < UCB
< .25	0	.25	0	0
.25 < .75	24	.75	24	12
.75 < 1.25	42	1.25	66	33
1.25 < 1.75	72	1.75	138	69
1.75 < 2.25	38	2.25	176	88
2.25 < 2.75	14	2.75	190	95
2.75 < 3.25	10	3.25	200	100

(b) The frequency distribution is constructed by extending vertical lines from the class boundaries to the appropriate frequency level for the class. For the cumulative distribution, values of the cumulative percentage of time < UCB are plotted at weld times corresponding to the UCB. For example, the frequency (12 percent) is plotted at UCB = .75 (as illustrated below).

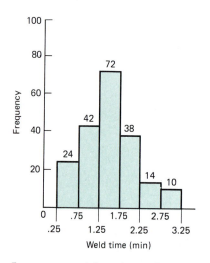
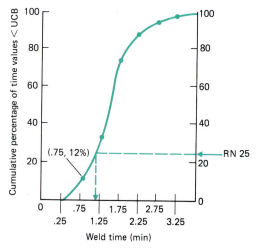

Frequency and Cumulative Distributions

(c) The simulated time for random number (RN) 25 is determined by entering the cumulative graph at 25 (as shown by the arrow) and proceeding horizontally to the curve and then down to the weld time. The resultant is a reading of 1.0 minute (rounded to the nearest .25 minute). Times for random numbers 90 and 59 are 2.5 and 1.5 minutes, respectively. (A larger graph would lend more accuracy.)

(d) From the cumulative distribution, about 12 percent of the times exceed 2.0 minutes.

11 *How simulated times can be used to gain a knowledge of the interface of two assembly activities* In an aircraft assembly operation, activity A precedes activity B, and inventory may accumulate between the two activities. With the use of random numbers, a simulated sample of performance times yielded the values shown (minutes) in the accompanying table.

Activity A		Activity B	
Random Number	Time (min)	Random Number	Time (min)
07	.3	63	.5
90	.8	44	.4
02	.2	30	.4
50	.5	98	.9
76	.6	30	.4
47	.5	72	.6
13	.3	58	.5
06	.3	96	.9
79	.7	37	.4

(a) Simulate the assembly of six parts, showing idle time in activity B, waiting time of each part, and number of parts waiting. *Note*: Omit the first random number of A so that activity B begins at time zero.

(b) What was the average length of the waiting line ahead of B (in number of units)?

(c) What was the average output per hour of the assembly line?

Solution

(a) Our interest lies in activity B, so we can set up a table (below) to show when parts arrive at B, how long it takes B to work on them, and the resultant idle and waiting times:

Part Number	Part Available for Activity B at Time	Activity B Beginning Time	Activity B Ending Time	Activity B Idle Time	Waiting Time of Part	Number Parts Waiting at B End Time
1	—	0	.5	0	0	0
2	.8	.8	1.2	.3	0	1
3	1.0	1.2	1.6	0	.2	1
4	1.5	1.6	2.5	0	.1	1
5	2.1	2.5	2.9	0	.4	2
6	2.6	2.9	3.5*	0	.3	2
7	2.9				1.0†	
8	3.2					

*Total run time.
†Total waiting time.

Activity B begins at 0, and it takes .5 minute to complete the first part. B is then idle for .3 minute until part 2 arrives from A at .8 minute. Part 2 takes .4 minute, so the ending time is .8 + .4 = 1.2 minutes. By this time part 3 has been waiting .2 minute because it became available at .8 + .2 = 1.0 minute, but work could not be begun on it until 1.2 minutes. However, before activity B is finished on part 3 at 1.6 minutes, part 4 has arrived (at 1.0 + .5 = 1.5 minutes), and so one part is waiting. We continue systematically in this manner through part 6, noting that when it is finished at time 3.5 minutes, there are two parts waiting, for their availability times were 2.9 minutes and 3.2 minutes, respectively.

(b) The average length of the waiting line (that is, average inventory) ahead of B can be expressed in equation form as follows:

$$\text{Average inventory} = \frac{\text{total waiting time}}{\text{total run time}}$$

$$= \frac{1.0 \text{ assembly minute}}{3.5 \text{ minutes}} = .29 \text{ assembly}$$

(c) Average output per hour:

$$\text{Units/hr} = \frac{6 \text{ units}}{3.5 \text{ min}} \left(\frac{60 \text{ min}}{\text{hr}}\right) = 102.9 \text{ units/hr}$$

QUESTIONS

5-1 What are the major steps in developing a new product?

5-2 Why is the distinction between production and marketing functions less definite for services than for goods?

5-3 Distinguish between the following: (a) Basic research and applied research; (b) CAD and CAM; (c) graphic and simplex methods of linear programming.

5-4 Explain what is meant by the "life cycle" of a product.

5-5   What key factors determine which products a firm should produce?

5-6   Why is linear programming a particularly suitable technique for product selection decisions? That is, how do the objectives and limitations of product selection decisions correspond to the assumptions underlying linear programming?

5-7   Explain how the process planning function differs for intermittent (such as jobshop) systems as opposed to continuous (line) systems.

5-8   Can robots "think"? Why do they pose a threat to American workers?

5-9   Distinguish between the following types of charts with respect to use: (a) assembly, (b) operations process, (c) flow process, (d) worker-machine, (e) activity.

5-10 In what respects is an equipment selection decision similar in concept to the initial steps in a break-even analysis?

5-11 What are the major reasons why production analysts might want to use simulation to analyze a production process?

5-12 Assume that you are an operations analyst and that you are asked to look into a problem of machine idle time. You are told that workers A and B both have mean operating times of 53 seconds and that machine X is set to perform an automatic welding cycle every 55 seconds. However, the machine often goes through an "empty" cycle, with a resultant loss of 55 seconds to all subsequent activities on the line. How would you go about resolving this problem?

PROBLEMS

1 A data processing manager wishes to formulate a linear programming model to help him decide how to use his personnel as programmers, (X_1) or systems analysts (X_2) in such a way as to maximize revenues (Z). Each programmer generates $40 per hour in income, and systems analysts bring in $50 per hour. Programming work during the coming week is limited to 50 hours, maximum. The production scheduler has also specified that the total of programming time plus two times the systems analysis time be limited to 80 hours or less. State the objective function and constraints.

2 Solve Prob. 1 via the graphic method, using X_1 for the horizontal axis and X_2 for the vertical axis.

3 Set up the initial simplex table for Prob. 1.

4 Suppose the optimal solution to Prob. 1 is as given in this simplex table.

C →		40	50	0	50	
↓		Decision Variables				Solution Values
	Variables in Solution	X_1	X_2	S_1	S_2	(RHS)
40	X_1	1	0	1	0	50
50	X_2	0	1	$-\frac{1}{2}$	$\frac{1}{2}$	15
	Z	40	50	15	25	2,750
	C − Z	0	0	−15	−25	

(a) How many hours of time should the manager schedule for systems analysis work?

(b) How many hours of time (in total) should be scheduled?

(c) How much revenue can the firm expect to gain from the optimal scheduling plan?

(d) How much more revenue would be gained if there were one more hour of programming work available?

(e) Assuming that programming work could be increased, how many more hours of programming time could profitably be added before other restrictions took effect? (That is, what is the upper sensitivity limit for the programming time constraint?)

(f) What is the shadow price associated with the 80-hour total time constraint?

Suppose the manager had to decrease the programming time by 1 hour (that is, gain 1 hour of slack programming time) for a maintenance activity.

(g) How much programming revenue (only) would be lost?

(h) By how much could the systems analysis time be increased?

(i) What would be the effect upon profits of such a change (that is, the dollar amount of increase or decrease)?

5 Sunstroke Paint Company makes a profit of $5 per gallon on its oil-base paint and $7 per gallon on its water-base paint. Both paints contain two ingredients, A and B. The oil-base paint contains 80 percent A and 20 percent B, whereas the water-base paint contains 40 percent A and 60 percent B. Sunstroke currently has 20,000 gallons of A and 8,000 gallons of B in inventory and cannot obtain more at this time. The company wishes to use linear programming to determine the appropriate mix of oil-base and water-base paint to produce to maximize its total profit.

(a) State the objective function and constraints.

(b) What is the slope of the objective function?

6 Maximize $Z = 4X + 2Y$
   subject to: $6X + 4Y \leq 12$
   $2X + 8Y \leq 16$

7 Precast Company can produce grade A material, which yields a profit of $1 per unit, and grade B material, which yields a profit of $2 per unit. Each unit of A requires 2 hours of machining and 1 hour of finishing. Each unit of B requires 1 hour of machining and 3 hours of finishing. Suppose 200 hours of machining capacity and 300 hours of finishing capacity are available.

(a) What amounts of A and B should be produced to maximize profits?

(b) What is the profit?

8 Minimize $C = \$10A + \$20B$
   subject to: $5A + 20B \geq 25$
   $15A + 5B \geq 30$

(Use the graphic method or computer solution.)

9 A company producing a standard line and a deluxe line of electric clothes dryers has the following time requirements (in minutes) in departments where either model can be processed:

Activity	Standard	Deluxe
Metal frame stamping	3	6
Electric motor installation	10	10
Wiring	10	15

The standard models contribute $30 each and the deluxe $50 each to profits. The motor installation production line has a full 60 minutes available each hour, but the stamping machine is available only 30 minutes per hour. There are two lines for wiring, so the time availability is 120 minutes per hour. What is the optimal combination of output in units per hour? (Solve graphically.)

10 Use the simplex method to solve Prob. 9 manually.

11 Solve Prob. 9 using a computer with an LP software package.

12 A food supplement for livestock is to be mixed in such a way as to contain exactly 25 pounds of vitamin A, at least 15 pounds of Vitamin B, and at least 40 pounds of vitamin C. The supplement is to be made from two commercial feeds. Each pound of feed #1 contains 2 ounces of A, 6 ounces of B, and 4 ounces of C, and costs $5. A pound of feed #2 contains 4 ounces of A, 1 ounce of B, and 3 ounces of C, and costs $3. Let X_1 be the pounds of feed #1 and X_2 be the pounds of feed #2.

(a) Formulate the objective functions and constraints for a linear programming problem that will minimize the cost of the food supplement while satisfying the vitamin content requirements.

(b) Solve the problem using an LP software package.

13 The initial matrix of a maximization linear programming problem with all ≤ constraints was found to be as follows:

$C \rightarrow$		187	45	95	0	0	0	
↓	Sol.	X_1	X_2	X_3	S_1	S_2	S_3	RHS
0	S_1	200	180	80	1	0	0	600
0	S_2	500	0	90	0	1	0	500
0	S_3	40	40	0	0	0	1	120
	Z	0	0	0	0	0	0	0
	$C - Z$	187	45	95	0	0	0	

(a) What is the objective function?
(b) What are the constraints?

14 Solve Prob. 13 using a computer with an LP software package.

15 A government agency has $800 million available to allocate among five recreational projects whose percent return on investment (ROI) and present value dollar costs (PV$_{cost}$) are shown below. The agency wishes to maximize its dollar value of return on investment [in other words, (ROI) (PV$_{cost}$)] subject to satisfying various requirements. Figures below are present value amounts in millions of dollars.

Project Type	X_1	X_2	X_3	X_4	X_5
ROI	.40	.15	− .05	.30	.25
PV_{cost}	280	210	150	230	180

All five projects are of a type that can be done "incrementally"—in other words, partial completion is worthwhile, but only one project of each type can be undertaken. At least $250 million (total) must be designated for projects 2 and 3, and no more than $300 million (total) can be allocated to projects 4 and 5. In addition, the expenditure on project 3 must be 50 percent of that allocated to project 1.

(a) State the objective function and constraints for a linear programming model that would determine what proportion of each project should be completed.

(b) Use an LP computer program to solve the problem for values of $X_1, \cdots, X_5$.

(c) What is the optimal dollar value return on investment expected?

16 Southern Oak Furniture Association (SOFA) has a plant in Arkansas which produces three models of chairs. The profit contributions per chair are as follows:

$$
\begin{aligned}
C &= \text{(Contemporary)} &= \$10 \\
D &= \text{(Danish)} &= 15 \\
E &= \text{(Early American)} &= 25
\end{aligned}
$$

The firm's dry-kiln capacity for green lumber limits the total production of any mix of chairs to 1,000 per day. If all production went into contemporary chairs and the dry kilns did not limit production, the firm could produce 1,500 chairs, but the Danish models take 1.5 times as long and the Early American models twice as long as the contemporary chairs. Also, the Danish models require special inlaid backs which come from a single supplier who cannot supply more than 500 per day. Assuming that the firm's retailers would accept any mix of models, *set up* (only) the objective function and the constraint equations that, if solved via linear programming, would result in an optimal selection of products to maximize profits.

17 Use the simplex method to solve Prob. 16.

18 Rework Solved Prob. 7 except with load times of 8 minutes, travel times of 6 minutes, and return times of 4 minutes. Assume 2-minute dump times.

(a) Find the length of the cycle.

(b) What is the idle time cost per hour?

19 A construction firm uses dump trucks to haul asphalt to a distant location, where a paving machine applies a four-inch layer to a new roadway. Trucks require 3 minutes for loading at the asphalt plant, 7 minutes to travel loaded to the new roadway, 10 minutes to dump the asphalt into the paving machine, and 5 minutes to return empty. The firm has only one paving machine, and it paves only while it is being fed (and pulled) by a truck during its dumping activity.

(a) How many trucks are required to pave the roadway as quickly as possible?

(b) Construct an activity chart for a two-truck, one-paving-machine arrangement.

(c) If the paving machine cost is $80 per hour and the truck cost is $34 per hour, how many trucks should be used to minimize the idle equipment cost?

20 A production analyst is planning for the manufacture of valve fittings. Each fitting must be milled on any one of three milling machines, X, Y, or Z. The setup and operating costs for each are as shown.

Machine	Setup Costs	Operating Costs
X	$10	$.30/unit
Y	30	.10/unit
Z	40	.05/unit

(a) Graph the cost structure for the three alternatives for volumes up to 250 units.

(b) For what *range* of outputs should the analyst specify the use of machine Y?

21 A Baltimore glass company can produce a certain insulator on any of three machines which have the charges shown. The firm has an opportunity to accept an order for either (1) 50 units at $20 per unit or (2) 150 units at $12 per unit.

Machine	Fixed Cost	Variable Cost
A	$ 50	$4/unit
B	200	2/unit
C	400	1/unit

(a) Prepare a chart showing the machine breakpoints.

(b) Which machine should be used if the 50-unit order is accepted?

(c) What profit would result if the 50-unit order is accepted?

(d) Which machine should be used if the 150-unit order is accepted?

(e) What profit would result if the 150-unit order is accepted?

(f) What is the incremental (profit) advantage of taking the 150-unit order over the 50-unit order?

(g) What is the break-even volume for machine B when revenue is $12 per unit?

22 A television cabinet assembly line is equipped with overhead carrier hooks at a spacing that is designed to carry a cabinet into a spray-painting booth every 30 seconds. The worker attaching the cabinets to the hooks has a normally distributed time with a mean of 24 seconds and a standard deviation of 4 seconds. What proportion of the time will the worker fail to get a cabinet hooked to the overhead carrier before the carrier hooks move on to the painting booth?

23 A promotional campaign is being planned where winners have an equal (uniform) chance of winning either 1, 2, 3, . . . up to 10 hours of professional instruction in small computer operations. Simulate the amount of time the firm will have to provide for the first five winners of the contest. Use the two-digit random numbers 94, 74, 62, 11, and 17 and round your simulated times to the nearest whole hour.

24 The time required to service a customer at the Pacific Airlines Counter is normally distributed with a mean of 2 minutes and standard deviation of .5 minute. Simulate the service times for three customers using a table of normally distributed random numbers. (Assume the numbers selected from the table at random are: − .48, 1.54, and − .22.)

25 A large grocery distribution center in Denver is computerizing its order service department. Orders from customers in Colorado (and adjacent states) will go via phone line directly into the company's main computer, which will generate "pick lists" with standard times to fill each order. To assist in planning for the proper number of delivery trucks, planners have collected the data shown below from the past year (300 days).

No. trucks required, X	20	21	22	23	24	25	26	27	28	29	30	31	32
No. days, frequency	0	4	18	25	28	41	68	56	31	22	5	2	0

(a) Simulate the demand for trucks over a 10-day period. (*Note:* Use the first three digits from column 6, Appendix I for your random numbers.)

(b) Compute the mean.

(c) Compute the standard deviation of your simulated sample.

26 Data were collected on the assembly times for 1,000 water valves (size 2-inch, 150 pounds) at the Drain Company, as shown in the table.

Time		Number of
LCB	UCB	Valves
1.0	Under 1.5 min	0
1.5	Under 2.0 min	20
2.0	Under 2.5 min	120
2.5	Under 3.0 min	280
3.0	Under 3.5 min	430
3.5	Under 4.0 min	120
4.0	Under 4.5 min	30
4.5	Under 5.0 min	0
		1,000

(a) Graph the data as a cumulative distribution.

(b) What percentage of the assembly times exceed 4.0 minutes?

(c) What would be the simulated assembly time for a random number of 44? (Estimate to the nearest half minute.)

27 In the meal preparation kitchens of New York International Airlines, dinners are prepared on an assembly line where there is limited space for an inventory of partially filled plates. A simulation of two adjacent workers (where Y is dependent upon X) developed the random numbers and times shown (in seconds).

X ──────────→ Y ───→

Activity X		Activity Y	
Random Number	Time	Random Number	Time
72	22	84	32
18	10	26	12
77	23	13	8
84	27	60	24
5	7	53	22
20	11	22	12
46	27	90	36

(a) Simulate the preparation of five meals, and determine the idle time for activity Y, the waiting time of each meal, and the number of meals waiting (omitting the first random number of X).

(b) What was the average length of the waiting line upstream from Y?

(c) What was the average output per minute of the production line?

REFERENCES

[1] Anderson, David R., Dennis J. Sweeney, and Thomas A. Williams: *Introduction to Management Sciences*, 2d ed., West, St. Paul, MN, 1979.

[2] Buffa, Elwood S.: *Modern Production/Operations Management*, 7th ed., Wiley, New York, 1984.

[3] Cook, Thomas M., and Robert A. Russell: *Contemporary Operations Management*, Prentice-Hall, Englewood Cliffs, NJ, 1980.

[4] Prospectus, ISC Systems Corporation, Spokane, WA, 1980.

[5] Joh, Sheyon: "Scent Strips Add New Dimension to Ads for Perfume, After-Shave," *The Spokesman-Review*, Spokane, WA, Aug. 25, 1985, p. C5.

[6] Norman, Richard: *Service Management*, Wiley, Chichester, England, 1984.

[7] "See Why Simulation at British Leyland," *P & IM Review 1986 Reference Guide and Directory*, T.D.A. Publications, Hollywood, FL, 1985, p. 54.

[8] "The Descendants of McDonald's," *USA Today*, Nov. 1, 1985, p. 7B.

[9] Timms, Howard L., and Michael F. Pohlen: *The Production Function in Business*, Richard D. Irwin, Homewood, IL, 1970.

SELF QUIZ: CHAPTER 5

Part I True/False [1 point each = 6]

1 _____ When developing new products, the product and process design phases are usually not completed until after feasibility studies have been made.

2 _____ Service-delivery systems are easier to plan and control than goods-manufacturing systems because most services are standardized.

3 _____ CAD/CAM systems work best when functional users (e.g., engineering and marketing) maintain their own information in the form that is most convenient to them—rather than in common.

4 _____ Robots are now negating the traditional distinction between intermittent and continuous systems by facilitating the production of made-to-order goods on continuous flow systems.

5 _____ Assembly charts use the symbols ▽ for storage, D for delay, and ▷ for transport.

6 _____ Simulation models do not necessarily reveal the best (optimal) solution to a problem (such as a linear programming model would).

Part II Problems [3 points each = 9. Calculate and select your answer.]

1 Betty Lou Cosmetics makes a profit of $1 on each tube of lipblush (X) and $8 on each bottle of lotion (Y). Requirements are:

	X Req.	Y Req.	Available/wk
A (mix hr)	6	—	42 hr
B (dry hr)	—	10	30 hr
C (package hr)	6	10	60 hr

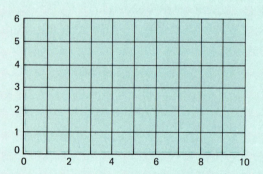

Using graphic linear programming, the optimal profit per week from X and Y is:
(a) $48.00
(b) $35.00
(c) $29.00
(d) $14.60
(e) None of the above.

2 The respective costs for the chart shown are $18 per hour for the operator and $90 per hour for each machine. What is the (steady state) idle time cost per hour?

(a) $ .11
(b) $ 2.00
(c) $ 6.67
(d) $14.40
(e) None of the above.

Load: 3 min
Unload: 1 min
Run: 5 min

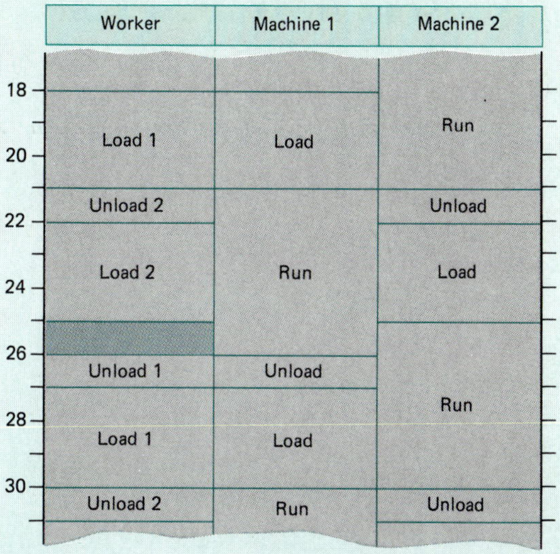

	Worker	Machine 1	Machine 2
18	Load 1	Load	Run
20			
22	Unload 2		Unload
	Load 2	Run	Load
24			
26	Unload 1	Unload	
28	Load 1	Load	Run
30	Unload 2	Run	Unload

3 A wave soldering machine opens to accept printed circuit boards every 2.20 minutes. The benchworker who feeds the machine must first install a resistor onto each circuit board, and her installation time is normally distributed with a mean of 2.02 minutes and standard deviation of .10 minute. If no inventory buildup is allowed, what percent of the time will she complete her installation on time to feed the board to the machine?

(a) 55.1 percent
(b) 84.1 percent
(c) 93.3 percent
(d) 96.4 percent
(e) None of the above.

CHAPTER 6
HUMAN RESOURCE MANAGEMENT

213-239, 243-247

INTRODUCTION

Xerox launched a massive effort to recapture some of the copier market it had lost to Japan—and with a good deal of success! How did they do it?

Xerox replaced much of their corporate bureaucracy with product-development and problem-solving "teams." Product quality and customer satisfaction were given increased importance in determining bonuses and promotions. Automated production and materials-handling equipment enabled the company to cut manufacturing employment in half while still maintaining a "cooperative" union relationship. This new "team" flexibility enabled Xerox to develop a new copier in 2½ years (instead of 5) using fewer than 350 people (instead of 1,500). In the words of Stephen Prokesch: "If the new corporate approach sounds similar to that of the Japanese, it is no coincidence, because Xerox has gone to extremes to study its Japanese competitors [19].

Farsighted firms like Xerox recognize that effective management of human resources is the key to their survival and success. This chapter directs our attention to managing human resources in the production system.

OVERVIEW OF JOB DESIGN AND WORK METHODS

Employees are the most valuable asset of an organization. No equipment can match their intrinsic worth nor their diversity of skills, emotions, and levels of performance. So it is true that "managing people" is frequently the most difficult aspect of an operations manager's job.

JOB DESIGN INPUTS AND OUTPUTS

Our study of human resource management is structured around the logical flow from product and process decisions to job design and work methods depicted in Fig. 6-1. *Jobs* are the activities performed by workers to meet organizational goals. Job designs dictate work methods, which in turn require some form of measurement and yield some degree of job satisfaction. Much of the managerial effort devoted to human resource management concerns these four areas: (1) job design, (2) job satisfaction, (3) work methods, and (4) work measurement.

In Fig. 6-1, note that the behavioral and *social* (priority) influences are again depicted on the left, and resources and *technical* (capacity) influences on the right, with a necessary *economic* balance in the center. This is consistent with the format we used earlier and with what will follow as we take up other topics.

For now, let us assume that the technical system is used to produce goods and services to satisfy needs arising from the social system. We will begin with a look into the philosophical and psychological makeup of the human resource. Then we will examine the elements of job design and work methods. Next we will review the commonly used techniques for setting labor standards. The chapter ends with some observations about employee safety and compensation. When you finish the

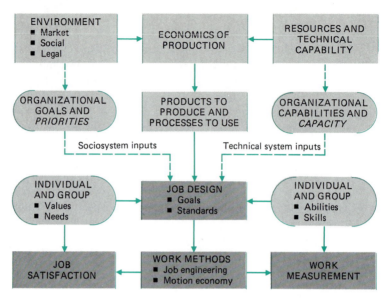

FIGURE 6-1   Elements of Job Design and Work Methods

chapter, you should know what considerations are involved in job design and work methods, and you should be able to compute labor standards.

POLICY FOUNDATIONS

Over the past 50 years, organizational theorists, behavioral scientists, and others have generated countless theories designed to explain and improve the management of the work force. We shall draw from these theories in this section. But first, let us recall the philosophical and psychological basis for a human resource management policy, which recognizes both (a) the human essence and (b) the levels of existence of employees.

Human Essence   All members of an organization share a *human nature*, or *essence*, that distinguishes them, as a class of beings, from rocks, plants, and other beings. In fact, this common nature of "humanness" is the basis for fairness and equal rights under the law for everyone in our society. We hold that the intrinsic value of human beings stems more from their human nature than it does from their accomplishments, position, or possessions. This essence of humanity thus establishes a minimal level of behavior for interactions with other humans. It implies that managers, workers, and all others associated with an organization should, at least as a bare minimum, *naturally* treat each other with respect as humans. As depicted in Fig. 6-2, this precept forms one cornerstone of a sound human resource management policy.

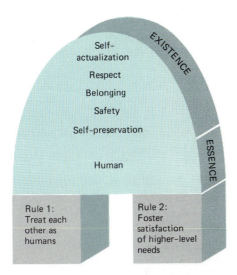

FIGURE 6-2   Foundations of Human Resource Management Policy

Levels of Existence   The psychologist A. H. Maslow has suggested that human beings have a hierarchy of needs, which are depicted in Fig. 6-2 [**25**]. The range extends from a minimal level of existence, or self-preservation, to a fuller psychological state of self-actualization [**15**].

These various needs are really integrated, for each higher-level need depends upon a minimal level of satisfaction of the preceding (lower-level) need. A full existence as a normal, healthy individual follows from the satisfaction, to at least some extent, of all five levels of need. First, people require (1) adequate compensation to satisfy their economic needs for food, shelter, and clothing. In addition, they need (2) some sense of safety and security, as well as (3) a genuine sense of belonging (such as to a group or organization), so that they can experience acceptance, love, and friendship. Finally comes the need for (4) respect and approval as a person and (5) some level of self-actualization.

The self-actualization need is complex. In Fig. 6-3 we see that its essential

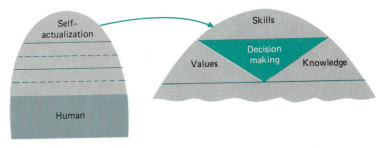

FIGURE 6-3   Components of Self-Actualization

components are *knowledge* (of facts, concepts, methodologies), *values* (love, beauty, emotions), *skills* (productive, artistic, athletic), and *decision-making* activities. The knowledge, value, and skill capabilities reflect a higher (spiritual) level of existence than simply a physical (material) presence. Knowledge relies upon the senses and the intellect, whereas values are more a product of inherent sensitivity and the will. Freedom, justice, and environmental tranquillity are some of the values we treasure. Skills arise primarily from training and practice. The ability to use knowledge, values, and skills to make decisions implies a degree of freedom and responsibility that is uniquely human.

Now let us relate the foregoing philosophical and psychological concepts more directly to work and organizations. At the start, individuals work to meet their basic needs. Some workers in third-world countries have difficulty progressing beyond this level. More often in our society, jobs link the individual with an organization that offers a sense of belonging.

As the lower-level needs of a person become satisfied, the intrinsic rewards of a job take on an increasingly significant role. Food and shelter are not enough; employees look to their organization for acceptance or respect and for the opportunity to make decisions. If activities take on more of a professional flavor, the job tends to become more absorbing and satisfying. Higher-order nonwage incentives, such as competency goals, replace more materialistic wage and status goals. This intrinsic element of satisfaction can emerge from both physical and mental assignments. For example, a welder may gain as much satisfaction from completing a difficult weld on a new skyscraper as did the architect from designing the building.

At the highest level of satisfaction, individuals use their unique knowledge and skills to accomplish meaningful tasks in a responsible way. At this stage the opportunity to make significant decisions that are consistent with one's value system can be very satisfying. Our second cornerstone of human resource management policy thus rests on the observation that employees have a hierarchy of needs, and jobs that satisfy higher-level needs are preferable to those that do not.

JOB DESIGN

APPROACHES TO JOB DESIGN

Job design is the conscious structuring of the content and methods of work effort. The design may specify *what* task is to be done, *how* to do it, and if necessary, *when* and *where* to do it. Job designs should be consistent with organizational objectives, and agreed upon by both employee and employer.

Figure 6-4 illustrates some differences in two approaches to job design [17:147]. The *objective approach* emphasizes the efficiency of getting the job done, whereas the *behavioral approach* focuses more on the individual doing the work. The objective (or efficiency) approach stems from Frederick Taylor's scientific management concepts and has given us quantitative measures such as time

Highly Behavioral	Job Design	Highly Objective
On individual hired	Emphasis	On job to be done
Unwritten	Job description	Written in detail
Widely diversified	Job assignments	Highly specialized
General—and continuous	Job training	Specific—and limited
Highly unspecified—much freedom	Job methods	Highly specified—no discretion
Measured over long run only	Performance	Immediate objective measure
Promotion, status	Rewards	Pay

FIGURE 6-4   A Comparison of Some Job Design Characteristics

studies, work sampling, and methods improvement studies. The behavioral emphasis has developed from the Hawthorn studies, and the work of Herzberg, Hackman, Oldham, and others, plus an analysis of Japanese management systems. Those using this approach claim that productivity and quality improvements result from having more broadly trained and highly motivated employees. Many firms have, of course, successfully blended appropriate elements of both systems.

WORK GOALS AND STANDARDS

Work Goals   Although the emphasis on goals differs from one firm to another, studies show that work goals are an important element of job design. People without clearly defined goals are more likely to work slowly, perform poorly, and accomplish less [24]. Work goals help structure activities and generate interest so that specific work is accomplished within designated time periods. Individual goals also help ensure that a person's efforts are channeled into productive activities which are consistent with organizational goals.

Denis Umstat has isolated three criteria which seem to be particularly important in utilizing goals at the job design level [24].

- *Goal clarity.* Clear and specific goals are most useful for directing work efforts.
- *Goal difficulty.* Moderately challenging goals are more effective than very easy or very difficult goals.
- *Goal acceptance.* Goals must be accepted to be useful—otherwise, they are worthless.

The chances for acceptance and commitment are enhanced by employee participation in setting the goals. The acceptance of clear and moderately difficult goals generally results in more effort, increased productivity, and improved performance.

Standards of Performance   Standards provide a basis for setting the (shorter-term) daily output or level of quality expected of the worker. They are not always specifically stated, but most firms have some form of understood or documented standards. Commonly used *labor standards* state the amount of time that should reasonably be used to perform a specified activity at a sustainable rate, using established methods under normal working conditions.

If a worker is trained (and matched) to a job and the standards for that job are realistic, standards can help both the worker and the organization. For the worker, they are a measure of performance whereby he or she can be motivated and rewarded for productive work. Standards can also be a measure of performance for the organization. In addition, they are used for scheduling work, costing operations, and other managerial purposes.

Many progressive firms, such as Westinghouse and IBM, have implemented systems whereby employees play a major role in designing their own jobs and setting their own standards—usually in conjunction with their supervisors. They have found that both productivity and morale are enhanced by gaining the active participation of workers in the job design (and redesign) process.

JOB SATISFACTION

The scientific management approach has, over the years, generated substantial efficiencies by delineating job activities, eliminating wasted motions, and fostering highly specialized jobs. The specialization of labor coupled with the use of highly automated assembly lines has, however, resulted in many repetitive and monotonous jobs. A good deal of assembly line work and monitoring work falls into this category. Turnover rates are often high, and quality levels may be low. Absenteeism in one major automobile manufacturing plant has run as high as 1 day in 5, or 20 percent. Employees tend to avoid dissatisfying jobs—or do them reluctantly, with a resulting low rate of productivity. Yet the jobs must be done. In some factories, many of these jobs are being transferred to robots. Where they are not, managers are faced with the problem of motivating their employees to do them.

Efforts to solve the motivation problem—and give workers more job satisfaction—are numerous. In addition to the traditional appeal of higher wages, organizations have developed a number of other motivational techniques. Figure 6-5 identifies three approaches which we shall discuss briefly.

JOB ENLARGEMENT AND ROTATION

Job enlargement programs are designed to increase the scope and complexity of a worker's job in order to make it more appealing. For example, machinists' jobs appear more interesting if the machinists do set-up and inspection activities as well as machine operations.

Numerous job enlargement experiments have been done, and with mixed results. In an insurance firm, productivity was increased and the number of errors decreased after workers were given responsibility for preparing a complete insurance policy rather than only one portion of it [5:412]. However, after an IRS

MOTIVATIONAL TECHNIQUE	FOCUS IS ON JOB	EFFECT ON JOB OR INDIVIDUAL
■ Job enlargement ■ Job rotation	V A R I E T Y	Additional tasks Rotation among different tasks

■ Flextime
 	
■ 4-day week
 	
■ Job sharing
	T I M E	Flexibility in setting arrival
		  and departure times
		
		Fewer days but longer hours per day
		
		Job shared between two (part-time)
		  workers

■ Job enrichment	P S Y C H O L O G Y	■ (Herzberg) Emphasis on motivational
		  factors (achievement, recognition, work
		  itself, advancement, growth)
		
		■ (Hackman–Oldham) Emphasis on
		  meaningfulness and responsibility
		  (skill variety, task identity, task
		  importance, autonomy, feedback)

FIGURE 6-5   Motivational Techniques Used in Job Design

redesign of clerical jobs, error rates were not lower, and production went down as a result of using more complicated methods [18:266].

Job rotation adds variety by enabling workers to perform different jobs, rather than adding more tasks to their current job. Some workers rotate on an hourly basis, while others rotate according to a daily or weekly schedule. A large number of firms use job rotations to reduce boredom and improve job satisfaction by fostering the development of new skills. Japanese firms often practice a lifelong job rotation of managers within their companies. This enhances employees' understanding of all operations and leads to better coordination of activities.

VARIABLE TIME APPROACHES

Variable time approaches are gaining popularity not only because they give the worker flexibility in scheduling his or her own hours but also because they help level the load on transportation routes, parking facilities, cafeterias, and so on. The *flextime* approach has been adopted by such major firms as Hewlett-Packard and has had favorable results. Depending upon the firm and the job, workers schedule their 8 hours of work to begin any time between 6:30 and 9:30 A.M. and end between 3 and 6 P.M.

Four-day workweeks (at 10 hours per day) offer employees the advantages of long weekends and fewer trips to work. But the necessity of having the firm available to suppliers and customers on a regular 8-hour-per day basis has caused some problems. Only a small percentage of the work force is on a 4-day workweek, and some firms that have tried it have reverted to the 5-day week.

In *job sharing,* two people share the same job by working alternate times (such as alternate days or morning-afternoon arrangements). It has some strong advocates among working mothers and those who wish to work only part-time, but problems can arise in allocating fringe benefits. A companion approach called *work sharing* is being used in some firms (for example, Motorola) as a means of avoiding layoffs during business downturns. With this approach a company that needs to reduce production 20 percent would ask its employees to work 4 days per week instead of 5. This avoids laying off 20 percent of the work force and makes it much easier (and less costly) to restore full-scale production when demand returns. A few states (for example, Arizona and California) even offer unemployment compensation for the percentage of time the employee is off work.

JOB ENRICHMENT

Unlike job enlargement, which involves a horizontal expansion of activities within a job classification, *job enrichment* is a systematic attempt to motivate employees by changing specific motivational factors. Job enrichment entails *vertical* job loading, thus giving employees an opportunity for growth and achievement beyond their current role. Enrichment efforts were initiated by IBM in the 1940s and have been enhanced by the work of Frederick Herzberg [12] and by Hackman, Oldham, Janson, and Purdy [11].

Herzberg Approach Herzberg observed that intrinsic "motivator" factors contribute to job satisfaction whereas what he terms "hygiene" factors contribute more to job dissatisfaction. In 12 investigations covering 1,685 employees, he found the primary *causes of satisfaction,* in decreasing order of importance, were (1) achievement, (2) recognition, (3) the work itself, (4) advancement, and (5) growth. These factors relate to an individual's ability to achieve and, through achievement, to experience psychological growth. This achievement and growth are a result of the *job content.*

The primary *causes of job dissatisfaction* were (1) company policy and administration, (2) supervision, (3) relationship with the supervisor, (4) work conditions, (5) salary, (6) relationship with peers, (7) personal life, (8) relationship with subordinates, (9) status, and (1) security. Herzberg identifies these "dissatisfiers" more with the *job environment* than with the job content.

Hackman-Oldham Approach Hackman and Oldham, writing for the *Journal of Applied Psychology* [10] have emphasized three psychological ingredients in motivation: (1) meaningful work, (2) responsibility for outcomes, and (3) knowledge of actual results. These three elements of motivation stem from jobs that have the desirable characteristics listed in Fig. 6-6.

- Skill variety: Require a variety of abilities and skills.
- Task identity: Plan for the whole job—from start to finish.
- Task importance: Make the job important and meaningful.
- Autonomy: Give the worker discretion in scheduling and accomplishing the work.
- Feedback: Give the worker quick and clear feedback about job performance.

FIGURE 6-6 Desirable Job Design Characteristics

To illustrate the Hackman-Oldham approach, consider the job of a computer data-entry clerk in the processing center of a large bank. Her skill variety is low—being limited largely to typing. If jobs are fragmented, she has little or no task identity. If she is one of several data-entry clerks recording volumes of transactions, the work may not appear especially meaningful. Control over her on-the-job time is likely to be strict, and her work is audited by others. The strongest motivational characteristic is probably feedback—and that may be demotivating if she is told only of her errors!

A more highly motivating job design would have the clerk responsible for obtaining the data for specifically assigned accounts, entering it, and ensuring its accuracy. It may not be feasible, however, to enrich jobs to an optimal level from a behavioral standpoint. Higher skill requirements usually result in higher wages. In addition, giving an employee a diversity of tasks may negate some of the economic benefits of specialization.

Furthermore, not everyone wants an enriched job. Some employees are more content with menial tasks that do not challenge them mentally or physically. For them, work tends to be more of a social occasion to chat with other workers about sports, soap operas, and the upcoming vacation.

Hackman and Oldham have supported their model with a carefully tested questionnaire called the Job Diagnostic Survey (JDS). The questions included measure job satisfaction in terms of the five characteristics they find important.[1] An abbreviated example is shown in Fig. 6-7.

THE SOCIOTECHNICAL SYSTEM

Much of the previously described background on motivational psychology has been incorporated into what Eric Trist and his associates have termed the *sociotechnical approach* [23,25]. In this view, a modern productive organization has two functioning systems: a technical system and an accompanying social system.

---

[1] Figure 6-7 is for illustrative purposes only. For more detail see J. R. Hackman and G. R. Oldham, "The Job Diagnostic Survey: An Instrument for the Diagnosis of Jobs and the Evaluation of Job Redesign Projects," Tech. Rep. 4, Yale University, Department of Administrative Sciences, New Haven, CT, 1974. The survey was tested on 658 employees in 62 different jobs in 7 different organizations. Survey results and reliability are reported in [10].

1 How much *variety* is there in your job, i.e., to what extent do you do different things requiring a variety of skills?

1 ...... 2 ...... 3 ...... 4 ...... 5 ...... 6 7

Very little, I do routine things.

Moderate variety.

Very much; I do different things requiring a variety of skills.

2 To what extent does your job involve a whole and *identifiable* piece of work?

1 ...... 2 ...... 3 ...... 4 ...... 5 ...... 6 7

I do a tiny part of the overall. My results are not visible in the final product or service.

I do a moderate amount of the overall work and my contribution can be seen in the final outcome.

I do the whole job from start to finish. My results are easily seen in the final product or service.

3 In general, how significant or *important* is your job?

1 ...... 2 ...... 3 ...... 4 ...... 5 ...... 6 7

Not very significant. My outcomes are not likely to have important effects on other people.

Moderately significant.

Highly significant. My outcomes can affect others in very important ways.

4 How much *autonomy* is there in your job?

1 ...... 2 ...... 3 ...... 4 ...... 5 ...... 6 7

Very little. Almost no "say" about how and when the work is done.

Moderate, autonomy. Many things are standardized but I can make some decisions about the work.

Very much. Almost complete responsibility for how and when the work is done.

5 To what extent does doing the job itself provide you with information about your performance—i.e., *feedback* from the actual work itself aside from that of coworkers or supervisors?

1 ...... 2 ...... 3 ...... 4 ...... 5 ...... 6 7

Very little. Job itself is such that I could work forever without finding out how well I am doing.

Moderately; sometimes doing the job provides feedback and sometimes not.

Very much. Job is set up so I get almost constant feedback as I work.

FIGURE 6-7   Questions from Job Diagnostic Survey

(Figure 6-1 at the beginning of the chapter incorporates these concepts.) The *technical system* includes the technological equipment and requisite skills underlying a given transformation process. The *social system* incorporates the formal and informal work-group organization. It influences productivity by the way it motivates workers and coordinates work activities.

People within Systems We tend to think of "assembly line" work as boring and monotonous—and much of it is. The effects are inattention to the job, higher costs, lower quality, and absenteeism. But such line work can also be stressful. And in the opinion of the director of the American Institute of Stress, "Stress is the No. 1 problem in the workplace today" [14]. It shows up in anxiety, depression, headaches, and hypertension, and in drug and alcohol abuse. *Monotony* and *stress* are both problems of matching (social) individuals to the pace of (technological) machines.

The sociotechnical approach is concerned with designing jobs in such a way that the social (human) qualities of workers and the technological pressures from the work environment are thoughtfully interfaced. Figure 6-8 identifies some of the contrasting factors that must be balanced in the job design.

Broadly defined and self-controlled jobs tend to be more motivating, whereas technologically paced work may have a short-term cost advantage. The "bottom line" is an economic balance, which seems to be moving toward the principle that machines should do what machines can do best, and people should do work that satisfies and challenges their human capabilities.

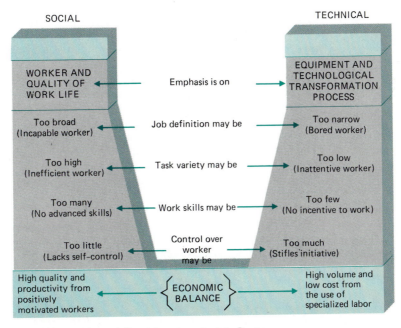

FIGURE 6-8   Some Sociotechnical Considerations in Job Design

Fortunately, the role of people in many systems is gradually changing from robotic-type work to monitoring, controlling, and managing the automatic equipment. Pehr Gellenhammer, chairman of Volvo, the largest employer in Sweden, has observed

The higher the technology, the more qualified the people need be because they must understand the system and be able to fix the system, not call for help from engineers or consultants. They should be the masters of the systems with which they work [22:48].

Sociotechnical Guidelines   In reviewing studies of sociotechnical systems, Richard Chase and Nicholas Aquilano have drawn from the work of Louis Davis [7] and F. E. Emery et al. [8] to develop some guidelines for job design at the individual and group levels [6:422]. These are summarized in Fig. 6-9.

Individual-Level Guidelines
1 Give workers an optimum level of variety of tasks within the job. Too great a variety is inefficient; too little results in boredom. The right amount gives workers a break from routine activity.
2 Arrange diverse but interdependent tasks into one meaningful pattern.
3 Give workers an optimum length of work cycle.
4 If feasible, give workers some responsibility in setting standards of quantity and quality, along with quick feedback on their job performance.
5 Include some auxiliary and preparatory tasks that extend the scope of the job and worker involvement in it.
6 Make the job tasks require sufficient skill, knowledge, or effort to generate respect within the workers' own work group.
7 Make the job show some contribution of value to the overall product or service being produced.

Group-Level Guidelines
8 Provide for interlocking tasks, job rotation, or physical proximity of workers. This is especially important in situations where (a) there is a necessary independence of jobs (in which it helps to create cooperation and better understanding among members of the work group); (b) the individual jobs involve a relatively high degree of stress (so that communication and interaction with others often lessen stress and reduce mistakes and accidents); and (c) individual jobs do not make an obvious, perceptible contribution to the end product.
9 Where the group has responsibility for a number of jobs that are linked together by interlocking tasks, its members should have some (a) perspective of the overall task to which they are contributing, (b) responsibility for setting standards and receiving feedback of results, and (c) control over "boundary tasks" (such as preparation and inspection activities).

FIGURE 6-9   Sociotechnical System Guidelines

Guidelines such as those in Fig. 6-9 may prove useful for integrating individual and group tasks by enhancing the meaningfulness of tasks and encouraging interest, responsibility, and respect for carrying them out. They also foster the cooperative benefits of work-group interaction, which has been one of the keys to the success of Japanese management systems. And they conform with Pehr Gellenhammer's advice that "work must be adapted to people, not people to machines" [22:48]. Gellenhammer is quite critical of industry's failure to make better use of workers' generally high level of education and training. "The most effective changes," he says, "are those in which the workers had the largest hand."

The sociotechnical orientation at Volvo has indeed been revolutionary and has attracted worldwide attention and admiration. Automobile assembly is done by work groups instead of by a long assembly line. Each group has about 20 workers and assembles an entire car. Teams set their own pace and break times and do their own inspections. The Volvo "experiment" has been sufficiently successful that General Motors drew upon Volvo ideas when they designed their new Saturn car plant in Tennessee. And GM was able to gain union cooperation for a labor agreement that called for workers to make design, marketing, and manufacturing decisions in an environment similar to Volvo's [16].

However, the sociotechnical guidelines are not necessarily appropriate for all circumstances, nor should they be implemented in a haphazard or arbitrary manner. Not all organizations are prepared to give work groups more decision-making responsibility, nor are the work groups prepared to accept it. Attempts to force changes prematurely by means of job design could do more harm to an organization than good. The sociotechnical challenge cannot be met overnight, and each organization's response must be tailored to its own circumstances and leadership style.

WORK METHODS AND MOTION ECONOMY

Work methods are simply ways of doing work. Sometimes they are specified as part of a job design, while at other times they are left to the discretion or experience of the worker.

As early as 1776, Adam Smith was promoting the "division of labor" as a means of developing higher skill levels in employees and allowing for the use of specialized machines. By the early 1900s, Frank and Lillian Gilbreth were performing extensive studies to define, classify, and economize work methods.

PRINCIPLES OF MOTION ECONOMY

As attention to work methods has continued, 22 widely accepted principles have evolved. These have been classified into three categories (see [2]):

- Human body (for example, begin and end motions of both hands at the same time)

- Work place   (provide a chair that permits good posture for every worker)
- Tools and equipment   (combine two or more tools wherever possible)

A systematic check through the list is likely to reveal even to an unskilled observer, some potential improvements in the work methods for any job. And if a task is highly repetitive, the benefits of a single improvement are multiplied many times.

Technology is, of course, a major source of motion economy today. Electronic controls and robotics are replacing the levers and fixtures of a few years ago, and push buttons, bar codes, and voice controls are eliminating the need for the physical force once required of workers.

METHODS IMPROVEMENT STUDIES

Figure 6-10 describes some widely accepted steps analysts have developed to establish and improve work methods. In the past, these steps were typically carried out by an "industrial engineering" or other staff group. Today, many companies are encouraging production workers to participate in internal (quality circle) groups to improve their own work methods.

Step 1   The *job to be studied* should be one that offers good potential for an improvement in working conditions or a reduction in costs. Examples are jobs that are:

- Time-consuming
- Frequently occurring
- Unsafe or unpleasant

- Bottlenecks in the work flow
- A source of rejects and rework
- A source of safety problems

It is usually preferable to begin methods improvement in areas where employees will readily accept and participate in implementing well-managed changes. Success in these areas will increase acceptance in other areas.

Step 2   *Documentation of the present method* consists of writing a step-by-step procedure describing the existing method in detail. The description can often be recorded by using a chart, such as a flow process chart, where the analyst can note any deviations in quality, quantity, sequence of operations, or tools used.

1 *Select* the job to be studied.
2 Document and *analyze* the present method.
3 *Develop* an improved method.
4 *Implement* the improved method.
5 *Maintain* and follow up on the new method.

FIGURE 6-10   Steps in Methods Improvement Study

Among the proven ways of analyzing the present method is a questioning technique which probes *every step* of the existing method, with two questions:

(a) What is its purpose?
(b) Why is it necessary?

Some flow process charts have a series of columns listing these questions and supplementary ones which ask if the activity can be eliminated, combined with another, changed in sequence, or simplified in any way.

A second technique of analysis uses a checklist to critically review every activity with respect to guidelines concerning materials flow, work-place design, hand and body movements, and so on. The principles of motion economy comprise one such checklist. Photographic methods of analysis may also be useful if the cost is justified and if employees do not object to being photographed.

Step 3 *Development of the improved method* flows from suggestions as to what activities can be combined or eliminated, which hand motions can be changed, which tools added, and so forth, to make the operation better.

New flow process charts of alternative methods should be prepared in order to compare these methods with the existing method. The total time required and total number of operations are often good indicators of improvement. After time, quality, cost, personnel effects, and any other relevant criteria have been considered with respect to the alternative methods, the best method should be selected and described in a summary report that delineates and justifies the proposed change.

Step 4 *Implementing a new method* is not an easy task. Assuming that the study was thorough and the proposal carefully prepared, the benefits of the changes must still be "sold" to both the appropriate line management and the employees. A major change may involve considerable training and should include line supervisor and employee suggestions on implementation. Few changes work smoothly from the very start, so the analyst, supervisor, and employees should all be prepared to make some modifications and spend some effort in overcoming the usual start-up problems.

Step 5 *Maintenance and follow-up of the new method* are essential to ensure that it is functioning according to plan. Such checking not only guards against a drift back to the older, more comfortable ways; it can also provide data and ideas for improvement elsewhere in the system.

PRODUCTIVITY IN OFFICE SYSTEMS

With automated equipment replacing labor, and service activities expanding at a rapid pace, the shift from factory to office activities is proceeding rapidly in the United States. A labor expert has observed that whereas blue-collar workers made up 31 percent of the nonfarm work force in 1981, their numbers will fall to 23 percent by the year 2000. And according to Henry Conn, former vice president for productivity at TRW, the 40 percent of TRW's workers who are currently involved in manufacturing will fall to 5 percent by the year 2000 [3].

This dramatic shift of the work force into nonmanufacturing activities explains why you are so likely to encounter advertisements for data processing equipment, networking facilities, and office automation systems as you page through many current business periodicals. Our society is rapidly shifting into "knowledge"-type activities. And the products and work environments that promise to improve the access and communication of information are important "methods improvement" techniques of today.

Conn has observed that office productivity improvements depend less on layouts and machine efficiency than on *how people use their time.* So one key to productivity improvement is the elimination of time-consuming searches for information, phone conversations, filing, and other distracting activities, such as attending meetings. TRW is experiencing a substantial increase in productivity from software writers who have been moved to soundproof, windowless offices with only relevant equipment such as a chair, bookshelves, a worktable, and a computer. All mail and messages are exchanged via computer. Says Conn, "You have to find activities where value is added, then eliminate everything else, either by automation or delegation" [3].

LABOR STANDARDS

Labor standards are declarations of the amount of time that should reasonably be used to perform a specified activity at a sustainable rate, using established methods under normal working conditions. Standards satisfy the needs of the worker, provide a measure of performance for the organization, and facilitate scheduling and costing of operations. Methods used to set standards include (1) historical, (2) time study, (3) predetermined time standards, and (4) work sampling.

HISTORICAL APPROACH

Not all firms have formal labor standards although studies suggest that over half of U.S. firms use some form of work measurement [21]. As suggested by Fig. 6-4, some firms prefer not to use formal standards. Many work activities, especially service and office jobs, are not easily measured. In other cases, firms may lack the capability of implementing standards.

Nevertheless, organizations that do not have explicit documented standards often have informal ones—perhaps even standards established by the workers themselves. These firms make do with simple judgmental estimates or historical data based upon the past output of an individual or a work center. Such estimates are inexpensive to derive; they are quickly and easily formulated, and they may be sufficiently accurate. In addition, they can build trust and individual responsibility for outcomes.

On the other hand, historical standards can be subjective, inconsistent, and susceptible to bias (they disregard rating factors and delays). For this reason, many firms prefer to have their standards rest upon a more formalized, organized database.

TIME-STUDY METHODS

Time-study methods were originally proposed by Frederick Taylor and were later modified to include a performance rating (PR) adjustment. They have now become one of the most widely used means of work measurement. Basically, by using time study, an analyst is taking a small sample of one worker's activity and using it to derive a standard for tasks of that nature. The only equipment needed is a stopwatch plus paper and pencil. The procedure is as summarized in Fig. 6-11 and described below.

Step 1 *Selecting the job.* Almost any repetitive short-cycle labor activity may be a candidate for time study. But a prerequisite of any study is that supervisors and workers be fully informed about the purpose and procedures of the study. An analyst should get acquainted with the operators and put them at ease as much as possible so that the study will be done under "normal" conditions, using the best methods available. Each element of the job should be a distinct operation and should be as short as possible—down to not less than 2 or 3 seconds in length.

1 Select the job, inform the worker, and define the best method.
2 Time an appropriate number of cycles (such as 25 to 50). $(10\text{-}25)$
3 Compute the average cycle time:

$$CT = \frac{\Sigma \text{ times}}{n \text{ cycles}} \tag{6-1}$$

4 Compute normal time:

$$NT = CT(PR) \tag{6-2}$$

5 Compute standard time:

$$ST = NT(AF) \tag{6-3}$$

where

$$AF = \frac{1}{1 - \% A} \tag{6-4}$$

FIGURE 6-11   Steps in Conducting a Time Study

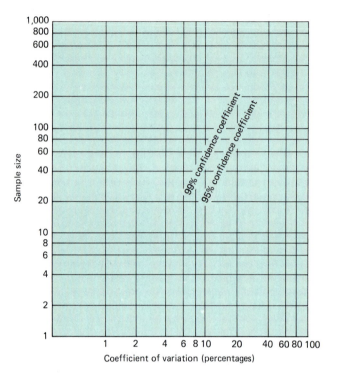

FIGURE 6-12 Time-Study Sample Size Chart (Chart is for ±5 percent accuracy for various coefficient of variation values.) *Source:* [1]

Step 2 *Timing the number of cycles.* The number of cycles to time actually depends upon how confident (statistically) the analyst wishes to be when inferring that the sample times are representative of actual on-the-job times. Since any operator's time may vary from one cycle to the next, the analyst must time enough cycles to obtain a valid estimate of the true average time. The sample size can be calculated from a knowledge of the distribution times, and the footnote on this page offers a formula to do that.[2] However, the numerous charts and graphs

---

[2] This equation does not necessitate that the standard deviation, *s*, be calculated first, but it does require that a preliminary sample of size *n′* be made. Then the time-study sample size *n* is:

$$n = \frac{Z^2[n' \ \Sigma x^2 - (\Sigma x)^2]}{h^2(\Sigma x)^2} \tag{6-5}$$

where *n′* = preliminary sample size
  x = recorded stopwatch times
  h = half the precision interval in % (for example, if ± 5%, then *h* = .05)
  Z = the standard normal deviate for the desired confidence level (for example, for 68.3%, *Z* = 1; for 95.5%, *Z* = 2; and for 99.7%, *Z* = 3)

Note: If the computed *n* is less than *n′*, the preliminary sample is large enough; otherwise, a larger sample must be taken.

available usually make this unnecessary. Figure 6-12 permits us to read the time-study sample size directly from a chart, once a value of the coefficient of variation, V, has been estimated from a preliminary or partial sample.

The *coefficient of variation* is an expression of the value of the sample standard deviation, s, divided by the sample mean, $\bar{x}$. It tells how much variability exists in the data relative to the value of the mean:

$$V = \frac{s}{\bar{x}} \qquad\qquad (6\text{-}6)$$

Figure 6-12 provides sample sizes which offer the analyst 95 or 99 percent confidence that the sample mean will be within ± 5 percent of the true population mean. The chart is entered at the base with the value of the coefficient of variation. Proceed up to the line depicting the desired confidence coefficient, and read the required sample size on the left-hand scale.

EXAMPLE 6-1

A preliminary sample showed a mean of 3.10 minutes and a standard deviation of .62 minute. How many cycles should be timed in order to be 95 percent confident that the resultant standard time is within 5 percent of the true population value?

SOLUTION

$$V = \frac{s}{\bar{x}} = \frac{.62}{3.10} = 20\%$$

Therefore, time $n \cong 58$ cycles (from Fig. 6-12).

Note that for a 20 percent coefficient of variation and 5 percent accuracy, the sample size in this case is slightly more than the 25 to 50 cycles stated initially in the summary of the procedure for time studies. Confidence levels of 95 percent and accuracies of ±5 percent and ±10 percent are widely used.

The timing activity then consists of actually clocking each element of the work cycle with a stopwatch and recording the times. Continuous or discrete times may be recorded. If readings are continuous, each reading must be subtracted from the subsequent reading in order to obtain incremental times for the cycle elements.

Step 3   *Computing average cycle time (CT).* Before averaging the cycle times, the readings for any nonrecurring or foreign elements should be deleted. The adjusted average cycle time is sometimes referred to as the *select time.*

Step 4   *Computing normal time (NT).* The normal time is the product of the cycle time multiplied by a performance rating factor (PR) which adjusts the standard so that it is not geared to the skill or effort level of the particular worker being studied. Then if the subject employee works at a faster pace than an average worker—for example, at 110 percent—the cycle time will be multiplied by 1.10

so that the resultant normal time will be longer and will still properly serve as a standard for an average worker.

Each element in a cycle can be rated with respect to performance during the time study. The rating factor is a subjective valuation by the analyst of how the individual worker compares with a concept of standard performance. Two measures of 100 percent performance are (1) walking at a steady pace of 3 miles per hour and (2) dealing 52 cards into four piles in .5 minute. Other appropriate working-activity standards have been filmed and are available from lending libraries and organizations such as the Society for the Advancement of Management. These films serve as a constant reference to ensure that analysts do not allow their perceptions of performance to drift from recorded standards. With practice, experienced analysts can rate workers within ± 5 percent about half the time and within ± 10 percent perhaps 75 percent of the time [20:113]. The farther a worker's performance is from 100 percent, the more difficult it is to get an accurate rating. Ratings for machine-controlled times of a cycle are normally assumed to be at 100 percent.

Step 5 *Computing standard time (ST).* The final computation of standard time makes allowances for personal time, fatigue, and unavoidable delays by including an allowance factor, AF. Many firms have a specified personal-time allowance for employees—for coffee breaks and the like. Often, specific allowances, such as 10 to 15 percent, are negotiated into collective bargaining agreements. Although a relatively scientific approach to fatigue allowances has been developed, most companies still set allowances on the basis of experience and subjective observation [6:465]. The personal, fatigue, and unavoidable-delay allowances are computed as a percentage of total on-the-job time.[3]

EXAMPLE 6-2

A job design to be time-studied has fatigue and delay allowances of 10 minutes per (8-hour) day and 25 minutes per day, respectively. The union contract further specifies that employees shall be allowed 25 minutes per day for personal time. Determine the allowance necessary to compute a standard time for this activity.

SOLUTION

$$\%A = \frac{\text{allowable time}}{\text{total time}}$$

$$= \frac{(10 + 25 + 25) \text{ min}}{(8 \text{ hr})(60 \text{ min/hr})} = 12.5\%$$

$$\therefore \text{AF} = \frac{1}{1 - \%A} = \frac{1}{1 - .125} = 1.143$$

---

[3] If the percent allowance is stated as a percentage of working time minus allowable time, it can be designated as $\%A_w$ and then $\text{AF} = 1 + \%A_w$. Thus, for Example 6-2, $\%A_w$ would be $60/(480 - 60) = .143$, and $\text{AF} = 1.0 + .143 = 1.143$ (same result).

Now that we have discussed the procedure for a time study, let us conclude with a slightly more comprehensive example.

EXAMPLE 6-3

A time study of a shop worker revealed the actual times shown. The standard deviation of the sample (with the 10.20-minute cycle omitted) was $s = .21$ minute. The analyst rated the worker at 90 percent PR and the company allows the following per 8-hour day:

Personal time: 20 min
Delay time: 30 min

Time (min/cycle)		
Worker	Machine	Total
2.30	.80	3.1
1.80	.80	2.6
2.00	.80	2.8
2.20	.80	3.0
1.90	.80	2.7
10.20*	.80	11.0
2.20	.80	3.0
1.80	.80	2.6

*Unusual, nonrecurring situation.

(a) Find the standard time.
(b) Determine whether the sample was of adequate size for the analyst to be 99 percent confident that the resultant standard time is within 5 percent of the true value. If it was not, how many cycles should have been time-studied to gain this level of confidence?

SOLUTION
(a) Cycle time should omit the unusual situation of a worker taking 10.20 minutes.

$$\text{Worker CT} = \frac{\Sigma \text{ times}}{n \text{ cycles}}$$

$$= \frac{2.30 + 1.80 + 2.00 + 2.20 + 1.90 + 2.20 + 1.80}{7}$$

$$= 2.03 \text{ min}$$

$$\text{Machine CT} = .80 \text{ min}$$

$$\text{NT} = \text{CT(PR)} = \underset{\text{(worker time)}}{2.03(.90)} + \underset{\text{(machine)}}{.80(1.00)} = 2.63 \text{ min}$$

$$\text{ST} = \text{NT(AF)}$$

$$\text{where } AF = \frac{1}{1 - \% A}$$

$$= \frac{1}{1 - \dfrac{20 + 30}{480}} = \frac{1}{1 - .1042} = 1.116$$

$$\therefore ST = 2.63 (1.116) = 2.94 \text{ min/cycle}$$

(b) Coefficient of variation:

$$V = \frac{s}{\bar{x}} = \frac{.21}{2.03} = 10.34\%$$

Using Fig. 6-12, $n \cong 40$ cycles would have been required. The 7 cycles were not adequate for 99 percent confidence.

PREDETERMINED TIME STANDARDS

A third method of setting labor standards is by using predetermined time values. This method consists of defining a job in terms of very small basic elements which have known (published) times. The times are then added until a total time value for the subject task is determined.

The advantages of this method are that (1) the standard can be determined from standard data which are universally available, (2) the standard can be completed before a job is done, (3) no performance rating is required, (4) it (the method) need not disrupt normal activities, and (5) it is widely accepted as a fair system of determining standards.

Several predetermined motion time systems have been developed, with two of the most popular being the *methods time measurement* (MTM) and *work factor* systems. The MTM system uses times measured in time-measurement units (TMU), where one TMU equals only .0006 minute. Figure 6-13 illustrates the measurement of move and grasp motions. Because about 200 elements of motion make up a minute of work, considerable time and skill are required to set a standard in this way.

WORK SAMPLING

The development of work sampling was a major advance in the techniques for establishing labor standards. The method was introduced by L. H. C. Tippett in 1934 for studying activities in the cotton industry. *Work sampling* consists of taking random observations of workers to determine the proportion of time they spend in specified activities. It is particularly useful for analyzing group activities, repetitive activities that take a relatively long time to complete, and activities that are not rigidly constrained from the time standpoint. Once data from a work-

FIGURE 6-13   Methods Time Measurement Values

TABLE I—MOVE—M

Distance Moved Inches	Time TMU				Wt. Allowance			CASE AND DESCRIPTION
	A	B	C	Hand In Motion B	Wt. (lb.) Up to	Dynamic Factor	Static Constant TMU	
3/4 or less	2.0	2.0	2.0	1.7				
1	2.5	2.9	3.4	2.3	2.5	1.00	0	A Move object to other hand or against stop.
2	3.6	4.6	5.2	2.9				
3	4.9	5.7	6.7	3.6	7.5	1.06	2.2	
4	6.1	6.9	8.0	4.3				
5	7.3	8.0	9.2	5.0	12.5	1.11	3.9	
6	8.1	8.9	10.3	5.7				
7	8.9	9.7	11.1	6.5	17.5	1.17	5.6	B Move object to approximate or indefinite location.
8	9.7	10.6	11.8	7.2				
9	10.5	11.5	12.7	7.9	22.5	1.22	7.4	
10	11.3	12.2	13.5	8.6				
12	12.9	13.4	15.2	10.0	27.5	1.28	9.1	
14	14.4	14.6	16.9	11.4				
16	16.0	15.8	18.7	12.8	32.5	1.33	10.8	
18	17.6	17.0	20.4	14.2				
20	19.2	18.2	22.1	15.6	37.5	1.39	12.5	
22	20.8	19.4	23.8	17.0				C Move object to exact location.
24	22.4	20.6	25.5	18.4	42.5	1.44	14.3	
26	24.0	21.8	27.3	19.8				
28	25.5	23.1	29.0	21.2	47.5	1.50	16.0	
30	27.1	24.3	30.7	22.7				
Additional	0.8	0.6	0.85		TMU per inch over 30 inches			

TABLE II—GRASP—G

TYPE OF GRASP	Case	Time TMU	DESCRIPTION	
PICK-UP	1A	2.0	Any size object by itself, easily grasped	
	1B	3.5	Object very small or lying close against a flat surface	
	1C1	7.3	Diameter larger than 1/2''	Interference with Grasp on bottom and one side of nearly cylindrical object.
	1C2	8.7	Diameter 1/4'' to 1/2''	
	1C3	10.8	Diameter less than 1/4''	
REGRASP	2	5.6	Change grasp without relinquishing control	
TRANSFER	3	5.6	Control transferred from one hand to the other.	
SELECT	4A	7.3	Larger than 1'' x 1'' x 1''	Object jumbled with other objects so that search and select occur.
	4B	9.1	1/4'' x 1/4'' x 1/8'' to 1'' x 1'' x 1''	
	4C	12.9	Smaller than 1/4'' x 1/4'' x 1/8''	
CONTACT	5	0	Contact, Sliding, or Hook Grasp.	

sampling study are available, they may be useful for methods analysis or cost analysis as well as for standard purposes.

Work-sampling methods have several advantages over time-study and predetermined time methods. Statistical sampling techniques are used so that sample sizes can be selected to provide the same specified level of confidence as with time studies. However, they can be used for a wider (less structured) range of activities, they can be done by less skilled (or part-time) observers, and they are less disturbing to workers. In general, work sampling has proved a very useful and economical technique and has found broad application in industrial plants, offices, hospitals, and other organizations.

The procedure for conducting a work-sampling study is summarized in Fig. 6-14.

As with any employee-centered study, it is important to gain worker cooperation before embarking on the study. Discussions with the workers will prove helpful in charting the work flow pattern and classifying work activities into major categories. They also give workers a fuller sense of participation in setting standards and of having a stake in their success.

Sample Size for Work Sampling   The sample size required for a work-sampling study is based upon the same statistical theory as that used for time studies. That is, we seek a *sample size n* that will be accurate within a specified range of *precision* (for example, ± 2 percent) at a desired level of *confidence* (for example, 95 percent).

---

1   Select the job to be studied, inform the workers, and prepare lists of their activities.
2   Determine the number of observations required, and prepare a tour schedule.
3   Observe, rate, and record worker activities per schedule.
4   Record starting time, stopping time, and number of acceptable units completed during the period.
5   Compute the normal time:

$$NT = \frac{(\text{total time})(\%\ \text{working})(PR)}{\text{number units completed}} \tag{6-7}$$

6   Compute the standard time:

$$ST = NT\ (AF)$$

where

$$AF = \frac{1}{1 - \%\ A}$$

FIGURE 6-14   Steps in Conducting a Work-Sampling Study

The sample size is computed by setting up an expression where half the precision interval (h) equals half the width of the confidence interval, which is the standard normal deviate, Z, times the standard error of proportion, s_p. Solving for the sample size n, we obtain the equation

$$n = \frac{Z^2 pq}{h^2} \qquad (6\text{-}8)$$

where p = value of sample proportion
$q = 1 - p$

EXAMPLE 6-4

A data processing manager estimates that the keypunch staff is idle 20 percent of the time and would like to do a work-sampling study that would be accurate within ± 4 percent. The manager wishes to have 95 percent confidence in the resulting study. How many observations should be made?

SOLUTION

$$n = \frac{Z^2 pq}{h^2}$$

where Z = 1.96 for 95% confidence
p = idle time estimate = .20
$q = (1 - p) = 1 - .20 = .80$
h = half the accuracy interval = .04

$$n = \frac{Z^2 pq}{h^2} = \frac{(1.96)^2(.20)(.80)}{(.04)^2} = 384 \text{ observations}$$

Note that we have used the estimate of idle time (20 percent) to calculate n. If early study results indicate that p will be outside the range of 20 percent ± 4 percent, then the number of observations may have to be adjusted as the study progresses.

Before proceeding, it is worth noting the (theoretical) distinction between the sample size calculations for work sampling and those for time study. Work-sampling studies typically yield proportionate times (for example, percentage of time in various activities), whereas time studies yield measurable times (for example, minutes). Thus the appropriate statistical distribution for work sampling is an attributes distribution (of proportions), whereas that for time studies is a variables distribution (of means). Figure 6-15 shows the comparable sample size expressions for attributes and variables data. Both computations require some preliminary estimate—either of p (for the proportions) or of s (for the means). You may wish to review Fig. 2-11, which gives a fuller description of the difference between these two distributions.

FIGURE 6-15 Sample Size Expressions for Attributes and Variables Data

Proportions (for example, work sampling)		Factor	Means (for example, time studies)	
Z = standard normal deviate		Measure of confidence	Z = standard normal deviate	
h = half the precision interval		Measure of precision	h = half the precision interval	
$s_p = \sqrt{\dfrac{pq}{n}}$	(2-11)	Standard error	$s_{\bar{x}} = \dfrac{s}{\sqrt{n}}$	(2-12)
$n = \dfrac{Z^2 pq}{h^2}$	(6-8)	Sample size	$n = \left(\dfrac{Zs}{h}\right)^2$	(6-9)

Making the Work-Sampling Observations   Once the number of observations has been determined, a tour schedule should be prepared showing when each observation is to be made. A good method of ensuring that observations are random is to use a random number table (Appendix I). If, for example, a work-sampling study is to be conducted over a 1-week period of five 8-hour workdays, the number of minutes available would be 60 minutes per hour times 8 hours per day times 5 days per week = 2,400 minutes. A four-digit column of random numbers could be used to select numbers between 0000 and 2,400. If, for example, 384 observations were required, then 384 random numbers would be chosen in this way (eliminating numbers greater than 2,400), and each would represent some minute of the 2,400-minute workweek when an observation should be made.

Figure 6-16 illustrates a tally table used to record work-sampling observations. In this study, the employee was working on an "other assignment" part of the time, so the percentage of working time, as used in Eq. (6-7), would be 80 percent.

FIGURE 6-16 Tally Table

Activity	Tally of All Observations (Total Time) Tally	Tally of All Observations (Total Time) Number	Working and Idle Time Only Number	Working and Idle Time Only Percent
Working	ԾԾԾԾԾԾԾԾԾ ԾԾԾԾԾ I	66	66	82.5
Idle	ԾԾ IIII	14	14	17.5
Other assignment	ԾԾԾԾ	20		
Total		100	80	100

An advantage of work-sampling studies is that the observations need not disturb the workers. One quick glance at a worker will generally be sufficient to identify which activity he or she is engaged in. Many analysts simply walk through a work area, mentally noting what the subjects of the study are doing, and then later convert this into a written tally. As the analysts observe the activities, they may also take note of the skill and effort level of their performance so that by the end of the period they have a representative performance rating (PR) for the subjects. Some analysts assume the PR is 100 percent unless it appears to be significantly above or below average.

After the data on times and units produced have been collected and tabulated, the normal time and standard time may be computed.

EXAMPLE 6-5

A work-sampling study of customer service representatives in a telephone company office showed that a receptionist was working 80 percent of the time at 100 percent PR. This receptionist handled 200 customers during the 8-hour study period. Company policy is to give allowances of 10 percent of total on-the-job time. Find the normal time and the standard time per customer.

SOLUTION

$$NT = \frac{(\text{total time})(\% \text{ working})(PR)}{\text{number units completed}}$$

$$= \frac{(480 \text{ min})(.80)(1.00)}{200} = 1.92 \text{ min/customer}$$

$$ST = NT \ (AF)$$

$$\text{where } AF = \frac{1}{(1 - \%A)}$$

$$= \frac{1}{1 - .10} = 1.111$$

$$\therefore ST = (1.92)(1.111) = 2.13 \text{ min/customer}$$

SAFETY, COMPENSATION, AND PRODUCTIVITY

Operations managers' responsibilities in the human resource area extend well beyond the measurement of job performance. We end this chapter with a brief mention of three concerns: (1) safety, (2) productivity, and (3) wages.

SAFETY CONSIDERATIONS

Safety is everyone's job. But accidents happen—from everyday cuts and bruises to such disasters as the poison gas leak at Union Carbide's plant in Bhopal, India, in

1984 (which killed over 2,000 people and injured nearly 200,000 others). In our society, about half of all males and a third of all females in the 17- to 24-year age group are injured annually. The U.S. Department of Labor estimates that work-related accidents or illnesses affect 2.5 million persons (or about 5 percent of employees) each year. In addition to untold grief, the lost work time has a staggering effect upon productivity.

Accidents are regarded as chance occurrences—due either to facility inadequacy or employee (or management) negligence. Some industries, such as nuclear power, require a thorough analysis of potential accidents well before plants go online. If serious accidents, such as the Three Mile Island (U.S.) and Chernobyl (U.S.S.R.) accidents, do happen, extensive investigations take place. In some cases, the prior chance (probability) of the accident happening can be analyzed on a statistical basis, using Bayes' rule and other concepts of probability. The purpose of such analysis is to assess responsibility and avoid similar accidents in the future.

What is done to enhance safety and reduce accidents? Most large firms promote safety programs, and many have their own safety standards and conduct plant safety inspections. The continuing enforcement of (and amendments to) the Occupational Safety and Health Act (OSHA) of 1970 has also encouraged widespread upgrading of industrial safety standards. In addition, many firms go beyond "safety compliance" to actively promote nutrition, exercise, and mental health programs for their employees.[4]

EMPLOYEE COMPENSATION

Wage Plans   Wages have always been the basic reward for labor in the United States. Wage levels depend upon both the industry (or technological skill classification) and the locality. Wage systems are often classified as (1) *time-based*, (2) *output-based*, or (3) some combination of the two. Most employees are paid on the basis of time (hourly or monthly), so their wages do not change as their productivity changes. Output-based systems offer some type of incentive either to an individual or to a work group. Some firms have realized substantial improvements in output by converting from a time-based system to a "usable output"–based pay system.

Wage incentives can help the organization save on total costs if they generate higher productivity. However, incentive plans cost money to administer, and they are difficult to apply to nonstandard (jobshop) activities and to machine-paced activities.

Other Monetary Incentives   The use of profit sharing as a group incentive has gained some popularity because all members tend to cooperate in order to share a

---

[4] Robots don't mind working in unsafe or hazardous environments—and they remain fast, efficient, and accurate. But they can cause accidents too! There have been five robot-related fatalities in Japan, and at least 25 robot-related accidents in the United States. However, robot vision is now helping them "see" what is going on around them. And one robot manufacturer has designed a voice-recognition safety system for a customer. It will halt the robot if a worker shouts, "Stop!" [4].

FIGURE 6-17   Types of Incentives Offered Employees

Incentive	Companies Offering Incentive (%)
Cash profit sharing	32
Lump-sum individual incentive	26
Productivity bonus	21
Team bonus	10

Source: Hewitt Associates, as reported in *The Wall Street Journal*, Nov, 20, 1985, p. 35.

bonus. As reported in Fig. 6-17, a significant proportion of companies in the United States now offer their employees a profit-sharing or cash-incentive award of some kind. This is in addition to regular merit increases or management bonuses.

Comparative Wages   Wages in many U.S. companies are high relative to those of foreign companies who compete in U.S. markets. The average pay of factory workers in the United States is in the neighborhood of $10 per hour and that of some unionized workers is $20 to $30 per hour. Laborers in some third-world countries make as little as $1 per hour—or perhaps only $1 per day! So there is an understandable tendency to blame U.S. economic problems on excessively high labor costs—and more specifically on union-enforced wages.

High wages have been instrumental in shifting many industries overseas, from toys and shoes to textiles and steel. Nonetheless, insofar as these jobs have been needed in the less-developed countries, this shift of productive facilities has helped stabilize the world's economic balance.

BARGAINING AND LABOR PRODUCTIVITY

Unions were initially formed as a (justified) reaction to the abuses of management. The National Labor Relations Act (1934) legitimized collective bargaining and did much to offset the power of management. And now, numerous collective bargaining agreements are concluded daily—over 95 percent of them without any work stoppage taking place. These negotiations are characterized by "give and take," with labor and management gradually moving closer together on wage and benefit issues.

Effects of Bargaining Power   The power of organized workers in the United States to command higher wages than nonunion workers (for equivalent work) has, however, had some far-reaching effects on society. Among the most noteworthy are (1) inflationary pressures, (2) income distribution effects, (3) employment effects, and (4) pressures for increased automation.

Inflationary pressures have arisen because companies were forced to pay wage increases greater than the increases in productivity (in other words, "more money" without more goods). As wage increases were transferred into product prices, exports of steel, autos, and other goods have declined, and the United States has incurred the largest negative balance of payments in its history. In the long term, this could undermine the stability of U.S. currency.

The *disparity of wages* between union and nonunion workers has also worsened the plight of lower-paid and less well organized employees. Census Bureau estimates place the median family income at approximately $26,500 per year. Even though the national average wage appears respectable, employees in many service industries (and some retired workers) are in a near-poverty income classification. Their plight has increased the social costs of state, federal, and charitable agencies.

Artificially high wages can also foster *unemployment*. They force companies to lay off workers so that they can pay premium wages to a smaller number of organized workers rather than average wages to a greater number of nonorganized workers.

Because of these and other perceptions, public approval of labor unions has declined over the last two decades. Gallup Poll surveys show the 70 percent approval rate in 1965 dropped to 55 percent in 1979 and 58 percent in 1985 (after a recession and some renegotiated wage contracts) [9].

Automation is increasing. High labor costs are prompting manufacturers to shift from labor-intensive to more capital-intensive production processes. Installations of automated and computer-controlled equipment are proceeding at an exponential pace, with over 8,000 robots already installed in U.S. factories [4]. The median investment (in company assets) per employee in the 500 largest employers in the United States is now nearing $50,000, with some of the oil companies averaging well over $400,000 per employee.

Reduction in Direct Labor Costs   As investment in equipment increases, a smaller proportion of production costs is attributable to labor. David Kearns, president of Xerox, has observed:

> The common wisdom is that labor accounts for the bulk of manufacturing costs. . . . At Xerox, our experience has been that direct workers, the people who actually build the products, are only a small part of the total unit manufacturing cost. We've found that our biggest labor cost is indirect workers, or overhead. They're the white-collar workers in management, sales, and administration who support the manufacturing function. . . . In our industry, as in most high-tech industries, 80 percent of unit manufacturing cost is parts and supplies. And a big factor in that cost equation is inventory [13].

Emphasis on Participation   The goals of managers can no longer be characterized as simple profit maximization, where the employee is viewed only as a labor resource or a direct labor cost. Nor are employees satisfied with a passive role. As a quality-of-worklife awareness permeates more U.S. companies, the confrontational nature of union–management relationships is being replaced with a participative philosophy of management. According to Kearns:

Somebody once said the best kind of efficiency is the spontaneous cooperation among people. Well, we've learned how true that is from firsthand experience since we started our employee involvement program three years ago. Employee involvement lets workers participate directly in solving any problems they have, or see, on the job. . . . We're getting our production employees involved in strategic business decisions. That was once the sole province of managers. . . . We have more than 60 percent of our people involved in some way—either on a team, on a committee or in a quality group. . . . An extraordinary change has taken place. People at Xerox believe in themselves again. They believe in what they're doing again. . . . I believe what's happening at Xerox is typical of what's happening all across American industry. There's a new vitality, a new sense of hope, a new confidence [13].

Of course, not all companies share the enthusiasm of Xerox. But participative programs have spread widely: The International Association of Quality Circles lists 2,000 American companies among its members [13].

SUMMARY

Human resources are among the most challenging inputs to manage because people are so much more complex than machines. Job design policies should recognize this humanness and foster satisfaction of higher-level needs. Work goals should be clear, moderately challenging, and accepted if they are to be useful.

A well-designed job should reflect both social (market) priorities and technical (organizational) capacities. Motivational techniques focus upon (1) *variety* (job enlargement adds more tasks, and job rotation adds variety because workers are rotated among tasks), (2) *time* (flextime, 4-day workweeks, and job sharing), and (3) *psychology* (enrichment).

The Herzberg enrichment approach emphasizes five motivational factors, and the Hackman–Oldham model stresses meaningfulness and responsibility. Hackman and Oldham have also developed a Job Diagnostic Survey, which measures skill variety, task identity, task importance, autonomy, and feedback. Finally, the sociotechnical approach is a view of production systems which incorporates much of this psychological knowledge into a working system that blends both social and technical components.

Work methods can often be improved by conducting a scientific study of present methods using well-developed questioning techniques and principles of motion economy. In office systems, significant productivity improvements can come from better information flows and better use of employee time.

Standards of performance should encourage the cooperation and participation of the workers to whom they will apply. Historical approaches, time studies, predetermined time methods, and work sampling are all useful ways of developing standards. Both time-study and work-sampling methods consist of sampling a worker's activities and subjectively rating the worker's performance level to determine a normal time (NT). Allowances are then taken into consideration and a standard time (ST) is determined. Work sampling is particularly suitable for analyzing less structured activities and group operations.

Every operations manager has opportunities to foster a favorable work climate among the employees by providing safe working conditions, just wages, and an environment that gives employees a stake in what the organization is doing. Many firms report favorable results from worker participation in problem-solving teams, quality circles, and other involvement programs.

SOLVED PROBLEMS

1 An analyst wants to obtain a cycle time estimate that is within ± 5 percent of the true value. A preliminary run of 20 cycles took 40 minutes to complete and had a calculated standard deviation of .3 minute. What is the value of the coefficient of variation to be used for computing the sample size for the forthcoming time study?

Solution

$$V = \frac{s}{\bar{x}}$$

where s = standard deviation of sample = .3 min/cycle

$$\bar{x} = \text{mean of sample} = \frac{\Sigma x}{n} = \frac{40 \text{ min}}{20 \text{ cycles}} = 2 \text{ min/cycle}$$

$$V = \frac{.3}{2} = .15, \text{ or } 15\%$$

2 How large a sample should be taken to provide 99 percent confidence that a sample value is within ± 5 percent of the true value if the coefficient of variation is estimated to be 15 percent?

Solution
From Fig. 6-12 for V = 15%, $n \cong 80$.

3 Past records of a certain work activity show that it has a mean time of 60 seconds and a standard deviation of 9 seconds. How many time-study observations should be made to be 95 percent confident that the sample mean is within 3 seconds (± 3) of the true population value?

Solution

$$V = \frac{s}{\bar{x}} = \frac{9}{60} = .15, \text{ or } 15\%$$

Figure 6-12 can be used because the 3-second accuracy required corresponds to 3/60 = 5 percent accuracy.

$$\therefore n \cong 35 \text{ observations}$$

4 Suppose we make a preliminary estimate that the standard deviation of an activity is 9 seconds. How many time-study observations should be made to be 95 percent confident that the sample mean is within 3 seconds (± 3) of the true population value?

Solution

Note the similarity between this and the previous problem. In this case we have no mean value available to estimate the coefficient of variation, so we must calculate the sample size instead of using Fig. 6-12. Our method is similar to that followed for the work-sampling Example 6-4 except in this case we are dealing with means ($\bar{x}$'s) rather than sample proportions (p's). Both situations rely on the sample means and proportions being normally distributed about the population parameters (that is, μ and π, respectively) if the sample size is sufficiently large (say 30 or more for means and 100 or more for proportions). In solving this problem we wish to set one-half the accuracy interval width equal to $Z (s/\sqrt{n})$ and use the resulting equation:

$$\therefore n = \left(\frac{Zs}{h}\right)^2 \qquad \text{where } h = 3 \text{ sec}$$
$$Z = 1.96$$
$$s = 9 \text{ sec}$$

$$n = \left(\frac{(1.96)(9)}{3}\right)^2$$

$$n \cong 35 \text{ observations}$$

Note that the chart method (Solved Prob. 3) and the calculation method (this problem) are essentially equivalent, but the chart is perhaps a little easier to use if V can be estimated.

5 A time-study analyst wishes to estimate the cycle time for an assembly operation within $\pm .03$ minute at a confidence level of 95.5 percent. If the cycle time standard deviation σ is known to be .08 minute, how many observations are required?

Solution

$$n = \left(\frac{Z\sigma}{h}\right)^2 \qquad \text{where } h = .03 \text{ min}$$
$$Z = 2.00$$
$$\sigma = .08 \text{ (Because } \sigma \text{ is known, we use it instead of } s.)$$

$$\therefore n = \left(\frac{2.00(.08)}{.03}\right)^2$$

$$= 28.4, \text{ say } 29 \text{ observations}$$

As the sample size gets below 30, the t is a more appropriate distribution than the normal. However, the normal approximation should be adequate here.

6 A time study of a restaurant activity yielded a cycle time of 2.00 minutes, and the waitress was rated at PR = 96 percent. The restaurant chain has a 20 percent allowance factor. Find the standard time.

Solution

$$CT = 2.00 \text{ min}$$

$$NT = CT(PR) = (2.00)(.96) = 1.92 \text{ min}$$

$$ST = NT(AF)$$

$$\text{where } AF = \frac{1}{1 - \%A} = \frac{1}{1 - .20} = 1.25$$

$$\therefore ST = 1.92(1.25) = 2.40 \text{ min}$$

7 An operator in a packing operation was clocked by an incremental reading stopwatch. The results are shown in the accompanying table. The allowance for this type of work is 15 percent.

	Minutes for Cycle					*Performance*
Element	*1*	*2*	*3*	*4*	*5*	*Rating*
1 Obtain 2 boxes.	.82	—	.80	—	.85	130
2 Pack 4 items/box.	.44	.42	.46	.40	.41	110
3 Set box aside.	.71	.67	.69	.71	.68	115

(a) Find the normal time per cycle.
(b) Find the standard time per cycle.

Solution
(a) $NT = CT(PR)$
    For element 1, each box suffices for 2 cycles.

$$NT = \frac{.82 + .80 + .85}{6} (1.30) = .535$$

For element 2:

$$NT = \frac{.44 + .42 + .46 + .40 + .41}{5} (1.10) = .469$$

For element 3:

$$NT = \frac{.71 + .67 + .69 + .71 + .68}{5} (1.15) = .796$$

$$\text{Total} = \overline{1.800}$$

$$\therefore NT = 1.80 \text{ min/cycle}$$

(b) $ST = NT(AF)$

$$\text{where } AF = \frac{1}{1 - \%A} = \frac{1}{1 - .15} = 1.18$$

$$ST = 1.80(1.18) = 2.12 \text{ min/cycle}$$

8 The State of Oreida Mental Health Division has a health care activity that has a normal time of 8 minutes, but the activity seems to have been prolonged recently by an increasing number of unavoidable delays. D. R. Mix, a management analyst called in to determine a new standard, conducted a work-sampling study and obtained the results shown in the accompanying table.

Activity	Number of Observations	Percentage of Observations
Working	585	78
Unavoidable delay	90	12
Personal time	75	10
Total	750	100

The Mental Health Division grants its workers a personal-time allowance of 8 percent of total time, and D. R. Mix wishes to retain that in the new standard.
(a) Incorporate the unavoidable-delay time, and determine a standard time for this activity.
(b) Determine how precise the estimate is of unavoidable time, assuming the analyst wishes to have 95 percent confidence in the estimate.
(c) State whether the same precision applies to the estimate of personal time.

Solution
(a) Allowances should now consist of:

Personal time	8 percent
Unavoidable delay	12 percent
Total	20 percent

$$\therefore AF = \frac{1}{1 - \%A} = \frac{1}{1 - .20} = 1.25$$

$$ST = NT(AF) = 8(1.25) = 10.0 \text{ min}$$

(b) For 95 percent confidence interval, $Z = 1.96$.

Half the interval width is: $\qquad h = Zs_p$

$$\text{where } s_p = \sqrt{\frac{pq}{n}} = \sqrt{\frac{(.12)(.88)}{750}} = .011$$

$$\therefore h = 1.96(.011) = .023$$

The interval is ± 2.3 percent—that is, the analyst could be 95 percent confident that the true unavoidable-delay time is between 9.7 percent and 14.3 percent of total time.

(c) The precision interval for the personal-time estimate would be slightly smaller (better) due to the use of 10 percent instead of 12 percent for the value of p. In general, for a given level of precision, the sample size required for various activities is governed by those activities with p values closest to .5.

9 *(Optional)* This problem illustrates the use of Bayes' rule of probability for analyzing the prior existence of an unsafe condition, given that an accident such as an airplane crash or refinery explosion has occurred. If we let θ represent the unsafe condition and A the occurrence of an accident, Bayes' rule—Eq. (2-8)—can be stated as:

$$P(\theta|A) = \frac{P(\theta)P(A|\theta)}{P(\theta)P(A|\theta) + P(\overline{\theta})P(A|\overline{\theta})}$$

Example

Let θ represent the probability of defective wiring and A represent an accidental fire. In a large old factory spot checks have established that $P(\theta) = .20$. Given that a plant has defective wiring, the probability of a fire occurring at some time during the year is .7 (that is, $P(A|\theta) = .7$), and if the wiring is not defective, the chance of a fire is reduced to .1 (that is, $P(A|\overline{\theta}) = .1$). A recent fire burned one employee severely and caused \$90,000 in damage. Although evidence is destroyed, the operations manager has been asked by an insurance company to estimate the likelihood that the fire was due to defective wiring.

Solution

$$P(\theta) = .2 \qquad \therefore P(\overline{\theta}) = 1 - .2 = .8$$

$$P(A|\theta) = .7 \qquad \therefore P(\overline{A}|\theta) = 1 - .7 = .3$$

$$P(A|\overline{\theta}) = .1 \qquad \therefore P(\overline{A}|\overline{\theta}) = 1 - .1 = .9$$

We wish to find the probability of defective wiring, θ, given the occurrence of the recent fire, A.

$$P(\theta|A) = \frac{P(\theta)P(A|\theta)}{P(\theta)P(A|\theta) + P(\overline{\theta})P(A|\overline{\theta})}$$

$$= \frac{(.2)(.7)}{(.2)(.7) + (.8)(.1)}$$

$$= .64, \quad \therefore 64 \text{ percent chance}$$

QUESTIONS

6-1   What two cornerstones of human resource management policy are brought out in the chapter?

6-2 Distinguish between highly behavioral versus highly objective job designs.

6-3 What aspects of goals are especially important when applying them at the job design level?

6-4 What are "variable time" approaches to motivation?

6-5 Distinguish between job enlargement and job enrichment.

6-6 What five factors does the Hackman–Oldham model of job enrichment emphasize?

6-7 What is the basis of the sociotechnical view of modern production organizations?

6-8 A consultant making a methods-improvement study has identified a problem and developed a written description of the present method of doing the job. What kinds of questions or principles would be most useful for analyzing the problem?

6-9 Request permission to conduct a methods-improvement study from the industrial relations manager of a local firm. Instead of instituting and maintaining new methods, provide the responsible manager (and your instructor) with a finished copy of your report and recommendations.

6-10 How are labor standards established, and what are their principal uses?

6-11 Distinguish between (a) cycle time, (b) normal time, and (c) standard time. Show the relationships between these times in your answer.

6-12 Under what circumstances would work sampling be preferable to time-study or predetermined time methods for developing labor standards?

6-13 The chapter contains statements from a former vice president of TRW and from the president of Xerox. What conclusions can you draw from them about the trend in direct labor as a percentage of total employment?

6-14 What has been the effect of higher wages without corresponding increases in productivity?

PROBLEMS

1 A garment workers' union in Atlanta has requested that a new time study be made of a skirt-sewing activity. Previous data indicate the activity has a mean time of $\bar{x} = 2.40$ minutes and a standard deviation of .90 minute. What is the best (preliminary) estimate of the sample size required in order to have 95 percent confidence in the result. (*Hint:* Use Fig. 6-12, and assume an accuracy of ± 5 percent.)

2 Fifty samples of a production cycle showed an average time of 2.30 minutes per piece. The performance rating was estimated at 90 percent, and allowances are set at 18 percent of the total time available. What is the standard time in minutes per piece?

3 A time study of an Idaho mining activity revealed a cycle time of 6.50 minutes for a worker rated at 108 percent. The allowances are as follows: personal time = 30 minutes per day, fatigue = 74 minutes per day, delay = 40 minutes per day. Determine the standard time for an 8-hour-per-day operation.

4 The standard time for a computer repair activity was determined to be 6.40 minutes from a study of a worker who was rated at 115 percent. If this standard includes a 20 percent allowance, what was the actual (cycle) time of the worker studied?

5 An activity has a select time of 4.00 minutes per cycle and a calculated normal time of 4.64 minutes per cycle. Allowances are 10 percent.
(a) What was the performance rating factor of the worker studied?
(b) What was the resultant standard time?

6 A time study of 30 cycles in a Syracuse machine shop showed these cycle times:

$$\text{Hand time} = .50 \text{ min/cycle}$$

$$\text{Machine time} = 1.80 \text{ min/cycle}$$

The worker was rated at 110 percent, and allowances for the operation, based on an 8-hour workday, are as follows: personal = 20 minutes per day, fatigue = 30 minutes per day, delay = 22 minutes per day. Calculate the standard time per cycle for the worker-machine operation (combined).

X7 Time-study data taken for a bulk-filling activity in a cannery in Topeka were recorded on a continuous basis, as shown in the accompanying table (that is, the times given are cumulative amounts).

	Cycle Time (sec)					
Activity	1	2	3	4	5	PR
Grasp bag	4	37	74	105	338	120
Locate for fill	16	51	84	117	352	120
Machine-fill	26	61	94	127	362	
Set on conveyor	34	68	102	334*	369	110

* Bag broke open due to presence of a foreign object on the conveyor.

The firm's labor contract requires a 5 percent allowance for all workers on the bulk-filling line. Compute the standard time for this activity.

8 A work-sampling study is to be made of a messenger system in a large metropolitan office building. The building manager feels the messengers are idle 30 percent of the time and wishes to have 95.5 percent confidence that the accuracy is within ±4 percent. How many observations should be made?

9 A management consultant for Quik Kut Shops wishes to develop a labor-time standard for a hair-cutting activity. The activity elements are (1) shampoo, (2) cut, and (3) blow dry. For element 2, the standard deviation is estimated to be $\sigma = 4.0$ minutes. To determine the cutting time to an accuracy of within ±1.5 minutes with 98 percent confidence, how large a sample should be taken?

10 Midwest Printers wishes to make a work-sampling study of a shop operation to develop standard costs. Estimates of the various element times, as provided by the shop manager, are as shown in the accompanying table. Management would like a 95.5 percent confidence-level estimate of the true proportion of time of the various elements within an accuracy of ±5 percent. How many samples should be taken to be sure the 95.5 percent confidence level holds for all elements?

Job Element	Estimated Time (%)
Planning and layout	20
Typesetting	55
Proofing and checking	15
Delay	10
	100

X 11   A work-sampling study was made of a Seattle dock operation for the purpose of developing a standard time. During the total 240 minutes of observation the employee under study was on the dock operation 80 percent of the time and loaded 20 pieces of cargo. The analyst rated the performance at 90 percent. If the firm wishes to incorporate a 10 percent allowance factor for fatigue, delays, and personal time, what is the standard time for this operation in minutes per piece?

X 12   A quality control operation at a defense plant was work-sampled over 2 days (16-hour total), during which time the employee inspected 40 vehicles. Actual working time was 90 percent of total time, and the performance rating was estimated to be 118 percent. If allowable time is set at 15 percent of the total time available, what is the standard time for this operation?

13   *Safety problem involving probabilities*   In a chemical plant, the probability of any given employee being injured from a fall is $P(F) = .005$, from chemical inhalation, $P(C) = .020$. If a worker falls, the probability of injury from chemical inhalation increases to $P(C|F) = .100$. What is the probability that an employee will be injured (a) by both a fall and chemical inhalation, (b) by either a fall or chemical inhalation?

*14   *Safety problem involving probabilities*   Company physicians have learned that the probability an executive's productivity is adversely affected by stress is $P(S) = .30$ and by a physical ailment $P(A) = .04$. If an executive is already under stress, the probability of his or her performance being affected by a physical ailment is increased to $P(A|S) = .10$. What is the probability that an executive will be affected by (a) both stress and a physical ailment, (b) by either stress or a physical ailment?

*15   *Safety problem involving use of Bayes' rule*   Let θ represent the probability of defective brakes and A represent a mining ore train accident. Inspection records reveal that $P(\theta) = .12$. Given that a train has defective brakes, the probability of an accident occurring sometime during the period of service is .30, that is $P(A|\theta) = .30$. If the brakes are not defective, the chance of an accident is only .05. A recent accident caused a fire which destroyed the evidence, but, as the mine operations manager, you have been asked by an insurance adjustor to estimate the probability that it was due to defective brakes.

REFERENCES

[1]   Abruzzi, A.: *Work Measurement*, Columbia University Press, New York, 1952.
[2]   Barnes, Ralph M.: *Motion and Time Study: Design and Measurement of Work*, 6th ed., Wiley, New York, 1968.
[3]   Brooks, Geraldine: "Faced with a Changing Work Force, TRW Pushes to Raise White Collar Productivity," *The Wall Street Journal*, Sept. 22, 1983.
[4]   Bulkeley, William: "Manufacturers Seek to Create More Safety-Conscious Robots," *The Wall Street Journal*, Oct. 4, 1985, p. 27.
[5]   Buffa, Elwood S.: *Modern Production Management*, 3d ed., Wiley, New York, 1969.
[6]   Chase, Richard B., and Nicholas J. Aquilano: *Production and Operations Management*, Richard D. Irwin, Homewood, IL, 1973 (also 1981).
[7]   Davis, Louis E.: *Job Satisfaction—A Socio-Technical View*, Report 575-1-69, University of California, Los Angeles, 1969.
[8]   Emery, F. E., E. Thorsud, and K. Lange: *The Industrial Democracy Project*, Report 2, Institute for Industrial and Social Research, Technical University of Norway, Trondheim, 1965.

[9] GallupPoll Info. Graphics from News America Syndicate, "Unions Gaining Back Support," *Spokesman Review,* Aug. 4, 1985, p. A12.

[10] Hackman, J. R., and G. R. Oldham: "Development of the Job Diagnostic Survey," *Journal of Applied Psychology,* vol. 60, 1975, pp. 159–170.

[11] Hackman, J. R., G. R. Oldham, R. Janson, and K. Purdy: "A New Strategy for Job Enrichment," *California Management Review,* vol. 17, 1975, pp. 57–71.

[12] Herzberg, Frederick: "One More Time: How Do You Motivate Employees?" *Harvard Business Review,* January–February 1968.

[13] Kearns, David T.: "Product Quality and Productivity," Rochester Institute of Technology, Rochester, NY, 1984.

[14] Lauerman, Connie: "Work-Stress Claims No Longer Laughing Matter," *Spokesman Review and Spokane Chronicle,* Nov. 24, 1985, p. C1.

[15] Maslow, A. H.: *Toward a Psychology of Being,* 2d ed., Van Nostrand, New York, 1968.

[16] Miller, Edward: "Assembly Line Falls from Grace," *Spokesman Review and Spokane Chronicle,* Nov. 24, 1985, p. C2.

[17] Monks, Joseph G.: *Schaums Outline Series. Operations Management,* McGraw-Hill, New York, 1985, p. 147.

[18] Moore, Franklin G., and Thomas E. Hendrick: *Production/Operations Management,* 8th ed., Richard D. Irwin, Homewood, IL, 1980.

[19] Prokesch, Steven E.: "Xerox Halts Japanese with Their Own Tactics," *Spokesman Review and Spokane Chronicle,* Nov. 10, 1985, p. B3.

[20] Radford, J. D., and D. B. Richardson: *The Management of Production,* Macmillan, London, 1968.

[21] Rice, Robert S.: "Survey of Work Measurement and Wage Incentives," *Industrial Engineering,* vol. 9, no. 7, July 1977, pp. 18–19.

[22] Roach, John M.: "Why Volvo Abolished the Assembly Line," *Management Review,* September 1977.

[23] Trist, E. L., et al.: *Organization Choice,* Travistock Institute, London, 1963.

[24] Umstat, D.: "Job Design," in D. Hellriegel and J. Slocum: *Organizational Behavior,* 2d ed., West Publishing, St. Paul, MN, 1979.

[25] Wales, C. E., and R. A. Stager: *Educational Systems Design,* 1974 (available from C. E. Wales and West Virginia University).

[26] Woodward, Joan: *Industrial Organization: Theory and Practice,* Oxford University Press, London, 1965.

SELF QUIZ: CHAPTER 6

Part I True/False [1 point each = 6]

1 _____ In job design, the market priorities and resource capacities are characterized as sociosystem and technical system inputs.

2 _____ One principle of job design is that work goals should be very difficult (in order to challenge the best employees).

3 _____ The Hackman–Oldham approach emphasizes the benefits of motivating employees through flextime, 4-day workweeks, and job sharing.

4 _____ As robots take over more activities, the jobs left for human workers are becoming more monotonous.

5 _____ The principles of motion economy refer to the three categories of human body, work place, and tools and equipment.

6 _____ Labor contracts that call for large hourly wage increases can foster higher levels of employment.

Part II Problems [3 points each = 9. Calculate and select your answer.]

1 The manager of Old South Bakeries wishes to do a new time study of a cake decoration activity that previously took 5.20 minutes ($s = .53$ minute). Approximately how many cycles should be timed? (She wishes to have 99 percent confidence that the resultant time is accurate to within $\pm.25$ minute.)
   (a) 15
   (b) 30
   (c) 60
   (d) 120
   (e) None of the above.

2 A fruit-packing activity in a plant near Sacramento is given a preliminary time study with results as shown ($s = .20$ minute).

Worker Time (min)	2.1	1.9	2.2	2.3	2.4	1.9	1.8	2.0	2.3	2.1
Machine Time (min)	.5	.5	.5	.5	.5	.5	.5	.5	.5	.5
Total	2.6	2.4	2.7	2.8	2.9	2.4	2.3	2.5	2.8	2.6

The worker was performance rated at 110 percent, and the company allows 30 minutes of time per 8-hour shift. The estimated standard time in minutes for this operation would be:
   (a) 2.10
   (b) 2.46
   (c) 2.86
   (d) 3.00
   (e) None of the above.

3 A work-sampling study is to be done of an office of the Indiana Motor Vehicles Division to determine the average waiting time of clerks in a licensing activity. A preliminary study suggests clerks are idle 30 percent of the time, and the office manager wishes to be accurate within ±5 percent. If a 92 percent confidence level is desired, how many observations should be made?
   (a) 227
   (b) 257
   (c) 323
   (d) 336
   (e) None of the above.

PART TWO
PRODUCTION AND INVENTORY CONTROL

PREVIEW: PRODUCTION AND INVENTORY CONTROL ACTIVITIES

A few years ago, a small test equipment manufacturer in California received a corporate directive to improve their business operations. With the help of a consultant, they decided to discard their manual production control system and undertake a five-phase program to gain better control of their costs. Here's what happened:

> First, the material requirements, estimated costs, and inventory records were computerized. Within four months, they began to check actual inventories against the computerized data base and analyze any variances. The general ledger and financial data were integrated into the system a month later. Ten months after that, the payroll and labor distribution information was transferred from their bank to the system; it was automatically interfaced to the job costing system. Finally, the order entry information and invoicing was incorporated. The manufacturing control system took about two years to implement and saved the firm $152,000 in the first year of operation. [*P&IM Review, 1986 Reference Guide*, p. 88]

P&IC Production and inventory control (P&IC) activities guide the flow of goods through the production cycle, from the initial purchase of raw materials to the final delivery of finished products. A major objective is to add value in a cost-effective and efficient way.

In recent years, some dramatic changes have enhanced the management of P&IC activities. Among them are the:

- Perfection of analytical techniques
- Widespread availability of online computer systems
- Increased professionalization of P&IC personnel

The American Production & Inventory Control Society (APICS) has helped significantly to improve the professionalism of P&IC activities. This has brought about an increased awareness of the interdependent nature of P&IC activities and has also generated financial and marketing benefits. Figure II-1 presents an overview of the production and inventory control topics discussed in Part Two of the text. As can be seen from the flowchart, the P&IC activities are highly interdependent.

FORECASTING (Chapter 7)

Demand is the vital link between a firm's production facilities and its customers in the market environment. If sufficient customer orders already exist, the firm can "produce to order." Otherwise, it produces "to stock" and stores the products in warehouses or distribution centers. Chapter 7 discusses techniques for analyzing past demand and projecting future demand on the P&IC system.

AGGREGATE PLANNING AND MASTER SCHEDULING (Chapter 8)

Forecasts of demand provide information for planning and scheduling what production is needed. Aggregate planning is concerned with whether the firm has the capacity to

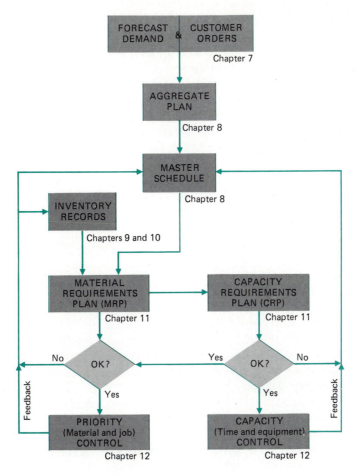

FORECAST DEMAND & CUSTOMER ORDERS

Chapter 7

AGGREGATE PLAN

Chapter 8

MASTER SCHEDULE

Chapter 8

INVENTORY RECORDS

Chapters 9 and 10

MATERIAL REQUIREMENTS PLAN (MRP)

Chapter 11

CAPACITY REQUIREMENTS PLAN (CRP)

Chapter 11

No   OK?   Yes   OK?   No

Yes   Yes

Feedback   Feedback

PRIORITY (Material and job) CONTROL

Chapter 12

CAPACITY (Time and equipment) CONTROL

Chapter 12

FIGURE II-1 Production and Inventory Control Flowchart

satisfy the expected demand or whether it should delay some production, or use overtime or subcontractors, and so forth. After a rough production plan is formulated, the master schedule is created to show the specific volume of end products that are scheduled according to the time periods in which they are to be completed.

INVENTORY MANAGEMENT (Chapters 9 and 10)

Inventories of raw materials, work-in-process, and finished goods play a critical role in the production process. An understanding of their costs and benefits is necessary. In Chapter 9 we take up the purchasing process and methods of selecting the most economic order quantities. Chapter 10 goes on to show how firms can use inventory management techniques to compensate for uncertainties in the forecast, to help stabilize production levels, and to provide customers with desired levels of service.

MATERIAL AND CAPACITY REQUIREMENTS PLANNING (Chapter 11)

The material requirements planning (MRP) system uses information from the master schedule and the inventory system. It breaks down the master schedule items into subassembly and raw material requirements, matches these against what is already on hand (or on order), and computes specific requirements (item by item) of everything needed. It also dictates when orders should be released (to purchasing or to the shop) so that the components will be available as specified in the proposed master schedule. If procurement or production time is inadequate, the master schedule may have to be revised.

After a preliminary material requirements plan is established, the time required to produce those materials is compared with the capacity of key work centers to determine whether sufficient labor and machine hours exist. This is the capacity requirements planning (CRP) function. If demands cannot be met, the master schedule must again be revised and the process repeated until an acceptable schedule is devised.

SCHEDULING AND CONTROLLING PRODUCTION ACTIVITIES (Chapter 12)

Scheduling and control activities are designed to ensure that (a) production orders are initiated at the proper time and that (b) capacity is effectively used to fill them. The principles and techniques used to plan, schedule, control, and evaluate production operations are referred to as *production activity controls* and encompass both priority and capacity features.

Priority control activities begin with releasing orders from the material requirements plan to the production center. The ensuing control over the status (that is, priority) of all orders is a major function of production activity controls. Schedulers use the priority data to sequence the flow of work orders through the production process.

Capacity control activities are concerned with monitoring the planned versus actual production rates in terms of hours of capacity available and hours used at the various work centers. One method of doing this is via weekly input-output reports. Control over both priorities and capacities must be maintained if the firm is to produce its goods on schedule and in an efficient manner.

OVERVIEW: PRIORITY AND CAPACITY CONCEPTS

As you work through the chapters of Part Two, you may find it intuitively helpful to think of some of the P&IC activities in terms of Fig. II-2. The master schedule, MRP, and priority control activities can be associated with physical "materials" or "jobs." After the master schedule is specified, the end-item requirements must be stated in terms of specific materials used in production. However, the raw materials soon become component parts and subassemblies under the classification of "shop orders" and "jobs." Thus the priorities of materials (under MRP) become transformed into priorities of jobs (on the shop floor) as the production process adds value in the form of assembled materials and labor.

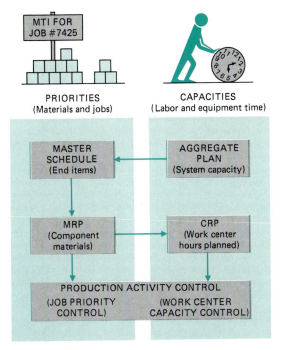

FIGURE II-2   Priorities and Capacities

Capacity concerns are reflected in aggregate planning, capacity requirements planning, and capacity control activities, which all possess a "time" dimension. Note, however, that although the term "MRP system" seems to focus attention on material requirements only, it is usually assumed to include capacity planning and control features as well.

Were it not for the computer and its ability to manipulate massive amounts of data in a few minutes, large companies would be unable to realize the production efficiencies they experience today. Nevertheless, not all firms need the same capabilities. Many firms have clerical or manual systems which suffice for their level of activity. With inexpensive minicomputers and microprocessors, however, nearly any firm can gain access to a suitable production and inventory control software package.

A major benefit of a computerized system is the *formality* or *discipline* it forces upon the organization. Formal systems offer predictable results that lend themselves to control and improvement over time. Informal systems often result in material shortages, overdue shipments, higher costs, and a good deal of buck-passing. They breed subjectivity and a resulting lack of confidence in the system.

We will begin our in-depth study of production and inventory control by examining the forecasting function. Forecasting provides the inputs for both priority and capacity planning activities.

CHAPTER 7

FORECASTING DEMAND

FORECASTING OBJECTIVES AND USES

Debbie Johnson is the forecasting manager at Nike's shoe headquarters in Beaverton, Oregon. Debbie's staff must project demand for hundreds of lines of shoes from proven court and running shoes to the hottest fall fashions. It's a tough job—shoe styles are not easy to predict. And Debbie has some busy and anxious days. Mistakes here can have disastrous effects. Their everyday decisions affect suppliers from Germany to Taiwan and retailers throughout the world. Fortunately they have some experienced forecasters, a good database, and some well-developed forecasting models.

WHAT IS A FORECAST?

Forecasts are estimates of the occurrence, timing, or magnitude of future events. They give operations managers a rational basis for planning and scheduling activities, even though actual demand is quite uncertain.

Some organizations claim they do not forecast at all, whereas others sport very sophisticated models. Organizations that pay no attention to forecasting are implicitly assuming that what has happened in the past will continue in the future. This is not necessarily an irrational approach, but it could certainly be improved upon by anticipating future events that are likely to happen.

WHY DO FIRMS FORECAST?

Figure 7-1 lists some of the ways firms benefit from forecasts. Accurate projections of future activity levels can minimize short-term fluctuations in production and help balance workloads. This lessens hiring, firing, and overtime activities and helps maintain good labor relations. Good forecasts also help managers have appropriate levels of materials available when needed. By anticipating employment and material needs, the forecasts enable managers to make better use of facilities and give improved service to customers.

COSTS OF FORECASTING

Forecasting activities can be costly, so it is important to assess their benefits versus their cost. Theoretically, there is an optimal level of activity where mar-

---

- Improved employee relations
- Improved materials management
- Better use of capital and facilities
- Improved customer service

FIGURE 7-1   Advantages of Good Forecasts

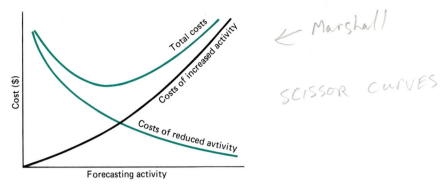

FIGURE 7-2   Cost of the Forecasting Activity

ginal benefit equals marginal cost, but in reality this level is difficult to find. Figure 7-2 illustrates.

As forecasting activity increases, data requirements increase, with the attendant costs of collection and analysis. The system for reporting and control must also be expanded. On the other hand, reduced activity may result in unplanned labor, materials, or capital costs, expediting costs, and—ultimately—lost revenues. The costs of not forecasting can be significant.

OUR APPROACH TO FORECASTING

In this chapter, we will try to gain an appreciation of the value of forecasting and an understanding of some of the more widely used techniques. In particular, we shall discuss (1) judgmental, (2) time series, (3) exponential smoothing, and (4) regression methods of forecasting. Examples will be discussed, and some refinements or extensions will be noted. The chapter ends with the reminder that the value of a forecasting technique lies in its ability to predict reliably and accurately. Thus it is important to measure forecast validity and control forecast error.

FORECASTING VARIABLES

Forecasting activities are a function of the (1) type of forecast, (2) time horizon being forecast, (3) database available, and (4) methodology employed. Let us explore each of these in more detail.

TYPE OF FORECAST

Most of the items used and produced by a firm do not need to be forecast in a formal way, because they are components, subassemblies, or required services that are part of a finished product. Forecasts should be used for end items and services that have uncertain demand. But there are other types of forecasts as well, and we discuss them in this section.

Purpose "Should we purchase a new computer system now, or wait until next year, when we might get more capacity and at a lower cost?" Managers must continually make decisions about purchasing new equipment, setting employment levels, carrying inventories, scheduling production, and so forth. Wise decisions in these areas depend upon a knowledge of current conditions and/or a prediction of future events. The *purpose* of forecasting activities is to make the best use of present information to guide decisions toward the objectives of the organization.

Types of Variables Being Forecast In their pursuit of corporate objectives, managers encounter two types of variables: *controllable* and *uncontrollable* (or random). Although we tend to think of numerous variables as random, many of them are only partly random. Sales, for example, is a function of both controllable variables (advertising effort, inventory levels) and uncontrollable variables (competition, raw material cost). In a sense, the "management game" consists of successfully managing the controllable variables, even though the uncontrollable variables may seem to mitigate against success.

Forecasting methodologies help by providing information about the uncontrollable variables. They cannot, of course, predict the value of inherently random components. But they can allow for random components, while basing projections primarily upon the nonrandom trends and relationships that exist in the data. Thus we find that the forecasting methods we study here are based primarily upon relationships that have been valid in the past. Computer programs are available for most methods [**6**].

Accuracy Forecasts tend to be more accurate (and easier) when the uncontrollable elements of a variable can be identified and isolated. Also, if demand can be decomposed into identifiable trends, or other components, this helps too. In general, the more the random effects can be isolated, the better the forecast will be.

Forecasts of product lines and groups of products take advantage of another aspect of randomness. Whereas individual product forecasts are strongly susceptible to error due to spontaneous random effects (which cannot be anticipated anyway), when several projects are aggregated together, the error effect is dissipated throughout the group, and compensating effects occur. One product's demand may exceed the forecast, while another's may fail to meet it. But as a whole, the aggregative forecast generally tends to be more accurate than individual product forecasts. Production planners take advantage of this knowledge by scheduling the use of production system capacities weeks before the specific end-item demand is firmed up.

Types of Forecasts The manager who must decide whether to invest in a computer system this year (or wait until next year) faces a different problem from the one who must decide how much inventory to place in stock. The former must grapple with the pace of technology whereas the latter must project future demand. Managers must select or develop those types of forecasts that will be most useful to them in their specific area of concern.

Forecasts of demand are especially important to operations managers because they guide the firm's scheduling and production control activities. Reliable forecasts enable managers to formulate material and capacity plans directing how their system will respond. And this response becomes the sales forecast or sales plan, from which financial, personnel, marketing, and other plans are derived.

Technological forecasts are concerned with the pace of new developments in technology, such as developments in storage devices that will increase the capacity and decrease the cost of computers. They are especially important to firms in technologically advanced industries, and some relatively sophisticated methods of extrapolating trends in innovation are in use.

Environmental forecasts are concerned with the social, political, and economic state of the environment. Nearly every major corporation now subscribes to an *econometric* forecasting service that provides forecasts of the gross national product, consumer prices, unemployment, housing starts, or other economic variables of particular interest to the firm.

TIME HORIZON

Forecasts are often classified according to time period. For example:

- Short-range—up to 1 year (typically 0 to 3 months)   *Operations*
- Medium-range—1 to 3 years   *Tactical*
- Long-range—5 years or more   *Strategic*

Short-range forecasts serve primarily as guides for current operations. Medium-range and longer-range forecasts are often of a more comprehensive or aggregated nature. A 3- to 5-year forecast may be necessary to support plant capacity decisions, whereas product-line and plant location decisions may require longer forecasts. Many firms find it necessary to use forecasts covering all three time periods. As might be expected, short-term forecasts are typically more accurate than long-term forecasts.

Product life cycle and seasonal factors affect the length of forecasts. Products in the early stages of their development will require longer forecasts than those in a declining stage. The forecasts are needed for planning different employment and inventory levels as the product passes through the various stages of growth and maturity. In a similar manner, forecast horizons are often geared to project the changes in production required to accommodate seasonal demand.

DATABASE: QUANTITATIVE AND QUALITATIVE

Most forecasting models rely upon quantitative data—it is the basis for scientific decision making. Quantification enhances the objectivity of the model and forces precision. However, problems arise when either the data or the model is inadequate. Some variables cannot be quantified, or the quantification process itself injects bias. In other cases, the models that a firm designs (or can afford) cannot accommodate the variables that the firm might like to include. Some judgmental

FIGURE 7-3   Forecasting Methodology

Description	Time and Application	Example	Relative Cost
Opinion and Judgment			
Ranges from simple subjective opinion to extensive analysis of historical data. Often is a collection of projections from sales coupled with judgment of higher-level management. Can incorporate aspects of other methodologies within its framework.	Short-range through long-range: e.g., for situations difficult to model, but good business judgment can help.	How much contract research can we obtain from the government next year?	Relatively low: Unless data used and analysis techniques are extensive.
Historical Analogy			
Comparison with stages in life cycle of comparable product (that is, introduction, growth, maturity, decline). Assume similar patterns.	Long-range: e.g., for new products.	How can we predict sales of our new shampoo?	Medium.
Delphi			
Panel of experts responds to series of questionnaires. Summary of responses is provided for panel and used to formulate next questionnaires. Each expert has access to all information. Assumes that the experts are knowledgeable.	Long-range: e.g., for facilities and new products.	Should our bank introduce a home video cash-management system next year?	Medium: Can be low if limited time spent on it.
Market Surveys			
Use of questionnaires, surveys, market panels for collecting data and testing hypothesis about consumer behavior. Assumes that the surveys are reliable and representative.	Usually long-range: e.g., new products, but also useful for short-range forecasts.	What level of services are city residents willing to pay for?	High: Due to survey cost and analysis.
Time Series			
Historical data on demand are decomposed to break out trend (T) and seasonal (S) factors, leaving cyclical (C) and random (R). Trend is typically isolated by either the least-squares equation or a moving average. Assumes time offers adequate explanation.	Short-range: e.g., for inventory and near term scheduling decisions. Also useful for long-range analysis of economic variables.	What is the demand pattern for soft drink aluminum cans?	Low: Based on historical data only, easily computerized.
Exponential Smoothing			
Use of exponentially weighted moving average, where new forecast lies between previous forecast and latest actual demand. Particularly suited to forecasting many items because computer storage space is minimized and tracking is simple. Assumes historical demand is indicative of future.	Short-range: e.g., inventory and near term scheduling decisions.	How much inventory of liquor is needed at the state liquor stores?	Low: Due to simplicity and updating via computer.

FIGURE 7-3   Forecasting Methodology (*Continued*)

Description	Time and Application	Example	Relative Cost
Regression and Correlation			
Use of one or more associative variables to forecast demands via a least-squares equation (regression) or via a close association (correlation) with an explanatory variable. Assumes logical (that is, explanatory) relationship exists.	Useful for short- and medium-range applications: e.g., existing products.	How do our sales of wood stoves relate to the price of fuel oil?	Low to medium, depending upon data needed and model used.
Econometric			
Use of an interdependent series of regression equations that typically relate to a broad range of economic activity. Assumes thorough identification of causal factors.	Short-range through long-range; e.g., whole product lines and corporate sales.	What effect will economic conditions have on our housing construction business?	High: Usually requires sophisticated computer model and current economic data.

allowance must be made for the model inadequacy. Even the most sophisticated models need the balance of good judgment.

Testing the model on past data or simulated data can be an effective check of its adequacy. And, as current data suggest changes, the model should be revised.

FORECASTING METHODOLOGY

The complexity of forecasting methodology sometimes tends to correspond to the extent to which future events are evaluated in an objective or professional manner. Subjective opinions may be adequate for less consequential or relatively certain situations. As the amount of uncertainty about future events increases, firms tend to rely more upon inferences and correlations based upon the present. When these inferences, in turn, come from the analysis of data, the methodology becomes more objective but also more complex. Complexity does not guarantee accuracy, however.

Figure 7-3 describes some of the more widely used approaches to forecasting. Some techniques are best suited to long-range or new-product forecasts, whereas others are more appropriate for production and inventory control. Instead of any one ideal method, several techniques are in common use. *Opinion methods*, although subjective, are widely used, especially by small firms. To a large extent they rely upon personal insights, imagination, or perhaps even guesswork. The cost is low, but accuracy is too. *Judgments* are an improvement over pure opinion in that they call on past experience, consensus with others, or perhaps knowledge of historically analogous situations. They may be the most economically feasible methods for some long-range and new-product marketing situations.

Time series methods, which capitalize upon the identification of trend and seasonal effects, are data-based and are likely to be more accurate than opinion methods. Nevertheless, they are based wholly upon time, and time series forecasts do not take specific account of outside or related factors. The basic assumption is that history follows a pattern that will continue. *Exponential smoothing methods* are of this same type, for they are trajectory, or trend-based. They are, however, readily adaptive to current levels of activity and have become increasingly popular in production and inventory control applications.

Regression and correlation methods are associative in nature and depend upon the causal relationship or interaction of two or more variables. They can be classified as statistical from an inferential standpoint, for we use one or more variables to infer something about the other. *Box-Jenkins* is a combination time series–regression approach (not listed here) that incorporates some advantages of both methods. The historical analogy, Delphi, market survey, and econometric methods are also useful, but they will not be covered in detail here either. Figure 7-3 presents some applications.

OPINION AND JUDGMENTAL METHODS

One of the most simple and widely used methods of forecasting consists of collecting the opinions and judgments of individuals who are expected to have the best knowledge of current activities or future plans. Some opinion and judgment forecasts are largely intuitive, whereas others integrate data and perhaps even some mathematical or statistical expectations into the forecast.

The employees with the most immediate knowledge of demand trends and customer plans are often company marketing representatives and division or product-line managers. Through regular contact with customers, the marketing and sales personnel are knowledgeable about individual industrial customers or retail market segments. Division management usually maintains broader market information on trends by product line, geographic area, and customer groups.

Judgmental forecasts often consist of one or more of the following:

- Forecasts by sales representatives, which are made up individually and aggregated for various products
- Forecasts by top management at the division or product-line level
- Forecasts based on the combined estimates of sales representatives and division or product-line managers

Figure 7-4 illustrates a combined-estimate approach (number 3) for a firm producing electric signs. Regional forecasts are from field sales representatives, who are in daily contact with their customers. Product-line sales forecasts are from the various product-line managers in the headquarters office. The estimates from both sources have been reconciled to arrive at the forecast shown. These values will be the sales "loadings" for the coming year. The next step will be to convert

FIGURE 7-4   Combined Forecast by Region and Product Line

		Forecast ($000) by Region					Product-Line Totals
Product Line / Region		Atlantic Coast	Central	South-west	Pacific Coast	Inter-national Division	
T27	Time and temperature	65	13	56	30	16	$180
S43	Stadium scoreboards	10	5	30	5	—	$ 50
M14	Message centers	—	—	16	64	10	$ 90
D70	Market display	—	10	5	—	—	$ 15
	Service parts	5	7	3	6	4	$ 25
Regional Totals		$80	$35	$110	$105	$30	$360

from the dollar amount of sales to specific number of units so that material and capacity requirements at the production plant can be projected.

Judgmental forecasts have the advantage that they can incorporate intangible factors and subjective experience as inputs along with objective data, if that is also available. However, if the forecasts prove to be inaccurate, there is no tangible, objective basis for improvement the next time around.

TIME SERIES METHODS

A *time series* is a set of observations of some variable over time. The series is usually tabulated or graphed in a manner that readily conveys the behavior of the subject variable. For example, assume that Fig. 7-5 presents the annual shipments (tons) of welded tube by an aluminum producer to machinery manufacturers. The graphs suggests that the series is time-dependent. The forecaster is interested in determining *how* the series is dependent on time and in developing a means of predicting future levels with some degree of reliability. The nature of the time dependence is often analyzed by decomposing the time series into its components.

COMPONENTS OF A SERIES

The components of a time series are generally classified as trend (T), cyclical (C), seasonal (S), and random (R) or irregular. In the classical model of time series analysis, the forecast (Y) is a multiplicative function of these components:

$$Y = TCSR \tag{7-1}$$

Year	Shipments (tons)
1977	2
1978	3
1979	6
1980	10
1981	8
1982	7
1983	12
1984	14
1985	14
1986	18
1987	19

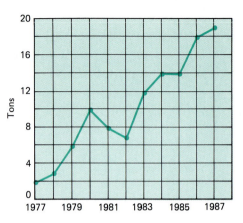

FIGURE 7-5 Aluminum Tube Shipments

The *trend* represents a long-term secular movement, characteristic of many economic series. *Cyclical* factors are long-term swings about the trend line and are usually associated with business cycles. *Seasonal* effects are similar patterns occurring during corresponding months of successive years. They can be hourly or weekly patterns as well, but these are not usually evident unless the data are plotted on an appropriate time scale. *Random or irregular* components are sporadic effects due to chance and unusual occurrences.

FORECASTING PROCEDURE

Most forecasting procedures that use time series data abstract the trend and seasonal factors. Some methods attempt to go beyond this and express a cyclical component, but it is usually evasive and somewhat subjective. The random component is inherently not predictable, so the forecasting procedure results in the procedure outlined in Fig. 7-6.

---

1 Plot historical data to confirm the type of relationship (for example, linear, quadratic).
2 Develop a trend equation to describe the data.
3 Develop a seasonal index (if desired).
4 Project the trend into the future.
5 Multiply the monthly trend values by the seasonal index.
6 Modify the projected values by a knowledge of:
    (a) Cyclical business conditions (C).
    (b) Anticipated irregular effects (R).

FIGURE 7-6 Forecasting Procedure for Using Time Series

METHODS OF ESTIMATING TREND

Several methods of estimating the trend of a time series are available. Some of these methods simply portray or describe the data, such as freehand curves and moving averages. Other approaches describe the data *and* provide a trend equation, such as the least-squares method. Let us refer to the data of Fig. 7-5 to illustrate.

Freehand   A freehand curve drawn smoothly through the data points is often an easy and perhaps adequate representation of the data. From Fig. 7-5 it appears that a straight line connecting the 1977 and 1987 shipments is a fairly good representation of the given data. The forecast can be obtained simply by extending the trend line. However, what appears to be a good fit for one individual may not be so for another, and this method suffers from subjectivity.

Moving Average   A moving average is obtained by summing and averaging the values from a given number of periods repetitively, each time deleting the oldest value and adding a new value.

$$\text{MA} = \frac{\Sigma X}{\text{number of periods}} \tag{7-2}$$

where one X value is exchanged each period.

EXAMPLE 7-1

Compute a 3-year moving average for the aluminum tube shipments of Fig. 7-5.

SOLUTION

Year	Shipments (tons)	Three-Year Moving Total		Three-Year Moving Average
1977	2	—		—
1978	3	11	÷ 3 =	3.7
1979	6	19		6.3
1980	10	24		8.0
1981	8	25		8.3
1982	7	27		9.0
1983	12	33		11.0
1984	14	40		13.3
1985	14	46		15.3
1986	18	51		17.0
1987	19	—		—

Note that the moving average is recorded in the center position of the data it averages. The 3.7-ton figure in the above example would thus be centered on July 1, 1978. The average effectively smooths out fluctuations while preserving the general pattern of the data. A graph of the moving-average values superimposed upon Fig. 7-5 would reveal this smoothing effect. Of course, the more components in the average (that is, the longer the period), the smoother will be the curve. It has the additional advantage that it can be applied to any data, whether they fit a precise mathematical curve or not.

The adaptability of the moving average is also the source of a major disadvantage, however, for there is no equation for forecasting. In place of an equation we use the latest moving-average value as the forecast for the next period. In Example 7-1 the next period (1988) forecast would then be 17 tons, which would probably be low in view of the strong trend. Moving averages lose data values at each end of the series and can be strongly affected by extreme values.

An adjustment to the moving-average (MA) method allows one to vary the weights assigned to components of the moving average; in this way, the most recent values can be emphasized.

$$MA_{wt} = \frac{\Sigma\ (wt)\ X}{\Sigma\ wt} \qquad (7\text{-}3)$$

This is often referred to as a *weighted moving-average method.* Weights can be percentages or any real numbers. In Example 7-1, if a weight of 3 is assigned to the 1987 shipments, 2 to 1986, and 1 to 1985, the weighted moving average is 17.8 tons.

Least Squares Least squares is one of the most widely used methods of fitting trends to data because it yields what is mathematically described as a "line of best fit." This trend line has the following properties: (a) the summation of all vertical deviations about it is zero, (b) the summation of all vertical deviations squared is a minimum, and (c) the line goes through the means $\overline{X}$ and $\overline{Y}$. For linear equations, it is found by the simultaneous solution for a and b of the two normal equations:

$$\Sigma Y = na + b\Sigma X$$

$$\Sigma XY = a\Sigma X + b\Sigma X^2 \qquad (7\text{-}4)$$

Where the data can be coded so that $\Sigma X = 0$, two terms in the above expressions drop out, and we have:

$$\Sigma Y = na$$

$$\Sigma XY = b\Sigma X^2 \qquad (7\text{-}5)$$

Coding is easily accomplished with time series data, for we simply designate the center of the time period as $X = 0$ and have an equal number of plus and minus periods on each side which sum to zero.

EXAMPLE 7-2   Use the least-squares method to develop a linear trend equation for the data of Fig. 7-5. State the equation complete with signature, and forecast a trend value for 1992.

SOLUTION

Year	X Year Coded	Y Shipments (tons)	XY	X²
1977	−5	2	−10	25
1978	−4	3	−12	16
1979	−3	6	−18	9
1980	−2	10	−20	4
1981	−1	8	−8	1
1982	0	7	0	0
1983	1	12	12	1
1984	2	14	28	4
1985	3	14	42	9
1986	4	18	72	16
1987	5	19	95	25
	0	113	181	110

Rearranging Eq. (7-5) we have:

$$a = \frac{\Sigma Y}{n} = \frac{113}{11} = 10.3$$

$$b = \frac{\Sigma XY}{\Sigma X^2} = \frac{181}{110} = 1.6$$

∴ The forecasting equation is of the form $Y = a + bX$

$$Y = 10.3 + 1.6X \qquad (1982 = 0, \ X = \text{years}, \ Y = \text{tons})$$

Forecast for 1992: Because 1992 is 10 years distant from the origin,

$$Y = 10.3 + 1.6(10) = 26.3 \text{ tons}$$

The above example assumes that a linear equation adequately describes the data. *The appropriateness of a linear function should always be checked first;* this can be done simply by graphing the data and observing whether a straight line would provide a satisfactory fit. If not, higher-order normal equations can be used, and these may be obtained from any good statistical reference text. The solution procedure for developing parabolic or exponential equations is similar, but slightly more tedious. However, computer programs are (also) available for fitting nonlinear data. Nevertheless, linear equations often suffice, for even though the data may be nonlinear in the long range, over the short range much data approximate linearity.

CHANGING THE ORIGIN AND SCALE OF EQUATIONS

When a moving average or trend value is reported, it is assumed to be centered in the middle of the month (fifteenth day) or the year (July 1). Similarly, the forecast value is assumed to be centered in the middle of the future period.

The reference point (origin) can be shifted or the X and Y units changed to monthly or quarterly values if desired. To shift the origin, simply add the desired number of periods to X in the original forecasting equation, or subtract the desired number of periods. Changing the time units from annual values to monthly values is accomplished by dividing X by 12. To change the Y units from annual to monthly values, the entire right-hand side of the equation must be divided by 12.

SEASONAL INDEXES

A *seasonal index* (SI) is a ratio that relates a recurring seasonal variation to the corresponding trend value at that given time. We are all familiar with the peaking of retail sales at Christmas and the decline in heating fuel consumption in summer. When data such as these are reported in monthly terms, and similar patterns occur during corresponding months of successive years, seasonal indexes of such patterns can be determined.

Several methods of computing seasonal indexes exist, but the most widely used is a *ratio-to-moving-average* method. The procedure is to tabulate the data in monthly terms and compute 12-month moving-average values over a period of several years. The 12-month moving average effectively dampens out all seasonal fluctuations. Actual monthly values are then compared with the moving average centered upon the actual month. For example, the 12-month moving average (that is, trend value) for heating fuel consumption for a plant in August 1986 may have been 40 gallons, but actual consumption was only 32 gallons. The ratio to moving average for August of 1986 is then 32 divided by 40 = .80. Values for August of other years are similarly computed, and all such values are averaged to get one seasonal index value for the month of August. The same is done for other months. Some monthly index values will exceed 1.00, but the total for all 12 months will be made equal to 12.00. See [2:682].

After valid seasonal indexes have been determined, they can be applied to forecasted trend values to obtain seasonalized (adjusted) forecast values (Y_{sz}).

Seasonalized forecast = seasonal index (trend forecast)

$$Y_{sz} = (SI)Y_c \tag{7-6}$$

EXAMPLE 7-3 The production manager of a natural gas pipeline company has projected trend values for next August, September, and October of 2.1, 2.2, and 2.3

million cubic meters, respectively. Seasonal indexes for the three months have been found to be .80, 1.05, and 1.20, respectively. What actual seasonalized (adjusted) production should the manager plan for?

SOLUTION

$$Y_{sz} = SI(Y_c)$$

For August: $= (.80)(2.1) = 1.68$ million cubic meters

For September: $= (1.05)(2.2) = 2.31$ million cubic meters

For October: $= (1.20)(2.3) = 2.76$ million cubic meters

After seasonal adjustments have been made, similar adjustments can be made for cyclical or irregular effects if data are available. For example, if a firm's business is closely tied to construction activity and economic indicators suggest a 20 percent drop in that activity over the next year, the firm may want to apply a .80 multiplier to its forecast of sales to the industry. Similarly, any irregular occurrence, such as a forthcoming strike, should be accounted for as much as possible.

EXPONENTIAL SMOOTHING

Exponential smoothing is a type of moving-average forecasting technique which weights past data in an exponential manner so that the most recent data carry more weight in the moving average. Simple exponential smoothing makes no explicit adjustment for trend effects, whereas adjusted exponential smoothing does take trend effects into account.

SIMPLE EXPONENTIAL SMOOTHING

With simple exponential smoothing, the forecast is made up of the last-period forecast plus a portion of the difference between the last-period actual demand and the last-period forecast.

$$F_t = F_{t-1} + \alpha(D_{t-1} - F_{t-1}) \tag{7-7}$$

where F_t = current-period forecast
F_{t-1} = last-period forecast
α = smoothing constant
D_{t-1} = last-period demand

Observe, from the equation, that each forecast is simply the previous forecast plus some correction for demand in the last period. If demand was above the last-period forecast, the correction will be positive; and if demand was below, the correction will be negative.

The smoothing constant, α, actually dictates how much correction will be made. It is a number between 0 and 1 used to compute the forecast F_t, which, in turn, is based upon previous forecasts where α was also used. By entering multiplicatively into all subsequent forecasts, an "exponential" weighting takes place.

If α were assigned a value as high as 1, each forecast would reflect a total adjustment to the recent demand, and the forecast would simply be last period's actual demand. Since demand fluctuations are typically random and sporadic, however, the value of α is often kept in the range of .005 to .30 in order to "smooth" the forecast. The exact value depends upon the response to demand that is best for the individual firm. We shall return to this consideration after an example.

EXAMPLE 7-4

A firm uses simple exponential smoothing with $\alpha = .1$ to forecast demand. The forecast for the week of February 1 was 500 units, whereas actual demand turned out to be 450 units.
(a) Forecast the demand for the week of February 8.
(b) Assume that the actual demand during the week of February 8 turned out to be 505 units. Forecast the demand for the week of February 15. Continue on forecasting through March 15, assuming that subsequent demands were actually 516, 488, 467, 554, and 510 units.

SOLUTION
(a) $F_t = F_{t-1} + \alpha(D_{t-1} - F_{t-1})$
$= 500 + .1(450 - 500) = 495$ units
(b) Arranging the procedure in tabular form, we have:

Week	Demand D_{t-1}	Old Fore-cast F_{t-1}	Forecast Error $D_{t-1} - F_{t-1}$	Correction $\alpha(D_{t-1} - F_{t-1})$	New Forecast (F_t) $F_{t-1} + \alpha(D_{t-1} - F_{t-1})$
Feb. 1	450	500	−50	−5	495
8	505	495	10	1	496
15	516	496	20	2	498
22	488	498	−10	−1	497
Mar. 1	467	497	−30	−3	494
8	554	494	60	6	500
15	510	500	10	1	501

In the accompanying example, an initial forecast value was available. If no previous forecast value is known, the "old forecast" starting point may be estimated or taken to be an average of the values of some preceding periods.

SELECTION OF THE SMOOTHING CONSTANT

Simple exponential smoothing does not extrapolate for trend effects, so no α value will fully compensate for a trend in the data. Low α values will result in more of a lag behind trend, however, because they give less weight to recent demand.

Low α values are particularly appropriate when product demand is relatively stable (that is, without trend or cyclical variation) but random variation (noise) is high. Higher values of α are more useful where substantive changes are likely to occur because they are more responsive to fluctuations in demand. For example, a higher α value may be appropriate for style goods industries that require a rapid and dramatic response. New-product introductions, promotional campaigns, and even anticipated recessions also suggest the use of higher α values.

A satisfactory value of α can generally be determined by trial-and-error testing of different smoothing constants to find one that results in the best fit (least error) when used on past data. As we saw earlier:

$$\text{Forecast error} = \text{demand} - \text{forecast} \tag{7-8}$$

The individual forecast errors are usually summarized in a statistic such as average error, mean squared error, or mean absolute deviation (MAD).

$$\text{MAD} = \frac{\Sigma |\text{error}|}{n} \tag{7-9}$$

where n = the number of periods.

The use of MAD for comparing forecasting models will be illustrated in the section on adjusted exponential smoothing.

Past data are not always available to experiment with. Some analysts recommend beginning with an α of .2 or .3 and watching the performance for a few periods. Others suggest picking an α value that approximates "a length of moving average that makes sense" [**7:15**]. An approximate equivalent to an arithmetic moving average, in terms of the degree of smoothing, can be estimated by

$$\alpha = \frac{2}{n + 1} \tag{7-10}$$

Thus, a 7-year moving average would correspond, roughly, to an α value of .25.

SEASONAL ADJUSTMENT TO EXPONENTIAL FORECAST

Where a seasonal pattern exists, it may be desirable to seasonally adjust an exponentially smoothed forecast, just as with a time series. The procedure is to (1) deseasonalize the actual demand, (2) compute a deseasonalized forecast, and (3) seasonalize (adjust) the forecast by multiplying by the seasonal index.

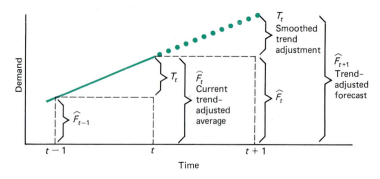

FIGURE 7-7   Components of a Trend-Adjusted Forecast

ADJUSTED EXPONENTIAL SMOOTHING[1]

The simple exponential smoothing forecast is really only a smoothed average centered on the current period—no projection is involved. It is used as a next-period forecast, but if a trend exists, the forecast will always lag the trend. Many firms do experience a growth trend; so it is important to recognize that in their forecasting activities.

Adjusted exponential smoothing models actually project into the future (for example, to time period $t + 1$) by adding a trend correction increment, T_t, to the current-period smoothed average, $\hat{F}_t$.

$$\hat{F}_{t+1} = \hat{F}_t + T_t \qquad (7\text{-}11)$$

Figure 7-7 depicts the components of a trend-adjusted forecast, $\hat{F}_{t+1}$. Like the simple exponential computation, the value $\hat{F}_t$, represents the current-period value of the smoothed average demand. However, we add a "hat" (^) to show that it is also adjusted for trend. Note that the same trend which is computed in the current period is simply advanced to the "$t + 1$" period.

Figure 7-8 describes the sequence for computing a trend-adjusted forecast. The current-period smoothed average, $\hat{F}_t$, includes the trend adjustment from the previous period, but it is still just an exponentially weighted average—not a projection.

Note that Eq. (7-13) for the trend adjustment, T_t, utilizes a second smoothing coefficient, β, which may be different from α. The β value determines the extent to which the trend adjustment relies upon the latest difference in forecast amounts $(\hat{F}_t - \hat{F}_{t-1})$ versus the previous trend, T_{t-1}. Thus it smooths much like α, except it works directly off the forecast difference and the previous trend.

---

[1] This material extends beyond that covered in some introductory texts. Computer programs are also available and widely used.

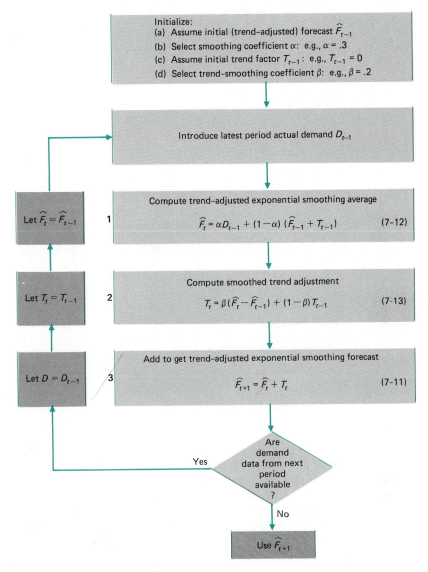

Initialize:
(a) Assume initial (trend-adjusted) forecast $\widehat{F}_{t-1}$
(b) Select smoothing coefficient α: e.g., $\alpha = .3$
(c) Assume initial trend factor T_{t-1}: e.g., $T_{t-1} = 0$
(d) Select trend-smoothing coefficient β: e.g., $\beta = .2$

Introduce latest period actual demand D_{t-1}

Let $\widehat{F}_t = \widehat{F}_{t-1}$ 1

Compute trend-adjusted exponential smoothing average

$$\widehat{F}_t = \alpha D_{t-1} + (1-\alpha)\,(\widehat{F}_{t-1} + T_{t-1}) \qquad (7\text{-}12)$$

Let $T_t = T_{t-1}$ 2

Compute smoothed trend adjustment

$$T_t = \beta\,(\widehat{F}_t - \widehat{F}_{t-1}) + (1-\beta)\,T_{t-1} \qquad (7\text{-}13)$$

Let $D = D_{t-1}$ 3

Add to get trend-adjusted exponential smoothing forecast

$$\widehat{F}_{t+1} = \widehat{F}_t + T_t \qquad (7\text{-}11)$$

Are demand data from next period available?

Yes

No

Use $\widehat{F}_{t+1}$

FIGURE 7-8   Computation of Trend-Adjusted Exponential Smoothing Forecast

EXAMPLE 7-5   Develop an adjusted exponential forecast for the week of 5/14 for a firm with the following demand. Let $\alpha = .1$ and $\beta = .2$. Begin with a previous average of $\hat{F}_{t-1} = 650$, and let the initial trend adjustment, $T_{t-1}, = 0$.

Week	3/19	3/26	4/1	4/9	4/16	4/23	4/30	5/7
Demand	700	685	648	717	713	728	754	762

SOLUTION

Following the procedure from Fig. 7-8, we have:

Week of 3/19

$$\hat{F}_t = \alpha D_{t-1} + (1 - \alpha)(\hat{F}_{t-1} + T_{t-1})$$
$$= .1(700) + .9(650 + 0) = 655.00$$
$$T_t = \beta(\hat{F}_t - \hat{F}_{t-1}) + (1 - \beta)T_{t-1}$$
$$= .2(655 - 650) + .8(0) = 1.0 + 0 = 1.00$$
$$\hat{F}_{t+1} = \hat{F}_t + T_t = 655 + 1 = 656.00$$

The 656.00 is the adjusted forecast for week of 3/26.

Week of 3/26

$$\hat{F}_t = .1(685) + .9(655 + 1.0) = 658.90$$
$$T_t = .2(658.9 - 655) + .8(1.0) = 1.58$$
$$\hat{F}_{t+1} = 658.9 + 1.58 = 660.48$$

The remainder of the calculations are in table form below. The trend-adjusted forecast for the week of 5/14 is $711.89 \cong 712$ units.

	(1)	(2)	(3)	(4)	(5)	(6)
						Next-
		Previous	Actual	Smoothed	Smoothed	Period
		Average	Demand	Average	Trend	Projection
	Week	$\hat{F}_{t-1}$	D_{t-1}	$\hat{F}_t$	T_t	$\hat{F}_{t-1}$
Mar.	19	650.00	700	655.00	1.00	656.00
	26	655.00	685	658.90	1.58	660.48
Apr.	2	658.90	648	659.23	1.33	600.56
	9	659.23	717	666.20	2.46	669.06
	16	660.20	713	673.09	3.35	676.44
	23	673.09	728	681.60	4.39	685.99
	30	681.60	754	691.79	5.74	698.53
May	7	692.79	762	704.88	7.01	711.89
	14		770			

As with α, the appropriate value to select for β can be determined by experimentation. A low β will give more smoothing of the trend and may be useful if the trend is not well established. A high β will emphasize the lastest trend and be more responsive to recent changes in trend. In Example 7-6 the forecast errors for three different smoothing coefficient possibilities are compared.

EXAMPLE 7-6   Use the demand data from Example 7-5 and a value of 770 for the week of May 14.

(a) Compute the mean absolute deviation (MAD) forecast error for the following:

Simple exponential smoothing ($\alpha = .1$)

Adjusted exponential smoothing ($\alpha = .1$ and $\beta = .2$)

Adjusted exponential smoothing ($\alpha = .1$ and $\beta = .8$)

(b) Compare the actual demand and the three forecasts on a graph.

SOLUTION

Computations of the forecast values for adjusted exponential smoothing ($\alpha = .1$; $\beta = .2$) are given in the previous example; computations for simple exponential smoothing and for $\alpha = .1$ and $\beta = .8$ are not shown, but the results are given below. The forecast error = demand − forecast and is computed as shown. The best fit of these models is $\alpha = .1$ and $\beta = .8$ for a MAD of 31.6. Figure 7-9 confirms that for these data, which have a strong trend, the higher value of β yields better results.

Week	Actual Demand	Simple: $\alpha = .1$ Forecast	Error	Adjusted: $\alpha = .1$; $\beta = .2$ Forecast	Error	Adjusted: $\alpha = .1$; $\beta = .8$ Forecast	Error
3/19	700	650	50	650	50	650	50
3/26	685	655	30	656	29	659	26
4/2	648	658	− 10	660	− 12	668	− 20
4/9	717	657	60	661	56	671	46
4/16	713	663	50	669	44	684	29
4/23	728	668	60	676	52	697	31
4/30	754	674	80	686	68	714	40
5/7	762	682	80	699	63	734	28
5/14	770	690	80	712	58	756	14
$\Sigma|\text{error}|$:			500		432		284
$\text{MAD} = \dfrac{\Sigma|\text{error}|}{9}$			55.6		48.0		31.6

Simple and adjusted exponential smoothing are sometimes referred to as *first-order smoothing* and *second-order smoothing*, respectively. One reason why they are widely used is that the forecast data can be computerized in a minimum amount of storage space and routinely updated. This is important to firms with thousands of items in inventory. Since each current forecast value contains all past forecast and demand data in its properly weighted (exponential) manner, there is no need to carry long records of historical data (as there is with arithmetic moving averages).

Exponential smoothing is an effective and efficient method of forecasting with a built-in means of tracking the average while discounting the erratic random

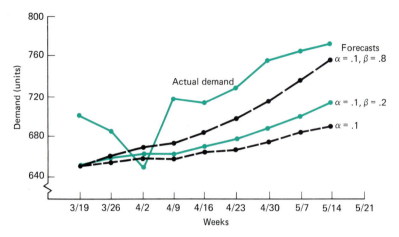

FIGURE 7-9   Forecast Results Using Simple and Trend-Adjusted Exponential Smoothing

fluctuations. Nevertheless, in some cases the sophistication gained by using adjusted exponential smoothing is simply not warranted. This may be true if, for example, users are *forced* to accept forecast values from a technique they do not understand.

REGRESSION AND CORRELATION METHODS

Time series and exponential smoothing methods describe the action of some variable over time, as if the variable were a function of time. Although this is often a useful relationship, it is sometimes more meaningful to relate the variable we are trying to forecast to other variables that are more suggestive of a causal relationship. Regression and correlation techniques are means of describing the association between two or more such variables. They make no claim to establishing cause and effect but instead merely quantify the statistical dependence or extent to which the two or more variables are related.

LINEAR REGRESSION

Regression means "dependence" and involves estimating the value of a *dependent variable*, Y, from an *independent variable*, X. In simple regression only one independent variable is used, whereas in multiple regression two or more independent variables are involved. The simple linear regression model takes the form $Y_c = a + bX$, where Y_c is the dependent and X the independent variable. A multiple linear regression equation may be of the form $Y_c = a + bX_1 + cX_2 + dX_3$, whereas a curvilinear relationship involving second- or higher-order functions might take the form $Y_c = a + bX + cX^2 + dX^3$. We shall limit consideration to simple linear regressions, which are often satisfactory for forecasting purposes. You may refer to a statistics text [2] for multiple regression and curvilinear regression models.

The forecasting procedure using regression is similar to that of time series in that data are first obtained and plotted to be sure the correct form of a model is chosen. A trend equation is then developed, and the equation is used for forecasting. The variables are not necessarily related on a time basis, so seasonal and cyclical adjustments are not usually made. However, the method of converting the data into a forecasting equation is the same in that the normal equations [see Eq. (7-4)] are used. Since the equations are always solved for the values of the slope b and intercept a, they are often rewritten in the more convenient form:

$$b = \frac{\Sigma XY - n\overline{X}\overline{Y}}{\Sigma X^2 - n\overline{X}^2} \qquad (7\text{-}14)$$

$$a = \overline{Y} - b\overline{X} \qquad (7\text{-}15)$$

where $\overline{X} = (\Sigma X)/n$ and $\overline{Y} = (\Sigma Y)/n$ are the means of the independent and dependent variables, respectively, and n is the number of pairs of observations made.

EXAMPLE 7-7

The general manager of a building materials production plant feels the demand for plasterboard shipments may be related to the number of construction permits issued in the county during the previous quarter. The manager has collected the data shown in the accompanying table.

Construction Permits (X)	Plasterboard Shipments (Y)
15	6
9	4
40	16
20	6
25	13
25	9
15	10
35	16

(a) Graph the data to see whether they can be satisfactorily described by a linear equation.
(b) Use the normal equations of (7-4) to derive a regression forecasting equation.
(c) Confirm the values of (b) and (a) using Eqs. (7-14) and (7-15).
(d) Determine a point estimate for plasterboard shipments when the number of construction permits is 30.

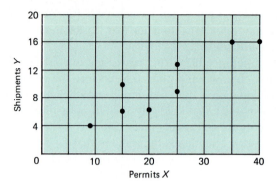

FIGURE 7-10   Plasterboard Shipments and Construction Permits

SOLUTION

(a) A scatter diagram (Fig. 7-10) shows that the data are not perfectly linear but approach linearity over this short range.

(b) See the accompanying table and calculations.

X	Y	XY	X²	Y²
15	6	90	225	36
9	4	36	81	16
40	16	640	1,600	256
20	6	120	400	36
25	13	325	625	169
25	9	225	625	81
15	10	150	225	100
35	16	560	1,225	256
184	80	2,146	5,006	950

$n = 8$ pairs of observations

$$\overline{X} = \frac{184}{8} = 23$$

$$\overline{Y} = \frac{80}{8} = 10$$

$$\begin{aligned}
\Sigma Y = na + b\Sigma X \longrightarrow \quad & 80 = & 8a + & 184b & (1)\\
\Sigma XY = a\Sigma X + b\Sigma X^2 \longrightarrow \quad & 2{,}146 = & 184a + & 5{,}006b & (2)
\end{aligned}$$

Multiplying (1) by (-23):* $\quad -1{,}840 = -184a - 4{,}232b \quad (3)$

Adding (2) and (3): $\quad 306 = \qquad\qquad 774b \quad (4)$

$$\therefore b = \frac{306}{774} = .395$$

Substituting in (1): $\quad 80 = 8a + 184(.395)$

$$8a = 80 - 72.7$$

$$a = \frac{7.3}{8} = .91$$

* Note that we are multiplying equation (1) by a number such that the coefficent for a will be the same value (but opposite sign) as that in equation (2). The 23 is obtained from $184 \div 8$ and assigned a negative value so that the a coefficient drops out upon addition.

Equation is $$Y_c = .91 + .395X$$

where X = permits and Y = shipments.

(c) Alternatively,

$$b = \frac{\Sigma XY - n\overline{XY}}{\Sigma X^2 - n\overline{X}^2} = \frac{2,146 - 8(23)(10)}{5,006 - 8(23)(23)} = .395$$

$$a = \overline{Y} - b\overline{X} = 10 - .395(23) = .91$$

(d) Letting $X = 30$,

$$Y_c = .91 + .395\,(30) = 12.76 \cong 13 \text{ shipments}$$

The regression line developed via the use of the normal equations has the characteristics of a line of best fit so that the sum of the squares of the vertical deviations from this line is less than the sum of the squares of the deviations from any other straight line through the same points. Any regression curve essentially describes the relationship between a given value of the independent variable, X, and the mean, $\mu_{Y \cdot X}$, of the corresponding probability distribution of the dependent variable, Y. Thus, for any value of X (such as 30 permits), there is a distribution of values of Y (many possible values), and our forecast, or point estimate of Y (the 13 shipments), is actually the mean of that distribution. See Fig. 7-11.

STANDARD DEVIATION OF REGRESSION

We can measure the dispersion around the regression line by subtracting the calculated trend value, Y_c, from each observation, Y, squaring and summing the

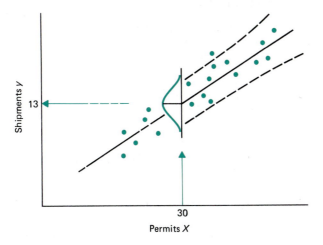

FIGURE 7-11 Regression Line

differences, and dividing by $n - 2$. If we take the square root of this, we obtain the standard deviation of regression, $S_{Y.X}$, read "S sub Y given X."

$$S_{Y.X} = \sqrt{\frac{\Sigma(Y - Y_c)^2}{n - 2}} \qquad (7\text{-}16)$$

This conditional standard deviation is similar to other standard deviation computations in that observed values (Y) are subtracted from the mean (Y_c), and the differences are squared and summed. The $n - 2$ in the denominator reflects a loss of 2 degrees of freedom because in this bivariate case we are using sample statistics for both the X and Y variables. A more difficult-looking equation, but one that is easier to use, will provide the same answer:

$$S_{Y.X} = \sqrt{\frac{\Sigma Y^2 - a\Sigma Y - b\Sigma XY}{n - 2}} \qquad (7\text{-}17)$$

EXAMPLE 7-8

Given the data on permits and shipments in the previous example, compute the standard deviation of regression ($S_{Y.X}$).

SOLUTION

$$S_{Y.X} = \sqrt{\frac{\Sigma Y^2 - a\Sigma Y - b\Sigma XY}{n - 2}}$$

$$= \sqrt{\frac{950 - (.91)(80) - (.395)(2,146)}{8 - 2}}$$

$$= 2.2 \text{ shipments}$$

PREDICTION INTERVAL ESTIMATES

We can use the standard deviation of regression to lend more precision to any point estimate of a forecast by stating the forecast as an interval. When working with large samples ($n \geq 100$) the approximate interval estimate for an *individual* value of Y is

$$\text{Prediction interval } Y_c = Y_c \pm ZS_{Y.X} \qquad (7\text{-}18)$$

where Y_c is the calculated trend value and Z represents the number of standard deviations for the specified interval. This formulation recognizes that for any given value of X (permits), the value of Y (shipments) can be expected to lie within the interval a designated proportion of the time.

This interval assumes that for a given X value, the Y values are normally distributed about the mean (that is, the regression line). Then, for example, 95.5 percent of the Y values are within $\pm 2S_{Y.X}$ of the regression curve, as shown by the dotted lines in Fig. 7-11. If the standard deviation of regression has been com-

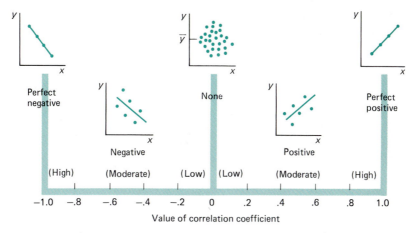

FIGURE 7-12   Interpretation of Correlation Coefficient

puted from a sample size of less than 100, the t rather than the normal Z distribution should be used and additional correction factors must be applied.[2] Equations for these situations can be found in any good statistics reference [2:537].

CORRELATION COEFFICIENTS: MEANING AND USE

We have seen that a *regression* curve expresses the *nature* (that is, intercept and slope) of the relationship between two or more variables. The regression equation states how the dependent variable changes as a result of changes in the independent variables.

Correlation is a means of expressing the *degree* of relationship between two or more variables. In other words, it tells how well a linear—or other—equation describes the relationship. Unlike regression, in correlation all the variables enjoy equal "status," so we do not consider one as dependent on another. Like regression, though, correlations may also be simple or multiple, linear or nonlinear, depending on the data. The correlation *coefficient* r is a number between -1 and $+1$ and is designated as positive if Y increases with increases in X and negative if Y decreases with increases in X. If $r = 0$, this indicates the lack of any relationship between the two variables.

Figure 7-12 illustrates the meaning of the linear correlation coefficient. If there were no correlation, our best estimate of Y, given any value of X, would probably be the mean of Y, or $\overline{Y}$. If X and Y were perfectly correlated, we would expect all values to lie on the regression line. Then, for any given value of X, we

[2] The more accurate expression of the prediction interval is $Y_c \pm tS_{\text{IND}}$, where

$$S_{\text{IND}} = S_{Y \cdot X} \sqrt{1 + \frac{1}{n} + \frac{(X - \overline{X})^2}{\Sigma(X - \overline{X})^2}} \qquad (7\text{-}19)$$

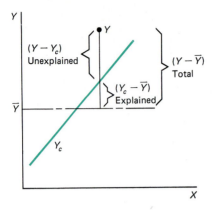

FIGURE 7-13   Deviation of Dependent Variable

could simply proceed up to the regression curve and over to the Y axis to read off the forecast value of Y.

The regression line thus justifies or explains why some value other than $\overline{Y}$ (the mean of Y) is to be expected when X takes on a specific value. The correlation coefficient is related to the percentage of the variation in Y that is explained by the regression line. Figure 7-13, which depicts only one of many possible points, relates the point of $\overline{Y}$ in terms of its deviation, or variation (that is, the summation of squared deviations):

$$\text{Total variation} = \text{explained} + \text{unexplained}$$

$$\Sigma(Y - \overline{Y})^2 = \Sigma(Y_c - \overline{Y})^2 + \Sigma(Y - Y_c)^2$$

The ratio of explained to total variation is called the *coefficient of determination*, r^2. It is effectively the percentage of variation in the dependent variable that is explained by the regression line.

Coefficient of determination:

$$r^2 = \frac{\Sigma(Y_c - \overline{Y})^2}{\Sigma(Y - \overline{Y})^2} \tag{7-20}$$

The square root of the coefficient of determination is the coefficient of correlation, r:

Coefficient of correlation:

$$r = \sqrt{\frac{\Sigma(Y_c - \overline{Y})^2}{\Sigma(Y - \overline{Y})^2}} \tag{7-21}$$

Because the explained variation as a percentage of the total is equal to total minus unexplained variation, the correlation coefficient is sometimes more conveniently written in the form

$$r = \sqrt{1 - \frac{\text{unexplained variation}}{\text{total variation}}} = \sqrt{1 - \frac{\Sigma(Y - Y_c)^2}{\Sigma(Y - \overline{Y})^2}} \qquad (7\text{-}22)$$

When the sample size is sufficiently large (for example, > 50), the value of r can also be computed more directly by the working equation:

$$r = \frac{n\Sigma XY - \Sigma X \Sigma Y}{\sqrt{[n\Sigma X^2 - (\Sigma X)^2][n\Sigma Y^2 - (\Sigma Y)^2]}} \qquad (7\text{-}23)$$

so there are a number of ways of arriving at the same value. Fortunately, most of these "arrivals" are normally accomplished on the firm's computer, for the equations are tedious.

When all points lie on the regression line, the unexplained variation is zero, and r takes on a value of 1. As the points deviate more and more, r gets closer to zero, and the regression equation is less useful as an explanatory model.[3]

EXAMPLE 7-9

A study to determine the correlation between plasterboard shipments, X, and construction permits, Y, revealed the following:

$$\Sigma X = 184 \qquad \Sigma X^2 = 5{,}006 \qquad \Sigma XY = 2{,}146$$

$$\Sigma Y = 80 \qquad \Sigma Y^2 = 950 \qquad n = 8$$

Compute the correlation coefficient.

SOLUTION

$$r = \frac{n\Sigma XY - \Sigma X \Sigma Y}{\sqrt{[n\Sigma X^2 - (\Sigma X)^2][n\Sigma Y^2 - (\Sigma Y)^2]}}$$

$$= \frac{8(2{,}146) - (184)(80)}{\sqrt{[8(5{,}006) - (184)^2][8(950) - (80)^2]}}$$

$$= \frac{2{,}448}{\sqrt{7{,}430{,}400}}$$

$$= .90$$

[3] The significance of any value of r can, however, be tested under a hypothesis that there is no correlation, that is, $H_0: r = 0$. The computed value of r is compared with a tabled value of r for a given sample size and significance level. If the computed value exceeds the tabled value, the hypothesis is rejected, and the correlation is deemed significant at the specified level. Critical values of r for 5 percent and 1 percent levels of significance are given in most standard statistics texts.

> *Optional* The .90 appears to be a significant correlation but could be tested using a significance test, or values from a statistical table of correlation coefficients. See [2]. (For a sample size of $n = 8$ at the 5 percent level, the tabled value of r is only .707. Since the calculated r of .90 is greater than .707, we could conclude that such high correlation would have occurred by chance less than 5 percent of the time.)

The correlation coefficient may be very useful in confirming the closeness of the relationship of two or more variables used in forecasting demand, inventory requirements, accident rates, and so forth. Many firms have identified so-called leading economic indicators, such as freight car loadings or machine-tool orders, that tend to precede and are highly correlated with their own business. Government statistics such as those covering the gross national product, disposable income, industrial production indexes, housing starts, and the like are available in regular publications such as *Survey of Current Business*, *Federal Reserve Bulletin*, and *Monthly Labor Review*.

APPLICATION AND CONTROL OF FORECASTS

Now that we have examined some forecasting methods, we will conclude the chapter with some observations about their applicability. At the beginning of the chapter, we noted the tradeoff between the costs and benefits of forecasting. No methods are totally accurate. Low-accuracy methods use little or readily available data, usually at a lower cost. Higher-accuracy methods require more effort/data and cost more to design and implement.

Each firm must assess its own accuracy-cost tradeoff. Often a simple, low-cost method seems to suffice.

SELECTION OF THE METHOD

We noted earlier that forecasting decisions were a function of (1) purpose and type, (2) time horizon, and (3) database. Let us now return to these determinants (but in reverse order).

Database *Qualitative data* in the form of experience, judgments, and insights about special events (for example, a recession) typically find their way into the judgmental, market survey, and Delphi approaches, which attempt to use the data in a logical way. *Quantitative data* permit the use of historical statistics and more analytical methods such as time series, regression, and econometric methods.

Time Horizon *Long-term forecasts*, which are used for location, capacity, and new-product decisions, require techniques with long-term horizons, such as Delphi, historical analogy, and econometric methods. *Short-term forecasts* are used in such areas as inventory and production control, labor levels, and cost control.

Introduction
- Data: No data available: rely on qualitative methods.
- Time: Need long horizon.
- Methods: Judgment, Delphi, and historical analogy were useful. Market surveys important.

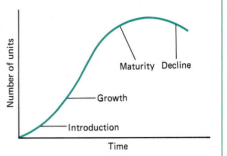

Growth
- Data: Some data available for analysis.
- Time: Still need long horizon; trends and cause-effect relationships important.
- Methods: Market surveys and historical comparison still useful. Regression and computer simulation models justified. Tracking product history now important.

Maturity
- Data: Considerable data available on demand, inventory levels, etc.
- Time: More uses of short-term forecasts; still need long-term projections, but trends change only gradually.
- Methods: Statistical and quantitative methods more useful. Time series help for trend, seasonal. Regression and correlation use associations and leading indicators. Exponential smoothing very useful. Econometric methods feasible.

Decline
- Data: Abundant data (but not necessarily on decline).
- Time: Shorter horizon.
- Methods: Continue use of maturity methods as applicable. Judgment, historical analogies, and market surveys may signal changes.

FIGURE 7-14   Life Cycle Effects upon Forecasting Methodology

Trends don't change much in the short run, so techniques that reflect recent history, such as time series and exponential smoothing, can be used.

Purpose and Type   The type of product (for example, good or service), its value (for example, high or low), its volume (for example, many TV sets or a few airplanes), and its life cycle (stage of maturity) also influence the forecasting technique. Figure 7-14 relates some life cycle effects.

LIFE CYCLE EFFECTS IN SERVICES

Changes in the demand for manufactured goods stem from deeper (or lesser) penetration of existing markets, expansion to new market areas, product innovations (or failure to innovate), and a number of other factors. The need for coordination of forecasting efforts among production, marketing, and distribution activities is thus obvious. But the difficulties of forecasting growth and decline effects in services can be even more severe than for goods [4].

As noted earlier, services involve the participation of customers in a social process—and that process is not as precisely specified nor as easily controlled as a manufacturing process. Thus the growth patterns in many service industries are less predictable than patterns in goods-producing industries. Although services *can* expand to large dominating giants, consumers object to being "monopolized." The trend is toward smaller, customized self-help services. Many service businesses, such as nursing care and fast food restaurants, have found that service economies of scale do not necessarily result from larger facilities but instead lie in the informational, policy, and managerial expertise. In the words of Richard Norman, "small is beautiful on a large scale" [4:85].

In service industries, growth frequently depends upon innovation and productivity improvement in the *service delivery system*. In this respect, factors in addition to technology, such as social trends and consumer lifestyles can significantly affect demand. A key factor in most services is, of course, the effectiveness of the (customer) communication and internal information systems.

FORECAST CONTROLS

No firm should forget about the forecast once it is completed; otherwise, a major benefit of forecasting is lost. A forecast is a plan of future activities. If activities don't conform to the plan, it is important to find out why and take corrective action if necessary.

In this section we will discuss controls for the time series, exponential smoothing, and associative forecasts. Figure 7-15 illustrates the concept underlying most forecast control. Limits are established around the forecast value, and data are collected to track the individual or cumulative error between the actual value and the forecast value. Both simple arithmetic totals and statistical measures of variation are used to describe and control forecast error.

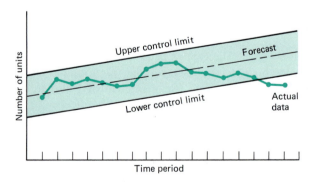

FIGURE 7-15   Control Limits for Forecasts

Controls for Simple Averages   The time series and simple averages methods of forecasting basically track the one variable of interest (that is, these methods are univariate in nature). A simple measure of forecast error is to compute the deviation of the actual from the forecast values for that variable. The deviations will vary from plus to minus, but they should tend to average out near zero if the forecast is on target.

A number of ways of establishing control limits about the forecast values have also been developed. Some of these are based on the range of difference and others on the standard deviation of values. Variations of actual values from the mean or average values can be quantified in terms of the standard deviation of forecast errors, S_F:

$$S_F = \sqrt{\frac{\Sigma \ (\text{actual} \ - \ \text{forecast})^2}{n \ - \ 1}} = \sqrt{\frac{\Sigma \ (X \ - \ \overline{X})^2}{n \ - \ 1}}$$

where X is the actual individual demand value, $\overline{X}$ is the average or forecast demand value, and n is the number of periods in the average.

Much variation tends to be normally distributed about the mean, and if this is a reasonably valid assumption, we might expect about 95.5 percent of the actual demand values to be within two standard deviations of the average value and 99.7 percent within three. When demand values occur outside these limits, they may be indicative of an unusual event or a substantial change (or possibly an invalid model) and should be investigated. If the limits are based upon data from a sample of less than 30, the t rather than normal Z distribution applies. Values for the area under the t distribution are available in most statistical reference texts.

Controls for Exponential Smoothing Forecasts   Several control systems have been developed for exponentially smoothed forecasts. Some of the most straight-forward and widely used systems make use of the same control concepts as used in other moving-average forecasts. Often, however, the forecast error is measured in terms of the mean absolute deviation (MAD) rather than standard deviation. MAD measures the average deviation of an actual from a forecast value, but it is easier to calculate than a standard deviation. It is related to the standard deviation by the approximation:

$$\sigma \cong 1.25 \ \text{MAD} \tag{7-24}$$

When the average deviation is divided into the cumulative deviation, the resultant is a "tracking signal."

$$\text{Tracking signal} = \frac{\text{cumulative deviation}}{\text{MAD}} \tag{7-25}$$

The tracking signal tells how well the forecast is predicting actual values, for it yields a measurement of the consistent difference between actual and forecast values by expressing the cumulative deviation in terms of number of average deviations. If the cumulative deviation is, say, 1,500 units, whereas the average MAD is 200 units, then the tracking signal for the period is 1,500 divided by 200 = 7.5. Suppose next period's tracking signal is 7.6, then perhaps 7.8 in the following period. This would indicate that demand was consistently greater than the forecast. Similarly, a negative tracking signal would be indicative of demand that tended to be less than the forecast. A good forecast should have about as much positive (over) as negative (under) deviation, which would result in a low cumulative deviation, or running sum of forecast error (RSFE).

Firms often set action limits for tracking signals so that when the tracking signal exceeds the limit, the situation will automatically be reviewed to determine if the forecast should be raised or lowered. If an action limit were set very low, it would require too much review for items that were being satisfactorily forecast. A signal set too high would not provide timely response and would limit the usefulness of the forecasting system in managing inventories. Acceptable maxima for tracking signal values are from 4 to 8 (Plossl and Wight suggest 4 for high-value items and up to 8 for low-value items) [5:107]. When the signal goes beyond this range, investigation and corrective action are called for.

The exponential smoothing technique also provides a means of continually updating the analyst's estimate of MAD. Thus, the current MAD_t is:

$$MAD_t = \alpha|\text{actual} - \text{forecast}| + (1 - \alpha) MAD_{t-1}$$

where α is a smoothing constant, and higher values of α will make the current MAD_t more responsive to current forecast errors.

Self-Adaptive Models

Considerable work has been done on computer models which are self-adjusting in response to changes in forecast accuracy. In adaptive models, the smoothing coefficients (α's and β's) become variables that are evolved or adjusted in an adaptive fashion. The models select a smoothing coefficient, use it on past (or simulated) data, and compute the forecast error. Then they do the same for other coefficients, or combinations. The objective is to derive adjusted coefficients in a fast, economical manner so as to minimize the error in the variable being forecast. Numerous models have been tested (for example, Trigg and Leach, Wybark, Winters, Chow), but no one has yet proved optimal for all demand patterns [1,7].

Controls for Associative Forecasts

The standard deviation of regression ($S_{Y.X}$) is the statistical measure of variation about the regression line and can be used as a means of control for forecasting methods involving two variables. In a manner similar to that used to establish reasonable limits for variation in demand about univariate averages, the probable limits for variation about the regression line can also be determined. Thus, we would expect 99.7 percent of the individual demand values to be within the control limits $Y_c \pm 3S_{Y.X}$ if the values are normally distributed about the regression line. When values fall outside these limits, we assume the system is out of control, investigate, and take appropriate action.

SUMMARY

Forecasts are estimates of the occurrence of uncertain future events or levels of activity. They help to improve the management of labor, materials, capital, and customer service.

Forecasting decisions are influenced by environmental and technological conditions and by consumer demand. Demand forecasts are used to plan marketing, financial, production, and other activities. The purpose, length of forecast, and database available all influence the methodology used.

Opinion and judgment methods are largely based on experience but often include the analysis of field sales data. *Time series* methods chart the action of a variable (usually demand) under the assumption that trend or seasonal patterns are a predictable function of time.

Exponential smoothing is a moving-average method of exponential weighting which allows recent data to exert a stronger influence in the forecast. Simple exponential smoothing makes use of a smoothing constant (α), which essentially dictates how much weight should be given to the past versus the current demand; a small α value yields a strong smoothing effect. Adjusted exponential smoothing adds a trend correction factor. Exponential smoothing requires relatively little computer storage space and is widely used for inventory management.

Regression and correlation methods rely upon the relationship of associated variables to make forecasts. A mathematical relationship is established via the normal equations or the coefficient of correlation. Then the action of an independent variable (in the case of regression) or an associated variable (in the case of correlation) serves as a basis for prediction. Interval estimates can be made to add more precision to the forecasts of mean and individual values.

Every forecasting system should have a means of tracking and controlling the forecast error. Common measures of variability are the standard deviation for univariate methods (for example, time series) and the standard deviation of regression for bivariate methods. Many firms using exponential smoothing calculate their tracking signals based upon mean average deviations (MADs) of actual from forecast values. When any variability or tracking signals exceed specified limits, investigative and corrective action should be taken.

SOLVED PROBLEMS

TIME SERIES ANALYSIS

1 A food processor uses a moving average to forecast next month's demand. Past actual demand (in units) is as shown in the accompanying table.
   (a) Compute a simple 5-month moving average to forecast demand for month 52.
   (b) Compute a weighted 3-month moving average where the weights are highest for the latest months and descend in order of 3, 2, 1.

Solution

(a) $MA = \dfrac{\Sigma X}{\text{number of periods}}$

$= \dfrac{114 + 121 + 130 + 128 + 137}{5}$

$= 126$ units

(b) $MA_{wt} = \dfrac{\Sigma\,(wt)(X)}{\Sigma\,wt}$

where $wt \times value = total$

$$
\begin{array}{rcrcr}
3 & \times & 137 & = & 411 \\
2 & \times & 128 & = & 256 \\
\underline{1} & \times & 130 & = & \underline{130} \\
6 & & & & 797
\end{array}
$$

$\therefore MA_{wt} = \dfrac{797}{6} = 133$ units

Month	Actual Demand
43	105
44	106
45	110
46	110
47	114
48	121
49	130
50	128
51	137
52	

2 The following forecasting equation has been derived by a least-squares method to describe the shipments of welded aluminum tube.

$$Y_c = 10.27 + 1.65X \qquad (1986 = 0,\ X = \text{years},\ Y = \text{tons/yr})$$

Rewrite the equation:
(a) Shifting the origin to 1991
(b) Expressing X units in months, retaining Y in tons/yr
(c) Expressing X units in months, and Y in tons/month

Solution

(a) $Y_c = 10.27 + 1.65(X + 5)$

$= 18.52 + 1.65X \qquad (1991 = 0,\ X = \text{years},\ Y = \text{tons/yr})$

(b) $Y_c = 10.27 + \dfrac{1.65X}{12}$

$= 10.27 + .14X \qquad (\text{July 1, 1986} = 0,\ X = \text{months},\ Y = \text{tons/yr})$

(c) $Y_c = \dfrac{10.27 + .14X}{12}$

$= .86 + .01X \qquad (\text{July 1, 1986} = 0,\ X = \text{months},\ Y = \text{tons/mo})$

EXPONENTIAL SMOOTHING

3 Lakeside Hospital has used a 9-month moving-average forecasting method to predict drug and surgical dressing inventory requirements. The actual demand for one item is as shown in the accompanying table. Using the previous moving-average data, convert to an exponential smoothing forecast for month 33.

Month	24	25	26	27	28	29	30	31	32
Demand	78	65	90	71	80	101	84	60	73

Solution

$$\text{MA} = \frac{\Sigma X}{\text{no. periods}} = \frac{78 + 65 + \cdots + 73}{9} = 78$$

∴ Assume $F_{t-1} = 78$.

$$\text{Estimate } \alpha = \frac{2}{n+1} = \frac{2}{9+1} = .2$$

$$F_t = F_{t-1} + \alpha(D_{t-1} - F_{t-1})$$

$$= 78 + .2(73 - 78)$$

$$= 77 \text{ units}$$

4   A shoe manufacturer, using exponential smoothing with $\alpha = .1$, has developed a January trend forecast of 400 units of a ladies' shoe. This brand has seasonal indexes of .80, .90, and 1.20, respectively, for the first three months of the year. Assuming actual sales were 344 units in January and 414 units in February, what would be the seasonalized (adjusted) March forecast?

Solution

(a) Deseasonalize actual January demand.

$$\text{Demand } D = \frac{344}{.80} = 430 \text{ units}$$

(b) Compute the deseasonalized forecast.

$$F_t = F_{t-1} + \alpha\,(D_{t-1} - F_{t-1})$$

$$= 400 + .1(430 - 400) = 403$$

(c) Seasonalized (adjusted) February forecast would be

$$F_{t(sz)} = 403(.90) = 363$$

Repeating for February, we have:

(a) Demand $D = \dfrac{414}{.90} = 460$ units

(b) $F_t = 403 + .1(460 - 403) = 409$

(c) $F_{t(sz)} = 409(1.20) = 491$

REGRESSION AND CORRELATION

5 Given the following:

$$\Sigma X = 80 \qquad \Sigma Y = 1{,}200 \qquad n = 20 \qquad \Sigma(Y - Y_c)^2 = 800$$
$$\Sigma X^2 = 340 \qquad \Sigma Y^2 = 74{,}800 \qquad \Sigma XY = 5{,}000 \qquad \Sigma(Y - \overline{Y})^2 = 2{,}800$$

(a) Find the linear regression equation.
(b) Find $S_{Y.X}$.
(c) Find r.

Solution

(a) $\Sigma Y = na \quad + b\Sigma X \rightarrow 1{,}200 = 20a + 80b$
   $\quad \Sigma XY = a\Sigma X + b\Sigma X^2 \rightarrow 5{,}000 = 80a + 340b$
   $\quad \therefore b = 10, \quad a = 20$
   $\quad Y_c = 20 + 10X$

(b) $S_{Y.X} = \sqrt{\dfrac{\Sigma(Y - Y_c)^2}{n - 2}} = \sqrt{\dfrac{800}{20 - 2}} = \sqrt{44.4} = 6.67$

(c) $r = \sqrt{1 - \dfrac{\Sigma(Y - Y_c)^2}{\Sigma(Y - \overline{Y})^2}} = \sqrt{1 - \dfrac{800}{2{,}800}} = \sqrt{.71} = .85$

APPLICATION AND CONTROL OF FORECASTS

6 Use the Lakeside Hospital data of Solved Prob. 3 to compute:
(a) A 3-month moving average (MA)
(b) The 90 percent control limits that could be expected for individual demand values (assuming a normal distribution)

Solution

(a) See the accompanying table.

Month	Actual Demand	3-Month MA	Forecast Demand	Deviation	(Deviation)²
24	78				
25	65	77.7			
26	90	75.3			
27	71	80.3	78	−7	49
28	80	84.0	75	5	25
29	101	88.3	80	21	441
30	84	81.7	84	0	0
31	60	72.3	88	−28	784
32	73		82	−9	81
					1,380

(b) $S_F = \sqrt{\dfrac{\Sigma(\text{actual} - \text{forecast})^2}{n - 1}} = \sqrt{\dfrac{1{,}380}{6 - 1}} = 16.6$

Because $n < 30$, we must use the t distribution rather than the Z for the control limits. Referring to any standard statistics text, we find that for $n - 1 = 5$ degrees of freedom at the 90 percent level, $t = 2.015$. The mean forecast value is:

$$\overline{X} = \frac{78 + 75 + 80 + 84 + 88 + 82}{6} = 81.2$$

$$\therefore \text{Control limits} = \overline{X} \pm tS_F$$

$$= 81.2 \pm 2.015(16.6)$$

$$= 47.8 \text{ to } 114.6$$

Note that the control limits explicitly recognize the variability in this data and, in turn, the uncertainty associated with trying to forecast it. A larger sample would yield tighter limits.

7 The moving-average forecast and actual demand for a hospital drug are as shown in the accompanying table. Compute the tracking signal, and comment on the forecast accuracy.

Month	Actual Demand	Forecast Demand	Deviation	Cumulative Deviation
27	71	78	−7	−7
28	80	75	5	−2
29	101	83	18	16
30	84	84	0	16
31	60	88	−28	−12
32	73	85	−12	−24

Solution

The deviation and cumulative deviation have already been computed above:

$$\therefore \text{MAD} = \frac{\Sigma|\text{actual} - \text{forecast}|}{n}$$

$$= \frac{7 + 5 + 18 + 0 + 28 + 12}{6}$$

$$= 11.7$$

$$\text{Tracking signal} = \frac{\text{cumulative deviation}}{\text{MAD}} = \frac{-24}{11.7} = -2.05 = |2.05|$$

The demand exhibits substantial variation, but a tracking signal as low as 2.05 (that is, $\leqslant 4$) would not suggest any action at this time.

QUESTIONS

7-1 Why are forecasts important to organizations?

7-2 Briefly summarize (in one or two sentences for each) the *essence* of the following forecasting methodologies: (a) judgmental, (b) time series, (c) exponential smoothing, and (d) regression and correlation.

7-3 What determines whether a forecast should be short-range or long-range?

7-4 The manager of a local firm says, "The forecasting techniques are more trouble than they are worth. I don't forecast at all, and I'm doing 20 percent more business than last year." Comment.

7-5 How do forecasting techniques predict the value of random fluctuations in demand? What effect do moving averages have on short-term fluctuations?

7-6 What do you see as the main problem with judgmental forecasts? Are they ever any better than "objective" methods?

7-7 Identify the classical components of a time series, and indicate how each is accounted for in forecasting.

7-8 A firm uses exponential smoothing with a very high value of α. What does this indicate with respect to the emphasis it places on past data?

7-9 Regression and correlation are both termed *associative* methods of forecasting. Explain how they are similar in this respect and also how they are different.

7-10 Explain what is meant by tracking a forecast. How does tracking relate to the concept of forecast reliability?

PROBLEMS

TIME SERIES ANALYSIS

1 A computer manufacturer has estimated the following number of high school students (in millions) were enrolled in computer-related courses during the years shown:

Year	1977	1978	1979	1980	1981	1982	1983	1984	1985	1986	1987
No. Students	.77	.82	.90	.90	.98	1.01	1.26	1.40	1.42	1.50	1.62

(a) If you were plotting a moving average, what 3-year moving-average values would correspond to the years 1979, 1980, and 1981?

(b) What would be the 5-year moving-average forecast for the next year in the future?

2 Use a weighted moving average to forecast the number of students enrolled in computer-related courses (Prob. 1) if the latest year is weighted 40 percent and each prior year's weight is reduced another 10 percent.

3 A Florida citrus processing cooperative is committed to accepting fruit from local producers and has experienced the following supply pattern (in thousands of tons per year and rounded).

Year	Tons	Year	Tons
1978	400	1983	600
1979	100	1984	400
1980	100	1985	400
1981	300	1986	800
1982	800	1987	800

The operations manager would like to project a trend to determine what facility additions will be required by 1992.

(a) Graph the data, and connect the points by straight-line segments.
(b) Sketch in a freehand curve, and extend it to 1992. What would be your 1992 forecast on the basis of the curve?
(c) Compute a 3-year moving average, and plot it as a dotted line on your graph.

4 Select a firm of your choice from the New York Stock Exchange, and locate an annual report which includes 9 years (or a minimum of 5 years) of sales or earnings per share.

(a) Graph the data.
(b) Using the normal equations, develop a least-squares forecasting equation, and state it, complete with signature.
(c) Use the equation to forecast a trend value 5 years into the future.
(d) Do you feel your linear equation satisfactorily represents your data? Discuss.

5 Use the data of Prob. 3 and the normal equations to develop a least-squares line of best fit. Omit the year 1978.

(a) State the equation, complete with signature, when the origin is 1983.
(b) Use your equation to estimate the trend value for 1992.

6 A trend equation describing plastic-pipe shipments was found to be:

$$Y_c = 42.8 + 3.2X \qquad (1986 = 0, \ X = \text{years}, \ Y = \text{tons})$$

Convert the equation to a 1989 = 0 base.

7 A forecasting equation is of the form:

$$Y_c = 720 + 144X \qquad (1988 = 0, \ X \text{ unit} = 1 \text{ yr}, \ Y = \text{annual sales})$$

(a) Forecast the annual sales rate for 1988 and also for 1 year later.
(b) Change the time (X) scale to months, and forecast the annual sales rate at July 1, 1988, and also at 1 year later.
(c) Change the sales (Y) scale to monthly, and forecast the monthly sales rate at July 1, 1988, and also at 1 year later.

8 An analysis of past data on the use of capacitors in an assembly operation revealed the following time series equation.

$$Y_c = 144 + 72X \qquad \left(\begin{array}{l} \text{Origin} = 1989, \quad X \text{ unit} = 1 \text{ yr} \\ Y = \text{annual consumption} \end{array} \right)$$

(a) On what day is the equation now centered?
(b) State the equation that would correspond to a signature:

(Origin = July 1, 1989; X unit = 1 month, Y = monthly consumption)

(c) Modify the equation as required, and use it to forecast the *annual* consumption rate (Y = annual consumption) during September 1989.

✗ 9 Data collected on the monthly demand for a housewares item were as shown in the accompanying table.

Month	Demand	Month	Demand
January	100	June	320
February	90	July	300
March	80	August	280
April	150	September	220
May	240		

(a) Plot the data as a 1-month moving average.
(b) Plot a 5-month moving average as a dotted line.
(c) What conclusion can you draw with respect to length of moving average versus smoothing effect?
(d) Assume the 12-month moving average centered on July was 250. What is the value of the ratio to moving average that would be used in computing a seasonal index?

10 An equation was developed to forecast demand for health care service as follows.

$$Y_c = 500 + 10X \qquad (1981 = 0, \ X = \text{years}, \ Y = \text{no. of patients annually})$$

The demand is seasonal, and the indexes for October, November, and December are .80, .90, and 1.10, respectively.
(a) Forecast the annual demand for 1991.
(b) Convert the X unit to months and the Y unit to monthly demand, and state the new equation complete with signature. (If necessary, shift the origin so that it is in mid-July 1981).
(c) Forecast the trend value for November 1989.
(d) Forecast the seasonalized (adjusted) value for November 1989.

11 The data shown in the accompanying table include the number of lost-time accidents for the Cascade Lumber Company over the past 7 years. (*Note*: The number of employees is shown for reference only. You will not need it to solve this problem.)
(a) Use the normal equations to develop a linear time series equation for forecasting the number of accidents. State the equation complete with signature.
(b) Use your equation to forecast the number of accidents in 1993.

Year	Number (000) of employees	Number of accidents
1981	15	5
1982	12	20
1983	20	15
1984	26	18
1985	35	17
1986	30	30
1987	37	35
		140

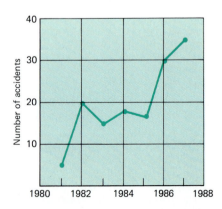

EXPONENTIAL SMOOTHING

12 The production supervisor at a fiberboard plant uses a simple exponential smoothing technique (α = .2) to forecast demand. In April, the forecast was for 20 shipments, and the actual demand was for 20 shipments. The actual demand in May and June was 25 and 26 shipments, respectively. Forecast the value for July.

13 A university registrar has adopted a simple exponential smoothing model (α = .4) to forecast enrollments during the three regular terms (excluding summer). The results are shown in the accompanying table.

Year	Quarter	Actual Enrollment (000)	Old Forecast (000)	Forecast Error (000)	Correction (000)	New Forecast (000)
1	1st	20.50	20.00	.5	.20	20.20
	2d	21.00				
	3d	19.12				
2	1st	20.06				
	2d	22.00				
	3d					

(a) Use the data to develop an enrollment forecast for the third quarter of year 2.
(b) What would be the effect of increasing the smoothing constant to 1.0?

X 14 A firm producing photochemicals plans to use simple exponential smoothing to forecast weekly demand and has collected the past data shown. Assume that the first-week forecast was for 20 units.

Week	1	2	3	4	5	6	7	8	9	10	11	12	13	14	15
Demand	30	34	22	16	10	10	14	20	30	36	30	10	12	20	30

(a) Compute the forecast values for α = .1.
(b) Compute the forecast values for α = .5.
(c) Plot the actual demand and forecast demands from (a) and (b).
(d) Comment on the difference in the reaction rate for α = .1 and α = .5. Round each new forecast value to one digit beyond the decimal point.

X 15 A city jail administrator has been using a 12-month moving average to forecast jail cell demand but wishes to convert to a simple exponential smoothing model. The current month's forecast is for 450 inmates.

(a) If the actual demand is 410, what should be the forecast demand for next month?
(b) If the actual demand for the next month is 520, what should be the following month's forecast?

16 A furniture company has developed a seasonal index where each month is expressed as a percentage of total annual sales and March = 8.0 percent, April = 10.0 percent, May = 9.5 percent. The forecast sales are for an average of 500 chairs per month, and the firm uses an alpha of .1. Prepare a seasonalized (adjusted) March forecast, then assume that actual March sales were 420, and develop a seasonalized simple exponential forecast for April.

17 In Example 7-4 assume that the actual demand for the next 3 weeks in the sequence is March 22 = 561, March 29 = 587, April 5 = 615.

(a) Extend the simple exponential forecast to cover these periods.

(b) Using a value of $\beta = .6$, compute the adjusted exponential forecast for the week of April 12th.

18 A governmental agency is using an adjusted exponential smoothing forecasting model with $\alpha = .1$ and a trend smoothing constant of $\beta = .3$. The most recent demand data have resulted in the following computations: trend-adjusted exponential smoothing average $\hat{F}_{t-1} = 500$; smoothed trend adjustment, $T_{t-1} = 120$; and demand, $D_{t-1} = 640$. Compute the trend-adjusted exponential smoothing forecast for the next period, $\hat{F}_{t+1}$.

19 A firm producing photochemicals has a weekly demand pattern as shown in Prob. 14. Using a smoothing constant of $\alpha = .5$ for both original data and trend, and beginning with week 1,

(a) Compute the simple exponentially smoothed forecast.

(b) Compute the trend-adjusted exponentially smoothed forecast for the first five periods.

REGRESSION AND CORRELATION

20 The data shown in the accompanying table include the number of lost-time accidents for the Cascade Lumber Company over the past 7 years. Some additional calculations are included to help you answer the following questions. X = number of employees (in thousands); Y = number of accidents.

Year	X	Y	X^2	Y^2	XY	$(Y - \bar{Y})$	$(Y - \bar{Y})^2$	Y_c	$(Y - Y_c)$	$(Y - Y_c)^2$
1981	15	5	225	25	75	−15	225	13.38	−8.38	70.22
1982	12	20	144	400	240	0	0	11.40	8.60	73.96
1983	20	15	400	225	300	−5	25	16.68	−1.68	2.82
1984	26	18	676	324	468	−2	4	20.64	−2.64	6.97
1985	35	17	1,225	289	595	−3	9	26.58	−9.58	91.78
1986	30	30	900	900	900	10	100	23.28	6.72	45.16
1987	37	35	1,369	1,225	1,295	15	225	27.90	7.10	50.41
	175	140	4,939	3,388	3,873		588			341.32

(a) Use the normal equations to develop a linear regression equation for forecasting the number of accidents on the basis of the number of employees. State the equation.

(b) Use the equation to forecast the number of accidents when the number of employees is 33(000).

21 Given the data of Prob. 20, answer the following questions:

(a) What is the standard deviation of regression?

(b) What percentage of the variation in number of accidents is explained by the employment level?

(c) What is the correlation coefficient between number of employees and number of accidents?

(d) (Optional) Is the correlation significant at the 5 percent level?

22 The two operations managers of a plastics firm have the responsibility of scheduling intermittent production runs of various grades of plastic pipe so as to maintain factory inventories at specified levels. They have formulated their own index (X)—from

published construction and employment data—which they feel may be useful in anticipating demand (tons) of class 160 PVC pipe (Y).

Index (X)	3	6	2	5	4
Demand in Tons (Y)	6	7	4	10	8

(a) Compute the regression equation.
(b) Determine the forecast values (Y_c) for each X and $\Sigma(Y - Y_c)^2$.
(c) Find $S_{Y \cdot X}$.
(d) What percentage of the variation in demand is explained by this index?
(e) Find r.

23 The Carpet Cleaner Company is attempting to do a better job of inventory management by predicting the number of vacuums the company will sell per week on the basis of the number of customers who respond to magazine advertisements in an earlier week. On the basis of a sample of $n = 102$ weeks, the following data were obtained.

$$a = 25 \qquad \Sigma(Y - Y_c)^2 = 22{,}500$$
$$b = .10 \qquad \Sigma(Y - \overline{Y})^2 = 45{,}000$$

(a) Provide a point estimate of the number of vacuums sold per week when 80 inquiries were received in the earlier week.
(b) Calculate the 95.5 percent confidence limits for the *mean* number of vacuums sold per week when 80 inquiries were received earlier. (*Note:* For estimating the *mean* number—rather than an individual prediction—use $S_{Y \cdot X}/\sqrt{n}$ in place of $S_{Y \cdot X}$.)
(c) State the value of the coefficient of determination.
(d) Explain the meaning of your r^2 value.

24 A recreation operations planner has had data collected on automobile traffic at a selected location on an interstate highway in hopes that the information can be used to predict weekday demand for state-operated campsites 200 miles away. Random samples of 32 weekdays during the camping season resulted in data from which the following expression was developed:

$$Y_c = 18 + .02X$$

where X is the number of automobiles passing the location and Y is the number of campsites demanded that day. In addition, the unexplained variation is $\Sigma(Y - Y_c)^2 = 1{,}470$, and the total variation is $\Sigma(Y - \overline{Y})^2 = 4{,}080$.
(a) What is the dependent variable (in words)?
(b) What is the value of the standard deviation of regression, $S_{Y \cdot X}$?
(c) Develop a point estimate of the demand for campsites on a day when 14,100 automobiles pass the selected location.

25 Given the data from the previous problem:
(a) What is the value of the coefficient of determination?
(b) Explain, in words, the meaning of the coefficient of determination.
(c) What is the value of the coefficient of correlation?

26 A management analyst has randomly selected 10 demand regions and determined

population values in order to establish a relationship that will help to predict sales. The resultant linear regression equation is:

$$Y_c = 2.02 + .80X$$

In addition the analyst has determined that the unexplained variation is .76 and that the total variation is 4.00. All population values should be entered into the equation in tens of thousands, and the resulting sales values are in thousands of dollars.
(a) Identify (in words) the dependent and independent variables.
(b) Give a point estimate of demand for a region with a population of 60,000.
(c) Calculate the coefficient of correlation, and explain its meaning.
(d) What relationship, in general, does *any* regression curve describe, and how does regression differ from correlation?

27 Solved Prob. 5 shows the computation of $S_{Y \cdot X}$ and r via the "definitional" type of equations. Use the data given to compute (a) $S_{Y \cdot X}$ and (b) r, using alternate methods.

CONTROL OF FORECASTS

✗ 28 Two "experienced" managers have resisted the introduction of a computerized exponential smoothing system, claiming that their judgmental forecasts are "much better than any impersonal computer could do." Their past record of prediction is as shown in the accompanying table.

Week	Actual Demand	Forecast Demand
1	4,000	4,500
2	4,200	5,000
3	4,200	4,000
4	3,000	3,800
5	3,800	3,600
6	5,000	4,000
7	5,600	5,000
8	4,400	4,800
9	5,000	4,000
10	4,800	5,000

(a) Compute S_F.
(b) Compute 95.5 percent control limits for the forecast, assuming that the forecast errors are normally distributed.
    (*Hint*: Since $n < 30$, the t rather than the normal distribution applies. When $n = 10$, for 95.5 percent limits, $t = 2.26$.)

✗ 29 Using the data from Prob. 28,
(a) Compute the MAD.
(b) Compute the tracking signal.
(c) On the basis of your calculations, is the judgmental system performing satisfactorily?

30 Use the data of Example 7-4 to compute the mean absolute deviation (MAD) of the difference between actual demand D and forecast F for (a) $\alpha = .05$, (b) $\alpha = .1$, and (c) $\alpha = .3$.

REFERENCES

[1] Dancer, R., and C. Gray: "An Empirical Evaluation of Constant and Adaptive Computer Forecasting Models for Inventory Control," *Decision Sciences*, vol. 8, no. 1, January 1977, pp. 228–238.

[2] Groebner, David F., and Patrick W. Shannon: *Business Statistics*, 2d ed., Charles E. Merrill, Columbus, OH, 1985.

[3] Makridakis, S., and S. C. Wheelwright: *Forecasting Methods and Applications*, Wiley, New York, 1978.

[4] Norman, Richard: *Service Management*, Wiley, Chichester, 1984.

[5] Plossl, G. W., and O. W. Wight: *Production and Inventory Control*, Prentice-Hall, Englewood Cliffs, NJ, 1967.

[6] Rice, Gillian, et al.: "A Directory of 132 Packages for Forecasting and Planning," *Journal of Business Forecasting*, Spring 1984, pp. 11–23.

[7] Whybark, D. Clay: "A Comparison of Adaptive Forecasting Techniques," *The Logistics Transportation Review*, vol. 8, no. 3, January 1973, pp. 13–26.

[8] Wight, Oliver W.: *Production and Inventory Management in the Computer Age*, Cahners Books, Boston, 1974.

SELF QUIZ: CHAPTER 7

Part I True/False [1 point each = 6]

1 _____ Forecasts are usually formulated by basing projections on the random components of a data set.
2 _____ The time horizon to forecast depends upon where the product currently lies in its life cycle.
3 _____ Opinion and judgmental forecasting methods sometimes incorporate statistical analysis.
4 _____ The most common method of calculating a 12-period moving average is by the "method of least squares."
5 _____ In exponential smoothing, low values of alpha result in more smoothing than higher values of alpha.
6 _____ A tracking signal action limit that is set too low would tend to overlook some forecast errors that should probably be investigated.

Part II Problems [3 points each = 9. Calculate and select your answer.]

1 Bellevue Software Company experienced the demand pattern shown. (Additional information also given.) Derive a least-squares linear forecasting equation and use it to forecast the sales (millions of dollars) for the year 1992.
(a) $15
(b) $19
(c) $23
(d) $45
(e) None of the above.

Year	Coded X	Sales ($ millions)		
1981	3	−9	9	
1982	4	−8	4	
1983	3	−3	1	
1984	4	0	0	
1985	9	9	1	
1986	11	22	4	
1987	15	45	9	
Total	49	56	28	

2 A regression analysis of the tons of ore shipped from a mine (Y) and the number of employees (X) revealed that:

$$\Sigma(Y - Y_c)^2 = 460,000 \quad \text{and} \quad \Sigma(Y_c - Y)^2 = 2,760,000$$

Using this data, what percentage of variation in ore output is associated with the number of employees?
(a) 3%
(b) 17%
(c) 86%
(d) 93%
(e) None of the above.

3 Below are the actual demand and exponential smoothing forecast for a new product $(\alpha = .2)$. Complete the July and August forecast amounts. What tracking signal value results from using the 6 months of data?
(a) 3.0
(b) 4.4
(c) 6.0
(d) 7.8
(e) None of the above.

Month	March	April	May	June	July	August
Forecast	110	86	90	100		
Actual	80	100	140	110	132	103

CHAPTER 8
AGGREGATE PLANNING AND MASTER SCHEDULING

INTRODUCTION: PLANNING AND SCHEDULING

When General Motors embarked on a highly touted joint venture with Toyota Motor Company to produce Novas in California, they expected the Nova to become the "flagship" of their small-car strategy. GM already had a plant with capacity to build about 20,800 Novas per month. Nevertheless, they planned for higher production in hopes of winning back some import buyers [4].

Unfortunately, early demand for the new cars failed to live up to expectations, and inventories were soon over 160 percent of normal levels. Some potential customers apparently preferred an "all Japanese" Toyota Corolla (at $7,148) to a General Motors/Toyota hybrid (at $7,435). With lower sales, production planners had to reassess their aggregate production plan and adjust their labor hours (and material purchases) accordingly.

Aggregate planning is the process of planning the quantity and timing of output over the intermediate time horizon (often 3 months to 1 year). Within that time frame, the maximum capacity of a production facility is relatively fixed. Given a forecast, planners are concerned with making the best possible use of the organization's labor, materials, and capital resources to respond to expected demand—which might be either higher or lower than expected.

Of course, demand cannot always be met. And options may exist to modify demand (such as by advertising, dealer incentives, or pricing strategies). But our main focus here will be on responding to irregular market demands by managing the controllable variables that affect supply, such as employment and inventory levels.

Figure 8-1 illustrates how aggregate planning links long-range and short-range planning activities. We use the term "aggregate" because the production plans at this stage are expressed in homogeneous units of output, such as number of automobiles or tons of steel.

Master scheduling follows aggregate planning and expresses the overall plan in terms of specific end items or models that can be assigned priorities. It is the major control over production activities.

Figure 8-2 illustrates a simplified aggregate plan and master schedule. Notice that whereas the aggregate plan simply expressses the end product as "motors," the master schedule specifies precisely how many of which type (or size) of motors will be produced, and when. This detail is necessary to plan for the material and capacity requirements.

This chapter defines the objectives of aggregate planning and identifies some of the more useful planning methods. Although a number of sophisticated planning models have been developed, studies suggest that none of them is widely used in industry [9]. Yet planning must be done. Our emphasis will be on identifying and analyzing the benefits and costs of the basic strategies.

In the second part of the chapter we discuss the objectives and methods of master scheduling. When you complete the chapter, you should understand the aggregate planning and master scheduling process. That will provide a good

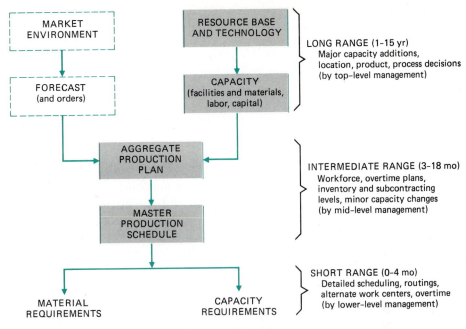

FIGURE 8-1   Flowchart of Aggregate Plan and Master Schedule

FIGURE 8-2   Aggregate Plan and Master Schedule

Aggregate Plan									
Month	J	F	M	A	M	J	J	A	S
Number of Motors	40	25	50	30	30	50	30	40	40

Master Schedule									
Month	J	F	M	A	M	J	J	A	S
AC motors:									
5 hp	15	—	30	—	—	30	—	—	10
25 hp	20	25	20	15	15	15	20	20	20
DC motors:									
20 hp	—	—	—	—	—	—	10	10	—
WR motors:									
10 hp	5	—	—	15	15	5	—	10	10

foundation for moving on to inventory management and to material and capacity requirements planning in the chapters that follow.

OBJECTIVES OF AGGREGATE PLANNING

In this section, we examine the aggregate planning problem, the variables subject to control, and the costs associated with various strategies.

THE AGGREGATE PLANNING PROBLEM

Good forecasts are helpful in planning future levels of production. But they still contain uncertainties. Trends and seasonal patterns change, and random variations are ever-present.

Planners must balance the demands against capacity to determine the extent to which the peaks and valleys of customer demand can be accommodated. Changing the volume of a production operation is not as simple as adjusting the rate of flow from a water faucet. Each production system is an intricate and interdependent mix of labor, materials, and equipment. When the rate of output is changed, the previous balance is lost, and the usage rate of the resources must be readjusted. If some equipment or human resources are idled (or overworked), new costs arise. And the guidelines are not always clear. Some firms recognize a moral (or perhaps even contractual) obligation to provide a secure and stable employment for their employees, whereas others do not.

Aggregate planning is one of the most integrative responsibilities of P&IC personnel. It requires an understanding of the organization's values and accurate information on productivity and inventories, plus an ability to formulate and evaluate the costs and benefits of alternative production plans. And its impact is significant. Aggregate planning decisions send repercussions throughout the firm—to personnel, finance, marketing, and other areas.

VARIABLES SUBJECT TO CONTROL

The variables subject to control are fundamentally the labor, materials, and capital inputs described in our production system model of Chapter 1. More labor effort is usually needed to generate more volume of output, so the *employment level* and use of *overtime* are highly relevant variables. Materials can also be used to regulate the flow of output from goods-producing firms by storing and depleting *inventories, back-ordering,* or *subcontracting* items to other firms. Finally, in addition to funding employment and inventory levels, the capital invested in plant and equipment represents a variable controlling the overall *plant capacity.*

These controllable variables constitute pure strategies by which fluctuations in demand and uncertainties in production activities can be accommodated. The strategies are illustrated in Fig. 8-3.

FIGURE 8-3   Pure Aggregate Planning Strategies

	Strategy	Vary Work-Force Size?	Use Over-time and Idle Time?	Carry Large Inventories?	Incur Stockout Costs?	Use Sub-contractors?	Adjust Capacity?
1	Employment	Yes	No	No	No	No	No
2	OT, IT, and PT	No	Yes	No	No	No	No
3	Inventories	No	No	Yes	No	No	No
4	Back orders	No	No	No	Yes	No	No
5	Subcontracting	No	No	No	No	Yes	No
6	Plant capacity	No	No	No	No	No	Yes

The first strategy suggests that a firm might simply vary the size of the work force by hiring and laying off in direct proportion to demand. A second pure strategy would be to maintain a stable work force but permit idle time (IT) when demand is slack and go to overtime (OT) when demand is strong. The service industries' strong use of part-time (PT) workers also falls into this category. The third strategy would be to have a constant work force and level production but carry sufficiently large amounts of inventory to absorb all demand fluctuations. This strategy is, of course, not available to service industries, such as hospitals and transportation firms, that cannot inventory their products.

A back-order strategy (number 4) assumes that customers are willing to wait for delivery, and this effectively smooths out production too—otherwise this strategy results in stockout costs. In essence, it is the strategy of negative inventory which acknowledges that some demands will not be satisfied. The subcontracting strategy would again permit level production, pushing the fluctuations off onto subcontractors. Finally, plant capacities can be adjusted in both the short term (by varying tooling and equipment capacities) and over the long run.

The appropriate strategy to follow depends upon the time frame over which the decision prevails and the costs/benefits that result. In the medium and short range additional strategies such as alternate routings or additional tooling may be considered. Other alternatives, such as buying components instead of making them and reallocating the work force to different jobs, also exist.

COSTS AND BENEFITS OF CONTROL

Every aggregate planning strategy has countervailing costs and benefits. The costs are largely a function of adjusting to increased or decreased demand, as depicted in Fig. 8-4. Surveys of major U.S. firms show a very strong preference for maintaining a stable work force even though demand fluctuates [9]. Employment fluctuations are also frequently limited by union contracts, which can require substantial unemployment benefits (up to 90 percent) for short-term layoffs (less

COSTS OF ADJUSTING TO INCREASED DEMAND	Via	COSTS OF ADJUSTING TO DECREASED DEMAND
■ Hiring and training ■ Use of less-efficient or less-skilled workers	Employment	■ Severance and unemployment insurance ■ Decreased employee morale ■ Loss of skilled personnel ■ Adverse community (and union) effects
■ OT shift premium	OT, IT, and PT	■ Fixed costs of underutilized workers
■ Carrying, storage, and tax ■ Increased purchasing, expediting, and transport ■ Reduced service level if safety stocks used up	Inventories	■ Carrying, storage, and tax ■ Obsolescence ■ Increased stock levels that may take up working space
■ Stockout costs of lost or dissatisfied customers	Backorders	■ Negligible
■ Cost premium ■ Decreased quality control	Subcontracting	■ Negligible
■ Overloaded facilities ■ Use of less-efficient machines ■ Increased maintenance and scrap ■ Decreased quality ■ Cost of new facilities	Plant capacity	■ Fixed costs of underutilized facilities ■ Obsolescence and deterioration

FIGURE 8-4   Costs of Adjusting to Demand

than 1 year). New employees may require expensive training and extra time to achieve high productivity levels.

Inventory strategies may also include the costs of advertising and promotional programs to dispose of inventories or shift the demand to slack periods. Shifting demand is also a viable strategy for service companies.

Plant capacity changes result from adding (or setting aside) machines, equipment, and other long-term assets. Some changes in this area require lead times longer than the normal aggregate planning horizon.

Combination   The most favorable solution to the nonuniform demand problem, however, does not usually result from a choice of one of the pure strategies. Indeed, the pure strategies are often infeasible from a practical standpoint.

Instead, a combination, or mix, is typically used. Very often the intention, and result, is not to respond totally to the random fluctuations but rather to generate a modified response that is judged to be best for the firm over the long run. So the mix may very well include some anticipated stockout costs (strategy 4). We will go into some examples of the uses of these strategies later in the chapter.

AGGREGATE PLANNING METHODS

Top management should (but sometimes does not) provide guidance for the aggregate planning activity because the planning decisions often reflect basic company policy. In this section some guidelines for aggregate planning and some methods of planning will be discussed.

POLICY GUIDELINES

While we cannot go into detail about the job of aggregate planning, selected guidelines are given in Fig. 8-5 and are discussed below.

Corporate Planning Policy All aggregate planning activities should rest firmly upon underlying corporate objectives, for they direct organization activities and dictate items of vital importance to employees, such as whether they will have steady work or will be laid off. Guides for such decisions should properly flow from corporate policy. Whether or not corporate policy explicitly recognizes the full interests of employees, society, stockholders, and others, these interests must be taken into account. This means that planning decisions may sometimes appear to be at variance with apparent standards of, say, short-term profits. Fostering the development of broadly based policy guidelines is an important aspect of the planners' job.

Forecast as a Basis for Planning A good forecast of demand is the basis for aggregate planning and serves as a target, or adjusting mechanism, to guide production activities. The forecast period and planning horizon should be suffi-

---

1 Determine corporate policy regarding controllable variables.
2 Use a good forecast as a basis for planning.
3 Plan in appropriate units of capacity.
4 Maintain as stable a work force as is practical.
5 Maintain needed control over inventories.
6 Maintain flexibility to change.
7 Respond to demand in a controlled manner.
8 Evaluate planning on a regular basis.

FIGURE 8-5   Aggregate Planning Guidelines

ciently long so that decisions such as hiring and laying off are optimal in the long run, and not only on a period-to-period basis. Forecast controls and validity checks should also be constantly maintained to justify faith in the system.

Appropriate Units of Capacity

Plant capacity is a relatively fixed asset which is often not fully utilized. Individual equipment capacities are not always balanced, and the product mix may have characteristics that limit the output of the system. Thus, aggregate planning decisions should be based on *system capacities* with allowance for normal system inefficiencies and learning effects. Plans themselves should be expressed in homogeneous units of production, worker-hours of production time, or other units that are common and manageable, rather than in monetary units.

Work-Force Stability

Work-force stability has become an increasingly important goal as firms have begun to accept a greater responsibility for their role in society. Employees give life to an organization, dedicate their work efforts to it, and are deserving of a just share of the benefits and the security it can provide. If workers are hired to satisfy a seasonal or demand peak, they should be made aware of the temporary nature of their employment before being engaged.

Effective Control over Inventories

Control over inventories is necessary if production control is to use them effectively. This means that having the authority to specify aggregate levels of raw materials, in-process, and finished-goods inventory is essential. One of the best ways to exercise control is, of course, to have the type of information that is available from online MRP systems.

Flexibility to Change

In the business realm change is inevitable. Systems should be designed to provide a fast reaction to change with as little disruption to the plant as possible. Subcontracting is one way of shifting fluctuations to the external environment. Internally, inventory fluctuations generally cause less disruption than does employee turnover. From a process planning standpoint a firm can improve its flexibility by making extensive use of standardized subassemblies and not committing component parts to a particular end item until as late in the process as possible.

Controlled Response to Demand

The controlled response to demand is an acknowledgment that demand fluctuations are in fact random deviations and should not be permitted to generate similar (or perhaps even amplified) fluctuations in the production rates at a manufacturing plant. Simulation studies have revealed that production distribution systems that involve factory, distributor, and retailer inventories can have substantial lag and pipeline effects. A 10 percent increase in retail sales, followed by normal inventory adjustments, can appear as a 40 percent increase by the time the demand information gets back to the factory.

Too rapid a response to demand, and overcorrection, can amplify demand fluctuations. Production controllers must guard against such effects by developing a good information base, assisting wholesalers and retailers with inventory control and production information, and making a controlled, or modified, adjustment to demand. The principle of modified response applies more to items produced for stock than to custom products made to order.

Evaluation of Planning Adequacy   Planning efforts are of no value unless the plans are implemented and do the job they are designed for. Control should be built into the aggregate planning system so that actual levels of activity are measured, the data are fed back to production control in a timely and accurate manner, comparisons are made of actual and planned levels, and corrections are authorized and made.

Production planning and control requires a broad knowledge of production operations. We now turn to some useful planning methods.

GRAPHIC AND CHARTING METHODS   *Know how this works*

No aggregate planning methods yield truly "optimal" rates of production. The graphic and charting techniques basically work with a few variables at a time on a trial-and-error basis. Some mathematical approaches also follow this pattern, whereas others begin with limiting (and sometimes unrealistic) assumptions and achieve a theoretical optimality. The problem then remains to reconcile this with the real-world situation.

Planning Charts and Workload Projections   Production requirements charts and cumulative workload projections are often the best means for conveying an initial understanding of the essence of an aggregate planning problem.

EXAMPLE 8-1

A firm has developed the following forecast (units) for an item which has a demand influenced by seasonal factors.

Jan.	220	July	378
Feb.	90	Aug.	220
Mar.	210	Sept.	200
Apr.	396	Oct.	115
May	616	Nov.	95
June	700	Dec.	260

(a) Prepare a chart showing the daily demand requirements. (*Note:* Available workdays per month are given below in column 2.)

(b) Plot the demand as a histogram and as a cumulative requirement.

(c) Determine the production rate required to meet average demand, and plot this as a dotted line on the graph.

SOLUTION

(a) See column 3 in Fig. 8-6.

FIGURE 8-6   Chart of Production Requirements

Month	(1) Forecast Demand	(2) Production Days	(3) Demand/Day (1) ÷ (2)	(4) Cumulative Production Days	(5) Cumulative Demand
January	220	22	10	22	220
February	90	18	5	40	310
March	210	21	10	61	520
April	396	22	18	83	916
May	616	22	28	105	1,532
June	700	20	35	125	2,332
July	378	21	18	146	2,610
August	220	22	10	168	2,830
September	200	20	10	188	3,030
October	115	23	5	211	3,145
November	95	19	5	230	3,240
December	260	20	13	250	3,500
	3,500	250			

(b) See Fig. 8-7.

(c) Average requirement $= \dfrac{\text{total demand}}{\text{total production days}} = \dfrac{3,500}{250} = 14$ units/day

The histogram and cumulative graphs illustrate the nature of the aggregate planning problem, for they show how the forecast deviates from average requirements. Some alternative means of meeting the forecast requirement are suggested by the pure strategies listed in Fig. 8-3. One plan might consist of varying the size of the work force by hiring and laying off as required. The production rate would then exactly follow the forecast requirement, as shown by the solid line in Fig. 8-7. Another alternative might be to follow strategy 3 and attempt to meet the requirement by inventory adjustments. In this case production could be at a steady rate, shown by the dotted line in Fig. 8-7. A third plan might be to follow strategy 5 and produce at some low, steady rate, perhaps five units per day, and subcontract all excess demand to other firms. Numerous other plans, consisting of other pure strategies (such as overtime, undertime, and back-ordering) and mixed strategies, could be proposed.

EXAMPLE 8-2

Use the data of Example 8-1 and determine the monthly inventory balances required to follow a plan of letting the inventory absorb all fluctuations in demand (strategy 3 of Fig. 8-3). In this case we have a constant work force, no idle time or overtime, no back orders, no use of subcontractors, and no capacity adjustment. Assume that the firm does not use safety stock to meet the demand.

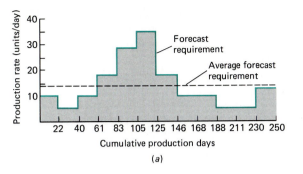
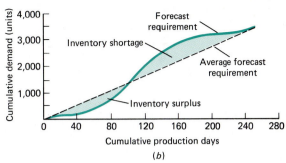

FIGURE 8-7   Histogram and Cumulative Graph of Forecast

SOLUTION

The firm can satisfy demand by producing at an average requirement (14 units/day) and accumulating inventory during periods of slack demand (periods below the dotted line in Fig. 8-7) and depleting it during periods of strong demand. Disregarding any safety stock, the inventory balance is:

$$\text{Inventory balance} = \Sigma \ (\text{production} - \text{demand}) \qquad (8\text{-}1)$$

	(1)	(2)	(3)	(4)	(5)
					Ending
				Ending	Balance
	Production	Forecast	Inventory	Inventory	with 566
Month	at 14/day	Demand	Change	Balance	on Jan. 1
January	308	220	+88	88	654
February	252	90	+162	250	816
March	294	210	+84	334	900
April	308	396	-88	246	812
May	308	616	-308	-62	504
June	280	700	-420	-482	84
July	294	378	-84	-566	0
August	308	220	+88	-478	88
September	280	200	+80	-398	168
October	322	115	+207	-191	375
November	266	95	+171	-20	546
December	280	260	+20	0	566
		3,500			

The pattern of demand is such that column 4 reveals that a maximum negative balance of 566 units exists at the *end* of July, so 566 additional units must be carried in stock initially if demand is to be met. Column 5 shows the resulting inventory balances required.

Cost Computation for Pure Strategies The above example requires that a substantial amount of inventory be carried, because it peaks at 900 units at the end of March and goes to zero in July. If the inventory requirements can be estimated like this, the carrying and storage costs can be computed and weighed against the costs of alternative plans. Carrying costs are based on average inventory levels, and storage costs on the maximum space needed.

EXAMPLE 8-3

Given the data of Example 8-1, the firm has determined that to follow a plan of meeting demand by varying the size of the work force (strategy 1) would result in hiring and layoff costs estimated at $12,000. If the units cost $100 each to produce, carrying costs per year are 20 percent of the average inventory value, and storage costs (based upon maximum inventory) are $.90 per unit, which plan results in the lower cost, varying inventory or varying employment?

SOLUTION

From Example 8-2:

Maximum inventory requiring storage = 900 units (from column 5)

$$\text{Average inventory balance} \cong \frac{654 + 816 + 900 + \cdots + 566}{12} \cong 460 \text{ units}$$

Plan 1 (varying inventory):

Inventory cost = carrying cost + storage cost

$$= (.20)(460)(\$100) + (\$.90)(900) = \boxed{\$10,010}$$

Plan 2 (varying employment): $\boxed{\$12,000}$

∴ Varying inventory is the strategy with the lower cost.

Cost Computation for Mixed Strategies The above example compared the costs of two pure strategies only. Other alternatives might be to make use of overtime, subcontract work, or follow a back-order strategy. The relevant costs of each alternative should be computed and compared. The best solution will most likely come in the form of a mixed strategy. Unfortunately, there are (theoretically) thousands of combinations of strategies that could be investigated. The realities of the situation will, however, generally help reduce the alternatives to a more manageable number. Example 8-4 carries forward with a simplified example of a mixed strategy.

EXAMPLE 8-4

Given the data from the previous examples, suppose the firm wishes to investigate two other alternatives. A third plan is to produce at a rate of 10 units per day and subcontract the additional requirements at a delivered cost of $107 per unit. Any accumulated inventory is carried forward at a 20 percent carrying cost (no extra storage cost).

The fourth plan is to produce at a steady rate of 10 units per day and use overtime to meet the additional requirements at a premium of $10 per unit. Accumulated inventory is, again, carried forward at a 20 percent cost.

SOLUTION

Plan 3 (produce at 10 units per day, carry inventory, and subcontract):

Referring to Fig. 8-6, a production rate of 10 units per day exceeds demand during only three months (February, October, and November). The inventory accumulated during these periods must be carried at a cost of (20 percent) ($100) ÷ 12 months = $1.67 per unit-month. Units are carried until they can be used to help meet demand in a subsequent month. Assume an equilibrium condition where the excess production from October and November (150 units) is on hand January 1.

Month	Demand	Production at 10/day	Inventory to Carry	Inventory Carried Until	Number of Months	Cost at $1.67 per Unit-Month
Initial			150	150 units to April	3	$ 750
Feb.	90	180	90	26 units to April	2	87
				64 units to May	3	320
Oct.	115	230	115	60 units to Dec.	2	200
				55 units to year end	3	275
Nov.	95	190	95	95 units to year end	2	317
						$1,949

Inventory cost (from above) $1,949

Add marginal cost of subcontracting:

$$\text{Number of units} = \text{demand} - \text{production}$$

$$= 3,500 - 10(250)$$

$$= 1,000 \text{ units}$$

$$\text{Cost/unit} = \$107 - 100 = \$7/\text{unit}$$

$$\text{Marginal cost} = (1,000 \text{ units})(\$7/\text{unit}) = \underline{\$7,000}$$

Total cost of plan 3 $8,949

Plan 4. This plan differs from plan 3 only in the marginal cost, which is now due to overtime rather than subcontracting.

Inventory cost (same as plan 3) $1,949

Add marginal cost of overtime:

1,000 units @ $10/unit   10,000

Total cost of plan 4 $11,949

Comparison of Plans

Plan		Strategy	Cost
1	(Pure)	Vary inventory	$10,010
2	(Pure)	Vary employment	12,000
3	(Mixed)	Subcontract and carry inventory	8,949
4	(Mixed)	Overtime and carry inventory	11,949

On the basis of this limited comparison, plan 3 has the lowest cost.

MATHEMATICAL PLANNING MODELS

The methods discussed previously certainly require mathematical computations, and the methods discussed below can also be facilitated by diagrammatic or chart representations. So it would be incorrect to place too much emphasis upon the distinction between charting and mathematical approaches. In general, however, the mathematical models attempt to refine or improve upon basic trial-and-error approaches. Some approaches are of an optimizing character. In this section we shall consider a modified response model, linear programming approaches, and the linear decision rule.

Magee's Modified Response Model   The modified response model [7:174] is of considerable conceptual value because it helps us to (schematically) visualize the production planning problem. In essence, the model is designed to help stabilize production activity in make-to-stock firms by limiting the firm's response to erratic fluctuations of demand. In this sense it is a strategy of inherently accepting stockout penalties. The model essentially bases the production order on a forecast, or budgeted, amount which is modified to make a partial adjustment for current demand and inventory levels [1]. Figure 8-8 is a schematic representation.

The model uses a control number, K, between zero and one which in effect directs that some portion of the production order is determined by current demand. It works like this. Inventory on hand and on order is matched against demand to determine how much additional production would seem to be warranted. However, only a fraction, K, of the resultant discrepancy is used. It is combined with a budgeted amount which has already been predetermined by the forecast. These two components constitute the production order (master schedule amount) which is issued to manufacturing for goods that ultimately go into inventory and to customers.

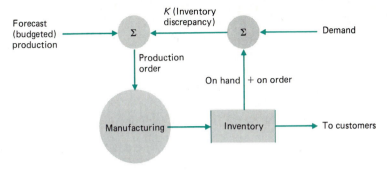

FIGURE 8-8 Modified Response Model

The value of K is, of course, a key determinant and should be based upon experience in the industry, a knowledge of costs and other operating parameters of the firm, and an appreciation of the market environment. It is essentially a smoothing factor which, if set equal to zero, would simply disregard demand and give total weight to the forecast. If set equal to one, it directs that production respond 100 percent to demand fluctuations. A value of $K = .10$ would thus provide a damped response yielding a mild adjustment to the random fluctuations of demand.

A simplified mathematical statement of the model [3:555] is shown below, where Δ represents a difference between planned and actual.

$$\text{Production level} = \text{plan or forecast production}$$
$$+ K[\Delta \text{ demand} + \Delta \text{ inventory} + \Delta \text{ deliveries}] \quad (8\text{-}2)$$

Computations are simplified if delivery requirements are automatically deducted from inventory and further simplified if the demand is essentially placed on the firm's inventory, as is often the case. The expression for the production level is then simply:

$$\text{Production level} = \text{plan or forecast} + K(\Delta D) \quad (8\text{-}3)$$

where ΔD is the difference between planned and actual demand.

In general, the incremental (Δ) amount of demand, inventory, or delivery is assigned a positive or negative sign in accordance with whether the compensating adjustment to production should be an increase or decrease in the level.

EXAMPLE 8-5 | An industrial chemicals producer has developed the accompanying forecast. The firm uses a modified response model (with a control number of $K = .8$) to set actual production levels. Since it takes almost 30 days of lead time to adjust production, the incremental response is effective after an intervening month.

Month	Forecast	Actual
April	12,000	11,500
May	16,000	
June	14,000	
July	10,000	

If the actual demand (which includes inventory and delivery changes) is 11,500 units in April, what "modified" production quantity should be scheduled for June?

SOLUTION

$$\text{Production level} = \text{forecast} + K(\Delta D)$$

$$\text{where } \Delta D = \text{actual} - \text{planned}$$

$$= 11,500 - 12,000 = -500$$

$$\text{Production level} = 14,000 + .8(-500)$$

$$= 14,000 - 400 = 13,600 \text{ units}$$

Linear Programming Approaches   If we view the aggregate planning problem as one of allocating capacity (supply) to meet forecast (demand) requirements, it can be structured and solved in a linear programming format. Both transportation and standard matrix approaches can theoretically be useful [10], but we shall concentrate upon the former for illustrative purposes. In this case the supply consists of the inventory on hand and units that can be produced via regular time (RT), overtime (OT), and subcontracting (SC). Demand consists of the individual month (or period) requirements plus any desired ending inventory. Costs associated with producing units in the given period or producing them and carrying them in inventory until a later period are entered in the small boxes inside the cells in the matrix. Solve by allocating supply to the least cost cells.

EXAMPLE 8-6

Given the accompanying supply, demand, cost, and inventory data for a firm that has a constant work force and wishes to meet all demand (that is, with no back orders), allocate production capacity to satisfy demand at minimum cost.

Supply Capacity (Units)

Period	Regular Time	Overtime	Subcontract
1	60	18	1,000
2	50	15	1,000
3	60	18	1,000
4	65	20	1,000

Demand Forecast

Period	Units
1	100
2	50
3	70
4	80

Additional Data

Inventory	Cost Data
Initial = 20	Regular time cost/unit = $100
Final = 25	(labor = 50 percent of the cost)
	Overtime cost/unit = $125
	Subcontracting cost/unit = $130
	Carrying cost/unit-period = $2

SOLUTION

The initial linear programming matrix in units of capacity is shown in Fig. 8-9, with entries determined as explained below. Because total capacity exceeds demand, a "slack" demand of unused capacity is added to achieve the required balance in supply versus demand.

- *Initial inventory.* 20 units available at no additional cost if used in period 1. Carrying cost is $2/unit per period if units are retained until period 2, $4/unit to period 3, and so on. If the units are unused during any period, the result is a cost of $8/unit.

	Supply, units from	Demand, units for					Capacity	
		Period 1	Period 2	Period 3	Period 4 and final	Unused	Total available	
	Initial inventory	0	2	4	6	8	20	
Period 1	Regular	100	102	104	106	50	60	
	Overtime	125	127	129	131	0	18	
	Subcontract	130				0	1,000	
Period 2	Regular		100	102	104	50	50	
	Overtime		125	127	129	0	15	
	Subcontract		130			0	1,000	
Period 3	Regular			100	102	50	60	
	Overtime			125	127	0	18	
	Subcontract			130		0	1,000	
Period 4	Regular				100	50	65	
	Overtime				125	0	20	
	Subcontract				130	0	1,000	
	Demand	100	50	70	105	4,001	4,326	

FIGURE 8-9 Linear Programming Format for Scheduling

■ *Regular time.* Cost/unit is $100 if units are used in the month produced; otherwise a carrying cost of $2/unit-month is added on for each month the units are retained. Unused regular time costs the firm 50 percent of $100 = $50.

■ *Overtime.* Cost/unit is $125 if the units are used in the month produced; otherwise a carrying cost of $2/unit-month is incurred, as in the regular-time situation. Unused overtime has zero cost.

■ *Subcontracting.* Cost/unit is $130 plus any costs for units carried forward. This latter situation is unlikely, however, for any reasonable demand can be obtained when needed, as indicated by the arbitrarily high number (1,000) assigned to subcontracting capacity. There is no cost for unused capacity here.

Note that if the initial allocations are made so as to use regular time as fully as possible, the solution procedure is often simplified. Overtime and subcontracting amounts can also be allocated on a minimum-cost basis.

■ *Final inventory.* The final-inventory requirement (25 units) must be available at the end of period 4 and has been added to the period 4 demand of 80 units to obtain a total of 105 units.

Since no back orders are permitted, production in subsequent months to fill demand in a current month is not allowed. These unavailable cells, along with the cells associated with carrying forward any subcontracted units, may therefore be blanked out, since they are infeasible. The final solution, following normal methods of transportation LP (or simply allocating supply to the least cost cells first) is shown in Fig. 8-10.

The optimal solution values can be taken directly from the cells. Thus in period 2, for example, the planners will schedule the full 50 units to be produced on regular time plus 12 units on overtime to be carried forward to period 4. This leaves 3 units of unused overtime capacity and no subcontracting during that period. Due to the similar carrying cost for units produced on regular time or overtime, it does not matter which physical units are carried forward, once overtime production is required.[1]

---

[1] This is reflected in the fact that different solutions (but with identical costs) may be obtained. Thus, the regular-time and overtime quantities for demand periods 3 and 4 may be rearranged as shown.

From

	100		102
	60		
	125		127
	10	8	

To

	100		102
	52	8	
	125		127
	18	0	

Note that the row and column totals still agree, and it is simply a matter of physical designation. The situation arises from what is referred to as a "degeneracy," where more than one arrangement is equally good. In transportation linear programming algorithms it can be remedied by assigning a small amount (approaching zero) to one of the cells, as shown in this footnote.

Supply, units from		Period 1	Period 2	Period 3	Period 4 and final	Unused	Total available
Initial inventory		0 · 20	2	4	6	8	20
Period 1	Regular	100 · 60	102	104	106	50	60
	Overtime	125 · 18	127	129	131	0	18
	Subcontract	130 · 2				998 · 0	1,000
Period 2	Regular		100 · 50	102	104	50	50
	Overtime		125	127	129 · 12	3 · 0	15
	Subcontract		130			1,000 · 0	1,000
Period 3	Regular			100 · 60	102	50	60
	Overtime			125 · 10	127 · 8	0	18
	Subcontract			130		1,000 · 0	1,000
Period 4	Regular				100 · 65	50	65
	Overtime				125 · 20	0	20
	Subcontract				130 · 0	1,000 · 0	1,000
Demand		100	50	70	105	4,001	4,326

FIGURE 8-10   Matrix for Planning Decision

The transportation linear programming approach can be extended to include back-order costs by entering them in the blanked-out portion of the matrix in the lower left corner. In this way, production in a later month can be allocated to supply a back-ordered demand from an earlier month at whatever stockout cost premium the firm chooses to assign. The planner must, of course, fill the back-ordered demand in subsequent periods. The format will still guarantee an optimal solution, but of course the solution is only as valid as the stockout cost assumptions that go into the matrix formulation. Solved Prob. 4 illustrates a back-order situation.

The transportation linear programming model illustrated above assumed a constant work force, so no hiring or layoff costs were involved. These and other costs can be expressed in the format of a standard or integer-type linear programming model. In theory, an aggregate plan might be expressed as shown below, where the following symbols refer to the costs shown:

RT = regular time	OT = overtime	SOC = stockout
H = hiring	IT = idle time	SC = subcontract
L = layoff	I_{cc} = inventory carrying	Cap = capacity change

$$\underset{(1)}{\qquad}\underset{(2)}{\qquad}\underset{(3)}{\quad}\underset{(4)}{\ }\underset{(5)}{\ }\underset{(6)}{\ }$$

$$\text{Min } C = (RT + H + L) + (OT + IT) + I_{cc} + SOC + SC + Cap$$

subject to constraints of:

- Meeting demand unless stockout costs are justified
- Limitations on regular time, hiring, layoff, overtime, subcontracting, and capacity
- Costs associated with production, employment, inventory, stockout, subcontracting, and changing capacity

The numbers in parentheses above the objective function correspond with the pure strategies of Fig. 8-3.

The interdependency of the controllable variables makes it difficult, if not impossible, to use the above linear programming model on most realistic problems. Relevant portions of the model have, however, been abstracted and formulated. Shore [10:399–346] has developed a model with an objective function of the general form as shown. The model essentially minimizes the costs of employment, overtime, and inventories subject to meeting demand in each period, i, by regular time, overtime, or carrying inventory forward to the next period. The double summation in the brackets arises from this inventory carryforward.

$$\text{Min } C = r\sum_{i=1}^{k} P_i + h\sum_{i=1}^{k} A_i + f\sum_{i=1}^{k} R_i + v\sum_{i=1}^{k} T_i + C\left[\sum_{i=1}^{k}\sum_{j=1}^{i}(P_i + T_i + D_i)\right]$$

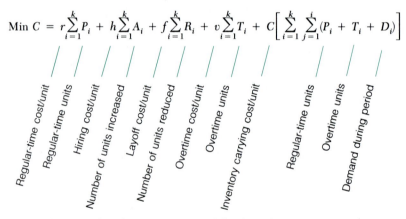

Regular-time cost/unit — Regular-time units — Hiring cost/unit — Number of units increased — Layoff cost/unit — Number of units reduced — Overtime cost/unit — Overtime units — Inventory carrying cost/unit — Regular-time units — Overtime units — Demand during period

The model includes the major parts of the first three pure strategies listed in Fig. 8-3. Other models have been developed which also include an idle-time cost and a back-order mechanism for handling demand variations. Although the simplex formulation of an aggregate planning situation may tend to increase the computational effort, it does facilitate more generalizations, such as the inclusion of costs which vary with time, planning production for more than one product, and costs associated with changes in the size of the work force. Nevertheless, the necessary assumptions limit the practical use of the standard linear programming model in realistic aggregate planning situations.

Theoretical Planning Models   One of the first widely publicized techniques for determining an optimum *production rate* and *work-force size* was the linear decision rule (LDR) developed by Holt, Modigliani, Muth, and Simon in 1955 [5]. Like many other models, the LDR depends upon first quantifying the relevant tangible (and less tangible) variables in terms of costs. But unlike many other models, the LDR requires that cost functions be in quadratic form (and therefore include one or more squared terms).

Relevant costs include regular payroll, hiring and layoff, overtime, and inventory-associated costs of holding, back-ordering, and setup. Other necessary inputs include a forecast for the forthcoming periods, the current size of the work force, and the inventory level during the last period. The model works by differentiating the quadratic cost functions with respect to each variable to ultimately derive two linear decision rules for computing W_t = work-force size required for forthcoming period and P_t = number of units to produce in forthcoming period.

The authors of the LDR applied the method to a paint company by reconstructing costs for a 6-year period of actual operation. They found that the quadratic cost structure and resultant LDRs gave them better (theoretical) performance than the actual company performance.

The assumptions underlying the model severely limit its application to industry, however. Aside from the cost quantification problem common to most models, many analysts hold that a quadratic function does not accurately represent the relevant costs, even though it may hold over a limited range. Often it appears that actual costs increase in a linear or step fashion. Also, there are no constraints on work-force size, overtime amount, inventory, and capital amounts. So the rule may yield impractical solutions. It has, nevertheless, helped focus attention on relevant cost relationships and has constituted a step forward toward understanding the aggregate planning problem.

Heuristic and Computer Search Models

Numerous heuristic, simulation, and computer search models have also been developed for production planning. The heuristics tend to simplify (or perhaps oversimplify) a complex situation by the use of guidelines or decision rules. While not necessarily optimizing per se, some heuristic methods tend to optimize given some basic cost and operational assumptions.

Bowman has proposed a *management coefficients model* [2] whereby decision rules for planning levels of production are based on the past performance of the managers. The model attempts to minimize the erratic or variable behavior of the managers. Regression analysis of their past behavior in similar situations is used to develop coefficients for each variable in the model. It is a unique way of incorporating experience or sensitivity into a formalized model, but its weakness is that it relies upon consistent decisions in the past.

Other approaches include a *simulation and search* procedure developed by Vergin [12], a *heuristic search procedure* by Taubert [11], and a goal programming approach suggested by Lee and Moore, [6]. Taubert's computer search method is designed to find minimizing cost coefficients, and requires the formulation of cost equations for work-force changes, overtime, back orders, and inventory. Costs are then evaluated over a forecast period, and the result is compared with previous results with different personnel, inventory levels, and so

FIGURE 8-11 A Summary of Some Mathematical Aggregate Planning Models

	Linear Programming	Linear Decision Rule	Management Coefficients	Computer Search Models
Application				
	Minimizes costs of employment, overtime, and inventories subject to meeting demand	Use quadratic cost functions to derive rules for work-force size and number of units	Develops regression model that incorporates managers' past decisions to predict capacity needs	Computer routine searches numerous combinations of capacity and selects the one of least cost
Strengths				
	▪ Understandable ▪ Yields optimal plan ▪ Powerful and inclusive ▪ Flexible	▪ Permits nonlinear cost functions ▪ Yields optimal plan ▪ Theoretical value	▪ No limitations on form of costs or constraints ▪ Incorporates past experience	▪ Accepts wide range of cost functions ▪ Flexible ▪ Easily changed
Limitations				
	▪ Requires linear cost functions ▪ Outputs require interpretation	▪ Complex—not easily understood ▪ Requires quadratic cost functions ▪ Outputs not always realistic (variables unconstrained)	▪ Nonoptimal, but reasonably close ▪ Relies on expertise of individual manager ▪ Model not directly transferable to others	▪ Nonoptimal, but does well compared with other rules ▪ Doesn't always locate global minimum

forth. The procedure is repeated in a systematic way until no better cost function can be determined.

Four of the mathematical aggregate planning models are summarized in Fig. 8-11. Unfortunately, much of this type of work is still academic, although the models are reaching the stage of being positively beneficial. A good deal of the benefit thus far has arisen from the detailed attention and careful analysis given to the relevant production parameters. In the future we may expect to see an increasing number of specialized models developed for the unique situations of individual organizations. Much of this work will be incorporated into management information systems which (appropriately) view the planning problems from a total systems perspective.

MASTER SCHEDULING OBJECTIVES

The master schedule (also known as the master production schedule, or MPS) formalizes the production plan and converts it into specific material and capacity

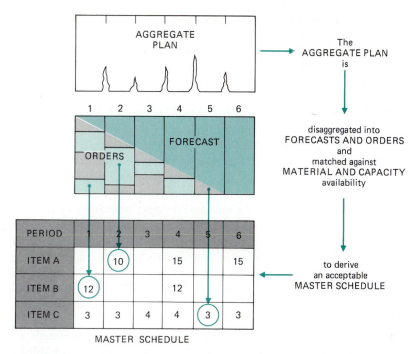

FIGURE 8-12   Master Scheduling Process

requirements, as suggested in Fig. 8-12. In this section we will identify the functions of the master schedule, its planning horizon, and its inputs and outputs.

FUNCTIONS OF THE MASTER SCHEDULE

The master production schedule (MPS) formalizes the production plan and converts it into specific material and capacity requirements. Labor, material, and equipment needs for each job must then be assessed. Thus the MPS drives the entire production and inventory system by setting specific production goals and responding to feedback from all downstream operations. Some key functions of a master schedule are listed in Fig. 8-13.

> 1 Translate aggregate plans into specific end items
> 2 Evaluate alternative schedules
> 3 Generate material requirements
> 4 Generate capacity requirements
> 5 Facilitate information processing
> 6 Maintain valid priorities
> 7 Effectively utilize capacity

FIGURE 8-13   Master Schedule Functions

1 *Translate aggregate plans.* The aggregate plan sets a level of operations that roughly balances market demands with the material, labor, and equipment capabilities of the firm. The master schedule translates this plan into specific numbers of end items or modules to be produced in specific time periods. Products are grouped into lot sizes that are economical to produce and realistically load (but not overload or underload) the firm's facilities. The master schedule is thus a manufacturing plan of what the firm actually intends to produce (and not a forecast of what it hopes to sell).

2 *Evaluate alternative schedules.* Master scheduling is a trial-and-error, work and rework activity. Many computerized P&IC systems have simulation capabilities that enable planners to "trial fit" alternative master schedules. Detailed material and capacity requirements are then derived, and the planner can see exactly what lead times and delivery schedules would result. When special promotional campaigns are being considered, a simulation can suggest how increased demand for one product might affect the production of others.

3 *Generate material requirements.* The master schedule is the prime input for the material requirements planning system. When end items appear on the master schedule, this signals the MRP system to purchase or produce the necessary components in sufficient time to meet the final assembly dates specified.

4 *Generate capacity requirements.* Capacity needs stem directly from material and job requirements, which in turn are established by the master schedule. Master scheduling is thus a prerequisite of capacity planning. The schedule should reflect an economical usage of labor and equipment capacities. When capacity requirements are inappropriate (either too little *or too much*), the master schedule should be revised.

5 *Facilitate information processing.* By controlling the load (and backlog) on the plant, the master schedule determines when deliveries will be made, both for make-to-stock and make-to-order items. It is also an important entry point for coordinating other management information such as marketing capabilities, financial resources (for carrying inventory), and personnel policies (for supplying labor).

6 *Maintain valid priorities.* Priorities can be *absolute* (relating to how far a job is behind or ahead of schedule), or they can be *relative* (that is, a rank in comparison with other jobs). In either case, they should reflect true needs if the supervisor and workers are to have confidence in the P&IC system. This means that the due date or rank should correspond with the time the order is actually needed. Customers may change their orders, and materials are sometimes scrapped. When components are not actually needed or end items cannot be produced because of a shortage of material, the master schedule should be adjusted to reflect this change.

7 *Effectively utilize capacity.* By specifying end-item requirements, the master schedule also establishes the load and the utilization parameters for labor and equipment. To utilize capacity most effectively, the master schedule may call for delaying some orders or building others ahead of demand.

TIME INTERVALS AND PLANNING HORIZON

The *time interval* used in master scheduling depends upon the type, volume, and component lead times of the products being produced. Firms often use weekly time intervals, which coincide with the time buckets used in most MRP systems. We will sometimes use monthly intervals in order to illustrate the length of the planning horizon without incorporating unnecessary detail.

The *time horizon* covered by the master schedule also depends upon product characteristics and lead times. Some master schedules cover a period as short as a few weeks. Others—for products with long lead times, such as steam generators—may cover a period longer than a year. The schedule must extend far enough in advance so that the lead times for all purchased and assembled components are adequately encompassed.

Figure 8-14 depicts an assembly that has a 10-week manufacturing lead time. The controlling (or critical path) item is component E; this component and C and D are assembled into subassembly A. If the 10 weeks posed a recurring problem, the planner might shorten it 3 weeks (to the dotted line) by stocking the purchased part (E). Other options include special handling of critical items or perhaps limited use of overtime in the machining or assembly activities.

Master schedules often have firm and flexible portions. Figure 8-15 illustrates a rolling master schedule for a make-to-stock furniture operation producing two types of tables and one type of lamp. As each week passes, the seventh week is advanced to the firm portion, and the flexible portion is rechecked. The furniture company has reasonably short lead times and uses a 13-week quarter for its

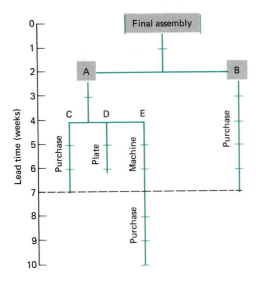

FIGURE 8-14   Assembly with 10-Week Combined Lead Time

Item	Week																	
	1	2	3	4	5	6	7	8	9	10	11	12	13	14	15	16	17	18
	←Firm→ (emergency changes only)						←Flexible→ (capacity firm and material ordered)							←Open→ (additions and changes OK)				
R28 Table	50		50	50		40			40	40		40	40			40		
R30 Table		80		20	60		80	80		60					80			
L7 Lamp	20		20		10	20			20	20	10	20	20	20				

FIGURE 8-15   Master Schedule for Make-to-Stock Furniture Company

planning period. Some firms use weekly intervals through 13 weeks and then use monthly units beyond that.

Changes in the master schedule affect lead times, work schedules, machine setups, and a multitude of other things such as distributor inventory levels. The "firm" portion will generally encompass the minimum lead times necessary for components and cannot be changed, except on a very high authority. Changes in the early weeks of the flexible portion are discouraged, but P&IC may change the *timing* of the jobs if average lead-time requirements are not violated. Any reasonable change can be made in periods that extend beyond the total average component lead-time horizon.

After the master schedule is prepared and accepted, it must be kept up to date. This means processing change orders as quickly as possible, rescheduling past-due orders, and incorporating new orders into the schedule. Fortunately, computerized systems can readily accept such changes.

MASTER SCHEDULE FORMATION: INPUTS AND OUTPUTS

In the introduction to this chapter, Fig. 8-1 illustrated how the market environment and resource base influence the aggregate production plan. These same forces penetrate to the master schedule. The market establishes priorities in terms of units of production. The resource base limits the capacity to produce, and economics dictate that production be accomplished in an efficient manner.

Figure 8-16 provides additional detail on how the market environment influences the master schedule. Notice that we are identifying two major sources of inputs: (1) forecasts and (2) customer orders. This corresponds (roughly) with make-to-stock and make-to-order items. This distinction is made because the master schedule for make-to-order items is sometimes more complex. Not all firms have both forecast and order information available for aggregate planning.

Make-to-Stock Items   For make-to-stock items, forecasts of demand are the major input for the master schedule. Requirements often flow from the need to

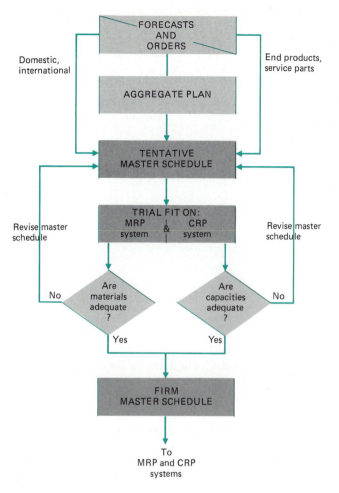

FIGURE 8-16 Market Influences on the Master Schedule

replenish plant or distributor inventories of end products or service parts. Figure 8-15 illustrates a master schedule for items made to stock.

Make-to-Order Items   Make-to-order items often require more detailed scheduling of the time and materials required because the quantities and/or items specified are unique to a particular customer order. And employee work time must be carefully balanced against the due date of the orders. If there is no work for some employees (such as painters), they cannot be "kept busy" producing items that can go into stock and eventually be sold.

Figure 8-17 illustrates a master schedule for a firm manufacturing kitchen cabinets, which are made to order in a plant which has 60 standard hours of

Kitchen cabinets— order group no.	Month and production days available						Standard hr/unit
	May (25)	June (25)	July (10)	Aug. (24)	Sept. (20)	Oct. (25)	
A110		15		15		15	24
B110	10				5		30
C130	24	28	20	24	24	24	32
D120		3		2		5	60
E110	22	2		5	13	5	20
Load							
Σ standard hr × no. of units	1,508	1,476	640	1,348	1,178	1,528	6-month load = 7,678 hr
Capacity							
Standard hr @ 60 hr/day	1,500	1,500	600	1,440	1,200	1,500	6-month capacity = 7,740 hr

FIGURE 8-17   Master Schedule for Make-to-Order Kitchen Cabinets

capacity available per day. The units in the cells are quantities of cabinets of a given order group. Thus, order group A110 will be produced in lots of 15 in June, August, and October. Units in group A110 require 24 standard hours to be produced.

Although the total load (7,678 hours) and capacity (7,740) are in good balance, the figures for the individual months vary. The schedule shows only 600 hours of capacity available in July (that is, 10 days at 60 standard hours per day) because of a vacation shutdown. With the July schedule somewhat overloaded because of a regular monthly commitment of 24 units of group C130, the scheduler has underloaded slightly in June and August to compensate. She is planning for 4 extra C130s in June (28 total) and only 20 in July. If the shop supervisor can begin work on the July orders during the last day or two of June, he will probably do so.

Customer orders for standard products that can be handled in much the same way as make-to-stock orders are no problem. In fact, the presence of firm customer orders (with long lead time) simplifies master scheduling because it removes uncertainties associated with the quantity demanded and options desired.

Serve-to-Order Items   In many service industries (such as banks, restaurants, and hospitals), demand can be very irregular and the time required to serve each customer can vary. This makes the task of gaining effective use of employee "on-the-job" time a major scheduling challenge. Aside from shifting demand (via appointments, published schedules, and so on), firms commonly schedule irregular working hours or assign lower priority duties (such as filing and maintenance activities) to employees during off-peak times.

Scheduling can have a significant impact upon the quality of service activities. This is because employee attitude and temperament is conveyed to customers in the social interactions that occur in service systems. If employees are bored or dissatisfied with their work, this disposition is likely to be perceived by customers as evidence of "poor" quality.

Trial-Fitting the Master Schedule Figure 8-16 also emphasizes the iterative nature of master scheduling. Once a tentative master schedule is developed, the end-item requirements can be extended (by computer) into material requirements and work center capacity requirements to determine how the production system will react to the proposed schedule. In this way, the master schedule can be used to evaluate customer delivery commitments before orders are accepted. It is much better to simulate the effect of changes and new orders on the computer (and make adjustments beforehand) than to blindly make commitments the firm cannot keep.

Trial-fitting the master schedule is a key feature of modern P&IC management. It allows the firm to develop a realistic schedule from the start and thereby fosters integrity in the whole P&IC system.

MASTER SCHEDULING METHODS

In the previous section we considered the functions and time horizons of make-to-stock and make-to-order master schedules and the need to distinguish between them. This section concludes with some policy guidelines and procedures for implementing and monitoring master schedules.

POLICY GUIDELINES

Although master scheduling depends upon the type of demand (forecasts versus firm orders) and the planning horizon, some scheduling guidelines have wide applicability. Figure 8-18 summarizes a few key points.

1 Work from an aggregate production plan.
2 Schedule common modules when possible.
3 Load facilities realistically.
4 Release orders on a timely basis.
5 Monitor inventory levels closely.
6 Reschedule as required.

FIGURE 8-18 Master Scheduling Guidelines

In addition to the *aggregate plan*, data should be available from forecasts and customer orders already received. By *scheduling items in modules* and/or at a point of high commonality of components, the immense problems of dealing with options are reduced. A *realistic load on facilities* means that the facilities are neither overloaded nor underloaded. Similarly, the *timely release of orders* to the production shop means offering a realistic delivery date that shop personnel can feel confident with. Close *monitoring of inventory levels* is necessary to avoid excess inventories on the one hand and stockouts on the other. *Rescheduling* capability acknowledges that changes do occur and permits the scheduler to keep priorities valid and capacities effectively utilized. Judgment must be exercised so that neither too many nor too few reschedules are permitted, however.

ASSEMBLY VERSUS PROCESS INDUSTRY SCHEDULING

Master scheduling is a logical process, but complicated by the need to deal with many *types of items* (as opposed to a high volume of one item) concurrently, while at the same time observing material and capacity limitations. Insofar as the master-schedule item is the entity that is "tracked" or monitored through the production process, it behooves planners to keep the number of master-schedule items down to the smallest number possible. The designation of "master-schedule items" can differ from one industry to another.

Manufacturing assembly activities typically begin with many raw materials and components that are combined into one or a few end items, such as a computer. As illustrated in Fig. 8-19*a*, master scheduling here starts with the few types of end items and works "upstream" to determine the raw material and component needs from the projected number of end items. Most computerized MRP systems are designed to accommodate this traditional type of scheduling logic. Firms that produce large volumes of a few items often produce for stock, and *material availability* is frequently a major concern in these firms.

Process industry manufacturing is almost the reverse of assembly manufacturing. It begins with one or a few types of raw materials that are sorted, milled, or somehow processed into multiple end items and by-products, such as the many petroleum products that come from crude oil. Figure 8-19*c* illustrates. In this situation, master scheduling begins at a raw-material (input) level and must plan for the materials and capacities needed for the various categories of output. When processes have uncertain yields, such as in many food processing plants, the scheduling and control over inventories can be a challenge. *Capacity* to handle the variable levels of materials is a major concern in process industries.

Figure 8-19*b* depicts an assemble-to-order situation where the master-schedule item is a major subassembly, but not necessarily the finished product. This is the approach followed by firms assembling a high volume of products that may offer options numbering in the thousands. In this situation, planners leave the end-item specification to an assembly sheet. [8:221] For example, an auto manufacturer may master schedule 30 percent of a production run to be a basic four-wheel drive subassembly (model) with a common engine size. The other 70

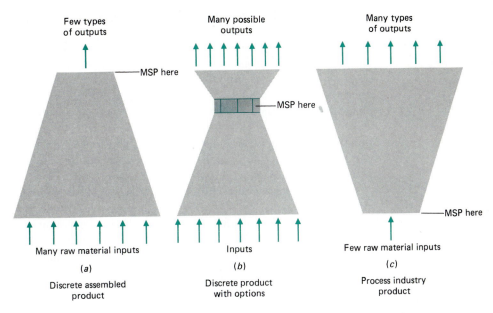

FIGURE 8-19   Master Scheduling in Discrete Assembly versus Process Industry.

percent will be another model. But the options to be included on each car will not be specified in the master schedule. They will be delineated on a specific car build (assembly) sheet that is released shortly before the car is actually put into production.

DETERMINING MASTER SCHEDULE REQUIREMENTS

The general procedure for master scheduling is to first consolidate all the (gross) requirements for the master-schedule item. This includes not only customer orders and forecasts of new demand, but also any service parts or interplant demand. The next step is to "net out" the requirements (that is, subtract on-hand inventory). The net requirements are then grouped (lot-sized) into planned orders to be released in a time-phased schedule. By working with planned orders, the schedulers can then check the planned workload against the time available at key work centers to ensure that capacity is adequate. If either the materials or capacity is insufficient, then the master schedule must be revised and the scheduling process repeated.

MONITORING THE MASTER SCHEDULE

As the key element of a firm's P&IC system, the master schedule should continually reflect what the firm can and will do. Once a schedule is set, planners are reluctant to change planned and released orders. However, some minor changes in demand can be accommodated by expediting or by the (judicious) use of overtime, safety stock, and other "relief" mechanisms.

Management consultants look for clues which tell them that a firm may have master scheduling problems. One of these is an excessively high current load and many past-due orders. Another is overloaded and/or underloaded facilities. Parts shortages at the assembly stage (and high inventories of the wrong items) also suggest master scheduling problems. In general, if the firm is unable to keep delivery promises to customers, it will become heavily reliant upon expediting, and informal systems will emerge. Supervisors and workers will lose confidence in the system. When this problem exists, master scheduling should be one of the first activities to examine.

Needless to say, the master schedule should be monitored by evaluating performance against the above criteria. Comparisons of master-scheduled output with actual output are useful, as are comparisons of the number of additions to the master schedule with the number of deletions (or setbacks). A high frequency of late releases may also be indicative of inefficiency stemming from special handling. A smoothly functioning master schedule will make a significant contribution toward maintaining valid priorities and effectively utilizing plant capacity.

SUMMARY

Aggregate planning involves adjusting controllable variables to respond to forecast and order fluctuations in a rational manner. Planning guidelines emphasize clearly delineated corporate goals and a reliable forecast, plus work-force stability, control over inventories, and flexibility to change. Planning should be done in units of capacity and evaluated on a regular basis.

The controllable variables include (1) employment, (2) overtime and idle time, (3) inventories, (4) back orders, (5) subcontracting, and (6) plant capacity. Each variable constitutes a pure strategy which can be evaluated on an economic basis by computing costs for alternative production plans, such as varying employment or carrying inventories. Most realistic situations will call for a mix of strategies. The number of alternative combinations may be large, and there is no guarantee that any particular plan is optimal. Nevertheless, the realities of the situation will (it is hoped) limit the alternatives.

Transportation linear programming methods have been applied to optimize production plans over several time periods when the controllable variables are regular and overtime employment levels and subcontracting and stockout (back-order) costs.

Linear decision rules, heuristic models, and numerous computer search and simulation approaches have also been developed to solve the aggregate planning problem, but much of this research is still theoretical.

Master scheduling follows aggregate planning and breaks the plan down into specific quantities of individual products to be produced in designated time periods (usually weeks). Material and capacity requirements are then evaluated, and the master schedule is revised if necessary. The immediate portion of the resultant schedule is usually firm, but changes can be accommodated in more distant (flexible) periods.

The actual master scheduling process consists of consolidating gross requirements, adjusting for inventory, and lot-sizing the net requirements into planned orders in a time-phased schedule.

SOLVED PROBLEMS

AGGREGATE PLANNING

1 High Point Furniture Company maintains a constant work force (no overtime, back orders, or subcontracting) which can produce 3,000 tables per quarter. The annual demand is 12,000 units and is distributed seasonally in accordance with the quarterly indexes: $Q_1 = .80$, $Q_2 = 1.40$, $Q_3 = 1.00$, $Q_4 = .80$. Inventories are accumulated when demand is less than capacity and are used up during periods of strong demand. To supply the total annual demand:
(a) How many tables must be accumulated during each quarter?
(b) What inventory must be on hand at the beginning of the first quarter?

Solution

Quarter	(1) Production at 3,000/Q	(2) Seasonal Demand $(SI)Y_c = Y_{sz}$	(3) Inventory Change	(4) Inventory Balance	(5) Balance with 600 on Jan. 1
1st	3,000	(.8)(3,000) = 2,400	600	600	1,200
2d	3,000	(1.4)(3,000) = 4,200	−1,200	−600	0
3d	3,000	(1.0)(3,000) = 3,000	0	−600	0
4th	3,000	(.8)(3,000) = 2,400	600	0	600

(a) The inventory accumulation is given in column 3.
(b) From column 4, the largest negative inventory is 600 units; therefore, 600 must be on hand on January 1. Column 5 shows the resulting balance at the end of each quarter.

2 Michigan Manufacturing produces a product which has a 6-month demand cycle, as shown. Each unit requires 10 worker-hours to be produced, at a labor cost of $6 per hour regular rate (or $9 per hour overtime). The total cost per unit is estimated at $200, but units can be subcontracted at a cost of $208 per unit. There are currenty 20 workers employed in the subject department, and hiring and training costs for additional workers are $300 per person, whereas layoff costs are $400 per person. Company policy is to retain a safety stock equal to 20 percent of the monthly forecast, and each month's safety stock becomes the beginning inventory for the next month. There are currently 50 units in stock carried at a cost of $2 per unit-month. Stockouts have been assigned a cost of $20 per unit-month.

	January	February	March	April	May	June
Forecast demand	300	500	400	100	200	300
Workdays	22	19	21	21	22	20
Worker hr at 8/day	176	152	168	168	176	160

Three aggregate plans are proposed.

Plan 1. Vary the work-force size to accommodate demand.

Plan 2. Maintain a constant work force of 20, and use overtime and idle time to meet demand.

Plan 3. Maintain a constant work force of 20, and build inventory or incur a stockout cost. The firm must begin January with the 50-unit inventory on hand.

Compare the costs of the three plans.

Solution

We must first determine what the production requirements are as adjusted to include a safety stock of 20 percent of next month's forecast. Beginning with a January inventory of 50, each subsequent month's inventory reflects the difference between the forecast demand and the production requirement of the previous month.

Month	Forecast Demand	Cumulative Demand	Safety Stock at 20 Percent Forecast	Beginning Inventory	Production Requirement (Forecast + SS − beginning inventory)
January	300	300	60	50	300 + 60 − 50 = 310
February	500	800	100	60	500 + 100 − 60 = 540
March	400	1,200	80	100	400 + 80 − 100 = 380
April	100	1,300	20	80	100 + 20 − 80 = 40
May	200	1,500	40	20	200 + 40 − 20 = 220
June	300	1,800	60	40	300 + 60 − 40 = 320

Plan 1 (Vary work-force size):

	January	February	March	April	May	June	Total
1 Production required	310	540	380	40	220	320	
2 Production hours required (**1** × 10)	3,100	5,400	3,800	400	2,200	3,200	
3 Hours available per worker at 8/day	176	152	168	168	176	160	
4 Number of workers required (**2** ÷ **3**)	18	36	23	3	13	20	
5 Number of workers hired		18			10	7	
6 Hiring cost (**5** × $300)		$5,400			$3,000	$2,100	$10,500
7 Number of workers laid off	2		13	20			
8 Layoff cost (**7** × $400)	$800		$5,200	$8,000			$14,000

Plan 2 (Use overtime and idle time):

	January	February	March	April	May	June	Total
1 Production required	310	540	380	40	220	320	
2 Production hours required (**1** × 10)	3,100	5,400	3,800	400	2,200	3,200	
3 Hours available per worker at 8/day	176	152	168	168	176	160	
4 Total hours available (**3** × 20)	3,520	3,040	3,360	3,360	3,520	3,200	
5 Number of OT hours required (**2** − **4**)		2,360	440			0	
6 OT premium* (**5** × $3)		$7,080	$1,320			0	$8,400
7 Number IT hours (**4** − **2**)	420			2,960	1,320		
8 IT cost (**5** × $6)	$2,520			$17,760	$7,920		$28,200

* Incremental cost of OT = overtime cost − regular-time cost = $9 − $6 = $3.

Plan 3 (Use inventory and stockout based on constant 20-worker force):

	January	February	March	April	May	June	Total
1 Production required	310	540	380	40	220	320	
2 Cumulative production required	310	850	1,230	1,270	1,490	1,810	
3 Total hours available at 20 workers	3,520	3,040	3,360	3,360	3,520	3,200	
4 Units produced (**3** ÷ 10)	352	304	336	336	352	320	
5 Cumulative production	352	656	992	1,328	1,680	2,000	
6 Units short (**2** − **5**)		194	238				
7 Shortage cost (**6** × $20)		$3,880	$4,760				$8,640
8 Excess units (**5** − **2**)	42			58	190	190	
9 Inventory cost (**8** × $2)	$84			$116	$380	$380	$960

Note that plan 3 assumes that a stockout cost is incurred if safety stock is not maintained at prescribed levels of 20 percent of forecast. The firm is in effect managing the safety stock level to yield a specified degree of protection by absorbing the cost of carrying the safety stock as a policy decision.

Summary:

> *Plan 1:* $10,500 hiring + $14,000 layoff = $24,500
> *Plan 2:* $8,400 overtime + $28,200 idle time = $36,600
> *Plan 3:* $8,640 stockout + $960 inventory = $9,600

Plan 3 is the preferred plan.

3　Idaho Instrument Company produces calculators in a Lewiston plant and has forecast demand over the next 12 periods, as shown. Each period is 20 working days (approx-

Period	Units	Period	Units	Period	Units
1	800	5	400	9	1,000
2	500	6	300	10	700
3	700	7	400	11	900
4	900	8	600	12	1,200

imately one month). The company maintains a constant work force of 40 employees, and there are no subcontractors available who can meet its quality standards. The company can, however, go on overtime if necessary and encourage customers to back-order calculators. Production and cost data are as follows:

Production capacity:

> Initial inventory: 100 units (final included in period 12 demand)
> RT hours: (40 employees)(20 days/period)(8 hr/day) = 6,400 hr/period
> OT hours: (40 employees)(20 days/period)(4 hr/day) = 3,200 hr/period
> Standard labor hours/unit: 10 hr

Costs:

> Labor: RT = $6/hr; OT = $9/hr
> Material and overhead: $100/unit produced
> Back-order costs: apportioned at $5/unit-period
> Inventory carrying cost: $2/unit-period

Option A. Assume that five periods constitute a full demand cycle, and use the transportation linear programming approach to develop an aggregate plan based on the first five periods only. (*Note:* A planning length of five periods is useful for purposes of methodology, but in reality the planning horizon should cover a complete cycle, or else the plan should make inventory, personnel, and other such allowances for the whole cycle.)

Option B. Determine the optimal production plan for the 12-period cycle using a transportation linear programming format. (*Note:* This more realistic option involves a substantial amount of calculation and should be done on a computer, using a transportation LP code if one is available.)

Solution (Option A)

> RT cap. avail./period = 6,400 hr ÷ 10 hr/unit = 640 units
> OT cap. avail./period = 3,200 hr ÷ 10 hr/unit = 320 units
> RT cost = (10 hr/unit)($6/hr) + $100 material and OH = $160/unit
> OT cost = (10 hr/unit)($9/hr) + $100 material and OH = $190/unit

Note that the back orders are shown in the lower left portion of the matrix.

Supply, units from	Period 1	Period 2	Period 3	Period 4	Period 5	Unused	Total available
	Demand, units for					Capacity	
Initial inventory	[0] 100	[2]	[4]	[6]	[8]	[10]	100
Period 1 — Regular	[160] 640	[162]	[164]	[166]	[168]	[60]	640
Period 1 — Overtime	[190]	[192]	[194]	[196]	[198]	[0] 320	320
Period 2 — Regular	[165] 60	[160] 500	[162] 60	[164] 20	[166]	[60]	640
Period 2 — Overtime	[195]	[190]	[192]	[194]	[196]	[0] 320	320
Period 3 — Regular	[170]	[165] 640	[160]	[162]	[164]	[60]	640
Period 3 — Overtime	[200]	[195]	[190]	[192]	[194]	[0] 320	320
Period 4 — Regular	[175]	[170]	[165] 640	[160]	[162]	[60]	640
Period 4 — Overtime	[205]	[200]	[195]	[190]	[192]	[0] 320	320
Period 5 — Regular	[180]	[175]	[170]	[165] 240	[160] 400	[60]	640
Period 5 — Overtime	[210]	[205]	[200]	[195]	[190]	[0] 320	320
Demand	800	500	700	900	400	1,600	4,900

Solution (Option B)

This solution is left as an exercise. See Prob. 13.

4 The High Point Furniture Company (of Solved Prob. 1) has decided to make a modified next-period response to demand fluctuations that deviate from the seasonalized forecast values, using a control number of $K = .4$. Actual demand during the four quarters turns out to be 2,800, 3,800, 3,500, and 2,200 units, respectively. The firm begins the year with 600 units on hand, excess inventory is carried forward, but unfilled demand is lost.
(a) By how much does actual total demand differ from the forecast?
(b) Show the respective inventory balances at the end of each quarter, and indicate how many unit sales are actually lost via stockout under this plan.
(c) Would the cost of such a plan be justified?

Solution

		Quarter			
	1st	2d	3d	4th	Total
1 Actual demand	2,800	3,800	3,500	2,200	12,300
2 Forecast demand	2,400	4,200	3,000	2,400	12,000
3 Difference (ΔD)	400	−400	500	−200	
4 $K(\Delta D)$, where $K = .4$	160	−160	200	−80	
5 Production adjustment	0	160	−160	200	
6 Actual production (3,000 + **5**)	3,000	3,160	2,840	3,200	12,200
7 Difference (**6** − **1**)	200	−640	−660	1,000	
8 Balance with 600 on January 1	800	160	−500*	1,000	

* No backlog allowed. ∴ these 500 units are lost sales.

(a) Actual − forecast = 12,300 − 12,000 = 300 units.
(b) Balances are shown in row 8. The 500 units represent lost sales. Note that the production adjustments take one quarter to implement.
(c) More information is desirable to determine the full economic value of the plan. Average inventory on hand is 490 units, and more units have been produced than forecast (12,200 versus 12,000). The costs of changing production levels, carrying inventory, and stockouts and the benefits of any additional profit should be compared with what would have occurred without modifying the response given the same actual demand.

MASTER SCHEDULING

5 An appliance manufacturer produces a motor assembly (X) that is used in several hand-held appliances. They currently have 60 units in stock and will manufacture more in production runs (lots) of 90 units. Develop a tentative master schedule for the demand shown below.

Initial inventory = 60 *Production run* = 90	*Week*									
	1	*2*	*3*	*4*	*5*	*6*	*7*	*8*	*9*	*10*
Customer forecast		5	30	40	50	40	50	50	50	50
Interplant forecast			5			5			5	
Customer orders	40	40	30	10	10	5				
Warehouse orders	15	10		5						

Solution

Consolidated requirements are determined by summing the forecast and order data.

$$\text{Week } 1 = 40 + 15 = 55$$
$$\text{Week } 2 = 5 + 40 + 10 = 55$$

Required production is determined by

$$\text{Production} = \text{beginning inventory} - \text{consolidated requirements}$$

$$\text{Week } 1 = 60 - 55 = 5 \quad \text{(No new production is needed.)}$$
$$\text{Week } 2 = 5 - 55 = (50) \quad \text{(Schedule a production run.)}$$

Ending inventory is determined by

$$\text{Ending inventory} = \text{beginning inventory} + \text{production} - \text{requirements}$$

$$\text{Week } 2 = 5 + 90 - 55 = 40$$

Initial inventory = 60 Production run = 90	Week									
	1	2	3	4	5	6	7	8	9	10
Requirements	55	55	65	55	60	50	50	50	55	50
Beginning inventory	60	5	40	65	10	40	80	30	70	15
Production required			90	90		90	90		90		90
Ending inventory	5	40	65	10		40	80	30	70	15	55

The "Production required" row shows the tentative master schedule amounts.

QUESTIONS

8-1   Distinguish between aggregate planning and master scheduling.

8-2   How would you classify aggregate planning activities in terms of their time horizon (long range versus short range), and level of management involvement?

8-3   Should a firm always attempt to "meet demand"? Why or why not?

8-4   What makes changing the volume of production operations such a difficult task?

8-5   Which of the controllable variables of aggregate planning do you feel are most difficult to quantify in terms of cost? Explain.

8-6   Give an example of a situation where a pure planning strategy would be infeasible from a practical standpoint.

8-7   In what way does Magee's modified response model attempt to respond to demand fluctuations?

8-8   How do the mathematical assumptions concerning costs differ with respect to linear programming techniques and the linear decision rule?

8-9   The master schedule is said to "drive" the whole production system. Identify some master scheduling functions that relate specifically (a) to priorities and (b) to capacities.

8-10 What determines the length of a master schedule time horizon? How can it be shortened?

8-11 Firms commonly experience rush orders, unexpected changes, and modifications of orders already booked. How do master schedulers handle last-minute changes in the production schedule?

8-12 What special problems does master scheduling pose for firms which manufacture specialized products to customer order on short delivery schedules?

8-13 How does the master scheduling function of planning for material and capacity requirements differ in manufacturing assembly versus process industry scheduling?

PROBLEMS

1   Rainwear Manufacturing, Incorporated, produces outdoor apparel which has a demand projected to be as shown. The plant has a 2-week vacation shutdown in July, so the available production days per month are 22, 19, 21, 21, 22, 20, 12, 22, 20, 23, 19, and 21, respectively.

January	4,400	April	6,300	July	1,200	October	9,200
February	4,750	May	4,400	August	3,300	November	7,600
March	6,300	June	2,000	September	5,000	December	7,350

(a) Prepare a chart showing the daily production requirements.
(b) Plot the demand as a histogram and as a cumulative requirement over time.
(c) Determine the production rate required to meet average demand, and plot this as a dotted line on your graph.

2 The Waterford Products planning department uses a forecasting equation of the form $Y = 320 + 10X$ (last quarter 1987 = 0, X = quarters, Y = units). The firm is currently studying production capacity requirements for the year 1992.
(a) Prepare a chart showing the quarterly production requirements for 1992.
(b) Determine the production rate required to meet average demand over the year, and plot this as a dotted line on your chart.

3 (*Statistical*) A governmental agency in a large city has a staff employed to provide financial and legal counseling to people who visit or phone for this service. The operations manager is reviewing the record of demand for the past several months (shown below) to help her plan for the appropriate number of counselors over the next few months.

(a) What is the mean and standard deviation of the frequency distribution of demand?
(b) If each counselor could service 10 customers per day, how many counselors would be required to handle the average (mean) demand?
(c) Assuming demand is normally distributed, how many counselors would be required to satisfy 90 percent of the requests for service?

Class Interval (Persons per day requesting help)	Frequency (Number of days this occurred)
0 to < 20	10
20 to < 40	52
40 to < 60	80
60 to < 80	44
80 to < 100	14
Total	200

4 Talking Toy Products Company has an 8-period demand cycle that has a repetitive pattern like that shown below (these are 45-day periods). The carrying cost for its major product is $4 per unit per period. Assuming the company can arrange to have whatever

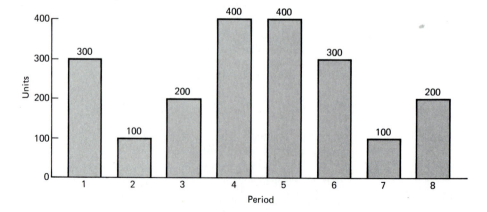

inventory level is required prior to period 1 at no additional cost, compute the total (carrying) cost of using a pure inventory strategy of producing at an average requirement.

5 The Speedee Bicycle Company makes 10-speed bikes that sell for $100 each. This year's demand forecast is as shown. Units not sold are carried in stock at a cost of 20 percent of the average inventory value per year, and storage costs are $2 per bike-year based upon maximum inventory.

Bike Demand Forecast

Quarter	Units
First	30
Second	120
Third	60
Fourth	70

(a) Plot the demand as a histogram on a quarterly basis, and show the average requirement as a dotted line on your graph.

(b) Assume that Speedee wishes to maintain a steady work force and to produce at a uniform rate (that is, with no overtime, back orders, subcontracting, or capacity changes) by letting inventories absorb all fluctuations. How many bikes must the company have on hand on January 1 in order to meet the forecast demand throughout the year?

(c) For an incremental amount of $400 in labor costs (total), Speedee can vary its workforce size so as to produce exactly to demand. Compare the costs of producing at a uniform rate and producing at a variable rate, and indicate which plan is less costly and the net difference in cost.

6 The Wexford Glass Company has a skilled work force capable of producing 2,000 sets of hand-cut crystal per month. The company has a highly seasonal annual demand of 24,000 sets, with quarterly indexes of $Q_1 = .30$, $Q_2 = .80$, $Q_3 = 1.90$, $Q_4 = 1.00$. The company policy is to do all the work in-house with its own steady work force on regular hours, and it does not accept back orders. The firm absorbs demand fluctuations by carrying inventory at a cost of $20 per set-year. To meet the demand,

(a) What inventory balance must be on hand by the end of each quarter?

(b) What is the average inventory balance?

(c) What is the cost for carrying the necessary inventory?

7 An aggregate planner at Duotronix has estimated the following demand requirements for forthcoming work periods, which represent one complete demand cycle for them. Duotronix is a "going concern" and expects the next demand cycle to be similar to this one.

Period	Forecast	Period	Forecast
1	400	6	1,200
2	400	7	600
3	600	8	200
4	800	9	200
5	1,200	10	400

Five plans are being considered:

Plan 1. Vary the labor force from an initial capability of 400 units to whatever is required to meet demand.

Amount of Change	Incremental Cost to Change Labor Force	
	Increase	Decrease
200 units	$ 9,000	$ 9,000
400 units	15,000	18,000
600 units	18,000	30,000

Plan 2. Maintain a stable work force capable of producing 600 units per period, and meet demand by overtime at a premium of $40 per unit. Idle-time costs are equivalent to $60 per unit.

Plan 3. Vary inventory levels, but maintain a stable work force producing at an average requirement rate with no overtime or idle time. The carrying cost per unit per period is $20. (The company can arrange to have whatever inventory level is required before period 1 at no additional cost.)

Plan 4. Produce at a steady rate of 400 units per period, and accept a limited number of back orders during periods when demand exceeds 400 units. The stockout cost (profit, goodwill, and so on) of lost sales is $110 per unit.

Plan 5. Produce at a steady rate of 200 units per period, and subcontract for excess requirements at a marginal cost of $40 per unit.

Graph the forecast in the form of a histogram, and analyze the relevant costs of the various plans. You may assume that the initial (period 1) work force can be set at a desired level without incurring additional cost. Summarize your answer in the form of a table showing the comparative costs of each plan.

8 Two mixed-strategy plans have been proposed for the Duotronix situation in the previous problem. Assume that the pattern inherent in the demand cycle given will be repeated in the next demand cycle.

Plan 6 (back orders and limited inventory). Produce at a steady rate of 400 units per period, and carry inventory at $20 per unit-period. Assume that 200 units of excess demand can be satisfied by back orders placed in period 4 and filled in period 8. A 200-unit inventory is available at the beginning of period 1 and should also be available at the beginning of the next cycle.

Plan 7 (subcontracting and limiting inventory). Produce at a steady rate of 400 units per period, and subcontract for excess requirements at a marginal cost of $40 per unit. A 400-unit inventory is available at the beginning of period 1 and should also be available at the beginning of the next cycle. Carry inventory at $20 per unit-period.

Determine the comparative costs of the two plans.

9 A relay manufacturer uses a modified response method to plan production for the upcoming months and has found that a control number of .2 is satisfactory. Given the forecast shown, if actual demands in January and February were 5,600 and 4,300 units, respectively, what modified production quantity should be scheduled for March? *Note*: Adjustments can be made almost instantaneously.

Forecast Demand

January	5,000 units
February	5,200 units
March	5,800 units

10 Burton Bag Company uses a modified response model with a 1-month lead time and a K factor of .6 for aggregate planning. Its model includes adjustments for demand (orders received but not yet filled) and inventory levels. The forecast production for April was 10,000 units. If February inventories were 2,000 units higher than planned and unfilled demand was 1,000 less than estimated, how many units should be scheduled for production in April?

11 Sun Valley Ski Company, which produces the famous Sun Ski, has a production cost of $60 per pair during regular time and $70 per pair on overtime. The firm's production capacity and forecast quarterly demands are shown below. Beginning inventory is 200 pairs, and stock is carried at a cost of $5 per pair-quarter. Demand is to be met without any hiring, layoff, subcontracting, or back orders. Unused regular time has a cost of $20 per pair.

Supply, units from		Demand, units for				Capacity	
		First quarter	Second quarter	Third quarter	Fourth quarter and final	Unused	Total available
Initial inventory							200
Period 1	Regular						700
Period 1	Overtime						300
Period 2	Regular						700
Period 2	Overtime						300
Period 3	Regular						700
Period 3	Overtime						300
Period 4	Regular						700
Period 4	Overtime						300
Forecast demand		900	500	200	1,900	700	4,200

(a) Develop the preferred plan, and present it in the form of a solved matrix.
(b) What is the minimum total cost of the plan? [Adapted from **10**:211.]

12 Set up and solve the following aggregate planning problem via the transportation linear matrix method.

	Regular	Overtime	Subcontracting
Production capacity/period	8,000 units	2,000 units	2,000 units
Production cost/unit	$7	$9	$10

Inventory: initial = 1,000 units. Carrying cost = $1 per unit-period. Demand in units per period: (1) = 6,000; (2) = 18,000; (3) = 3,000; (4) = 10,000. Back orders are not allowed, and unused regular time has a cost of $4 per unit.
(a) Show your solution matrix.
(b) Tabulate the total cost of your plan.

13 Complete option B of Solved Prob. 3.
14 Using the data from Solved Prob. 4,
   (a) Compute the number of units lost via stockout if the actual demand is as given and no modified response is made.
   (b) Compute the number of units that are actually sold under the original (constant work force) plan versus the modified response plan.
15 Shown below is the expected demand for bank card machine keyboards manufactured at a plant in Minneapolis. The firm produces in lots of 50 units and currently has 40 units on hand. It plans to keep a reserve amount of 30 units on hand as safety stock (SS) for periods of unusually heavy demand. Develop a tentative master schedule for the keyboards (in other words, one that doesn't allow ending inventories to drop below 30 units).

Initial inventory = 40	Week									
Production run = 50	1	2	3	4	5	6	7	8	9	10
Customer forecast			5	10	5	5	10	10	15	10
Service forecast			5		10			10		
Domestic orders	10	15	10	10						
International orders		5	5			5				

16 Solar Products Company produces five types of solar panels to customer order. The standard hours to produce each type of panel are as follows:

$$SP7A = 20 \text{ hr} \qquad S12B = 40 \text{ hr} \qquad S25C = 90 \text{ hr}$$
$$SP8A = 32 \text{ hr} \qquad S15B = 60 \text{ hr}$$

The company has 110 standard hours of capacity available and plans on 22 workdays per month. A consultant has developed the following tentative plan for production (in units).

Panel	Jan.	Feb.	Mar.	Apr.	May	June
SP7A	50	45	45	55	50	60
SP8A	—	11	20	15	—	20
S12B	25	—	—	5	10	—
S15B	—	—	15	—	—	—
S25C	5	24	—	—	15	—
Total units	80	80	80	75	75	80

(a) Arrange the plan into a master schedule format for make-to-order products.
(b) What is the ratio of the 6-month load to the 6-month capacity—that is, what is the expected utilization percentage of the capacity?
(c) Does the schedule appear to be satisfactory?

17 Clear Lake Foundry produces three types of castings (A, B, C) to customer order. The standard hours per unit and proposed delivery schedule over the next five periods are as shown below.

Product	Standard hr/unit	Demand, units/period				
		1	2	3	4	5
A	10	8	10	10	8	10
B	60	4	8	2	—	2
C	30	10	6	—	30	20

Plant capacity is set at 620 standard hours per period, based on a single-shift operation.
(a) Arrange the data into a tentative master schedule in a make-to-order format.
(b) What changes would you recommend in order to better utilize the plant capacity?

18 Medical Instruments Company markets two ultrasonic cardiograms to an international market: ECHO 27 and VUE 5. The anticipated demand over the next six periods is as follows:

	Expected Demand during Period					
	1	2	3	4	5	6
Domestic orders						
ECHO 27	20	20	15	10	5	5
VUE 5	35	30	20	20	10	—
International orders						
ECHO 27	8	6	4	—	—	2
VUE 5	12	5	7	5	—	—
Forecast						
ECHO 27	5	3	10	20	30	30
VUE 5	—	5	5	10	10	30

Additional data:

	Beginning Inventory	Lot Size	Safety Stock
ECHO 27	64	40	10
VUE 5	50	60	20

Develop a tentative master schedule based upon the data given.

REFERENCES

[1] Abramowitz, Irvin: *Production Management*, Ronald Press, New York, 1967.
[2] Bowman, E. H.: "Consistency and Optimality in Managerial Decision Making," *Management Science*, vol. 4, Jan. 1963, pp. 100–103.
[3] Garrett, Leonard J., and Milton Silver: *Production Management Analysis*, 2d ed., Harcourt Brace Jovanovich, New York, 1974.
[4] Guiles, Melinda Grenier: "GM's Chevrolet Nova is Part Japanese, But Car Buyers Prefer the Real Thing," *The Wall Street Journal*, Dec. 13, 1985, p. 31.
[5] Holt, C. C., F. Modigliani, J. F. Muth, and H. A. Simon: *Production Planning, Inventories, and Work Force*, Prentice-Hall, Englewood Cliffs, NJ, 1960.
[6] Lee, S. M., and L. J. Moore: "A Practice Approach to Production Scheduling," *Production and Inventory Management*, 1st quarter 1974, pp. 79–92.
[7] Magee, J. F.: *Production Planning and Inventory Control*, McGraw-Hill, New York, 1958.
[8] Moore, Franklin G., and Thomas E. Hendrick: *Production/Operations Management*, 9th ed., Richard D. Irwin, Homewood, IL, 1985.
[9] Shearon, Winston T.: "A Study of the Aggregate Planning Production Problem," Ph.D. dissertation, Colgate Darden Graduate School of Business Administration, University of Virginia, 1974.
[10] Shore, Barry: *Operations Management*, McGraw-Hill, New York, 1973.
[11] Taubert, William H.: "A Search Decision Rule for the Aggregate Scheduling Problem," *Management Science*, February 1968, pp. 343–359.
[12] Vergin, R. C.: "Production Planning under Seasonal Demand," *Journal of Industrial Engineering*, May 1966, pp. 260–266.

SELF QUIZ: CHAPTER 8

POINTS: 15

Part I True/False [1 point each = 6]

1. __F__ The purpose of aggregate planning is to adjust production so as to satisfy all customer demand.
2. __T__ A back-order strategy assumes that customers are willing to accept delivery in a later time period.
3. __F__ The transportation linear programming approach to aggregate planning can accommodate overtime and subcontract strategies, but not back-order strategies.
4. __F__ The linear decision rule (LDR) is the most widely used of the numerous aggregate planning methods available to managers.
5. __T__ Service industries do not typically have all of the same aggregate planning strategies that are available to manufacturing industries.
6. __F__ Both manufacturing assembly and process industry master schedules begin with the end items and work backward to determine the material and capacity required to produce those end items.

Part II Problems [3 points each = 9. Calculate and select your answer.]

1. Snow-Dasher, Inc. produces snowblowers in a Madison shop with a steady work force on regular hours (no back orders). A quarterly demand of $Q_1 = 500$, $Q_2 = 100$, $Q_3 = 200$, and $Q_4 = 800$ is to be met using a pure inventory strategy where the carrying cost is $80 per unit per year. Assuming adequate inventory is on hand at the start of Q_1, what annual inventory carrying cost is incurred?
   - (a) $18,000
   - (b) $20,000
   - (c) $22,500
   - (d) $72,000
   - (e) None of the above.

2. Northeast Building Products uses a modified response model that includes an adjustment for unfilled orders and inventory on hand. The model uses a 1-month lead time and a control factor (K) of .4. Suppose the forecast production for August is 500 units. If unfilled orders in June were 80 units higher than planned, and inventories 120 units lower than planned, how many units should actually be scheduled for production in August?
   - (a) 300
   - (b) 420
   - (c) 500
   - (d) 580
   - (e) None of the above.

3. A firm producing two lines of custom-designed sportswear has 60 hours of sewing machine time available per day (5 days per week). The firm is tentatively scheduled to produce 22 cartons of jeans (J4s) and 108 cartons of a new line of jackets (J17s) during the 5 weeks as shown in the "trial" master schedule below. What is the ratio of cumulative hours of load to cumulative capacity?

   - (a) 86%
   - (b) 116%
   - (c) 130%
   - (d) 134%
   - (e) None of the above.

	Units Scheduled to Be Produced during Week					
	1	*2*	*3*	*4*	*5*	*Std Hr/Unit*
J4 jeans (22)	5	—	10	—	7	30
J17 jackets (108)	20	28	15	25	20	10
Total load (std hr)						Cumulative
Capacity available						Cumulative

CHAPTER 9
MATERIALS MANAGEMENT: PURCHASING AND INVENTORY ACQUISITION

INTRODUCTION

In a dramatic switch of philosophy, the Huffy Corporation decided to give up having their warehouses fully stocked with assembled bicycles. Instead they planned to satisfy demand by assembling the bicycles as needed. This meant getting parts from suppliers, assembling the bicycles, and shipping them to the retail stores without any hitches. Any time Huffy ran out of stock, they risked losing sales. But the costs of trying to carry about $70 million of inventory and the availability of computerized controls prompted Huffy management to risk the change. And within 2 years, Huffy had cut its investment almost in half. According to *The Wall Street Journal*,

> So far, the lean-inventory strategy is working fairly well at Huffy and most companies. They are saving millions of dollars in interest and storage costs by keeping the lowest inventory-to-sales ratios in more than a decade. And in doing so, they are losing remarkably few sales [5].

Other companies report similar moves that are hailed as "very positive." A typical annual report says, "Our inventories continue to decrease. In the past year, we have brought them down from $68 to $45 million, a reduction of 34 percent. We expect to continue to reduce our inventories" [4].

But the impact of inventory modernization programs is not always limited to the companies producing the finished goods. General Motors' electronic systems division (Delco Electronics) has switched to the "just-in-time" inventory philosophy used by their Japanese competitors. Now their 800 materials suppliers must deliver materials as needed, but in smaller batches and more frequently than before. This enables Delco to avoid costly inventory accumulations while still retaining the flexibility to respond quickly to its market. However, it has also prompted some Delco suppliers to relocate closer to Delco's central manufacturing plant, lest they lose out to suppliers who can offer better service [2].

SCOPE OF MATERIALS MANAGEMENT

MATERIALS

Materials are the raw materials, components, subassemblies, and supplies used to produce a good or service. Most materials are transformed into finished products, but supplies are consumed in daily operations. Materials become direct costs, whereas supplies are often classified as overhead.

Manufacturing Firms For many manufacturing firms, materials account for one-half to three-quarters of their product cost. And as production activities become more highly automated (and use less direct labor), the materials proportion of the product cost tends to increase. Meanwhile, the supplies of many natural resources are diminishing while the costs to acquire them are spiraling. This supply-demand imbalance has put pressures on materials managers in manufacturing firms.

Service Firms Service systems typically use fewer raw materials and components but more consumable supplies and service parts. The proportion of their material costs is lower—and may even approach zero. Hospitals, legal services, and airlines are examples of firms that do not produce physical products. Still, these and other service organizations are concerned with the acquisition, storage, and security of their supplies. So good materials management procedures are important to them as well. Such control is also important to wholesalers and retailers, who warehouse and distribute products rather than creating them. In summary, anyone investing funds in materials and supplies should have an interest in the effective management of those materials.

MATERIALS MANAGEMENT

Materials management is the planning, organizing, and controlling of the flow of materials, from their initial purchase through internal operations to the distribution of finished goods. Figure 9-1 identifies the major concerns of materials

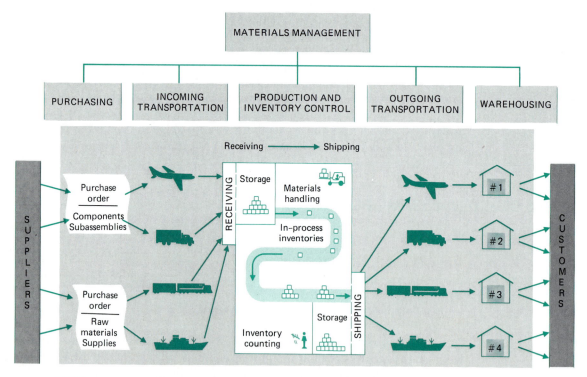

FIGURE 9-1 Major Elements of Materials Management Systems

management as (1) purchasing, (2) transportation (incoming and outgoing), (3) control through production and inventory management (includes receiving, storage, shipping, materials handling, and inventory counting), and (4) warehousing and distribution.

As is evident from Fig. 9-1, materials management is not always a clear and distinctive activity. And not all organizations have a formally designated "materials manager." In those firms that do, the manager may have responsibility for the flow of materials through the entire organization. He or she must then ensure that the right materials are available at the right time and in the right place. This means avoiding an excess of materials that would tie up unnecessary funds (and space) while at the same time precluding shortages that might cause a halt to production. By coordinating the interests of production, financial, and marketing managers, a materials manager can make the best use of the organization's investment in materials.

FOCUS OF THIS CHAPTER

We begin this chapter with a description of the purchasing process and some techniques for evaluating make versus buy decisions. Some guidelines for materials handling are reviewed next, as well as some reasons for carrying inventories. Then we take up the cost components of inventories and what quantities are most economical to order (or to produce). We end the chapter with some comments on inventory classification and counting systems.

The chapter is relatively condensed, but upon completing it you should be able to describe the materials management function and know how to calculate the major costs associated with managing inventories.

PURCHASING

THE PURCHASING PROCESS

Purchasing is the acquisition of goods or services in exchange for funds. Figure 9-2 depicts the purchasing process in schematic form. Some common materials and supplies are purchased by simply picking up the phone and giving the vendor an order. Other, more specialized or higher-valued purchases may warrant obtaining competitive bids from several suppliers. After bids are received, they are carefully evaluated, orders are placed, and the goods or services are ultimately delivered to the requisitioning department. The vendor's shipping invoice then signals the accounting department to pay for the goods or services.

Orders   The process of obtaining quotations and placing orders depends upon the category of item purchased.

- For *normal items*, buyers issue a request for quotation (RFQ), and vendors respond with a bid which gives the price, delivery terms, and terms of

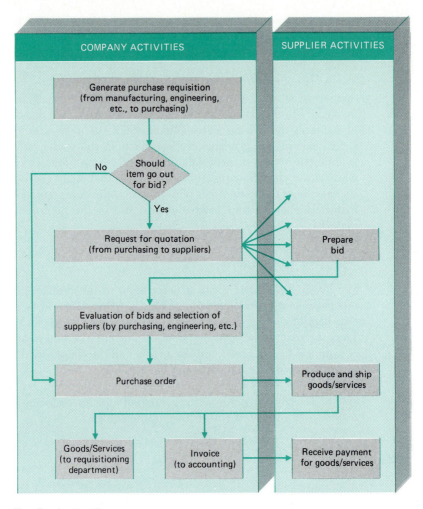

FIGURE 9-2   The Purchasing Process

payment. The buyer evaluates the sellers' offers, selects one on the basis of an established set of criteria, and issues a purchase order (P.O.)

■ *High-volume items* that will be used continuously are often supplied under a blanket purchase order, which usually establishes a firm price for a large volume of items. It provides for delivery at future times as specified by the buyer. For example, a blanket P.O. would enable a producer of furnaces to ensure an annual supply of 12,000 electric fan motors at a quantity discount price. The furnace manufacturer would issue release orders as needed to meet the production schedule during the year.

■ *High-value items* that are infrequently purchased, such as large computers, turbine generators, and specialized equipment, often require the consultation of company engineers and vendor specialists. The purchasing department coordinates these contacts.

- *Low-value items* such as stationery may cost less than the cost of processing an order, which may run as high as $50 or $60. Such items are often supplied under *open purchase orders* by local suppliers. Individual departments of a firm sometimes obtain these supplies directly (without involving the purchasing department), but transactions are typically limited in the total amount, for example, up to $100.

PURCHASING RESPONSIBILITIES

Purchasing responsibilities extend beyond the limited "buying" of a product. Professional buyers must have specialized knowledge about selected product lines and be familiar with engineering specifications, contract law, shipping regulations, and a myriad of related factors. Figure 9-3 outlines the major responsibilities of purchasing department personnel.

Alternative sources of supply help ensure competitive prices and reduce the risk of materials shortages. But having too many suppliers is not always best either. Close working relations with a few (certified) suppliers can give the firm more consistent, high-quality supplies and better coordination of deliveries. Reliable supplies are essential to firms moving toward low inventory (or "stockless") positions in their own plants.

Important variables to consider in selecting suppliers include: (1) price, (2) delivery, (3) quantity, (4) quality, (5) service, (6) maintenance, (7) technical support, (8) financial stability, and (9) terms of purchase. Trade discounts (based upon whether the buyer is a manufacturer, distributor, or user), cash discounts (for prompt payment), and shipping terms (for instance, F.O.B. shipping point) all affect cost. In some cases, suppliers are ranked on the basis of several criteria, which are assigned importance ratings of 1 to 10.

$$\text{Expected score} = \Sigma \text{ (importance rating} \times \text{criteria value)} \qquad (9\text{-}1)$$

EXAMPLE 9-1

A municipal utility in Texas has four suppliers for watt-hour meters. The company's computer has recognized a low-stock situation and must issue a

---

1. Identify and develop sources of supply.
2. Select suppliers and negotiate contracts.
3. Maintain working relations and control vendor performance.
4. Evaluate supply-demand economics and initiate cost and make-or-buy studies.
5. Maintain supply system database.

FIGURE 9-3 Purchasing Department Responsibilities

purchase recommendation to the buyer on the basis of the criteria shown. What rank will the computer give to the respective vendors?

	Importance Rating (1–10)	Vendor			
Criterion		(A) Western Supply	(B) Central Electric	(C) Roundy Corp.	(D) Ohio Meters
1 Price	6	.4	.4	.6	.7
2 Field service	3	.7	.7	.3	.2
3 Delivery reliability	4	.8	.9	.2	.3
4 Delivery time	1	.5	.3	.2	.2
5 Ease of maintenance	8	.6	.4	.3	.3
6 Computer adaptability	2	.5	.6	.0	.9
7 Product life	3	.5	.4	.3	.3

SOLUTION

The computer will sum the weighted scores for each potential vendor and print out a list of ranks, with "1" being the highest and "4" being the lowest.

Supplier A = 6(.4) + 3(.7) + 4(.8) + 1(.5) + 8(.6) + 2(.5) + 3(.5) = 15.50
Supplier B = 6(.4) + 3(.7) + 4(.9) + 1(.3) + 8(.4) + 2(.6) + 3(.4) = 14.00
Supplier C = 6(.6) + 3(.3) + 4(.2) + 1(.2) + 8(.3) + 2(.0) + 3(.3) = 8.80
Supplier D = 6(.7) + 3(.2) + 4(.3) + 1(.2) + 8(.3) + 2(.9) + 3(.3) = 11.30

Ranks are 1 = supplier A, 2 = supplier B, 3 = supplier D, 4 = supplier C.

In an effort to exert extra influence, suppliers frequently offer buyers free lunches, gifts, and entertainment. In some foreign countries, extra concessions (bribes and kickbacks) are accepted as a way of doing business. However, many U.S. firms have adopted strict codes of conduct to ensure that their buyers do not become obligated to overly aggressive sales representatives.

Political situations are an ever-present influence on sources of supply. This is especially true as the United States, European Economic Community, and other countries resort to more use of economic sanctions to achieve political objectives such as discouraging segregation, terrorism, or military aggression. Reciprocity also influences the choice of supplier, although firms do not always recognize or acknowledge it. For example, when a copper producer buys electric motors, it seems to make good business sense to buy from a supplier who is a large user of its copper. However, when the (unwritten) purchasing behavior reaches a point where reciprocal purchases constitute conditions for future business, it becomes an issue of ethical and legal concern to responsible purchasing personnel. In general, the legal codes are designed to preserve a condition of "fairness" by promoting free and open competition among suppliers.

As suggested in Fig. 9-3, purchasing department responsibilities also extend to studies of supply-demand economics and other analytical efforts aimed at

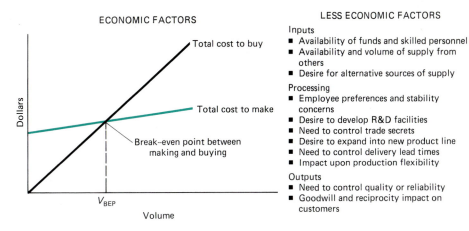

FIGURE 9-4   Economic and Less Economic Factors Influencing Make-or-Buy Decisions

improving purchasing effectiveness. This includes projections of long-range needs, compilations of data on price and delivery trends, value analysis, and make-or-buy comparisons (which we will take up next). *Value analysis* is an attempt to reduce costs by using more cost-effective materials or components. Buyers sometimes work with value engineers here to see if costs can be reduced by eliminating, simplifying, combining, or substituting less expensive materials or components, without affecting performance of the item being purchased.

Computerized inventory systems (such as MRP systems) are designed to integrate purchased parts into the normal flow of a firm's internal production schedule. This means that full, accurate, and up-to-the-minute data on vendor-supplied items are essential. Specifications, quantities, and delivery dates must be just as error-free as for internally made components. In essence, the suppliers' plants are "outside factories" that are like extensions of a firm's own production operations.

MAKE-OR-BUY DECISIONS

Decisions concerning whether to make or buy components involve both economic and noneconomic considerations. Economically, an item is a candidate for in-house production if the firm has sufficient capacity and if the component's value is high enough to cover all the variable costs of production plus make some contribution to fixed costs. Low volumes of usage favor buying, which entails little or no fixed costs. Figure 9-4 illustrates.

EXAMPLE 9-2 | Auburn Machine Company produces parts that are shipped nationwide. It has an opportunity to produce plastic packaging cases which are currently purchased at $.70 each. Annual demand depends largely on economic conditions, but long-run estimates are as shown.

Demand (units)	20,000	30,000	40,000	50,000	60,000
Chance (%)	10	30	40	15	5

If the company produces the cases itself, it must renovate an existing work area and purchase a molding machine which will result in annual fixed costs of $8,000. Variable costs for labor, materials, and overhead are estimated at $.50 per case.

(a) Should Auburn Machine make or buy the cases?

(b) At what volume of production is it more profitable to produce in-house rather than purchase from an outside supplier?

SOLUTION

(a) *First*, determine the expected volume by treating the percentage of chance as an empirical probability. Thus, $E(D) = 37,500$ units.

Demand D	Chance P(D)	$D \cdot P(D)$
20,000	.10	2,000
30,000	.30	9,000
40,000	.40	16,000
50,000	.15	7,500
60,000	.05	3,000
		37,500

Next, Auburn Machine should produce the cases if the expected cost to produce is less than the expected cost to purchase.

Expected cost to produce:

$$TC = FC + VC(V) = \$8,000 + (\$.50/\text{unit})(37,500 \text{ units}) = \$26,750$$

Expected cost to purchase:

$$TC = (\text{price})(V) = (\$.70/\text{unit})(37,500 \text{ units}) = \$26,250$$

Conclusion. Continue to purchase the cases.

(b) The break-even point is the volume of production where the total costs to make equal the total costs to buy:

TC to make = TC to buy

$$FC + VC(V) = P(V)$$

$$\$8,000 + (\$.50)V = (\$.70)V$$

$$\$.20V = \$8,000$$

$$V = 40,000 \text{ units}$$

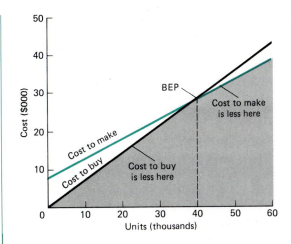

For volumes above 40,000 units, it is more economical to make the cases in-house.

The economic analysis becomes more complex as we begin to consider the extent to which a product will be using capacity that could be used to produce other products, that is, the *opportunity cost* of producing rather than buying. Often the fixed costs of plant and equipment depreciation are irrevocable ("sunk" costs), so the extent to which a product covers these costs is less significant. Or more than one product can be a candidate for carrying the fixed costs (see Solved Prob. 1).

MATERIALS HANDLING, STORAGE, AND RETRIEVAL

Materials handling is the movement of materials from receiving, through operations, to final shipment. It often represents a significant part of the cost-of-goods-sold, but it adds no tangible value to the product. Conventional systems use workers, assisted by trucks, fork lifts, cranes and hoists, conveyors, pipelines, and other equipment. Automated systems use robots and computer-guided vehicles. About one-third of all robots are used for materials handling. Some of the automatically guided vehicle systems are directed by software commands emitted from wires buried in the shop or warehouse floor.

Figure 9-5 lists some guidelines for conventional systems.

Service industries are typically more concerned with the flow of personal effects than with the flow of materials. For example, airports must accommodate the handling of luggage, and subways are designed for the flow of people.

Automated storage and retrieval systems (AS/AR) are computer-controlled materials-handling systems which receive, store, and deliver inventory to high, cube-storage locations in quantities specified by the computer. Highly automated systems are integrated with production so that material requirements are automatically identified from the bill-of-material database. Items are selected by part-

1 Plan handling as a complete system.
2 Minimize handling volume and frequency.
3 Optimize load size and weight.
4 Use direct, rapid, steady flows.
5 Minimize idle time of equipment and operators.
6 Allow for breakdowns, changes, and maintenance.

FIGURE 9-5   Materials-Handling Guidelines (Conventional Systems)

retrieval robots. Then computer-controlled stackers and conveyors move them to appropriate collection (or kitting) locations or work stations. In addition, inventory, work-in-process, and material-requirements-planning (MRP) records are automatically updated.

PURPOSE OF INVENTORIES

Inventories are idle resources that possess economic value. They are vitally important to manufacturing firms, of course, because they store the value of the labor and processing activities used to make their products. For accounting purposes, firms often classify their inventories as either (1) raw materials, (2) work-in-process, or (3) finished goods.

Adequate inventories facilitate production activities and help to assure customers of good service. On the other hand, carrying inventories ties up working capital on goods that sit idle—not earning any return on investment. Hence the major problem of inventory management is to maintain adequate, but not excessive, levels of inventories. Figure 9-6 summarizes some of the major reasons for holding inventories.

1 *Service customers* with variable (immediate and seasonal) demands.
2 *Protect against* supply errors, shortages, and stockouts.
3 *Help level production activities*, stabilize employment, and improve labor relations.
4 *Decouple successive stages* in operations so breakdowns do not stop the entire system.
5 *Facilitate the production of different products* on the same facilities.
6 Provide a means of obtaining and handling materials in economic lot sizes and of *gaining quantity discounts*.
7 Provide a means of *hedging against future price and delivery uncertainties*, such as strikes, price increases, and inflation.

FIGURE 9-6   Reasons for Carrying Inventories

DEPENDENT AND INDEPENDENT DEMAND

If inventories are to achieve the purposes listed above, someone must decide *how much* to order and *when* an inventory is required. The "how much" question is largely a function of costs, and our inquiry here will extend to the concept of an economic order quantity. The "when to order" question is a function of the firm's forecast or scheduled requirements. If the item is a finished product and has a demand that is "independent" of the demand for other items, an order point (or reorder point) technique can help to answer the question.

On the other hand, most items brought into inventory in manufacturing firms are components or subassemblies of finished products. Their demand is "dependent" upon the finished-product demand, and although the finished-product demand may be uncertain, the requirements for components vis-à-vis other components are fixed by design. There is no need to consider each component as an entity with independent demand characteristics—in fact, it is better not to do so. In this situation, the "when to order" question is best answered by an MRP approach.

Dependent demand inventory consists of the raw materials, components, and subassemblies that are used in the production of parent or end items. For example, the demand for computer keyboards depends on the demand for the parent item, computers. *Manufacturing inventory* is largely dependent and predictable.

Independent demand inventory consists of the finished products, service parts, and other items whose demand arises more directly from the uncertain market environment. Thus, *distribution inventories* often have an independent and highly uncertain demand. Dependent demands can often be calculated, whereas independent demands usually require some kind of forecasting.

INVENTORY COSTS AND ORDER QUANTITIES

The major costs associated with procuring and holding inventories are as follows:

- *Ordering and setup costs* for placing orders, expediting, inspecting, and changing or setting up facilities to produce in house
- *Carrying costs* on invested capital, handling, storage, insurance, taxes, obsolescence, spoilage, and data-processing costs[1]
- *Purchase costs* including the price paid, or the labor, material, and overhead charges necessary to produce the item

TOTAL COSTS AND THE EOQ MODEL

The total cost (TC) of stocking inventory is the sum of the cost of ordering, plus the cost of carrying, plus the purchase cost. If D equals demand in units on an annual

---

[1] An in-depth study by Lambert suggested firms tend to underestimate their carrying costs. His studies revealed rates of 14 to 35 percent [3].

basis, C_o equals cost to prepare or set up for an order, C_c equals cost to carry a unit in stock for a given time period, P equals purchase cost, Q equals lot size, and $Q/2$ equals average inventory, then the relationship can be expressed mathematically:

$$\text{Total cost} = \text{ordering cost} + \text{carrying cost} + \text{purchase cost}$$

$$\text{where} \quad \text{Ordering cost} = \left(\frac{C_o\$}{\text{order}}\right)\left(\frac{\text{order}}{Q \text{ units}}\right)\left(\frac{D \text{ units}}{\text{yr}}\right)$$

$$\text{Carrying cost} = \left(\frac{C_c\$}{\text{unit-yr}}\right)\left(\frac{Q \text{ units}}{2}\right)$$

$$\text{Purchase cost} = \left(\frac{P\$}{\text{unit}}\right)\left(\frac{D \text{ units}}{\text{yr}}\right)$$

$$\therefore \text{TC} = C_o \frac{D}{Q} + C_c \frac{Q}{2} + PD \tag{9-2}$$

Differentiating with respect to the order quantity, Q, yields the slope of the TC curve. [*Note:* Those whose calculus is a bit rusty may skip down to Eq. (9-3) or refer to Solved Prob. 4 for the differentiation explanation.]

$$\frac{d\text{TC}}{dQ} = -C_o DQ^{-2} + \frac{C_c Q^0}{2} + 0$$

Setting this first derivative equal to zero identifies the point where the TC is a minimum.

$$0 = -\frac{C_o D}{Q^2} + \frac{C_c Q^0}{2} + 0$$

$$\therefore Q = EOQ = \sqrt{\frac{2C_o D}{C_c}} \tag{9-3}$$

Equation (9-3) is known as the economic order quantity (EOQ) or economic lot size (ELS) equation. It is used to determine the order quantity that will satisfy estimated demand at the lowest total cost. Note that although the purchase price, P, is an important component of total cost, the term drops out upon differentiating. Thus, so long as the purchase price does not vary with the quantity ordered, it should not directly affect the decision as to what is the most economical lot size to purchase. Figure 9-7 describes the relationship between the relevant ordering and carrying costs. Note also that the total-cost curve is relatively flat in the area of the EOQ, so small changes in the amount ordered do not have a significant effect on total costs.

Once the economic order quantity, Q, has been determined, the minimum inventory cost can be computed by substituting this Q value into the total-cost equation—Eq. (9-2). The number of orders per year required is:

$$\text{Orders/yr} = \frac{D \text{ units/yr}}{Q \text{ units/order}} = \frac{D}{Q} \tag{9-4}$$

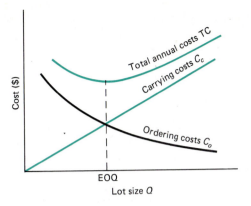

FIGURE 9-7 Economic Order Quantity (EOQ)

EXAMPLE 9-3

Overland Motors uses 25,000 gear assemblies each year and purchases them at $3.40 each. It costs $50 to process and receive an order, and inventory can be carried at a cost of $.78 per unit-year.
(a) How many assemblies should be ordered at a time?
(b) How many orders per year should be placed?

SOLUTION

(a) $\text{EOQ} = \sqrt{\dfrac{2C_oD}{C_c}} = \sqrt{\dfrac{2(50)(25,000)}{.78}} = 1,790$ assemblies

(b) $\text{Orders/yr} = \dfrac{D}{Q} = \dfrac{25,000}{1,790} = 14$ orders/yr

Carrying costs are sometimes denoted as an annual percentage (%) of the purchase price P. If so, $C_c = (\%)(P)$ and is still expressed in dollars per unit-year. The time unit used (for example, year) can vary, but both D and C_c must be in the same time units. (See Solved Prob. 6.)

ASSUMPTIONS OF THE BASIC EOQ MODEL

The EOQ equation is a convenient and widely used expression for determining optimal order quantities when the actual cost components and purchase conditions happen to coincide with the variables of the EOQ model. Order tables and nomographs have also been developed that offer a quick and even simpler means of determining the EOQ without necessitating calculations. However, it is well to keep in mind that in a manufacturing operation, obtaining an order at the right time (scheduling) is usually far more crucial than obtaining the exact order quantity. The enthusiastic and sometimes blind acceptance of the EOQ model has tended to obscure this fact in the past.

Aside from the real-world problems of constantly changing requirements, expediting partial shipments, splitting lots, and so on, there are several assumptions underlying the basic EOQ model. Four of them are as follows.

1 Demand and lead time are known and constant.
2 Replenishment is instantaneous at the expiration of the lead time.
3 Purchase costs do not vary with the quantity ordered.
4 Ordering and carrying-cost expressions include all relevant costs (and these costs are constant).

Much of inventory theory is concerned with how to adjust for situations in which the above assumptions do not hold. Chapter 10 is concerned with assumption 1—how to deal with uncertainties in demand and lead time. Assumptions 2 and 3 are the subject of the next two sections of this chapter; we take up the noninstantaneous replenishment situation first and then the situations where purchase costs *do* vary with the quantity ordered. With respect to the inclusion of all relevant costs, assumption 4, the addition of other costs can best be handled by going back to the original total-cost equation—Eq. (9-2). Solved Prob. 4 shows how the EOQ formula changes when storage costs, based upon total rather than average inventory, are included in the model.

ECONOMIC RUN LENGTHS

When a firm is producing its own inventory rather than purchasing it, the order costs are replaced by manufacturing setup costs. (Setup costs are of a fixed nature, like order costs. They represent the one-time costs for machine adjustments, paperwork, scheduling efforts, and the like, to begin production of a different item.) The EOQ equation must also be modified to account for the time it takes to produce items, of which only a portion go into inventory. The other portion is used concurrently in the production process or is sold as produced. The *production rate p*, is, of course, noninstantaneous and must be greater than or equal to the *demand rate d*.

Figure 9-8 illustrates the difference between the instantaneous and noninstantaneous supply situations. With the basic EOQ, all goods go into inventory

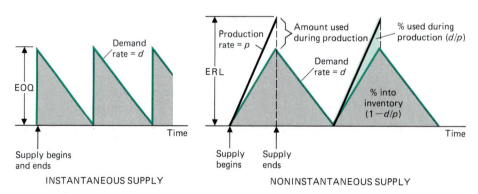

FIGURE 9-8 Inventory Quantities in EOQ and ERL Models

when received (instantaneously) and are withdrawn, or used, at a demand rate of d units per period. Carrying costs apply to the whole EOQ amount.

The modification to the EOQ equation for noninstantaneous supply does not affect C_o (which now becomes the setup cost) or the total demand, D. But it acts to reduce the carrying cost, C_c, by deleting the carrying charge on that portion of the production run that does not go into inventory. If d = demand per day and p = production per day, the ratio d/p represents the proportion of production that is allocated to daily demand, and $1 - (d/p)$ represents that portion of the production run that goes into inventory. For example, if d = 75 units per day and p = 100 units per day, then d/p = 75/100; 75 percent is allocated to daily demand, and $1 - .75$, or 25 percent, goes into inventory.

If we take into account the decreased carrying cost of this reduced level of inventory, the economic run length (ERL) in number of units to produce per production setup is:

$$\text{ERL} = \sqrt{\frac{2C_oD}{C_c\,[1 - (d/p)]}} \tag{9-5}$$

where C_o = setup cost in \$/setup
D = annual demand in units/yr
C_c = carrying cost in \$/unit-yr
d = demand rate, for example, units/day
p = production rate, for example, units/day

Note that when the demand rate just equals the production rate, there is no carrying cost, and the run length is continuous. Also, the two rates can be in other time period units so long as they are consistent units.

As suggested in Fig. 9-8 and by Eq. (9-5), if all other factors were constant, the ERL would be greater than the EOQ. This is because the carrying cost does not apply to the total production; it applies only to that amount going into inventory.

EXAMPLE 9-4

A plastics molding firm produces and uses 24,000 Teflon bearing inserts annually. The cost of setting up for production is \$70, and the weekly production rate is 1,000 units. If the production cost is \$5.50 per unit and the annual carrying cost is \$1.50 per unit, how many units should the firm produce during each production run?

SOLUTION
The demand and production rates must be in the same units, so we arbitrarily put both into annual terms, assuming a 52-week year.

$$\text{ERL} = \sqrt{\frac{2C_oD}{C_c[1 - (d/p)]}} = \sqrt{\frac{2(70)(24{,}000)}{1.50[1 - (24{,}000/52{,}000)]}} = 2{,}040 \text{ inserts}$$

At a production rate of 1,000 units per week each production run will last about 2 weeks, so the firm will be producing inserts about every month.

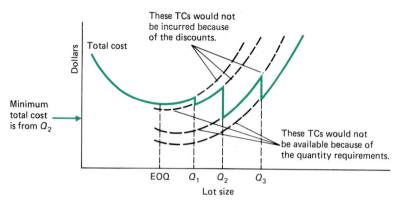

FIGURE 9-9   Quantity Discount Situation

QUANTITY DISCOUNTS

Manufacturers often provide a price discount for buyers who purchase in large volumes. A firm should take advantage of these quantity discounts to the point at which the incremental increase in their annual carrying costs will just equal the savings in purchase cost. The assignment of a different purchase price, depending on the quantity purchased, now makes the price a function of lot quantity Q, with the result that the total-cost function becomes discontinuous, as shown in Fig. 9-9.

A mathematical expression for the optimal order quantity in a discount situation can be derived on the basis of minimizing total costs. However, the most expedient approach to finding an optimal order quantity when a discount is involved is to follow these steps:

1   Determine the EOQ on the basis of the nondiscounted base price.
2   Compare the total cost at this EOQ point with that for price breakpoints at higher volumes.
3   If the EOQ happens to fall in a quantity discount range, recalculate it using the quantity discount price and recheck to see if the revised EOQ or a price breakpoint (to the right) has the lower total cost.

Referring to Fig. 9-9, the lot size designated as EOQ represents the point of minimum slope on the total-cost curve. Thus there is no more optimal order quantity of fewer units. However, because of the discontinuities in the TC curve, points to the right, representing larger lot sizes, may also represent lower total annual costs. The shape of the TC curve will obviously differ from one firm to another, depending upon the firm's cost of capital, ordering costs, and so on, as well as on the price discount rates. For the specific case in Fig. 9-9, the calculation of the total costs [Eq. (9-2)] at the initial EOQ point, as well as at the price breakpoints (Q_1, Q_2, and Q_3), would reveal that Q_2 has the minimum annual total cost. This may suggest, for example, that it is more economical to accept a 10 percent discount on a 5,000-unit purchase and carry a larger average inventory than it is to purchase a smaller EOQ lot size with no discount applied.

EXAMPLE 9-5

A producer of photo equipment buys lenses from a supplier at $100 each. The producer requires 125 lenses per year, and the ordering cost is $18 per order. Carrying costs per unit-year (based on average inventory) are estimated to be $20 each. The supplier offers a 6 percent discount for purchases of 50 lenses and an 8 percent discount for purchases of 100 or more lenses at one time. What is the most economical amount to order at a time?

SOLUTION

Disregarding quantity discounts, the EOQ amount would be:

$$EOQ = \sqrt{\frac{2C_oD}{C_c}} = \sqrt{\frac{2(18)(125)}{20}} = 15 \text{ lenses}$$

And the total annual cost associated with this EOQ is:

$$TC = \text{ordering} + \text{carrying} + \text{purchase}$$

$$= C_o\frac{D}{Q} + C_c\frac{Q}{2} + D(P)$$

$$= 18\left(\frac{125}{15}\right) + 20\left(\frac{15}{2}\right) + 125(100) = \$12,800$$

For a 50-unit order, the purchase cost is reduced by 6 percent of $100, or $6. Assuming that the ordering and carrying costs remain constant, the total annual cost associated with a 50-unit order is:

$$TC = 18\left(\frac{125}{50}\right) + 20\left(\frac{50}{2}\right) + 125(100 - 6) = \$12,295$$

Similarly, the total annual cost associated with a 100-unit order is:

$$TC = 18\left(\frac{125}{100}\right) + 20\left(\frac{100}{2}\right) + 125(100 - 8) = \$12,522$$

The 50-unit lot size results in the lowest total annual cost. Although the purchase price per unit is less with the 100-unit order, the carrying costs begin to outweigh such savings. The costs and direction of change up (↑) or down (↓) are shown below.

Order Quantity	Ordering Cost	+ Carrying Cost	+ Purchase Cost =	Total
15-unit order	$150	$ 150	$12,500	$12,800
50-unit order	45 ↓	500 ↑	11,750 ↓	12,295 ↓
100-unit order	22 ↓	1,000 ↑	11,500 ↓	12,522

In the previous example we assumed that carrying costs remained the same after the discount was applied. Since the discount reduces the amount of invested capital (that is, with the 6 percent discount the purchase price per unit is only $94 instead of $100), the per-unit carrying cost ($20 in this case) will most likely be reduced by some small but proportionate amount. This correction should be accounted for if it is significant.

INVENTORY CLASSIFICATION AND COUNTING

Materials managers responsible for 50,000 or more items of inventory must have well-organized methods of control. This last section of the chapter describes how materials are categorized, coded, counted, and warehoused.

ABC CLASSIFICATION SYSTEM

The time and record-keeping activities required to control thousands of materials cost a good deal of money. Some items of low unit cost, such as bolts and paper clips, may not warrant the expense of exacting control, whereas others do. Typically a small percentage of the items usually accounts for a large percentage of the value of items in stock. This widely recognized characteristic has led many firms to classify their material inventories into three groups, designated as A, B, and C. Figure 9-10 summarizes the key characteristics of this system.

Although the ABC classification system is not precise, it is a useful way of focusing control and is widely used. It does not suffice, however, for all situations. If a manufacturing firm has a computerized inventory system that is highly dependent upon the accuracy of *all* items that are supposed to be in stock (including C items), then close control of all items may be necessary.

BAR CODING

Bar codes are the alternating vertical dark and light spaces that label inventory items with digitally encoded information—usually the number printed below the bar code. They have become such a widely used method of marking goods that

GROUPS	QUANTITY (% of items)	VALUE (% of $)	DEGREE OF CONTROL	TYPES OF RECORDS	SAFETY STOCK	ORDERING PROCEDURES
A items	10–20%	70–80%	Tight	Complete accurate	Low	Careful, accurate; frequent reviews
B items	30–40%	15–20%	Normal	Complete accurate	Moderate	Normal ordering; some expediting
C items	40–50%	5–10%	Simple	Simplified	Large	Order periodically: 1- to 2-year supply

FIGURE 9-10   Characteristics of the ABC Classification System

they now appear on everything from breakfast cereals and missile parts to employee identification cards.

Bar codes are read with optical scanners (wands or light pens) that are linked to computers. You have no doubt encountered bar code readers at supermarkets and retail stores, where they are used to convey the number (code) of an item to the store's computer. The computer might then describe the item and list its price (on your sales receipt), and subtract the quantity you purchase from the total inventory count it keeps of the items in the store.

Bar codes have been one of the most significant advances in automatic identification systems to date. They are an inexpensive and versatile means of automating data so that a firm can identify inventory items, compute their cost, locate them, and keep track of other useful information. And their acceptance in industry is extensive [1]. For example, at Renault's automobile plant in France, they are used to identify and dispatch windshields to the proper destination so they are installed on the right model car. Bar codes keep records of employee time and attendance data at the Westinghouse Specialty Metals facility in Pennsylvania. And at Apple Computer's Macintosh plant in California, bar codes are used to track parts through the whole manufacturing operation, including quality control inspection. They can be used to identify the source of items, what work had been done (or needs doing), who did it, and a myriad of other information.

INVENTORY COUNTING

Today's automated production systems demand that inventory records be highly accurate (for example, 98 percent correct or better). If records are not accurate, the firm may be paying carrying charges for obsolete items, or forced to explain late deliveries to irate customers. To ensure accuracy, all receipts and disbursements of materials are recorded. In addition, the inventory levels are physically counted to check records against actual on-hand balances. Two methods of counting inventory are by (1) periodic physical counting and (2) cycle counting.

- *Periodic physical counting* is frequently a once-a-year activity that uses almost anyone who is available (often on an overtime basis) to help count all inventories in stock. It is a satisfactory method of measuring material quantities in some businesses, particularly those with relatively few items in stock. Industrial plants and warehouses with thousands of items in stock, however, must take a more professional approach to inventory counting.
- *Cycle counting* is the continuous physical counting of inventory so that all items are counted at a specified frequency, and inventory records are periodically reconciled with actual data. Cycle counters are employees who are familiar with storeroom operations, locations, identity codes, and transaction records. They spend their time counting inventory, doing recounts (on items with questionable variation), and location audits, which may reveal other items to be counted. They also analyze transactions to locate causes and implications of errors.

For firms moving toward computerized inventory systems, inventory record inaccuracy is one of the first hurdles to overcome. Record accuracy is measured by first establishing an allowable tolerance (or specified percentage or dollar value) regarding the difference between the actual count and the record. The quantity on the record will be considered accurate if it is within this tolerance. The accuracy of inventory is then expressed as the percentage of items whose actual count turns out to be within this tolerance. For firms just beginning to implement a cycle counting system, dramatic improvement (for example, from 60 percent accuracy to over 90 percent accuracy) may come about in a short time, say a few months. Reaching 100 percent accuracy is much more difficult.

The procedure for determining the number of items to count per day (on average) is relatively simple. A *cycle* is the time required to count all items in inventory at least once. This is often a year. The count frequency is the number of times an item is counted in each cycle.

$$\text{Number of items counted/day} = \frac{\Sigma(\text{number of items})(\text{count frequency})}{\text{number of workdays/cycle}}$$

Items of higher value or that are subject to a higher risk of error should be counted more frequently. For example, A items may be counted monthly, B items quarterly, and C items annually. An example will illustrate.

EXAMPLE 9-6

Empire Building Supply has 6,400 items in stock; 400 are class A items, 1,000 are B items, and 5,000 are C items. The company operates 250 days per year and wishes to count A, B, and C items with a relative frequency of 5, 2, and 1 times a year. How many items should the company count per day, on the average?

SOLUTION

Type	Item Number	Count Frequency	Total Counts
A	400	5	2,000
B	1,000	2	2,000
C	5,000	1	5,000
			9,000

$$\frac{\text{Number of items}}{\text{counted/day}} = \frac{\Sigma \text{ total counts}}{\text{number of days}} = \frac{9,000 \text{ counts}}{250 \text{ days}} = 36 \text{ items counted/day}$$

Note: In a well-disciplined inventory management system, a cycle counter may be able to count and reconcile as many as 40 items per day, so this *may* be within the capacity of one cycle counter at Empire Building Supply.

WAREHOUSING

Warehousing is concerned with receiving and storing finished goods, and distributing them to customers. Major decisions relate to (1) the location and size of warehouses, (2) ordering and handling materials, and (3) record keeping. To provide the same level of protection against running out of stock, a smaller amount of extra (or safety) stock is needed for one location than when several locations are used. Assuming that statistical variations are independent across warehouses, the combined effect (standard deviation, or SD) of safety stocks in several locations is the square root of the sum of the individual effects.

$$\text{Combined effect (SD)} = \sqrt{\Sigma \, (SD)^2}$$

EXAMPLE 9-7

The sketch below depicts the safety stock (SS) amounts in four warehouses in Ohio. Show that one central warehouse or back-up supply at the factory could provide the same service with less stock.

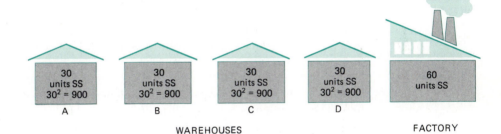

WAREHOUSES   FACTORY

SOLUTION

$$\text{Combined effect (SD)} = \sqrt{\Sigma \, (SD)^2} = \sqrt{900 + 900 + 900 + 900}$$
$$= \sqrt{3,600} = 60 \text{ units}$$

The equivalent effect at the central warehouse can be obtained by stocking 60 units.

The assumption here is, of course, that the same stock can be shipped just as quickly from the central warehouse without any adverse time loss due to transportation.

SUMMARY

Materials management is the planning, organizing, and controlling of the flows of materials, from their initial purchase through internal operations to the distribution of finished goods. Materials responsibilities overlap financial, marketing, production, and other areas.

Purchasing is concerned with identifying sources of supply, selecting suppliers, controlling vendor peformance, continually evaluating supply-demand relationships, and maintaining the supply system database. Professional buyers typically evaluate suppliers on the basis of several criteria (in addition to price), and are sometimes faced with decisions whether to make or buy selected components.

Materials handling is a central responsibility of materials management. Many firms are moving toward highly automated materials-handling systems today.

Inventories are idle resources that have economic value. They enable firms to give better service to customers and protect against stockouts. In the production area, they can be used to help stabilize employment and to decouple operations, so different products can be produced on the same facilities. They also enable firms to do more economic purchasing and hedge against price and delivery uncertainties.

Inventory managers attempt to realize the benefits of inventory while minimizing the total costs necessary to provide for a specified level of service. The basic EOQ equation simply minimizes the ordering and carrying costs. The ERL equation is similar except that setup costs replace ordering costs, and the carrying charge is applied to only that proportion of production that goes into inventory. When the purchase price is a function of quantity, annual costs at the price breakpoints must be compared with the EOQ to determine the optimal order quantity.

Experience has shown that a small percentage of materials (10 to 20 percent) typically accounts for a major portion (70 to 80 percent) of the value of materials in stock. This disproportion has led firms to use the ABC system of classification, which enables them to have closer control over the high-value and critical items.

Accurate records of on-hand quantities are necessary today because of the dependence of computer systems on reliable information. Bar codes are used throughout manufacturing (factories) and service industries (such as hospitals) to track all types of inventory (and other) information. Industrial firms are also finding some success in adopting full-time cycle counting programs.

Warehousing is the last step in the materials management chain before goods go to customers. Careful attention to handling and stock-level decisions can generate savings here, by identifying appropriate stock-level tradeoffs between factory and warehouse locations.

SOLVED PROBLEMS

MAKE-OR-BUY DECISIONS

1 The Evergreen Garden Tractor Company has extra capacity that can be used to produce gears that the company has been buying for $10 each. If Evergreen makes the gears, it will incur materials costs of $3 per unit, labor costs of $4 per unit, and variable overhead costs of $1 per unit. The annual fixed cost associated with the unused capacity is $8,000. Demand over the next year is estimated at 4,000 units.

(a) Would it be profitable for the company to make the gears?

(b) Suppose the capacity could be used by another department for the production of some sports equipment that would cover its fixed and variable costs and contribute $3,000 to profit. Which would be more advantageous, gear production or sports equipment production?

Solution

(a) In this part we assume that the unused capacity has no alternative use.

$$\text{Cost to make:} \quad \text{VC/unit} = \text{materials} + \text{labor} + \text{overhead}$$
$$= \$3 + \$4 + \$1 = \$8/\text{unit}$$

TVC = (4,000 units)($8/unit)		= $32,000
Add: FC		+8,000
	Total costs	$40,000

Cost to buy: Purchase cost = (4,000 units)($10/unit)	=	$40,000
Add: FC		+8,000
	Total costs	$48,000

Making the gears is advantageous because it can be done for $32,000 in variable costs versus the $40,000 cost of purchasing the gears. The $40,000 total cost to make the gears covers both fixed and variable costs, whereas the $40,000 purchase cost does not help cover any fixed cost. Yet the fixed cost must be covered.

(b)

	Make Gears	Purchase Gears and Make Sports Equipment*
TVC	$32,000	$40,000†
FC	8,000	0
Total costs	$40,000	$40,000
Less: Contribution to profit	0	3,000
Net relevant cost	$40,000	$37,000

* TVC of sports equipment are unknown, but TVC and FC of $8,000 are covered by the sports equipment because a $3,000 profit is realized.
† For purchase of gears.

If the company makes the gears, the total cost is $40,000 (that is, TVC + FC). If it makes the sports equipment, the relevant variable cost rises to $40,000, which is the purchase price of the gears. Because the fixed cost is now covered by the sports equipment, the total cost to purchase remains at $40,000. However, the profit contribution from the sports equipment makes it advantageous to produce the sports equipment and buy the gears.

2 Northwest Products Company has received an order for 800 portable heating cells from a military agency. The heaters have a special casing that must be molded to such close tolerances that some of them don't fit and must be reworked. The percentages of defectives, along with the probabilities of occurrence, are as shown.

% Defective D	Probability P(D)
0	.60
1	.20
2	.10
3	.05
4	.03
5	.02

The casings cost $60 to make and $50 each to rework. A buyer in the purchasing department has located a potential supplier who will agree to supply 100 percent acceptable casings at a cost of $62 per casing. We must now determine whether the company should purchase the casings or produce them.

(a) What is the break-even point in the proportion of defectives such that the cost of making the casings would be equal to the cost of buying them?
(b) What proportion of defectives can be expected if the firm produces its own casings?
(c) On the basis of this data, should Northwest make or buy the casings?

Solution

(a) Let P = the proportion of defectives where cost to make equals cost to buy. Then

$$\text{Production cost to make} = \text{purchase cost to buy}$$

$$\text{Initial cost} + \text{rework cost} = (\text{price})(\text{volume})$$

$$(\$60/\text{unit})(800 \text{ units}) + P(\$50/\text{unit})(800 \text{ units}) = (\$62/\text{unit})(800 \text{ units})$$

$$\$48,000 + \$40,000\ P = \$49,600$$

$$\therefore P = \frac{\$1,600}{\$40,000} = .04 = 4\%$$

(b) The expected proportion of defectives is found as follows:

$$E(D) = \Sigma\ D \cdot P(D)$$

$$= 0(.60) + .01(.20) + .02(.10) + .03(.05) + .04(.03) + .05(.02)$$

$$= 0 + .002 + .002 + .0015 + .0012 + .001$$

$$= .0077 = .77\% \text{ (that is, less than 1\% defective)}$$

(c) The company should make the casings because it produces less than 1 percent defective casings on the average, and it is more profitable to make them until the defect rate is greater than or equal to 4 percent.

MATERIALS HANDLING, STORAGE, AND RETRIEVAL

3 Lakeview Lumber uses forklift trucks to transport lumber from the mill to a storage warehouse .3 mile away. The lift trucks can move three loaded pallets per trip and

travel at an average speed of 6 miles per hour (allowing for loading, delays, and travel). If 420 pallet loads must be moved during each 8-hour shift, how many lift trucks are required?

Solution

$$\text{Distance/trip} = .3(\text{over}) + .3(\text{return}) = .6 \text{ mile}$$

$$\text{Time/trip} = .6 \text{ mile} \div 6 \text{ miles/hr} = .1 \text{ hr}$$

$$\text{Capacity/trip} = 3 \text{ pallets}$$

$$\text{Capacity/shift} = \left(\frac{3 \text{ pallets}}{.1 \text{ hr}}\right)\left(\frac{8 \text{ hr}}{\text{shift}}\right) = 240 \text{ pallets/shift per lift truck}$$

$$\text{Number of lift trucks} = \frac{420 \text{ pallets/shift}}{240 \text{ pallets/shift/lift truck}} = 1.75 \text{ lift trucks (use 2 lift trucks)}$$

TOTAL COSTS AND THE EOQ EQUATION

*4 *Calculus explanation and derivation* If carrying costs consist of two components—(1) C_i = interest cost per unit-year on the average inventory investment and (2) C_S = storage space cost per unit-year to accommodate Q units—set up an equation for total costs, and derive an expression for the EOQ which includes both these terms.

Solution

$$\text{TC} = \text{ordering} + \text{interest} + \text{storage} + \text{purchase}$$

$$= C_o\left(\frac{1}{Q}\right)D + C_i\frac{Q}{2} + C_sQ + \text{PD}$$

The TC equation can be differentiated by standard calculus methods, where the differential of $Y = X^n$ is

$$\frac{dY}{dX} = nX^{n-1}$$

and when a constant, a, is included, the differential of Y with respect to X is

$$Y = aX^n$$

$$\frac{dY}{dX} = naX^{n-1}$$

The differential of a constant (by itself) is, of course, equal to zero; so, for example, if $Y = 4 + 5X^3$,

$$\frac{dY}{dX} = 0 + 15X^2$$

The differential of TC with respect to Q can be obtained most easily if we first move the Q's into the numerator (by adjusting to a negative exponent) so that

$$\text{TC} = C_o DQ^{-1} + \frac{C_i Q}{2} + C_s Q + PD$$

Upon differentiating, the purchase cost is a constant and drops out:

$$\frac{d\text{TC}}{dQ} = -C_o DQ^{-2} + \frac{C_i Q^0}{2} + C_s Q^0 + 0$$

Recognizing that any variable to the zero power equals 1, and setting the first derivative equal to zero, the order quantity is now

$$0 = -\frac{C_o D}{Q^2} + \frac{C_i}{2} + C_s$$

$$\frac{C_o D}{Q^2} = \frac{C_i + 2C_s}{2}$$

$$Q = \sqrt{\frac{2C_o D}{C_i + 2C_s}} \qquad (9\text{-}6)$$

5 An inventory manager is reviewing some annual ordering data for 3 years ago, when the firm used only 2,000 cases and had carrying charges of only 6 percent of the $20 per case purchase price. At that time it cost the firm only $10 to write up an order. The manager has come across the following equation.

$$Q = \sqrt{\frac{2(10)(2,000)}{1.20}} = \sqrt{\frac{2(\;)\,10(\;)\,2,000(\;)}{1.2(\;)}}$$

Identify the units associated with the numbers used in the equation, and show what units Q results in.

Solution

$$Q = \sqrt{\frac{2\left(\dfrac{\text{pure}}{\text{number}}\right)10(\$)\,2,000\left(\dfrac{\text{cases}}{\text{yr}}\right)}{120\left(\dfrac{\$}{\text{case-yr}}\right)}} = 183 \text{ cases}$$

Note that the $ and yr units cancel, leaving cases^2, so the answer is in cases.

6 A San Antonio stockyard uses about 200 bales of hay per month. It pays a broker $80 per order to locate a supplier and handle the ordering and delivery arrangements. Its own storage and handling costs are estimated at 30 percent per year. If each bale costs $3, what is the most economical order quantity?

Solution

The purchase price is relevant for computing carrying charges (only), and they must be in the same units as demand. We will (arbitrarily) use months.

$$EOQ = \sqrt{\frac{2C_oD}{C_c}}$$

where $C_c = (\%)(P) = (.30/\text{yr})(\$3/\text{unit}) = \$.90/\text{unit-yr} = \$.90/12 = \$.075/\text{unit-mo.}$

$$EOQ = \sqrt{\frac{2(\$80)(200)}{\$.075}}$$

$$= 653 \text{ bales}$$

7 Far West Freeze Dry purchases 1,200 tins of tea annually in economic order quantity lots of 100 tins and pays \$9.85 per tin. If processing costs for each order are \$10, what are the implied carrying costs of this policy?

Solution

$$Q = \sqrt{\frac{2C_oD}{C_c}}$$

Solving for C_c we have:

$$C_c = \frac{2C_oD}{Q^2} = \frac{2(10)(1,200)}{(100)^2} = \$2.40/\text{tin-yr}$$

8 A manufacturer requires 600 printed circuit boards per year and estimates an ordering cost of \$20 per order. Inventory is financed by short-term loans at approximately 10 percent, which work out to a carrying charge of \$.10 per unit-year based upon the average inventory. Storage costs, based upon adequate space for maximum inventory, are \$.025 per unit-year, and the purchase price is \$1 per unit.
(a) What is the most economical order quantity?
(b) What is the total annual cost of the inventory?
(c) How many orders are placed per year?

Solution
(a) The EOQ can be determined from the total-cost expression:

$$TC = \text{ordering} + \text{interest} + \text{storage} + \text{purchase}$$

$$= \frac{\$20(600)}{Q} + \frac{\$.10}{\text{unit-yr}}\left(\frac{Q}{2}\right)\text{units} + \frac{\$.025Q}{\text{unit-yr}} + \$1.00(600)$$

$$= \frac{12,000}{Q} + .05Q + \$.025Q + 600$$

$$= \frac{12,000}{Q} + \$.075Q + 600$$

Differentiating, we have:

$$\frac{d\text{TC}}{dQ} = \frac{-12,000}{Q^2} + .075$$

Setting the first derivative $= 0$,

$$Q = \sqrt{\frac{12,000}{.075}} = 400 \text{ units/order}$$

Alternatively, we could use Eq. (9-6):

$$Q = \sqrt{\frac{2C_oD}{C_i + 2C_s}} = \sqrt{\frac{2(20)(600)}{.10 + 2(.025)}} = 400 \text{ units/order}$$

(b) Substituting $Q = 400$ into the TC expression, we have:

$$\text{TC} = \frac{12,000}{400} + .075(400) + 600 = \$660$$

(c) Orders/yr $= \dfrac{D}{Q} = \dfrac{600}{400} = 1.5$ orders/yr $= 3$ orders every 2 yr

ECONOMIC RUN LENGTHS

9   The Finnish Creamery Company produces ice cream bars for vending machines and has an annual demand for 72,000 bars. The company has the capacity to produce 400 bars per day. It takes only a few minutes to adjust the production setup (cost estimated at \$7.50 per setup) for the bars, and the firm is reluctant to produce too many at one time because the storage cost (refrigeration) is relatively high at \$1.50 per bar-year. The firm supplies vending machines with its "Finn-Barrs" on 360 days of the year.
(a) What is the most economical number of bars to produce during any one production run?
(b) What is the optimal length of the production run in days?

Solution

(a) ERL $= \sqrt{\dfrac{2C_oD}{C_c[1 - (d/p)]}}$

where C_o = setup cost = \$7.50
D = annual demand = 72,000 bars/yr
C_c = carrying cost = \$1.50/bar-yr
d = daily demand rate = $\dfrac{72,000}{360}$ = 200 bars/day
p = daily production rate = 400 bars/day

$$ERL = \sqrt{\frac{2(7.50)(72,000)}{1.50[1 - (200/400)]}}$$

$$= 1,200 \text{ bars/run}$$

(b) Optimal number of days of the run is

$$\text{Number of days} = \frac{1,200 \text{ bars}}{400 \text{ bars/day}} = 3 \text{ days}$$

10 A firm has a yearly demand for 52,000 units of a product which it produces. The cost of setting up for production is $80, and the weekly production rate is 1,000 units. The carrying cost is $3.50 per unit-year. How many units should the firm produce on each production run?

Solution

$$Q = \sqrt{\frac{2C_oD}{C_c[1 - (d/p)]}} = \sqrt{\frac{2(80)(52,000)}{3.50[1 - (1,000/1,000)]}} = \sqrt{\infty} = \infty$$

Note that the demand and production rates in this problem are equal and the equation (rightly) suggests they should have an infinite (continuous) run.

QUESTIONS

9-1 Define materials management. What is included in the term "materials"?

9-2 To what extent are service system managers involved in materials management activities?

9-3 How does a materials manager's responsibilities differ from the responsibilities of other functional managers, such as the marketing manager, with respect to the scope of responsibility?

9-4 Do industrial buyers go "out for bid" on all items? Why or why not?

9-5 Briefly identify the purchasing department responsibilities.

9-6 What are some of the key factors to consider in the selection of suppliers?

9-7 How do the cost components for making a product differ from those for buying it?

9-8 How do materials-handling applications in service industries differ from manufacturing applications?

9-9 Identify the major reasons why firms carry inventories.

9-10 Demand for a product doubled during a 3-year period. At a management meeting, the inventory manager was asked to explain why his order size for this product had failed to increase in a proportional (linear) amount to demand. How should he respond?

9-11 The standard "cookbook" EOQ formula does not include the purchase price of an item. Why is this so? When is it important to consider purchase price in computing the most economic lot size?

9-12 In the economic-run-length equation, what is the effect of letting the production rate get increasingly faster than the demand rate (in other words, to the point where goods are produced almost instantaneously)?

9-13 Why do firms classify their materials according to the ABC method of classification?

9-14 Why do industrial firms use cycle counting rather than periodic physical counting?

PROBLEMS

1 The Madison headquarters of Fred's Fast Foods must select a national grocery chain to supply its fast-food chains with fresh vegetables on a nationwide basis. It has developed the following criteria and scores for prospective vendors. Which supplier has the highest expected score, and what is its value?

	Value Rating (1–10)	Potential Suppliers of Vegetables		
		Food Fair	A & R	SaleWay
Price	8	.7	.3	.5
Quality	3	.2	.8	.5
Delivery	5	.5	.4	.4
Location	2	.1	.7	.6

2 A city operations manager must decide whether to extend city garbage collection services to a new 300-home subdivision or purchase the service from a rural collection agency which would charge $150 per year for each home. If city service is extended to the subdivision, fixed costs would increase by $10,000 per year. Variable costs of collection are estimated at $80 per house per year. Which is the best course of action for the manager to recommend (on an economic basis): to supply the collection service or purchase it from the rural agency?

3 Banktel Inc. produces an automatic cash machine in leased facilities in an industrial park. The product uses some special-purpose punch keys which the firm currently purchases at $4.20 each. It is considering leasing additional space and producing the keys itself. The long-term lease would result in annual costs of $4,800. The labor, materials, and variable overhead are estimated at $2.80 per key, and fixed overhead would be an additional $1,080 per year. Demand is estimated as shown.

Demand D	Probability P(D)
2,000	.05
3,000	.10
4,000	.30
5,000	.40
6,000	.15

(a) Should Banktel produce the keys?

(b) What is the break-even volume where it becomes profitable to produce them rather than buy from a supplier?

4 South Bend Gear Works has received an order from a tractor manufacturer for 500 spur gears which can either be produced in its own plant for $29.40 each or subcontracted at $30 each. Its own gear-hobbing machine requires frequent adjustment

and produces defective gears with the probabilities shown. Any defects must be reworked at a cost of $10 per gear. Gears obtained from the subcontractor are guaranteed to be free of defects.

Percentage of Defectives p	Probability $P(p)$
2	.10
5	.60
10	.30

Assume that the manager must choose a course of action without any additional information and that he bases his choice on a comparison of the expected cost of using the firm's own machine versus the cost of subcontracting.
(a) What is the break-even point (BEP) in the proportion of defectives where the firm is indifferent about whether to produce the gears itself or subcontract?
(b) What is the expected proportion of defectives if the company produces on its own machine?
(c) On the basis of the BEP, should the firm make the gears itself or buy them from a subcontractor?
(d) What other factors should be considered in this type of make-or-buy decision?

5 The warehouse manager at the Textile Import Center estimates that the purchase of a $70,000 forklift would save 2 hours per shift of labor time. The firm works 2 shifts per day and 300 days per year. If the labor cost to the firm (including benefits) is $32 per hour, how long would it take for the forklift to pay for itself?

6 (Requires use of discount tables) Napa Packing Company is considering the purchase of a conveyor system if the savings in labor costs justify it. The conveyor would cost $80,000 and would be expected to last 10 years, after which the salvage value would be $8,000. Operation and maintenance costs would be $4,000 per year.
(a) Assuming that the firm uses an 18 percent cost of capital, compute the equivalent annual cost of the conveyor.
(b) The conveyor is expected to reduce the existing $120,000-per-year labor cost by 25 percent. Does that savings justify the purchase of the conveyor system?

7 The hospital operations manager at St. Ann's has asked the stores department to begin ordering inventory on an economic lot size basis. The hospital uses 900 electrocardiogram tape rolls per year, has an ordering cost of $15 per order, and estimates carrying costs at $.45 per unit-year. How many tapes should be ordered each time?

8 Discount Appliances has an annual demand represented by the probability distribution shown.

Demand	Probability
200	.10
400	.20
600	.30
800	.40

The distributor operates 250 days per year and carries a safety stock of 30 toasters. Each toaster costs $8.75, but ordering costs are $15 per order, so it is not profitable to order a few toasters. In addition, carrying and storage costs are $1.50 per toaster per year. The time from placing an order until delivery from the supplier is approximately 10 days. What is the most economical number of toasters to order at one time?

9 Factory Built Homes, Inc. (FBH) purchases paneling components from a nearby western New York mill for $5 per unit. It expects to use about 4,000 units during the coming year. FBH estimates that it costs $30 to place an order and $1.50 per unit-year for carrying and storage costs. The mill can provide FBH with immediate delivery of any reasonable quantity.

(a) What is the most economical quantity for FBH to order?
(b) How many orders per year should be placed?
(c) What is the total yearly cost associated with ordering, carrying, and purchasing the EOQ amount?

10 A farm machinery manufacturer requires 7,000 air filters per year as replacement parts on mechanical harvesters. The filters cost $3 each and are stored in rented facilities at a cost of $.35 per unit-year, with storage requirements based upon the maximum number of units purchased at one time, Q. The interest (carrying) costs, based upon average inventory, are $.30 per unit-year, and the firm uses $35 per order as the ordering cost. What is the most economical order quantity? (*Hint*: See Solved Prob. 4.)

11 Golden Valley Cannery uses 64,000 size 7X cans annually and can purchase any quantity up to 10,000 cans at $.040 per can. At 10,000 cans the unit cost drops to $.032 per can, and for purchases of 30,000 it is $.030 per can. The costs of ordering are $24 per order, and interest costs are 20 percent of the price per can and apply to the average inventory. Storage costs are $.02 per can-year and are based upon maximum inventory. (Disregard safety stock costs.)

(a) What is the EOQ, disregarding the quantity discounts?
(b) What is the most economical order quantity, considering the quantity discounts?

*12 *Optional.* Derive an equation for the most economic lot size when the following costs apply:

Ordering: C_o $/order
Stockout: C_e $/exposure (where each order cycle constitutes an exposure)
Interest: C_i $/unit-yr (based upon average inventory)
Storage: C_s $/order (based upon maximum inventory)
Purchase: P $/unit (based upon annual demand, D)

Hint: The C_o and C_e costs should end up combined as $(C_o + C_e)$.

13 An electronics firm produces calculators at a rate of 100 per week (5-day week and 50 weeks per year). Each calculator requires two nickel-cadmium batteries (10,000 per year total), which are also produced internally at a rate of 500 per day. Setup costs for battery production are estimated at $230 per run, and the production analyst estimates carrying and storage costs for each battery at $.20 per unit-year. What is the most economical run length for batteries?

14 Spokane Public Power Co. purchases transformers at a cost of $330 and uses an ordering cost of $45 per order. Inventory is carried at a cost of 10 percent of the per-unit price (based on average inventory). Storage costs, based upon adequate space for maximum inventory, are $6 per transformer. Annual demand is 800 units.

(a) Compute the total yearly cost if the firm orders in EOQ amounts.
(b) The supplier has offered the power company a 10 percent discount for purchasing in quantities of 200. Assuming this affects all costs except ordering and per-unit storage costs, compute the total yearly cost for this quantity discount situation.

15 A governmental supply warehouse is implementing a cycle counting system whereby class A items are counted monthly, B items quarterly, and C items annually. Of the 6,300 items in inventory, 900 are in class A, 2,100 are in class B, and the remainder are in class C. Assuming that there are 250 workdays per year, how many items should be counted per day?

16 National Restaurant Supply Corporation (NRSCO) has divided its market area into geographic regions. The southwest region has a central warehouse in Oklahoma City and eight satellite warehouses. NRSCO currently carries 17 replacement microprocessors for its computerized cash registers in the Oklahoma City warehouse. Each microprocessor represents a $300 investment. A member of the board of directors has suggested that replacement stock be shifted to the satellite warehouses to provide faster service. How much additional investment, if any, would be required? Assume that the stock amounts represent one standard deviation of demand on the Oklahoma City warehouse and that the satellite warehouses are to provide an equivalent amount of coverage.

REFERENCES

[1] American Production and Inventory Control Society, *P&IM Review 1986 Reference Guide and Directory*, T.D.A. Publications, Hollywood, FL.

[2] Johnson, Robert: "An Idea from Japan May Offer Cities a Way of Recruiting Industry," *The Wall Street Journal*, Aug. 23, 1983, p. 1.

[3] Lambert, Douglas M.: *The Development of an Inventory Costing Methodology: A Study of the Costs Associated with Holding Inventory* (research report), National Council of Physical Distribution Management, Chicago, 1975.

[4] Omark Industries, Portland, OR, Third Quarter Report, 1983.

[5] Winter, Ralph E.: "Firms Cut Inventories Down to Low Levels, but Major Test Looms," *The Wall Street Journal*, Mar. 29, 1984, p. 1.

SELF QUIZ: CHAPTER 9

Part I True/False [1 point each = 6]

1 _____ Materials management procedures do not apply to service industry firms (such as hospitals and airlines.

2 _____ A blanket purchase order fixes a price but allows for variable delivery times as specified by the buyer.

3 _____ Most manufacturing inventory tends to have a "dependent" demand, whereas distribution inventories are more likely to have an "independent" demand.

4 _____ According to the basic EOQ model (and if other factors are constant), increasing the ordering cost tends to decrease the quantity ordered.

5 _____ In the ERL model, if the demand rate is 60 units per month and the production rate is 200 units per month, then 70 percent of production goes into inventory.

6 _____ In make-or-buy analysis, the slope of the total cost line to "make" a product is usually greater (or steeper) than the slope of the total cost line to buy the product.

Part II Problems [3 points each = 9. Calculate and select your answer.]

1 A sporting goods company can either purchase a shotgun part for $15 each, or produce it (where FC = $45,000 and VC = $10/unit). They figure a 70 percent chance demand will be 4,000 units and a 30 percent chance it will be 6,000 units. The economic advantage of buying the part (instead of making it) is:
   (a) Negative (in other words, make it)
   (b) From $0 to < $2,000
   (c) From $2,000 to < $5,000
   (d) From $5,000 to < $20,000
   (e) > $20,000

2 A manufacturer of bar code readers purchases a component (a modem) from a supplier for $40 each. Their annual demand is 2,028 modems and they have an ordering cost of $50 per order and a carrying cost of $12/unit-yr. If the modem supplier offered a 10 percent discount for purchasing in lots of 200, what would be the annual savings over ordering in EOQ amounts?
   (a) No savings
   (b) $1,147
   (c) $5,020
   (d) $7,965
   (e) None of the above

3 Melody Instrument Company has an inventory of 200 class A items, 700 class B items, and 1,500 class C items. If they wish to cycle count the A, B, and C items with a relative frequency of six, four, and two times per year respectively and they work 260 days per year, how many items should they average per day?
   (a) < 20 items
   (b) 20 to 24 items
   (c) 25 to 29 items
   (d) 30 to 34 items
   (e) > 30 items

CHAPTER 10
INVENTORY CONTROL: SAFETY STOCKS AND SERVICE LEVELS

INTRODUCTION

As may already be apparent, inventory control is one of the most vital responsibilities of an operations manager. Insufficient inventories hamper production and limit sales, whereas excessive inventories tie up cash that may be urgently needed elsewhere. It is no surprise, then, that inventory control has been the key to the success of many firms as well as the cause of failure of numerous others. An example of a large distributor of supermarket supplies will illustrate.

INVENTORY PROBLEM

Over several years, a grocery products distributor built up a large business in a four-state area. It maintained a $15 million stock of inventory (everything from cornflakes to dog food) in a huge warehouse. Customer orders came in via phone directly to the warehouse computer, where they were given to forklift truck drivers, filled, and loaded into one of the company's 75 trucks. Over 80 percent of the goods requested could be shipped from stock with no delay.

However, a competitive distributor came on the scene—and began promising that he could deliver over 95 percent of the goods from stock. The first reaction of the established distributor was to "overstock" some items. But the financial manager felt the company already had "too much money tied up in inventory," because cash flow was diminished and profits were low.

SOLUTION

An alert company vice president took the initiative to start an "inventory project." With the help of some part-time (student) employees, he began putting the demand history of each product on the firm's computer. After doing some statistical analysis of their demand patterns, he established stock levels on the basis of meeting demand a specified proportion of the time. Within 6 months, the service rate had improved, even though the total investment in inventory had gone down. And inventory "turnover" (the average number of times inventory is sold during the year) was up. With better service, customers were secure and profits were edging higher. The "inventory project" had made the difference depicted in Fig. 10-1.[1]

Our Focus The problems of inventory management cannot simply be ignored in the hope that they will go away. Neither can one rely upon intuitive methods of setting inventory stock levels. Competition will not permit that. Someone must intelligently set policies, establish guidelines for inventory levels, and ensure that control systems are functioning properly.

This chapter continues the exploration of inventory theory begun in the previous chapter. In that chapter, we addressed the question of *how much to*

---

[1] Unfortunately, however, the firm soon lost this vice president to another organization in search of a president.

- Excess stock
- Poor service
- Low cash flow
- Low profits

POOR INVENTORY CONTROL

- Adequate stock
- Good service
- Higher cash flow
- Better profits

GOOD INVENTORY CONTROL

FIGURE 10-1   Advantages of Good Inventory Control

order. Here we focus upon the more difficult question of *how much to retain in stock* in order to offset the uncertainties of an unpredictable demand (or lead time).

We first recall the distinction between manufacturing and distribution inventories. Then we identify the inventory variables that can be controlled and explore some alternative methods of using those variables to handle uncertainties in demand (or lead time). The chapter ends with a summary of some basic types of inventory control systems. Upon completion of the chapter, you should be able to explain how the various inventory variables are related and be able to compute appropriate levels of safety stock for any desired level of customer service.

INVENTORY TYPES AND SYSTEM VARIABLES

MANUFACTURING VERSUS DISTRIBUTION INVENTORY

We saw earlier (Chapter 9) that *manufacturing inventories* are the raw materials, components, and work-in-process maintained to support planned manufacturing operations. These materials and components are classified as *dependent* demand because the number required *depends upon* the number of end items scheduled for production. Once a production plan has been formulated, the requirements for the components that are assembled into finished products can be calculated (for example, by an MRP system).

In manufacturing, then, the timing of the arrival of materials and components is often more important than having an extra stock of those materials on hand. This is not to suggest that certain manufacturing activities do not warrant some reserve for scrap losses, breakdowns, and so on. However, for the most part, manufacturing requirements are predictable.

Distribution inventories are the finished goods flowing from the manufacturing process. As in the grocery distribution system described in the example at the beginning of this chapter, these goods are maintained to satisfy customer needs—which may be very uncertain. We typically classify finished goods as having *independent* demand. Independent demand can occur randomly and is not as predictable, so having a reserve stock of inventory on hand to compensate for uncertainties is usually desirable.

In this chapter, we deal primarily with *independent* demand items, for which the demand can be considered probabilistic. The next chapter focuses upon *dependent* demand inventories that exist in a manufacturing setting, where the timing of arrivals of stock is more critical.

SAFETY STOCKS, ORDER POINTS, AND SERVICE LEVELS

Safety Stock   *Safety stocks* (SS) constitute one of the major means of dealing with the uncertainties associated with variations in demand and lead time. They are amounts of inventory held in excess of regular usage quantities in order to provide specified levels of protection against stockout. Figure 10-2 illustrates a varying demand and lead time and the use of safety stock for an inventory system that is replenished by a fixed size of order, Q. In this type of system the order point (OP) is the inventory level at which a replenishment order is placed. As illustrated in the figure, it should include a sufficient quantity to handle demand during the lead time (D_{LT}) plus a designated margin of safety stock.

$$OP = D_{LT} + SS \qquad (10\text{-}1)$$

EXAMPLE 10-1

A nationwide trucking firm has an average demand of 10 new tires per week and receives deliveries from a Dayton, Ohio, tire company about 20 business days (5 days per week) after placing an order. If the firm seeks to maintain a safety stock of 15 tires, what is the order point?

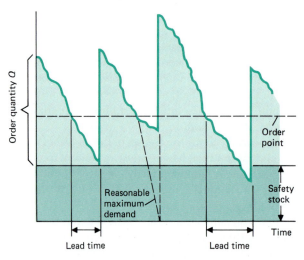

FIGURE 10-2   Inventory Variables

SOLUTION

$$OP = D_{LT} + SS$$

$$= (10 \text{ tires/week})(4 \text{ weeks}) + 15 \text{ tires}$$

$$= 55 \text{ tires}$$

Stockouts If no safety stock were carried and reorders were placed so that inventory was scheduled to arrive (on the average) when the previous inventory was used up, the organization would run out of stock on about half of the order cycles. In manufacturing organizations, stockouts can halt production, idling expensive labor and facilities. Other costs of being out of stock include the cost of expediting replacement inventory, the cost of a loss of sales and a loss of goodwill, and other intangible costs.

The basic EOQ model assumes demand is known and constant, so it does not include any provision for stockout costs. If they were to be recognized in the EOQ equation, one method would be to include them like an order cost that is incurred each order cycle. The effect of including stockout costs this way would be to increase the order quantity, Q, which decreases the frequency of exposure to the risk (cost) of the stockout. If we let C_e be the cost of exposure to a stockout (SO), the EOQ equation would take the form:

$$EOQ \text{ (with SO)} = \sqrt{\frac{2D(C_o + C_e)}{C_c}} \qquad (10\text{-}2)$$

Stockout costs are essentially offset by the cost of carrying inventory beyond that required to meet average demand, so we can use carrying costs to imply something about stockout costs. If a preliminary calculation of the EOQ can be made (without including C_e), then an approximation of the number of orders per year can be calculated. Dividing the total annual carrying cost by this estimated number of orders yields an approximation of what the firm is paying for carrying costs (dollars per order). If we assume that the firm is willing to carry inventory up to the point where this carrying cost is just offset by the stockout cost, then that same cost per order can be used as our estimate of the stockout cost C_e. We could then recalculate the EOQ using this estimate of C_e. A more accurate estimate would, of course, entail more advanced mathematics, which is beyond our scope here. But further iterations could be made to improve the estimate.

EXAMPLE 10-2

A glasswear manufacturer with an annual demand of 500 units has ordering costs of $45 per order and carrying costs of $15 per unit per year.
(a) Compute the implied stockout cost.
(b) Use it to compute a revised EOQ that incorporates a rough approximation of stockout costs.

SOLUTION

(a) Our preliminary estimate of the EOQ is:

$$EOQ = \sqrt{\frac{2C_o D}{C_c}} = \sqrt{\frac{2\,(45)(500)}{15}} = 55 \text{ units}$$

$$\text{Orders/yr} = \frac{D}{Q} = \frac{500 \text{ units/yr}}{55 \text{ units/order}} = 9 \text{ orders/yr}$$

$$\text{Implied SO cost/order} = \frac{\text{carrying cost/yr}}{\text{orders/yr}} = \frac{C_c(Q/2)}{\text{orders/yr}}$$

$$= \frac{(\$15/\text{unit-yr})(55 \div 2 \text{ units})}{9 \text{ orders/yr}} = \$46/\text{order}$$

(b) $$\text{EOQ} \atop \text{(with SO)} = \sqrt{\frac{2D(C_o + C_e)}{C_c}} = \sqrt{\frac{2\,(500)(45 + 46)}{15}} = 78 \text{ units}$$

Equation 10-2 is conceptually helpful in that it is a mechanism for relating stockout costs to inventory carrying costs. However, the equation per se is not widely used to establish safety stock levels. The amount of safety stock inventory that is necessary is generally considered to be that quantity which is necessary to meet any reasonable maximum demand during the lead time. This is shown by dotted lines in the second reorder cycle of Fig. 10-2. "Reasonable maximum demand" is, however, open to much interpretation. More precisely, the quantity should be determined on the basis of knowledge of the frequency distributions of demand and lead time (and the cost of carrying the stock).

Later in the chapter we shall deal with setting safety stock levels on the basis of actual empirical data, and then on the basis of known statistical distributions. Before embarking on that, however, we need to finish this section with a more precise definition of the concept of a service level, and we need to consider some other (recognized) methods of handling inventory uncertainties.

Service Level The *service level* (SL) of an inventory is a number that represents the percentage of units or the percentage of order cycles in which all demand requests can be supplied from stock. The converse of service level is a percentage figure representing the stockout risk (SOR).

$$SL = 100\% - SOR \tag{10-3}$$

Customers would like 100 percent service, but production economics usually dictate that firms provide something less, perhaps in the range of 75 to 99.7 percent service. We shall return to the question of setting the stockout risk shortly.

METHODS OF HANDLING INVENTORY UNCERTAINTIES

OVERVIEW OF METHODS

The major uncertainties associated with managing inventories are variability of demand and variability of lead time. Most of the approaches to handling these uncertainties make use of safety stock, but other ratio, expected value, and incremental techniques are in use. Figure 10-3 summarizes some of the methods on which we will focus for the remainder of the chapter. In the figure, D_{ave} represents an average demand during a specified period, such as a lead time.

INFORMAL DECISION RULES

A number of informal (and intuitive) decision rules are used—and some appear satisfactory. However, they offer little in the way of quantifying the level of service and they are frequently unsatisfactory for large-scale business operations.

FIGURE 10-3 Methods of Protecting Against Shortages and Stockouts[2]

Method	Description
Informal decision rules	1 *Ratios:* Order stock on basis of ratio (e.g., 300 percent of the expected usage during LT). 2 *Ultraconservative:* Provide stock for largest daily usage × longest LT. 3 *Safety stock percentage:* Let SS = D_{ave} plus a 25–40 percent safety factor. 4 *Square root of LT:* Less SS = $\sqrt{D_{\text{ave}} \text{ during LT}}$.
Expected value approach	Construct payoff and expected value tables where alternatives are amounts of inventory to stock and uncontrollable variable is D or LT (especially suitable for handling perishable inventories).
Incremental approach	Add inventory to point where Incremental cost = incremental gain × P (gain). 1 *Single-period model:* Use understocking cost per unit and overstocking cost per unit for one time demand. 2 *Multiple-period model:* Use stockout cost per unit and carrying cost per unit for multiple period demands.
Safety stock (statistical)	1 *Empirical:* Use empirical data to formulate a probability distribution of D or LT and compute required SS for specified service level (where service level is based on percentage of order cycles in stock). 2 *Known distribution:* Use known (or assumed) statistical distribution of D or LT and compute required SS for specified service level (where service level is based on percentage of order cycles in stock).

[2] Some instructors may place less emphasis (or skip) some of these methods.

EXAMPLE 10-3 | A supplier of air conditioners has had weekly demands from zero to 14 units with $D_{ave} = 3$, and has experienced lead times of from 4 weeks to 20 weeks. What amount of stock would be carried under a decision rule of (a) maintaining a ratio of three times the average usage during the average lead time, or (b) stocking for the largest weekly usage multiplied by the longest lead time? How much safety stock should be maintained for (c) SS of average demand per week plus a 25 percent safety factor, and (d) SS equal to the square root of average demand during lead time [3]?

SOLUTION

(a) Using the LT midpoint as the LT_{ave},

$$LT_{ave} = \frac{4 + 20}{2} = 12 \text{ wk}$$

$$\text{Stock} = 300\% \, (D_{ave})(LT_{ave}) = 3.00(3 \text{ units/wk})(12 \text{ wk}) = 108 \text{ units}$$

(b) Stock = $(D_{max})(LT_{max}) = (14 \text{ units/wk})(20 \text{ wk}) = 280 \text{ units}$

(c) SS $= D_{ave} + .25(D_{ave}) = 3 + .25(3) = 3.75$, say 4 units

(d) SS $= \sqrt{D_{ave} \text{ during } LT_{ave}} = \sqrt{(3)(12)} = \sqrt{36} = 6 \text{ units}$

EXPECTED VALUE APPROACH

Expected value approaches have been applied to situations in which revenues and costs can be measured as a result of having or not having stock on hand. Products that lose value if not immediately used or sold (for example, fresh produce) are particularly suitable for this type of analysis. The analysis frequently involves the construction of payoff tables and expected value tables. In general, the controllable (action) alternatives consist of the choice of how much inventory to stock, and the uncontrollable (state of nature) variable is the demand or lead time.

INCREMENTAL APPROACH

Theoretically, a firm should continue to add inventory to the point at which the incremental cost of more inventory equals the incremental gain from having it times the probability that the gain will be realized. This can be expressed in traditional economic terms by saying that inventory should be added to the point at which its marginal cost (MC) equals the marginal revenue (MR) times the probability that the items will be demanded, $P(D)$, during that period. Thus we have:

$$MC = MR \times P(D)$$

Solving for $P(D)$ yields a measure of the likelihood of sale, where the incremental gain from selling an item just offsets the incremental cost of acquiring and holding the item for sale. Recognizing that the marginal revenue includes both marginal cost (MC) and marginal profit (MP), we have, for a one-time demand:

$$P(D) = \frac{MC}{MR} = \frac{MC}{MC + MP} \qquad (10\text{-}4)$$

where $P(D)$ represents the cumulative probability of needing the *next* unit.

EXAMPLE 10-4

An item costs $6 to produce, sells for $10, and has an estimated cumulative probability distribution of demand during the next period as shown below.

Unit Number	1	2	3	4	5	6	7	8
P(selling ≥ this unit)	1.00	.92	.82	.75	.62	.40	.15	.10

How many units should be ordered?

SOLUTION

$$P(D) = \frac{MC}{MC + MP}$$

where   MC = $6
        MP = $10 − $6 = $4

$$P(D) = \frac{\$6}{\$6 + \$4} = .60$$

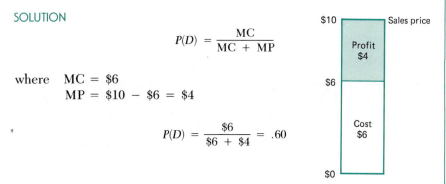

Therefore, order 5 units when P(selling ≥ 5 units) of .62 is just greater than the equating probability of .60. It seems intuitively correct that since the cost ($6) represents 60 percent of the value of the item, the likelihood of sale, $P(D)$, should also equal 60 percent. If the cost were a higher proportion (for example, 82 percent), then fewer units would be justified (3 units) because the marginal cost is higher.

The marginal (theoretical) analysis above can be extended to apply to realistic inventory situations by incorporating the carrying and stockout costs we have worked with previously. In this case, the analysis is made in an attempt to balance the costs of carrying excess stock (C_{os} = overstocking) against the stockout costs of having too little stock (C_{us} = understocking). Figure 10-4 illustrates the balancing act required. The C_{os} is the price of the unit less any salvage value. In the long run, this cost would also include carrying and storage costs. The C_{us} is an opportunity cost of the contribution to profit that could have resulted from the availability of a unit.

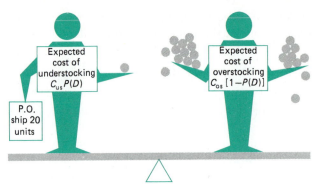

FIGURE 10-4   Balancing Costs of Understocking and Overstocking

Two models apply. The *single-period model* applies to situations in which unused items are not normally carried forward from one period to the next, or a penalty exists for doing so. *Multiple-period models* apply to the bulk of continuous-production operations, which have recurring demand.

Single-Period Models   Single-period models assume that (1) demand can be estimated, (2) purchase quantity is limited and may not be increased beyond the initial amount, and (3) individual per-unit costs are available for overstocking and understocking. Here we let $P(D)$ be the cumulative probability of demand being greater than or equal to the individual demand values, d. At the (optimal) balance point, the expected cost of understocking, $C_{us}P(D)$, equals the expected cost of overstocking, $C_{os}[1 - P(D)]$. Solving for the cumulative probability value, $P(D)$, we have:

$$C_{us}P(D) = C_{os}[1 - P(D)]$$

Single-period:

$$P(D) = \frac{C_{os}}{C_{os} + C_{us}} \qquad (10\text{-}5)$$

The value of $P(D)$ is then the balance point at which the two costs (overstocking and understocking) are equal. By relating the value of $P(D)$ to the cumulative distribution table (or curve), we can find (on the horizontal axis) the most economical level of stock for any combination of C_{us} and C_{os} costs.

EXAMPLE 10-5   An operations manager of Nationwide Car Rentals must decide on the number of vehicles of a certain model to allocate to his agency in the Nashville area on a one-time basis. The cars are obtained from an auto leasing firm at a cost of $20 per day. Nationwide rents the cars to its customers for $30 per day. If a car is not used, the auto leasing firm will give Nationwide an $8 rebate.

Records of past demand have yielded the empirical probability distribution shown. How many units of this model should Nationwide stock if it seeks to balance the costs of overstocking and understocking?

Demand d (No. of cars)	Probability of Demand P(d)	Cumulative Probability P(D ≥ d)
6 (or less)	0	1.00
7	.03	1.00
8	.07	.97
9	.15	.90
10	.20	.75
11	.23	.55
12	.15	.32
13	.12	.17
14	.05	.05
15 (or more)	0	0

SOLUTION

The cumulative probability, $P(D)$, that demand will be at least the amount d is shown in the column on the right. It is computed by recognizing that 100 percent of the time demand was greater than or equal to 7 cars (therefore $P(D) = 1.0$). Because the $P(d = 7 \text{ cars}) = .03$, the cumulative $P(D) \geq 8$ cars is $1.00 - .03 = .97$. Other values follow by subtraction in a similar manner. The equating probability is:

$$P(D) = \frac{C_{os}}{C_{os} + C_{us}}$$

where $C_{os} = \$20 - \$8 = \$12$

$C_{us} = \$30 - \$20 = \$10$

$\therefore P(D) = \frac{12}{12 + 10} = .545$

We choose to stock 11 cars because our calculated $P(D)$ value of .545 is closer to the $P(D \geq d)$ value of .55 than to any other cumulative value. See sketch. For cumulative values midway between the cumulative values, we would be inclined to stock less rather than more because the cost of overstocking (\$12) is greater than the cost of understocking (\$10).

Insofar as $P(D)$ is the cumulative probability that demand will be exceeded, it also represents the stockout risk (SOR) associated with the corresponding level of stock.

Single-period:
$$\text{SOR} = \frac{C_{os}}{C_{os} + C_{us}} \tag{10-6}$$

Thus, in Example 10-5, a stock of 11 cars would yield a SOR equal to $P(D)$ of approximately .545. And because the SOR is the complement of the service level, we have:

$$\text{SL} = 100\% - \text{SOR}\% = \frac{C_{us}}{C_{os} + C_{us}} \tag{10-7}$$

and the service level in Example 10-5 would be $1.000 - .545 = .455$.

Example 10-5 illustrated the use of the single-period model for finding the optimum stocking level, given some historical (empirical) demand. The model can also be used for data that are known to follow standard statistical distributions. Solved problems at the end of the chapter illustrate the use of this incremental approach when the data are distributed in a uniform, normal, or Poisson manner.

Multiple-Period Models   Multiple-period models apply to continuous production operations and are also useful where one wishes to incorporate an *individual stockout cost per unit*. Purchase quantities may be calculated by standard equations, or influenced by the type of inventory (dependent versus independent), the type of inventory classification (A, B, or C), the associated costs of ordering, carrying, and purchasing, or the type of inventory control system used. We simply enter the order quantity being used as Q in the equation below.

The overstocking and understocking costs of the single-period model are replaced by per-unit carrying costs C_c and per-unit stockout costs C_{so}. We assume that carrying costs per unit are known (not probabilistic). Stockout costs per unit must be multiplied by the number of opportunities for stockout, or order cycles, D/Q. The multiple-period SOR is thus:

$$\left(\begin{matrix}\text{Expected stockout}\\ \text{cost/unit}\end{matrix}\right) \times \left(\begin{matrix}\text{number of order}\\ \text{cycles this occurs}\end{matrix}\right) = \left(\begin{matrix}\text{carrying cost}\\ \text{of the unit}\end{matrix}\right)$$

$$\underbrace{\left(\begin{matrix}\text{Probability}\\ \text{of stockout}\end{matrix}\right) \times \left(\begin{matrix}\text{stockout}\\ \text{cost/unit}\end{matrix}\right)} \times \left(\frac{D \text{ units/yr}}{Q \text{ units/order}}\right) = \left(\begin{matrix}\text{carrying cost}\\ \text{per unit-yr}\end{matrix}\right)$$

In symbols:

$$(\text{SOR}) \quad \times \quad (C_{so}) \quad \times \quad D/Q \quad = \quad C_c$$

Therefore:

Multiple-period:
$$\text{SOR} = \frac{C_c}{C_{so}}\left(\frac{Q}{D}\right) \tag{10-8}$$

Note that Eq. (10-8) applies to situations in which individual stockout costs *per unit* are known (or estimated). This is in contrast to the stockout cost *per order cycle* of Eq. (10-2).

EXAMPLE 10-6

A construction equipment dealer experiences an annual demand of about 300 electric generators and orders in quantitives of 50 units per order. Carrying costs are $900 per unit-year, and stockout costs are estimated at $2,000 per unit. What optimum probability of stockout should be used to determine the appropriate inventory-stocking level?

SOLUTION

$$\text{SOR} = \frac{C_c}{C_{so}}\left(\frac{Q}{D}\right) = \left(\frac{\$900/\text{unit-yr}}{\$2,000/\text{unit-order}}\right)\left(\frac{50 \text{ units/order}}{300 \text{ units/yr}}\right) = .075$$

The stock should be enough that demand is exceeded only 7.5 percent of the time. If the cumulative distribution of demand were available to us (as in the previous problem) we would then use it to find the stock level that is exceeded only 7.5 percent of the time and designate this as our optimal stocking amount.

USING EMPIRICAL DATA TO SET SAFETY STOCK LEVELS

Empirical data describing past demand, and lead-time variations, may be used to establish safety stock levels if the service level and carrying cost of inventory is specified. First, we assume that demand is variable and that lead times are constant. Once the stockout risk is established, and data collected on past demand, a cumulative distribution of demand can be formulated, and the maximum demand for a given stockout risk (D_{SOR}) can be obtained directly from the cumulative distribution. The required safety stock is then the difference between this maximum demand (D_{SOR}) and the average demand (D_{ave}).

$$\text{SS} = D_{SOR} - D_{ave} \tag{10-9}$$

In the example that follows (Example 10-7), the service level (SL) represents the *percentage of order cycles* that demand is met from stock on hand. This is a major difference between the methods in this section and the incremental methods discussed above.

EXAMPLE 10-7

The data below represent weekly demand on a $250 item which has a constant lead time of 1 week. The firm has a 20 percent per-year cost for carrying inventory. Determine the safety stock level and carrying cost for providing a service level of (a) 90 percent and (b) 95 percent.

Weekly Demand (Number of units)	Frequency (Number of weeks this demand occurred)	Cumulative Frequency (Number of weeks demand exceeded lower class boundary)	Cumulative Percentage (Percentage of weeks demand exceeded lower class boundary)
0 < 50	1	104	100.0
50 < 100	7	103	99.0
100 < 150	11	96	92.3
150 < 200	16	85	81.7
200 < 250	19	69	66.3
250 < 300	20	50	48.1
300 < 350	14	30	28.8
350 < 400	9	16	15.4
400 < 450	5	7	6.7
450 < 500	2	2	1.9
	104		

SOLUTION

The 90 percent and 95 percent service levels represent stockout risks of 10 percent and 5 percent, respectively [per Eq. (10-3)]. We can formulate a frequency distribution (histogram) and cumulative distribution (ogive) of demand as shown in Fig. 10-5.

Because it is readily available and sufficiently representative of the central tendency of the data, we use the median (the fiftieth percentile value) of the cumulative distribution as our estimate of average demand.

$$D_{ave} = \text{average demand} \cong 240 \text{ units}$$

(a) 90 percent service level (10 percent SOR):

$$D_{SOR} = \text{demand level corresponding to 10 percent risk of stockout}$$

$$\cong 385 \text{ units (from graph)}$$

$$SS = \text{safety stock level} = D_{SOR} - D_{ave} = 385 - 240 = 145 \text{ units}$$

$$SS \text{ cost} = \left(\frac{\$250}{\text{unit}}\right)\left(\frac{20\%}{\text{yr}}\right)(145 \text{ units}) = \$7,250/\text{yr}$$

(b) 95 percent SL (5 percent SOR):

$$D_{SOR} = \text{demand level corresponding to 5 percent risk of stockout}$$

$$\cong 430 \text{ units (from graph)}$$

$$SS = D_{SOR} - D_{ave} = 430 - 240 = 190 \text{ units}$$

$$SS \text{ cost} = \left(\frac{\$250}{\text{unit}}\right)\left(\frac{20\%}{\text{yr}}\right)(190 \text{ units}) = \$9,500/\text{yr}$$

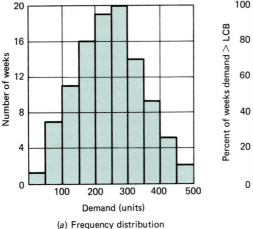

(a) Frequency distribution

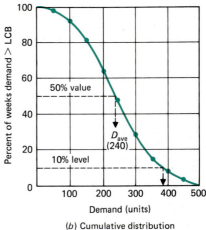

(b) Cumulative distribution

FIGURE 10-5   Distributions of Demand

Note the nonlinearity of the cumulative distribution in Fig. 10-5, especially at the upper end of the curve. Higher levels of service require an increasingly larger (and more costly) amount of safety stock. Thus it costs $7,250 to carry enough safety stock to provide 90 percent service. But to increase service by 5 percent (that is, to 95 percent service) required a 31 percent increase in cost (to $9,500).

Variations in lead time are the second major cause of uncertainty in inventory management, although lead times are generally more controllable than demand. As with variations in demand, the lead-time uncertainty can be handled by developing cumulative frequency or probability distributions depicting the relative occurrence of different lead times for the given inventory item or group of items. By referring to the cumulative distribution, the safety stock level (as in weeks of usage) required to guard against this uncertainty can be determined. This is done by using the cumulative distribution to find the lead time required to limit the stockout risk to a given level (LT_{SOR}) and subtracting the average lead time (LT_{ave}) from LT_{SOR}.

$$SS = LT_{SOR} - LT_{ave} \qquad (10\text{-}10)$$

STOCKOUT RISK AND ITS EFFECT UPON ORDER QUANTITIES

Because of the intangible nature of stockout costs associated with such concerns as loss of potential business or customer goodwill, management is often unprepared or reluctant to assign a cost to being out of stock. The above methods of setting safety stock levels in the face of uncertain demand (or lead time) approach the problem of stockout costs from a slightly different perspective. Instead of asking the manager, "What does it cost you to be out of stock?" the above approach seeks an answer to the question, "What would you be willing to pay *not* to be out of stock 90 percent of the time, or 95 percent of the time, or some other specified service level?" If, for example, the responsible manager is not willing to allocate as much as $9,500 per year to ensure that there is stock on hand 95 percent of the order cycle times, the cumulative distribution curves can be used to identify the level of service a manager can expect for any lower (or higher) carrying cost.

EXAMPLE 10-8

Given the data from Example 10-7, suppose the manager is willing to allocate only $3,000 per year to the carrying of safety stock for the $250 item. For what percentage of order cycles can he or she expect to run out of stock?

SOLUTION

We can compute how much safety stock the $3,000 would fund by dividing the $3,000 by the carrying cost per unit-year.

$$SS = \frac{\$3,000 \text{ allocated/yr}}{\$250/\text{unit } (20\%/\text{yr})} = 60 \text{ units}$$

The stockout risk corresponding to SS = 60 units is:

$$SS = D_{SOR} - D_{ave}$$

$$\therefore D_{SOR} = SS + D_{ave} \qquad [\text{where } D_{ave} = 240 \text{ units (from Figure 10-5)}]$$

$$= 60 + 240 = 300 \text{ units}$$

From the cumulative distribution (Fig. 10-5), a demand of 300 units corresponds to a percentage value of approximately 29 percent. Therefore the manager may expect to run out of stock on approximately 29 percent of the order cycles. That is, if the firm places an order each week, it may run out of stock on $(.29)(52) \cong 15$ occasions. Knowng this, the manager may want to reconsider the $3,000 allocation.

INTERDEPENDENCY OF INVENTORY VARIABLES

The order point, order quantity, demand, lead time, and safety stock levels are all interdependent variables. Each can influence the risk of stockout. The *order point establishes the amount of risk of stockout*, for it includes safety stock plus demand during lead time. Thus, the higher the order point, the more inventory is carried in stock and the less the risk of stockout (although the greater the carrying cost). The *order quantity establishes the frequency of exposure to risk of stockout*, or number of trials to run out of stock. An order quantity equal to annual demand would limit the number of stockout risks, or trials, to one per year. On the other hand, carrying such a large average inventory for a long period of time could result in high carrying costs.

In terms of the EOQ model, ordering and stockout costs act to increase the quantity ordered so that the frequency of orders and exposures to stockout is reduced. Quantity discounts also tend to increase Q. Carrying and storage costs exert the opposite effect of tending to reduce order quantities.

We have seen how safety stock levels can be set using empirical data of actual demand or lead times. When the demand or lead-time pattern follows a known statistical pattern, the problems of setting safety stock levels are simplified, for we need not go through the extra work of formulating cumulative distributions of actual data.

USING STATISTICAL DISTRIBUTIONS TO SET SAFETY STOCK LEVELS

Sometimes the frequency pattern of demand or lead time follows a known statistical distribution such as the normal or Poisson. If, as with stock levels set using empirical data, a desired service level can be ascertained (a management decision), then the safety stock levels and appropriate order points can be determined quite easily.

INVENTORY LEVELS UNDER NORMALLY DISTRIBUTED DEMAND

If the distribution of demand during lead time is symmetrical and unimodal, the normal distribution may satisfactorily describe it. Figure 10-6 depicts a normal distribution of demand during lead time. Note that an average demand would just use up the cycle (that is, non–safety stock) inventory during the lead time. If no safety stock were carried, we would expect the firm to run out of stock on about 50 percent of the order cycles.

The standard deviation (σ) or mean absolute deviation (MAD) is a useful measure of dispersion of individual demand values from the mean value. We have seen previously that:

$$\sigma = \sqrt{\frac{\Sigma\,(X - \mu)^2}{N}} \quad \text{and} \quad \text{MAD} = \frac{\Sigma|X - \mu|}{N}$$

$$\sigma \cong 1.25\ \text{MAD}$$

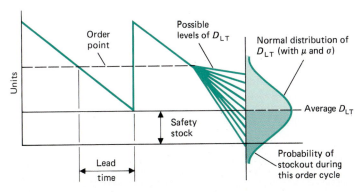

FIGURE 10-6   Normal Distribution of Demand during Lead Time

By expressing the service level as a percentage of the area under the normal curve, it is possible to calculate the safety stock required to provide a given level of service in terms of deviations from the mean. Conversely, if the number of units of safety stock is specified, we can determine how much protection against stockout (that is, the percentage of service) the safety stock provides. A table of safety stock level factors (SF) for normally distributed variables is given in Fig. 10-7. The

FIGURE 10-7 Safety Stock Level Factors for Normally Distributed Variables

$$SS = SF_\sigma(\sigma) \quad \text{or} \quad SS = SF_{MAD}(MAD)$$
$$OP = D_{LT} + SS$$

	Safety Factor Using	
Service Level (percentage of order cycles without stockout)	Standard Deviation SF_σ	Mean Absolute Deviation SF_{MAD}
50.00	.00	.00
75.00	.67	.84
80.00	.84	1.05
84.13	1.00	1.25
85.00	1.04	1.30
89.44	1.25	1.56
90.00	1.28	1.60
93.32	1.50	1.88
94.00	1.56	1.95
94.52	1.60	2.00
95.00	1.65	2.06
96.00	1.75	2.19
97.00	1.88	2.35
97.72	2.00	2.50
98.00	2.05	2.56
98.61	2.20	2.75
99.00	2.33	2.91
99.18	2.40	3.00
99.38	2.50	3.13
99.50	2.57	3.20
99.60	2.65	3.31
99.70	2.75	3.44
99.80	2.88	3.60
99.86	3.00	3.75
99.90	3.09	3.85
99.93	3.20	4.00
99.99	4.00	5.00

Source: Adapted from G. W. Plossl and O. W. Wight, *Production and Inventory Control: Principles and Techniques,* 1967, p. 108. Reprinted by permission of Prentice-Hall, Englewood Cliffs, NJ.

factors are simply the number of standard (and mean absolute) deviations required to include the specified percentage of area under the normal curve cumulated in the positive direction.

EXAMPLE 10-9

The demand for a product during its lead time is normally distributed, with mean $\mu = 1,000$ units and standard deviation $\sigma = 40$ units. What percentage of service can a firm expect to offer if (a) it provides for average demand only and (b) it carries 60 units of safety stock?

SOLUTION

(a) Average demand (1,000 units) would include no safety stock. Therefore, service = 50 percent.
(b) With 60 units of SS:

$$SF_\sigma = \frac{SS}{\sigma} = \frac{60}{40} = 1.5$$

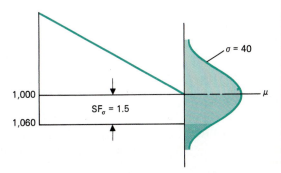

Therefore, from Fig. 10-7 the service level = 93.32 percent.
Note that the same result would be obtained from using any table of the normal distribution where

$$Z = \frac{X - \mu}{\sigma} = \frac{1,060 - 1,000}{40} = 1.5$$

The service level corresponds to the shaded area under the normal curve in Fig. 10-8.

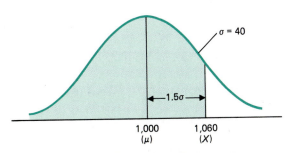

FIGURE 10-8 Service Level Shown as Area under the Normal Curve

EXAMPLE 10-10
(Using σ)

A firm has a normal distribution of demand during a (constant) lead time, with σ = 250 units. The firm wants to provide 98 percent service.
(a) How much safety stock should be carried?
(b) If the demand during the lead time averages 1,200 units, what is the appropriate order point?

SOLUTION
(a) SS = $SF_\sigma(\sigma)$ = (2.05)(250) = 512 units
(b) OP = D_{LT} + SS = 1,200 + 512 = 1,712 units

As indicated previously, the service level is a statement of the percentage of order cycles that do not experience a stockout. If the number of stockouts allowed per time period is designated, it can easily be expressed as a service level. We first estimate the number of reorder cycles. Then we express the number of cycles the stock is adequate as a percentage of the total number of cycles. If, for example, a firm places an order about every week and wants to limit the number of stockouts to one per year, this means it must have sufficient safety stock to supply it during 51 of the 52 order cycles. The ratio 51/52 would then constitute a 98 percent service level.

EXAMPLE 10-11
(Using MAD)

A firm has a normally distributed forecast of demand, with MAD = 60 units during the fixed lead time of 1 week. It desires a service level which limits stockouts to one order cycle per year.
(a) How much safety stock should be carried?
(b) If D_{LT} averages 500 units, what is the appropriate order point?

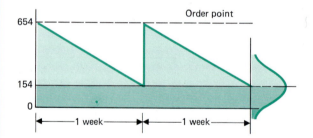

SOLUTION
(a) SS = $SF_{MAD}(MAD)$

where SF_{MAD} depends upon the service level:

1 week's supply/order = 52 orders/yr

1 stockout in 52 = $\frac{51}{52}$ in stock = 98 percent service

∴ SF_{MAD} = 2.56   (from Fig. 10-7)

SS = 2.56(60) = 154 units

(b) OP = D_{LT} + SS

= 500 + 154 = 654 units

LEAD TIMES DIFFERENT FROM THE DEMAND PERIOD[3]

In the previous example, the lead time and order cycle (or demand period) were both 1 week. What changes are necessary to accommodate situations in which lead times are (1) shorter than the order cycle or (2) longer than the order cycle? Remember, we are still assuming that lead times are constant.

LT < Order Cycle

We have already illustrated the situation in which lead times are shorter than the order cycle. (See Fig. 10-6.) No special adjustments are necessary because our uncertainty is confined to the latter phase of the demand cycle, that is, the time after reaching the order point. We can use the data from Example 10-11 to show that no change in safety stock level is necessary to yield the same level of service for longer order cycles.

EXAMPLE 10-12

Suppose the firm in Example 10-11 (where LT = 1 week, D_{LT} = 500 units, MAD = 60 units) ordered a 5-week supply rather than a 1-week supply. For the same level of service (98 percent):
(a) How much safety stock should be carried?
(b) What is the appropriate order point?

SOLUTION
(a) SS = SF_{MAD}(MAD) = 2.56(60) = 154 units
(b) OP = D_{LT} + SS = 500 + 154 = 654 units
As is evident, the safety stock is a direct function of MAD, which is unchanged for this situation.

As another example, suppose the firm in Example 10-12 wished to use the criterion (as in Example 10-11) of limiting stockouts to one order cycle per year. The 5-week supply would necessitate placing only 52/5 = 10.4 orders per year. Being out of stock one time would result in 9.4/10.4 ≅ 90 percent service. Using Fig. 10-7, the safety stock required would be only SS = 1.60(60) = 96 units (as compared with 154 units for 98 percent service). Figure 10-9 illustrates this situation.

Figure 10-9 assumes that there is a constant monitoring of demand so that uncertainty is limited to the demand during the last (5th) week, when a reorder has been placed but has not yet arrived. Unfortunately, the safety stock is carried (at a cost) for the first 4 weeks too, even though it is not needed then. Time-phased and MRP systems attempt to reduce this unnecessary inventory by scheduling materials to arrive as needed. We shall go into more detail on this later.

---

[3] This material extends beyond that covered in some introductory texts.

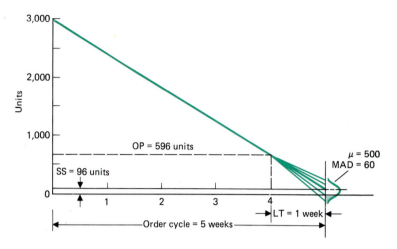

FIGURE 10-9   Product with 5-Week Order Cycle and 1-Week Lead Time (90% SL)

LT > Order Cycle   This type of situation arises when smaller shipments are ordered at frequent intervals, but delivery time is long. High carrying costs (or a tight cash position) may prompt a firm to follow this course of action. For example, a tire distributor may find that it is more economical to place replenishment orders on a weekly basis rather than every few weeks. Even though it takes 4 weeks for the tires to arrive from the factory, the weekly orders are easier to store and don't require so much cash outlay at one time.

Figure 10-10 illustrates a LT > order cycle situation. Each of the individual order cycles within the span of the lead time adds some of its own demand uncertainty to the ending distribution. However, the increase required in safety stock is not directly proportional to the increase in lead time.

As you may recall from your statistics, standard deviations (σ's) are not additive, but variances (σ^2) are additive. However, we want to end up with an

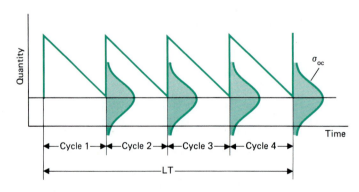

FIGURE 10-10   Lead Time Containing Four Order Cycles

aggregated standard deviation of demand during lead time, σ_k. Therefore, we convert the individual standard deviations of the order cycle (σ_{oc}) into variances (σ_{oc}^2), add the variances ($\Sigma\sigma_{oc}^2$), and take the square root ($\sqrt{\Sigma\sigma_{oc}^2}$). Recognizing our assumption of a constant lead time and that this lead time has n independent order cycles, each of which has a similar normally distributed demand, we can eliminate the summation step and simply multiply the variance of the (average) distribution by the number of demand cycles, n.

Thus, for constant LTs > order cycles, we can estimate the standard deviation of demand during the lead time, σ_k, as

$$\sigma_k = \sqrt{n\sigma_{oc}^2} \tag{10-11}$$

where n = number of order cycles in the lead time

σ_{oc}^2 = variance of an order cycle (that is, a representative variance)

EXAMPLE 10-13 | A tire distributor has a weekly order cycle and has experienced a normally distributed demand with a mean of 40 units per week and a standard deviation of 5 units per week. Lead time is constant at 6 weeks. The distributor wishes to provide 90 percent service.
(a) How much safety stock should be carried?
(b) How much stock is on hand when the reorder is placed?

SOLUTION
(a) $\text{SS} = \text{SF}_\sigma(\sigma)$

where SF for 90% = 1.28

σ = the σ_k of demand during the 6-week LT

$= \sqrt{n\sigma_{oc}^2}$
where $n = 6$
$\sigma_{oc}^2 = 5^2$
$= \sqrt{6(5)^2}$
$= 12.25$ units

$\therefore \text{SS} = (1.28)(12.25)$
$= 15.68$, say 16 units (tires)

(b) The safety stock of 16 units is designed to protect the distributor over 6 order cycles of demand uncertainty (and it is assumed that the lead time of 6 weeks is constant). Therefore the distributor can work with an order plan based upon the amount used during one order cycle, D_{oc}. The actual (physical) inventory on hand, I_{oh}, when the distributor places an order will be:

$$I_{oh} = D_{oc} + \text{SS} = 40 + 16 = 56 \text{ tires}$$

Note, however, that in terms of units on hand *and on order* the (book value) order point would be substantially higher, for it would be triggered by 6 weeks of demand at 40 units per week plus the 16 units of safety stock, or OP = 6(40) + 16 = 256 units.

In Example 10-13, if the lead time were only 1 week, only $(1.25)(5) = 6.4$, say 7 units of safety stock would have been required. The extended lead time has thus more than doubled the safety stock requirement.

If the variability of demand during the lead time is expressed in MAD rather than σ values, it can be converted into σ's.

OTHER DEMAND AND LEAD-TIME DISTRIBUTIONS

Previous examples have assumed a constant lead time and variable demand. If demand were constant and lead time varied, the same theory would hold. However if both demand and lead time vary simultaneously, the combined distribution is likely to be of some nondeterminant form, and computer simulation may be the most effective way of estimating an appropriate level of safety stock. One conservative approach is to use the longest normal lead time.

Many demands have a normal distribution at the production-plant level and a Poisson distribution at the retail level. The Poisson distribution also has some applicability in estimating lead time.

INVENTORY CONTROL SYSTEMS

Inventory control systems are the ordering and monitoring techniques used to control the quantity and timing of inventory transactions. The traditional inventory control systems are classified as either perpetual (continuously monitored) or periodic. However, other inventory control measures are used (such as inventory "turns"), and numerous combinations exist (for example, a base stock system). In addition, many broad-based scheduling systems incorporate inventory control activities as an integral part of the larger systems. The Japanese have introduced the world to just-in-time (JIT) inventory management systems with Kanban material movement subsystems. And the computerized MRP systems, developed largely in the United States, are very highly integrated production and inventory control systems.

Space does not permit a detailed description of the numerous types of inventory control systems in use today, but we shall take a brief look at (1) perpetual, (2) periodic, (3) just-in-time, and (4) MRP and related systems.

The perpetual and periodic systems, by themselves, are essentially only *order launching* techniques. They also tend to look *back* at historical averages rather than *ahead* to a forecast of material requirements. Nevertheless, they are still widely used as a basis for releasing orders because they answer the basic questions of *how much* to order and *when*. This is often satisfactory for distribution inventories (such as we have dealt with in this chapter) but is usually unsatisfactory for manufacturing inventories. MRP systems (for manufacturing) are the subject of the next chapter.

PERPETUAL (FIXED ORDER-QUANTITY) SYSTEMS

Perpetual inventory systems are often referred to as fixed-quantity systems. They keep a current (perpetual) record of the amount of inventory in stock at all times. A fixed quantity Q is ordered when the order point is reached (that is, when the amount on hand, without using the safety stock, will just meet the average demand during the lead time). This type of system, illustrated in Fig. 10-11, lends itself to the use of EOQ purchasing methods. The system requires continuous monitoring of inventory levels, which can easily be done if the system is computerized. Because of this, it is often used for inventories that have large, unexpected fluctuations in demand, such as end-item inventories.

PERIODIC (FIXED ORDER-INTERVAL) SYSTEMS

Periodic systems are often referred to as fixed-interval systems. They review the amount of inventory in stock at periodic intervals, such as weekly or monthly. A variable quantity Q is then ordered on a regular basis. The order quantity is the estimated quantity needed to bring the inventory on hand and on order up to a specified level. Because the safety stock must provide protection over the entire cycle (that is, from time period t_1 to t_2), it is typically larger than would be required under a fixed order-quantity system, where the safety stock must protect over the lead time only. This system does not, however, require continuous monitoring, and it is especially useful for processes that call for a consistent use of material. It also lends itself to conditions where a single review period can be used

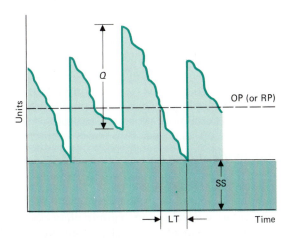

FIGURE 10-11   Perpetual (Fixed-Quantity) System

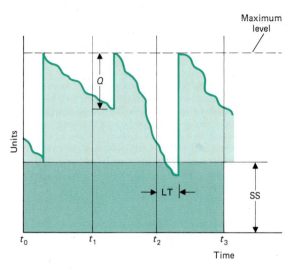

FIGURE 10-12 Periodic (Fixed-Interval) System

to identify several items, which can then be ordered at one time, with a possible savings in the ordering cost.

Fixed order-interval systems, also called *fixed order-period systems*, lend themselves to situations in which periodic physical counting of on-hand materials is more practical than maintaining a perpetual count. (See Chapter 9 for more on inventory counting.)

In fixed order-interval systems, the order point is often associated with a time period rather than with a quantity. Thus, in Fig. 10-12 the order points are at t_1, t_2, and t_3. (In order to avoid confusion, we shall continue to assume that order points relate to quantities, as in fixed order-quantity systems, unless specified otherwise.)

Combinations of the two systems described above are prevalent. The base stock system is one of many combinations of inventory systems and has elements of both the fixed order-quantity and fixed order-interval systems. In this system, inventory levels are reviewed periodically, but orders are placed only when the stock is below some specified level. The system thus provides some of the control aspects of periodic review systems but would typically result in the placement of fewer orders, and orders of a more economic lot size.

JUST-IN-TIME INVENTORY SYSTEMS

Just-in-time (JIT) is a manufacturing philosophy developed in Japan for the high-volume production of discrete units (such as Toyota automobiles). It is sometimes described as an inventory control system because of its inherent tight control over inventory (a better term might be "restriction of inventory"). In the original JIT systems, inventory is controlled by a visual (Kanban) system that virtually assures that work-in-process will be kept to a minimum.

- Have a flexible work force capable of using multiple skills.
- Strive for very short setup times and very small lot sizes.
- Work for a relatively constant (stabilized) master schedule.
- Insist that defect-free materials and supplies be delivered when needed.
- Use a Kanban or comparable system to pull needed inventory through the system (in response to final assembly schedule).
- Develop necessary support (reliable vendors, employee cooperation, outstanding maintenance program, spare capacity, and so on).

FIGURE 10-13   Key Elements in a JIT System

Figure 10-13 summarizes some of the key features of JIT systems. A major tenet is to avoid holding any unnecessary inventory [4:469]. Instead, the firms rely upon the careful scheduling of work, on-time delivery of (zero-defect) supplies, and skilled workers who are capable of handling any problems that may arise during production (such as shortages or breakdowns).

The absence of unnecessary inventory forces JIT systems to become very flexible to change—for example, to be able to produce a different part or model on a moment's notice. Setup and "model change-over" times in JIT plants are typically reduced from hours to minutes. (This in turn can save millions of dollars in idle time costs.) As is evident, teamwork and close cooperation of everyone is vital. Suppliers even cooperate to deliver parts several times per day, just as if they were extensions of the main production plan.

Kanban Systems   In JIT systems, inventory is viewed as a waste. It just sits there tying up funds and taking up space (a problem which the Japanese take seriously). Instead of using inventory as a protection against emergencies, JIT systems "cut it to the bone" so as to expose the scheduling, materials, or other problems in the system—which are then attacked and corrected.

The heart of the materials control system is a rather simple physical card and container system that replaces the paperwork used in most shops. The cards, or markers, limit inventory to that needed to support current production. Two main types of cards are used: (1) production Kanbans and (2) move Kanbans. *Production Kanbans* authorize the production of the number of parts needed to fill a limited size container (such as 25 gears). *Move, or withdrawal, Kanbans* authorize the movement of containers from the output of one work center (WC) to the input of the next.

Figure 10-14 illustrates the inventory flow in a portion of an assembly line with three work centers. The daily production schedule is given to the final assembly line (on the right) and to outside suppliers. Assume it authorizes production at WC 3 and in doing so uses up a full container of parts. The empty container, and a move Kanban are returned to the output area of WC 2, which has a full container (with a production Kanban attached). The production Kanban in the full container is removed and placed on a receiving post at WC 2 (signaling the

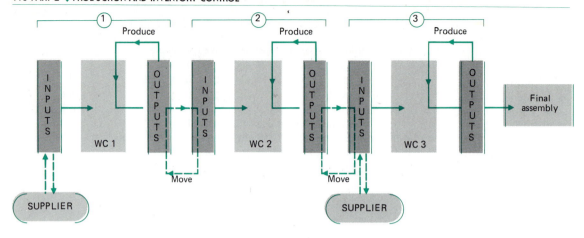

FIGURE 10-14   Partial Kanban System (Adapted from [1])

authorization to produce another container of parts). The move Kanban from the empty container is then transferred to the full container, which is moved back to the input area of WC 3. As WC 2 needs more inputs, its supply requirements are in turn transmitted back to WC 1 (and possibly to outside suppliers).

Kanban systems might be characterized as deceptively simple and yet elegantly effective. Although they do seem to require unnecessary worker involvement in materials handling, they foster cooperation and avoid unnecessary paperwork. And as improvements in setup and production times are realized, inventory levels can be further reduced by removing some of the available containers.

MRP AND OTHER SYSTEMS

Many firms have thousands of items of inventory which require some form of control. The usage calculations and record-keeping chores would soon become overwhelming were it not for the computer and its unique information storage and retrieval capabilities. Inventory control is so ideally suited to computerization that it is usually one of the first and most important tasks to gain priority on an organization's computer. Most computer manufacturers offer software packages of inventory control systems and will provide technical assistance for setting up a computerized control system.

Computerization of the inventory control system rests upon the application of the inventory theory presented earlier in this chapter. There is no inherent magic that automatically solves inventory problems. The computer keeps a record of prices paid, quantities in stock, and so forth. The firm's management must specify service levels desired, stockout costs, carrying costs, usage expectations, and the like. From there on, the computer can calculate demand patterns, variances, and lead-time statistics, and it can print out recommended order quantities on appropriate dates. It does the tedious calculations for thousands of items which would be impractical to do by hand. In some cases its low-cost data storage capabilities have eliminated the need for traditional classifications of inventory, such as the ABC system. When working with families of items, simple EOQs may not result in the optimal number of orders or machine setups. Computerized methods have also been developed to determine the most economic lot sizes while staying within given set-up hour limitations and still balancing ordering and inventory carrying costs [2:75].

With the availability of small business computers (with large processing capability and memory), nearly any firm can computerize its inventory system. Inexpensive inventory programs are often wholly adequate for small firms. Complete and more comprehensive inventory packages are available from such firms as IBM, Xerox, Honeywell, and Boeing.

Time-phased MRP systems are the last distinctive type of inventory system that we shall discuss (see Chapter 11). MRP systems can handle all inventory items, but they are particularly well suited to dependent-demand items, whereas the order point systems are not. Unfortunately, many firms have tried to force dependent-demand inventories into an order point format for years, and it has never worked well for that. Like JIT systems, MRP is really more than an inventory system—it represents a whole new capability for scheduling as well as for inventory management.

SUMMARY

This chapter is concerned primarily with distribution (*independent demand*) inventories that must respond directly to varying patterns of customer demand. (Manufacturing inventories are largely dependent and there is less need for carrying extra (safety) stock.) The EOQ formula can be adjusted to incorporate stockout costs when they are available.

Four methods of protecting against stockouts are (1) informal decision rules, (2) expected value approaches, (3) incremental approaches, and (4) statistical methods of setting safety stocks. Other than the informal decision rules, the methods basically attempt to balance the advantage of having some inventory against the cost of carrying it. The expected value approach is most useful for inventory items that drop in value if not used right away.

A major difference between the other two approaches is in how the stockout cost is applied. In the incremental models of method 3, the stockout costs pertain to individual units; whereas in the statistical models of method 4, costs are stated in terms of order cycles, so in method 4 there is no adjustment for whether the shortage is 2 units or 20.

The *single-period incremental model* uses the overstocking and understocking costs of individual units to derive a balance point at which the two costs are equal. The balance point, $P(D)$, is then the cumulative probability that demand will be a certain amount, d, and so we choose to stock that amount. The $P(D)$ also equals the stockout risk (SOR). In the *multiple-period incremental model* the overstocking and understocking costs are replaced by per-unit carrying and stock-out costs. The model is also adjusted to reflect the number of orders placed, D/Q. But the formula for calculating the stockout risk is relatively simple.

When using the *statistical models* of method 4, the service level indicates the percentage of order cycles that the firm will be able to supply inventory from stock. Historical demand (or lead-time) data can be used to formulate *empirical* cumulative distributions which reveal how much safety stock is needed to maintain a specified service level. The appropriate reorder point is then simply the average demand during the lead time plus the safety stock.

When demand distributions follow a *normal* distribution, the calculations for setting safety stock levels are simplified. We just compute the number of standard deviations (σ's) or mean absolute deviations (MADs) required to provide a given service level and express this in units of inventory. Using safety stock level factors from a table of σ or MAD values further simplifies the calculations. When the lead time exceeds the order cycle, however, more safety stock is required.

Good inventory management is essential in both manufacturing and distribution situations. Distribution inventories tend to be more suited to controls which key off an order point. Perpetual (fixed-quantity) and periodic (fixed-interval) systems are two of the most popular order-launching systems. The fixed-quantity systems require continuous monitoring but can accept EOQ ordering and lend themselves to computerized control.

Just-in-time (JIT) and MRP systems are more suitable for handling dependent-demand (manufacturing) inventories. JIT systems strive to reduce inventories to a bare minimum, depending upon good scheduling and skilled, cooperative workers to handle any difficulties. Inventory control is sometimes accomplished by use of a Kanban system that offers a visual control via the use of cards and containers. MRP systems are the subject of the next chapter.

SOLVED PROBLEMS

SAFETY STOCKS, ORDER POINTS, AND SERVICE LEVELS

1   A producer of Sun-Stop suntan lotion uses 400 gallons per week of a chemical which is ordered in EOQ quantities of 5,000 gallons at a quantity discount cost of $3.75 per gallon. The procurement lead time is 2 weeks, and a safety stock of 200 gallons is maintained. The storage cost is $.01 per gallon-week. Find (a) the maximum inventory on hand (on the average), (b) the average inventory maintained, and (c) the order point (in units).

Solution

(a) Maximum inventory: I_{max} = safety stock + EOQ

$$= 200 + 5,000 = 5,200 \text{ gal}$$

(b) Average inventory: $I_{ave} = \dfrac{I_{max} + I_{min}}{2} = \dfrac{5,200 + 200}{2} = 2,700 \text{ gal}$

(c) Order point:
$$OP = D_{LT} + SS$$
$$= (400)(2) + 200 = 1,000 \text{ units}$$

2   A firm has an annual demand of 1,000 units, ordering costs of $10 per order, and carrying costs of $10 per unit-year. Stockout costs are estimated to be about $40 each time the firm has an exposure to stockout. How much safety stock is justified by the carrying costs?

Solution

$$Q = \sqrt{\frac{2D(C_o + C_e)}{C_c}} + \sqrt{\frac{2(1,000)(10 + 40)}{10}} = 100 \text{ units}$$

$$\therefore \text{ Orders/yr} = \frac{D}{Q} = \frac{1,000 \text{ units/yr}}{100 \text{ units/order}} = 10 \text{ orders/yr}$$

Stockout costs are ($40/trial)(10 trials/yr) = $400/yr. At carrying costs of $10/unit-yr, the $400 will fund:

$$\frac{\$400/\text{yr}}{\$10/\text{unit-yr}} = 40 \text{ units of safety stock}$$

3   A container manufacturer produces corrugated bales of pressboard on a multipurpose production line at a rate of 50 bales per week. The cost to set up for production of bales is $3,000. The bales are used in another part of the plant at a rate of 20 bales per week (1,000 per year), and the firm uses a cost of $9,000 for being out of stock. If carrying costs are $140 per bale per year, what is the most economic production run length?

Solution
This problem necessitates that we modify Eq. 10-2, adjusting it for a noninstantaneous supply:

$$\text{ERL (with SO)} = \sqrt{\frac{2D(C_o + C_e)}{C_c(1 + d/p)}}$$

$$= \sqrt{\frac{2(1,000)(\$3,000 + \$9,000)}{\$140(1 - 20/50)}} = 535 \text{ bales}$$

4   *Informal decision rules*   Trident Valve Company has experienced a demand pattern of a maximum of 40 units/day, a minimum of 10 units/day, and $D_{ave} = 21$ units/day. Lead times for reorders vary from 2 to 8 days.
  (a) What amount of stock would be carried under a decision rule of largest daily usage times longest lead time?
  (b) How much safety stock would be carried under a rule of average demand plus 30 percent safety factor?
  (c) How much under a rule of the square root of average demand during lead time?

Solution

(a) Stock $= (D_{max})(LT_{max}) = (40 \text{ units/day})(8 \text{ days}) = 320 \text{ units}$

(b) $\quad SS = D_{ave} + 30\%(D_{ave}) = 21 + .30(21) = 27.6 \qquad \therefore \text{ Use 28 units.}$

(c) $\quad SS = \sqrt{D_{ave} \text{ during } LT_{ave}}$

$$\text{where} \qquad LT_{ave} = \frac{2 + 8}{2} = 5 \text{ days}$$

$$D_{ave} \text{ during } LT = \left(21\frac{\text{units}}{\text{day}}\right)(5 \text{ days}) = 105 \text{ units}$$

$$SS = \sqrt{105} = 10.25 \qquad \therefore \text{ Use 11 units.}$$

5   *Expected value approach*   Idaho Potato Company believes that next period's demand can be approximated from past data as shown below. The selling price is $100 per thousand pounds, cost is $60 per thousand pounds, and any potatoes not sold are used for hog feed at $10 per thousand pounds.

Demand X (lbs)	20,000	25,000	40.000	60,000
Frequency (no. periods)	10	20	50	20

(a) Develop a payoff matrix.

(b) What is the expected profit matrix?

(c) What amount of potatoes should be stocked to maximize expected profits?

Solution (*all values in thousands of pounds*)

(a) The payoff matrix shows the *state of nature* (demand) on the horizontal scale and *action* of stocking various amounts of inventory (supply) on the vertical. Each cell's payoff value is systematically computed recognizing that the profit (on units sold) and loss (on unsold units) are

$$\text{Profit} = \text{sales revenue} - \text{cost} = \$100 - \$60 = \$40$$

$$\text{Loss} = \text{cost} - \text{revenue from hog feed} = \$60 - \$10 = \$50$$

Thus for the cell of:

     Stock 20, demand 20:   profit $= 20(\$40) = \$800$
     Stock 20, demand 25:   profit $= 20(\$40) = \$800$
     Stock 25, demand 20:   profit $= 20(\$40) - 5(\$50) = \$550$
     Stock 40, demand 20:   profit $= 20(\$40) - 20(\$50) = -\$200 \text{ (loss)}$

Payoff Matrix

		State of Nature (demand)			
		20	25	40	60
Action (supply)	20	800	800	800	800
	25	550	1,000	1,000	1,000
	40	(200)	250	1,600	1,600
	60	(1,200)	(750)	600	2,400

(b) Expected values are computed by multiplying the payoff value X by its probability of occurrence $P(X)$. Thus for the cell:

Stock 20, demand 20: $E(X) = 800(.1) = 80$
Stock 20, demand 25: $E(X) = 800(.2) = 160$

Expected Profit Matrix

			State of Nature (demand)			
		(.1) 20	(.2) 25	(.5) 40	(.2) 60	Expected Profit
Action (supply)	20	80	160	400	160	800
	25	55	200	500	200	955
	40	(20)	50	800	320	1,150
	60	(120)	(150)	300	480	510

The expected value for each course of action is the summation of the cell row expected values, or $\Sigma\,[XP(X)]$. Thus for the course of action:

Stock 20: $\Sigma[XP(X)] = 800(.1) + 800(.2) + 800(.5) + 800(.2) = 800$

Stock 25: $\Sigma[XP(X)] = 550(.1) + 1,000(.2) + 1,000(.5) + 1,000(.2) = 955$

(c) The maximum expected value is from stocking 40 (thousand) pounds for $1,150.

6 *Incremental approach: Single-period model uniformly distributed* The *City Chronicle* has a daily newspaper demand that varies uniformly between 20,000 and 24,000 copies per day. The paper costs 8 cents per issue to produce and generates a revenue of 20 cents per issue. Unsold papers have no value.
(a) What is the optimal level of papers to stock?
(b) What service level would that optimal level correspond with?

Solution

(a) This is a problem of balancing the cost of understocking inventory C_{us} with that of overstocking C_{os}. From Eq. 10-5 the balance point is where the cumulative probability of demand $P(D)$ establishes the equality of

$$C_{us}P(D) = C_{os}[1 - P(D)]$$

Thus
$$P(D) = \frac{C_{os}}{C_{os} + C_{us}}$$

where C_{os} = cost/unit − salvage value = $.08 − 0 = $.08

C_{us} = revenue/unit − cost/unit = $.20 − $.08 = $.12

Therefore,
$$P(D) = \frac{.08}{.08 + .12} = .40$$

Because demand is uniform, we can depict it with a straight (linear) line from the minimum demand (20,000) to the maximum demand (24,000). Going into the curve (below) from .4 and down to the horizontal axis yields an optimal value of 22,400.

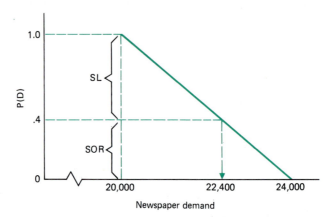

Newspaper demand

(b) The .40 is the equating probability that demand will be exceeded, and represents a stockout risk established on the basis of the costs given. Thus the corresponding service level is:

$$SL = 1 - SOR = 1 - .4 = .6$$

Note: Algebraically, the point representing a 60 percent service level is an inventory of:

$$I_{OPT} = D_{min} + \%SL(\Delta \text{ inventory}) = 20,000 + .60(24,000 - 20,000) = 22,400 \text{ units}$$

7 *Incremental approach: Normally distributed demand* Demand for a chemical product is normally distributed with μ equals 80 gallons per week and σ equals 5 gallons per week. If C_{os} is $.15 per gallon and C_{us} is $.50 per gallon, what is the optimal level to stock?

Solution

$$P(D) = \frac{C_{os}}{C_{os} + C_{us}} = \frac{.15}{.15 + .50} = .231$$

$$I_{opt} = \mu + Z\sigma$$

where Z is for a probability area of $.500 - .231 = .269$. Therefore $Z = .73$.

$$I_{opt} = 80 + .73(5) = 83.65 \text{ gal}$$

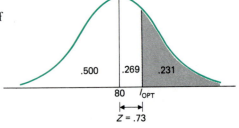

Note: The solution above corresponds to an SL of $1 - \text{SOR} = 1.00 - .231 = .769 = 76.9$ percent. Some analysts compute the SL percentage directly by reversing the equation for $P(D)$ to:

$$\text{SL\%} = \frac{C_{us}}{C_{os} + C_{us}} = \frac{.50}{.15 + .50} = .769$$

8 *Incremental approach: Poisson demand* A large city hospital has determined that the demand for ambulances can be approximated by a Poisson distribution with a mean of 6 per day. The cost for having an ambulance available is $460 per day, and its life-support value, when used, is placed at $2,000 per day. If unused, of course, its service value is zero. What is the optimum number of ambulances to maintain?

Solution

The two expected costs are equal for the cumulative probability:

$$P(D) = \frac{C_{os}}{C_{os} + C_{us}}$$

where C_{os} = cost/unit − salvage = $460 − 0 = $460
$\quad\quad\;\; C_{us}$ = value/unit − cost/unit = $2,000 − $460 = $1,540

$$P(D) = \frac{\$460}{\$460 + \$1,540} = .23$$

Thus, SL = $1.00 - .23 = .77$.

Cumulative probabilities for a Poisson distribution with a mean of 6.0 are then obtained from Appendix E, as $P(X|\lambda = 6)$.

Demand (Ambulances per day)	0	1	2	3	4	5	6	7	8	9
Cumulative Probability	.002	.017	.062	.151	.285	.446	.606	.744	.847	...

Seven ambulances would closely approximate the service level which balances the expected costs and benefits (that is, 77 percent), but eight would be required to equal or exceed the 77 percent.

9 *Incremental approach: Multiple-period model, normally distributed demand, individual-unit stockout costs* Supermarket Supply Company distributes grocery products to customers in Arizona, New Mexico, Texas, and Oklahoma. Demand for canned corn averages 280 cases per month. Lead time to obtain a shipment is about a month, and demand during the lead time is normally distributed with a standard deviation of 60 cases. The company estimates their ordering cost at $8.00 per order, carrying cost at $2.40 per case-year and stockout cost is $2.00 per case.
(a) Find the EOQ disregarding stockout costs.
(b) What is the number of orders per year if the EOQ is used?
(c) Find the optimum level of SOR.
(d) Find the reorder point.

Solution

(a)
$$\text{EOQ} = \sqrt{\frac{2C_oD}{C_c}} = \sqrt{\frac{2(8)(280 \times 12)}{2.40}} = 150 \text{ cases/order}$$

(b)
$$\frac{\text{Orders}}{\text{Year}} = \frac{D}{Q} = \frac{(280 \times 12) \text{ cases/yr}}{150 \text{ cases/order}} = 22.4 \text{ orders/yr}$$

(c)
$$\text{SOR} = \frac{C_c}{C_{so}}\left(\frac{Q}{D}\right) = \left(\frac{\$2.40/\text{case-yr}}{2.00/\text{case-order}}\right)\left(\frac{150 \text{ cases/order}}{3,360 \text{ cases/yr}}\right) = \begin{array}{l}.054, \text{ or } 5.4\% \text{ risk} \\ \text{of stockout}\end{array}$$

Thus, $\text{SL} = 1.00 - .054 = .946 = 94.6$ percent.

(d) $\text{RP} = D_{LT} + \text{SS}$

where $\text{SS} = \text{SF}_\sigma(\sigma) = 1.56(60) = 94$ cases

$\text{RP} = (280 \text{ cases/month})(1 \text{ month LT}) + 94 \text{ cases} = 374 \text{ cases}$

SAFETY STOCK USING KNOWN DISTRIBUTIONS

10 *Normal distribution: LT greater than order cycle* Robotic Devices, Inc. produces a microprocessor which has an average demand of 600 units per work day, with $\sigma = 40$. The production rate is 2,000 per day, and each run costs \$325 to set up and requires a 4-day scheduling and setup time. The company works 250 days a year, and carrying costs for the microprocessor are \$8.00 per unit-year.
(a) Find the optimal production quantity.
(b) What reorder point will give the firm a 95 percent chance of meeting any customer demand that occurs during the 4-day lead time? Assume that demand during the setup time is normally distributed and independent from one day to the next.

Solution

(a)
$$\text{ERL} = \sqrt{\frac{2C_oD}{C_c(1 - d/p)}} = \sqrt{\frac{2(\$325)(600 \times 250)}{\$8[1 - (600/2,000)]}} = 4,173 \text{ units}$$

(b)
$$\text{OP} = D_{LT} + \text{SS}$$

where $\text{SS} = \text{SF}_\sigma(\sigma)$, and in this case;

$$\sigma = \sigma_k = \sqrt{n\sigma_{oc}^2} = \sqrt{4(40)^2} = 80$$

$$\text{SF}_\sigma \text{ for 96\% SL} = 1.75 \quad \text{(from Fig. 10-7)}$$

$$\text{SS} = (1.75)(80) = 140 \text{ units}$$

$$\therefore \text{OP} = (600)(4) + 140 = 2,540 \text{ units}$$

The firm should begin preparations for a production run of 4,173 units whenever existing inventory levels drop to 2,540 units.

*11 *Poisson distribution* An inventory analyst has determined that the lead time for a certain item is distributed as Poisson with a mean $\mu = 1.8$ weeks. Each week the firm uses 200 of these items, and the analyst wishes to establish a safety stock level that gives 99 percent assurance that the item will be in stock when it is needed. How many units of safety stock should be kept on hand to provide this level of service? (Round any fractional weeks of lead time to the next highest number; for example, $7+$ weeks $= 8$ weeks.)

Solution

Using a cumulative Poisson distribution, we need to find a numerical value for X such that

$$P(X \geq ? \mid \mu = 1.8) = .01$$

where .01 is the SOR and 1.8 is the mean, μ.

From the Poisson distribution table, Appendix E, we find

$$P(X > 5 \mid \mu = 1.8) = .01$$

$$\therefore \text{ Maximum value (that is, } > 5) = 6$$

Thus, the lead time that will be exceeded only 1 percent of the time is 6 weeks.

$$\text{SS} = L_{\text{SOR}} - L_{\text{ave}}$$

$$= 6.0 - 1.8 = 4.2 \text{ weeks}$$

$$\text{Number of items} = (4.2 \text{ weeks}) \left(\frac{200 \text{ items}}{\text{week}} \right) = 840 \text{ items of SS}$$

QUESTIONS

10-1 Distinguish between dependent and independent inventories.

10-2 What effect does the inclusion of stockout costs have upon the economic order quantity?

10-3 What are the two major uncertainties encountered in managing inventories and what is usually done to compensate for those uncertainties?

10-4 Using the accompanying diagram, identify the following by letter:
(a) ____ reorder point
(b) ____ lead time
(c) ____ order cycle
(d) ____ order quantity
(e) ____ safety stock

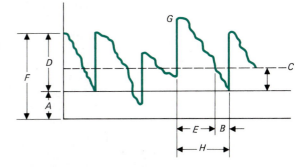

10-5   List one advantage and one disadvantage of using an informal decision rule for helping set an inventory level.

10-6   Using the logic of an incremental approach, what should be the cumulative probability of demand, $P(D)$, for the last item added to inventory, if the marginal cost is 75 percent of the value of the item?

10-7   How do the two major costs in the single-period and the multiple-period models (of the incremental approach) differ with respect to (a) the content (or designation) of what the costs are and (b) the probabilistic nature of the costs?

10-8   What is the major distinction between the incremental approaches and the safety stock (statistical) approaches with respect to how the stockout cost enters into the model? That is, where does it apply on a *per-unit* basis versus a *per-order-cycle* basis?

10-9   Suppose you are assigned the task of setting up safety stocks for generator spare parts for a municipal power company. How might you go about establishing a stockout cost?

10-10   Contrast the perpetual (fixed order-quantity) and periodic (fixed order-interval) inventory control systems, pointing out (a) what the interrelated variables are, (b) briefly how each system functions, and (c) what kinds of uncertainties the systems are designed to cope with.

10-11   Why does a Kanban inventory system appear to "fit" so well into the just-in-time (JIT) manufacturing philosophy?

PROBLEMS

1   Lowell Equipment Company supplies auto parts stores with oil filters and has experienced an average demand of 32 per week. They purchase the filters from a supplier who generally delivers them three weeks after Lowell mails the order. If Lowell Equipment trys to maintain a safety stock of two dozen filters, what should be their order point?

2   A soft drink producer receives bottles in economic lot quantities of 10,000 units per order and uses them at a rate of 400 per day. If the lead time is 15 working days, and the producer carries a safety stock of 2,000 bottles, what is the appropriate order point?

3   An Indiana bakery orders a raw material in quantities of 4 tons per order from a supplier who always delivers in 1 month. The price is $600 per ton, and the carrying and storage cost is 30 percent per year. The bakery uses 24 tons per year and tries to maintain a safety stock of 2 tons. Find (a) the maximum inventory on hand, I_{max}, (b) the average inventory maintained, I_{ave}, (c) the annual carrying and storage cost, and (d) the order point.

4   A distributor with an annual demand of 800 appliances has ordering costs of $60 per order and carrying costs of $40 per unit per year. Use the carrying costs to imply a stockout cost and develop an approximate EOQ (with stockout cost).

5   Medical Supply Company (of Wayne, Michigan) stocks a hospital item at an estimated carrying cost of $6 per unit-year. Their annual demand is only for 140 units, but stockout costs are set at $200 each time the company has an exposure to stockout. If ordering costs are estimated to be $50 per order, how much safety stock is justified by the carrying costs?

6   Maintenance Supply Company has an annual demand of 400 motors, which cost them $1,020 each. Ordering costs are $38 per order, and carrying costs are $200 per motor-

year. Stockout costs are approximately $90 per exposure to stockout. How much safety stock is justified by the carrying costs?

7   A lumber distributor orders plywood sheets in economic lot sizes of 2,000 sheets per order, and it takes 10 days before the mill delivers the plywood. The distributor sells roughy 40 sheets per day (12,000 per year) and maintains a safety stock of 300 sheets.
    (a) What is the lead time?
    (b) What is the appropriate order point?
    (c) If it costs the firm $30 to place an order, what is the implied holding (including storage) cost?

8   For the following data, find
    (a) The stock justified under a decision rule of largest daily usage times longest lead time.
    (b) The safety stock under a rule of square root of average demand during lead time.

$$D_{max} = 60 \text{ units/wk} \qquad D_{ave} = 18 \text{ units/wk}$$

$$D_{min} = 9 \text{ units/wk} \qquad \text{LT range} = 4\text{--}10 \text{ wk}$$

*9   *Expected value approach*   Evergreen Nursery Company has established the demand pattern shown below for a product that costs $40 each, sells for $90 each, and (if not sold immediately) has a salvage value of $10. Use a payoff and an expected value matrix to determine what amount of the product should be stocked to maximize expected profits.

Demand X (in units)	10	20	30
Frequency (no. periods)	30	60	10

10   Suppose demand for Christmas trees was estimated to be as follows:

Tree Number	30	32	34	36	38	40	42	44	46	48	50
P (selling ≥ this tree)	.95	.85	.75	.65	.55	.45	.35	.25	.15	.10	.05

If the trees cost $7 to obtain and market, and they sell for $27 each, what amount of stock would be most advantageous to order?

11   New England Grocery Supply Company has collected the historical data shown on weekly demand for a line of breakfast cereals. An operations analyst estimates that it costs the company $1.50 per case per week to be overstocked because of spoilage and carrying costs. Being understocked results in lost profits of $2.40 per case.

Weekly Demand (No. of cases)	Probability of Demand P(d)
500	.10
600	.20
700	.30
800	.30
900	.05
1,000	.05

(a) Compute the cumulative probability of demand that equates the cost of understocking with the cost of overstocking.

(b) Assuming that the company must purchase in lots of 100, how many lots should it stock?

*12 Demand during lead time varies uniformly between 8,000 units and 12,000 units. Each unit costs $3.00, sells for $4.00, and has a salvage value of $1.20 if not sold. Use the single-period model to find the optimal level of inventory to stock.

*13 A raw material has a normally distributed demand during lead time with $\mu = 200$ (lb/ week, $\sigma = 10$ lb/week, $C_{os} = \$.80/lb$, and $C_{us} = \$3.20/lb$. Find the optimal level to stock, assuming the single-period model applies.

*14 A Poisson-distributed demand with a mean of 8 per week has an acquisition cost of $80, an unused salvage value of $10, and a sale price (benefit value) of $640. How many units of the product should be stocked to balance the expected costs and benefits of overstocking and understocking?

15 *Multiple-period model with individual unit stockout costs*   Muffler Installations, Inc. has an annual demand of about 7,500 mufflers per year. Demand during the 2-week lead time is normally distributed with a mean of 300 and standard deviation of 50. The firm estimates its ordering cost at $20 per order, holding cost at $10 per unit-year, and stockout cost at $15 for each lost muffler sale. The operations manager would like to establish a fixed-quantity inventory system that would carry an optimal amount of safety stock, in other words, where the cost of adding one more unit of stock just equals the expected gain from adding that unit.

(a) How many mufflers should be ordered at one time?

(b) How much safety stock should be carried?

(c) What reorder point should the company use?

16 Demand for a particular type of transformer bushing varies according to the schedule shown. The manufacturer purchases bushings from an outside supplier at $200 per bushing and estimates that it costs 20 percent of the purchase price to carry a bushing in stock for a year. Lead time is 1 week.

Weekly Demand (No. bushings)	Frequency (No. weeks)
0 < 10	5
10 < 20	10
20 < 30	35
30 < 40	20
40 < 50	15
50 < 60	10
60 < 70	5

(a) Compute the cumulative distribution of demand, and plot the curve.

(b) What is the median number of bushings needed per week and the cost per year of carrying this amount (that is, the median amount) on a continuing basis?

(c) Estimate the service level provided by carrying a safety stock of 30 units.

(d) What is the total carrying cost ($/yr, including average inventory and safety stock) required to limit the risk of stockout to 5 percent of the order cycles?

(e) How many units of safety stock are required to provide the firm with a 50 percent service level?

17 A Kansas City feedlot operator supplies beef to several meat packing plants. The steers have an average value of $450, and the operator finances them through a local bank, paying 10 percent interest on the borrowed funds. The data given represent the weekly demand over the past 100 weeks.

Weekly Demand (No. steers)	Frequency (No. weeks)
0 < 100	10
100 < 200	35
200 < 300	40
300 < 400	10
400 < 500	5
	100

(a) Prepare a histogram of the frequency distribution of demand.
(b) Graph the cumulative distribution of demand.
The feedlot operator wishes to keep enough stock in the lot to supply weekly demand 90 percent of the time. Feed costs to "maintain" a steer at a prescribed weight are $5 per week.
(c) What level of safety stock (that is, how many steers) should the operator carry to provide the 90 percent service level?
(d) What is the annual cost of carrying this safety stock?

18 Demand for a piping component during its 2-week lead time is normally distributed, with a mean of 500 units and standard deviation of 20. The firm wishes to limit stockouts to an average of 1 in every 20 reorder cycles. What order point should be used?

19 A manufacturer of water filters purchases components in EOQs of 850 units per order. The total need (demand) averages 12,000 components per year, and MAD = 32 units during the lead time. If the manufacturer carries a safety stock of 80 units, what service level does this give the firm? Assume a normal distribution of D_{LT}.

20 A franchised restaurant drive-in operation in Chicago operates 50 weeks per year and is closed 2 weeks for vacation. The restaurant gets its hamburger directly from a meat packer but must order a week in advance of shipment. The current forecast of demand is 600 pounds per week, and the mean absolute deviation (MAD) is 40 pounds during the lead time. The operations manager wishes to carry enough hamburger to limit the stockouts to two times per year.
(a) If the order quantity is 600 pounds per order, how many extra pounds of hamburger (safety stock to the nearest pound) should be carried?
(b) What is the appropriate order point?
(c) Estimate the standard deviation (σ) of demand.

*21 The same restaurant mentioned in the previous problem (demand = 600 pounds per week, lead time = 1 week, MAD = 40 pounds) is expecting a beef shortage and plans to begin ordering a 4-week supply (2,400 pounds) rather than a 1-week supply. How much safety stock should now be carried to have the same service level (%) as before? (Lead time remains constant.)

*22 The restaurant mentioned in Prob. 20 (demand = 600 pounds per week, lead time = 1 week, MAD = 40 pounds) has received word from the meat packer that orders must now be placed 5 weeks in advance of shipment instead of 1 week. Due to limited freezer space, the restaurant will continue to order only a 1-week supply (600 pounds) at a time, and MAD remains at 40 pounds during the 1-week order cycle. Assume that the lead time is now constant at 5 weeks and that the restaurant wishes to carry enough hamburger to limit stockouts to two times per year.

(a) How much safety stock should be carried?

(b) At what (physical) stock level is it necessary to reorder?

(c) At what (accounting) stock level of on-hand and on-order inventory should the reorder be placed?

23 The Hotel-Restaurant Supply Company orders potatoes in units of 500 bags per order and receives them 10 days later. Its deliveries and usage average 20 bags per day, and it maintains an extra rotating stock of 40 bags to be sure it does not run out of stock. Assume that the demand is normally distributed during the lead time, with $\sigma = 16$ bags.

(a) What is the lead time?

(b) What is the order point?

(c) What service level does the safety stock provide?

(d) Suppose the firm's management felt that running out of stock during two order cycles of the year was acceptable. By how much could the safety stock be reduced? Assume that there are 250 working days per year.

24 Swensen Supply Company distributes 31,200 electric switches per year and orders in economic lot sizes of 6,000 switches per order. A safety stock level of 4,000 has been set by management. The lead time is typically 10 calendar days, and the firm operates 6 days per week, 52 weeks per year.

(a) Under a fixed order size system, what is the appropriate order point?

(b) If the firm switched to a fixed order interval system, would it still order an economic lot size amount each time?

(c) What would be the reorder interval under a periodic system (assuming that the same safety stock of 4,000 were maintained)?

REFERENCES

[1] Hall, Robert W.: *Driving the Productivity Machine: Production Planning and Control in Japan*, American Production and Inventory Control Society, Falls Church, VA, 1981.

[2] Plossl, G. W., and O.W. Wight: *Production and Inventory Control*, Prentice-Hall, Englewood Cliffs, NJ, 1967.

[3] Riggs, James L.: *Production Systems: Planning, Analysis, and Control*, 2d ed., Wiley, New York, 1982.

[4] Schroeder, Roger G., *Operations Management: Decision Making in the Operations Function*, 2d ed., McGraw-Hill, New York, 1985.

SELF QUIZ: CHAPTER 10

Part I True/False [1 point each = 6]

1 _____ Distribution inventories usually experience more uncertain (probabilistic) demand than the bulk of manufacturing inventories.

2 _____ If the marginal cost of an item is $40 and the marginal profit is $20, the firm should theoretically add inventory until the cumulative probability of selling the next unit is .67.

3 _____ The incremental approach to handling inventory uncertainty is based upon stockout costs that apply to each order cycle (in other words, regardless of how many units are out of stock).

4 _____ As the desired level of service (from inventory) increases, the amount of safety stock required typically increases in direct linear proportion.

5 _____ In fixed order quantity systems, the usual practice is to place orders when the safety stock level is reached, rather than before or after.

6 _____ Kanban systems "pull" inventory through the system because the "production" and "move" Kanbans are activated in response to the final assembly schedule.

Part II Problems [3 points each = 9. Calculate and select your answer.]

1 A producer of cake mixes purchases flour in 100-pound bags as follows:

Price	$10/bag	Ordering cost	$20/order
Annual usage	3,125 bags	Carrying cost/yr	20% of price
Safety stock	90 bags	EOQ (1st estimate)	250 units

Assuming that the carrying cost on the safety stock is an acceptable approximation to the stockout cost per exposure, what is the implied EOQ (or, the first approximation with stockout cost included)?
(a) 250 units
(b) 278 units
(c) 328 units
(d) 400 units
(e) None of the above.

2 A firm purchasing computer chips wishes to use the multiple-period model to derive a reorder point. It has a (normally distributed) demand that averages 30 units during its 1-month lead time ($\sigma = 4.3$). Their ordering cost is $20 per order, their carrying cost is $10 per unit, and the stockout cost is known to be $35 per chip. What reorder point is appropriate for the optimum level of stockout risk?
(a) 38 chips
(b) 42 chips
(c) 58 chips
(d) 60 chips
(e) None of the above.

3 Demand during a 1-week lead time is normally distributed with a mean of 600 units and MAD = 50 units. If the firm places orders weekly and desires a service level that allows two stockouts per year, what is the appropriate order point?
(a) 650 units
(b) 688 units
(c) 710 units
(d) 728 units
(e) None of the above.

CHAPTER 11

MATERIAL AND CAPACITY REQUIREMENTS PLANNING

OVERVIEW: MRP AND CRP

Suppose you were in charge of production at one of General Motors' automobile plants for the coming month. Your aggregate plan and master schedule have spelled out what models and how many to produce. And your inventory system can tell you what materials are on hand. So now comes the next step. Build the cars—just build the cars.

All of a sudden the pressure is on! Each car has hundreds of components. A quick check reveals inventories of parts are purposely low. You have neither the storage space nor the financial luxury for stocking inventory that "might" be needed in a few weeks. How will you ever arrange to have the right amount of steel, windshields, and tires available at the right time? Even if the steel is available, how can you be sure your numerous machine shops can grind out the door panels, fenders, and engine blocks when you need them? Cars don't run very well without engine blocks. One little shortage and you're in trouble. Your mile-long production shop could be shut down in 2 minutes—perhaps less.

What Are MRP and CRP?   Companies that produce end products from purchased and/or manufactured components need a systematic method of planning for their material and capacity requirements.

> **Material requirements planning** (**MRP**) is a technique for determining the quantity and timing for the acquisition of dependent demand items needed to satisfy master schedule requirements.
>
> **Capacity requirements planning** (**CRP**) is a technique for determining what personnel and equipment capacities are needed to meet the production objectives embodied in the master schedule and the material requirements plan.

Together, MRP and CRP establish specifically what materials and capacities are needed and when they are needed. Firms such as General Motors take full advantage of such techniques. So do Hewlett-Packard, Corning Glass, Westinghouse, and thousands of smaller manufacturing companies. Otherwise they simply could not survive in today's market.

MRP and MRP II   Whereas MRP focuses upon the priorities of *materials*, CRP is concerned primarily with *time*. Nevertheless, both the material and time requirements must be integrated within one system, and CRP activities are often assumed to be included within the concept of "an MRP system." Beyond this, the term "MRP II" has been coined to "close the loop" by integrating financial, accounting, personnel, engineering, and marketing information—along with the production planning and control activities of basic MRP systems. This broad-based coordination of various information systems within the context of the corporate business plan has been labeled *manufacturing resource planning* (*MRP II*). For many manufacturing firms, MRP II is the "heart" of their corporate Management Information System.

What Do MRP and CRP Accomplish?   At a display terminal manufacturing firm in Minneapolis, an MRP system improved inventory accuracy from 30 percent to 97 percent [1:68], and at a valve manufacturer it reduced production lead times by 40 percent [1:92]. With MRP, an aerospace manufacturer in Tennessee reduced work-in-process inventories by $4 million while improving its delivery performance by 60 percent [1:90]. At an instrument company, inventories were reduced by 20 percent the first year, while lead times for shipments went from 13 weeks to less than 2 weeks [1:60]. According to the president of a firm that supplies Caterpillar Tractor Company,

> MRP has been revolutionary here at Balderson Inc. Not only has it brought about new ways of doing things, it also nearly produced a revolution! It is an incredibly simple idea and yet is a very difficult system to implement. The benefit to us has been significant in many tangible ways; productivity increases, reduced purchases, greater customer service, and more. But the greatest benefit, in my mind, is that MRP has brought us all together in a common effort. Because we involved everyone, it has become everyone's system. Because we educated everyone, employees in every area of the company understand our dependency on each other. And finally, because we communicate continually about our goals, performances, weaknesses, and strengths, we have together improved our product, our productivity, and our profitability. [1:121]

But MRP systems aren't all roses. They can be difficult to implement—and they can be costly (from thousands of dollars to over a million dollars for some firms). Nor are many systems wholly successful; some analysts think 50 percent fall into this category. Nevertheless, the benefits of successful installations are often remarkable, mostly in (1) reducing inventory costs, (2) improving scheduling effectiveness, and (3) responding more quickly to market demands. The end result of a successful system is improved productivity and profitability.

Focus of the Chapter   We begin this chapter by reviewing some necessary terminology and examining a flowchart that displays the role of MRP and CRP in the context of the forecasting, aggregate planning, and inventory topics we have already studied. In addressing the inputs to an MRP system we give special attention to the product structure file. Then we will go into some detail about the MRP processing logic. As we shall see, the calculations are really quite simple. But they are nearly always done on computer because they may have to be repeated for 10,000 or 20,000 items (or more).

The latter part of the chapter takes up the concepts underlying capacity requirements planning. Upon completing the chapter you should be able to develop a material requirements plan given specified end-item requirements. You should also be able to describe capacity planning activities.

MRP: UNDERLYING CONCEPTS

Before the 1960s there was no satisfactory method available for handling the inventory of dependent-demand items. A firm's formal inventory system was often patterned after order points and was either misapplied or broken down into a maze of informal methods when it came to handling dependent items. There was no feasible method of keeping accurate records of thousands of inventory items that went into finished products, so firms relied upon the safety stocks of the order point model to keep them out of too much scheduling trouble. Unfortunately, they did not always achieve that objective, but they did always make a healthy contribution to the inventory carrying and storage costs. In essence, the manual and informal control systems in use before 1960 (and still in use in some firms today) could not adequately cope with a multitude of items and with the complex scheduling activities that took place in an average-size manufacturing concern.

DEFINITIONS AND TERMINOLOGY

During the 1960s, the computer opened the door to an inventory system that could keep up-to-date records on the status of all inventory in stock. This brought a better understanding of production operations and new ways of managing production. It also brought out some new terminology, such as priority and capacity planning. The American Production and Inventory Control Society (APICS) has done much to standardize the terminology in this field.

Figure 11-1 describes a few of the key terms we will need. Many of them are used to express material requirements in a "time-phased" format so that orders for materials and parts are released with sufficient lead time to ensure that the items are received as planned (and needed) for production.

FLOWCHART OF MRP AND CRP

Figure 11-2 describes MRP and CRP activities in schematic form. Forecasts and orders are combined in the production plan, which is formalized in the master production schedule (MPS). The MPS, along with a bill-of-material (BOM) file and inventory status information, is used to formulate the material requirements plan. The MRP determines what components are needed and when they should be ordered from an outside vendor or produced in-house.

The CRP function translates the MRP decisions into the hours of capacity (time) needed to do the anticipated work. If materials, equipment, and personnel are adequate, orders are released, and the workload is assigned to the various work centers.

MRP SYSTEM INPUTS

As indicated in Fig. 11-2, the three major inputs for an MRP system are from (1) the master production schedule, (2) the inventory status file, and (3) the product structure file.

MRP. A technique for determining the quantity and timing of dependent-demand items.

Parent and component items. A *parent* is an assembly made up of basic parts, or *components*. The parent of one subgroup may be a component of a higher-level parent.

Dependent demand. Demand for components that is derived from the demand for other items.

Lot size. The quantity of items required for an order. The order may be either purchased from a vendor or produced in-house. Lot sizing is the process of specifying the order size.

Time phasing. Scheduling to produce or receive an appropriate amount (lot) of material so it will be available in the time periods when needed—not before or after.

Time bucket. The time period used for planning purposes in MRP—usually a week.

Requirements. Projected needs for raw materials, components, subassemblies, or finished goods. Gross requirements are total needs from all sources, whereas net requirements are "net" after allowing for available inventory.

Requirements explosion. The breaking down (exploding) of parent items into component parts that can be individually planned and scheduled.

Bill of materials. A listing of all components (subassemblies and materials) that go into an assembled item. It frequently includes the part numbers and quantity required per assembly.

Scheduled receipt. Materials *already on order* from a vendor or in-house shop. The MRP shows both the quantity and projected time of receipt.

Planned receipt. Materials that *will be ordered* from a vendor or in-house shop. Otherwise it is similar to a scheduled receipt. (*Note:* Some MRP formats do not distinguish between scheduled receipts and planned receipts.)

Lead-time offset. The supply time, or number of time buckets between releasing an order and receiving the materials.

Planned order release. The plan (that is, quantity and date) to initiate the purchase or manufacture of materials so that they will be received on schedule after the lead-time offset.

FIGURE 11-1   MRP Terminology

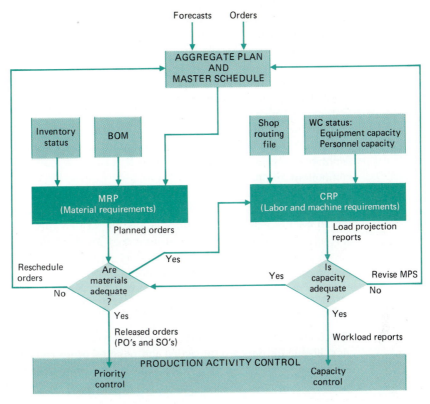

FIGURE 11-2 Material and Capacity Planning Flowchart

Master Production Schedule (MPS) As discussed in Chapter 8, the MPS specifies what end items are to be produced and when. Recall that it is a specific production plan derived from forecast and firm customer orders—and not necessarily a sales forecast. The planning horizon should be long enough to cover the cumulative lead times of all components that must be purchased or produced to satisfy the end-item requirements.

The MRP system accepts whatever the master schedule demands and translates the MPS end items into specific component requirements. Most systems then make a simulated "trial run" to determine whether the proposed master schedule can be satisfied. If either materials or capacity is inadequate, the MPS is revised until an acceptable "authorized" master schedule is developed.

Inventory Status File Every inventory item being planned must have an inventory status file, which gives full and up-to-date information on the on-hand quantities, gross requirements, scheduled receipts, and planned order releases for the item. In addition, the inventory status file includes planning information such as lot sizes, lead times, safety stock levels, and scrap allowances. Subsidiary data covering open orders, change orders, firm planned orders, unfilled purchase requisitions, and accumulators to record usage patterns and measure forecast accuracy may also be included. The inventory status records should be updated frequently (for example, daily) as changes occur.

Product Structure File   To schedule the production of an end product, an MRP system must plan for all the materials, parts, and subassemblies that go into that end product. The bill-of-material file in the computer system provides this information. The BOM file identifies each component by a unique part number and facilitates processing by a process which "explodes" end-item requirements into component requirements.

The bill-of-materials processor is a software package that maintains and updates the BOM listing of all components that go into end products. It also links the BOM file with the inventory status file so that the requirements explosion correctly accounts for the current inventory levels of all components [3].

A good understanding of the product structure file is important, so we shall examine it in more detail in a moment.

MRP SYSTEM OUTPUTS

The major outputs from an MRP system are depicted in Fig. 11-3. Perhaps the most visible outputs are the actual and planned order releases that go to *purchasing and in-house production shops*. They result from exploding end-item require-

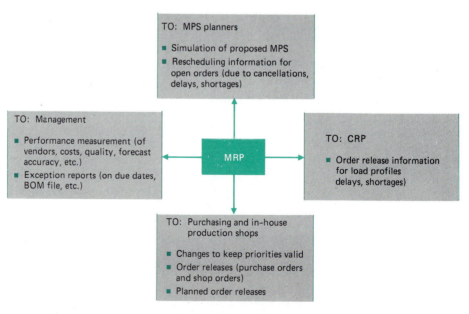

FIGURE 11-3   Outputs from an MRP System

ments into components via the BOM file and then using the inventory status file to determine net requirements and release dates. By making due dates and need dates coincide, the MRP system helps keep priorities valid.

The second category of output is that used for *capacity requirements planning*. This includes a sufficiently long planning horizon of open and planned orders so that loading profiles can be established for key work centers.

The MRP system supplies the *master production schedule planners* with the simulated results of a proposed master schedule and identifies what changes in order due dates would be needed to accommodate the proposed change. This simulation capability can be used in other ways too. For example, if marketing must make a delivery concession to secure a large order, the impact of that order upon other open orders can be assessed before the order is accepted. The MRP system also gives MPS planners information about predicted shortages, delays, and scrapped orders so the open orders can be rescheduled. Once the authorization from the MPS is received, MRP can accept the new schedule.

Finally, the MRP system can provide *management* with valuable measures of performance, for example, of cost, quality, and vendor activity. Thus, it can collect data on material receipts by vendor and develop measures of lead time variability, forecast error, and preferred suppliers. Other reports, such as those concerning invalid due dates, inaccurate BOMs, and inventory discrepancies, also help ferret out difficulties needing attention.

TIME-PHASING CONCEPTS

We have seen previously that end items in warehouses, such as TV sets, have an *independent* demand that is closely linked to the ongoing needs of consumers. It is random but relatively constant. But the components used in manufacturing the TV set, such as 24-inch picture tubes, have a *dependent* demand that is linked more closely to the production process itself. This is because many firms use the same facilities (and workers) to produce different products. It is economical for them to produce large lots once the setup costs are incurred. They may first produce 24-inch sets and then, after building up enough inventory, set up to produce portables or possibly video disk players.[1]

Lumpy Demand   Demand that is governed by the lot size of the particular run is predictable but tends to be "lumpy." Figure 11-4 illustrates the difference between on-hand inventory levels (*a*) under independent demand and (*b*) under dependent demand.

If the inventory of parts for manufacturing a product was maintained on a traditional order point basis, the inventory level in Fig. 11-4*b* would not be allowed to drop to zero (as it does) because parts would automatically be reordered whenever the reorder point was reached. With time phasing, however, the

---

[1] Recall that the JIT production system attempts to overcome this inventory buildup by striving to reduce the setup time so that very small lot sizes (even of one unit) can be economically produced.

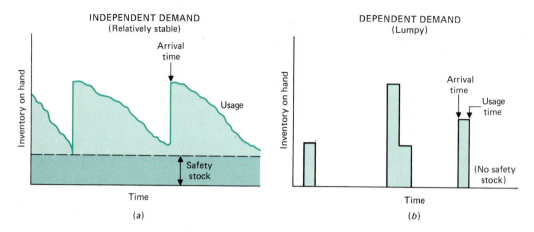

FIGURE 11-4   Inventory Levels under Independent and Dependent Demand
(*a*) Demand for end item (TV sets)
(*b*) Demand for component (picture tubes)

inventory is scheduled to arrive (or be available) only a short time before it is needed. So time phasing reduces the length of time that funds are invested in inventory. The savings on the carrying cost of inventory under an MRP system, over the comparable cost in a traditional order point system, is of course one of the major (financial) benefits of MRP systems. An example will illustrate.

EXAMPLE 11-1   Suppose the use of traditional order point techniques for a component resulted in carrying an average inventory of 60 units of that component. By time phasing the receipt of inventory, the average level could be dropped to 15 units. Assuming an item value of $20 and a carrying charge of 30 percent per year:

(a) How much annual carrying cost C_{AC} could be saved by time phasing this item?

(b) What would be the impact of extending this same savings to 2,000 components?

SOLUTION

(a) *Inventory Cost (Order Point)*   *Inventory Cost (Time Phased)*

$$C_{AC} = I_{ave}(\text{item value})(\%)$$ $$C_{AC} = I_{ave}(\text{item value})(\%)$$

$$= 60 \text{ units}(\$20/\text{unit})(.30/\text{yr})$$ $$= 15 \text{ units}(\$20/\text{unit})(.30/\text{yr})$$

$$= \$360/\text{yr}$$ $$= \$90/\text{yr}$$

$$\therefore \text{ Savings} = \$360/\text{yr} - \$90/\text{yr} = \$270/\text{yr}$$

(b) Savings = 2,000 items ($270/item-yr) = $540,000/yr

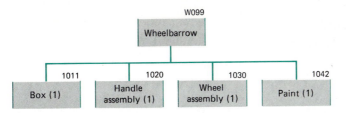

FIGURE 11-5   Product Structure Diagram for a Single-Level Bill of Material

BILL OF MATERIALS (BOM)

The product structure, or BOM, file defines products in very precise and unambiguous terms so that the component requirements are clearly delineated. Two methods of specifying component requirements are (1) using single-level bills of material with reference pointers and (2) using indented bill-of-material files [8].

Single-Level Bills of Material   A single-level BOM specifies requirements for only the immediate or next-level components that are needed to assemble a parent item. For example, suppose a firm produced wheelbarrows that were assembled from a box, a handlebar assembly, a wheel assembly, and some paint. The product structure for a single-level BOM would contain only a single level of components below the finished product, as depicted in Fig. 11-5. The numbers in parentheses inside the boxes tell how many of the component items are needed for one end item, and the numbers above each box are the reference part numbers, or pointers.

Figure 11-6 is a single-level BOM as it might be stored in a computer. It completely specifies the subassemblies (or components) that are needed to produce the parent item (wheelbarrow), and the quantity required. By including the part number pointers, the computer can track down all the component needs of all the subassemblies as well. For example, by referencing part number 1030, the computer can determine all the components that go into the wheel assembly.

Different end products often use the same components. For example, the

BILL OF MATERIAL

Part No. W099: Wheelbarrow

Part No.	Description	Quantity/Assembly	Units
1011	Box: deep size, aluminum	1	each
1020	Handle assembly	1	each
1030	Wheel assembly	1	each
1042	Paint: blue	1	pint

FIGURE 11-6   Single-Level Bill of Material for a Wheelbarrow

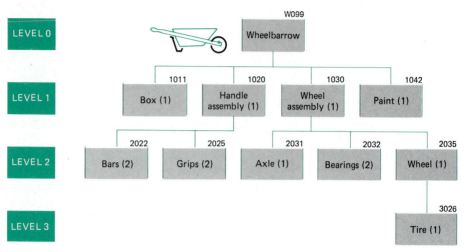

FIGURE 11-7 Product Structure Tree Showing BOM Levels for a Wheelbarrow

wheel assembly is an identifiable subassembly of the wheelbarrow, and it may also be used on other products, for example, on garden tractors. By maintaining a unique part number for each subassembly such as this, and for each component, all the end-product requirements can be translated into specific component requirements. Then orders for the components are sized and timed to satisfy the total requirements for each component, regardless of where it ends up being used.

Indented Bills of Material   For material planning purposes, BOMs are often structured to show the manufacturing sequence of the parent item. This enables planners (and the computer) to more readily identify components which must be available to make subassemblies prior to the assembly of the end product. Figure 11-7 illustrates the hierarchy of component levels for the wheelbarrow. In this figure, the components which make up the handlebars and wheel subassemblies are included.

Note that the final assembly (parent item) is positioned at level 0 and that all the components that go into the final assembly are assigned to level 1. Components that are used for the level 1 subassemblies are assigned to level 2. If the same component happened to exist on more than one level of the product structure tree (for example, on both level 2 and level 3), it would be assigned the lowest level (that is, level 3). (The coding is recorded on the item record in the computer.) This process is referred to as *low-level coding* because the level number farthest from the top is used. Remember, the code for the highest level is zero.

The MRP explosion process starts at the top level; the net requirements for the parent-level item are determined before moving on to its components. Then, at each of the lower levels, the components required for each item are quickly determined. Even when different end products use the same components, the

BILL OF MATERIAL

Part No. W099: Wheelbarrow   Level 0

Part No.			Description	Quantity/Assembly	Units	Level
1011			Box: deep size, aluminum	1	each	1
1020			Handle assembly	1	each	1
	2022		Aluminum bars	2	each	2
	2025		Grips: neoprene	2	each	2
1030			Wheel assembly	1	each	1
	2031		Axle	1	each	2
	2032		Bearing: normal–duty	2	each	2
	2035		Wheel	1	each	2
		3026	Tire: size A	1	each	3
1042			Paint: blue	1	pint	1

FIGURE 11-8   Indented Bill of Material for a Wheelbarrow

computer can readily scan the requirements and quickly determine the total needs for any given item because *processing on all items is delayed until all requirements from higher levels have been determined.*[2]

A product structure form of a BOM differs from a product summary form (parts list) in the way it is structured. A convenient way to capture the hierarchical structure while still enabling the computer to handle the massive data processing chore is by means of an "indented" listing. An indented BOM shows how many levels a component or assembly is from the end item because each level is offset (or specified), as shown in Fig. 11-8.

A good BOM format can be useful to engineering, accounting, maintenance, and other departments as well as to production planning and control. It should easily reveal the hierarchical structure so that end items and common parts can be identified. It should also be easy to change and update. And no part number should identify more than one unique item (or assembly). Thus, if material goes from raw to finished stock, or if components are added or deleted, different part numbers should be used.

Closing the Loop   The information on a BOM concerning a specific part number is, of course, only part of the total information retained about that part in the computer's database. Cost, manufacturing time, inventory levels on hand, lot size, safety stock, and other information are tracked as well. If the firm progresses toward MRP II, broader-based financial, personnel, and marketing information will then become integrated into the network. When an item is produced, the labor and material costs are assessed, cash flow changes are recognized, marketing is notified that the item is in stock, and so on. This is referred to as "closing the loop." In the future, we will see computer-integrated manufacturing (CIM) systems.

[2] Computer programs do this by requiring all identical items to have the same level in the part number coding. This permits the computer to sum requirements across a single level of the BOM.

BOMs are frequently the responsibility of a manufacturing or production engineering group, and accuracy is essential. Audits are performed regularly to ensure BOM accuracy. Some firms even base the merit wage increase of their bill-of-material technicians on the extent to which they maintain accuracies of 99 percent and higher on the BOMs for which they are responsible.

Final Assembly Bills of Material Not every end item is assigned a BOM or part number—especially those that come with numerous options such as automobiles. For many such products, there might be millions of different combinations possible. The IBM Selectric typewriter formerly used 2,700 parts and came in 55,000 combinations (and 36 color choices) [6]. The amount of record keeping for something like this would be overwhelming (even for a computer). A simple example will illustrate.

EXAMPLE 11-2

A manufacturer of wheelbarrows has developed the list of part numbers shown in Fig. 11-9.

(a) If every option was considered a master schedule item, how many items

ITEM DESCRIPTION	PART NUMBER FOR ITEM ON			
	Level 0	Level 1	Level 2	Level 3
Wheelbarrow	0099			
Box: Deep, steel		1010		
Deep, aluminum		1011		
Shallow, steel		1012		
Shallow, aluminum		1013		
Shallow, poly.		1014		
Handle assembly		1020		
Bar: Steel			2121	
Aluminum			2022	
Oak			2023	
Grips			2025	
Wheel assembly		1030		
Axle			2031	
Bearing: Normal			2032	
Heavy			2033	
Wheel			2035	
Tire: Size A				3026
Size B				3027
Size C				3028
Paint: Red		1040		
Green		1041		
Blue		1042		
Black		1043		
Orange		1044		

FIGURE 11-9 Part Numbers for Wheelbarrow Components

would the master schedule have to accommodate for this product (wheelbarrows) alone?

(b) What would be the effect of offering the choice of a white stripe on the front?

SOLUTION

(a) There are 5 options for boxes, 3 for handlebars, 6 for wheel assemblies (that is, 3 sizes of tires and a choice of normal or heavy-duty bearings on each), and 5 for paint, so there are $5 \times 3 \times 6 \times 5 = 450$ combinations. The grips, axle, and wheel are "common" parts used on all wheelbarrows.

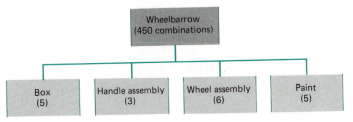

(b) Offering the choice of a stripe would mean that each end item could come either with or without the stripe, so the effect would be to double the potential number of end items to 900.

$$\underset{\text{without stripe}}{450 \text{ wheelbarrows}} + \underset{\text{with stripe}}{450 \text{ wheelbarrows}} = 900$$

If the planner (in the example above) scheduled items at the finished wheelbarrow level (that is, level 0), the firm's computer would have to contain all 900 bills of material. Instead, master schedulers often plan requirements in basic units or major subassemblies. Then the final configuration of each end item (such as each wheelbarrow) is left to a *final assembly bill of materials*, or "assembly bill." An illustration in the next chapter (Fig. 12-16) will show how a car manufacturer uses a "car build sheet" as an assembly bill to specify options just before the car is put into production. (The choices selected on that form represent 2.5×10^{14} options.)

If the planner scheduled the wheelbarrow at level 1 rather than level 0, then only 19 master schedule BOMs would have to be scheduled (that is, 5 types of boxes, 3 handlebar assemblies, 6 wheel assemblies, and 5 colors of paint). This also eases the load on the computer. Instead of maintaining a separate BOM number for each of the many options available, the final configuration of each end item is left to the assembly bill, or build sheet.

Relationship of BOM to the Master Schedule   For scheduling purposes, planners usually use major subassemblies or common groupings of one type or another as the master schedule items. This is especially true if the firm offers many end

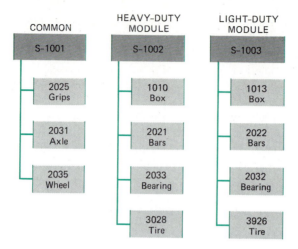

FIGURE 11-10   Some Planning Bills for a Wheelbarrow

items. The *point of greatest commonality* usually eliminates color, brand differences, packaging, and other marketing-influenced options that can be assigned to the final assembly order in the last week or day before manufacturing.[3]

Planning Bills and the Master Production Schedule   Reducing the number of master-scheduled items from 450 to 19 is an improvement. But for firms that have many end products, each with several options, the problem of master scheduling is still complex. One method of further reducing the number of master-scheduled items is via the use of *planning bills*. These are "phantom" or "pseudo" bills of materials that combine parts and assemblies into artificial units created just to facilitate planning. They are created specifically by production control for master scheduling purposes, and they are stored in the master production file, not in the engineering BOM file.

Figure 11-10 illustrates some planning bills for the wheelbarrow example discussed above. Note that the planning bills have been used to segregate common parts from unique (or optional) parts and to group components by use. For this product, planners have found it useful to group components into common, heavy-duty, and light-duty modules. Minor assembly items, such as the bolts and nuts for a wheelbarrow, can be handled as a "kit" or bag of materials, which can be treated as an assembly item for purposes of the master schedule.

Planning bills can be very useful—even though they do not always constitute a buildable combination of items. *First*, they can be used to determine the material requirements in the same way as any other BOM can be used. *Second*, they can help isolate uncertainty about what items will be needed. And *third*, they

[3] At this point you may wish to review the sketch for master scheduling discrete products with options (Fig. 8-19) that we discussed in the chapter on master scheduling. The point of greatest commonality is the narrowest point in the figure.

offer the planner a way of scheduling quantities for option items. Let us explore reasons two and three a bit further.

By separating common and optional modules, planners can reduce the uncertainty of demand to only those components for which the demand is really uncertain. For example, if all wheelbarrows use a No. 2031 axle, the axle demand is known once the end-item quantities are set. But if the proportion of heavy-duty models is not firmed up until dealer orders arrive, then the planners may not know whether to schedule production of box 1010 or box 1013.

Requirements for the options are usually handled on a "percentage of end item" basis. That is, if the scheduler knows, historically, that 30 percent of the products call for a certain option (for example, heavy-duty option), he or she will master schedule to produce that proportion of components by specifying the heavy-duty planning module for 30 percent of the output. But orders may not be firmed up until just before production is to start. Because of the risk of error, firms typically carry some safety stock of option items. As with other independent demand items, the safety stock can be established on the basis of a service level related to the standard deviation (or MAD) applicable to the past demand for the given option.

In-Process Bills An *in-process* or transition bill of materials is also used by some firms. It identifies subassemblies that are built on feeder lines but are not normally stocked. In-process bills usually relate to parts that are in process and can quickly be finished to customer order. The in-process bill permits planners to move parts into and out of stock and use on-hand assemblies without creating or modifying the permanent BOM file.

SYSTEM PARAMETERS

Before we trace the actual logic of MRP, let us briefly consider a few remaining parameters of MRP systems—in particular, (1) the planning horizon and replanning function, (2) lead times and safety stocks, and (3) lot-sizing considerations.

PLANNING HORIZON AND REPLANNING

The master schedule incorporates both forecasts and firm orders in the tentative plan that goes to the MRP system. The planning horizon may be 10 weeks, 26 weeks, or even 52 weeks—it depends upon the type of firm and the products involved. However, it should equal or exceed the cumulative lead times for the longest time sequence required by any parent-component relationship. Otherwise it will be inadequate, as depicted in Fig. 11-11. The result may then be late orders and costly or disruptive expediting activities.

Once the MRP is "run" (on the computer), orders are released, and goods are produced. As time passes, the status of orders changes, and the MRP system must be updated. With *regenerative MRP systems*, replanning is commonly done on a

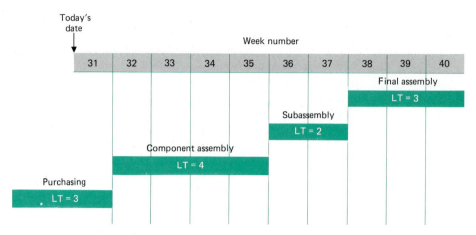

FIGURE 11-11 Inadequate Planning Horizon

weekly basis. It can be costly to replan too frequently and self-defeating to have too long of an updating interval. If the replanning period is greater than a week (or perhaps 2 weeks), schedulers are sometimes inclined to circumvent the MRP system with informal solutions to problems. This is a sure way to cause the whole system to collapse.

LEAD TIMES AND SAFETY STOCKS

The MRP system uses planned lead times for scheduling order releases, but the actual lead times do not always correspond to the plan. When actual times differ, sometimes materials can be expedited or received earlier without affecting the job priority. If not, the actual lead-time data should be fed into the MRP system so that the replanning of all affected jobs can be accomplished.

Safety stocks have been associated primarily with independent demand, but we also noted that they were used to help manage the uncertainty associated with "option" items. In effect, they can be used anywhere within the MRP system where the expected cost of uncertainty justifies their use. In tightly controlled production schedules, safety stocks may be justified to circumvent the potentially detrimental effects of delayed lead times, scrap losses, and change orders.

LOT-SIZING CONSIDERATIONS

Released orders must specify a discrete size of lot to purchase or produce. Figure 11-12 summarizes some of the lot-sizing methods available to planners [7:120].

The fixed order quantity and EOQ methods are readily adaptable to MRP systems and widely used. But for discontinuous and nonuniform demand, they can be ineffective. The lot-for-lot technique is probably the simplest of the variable ordering techniques. It minimizes inventory carrying costs and is especially

- *Fixed order quantity.*   Order a specified amount, for example, 40 units.
- *Economic order quantity (EOQ).*   Order an EOQ or ERL amount.
- *Lot for lot (LFL).*   Order the exact amount of the net requirements each period.
- *Fixed period requirements.*   Order a supply for a given number of periods each time (for example, a 2-month supply).
- *Period order quantity (POQ).*   Divide the EOQ into the annual demand, and order that many times per year.
- Least cost approaches:
  Least unit cost (LUC).   Order the net requirements for the current period, or current plus next, or current plus next two, and so on, depending upon which gives the lowest unit cost (that is, of setup and carrying costs).
  Least total cost (LTC).   Order the quantity that minimizes the total set-up and carrying costs over the planning horizon.
  Part-period algorithm (PPA).   Use the ratio of ordering and carrying costs to derive a part-period number and use the number as a criterion for cumulating requirements.

FIGURE 11-12   Lot-Sizing Methods Available to Planners

effective for highly discontinuous demand. The part-period algorithm is one of the more widely used "complex" methods—although it is not difficult for a computer to calculate. A solved problem illustrates this method. In general, however, MRP tends to capitalize more upon the benefits of the timing of orders than it does upon the accuracy of order quantities.

MRP LOGIC

The master production schedule dictates *gross or projected requirements* for end items to the MRP system. (Gross requirements do not take account of any inventory on hand or on order.) The MRP computer program then "explodes" the end-item demands into requirements for subassemblies, components, and materials by processing all relevant bills of materials on a level-by-level basis. *Net requirements* are then calculated by adjusting for existing inventory and items already on order, as recorded in the inventory status file.

$$\begin{matrix} \text{Net} \\ \text{requirements} \end{matrix} = \begin{matrix} \text{projected gross} \\ \text{requirements} \end{matrix} - \left(\begin{matrix} \text{inventory} \\ \text{on hand} \end{matrix} + \begin{matrix} \text{scheduled} \\ \text{receipts} \end{matrix} \right)$$

$$NR = PR - (OH + SR) \tag{11-1}$$

Order releases are planned for components in a time-phased manner (using lead-time data from the inventory file) so that materials will arrive precisely when needed. At this stage the material is referred to as a *planned order receipt*. When the orders are actually issued to vendors or to in-house shops, the planned receipt technically becomes a *scheduled receipt*. Some MRP formats maintain separate lines for planned and scheduled receipts, whereas others combine them under the single heading of receipts, as we will do in this text.

EXAMPLE 11-3

A firm producing wheelbarrows is expected to deliver 40 wheelbarrows in week 1, 60 in week 4, 60 in week 6, and 50 in week 8. Among the requirements for each wheelbarrow are two handlebars, a wheel assembly, and one tire for the wheel assembly. Order quantities, lead times, and inventories on hand at the beginning of period 1 are shown below.

Part	Order Quantity	Lead Times (wk)	Inventory on Hand
Handlebars	300	2	100
Wheel assemblies*	200	3	220
Tires	400	1	50

*90 wheel assemblies are also needed in period 5 for a garden tractor shipment

A shipment of 300 handlebars is already scheduled to be received at the beginning of week 2. Complete the material-requirements plan for the handlebars, wheel assemblies, and tires and show *what quantities* of orders must be released and *when* they must be released in order to satisfy the MPS.

SOLUTION

Figure 11-13 depicts the master schedule and component part schedules. We shall assume that the customer completes the final assembly, so no time allowance is required there. Note that because each wheelbarrow requires two handlebars, the projected material requirements for handlebars are double the number of end products. The projected requirements of 80 handlebars in period 1 are adequately satisfied by the 100 units on hand at the beginning of period 1, leaving 20 on hand at the end of period 1. On-hand materials can be calculated with the following equation:

$$\begin{array}{ccc} \text{On hand at} \\ \text{end of period} \end{array} = \begin{array}{c} \text{on hand at} \\ \text{end of previous period} \end{array} + \text{receipts} - \begin{array}{c} \text{projected} \\ \text{requirements} \end{array}$$

$$OH_t = OH_{t-1} + R_t - PR \qquad (11\text{-}2)$$

With the receipt of 300 handlebars in period 2, the on-hand inventory will be adequate until week 8, which at first glance will be 20 units short. To overcome this, a planned order release for the standard order quantity (300) has been scheduled for week 6, because handlebars have a 2-week lead time. The planned receipt of 300 in week 8 will thus result in an end-of-period inventory of 280 units.

Moving on to the wheel assemblies, note that each end item requires one wheel assembly, so the projected requirements coincide with end-

FIGURE 11-13   MRP Master Schedule and Component Plans

End-Item Master Schedule: Wheelbarrows

Week No.	1	2	3	4	5	6	7	8
Requirements	40			60		60		50

Component Materials Plan: Handlebars

Order quantity = 300 Lead time = 2 weeks		Week							
		1	2	3	4	5	6	7	8
Projected requirements		80			120		120		100
Receipts			300						300
On hand at end of period	100	20	320	320	200	200	80	80	280 −20
Planned order release							(300)		

Negative amount
(∴ place order
in week 6)

Component Materials Plan: Wheel Assemblies

Order quantity = 200 Lead time = 3 weeks		Week							
		1	2	3	4	5	6	7	8
Projected requirements		40			60	90*	60		50
Receipts							200		
On hand at end of period	220	180	180	180	120	30	170 −30	170	120
Planned order release				(200)					

*Requirements from another product (garden tractor) that uses the same wheel assembly.

Subcomponent Materials Plan: Tire for Wheel Assembly

Order quantity = 400 Lead time = 1 week		Week							
		1	2	3	4	5	6	7	8
Projected requirements				200					
Receipts				400					
On hand at end of period	50	50	50	250 −150	250	250	250	250	250
Planned order release			(400)						

product demand. In addition, the 90 wheel assemblies needed for the garden tractor in week 5 are automatically incorporated into the projected requirements. The on-hand stock is adequate until week 6, when quantities will drop to -30 unless a planned order is released in week 3.

The bottom chart of Fig. 11-13 illustrates the MRP for tires, which are a subcomponent of the wheel assemblies. Note that the planned order release of 200 units from the above wheel assemblies plan shows up as a projected requirement for 200 tires in the same week (week 3) on the subcomponent plan. Since on-hand inventory is inadequate to supply this need, a planned order release is scheduled for week 2. It should ensure that an order of 400 tires will be available by the beginning of week 3.

SYSTEM REFINEMENTS

Key features of MRP systems are (1) generation of lower-level requirements, (2) time-phasing those requirements, (3) planned order releases, and (4) the rescheduling capability provided. However, many firms take advantage of additional capabilities such as (5) utilizing firm planned orders, (6) pegging capability, and (7) various priority planning activities.

FIRM PLANNED ORDERS

Regular MRP logic automatically (and continually) controls the quantity and timing of planned order releases for components. But conditions change. Machines break down, customers want larger quantities than originally ordered, or marketing "absolutely must" quote an earlier than normal delivery to secure a vital order. In addition, some firms have seasonal peaks which may extend beyond their computer's MRP planning horizon. Aggregate planners know they should be building up inventories well in advance of the need, but the computer may not see that far into the future.

These "special circumstances" are normal routine for many production planners. They know that they cannot allow the automated processes of their computer to overrule their good judgment. Yet they do not want to circumvent the system with informal methods—that is one of the fastest ways to bring it crashing down.

Fortunately, systems designers have developed a way of instructing the computer to accept and hold firm to certain requirements, even though normal MRP logic would automatically delay or reschedule such orders. Planners can gain this added control over planned orders by designating them as "firm planned orders." Then the computer will not automatically change the release date, the planned order receipt date, or the order quantity. In addition, the system will not allow another planned order into the designated "time fence" or "frozen" period around the planned order release date [6:24].

EXAMPLE 11-4

Several weeks ago an appliance manufacturer accepted an order from a distributor for 40 appliances (A) to be shipped in week 27 and 40 more to be shipped in week 31. Each end item has a motor component (M). One week is needed for final assembly, so the motors are needed in weeks 26 and 30, as shown in the MRP plan for M below:

Component M

Order quantity = 40 Lead time = 3 weeks		Week									
		24	25	26	27	28	29	30	31	32	33
Projected requirements				40				40			
Receipts								40			
On hand at end of period	40	40	40	0	0	0	0	0	0	0	0
Planned order release				40							

Marketing now urgently requests that the order quantity for the first shipment be increased from 40 to 60, even though it is "a little late." How would the situation be handled as a firm planned order?

SOLUTION

We shall assume that the planner first tried to identify alternative solutions—for example, Can substitute parts be used? Are components available elsewhere? (One alternative is to refuse the order.) We will also assume that other components needed for the appliances are in stock and that the best solution is to deliver the 60 motors in week 26.

Note that the 40 motors originally needed in week 26 are already on hand. But the lead time to produce 20 more motors is 3 weeks, and only 2 weeks are available. A requirement of 60 in week 26 would normally generate a reschedule message from the computer because the on-hand stock would drop to −20 motors.

Suppose the planner checks with the shop and verifies that it is feasible to compress the planned lead time for M into 2 weeks. She could then enter the order as a firm planned order in week 24 as shown below. She also designates a time fence over weeks 24 to 26 so that the computer will not allow any other planned orders for motors to be generated during those weeks. Once the firm planned order is entered, any subsequent MRP replanning cycle will not automatically change either the quantity or the scheduled dates of the order.

Component M

Order quantity = 40 Lead time = 3 weeks		Week									
		24	25	26	27	28	29	30	31	32	33
Projected requirements				60				40			
Receipts				20F				40			
On hand at end of period	40	40	40	0	0	0	0	0			
Planned order release		20F			40						

Time fence

PEGGING OF REQUIREMENTS

Pegging refers to the ability to identify the parent item or items that generated the component requirements. For example, suppose a firm purchases large lots of small switches that are used in the production of several different products. The firm has just received word that a needed shipment of switches was lost in transit. The pegged requirements file would permit it to identify each end item that is relying upon that shipment. Then changes can be made to rectify the problem.

Pegging capability begins with the creation of a special "where-used" file. It lists *only* those parents that have planned or open orders in their records—not all parent-component relationships. Inventory planners can then trace requirements *upward* in the product structure to determine what parents currently on order are dependent upon a given component. This capability is valuable in numerous ways—from rescheduling current operations to identifying which end items might be affected by defective components, such as defective brakes in certain models of automobiles.

PRIORITY PLANNING AND CONTROL

Priority planning involves assigning a measure of importance (that is, a rank or completion date) to quantities of items that are to be produced. MRP systems have valid priorities when the quantity and "due date" on the orders agree exactly with what is really needed.

Maintaining valid open-order due dates is vital. So it is essential to keep updating the MRP system with the latest open-order status information from vendors and from the firm's own shops. Most systems will then automatically reevaluate all open-order due dates. If the system detects a difference, it signals the planner. The planner may wish to investigate the possibility of expediting (or deexpediting) some materials, purchasing on the outside, subcontracting, or other strategies, but his or her responsibility is to reschedule the system in a valid, credible way. Otherwise, the supervisor and workers whom the planner is planning for will disregard the plan and eventually circumvent the system.

Priority planning is the most straightforward for one-piece make-to-order products. When goods are made for stock, the priorities become slightly more complex because they depend upon the variable demand from the customer. Assembled products that are made to order present a more complex problem because their components have horizontally dependent priorities. That is, components are needed only when co-components of the common parent are available. If there is a delay in getting a co-component, the real priority of the component may have dropped, even though the formal priority (that is, the priority assigned initially by the system) remains the same.

Assembled products made to stock present the most complex problem because their real priority depends upon the available stock of the parent item (as influenced by demand) as well as on the availability of co-components needed to assemble the parent item. But whatever the cause (or level) of priority change, the important point is to feed that input into the MRP system in a timely manner.

Priority control ensures that the priority plans are carried out. That is the task of production activity control, which we shall take up in the next chapter. The link between the two is, however, direct and vital. Priority planning supplies the priorities on materials and jobs so that priority control can actually make up schedules and dispatch lists that sequence the work flow on the basis of those priorities. Together, these two functions have a tremendously far-reaching effect upon productivity.

MRP IMPLEMENTATION

Implementing an MRP system usually requires a strong educational effort throughout the organization and the full commitment of top management. Figure 11-14 outlines some essential steps—which often take up to a year or more to accomplish. Many of them have already been mentioned.

Performance Measurement   In addition to education and commitment, one of the most essential ingredients of a successful MRP system is a comprehensive method of measuring the performance of all elements of the system. This includes inventory accuracy, production plan and master schedule accuracy, bills-of-material accuracy, and so forth. Goals should be set (such as ≥ 95 percent on-time delivery performance) and performance measured against these goals on a regular monthly basis.

Computers and Consultants   Most of the major computer manufacturers offer MRP software packages—many of which incorporate everything from sales forecasting to production activity controls. In addition, now that the memory and

---

1 Initial education
2 Justification, commitment, and assignment of responsibility
3 Detailed educational plan (for management, P&IC, engineering, data processing, shop, etc.)
4 Upgrading inventory records to ≥ 95 percent accuracy
5 Bill-of-material restructuring and accuracy
6 Item analysis of OQ, LT, SS, coding, and use patterns
7 Master schedule preparation policy and procedures
8 Systems design and software selection
9 Preinstallation procedures for rescheduling, order release, and shop floor relations
10 Pilot program trial run on several hundred part numbers
11 Cut over to all product lines and other divisions
12 Capacity requirements planning
13 Production activity control

FIGURE 11-14   MRP Implementation Steps [4]

processing capabilities of microcomputers is so large, MRP packages are also available on personal computer systems.

Finding the right computer system for a given firm may require a fairly extensive review of possibly 20 or 30 types of systems on the market. Then the system must be adapted to the specific environment of the firm. Many firms have found it advantageous to make use of industry consultants who have had experience implementing MRP systems in other firms.

Regenerative and Net Change Systems When MRP systems were first introduced, they were designed for batch processing of data on a periodic basis. These *regenerative* systems do a full explosion of all items (usually over the weekend) to create an entirely new material requirements plan each period.

Today, more firms are installing net change MRP systems. *Net change* MRP is an online system that continuously reacts to changes in the master schedule, inventory additions, and other transactions. It uses the same type of MRP logic, but net change systems replan only those items that are changed or were not previously planned. This (partial) explosion of only the affected BOMs is more sophisticated to maintain, but it keeps the database more current and can save computer time. A complete regeneration of the whole system may, however, still be desirable on a regular basis (perhaps every few months) to locate errors and purge unused files.

A net change system was implemented in a Portland, Oregon, firm which utilizes 30,000 part numbers and 70,000 BOMs. The firm now maintains a 97 percent inventory record accuracy. All parts are planned nightly, and shop orders are dispatched daily. The system reduced inventories by over 85 percent compared with what they could have been, given the sales increase experienced by the firm. Lead time from the plant has been cut 63 percent, and shop orders held because of raw material shortages dropped from 1,100 to 10.

MRP systems can do an outstanding job of ensuring that materials will be available at appropriate times. But material supplies are of little value unless capacity is available to work on them. We will now focus upon capacity concepts—more specifically, upon capacity requirements planning (CRP).

CAPACITY MANAGEMENT

Capacity is a measure of the productive capability of a facility per unit of time. Capacity decisions begin with the initial facility layout and extend to aggregate planning, master scheduling, capacity requirements planning, and capacity control activities. In this section we review some terminology and focus upon the capacity requirements planning (CRP) process by looking specifically at the inputs, planning activity, and outputs of CRP.

CAPACITY CONCEPTS IN REVIEW

Some measures of capacity were introduced in Chapter 3 (that is, design capacity, system capacity, and output capacity). It was noted that capacity is typically measured in common denominator units, such as tons, pieces, or work time available. For capacity planning purposes, time units (for example, hours, days, weeks) are often most useful. And unless otherwise stated, we will assume that capacity refers to the actual capacity as measured from the average of past labor reports or work center records. If they are not available, the "rated capacity" is estimated.

$$\text{Rated capacity} = \binom{\text{number of}}{\text{machines}} \binom{\text{machine}}{\text{hours}} \binom{\text{percentage of}}{\text{utilization}} \binom{\text{system}}{\text{efficiency}} \quad (11\text{-}3)$$

EXAMPLE 11-5

A work center operates 6 days per week on a two-shift per day basis (8 hours per shift) and has four machines with the same capability. If the machines are utilized 75 percent of the time at a system efficiency of 90 percent, what is the rated output in standard hours per week?

SOLUTION

$$\text{Rated capacity} = \binom{\text{number of}}{\text{machines}} \binom{\text{machine}}{\text{hours}} \binom{\text{percentage of}}{\text{utilization}} \binom{\text{system}}{\text{efficiency}}$$

$$= (4)(8 \times 6 \times 2)(.75)(.90) = 259 \text{ standard hr/week}$$

Note that capacity is expressed as a rate (for example, standard hours per week). In concept, it is a limiting factor much like the drainpipe on a bathtub. The drain limits the output of water regardless of whether the tub is half full or full. In this case the flow rate would be expressed in gallons per minute, and the water in the tub would be the "load."

Capacity Variables   Some factors affecting capacity are more controllable than others [1]. Controllable factors include the amount of labor, facilities, machines, tooling, shifts worked per day, days worked per week, overtime, subcontracting, alternative routings of work, preventive maintenance, and number of setups. Less controllable factors include absenteeism, labor performance, machine breakdowns, material shortages, scrap and rework, and unexpected problems.

Capacity in Goods and Services   Capacity problems may be evidenced in the long lead time for many goods and in the queues at service facilities such as doctors' offices, banks, and some retail stores. Underutilized facilities are also part of the capacity problem. It is important to recognize capacity problems for what they are; otherwise, we may tend to work on the symptom rather than the problem. If the load is too large for a facility to handle, a capacity problem exists. Assigning priorities (or giving special attention) to selected jobs does not solve the capacity problem. Both priority and capacity planning systems are vital and need to be coordinated. But they address different problems.

CAPACITY TIME HORIZONS

Figure 11-15 depicts some capacity management responsibilities classified according to the time horizon of the decision.

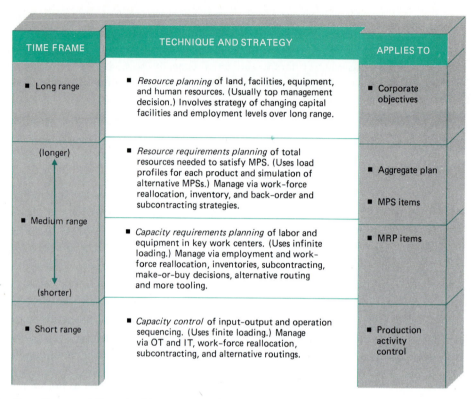

FIGURE 11-15 Time Frame of Capacity Management Decisions

- *Long range.* In the long range, management must plan for the human, material, and financial resources that will give their organization the capacity appropriate for their corporate goals. This requires a broad-based knowledge of the economic, technological, and competitive variables that exist in their operating environment.
- *Medium range.* In the medium range, planners are concerned with having the capacity to do the work embodied in the aggregate plan and the MPS. This means converting material and job requirements into standard hours of labor and machine time and developing loads for the firm's work centers that are in balance with the work center capacities.
- *Short range.* In the short range, the capacities are used to do the jobs assigned by the capacity requirements plan. This means controlling the flow (input-output) of work, comparing results with standards, and taking corrective action when necessary. (Capacity control techniques will be covered in depth in the next chapter.)

CRP ACTIVITIES

CRP activities are perhaps best described by following the chronological flow of orders and information—from inputs through the planning activity to outputs. We will begin with an overview.

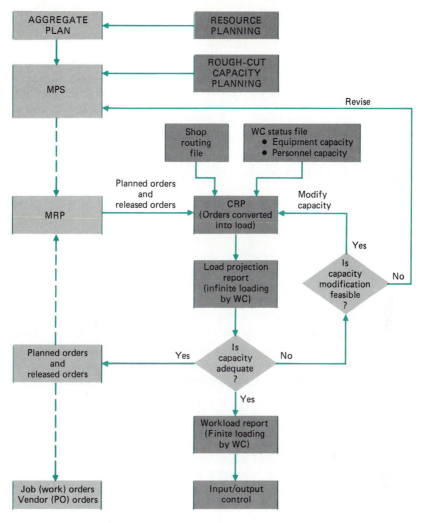

FIGURE 11-16   Flowchart of the CRP Process

OVERVIEW OF THE CRP PROCESS

Figure 11-16 describes the CRP process in schematic form. End-item requirements arising from the aggregate plan and MPS are exploded into tentative planned orders for components by the MRP system. The CRP system then converts these orders into standard labor and machine hours of load on the appropriate workers and on the machines as identified from the work center status and shop routing files. The output is a load projection report by work center. If work center capacities are adequate, the planned order releases are verified for the MRP system, and released orders become purchase and shop orders. Workload reports are also made for use in input/output control. If some initial load projection reports reveal inadequate capacity, either the capacity must be modified (for example, by using overtime or shifting personnel) or the master schedule revised.

CRP INPUTS

As depicted in Fig. 11-16, the major inputs for the CRP process are [2]:

1 Planned orders and released orders from the MRP system
2 Loading information from the work center status file
3 Routing information from the shop routing file
4 Changes which modify capacity, give alternative routings, or alter planned orders

All these must be timely if the system is to function effectively.

PLANNING ACTIVITY: INFINITE AND FINITE LOADING

The released and planned orders from the MRP system are converted into standard hours of load by the CRP system. Figure 11-17 illustrates the process. It shows the transition from the planned order release for 300 handlebars in period 6 (from Fig. 11-13) to 6.2 standard hours in work center (WC) 4. These hours and the hours for other jobs planned for WC 4 during period 6 plus the hours for orders already released constitute the total expected load of 185 standard hours. Note that some time (20 hours) has been allowed for unplanned or emergency jobs.

MRP systems assume that capacity is available when needed unless otherwise indicated. Thus, if the planned order release for handlebars in period 6 was for 3,000 units instead of 300 units, the additional load would still show up in period 6. If the total load is greater than available capacity, then either the capacity must be changed or the MPS revised. Thus CRP is an iterative process that first simulates loads on the work centers and relies upon planners to suggest changes if the plan cannot be met.

When planning capacity, it is not necessary to plan every work center in detail. Work centers that have known excess capacity will not be bottlenecks and so will not necessitate changes to the master schedule. (However, it may be desirable to plan these work centers for purposes of control.)

The process of loading work centers with all the loads when they are required without regard to the actual capacity of the work centers is called *infinite loading*. Infinite loading gives planners a good grasp of the actual released order demand upon the system so that they can make decisions about using overtime, using alternative routings, delaying selected orders, etc. CRP really goes beyond infinite loading, however, for it includes planned orders as well as released orders and involves an iterative plan-replan process. The replanning is continued until a realistic load is developed.

Figure 11-18 illustrates the lumpy nature of an infinite loading profile for a work center that has a substantial amount of "past due" work included with the

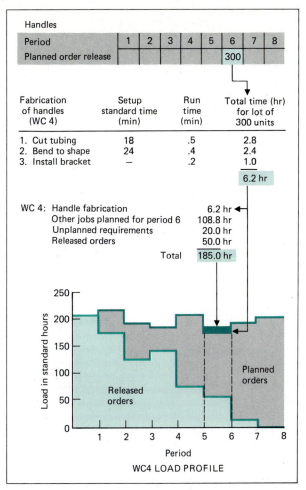

FIGURE 11-17 Transition of Planned Order Release from MRP to Load in CRP System

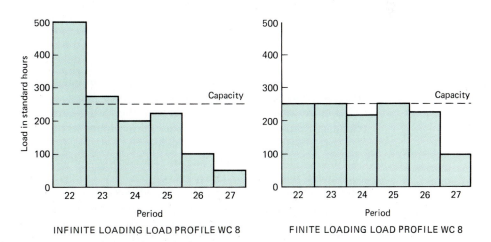

FIGURE 11-18 Infinite and Finite Loading Profiles

463

current period. Although many firms continue to function with this kind of load, it is obviously unrealistic. Systems that plan like this lack credibility and will not be relied upon or adhered to. This loading plan needs to be revised so that requirements are brought more into line with capacity.

The profile on the right in Fig. 11-18 illustrates the principle of *finite loading*. Finite loading can be done automatically by computerized loading systems; they simply limit the amount of load assigned to a work center in each period (250 standard hours in Fig. 11-18). However, finite loading does not usually work well at the CRP stage because it forces "mechanical" changes back onto the master schedule that are not always the best solutions to the scheduling problem. Finite loading tends to be more useful for single work centers in the capacity control stage where jobs are being scheduled.

Most firms have found that infinite loading, coupled with the inclusion of planned orders, works well when the CRP process is done in an iterative way. Then the MPS is not "authorized" until both priorities and capacities are in balance.

CRP OUTPUTS

Aside from the rescheduling messages which call for capacity modification or revision of the MPS, the major outputs of the CRP system are the verification of planned orders for the MRP system and the load reports. Good load reports have three characteristics [9]:

1 They are complete—that is, they have both planned and released orders.
2 They are based upon valid priorities (which are up to date).
3 They facilitate planning for the future.

The firm can plan for the average amount of labor and equipment that is expected, without actually designating the capacity for specific orders.

SUMMARY

Material requirements planning (MRP) is a technique for determining the quantity and timing of dependent-demand items. Capacity requirements planning (CRP) takes material requirements from the MRP system and converts them into standard hours of load on the labor and machines in the various work centers.

MRP permits planners to schedule the individual requirements of thousands of items in a time-phased format. For dependent items that have a "lumpy" demand, scheduling the receipt of components "as needed" minimizes the costs of holding inventory. The savings over traditional order point systems can be significant. Independent-demand items can also be time-phased.

A well-designed bill of material is essential for realistic master scheduling—which in turn is vital to MRP and CRP systems. Indented bills showing the hierarchical levels of components are most useful. For option items, firms use planning bills (or modules) and separate assembly schedules. Modules simplify master scheduling by reducing the number of master schedule end items.

The master schedule drives the MRP system. Other inputs come from the bill of materials (BOM) and the inventory status file. During the MRP computer run, all requirements are exploded into their component parts, beginning at the highest level (level 0) and extending to the lowest-level items.

MRP outputs are (1) released orders which go to purchasing and in-house production shops, (2) planned orders which are used for CRP, (3) rescheduling information used by master schedulers, and (4) reports and performance measurement information. Most MRP systems also have other features which enable them to use firm planned order and pegging capabilities.

Capacity management concerns extend from long-range resource-planning activities (involving corporate objectives) to medium-range decisions (involving the aggregate plan, master schedule, and CRP) to short-range decisions (capacity control). For CRP, the requirements dictated by the MRP are usually translated into loads on key work centers via an infinite loading technique. If capacities are inadequate, they must be modified, or the MPS must be revised. After acceptable loads have been established, the workloads can be assigned to work centers on a finite loading basis.

MRP is the "heart" of today's computerized inventory and scheduling activities. Thousands of firms have adopted MRP systems, and many more are in the implementation stage. MRP can be expected to give our nation's productivity a substantial boost in the future as more firms bring their systems on-line.

SOLVED PROBLEMS

BILL OF MATERIALS (BOM)

1 A BOM is desired for a bracket (Z100) that is made up of a base (A10), two springs (B11), and four clamps (C20). The base is assembled from one clamp (C20) and two housings (D21). Each clamp has one handle (E30), and each housing has two bearings (F31) and one shaft (G32).

(a) Design a product structure tree that includes the level coding information.

(b) Show the data in the form of an indented BOM.

Solution

For this BOM, level 0 will be the highest (end-item code) and level 3 the lowest (see Fig. 11-19). Note that the four clamps are a component of the end-item bracket but are also a component of the base. To facilitate calculation of net requirements, the product tree has been restructured: the clamp components have been moved from where they might have been (shown dashed) to the lower level consistent with the other (identical) clamp.

2 Determine the quantities of A10, B11, C20, D21, E30, F31, and G32 needed to complete 50 of the Z100 brackets of Solved Prob. 1. (For simplicity, use A, B, . . . , E as part numbers.)

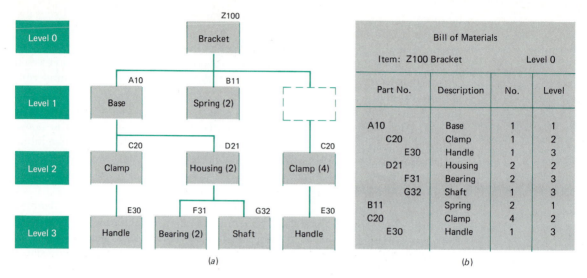

FIGURE 11-19 (a) Product structure tree. (b) Indented bill of materials.

Solution

First determine the requirements for one bracket as shown below and then multiply by 50. Note that parts C and E are used in two different subassemblies, so their separate amounts must be summed. For 50 brackets, each of the requirements column amounts must be multiplied by 50 to obtain the gross requirements.

Component	Dependency Effect	Requirements
A (Base)	1A per Z	1
B (Spring)	2B's per Z	2
C (Clamp)	(1C per A) · (1A per Z) + (4C's per Z)	5
D (Housing)	(2D's per A) · (1A per Z)	2
E (Handle)	(1E per C) · (1C per A) · (1A per Z) + (1E per C) · (4C's per Z)	5
F (Bearing)	(2F's per D) · (2D's per A) · (1A per Z)	4
G (Shaft)	(1G per D) · (2D's per A) · (1A per Z)	2

3 A flashlight is assembled from three major subassemblies: a head assembly, two batteries, and a body assembly. The head assembly consists of a plastic head, a lens, a bulb subassembly (comprising a bulb and bulb holder), and a reflector. The body assembly consists of a coil spring and a shell assembly, which in turn is made up of an on-off switch, two connector bars, and a plastic shell. The on-off switch is assembled from a knob and two small metal slides. The plastic head is made from one unit of orange plastic powder, and the plastic shell is made from three units of orange plastic powder. Develop a product structure tree of the flashlight, and include the level coding for each component.

Solution

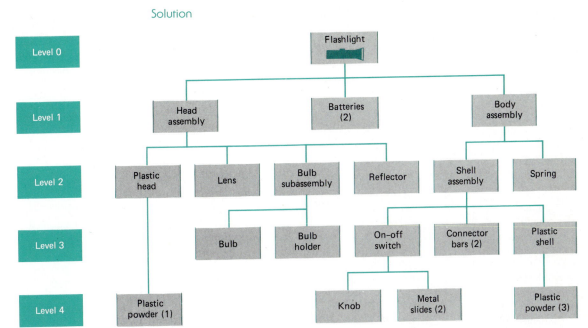

Level 0 — Flashlight

Level 1 — Head assembly | Batteries (2) | Body assembly

Level 2 — Plastic head | Lens | Bulb subassembly | Reflector | Shell assembly | Spring

Level 3 — Bulb | Bulb holder | On-off switch | Connector bars (2) | Plastic shell

Level 4 — Plastic powder (1) | Knob | Metal slides (2) | Plastic powder (3)

4 Design an indented bill of materials for the flashlight in Solved Prob. 3. (*Note:* Assign appropriate four-digit part numbers to the components.)

Solution

Bill of Materials			
Item: 0010 Flashlight			Level: 0
Part No.	Description	No.	Level
1001	Head assembly	1	1
2001	Plastic head	1	2
4001	Plastic powder	1	4
2002	Lens	1	2
2003	Bulb assembly	1	2
3001	Bulb	1	3
3002	Bulb holder	1	3
2004	Reflector	1	2
1002	Batteries	2	1
1003	Body assembly	1	1
2005	Shell assembly	1	2
3003	On-off switch	1	3
4002	Knob	1	4
4003	Metal slides	2	4
3004	Connector bars	2	3
3005	Plastic shell	1	3
4001	Plastic powder	3	4
2006	Spring	1	2

GROSS AND NET REQUIREMENTS

5   The company that produces flashlights (Solved Prob. 3) has an order for 200 end items (flashlights). They have on hand 10 head assemblies (no. 1001), 12 lenses (no. 2002), 50 springs (no. 2006), and 15 on-off switches (no. 3003). Compute the gross requirements and the net requirements to satisfy the order.

Solution

See Fig. 11-20.

FIGURE 11-20

Part No.	Description	Gross Requirements	On Hand	Net Requirements
0010	Flashlight	200	0	200
1001	Head assembly	$1 \times 200 = 200$	10	190
1002	Batteries	$2 \times 200 = 400$	0	400
1003	Body assembly	$1 \times 200 = 200$	0	200
2001	Plastic head	$1 \times 1 \times 200 = 200$	10	190
2002	Lens	$1 \times 1 \times 200 = 200$	22	178
2003	Bulb assembly	$1 \times 1 \times 200 = 200$	10	190
2004	Reflector	$1 \times 1 \times 200 = 200$	10	190
2005	Shell assembly	$1 \times 1 \times 200 = 200$	0	200
2006	Spring	$1 \times 1 \times 200 = 200$	50	150
3001	Bulb	$1 \times 1 \times 1 \times 200 = 200$	10	190
3002	Bulb holder	$1 \times 1 \times 1 \times 200 = 200$	10	190
3003	On-off switch	$1 \times 1 \times 1 \times 200 = 200$	15	185
3004	Connector bars	$2 \times 1 \times 1 \times 200 = 400$	0	400
3005	Plastic shell	$1 \times 1 \times 1 \times 200 = 200$	0	200
4001	Plastic powder	$(1 \times 1 \times 1 \times 200) + (3 \times 1 \times 1 \times 1 \times 200) - 10 = 790$	0	790
4002	Knob	$1 \times 1 \times 1 \times 1 \times 200 = 200$	15	185
4003	Metal slides	$2 \times 1 \times 1 \times 1 \times 200 = 400$	30	370

Gross requirements are the total quantities needed to produce the 200 flashlights, whereas *net* requirements are the quantities needed in addition to existing inventory levels (or scheduled receipts). The net requirements must therefore take into account the components already assembled (or hidden) in completed assemblies.

We shall first determine the gross requirements by taking account of all dependencies. For example, the gross requirements of connector bars (no. 3004) are (2 connector bars per shell assembly) times (1 shell assembly per body assembly) times (1 body assembly per flashlight) times (200 flashlights), or $2 \times 1 \times 1 \times 200 = 400$. See Fig. 11-21.

Then we compute the on-hand inventory by totaling both the individual stock items on hand plus any units of the same item that are already in subassemblies or assemblies. For example, the on-hand inventory of lenses consists of 12 lenses in stock plus 10 lenses already installed in the head assemblies. Requirements will be computed on a level-by-level basis so that components used in more than one subassembly (such as the plastic powder, no. 4001) can be combined.

LOT SIZING: PART-PERIOD ALGORITHM (PPA)

*6 The ordering cost to order an item is $225 and carrying cost is $.75 per period. Net requirements per month are as shown below. Use the part-period algorithm to determine the size and timing of orders.

Month	1	2	3	4	5	6	7	8	9
Requirement	250	150	300	150	100	400	250	200	300

Solution

First, express the *ordering cost* in terms of an equivalent number of part-periods of carrying cost by dividing the order cost, C_o, by the carrying cost, C_c.

$$\text{PPA order cost} = \text{PPA } C_o = \frac{C_o}{C_c} = \frac{\$225}{\$.75} = 300 \text{ part-periods}$$

Next, express the *carrying cost* in terms of part periods by assigning one part-period cost for each time period a unit is held in stock (that is, weight each unit by the number of periods it is carried).

$$\text{PPA carrying cost} = \text{PPA } C_c = 0/\text{unit if units used during period they arrive}$$
$$= 1/\text{unit for units carried forward 1 period}$$
$$= 2/\text{unit for units carried forward 2 periods, etc.}$$

Next, cumulate requirements until the part-period carrying cost PPA C_c is as close as possible to the part-period ordering cost PPA C_o. Do not divide a period's requirements. Begin with an order to be received in period 1 for the period-1 requirements. Multiply the number of units required times PPA C_o of zero, and add other periods (appropriately weighted).

Cumulate requirements until Σ PPA C_c is closest to 300.

	Month 1	Month 2	Month 3
No. required × PPA C_c	250 × 0 = 0	150 × 1 = 150	300 × 2 = 600
Cumulative total	0	150	750

The value nearest 300 is 150 (see Month 2). The first order will include requirements for months 1 and 2 only (400 units).

Next, continue by reassigning the next (unfilled) order a PPA C_c of zero, and repeat the previous step until the allocation is complete. For convenience we can arrange the results of this procedure in table form, where each additional row identifies another order. See table on next page.

Order No.	Month: No. required	1 250	2 150	3 300	4 150	5 100	6 400	7 250	8 200	9 300
1	No. × PPA C_c Cum. Total	250 × 0 0	150 × 1 150	300 × 2 750						
2	No. × PPA C_c Cum. Total			300 × 0 0	150 × 1 150	100 × 2 350				
3	No. × PPA C_c Cum. Total						400 × 0 0	250 × 1 250	200 × 2 650	
4	No. × PPA C_c Cum. Total								200 × 0 0	300 × 1 300
Order size		400		550			650		500	

Conclusion: Order 400 units in period 1, 550 in period 3, 650 in period 6, and 500 in period 8.

MRP LOGIC

7   Complete the material requirements plan for item X shown below. Note that this item has an independent demand that necessitates that a safety stock of 40 units be maintained.

Order quantity = 70 Lead time = 4 weeks Safety stock = 40		Week											
		1	2	3	4	5	6	7	8	9	10	11	12
Projected requirements		20	20	25	20	20	25	20	20	30	25	25	25
Receipts			70			70			70			70	
On hand at end of period	65	45	95	70	50	100	75	55	105	75	50	95	70
Planned order release		70			70			70					

Solution

Order quantity = 70 Lead time = 4 weeks Safety stock = 40		Week											
		1	2	3	4	5	6	7	8	9	10	11	12
Projected requirements		20	20	25	20	20	25	20	20	30	25	25	25
Receipts			70			70			70			70	
On hand at end of period	65	45	95	70	50	100 / 30	75	55	105 / 35	75	50	95 / 25	70
Planned order release		70			70			70					

8 Clemson Industries produces products X and Y, which have demand, safety stock, and product structure levels as shown. The on-hand inventories are as follows: X = 100, Y = 30, A = 70, B = 0, C = 200, and D = 800. The lot size for A is 250, and the lot size for D is 1,000 (or multiples of these amounts); all the other items are specified on a lot-for-lot (LFL) basis (that is, the quantities are the same as the net requirements). The only scheduled receipts are 250 units of X due in period 2. Determine the order quantities and order release dates for all requirements using an MRP format.

Product	SS	Demand in period							
		1	2	3	4	5	6	7	8
X	50			300			200		250
Y	30							400	

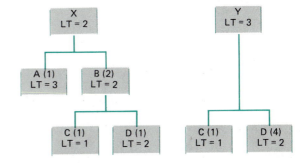

Solution

(a) First, establish the codes (lowest level) applicable to each product. Items C and D appear both at level 1 in product Y and at level 2 in product X, so they are assigned to level 2. Thus their requirements are not netted out until all level 0 and 1 requirements have been netted out.

Item	Low-Level Code
X	0
Y	0
A	1
B	1
C	2
D	2

(b) Next, set up an MRP format for all items (see Fig. 11-21), and enter the end-item gross requirements for X and Y. They both have low-level codes of 0 and so can be netted out using order quantities that match their requirements (preserving safety stocks, of course). This results in planned order releases of 200 and 250 units for X (periods 4 and 6) and 400 units for Y (period 4).

(c) Next, explode the planned order releases for X and Y (that is, multiply them by the quantities required of the level 1 items, A and B). (Note that C and D are not level 1 items.) Projected requirements for A (200 and 250 units) are direct results of the planned order releases for X. Two units of B are required for each X, so item B's projected requirements in periods 4 and 6 are 400 and 500, respectively. Items A and B are then netted, and the order release dates and amounts are set.

(d) Next, explode the level 2 planned order releases to the level 3 items. The arrows in

FIGURE 11-21 MRP Plan for X and Y

		Period							
		1	2	3	4	5	6	7	8

X: OQ = LFL; LT = 2; SS = 50

	1	2	3	4	5	6	7	8
Projected requirements			300			200		250
Receipts		250				200	250	
On hand at end of period	100	100	350	50	50	50	50 / -150	50	50 / -200
Planned order release				200		250		

Y: OQ = LFL; LT = 3; SS = 30

	1	2	3	4	5	6	7	8
Projected requirements							400	
Receipts							400	
On hand at end of period	30	30	30	30	30	30	30	30	30
Planned order release				(400)				

A: OQ = 250; LT = 3

	1	2	3	4	5	6	7	8
Projected requirements				200		250		
Receipts				250		250		
On hand at end of period	70	70	70	70	120 / -130	120	120	120	120
Planned order release		250		250				

B: OQ = LFL; LT = 2

	1	2	3	4	5	6	7	8
Projected requirements				400		500		
Receipts				400		500		
On hand at end of period	0	0	0	0	0 / -400	0	0 / -500	0	0
Planned order release			(400)		(500)			

C: OQ = LFL; LT = 1

	1	2	3	4	5	6	7	8
Projected requirements			400		900			
Receipts			200		900			
On hand at end of period	200	200	0 / -200	0	0 / -900	0	0	0	0
Planned order release		200		900				

D: OQ = 1,000; LT = 2

	1	2	3	4	5	6	7	8
Projected requirements			400		2,100			
Receipts					2,000			
On hand at end of period	800	800	400	400	300 / -1,700	300	300	300	300
Planned order release			2,000					

Figure 11-21 show that requirements for C and D come from planned order releases for both B and Y. End item Y requires 4 units of D, so the projected requirements in period 4 are 2,100 units, with 1,600 from Y (that is, 4 × 400) and 500 from B. Together, they generate a planned order release for 2,000 units of D in period 2.

CAPACITY MANAGEMENT

9 A work center operates 6 days per week on a two-shift-per-day basis (8 hours per shift) and has four machines with the same capability. If the machines are utilized 75 percent of the time at a system efficiency of 90 percent, what is the rated output in standard hours per week?

Solution

$$\text{Rated capacity} = \left(\begin{array}{c}\text{number of}\\\text{machines}\end{array}\right)\left(\begin{array}{c}\text{machine}\\\text{hours}\end{array}\right)\left(\begin{array}{c}\text{percentage of}\\\text{utilization}\end{array}\right)\left(\begin{array}{c}\text{system}\\\text{efficiency}\end{array}\right)$$

$$= (4)(8 \times 6 \times 2)(.75)(.90) = 259 \text{ standard hr/week}$$

10 The Metric Instrument Company uses an MRP system and plans to adjust capacity when the cumulative deviation exceeds one-half of the forecasted average per week. They have calculated capacity requirements per week for their testing laboratory over the next 8 weeks as shown below. Graph the capacity requirements, showing the average requirement as a dotted line.

Week No.	1	2	3	4	5	6	7	8
Hours Required	400	380	210	530	420	410	500	350

Solution

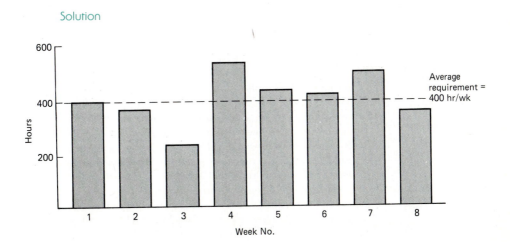

QUESTIONS

11-1   Define (a) MRP, (b) CRP, and (c) BOM.

11-2   Why did firms experience so much difficulty in scheduling dependent-demand items prior to the 1960s?

11-3   Rank the following terms in the appropriate sequence:
  (a) Released orders   (e) Master schedule
  (b) Aggregate plan   (f) Are materials adequate?
  (c) Is capacity adequate?   (g) MRP
  (d) CRP   (h) Vendor purchase order

11-4   Distinguish between a planned receipt and a scheduled receipt.

11-5   Explain what is meant by "time phasing."

11-6   What are the major outputs from an MRP system?

11-7   Explain how time-phasing concepts (in contrast to traditional order point techniques) can generate inventory cost savings when applied to items with dependent ("lumpy") demand.

11-8   In what way do MRP benefits extend to inventories, priorities, and capacities?

11-9   Differentiate between the following: (a) single-level BOM, (b) indented BOM, (c) planning BOM, (d) assembly BOM.

11-10   Master schedules do not always include the end items which will ultimately be produced for customer orders. Explain why this is so and what is done to ensure that the customers' orders are taken into account.

11-11   How long should the MRP planning horizon be, and what can be done if a cyclical demand needs attention but falls outside the horizon?

11-12   What is meant by (a) lot-for-lot ordering, and (b) pegging?

11-13   What are the inputs for the CRP process?

11-14   Distinguish between infinite loading and finite loading. Where is each best used?

PROBLEMS

1   A firm investigating the possibility of installing an MRP system maintains an average inventory of 50 units of a dependent-demand item that costs them $60 to purchase. They estimate that by time phasing the receipt of that item, the average inventory would drop in half. If they use a carrying charge of 32 percent per year, how much annual savings would result from time phasing this item?

2   By using a time-phased plan for component inventories, a firm producing robotic parts can reduce average inventory levels from 65 units to 35 units. If the average value of an item is $7 and the reduction applies to 2,000 components, how much savings would result? Assume inventory carrying costs of 25 percent per year.

3   Given the product structure tree shown, compute the net requirements of A, B, C, D, E, and F to produce 10 units of end item X. No stock is on hand.

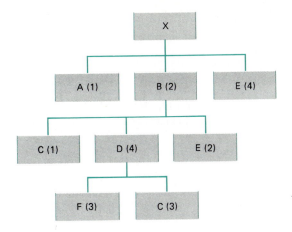

4 Given the product structure for end product X, what product level codes would be assigned to the end product and components for BOM planning purposes?

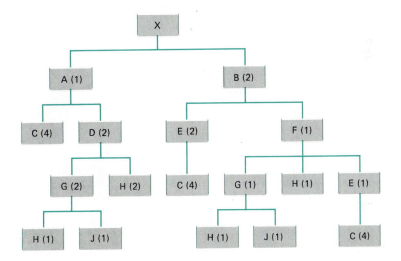

5 Given the product structure tree shown in Prob. 4, compute the net requirements to produce 100 units of subassembly A. No stock is on hand or on order.

6 Given the product structure tree shown in Prob. 4, compute the net requirements to produce 100 units of subassembly B. No stock is on hand or on order.

7 End item X is assembled from three major assemblies: A, B, and C. Subassembly A consists of two units of D, two units of E, and one F. To make B, component G and three units of H are needed. Subassembly C requires two units of J and one F. Component D requires two units of J and one unit of K.

(a) Construct a product structure tree for X.

(b) What quantities of A, B, C, D, E, F, G, H, J, and K are required to produce 100 units of X?

8 An end item Y is assembled from one unit of A and two units of B. Each A is composed of 2 units of H. The B is composed of 3 C's and 1 E. Each C is made up of 4 H's and 3 D's.

   (a) Construct a product structure tree that shows the components arranged properly for low-level coding. (Show the coding levels.)

   (b) What quantities of H are required to produce 100 units of Y?

   (c) Suppose 50 B's are already on hand. Then how many H's would be required?

9 Determine the net requirements for the two items below.

	20-hp Motors	Size II Controllers
Projected (gross) requirements	30	45
On-hand inventory	12	22
Inventory on order (scheduled receipts)	10	0

10 Given the following product structure tree, compute the net requirements for A, B, C, and D to produce 20 units of product X.

Component	Inventory On Hand and On Order
A	10
B	5
C	10
D	10

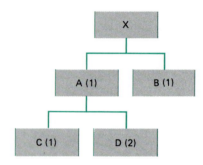

11 Determine the net requirements for the three items shown.

	Switches	Microprocessors	Keyboards
Projected (gross) requirements	55	14	28
On-hand inventory	18	2	7
Inventory on order (scheduled receipts)	12	12	10

12 Given the product structure tree shown in Prob. 4, what net amounts of C are required to produce 140 units of X if the only on-hand inventory is 120 units of subassembly B and 40 units of subassembly F?

13 A skateboard consists of one baseplate and two wheel assemblies. Each wheel assembly is comprised of 1 mounting bracket, 1 axle, and 2 wheels. Each wheel has 1 bearing and 1 steel shell.

   (a) Draw the product structure tree showing the BOM levels.

   (b) Assume the firm has an order for 300 skateboards and has 200 completed skateboards on hand, plus 40 wheel assemblies and 50 bearings. How many *more* bearings (net requirements) are needed?

14 The Little Red Wagon Company produces wagons (W) consisting of the following parts:

A001 Box (1) C003 Wheel assembly (4) E005 parts kit (1)
B002 Handle (1) D005 axle (2)

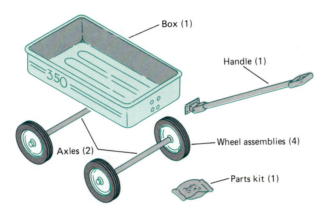

Each wheel assembly is composed of: F006 Wheel (1)
G007 Bearing (2)

The wheel, in turn, is composed of: H008 Disk (1)
I009 Tire (1)
J010 Bearing housing (1)

Each parts kit contains: K011 Washer (4)
L012 Snap ring (4)

Each wagon is painted with: P013 Red paint ($\frac{1}{2}$ pint)

(a) Construct a product structure tree showing the BOM levels for the wagon.
(b) Construct an indented BOM for the wagon.
(c) Suppose the company offers 3 different sizes of boxes, 2 different sizes of wheels, and a choice of 10 different color schemes. How many end-product combinations could result?

* 15 *Part-period algorithm* The cost of placing an item on order is $90, and the per-unit carrying charge is $.45 per month. Net requirements per month are as shown below. Use the part-period algorithm to determine the size and timing of orders.

Month	1	2	3	4	5	6	7	8
Requirement	180	150	250	450	125	50	200	210

16 Complete the material requirements plan shown below and find the amount of inventory on hand at the end of week 8.

Order quantity = 500 Lead time = 4 weeks		Week							
		1	2	3	4	5	6	7	8
Projected requirements		150	150	150	150	200	200	180	320
Receipts				500					
On hand at end of period	300	150	0	350	200				
Planned order release									

17 Complete the MRP format shown below. How many units are on hand at the end of period 8?

Order quantity = 200 Lead time = 3 weeks		Week							
		1	2	3	4	5	6	7	8
Projected requirements		40	85	10	60	130	110	50	170
Receipts									
On hand at end of period	140								
Planned order release									

18 The forecast below is for an option item, so the firm maintains a safety stock of 25 units. Complete the MRP and determine the inventory on hand at the end of period 10.

Order quantity = 60 Lead time = 2 weeks Safety stock = 25		Week									
		1	2	3	4	5	6	7	8	9	10
Projected requirements		20	20	20	30	20	20	20	55	20	45
Receipts			60								
On hand at end of period	50										
Planned order release											

19 A master scheduler would like to determine whether an order for 200 units of product A can be supplied in period 8. No stock of any components is on hand or on order, and all order sizes are lot-for-lot. Determine the amount and date of the planned order releases for all components.

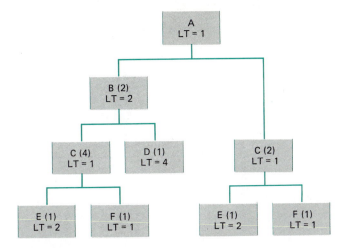

20 A master schedule calls for 50 units of F in period 6 and 60 in period 8. On-hand levels are G = 20, H = 60, E = 0, J = 30, and C = 100. Another 200 units of C are scheduled for receipt in period 2. Order quantities are all lot-for-lot except for C, which has an ERL of 200 (or multiples of that).

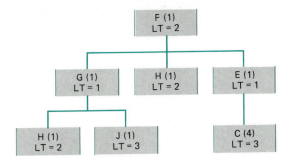

(a) Use an MRP format to determine the order size for all components and when each order should be released.

(b) Suppose the scheduler wanted to move both orders for F ahead by 1 week. Could it be done? If not, what components are limiting items?

21 Industrial Supply Company produces a maintenance and repair parts cart (MRP cart) for use in warehouses. The cart design and product structure are as shown below. The firm has 2 axles (number 2005) and 1 wheel assembly (number 2006) in stock.

(a) Construct an indented BOM.

(b) The firm has an order for 3 carts in period 10. Use an MRP format to determine the order size for all components and when each order should be released.

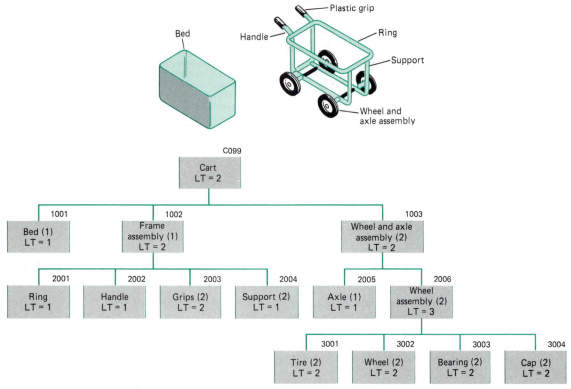

22 The inventory manager of Office Fixtures is attempting to plan material requirements for the production of one of the firm's desk lamps over the next 8 weeks. Each lamp consists of a metal base, a tube steel frame, and two light assemblies. The light assemblies are, in turn, each made up of a switch and tube holder. Details on the end-item requirements and component parts are given below. Develop a material requirements plan (MRP) for the various inventory components showing (1) the time-phased requirements, (2) the scheduled receipts, (3) the on-hand inventory, and (4) the planned order release information.

End-Item Requirements

Week	1	3	6	8
Number	120	80	100	120

The component part data are shown in the following table:

	Base	Frame	Light Assembly (Complete)	Light Assembly Components	
				Switch	Tube Holder
Order quantity*	200	350	150	500	600
Lead time (weeks)	5	3	4	2	2
On hand	250	200	420	340	550

* Order quantities may be doubled if requirements exceed these amounts.

23 An office furniture manufacturer has a work center with 3 metal presses which are each operated 7½ hours per shift on a 3-shift-per-day, 6-day-per-week basis. The presses are allocated to furniture production 80 percent of the time, with the remainder reserved for special-order jobs. If the machine efficiency is 95 percent, what is the rated output for furniture production in standard hours per week?

24 Culver Electronics has a capacity of 300 hours per week in work center 2. At the end of week 53 the workload is as shown. Prepare (a) an infinite loading load profile and (b) a finite loading load profile for weeks 54 through 58. Use the first letter of the job number to show when the various jobs are scheduled under each loading profile.

Workload for Work Center 2

Job Number	Hours Required	Week Due
A10	180	52
B11	120	53
C12	140	54
D12	155	54
E13	290	55
F13	60	55
G14	100	56
H15	140	57
I16	50	58

REFERENCES

[1] American Production and Inventory Control Society, *1986 P&IC Reference Guide and Directory*, T.D.A. Publications, Hollywood, FL.

[2] *Capacity Management Certification Program Study Guide*, American Production and Inventory Control Society (APICS), Washington, DC, 1981.

[3] Jackson, Larry C.: *Bills-of-Material*, APICS training aid, APICS, Washington, DC.

[4] Landvater, Darryl: *MRP Detailed Implementation Plan*, Williston, VT, 1975.

[5] Marcom, John, Jr.,: "IBM is Automating, Simplifying Products to Beat Asian Rivals," *The Wall Street Journal*, April 14, 1986, p. 1.

[6] *Material Requirements Planning*, APICS training aid, APICS BUCS-MONT Chapter, Washington, DC.

[7] Orlicky, Joseph A.: *Material Requirements Planning*, McGraw-Hill, New York, 1975.

[8] Orlicky, Joseph A., George W. Plossl, and Oliver W. Wight: "Structuring the Bill of Materials for MRP," *Production and Inventory Management*, December 1972, pp. 19–42.

[9] Wight, Oliver W.: *Production and Inventory Management in the Computer Age*, Cahners Books, Boston, 1974.

SELF QUIZ: CHAPTER 11

Part I True/False [1 point each = 6]

1 _____ The major inputs to MRP are the master production schedule, the bill-of-materials file, and inventory status information.

2 _____ Manufacturing inventory tends to have a dependent demand that is more "lumpy" than end-item inventory (which is independent).

3 _____ The use of BOMs should be limited to product configurations that are buildable; otherwise the BOMs are of no value.

4 _____ In MRP, the computer database must have a BOM number on file for every option available in the final assembly of a product.

5 _____ Pegging refers to the ability of the MRP system to accept and plan for certain orders even though normal MRP logic would automatically reschedule such orders.

6 _____ CRP is an iterative process whereby the computer first simulates loads on the work centers, and then relies upon planners to suggest changes if the plan cannot be met.

Part II Problems [3 points each = 9. Calculate and select your answer.]

1 End item A has a BOM as shown, where the numbers are amounts required. There are 25 units of B and 900 units of H in stock. What net requirements of H are needed to supply 300 units of A?

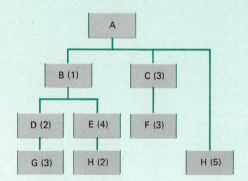

(a) 1,500
(b) 2,100
(c) 2,800
(d) 3,700
(e) None of the above.

Master Schedule for A

Week number	1	2	3	4	5	6	7	8
Requirements			20		85			25

B: OQ = 100 LT = 1

		1	2	3	4	5	6	7	8
Projected requirements				20		85			25
Receipts						100			100
On-hand end of period	25	25	25	5	5	20	20	20	95
Planned order release					100			100	

E: OQ = LFL LT = 2

		1	2	3	4	5	6	7	8
Projected requirements					400			400	
Receipts			200		200			400	
On-hand end of period	0	0	200	200	0	0	0	0	0
Planned order release			200			400			

H: OQ = 1,000 SS = 500 LT = 1

		1	2	3	4	5	6	7	8
Projected requirements				400	100		125		125
Receipts					1000		1000		
On-hand end of period	900	900	500	1400	1400	1175	1175	1175	1050
Planned order release				1000		1000			

2 Suppose the MPS for A is as shown above. Complete the MRP for B using the data given. What inventory is on hand at the end of period 8?
 (a)   0
 (b) 95
 (c) 100
 (d) 120
 (e) None of the above.

3 Complete the charts shown for E and H. What is the ending inventory for H?
 (a)   75
 (b) 175
 (c) 675
 (d) 1,050
 (e) None of the above.

CHAPTER 12
SCHEDULING AND CONTROLLING PRODUCTION ACTIVITIES

INTRODUCTION

Take a moment to look at the people and products around you. You're likely to see a number of "walking billboards" promoting everything from Apple computers and Stanford University to Miller beer and Porsche automobiles—plus a few fun runs and vacation spots. And you're likely to see a number of designer-label and special option products ranging from jeans and jackets to salad bars and cars. As Americans, we seem to like to trademark ourselves with distinguishing labels and products that enable us to say, "I'm different—but in a quality way."

The availability of specialized products and options has become an inherent part of competition in U.S. industry today. A consulting firm studying the smorgasbord of automobile products available found that, given the possible combinations of engines, transmissions, and optional accessories, a Chevrolet Citation came in more than 32,000 versions. And a Ford Thunderbird was available in more than 69,000 varieties. (Though the Honda Accord was sold in only 32 versions in the United States [**6**:31].)

It costs money and takes a great deal of coordination of materials and labor effort to provide options in a manufacturing plant. The consultant mentioned above estimated that over the past 20 years, the expansion of product lineups in the automobile industry in the United States has added well over $1,000 in overhead to the cost of the average car. In operational terms, it has meant that production activities must be more precisely controlled. With high-volume production of customized products, there is not much leeway for foul-ups. Things must happen on time, as scheduled!

In Chapter 11 we saw that the MRP system specifies what products (or components) are needed, in what quantities, and when they are required. Production activity controls then take over to deliver the goods. They direct how, when, and where the products should be made. Thus they bridge the gap between the material and capacity *plans* (discussed earlier) and the finished *products*.

Production activity controls (PAC) are the priority and capacity management techniques used to schedule and control production operations. Figure 12-1 depicts these two major concerns of PAC systems.

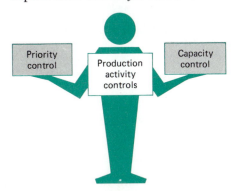

FIGURE 12-1   Major Concerns of Production Activity Control

Priority control ensures that production activities follow the priority plan (the material requirements plan) by controlling the orders to vendors and in-house production shops. *Capacity control* helps by monitoring work centers to ensure that they are providing the amount of labor and equipment time that is necessary (and was planned) to do the scheduled work.

Although the material in this chapter applies most directly to manufacturing facilities, many of the concepts apply equally well to service systems. Because they are consumed as they are produced, services do not accumulate inventories in the same sense as manufacturing firms. However, the concepts of priority control (such as of medical care in hospitals), and capacity control (such as in the utilization of beds and operating rooms) still apply. The unique problems of services and large-scale projects will be dealt with in a later chapter.

Before commencing your study of this chapter, scan the list of terms defined in Fig. 12-2. You may find it helpful to refer to them later.

PAC OBJECTIVES AND DATA REQUIREMENTS

SYSTEM OBJECTIVES

The objectives of PAC systems are heavily dependent upon the timely flow of accurate information:

1   *Know the current job status* (what jobs are running and where they are located).
2   *Guide future job operations* (determine what jobs should be next and in what work centers).
3   *Ensure the adequacy of materials and capacities* (make sure that correct quantities of materials are in the right place at the right time and that capacity and tooling are available to work on them).
4   *Maximize operational efficiency* (maximize labor and machine utilization and minimize inventory, set-up, and other costs while meeting master schedule service objectives).
5   *Maintain operational control* (monitor job status and lead times, measure progress, and signal corrective action when necessary).

Taken together, the five objectives constitute the requirements for a formal system that integrates and coordinates the human and machine resources of an organization. Let us identify some desirable characteristics of such a system.

SYSTEM CHARACTERISTICS

Production activity control responsibility normally rests with the director of manufacturing or the production control manager. It is usually a staff function. A centralized production control department typically coordinates activities, sets

1 *Control* (as related to the type of system):
Flow. Control of *continuous operations* by setting common production rates for all items, feeding work into the system at a specified rate, and monitoring the rate.
Order. Control of *intermittent operations* by monitoring the progress of each individual order through successive operations in its production cycle.

2 *Control* (as related to jobs and time):
Priority. Control over the status of jobs and work activities by specifying the order in which materials or jobs are assigned to work centers.
Capacity. Control over the labor and machine *time* used for jobs and work activities by planning and monitoring the time requirements of key work centers.

3 *Critical ratio.* A dynamic scheduling technique. Priority index numbers are calculated for ranking jobs according to which are in most urgent need of work time so that orders can be shipped on schedule.

4 *Dispatching.* Selecting and sequencing jobs to be run at individual work centers and actually authorizing or assigning the work to be done. The dispatch list is the primary means of priority control.

5 *Expediting.* Finding discrepancies between planned and actual work output and correcting them by attempting to speed up the processing in less than the normal lead time.

6 *Input control.* Control over the work being sent to a supplying facility, whether this is the shop itself or an outside vendor.

7 *Lead time.* The period between the decision to release an order and the completion of the first units. Includes wait, move, set-up, queue, and run time.

8 *Line of balance.* A charting technique that uses lead times and assembly sequencing to compare planned component completions with actual component completions.

9 *Loading.* Assigning hours of work to work centers in accordance with the available capacity of the work centers.
Finite capacity. Work is rescheduled into other periods if insufficient capacity exists in the required time period.
Infinite capacity. Work is assigned to the given time period whether or not sufficient capacity exists.

10 *Output control.* Dispatching, expediting, and any other follow-up necessary to get scheduled work from a work center or vendor.

11 *Priority decision rules.* Rules used by a dispatcher to determine the sequence in which jobs will be done.

12 *Routing.* The determination of which machines or work centers will be used to manufacture a particular item. Routing is specified on a route sheet; the route sheet identifies operations to perform, sequence, and possibly materials, tolerances, tools, and time allowances.

13 *Scheduling.* Setting operation start dates for jobs so that they will be completed by their due date.
Forward scheduling. Starting with a known start date and proceeding from the first operation to the last to determine the completion date.
Backward scheduling. Starting with a given due date and working backward to determine the required start date.

14 *Set-up time.* The time required to adjust a machine and attach the proper tooling to make a particular product.

15 *Shop order (manufacturing order).* A document conveying the authority to produce a specific quantity of a given item. It may also show the materials and machines to use, the sequence of operations, and the due dates that have been assigned by the scheduler.

16 *Work center.* An area or work station where a particular type of work is performed.

Source: The definitions are taken largely from the *American Production and Inventory Control Society (APICS) Dictionary*, 5th ed., 1984 (modified and/or condensed).

FIGURE 12-2 Production Activity Control Terms

schedules, and reviews results. Dispatchers on the shop floor follow the status of jobs and recommend adjustments where they are needed.

The production planner plays a vital role in controlling shop activities. Duties include coordinating inputs from purchasing and materials management plus planning the sequence of operations for the shop. This means working with the shop supervisor to ensure that jobs are done on schedule. If significant delays result or capacity levels are inappropriate, the planner must feed that information back to the master scheduler so that corrective action can be taken right away.

In some firms, production controls are simple (perhaps even manual) schedules or records of jobs assigned to production facilities. Other firms integrate their controls with computerized MRP and CRP systems. However, considerable differences in system design exist, depending on the nature of the product (whether it is standard or custom-built), the plant layout and process (whether it is continuous or intermittent), the volume of production, and whether items are produced for order or for stock.

Before effective control activities can commence, the work centers, routings, and manufacturing lead times must be well defined. Each work center's capacity and efficiency vis-à-vis standard capability should be known. Routing essentials include what is to be done (operation), where it is to be done (work center), and how long it should take (standard). Lead times such as times used for setup and transit must also be known.

Experience suggests some qualities which are desirable to make any PAC system run effectively [2]. These RUN characteristics, identified in Fig. 12-3, include making the system

- *Realistic*. Schedules should reflect what can realistically be accomplished. They can be "tough" goals that promote efficient use of firm's resources. But they should also be feasible, not only in terms of time standards but in terms of allowance for errors in lead times and stock levels. Otherwise, supervisors and workers will lose confidence in the schedules and circumvent the system.
- *Understandable*. The system should become a reliable communication medium and support (not threaten) operating personnel. Simplicity of operation will enhance understanding and acceptance by both management and shop personnel.
- *Necessary*. Accuracy, timeliness, and flexibility are key characteristics for generating confidence in the system. Systems that are accurate and timely become more indispensable over time. Flexibility will permit replanning and

FIGURE 12-3 PAC RUN Characteristics

last-minute schedule modification, so planners can use actual order information (if available) rather than forecast data.

PRIORITY AND CAPACITY CONTROL ACTIVITIES

Priority and capacity controls receive their inputs from the MRP and CRP systems. They attempt to ensure that the production quantities specified in the material requirements plan are completed as scheduled within the hourly time estimates established by the capacity requirements plan.

Figure 12-4 depicts the major priority and capacity control functions. Priority control activities include order release, dispatching, and status control. We shall treat each function in depth later in the chapter. For now, note that the priority control system is concerned with the proper sequencing of jobs in work centers. It should be flexible enough to allow for the updating of priorities whenever quantities or due dates change. That is, it should always reflect valid priorities whether higher *or lower* than previously planned.

For capacity control, the major concerns are lead-time control, balance of workload, and input/output control. The load on the shop (in unit hours) determines how long it takes to produce an item (that is, the lead time). By controlling the rate at which orders are released to the shop, lead times can be controlled, and capacity can be more effectively utilized.

DATA REQUIREMENTS

A well-organized database is essential to a workable PAC system. Figure 12-5 identifies some key requirements in terms of planning and control functions [8:3–7].

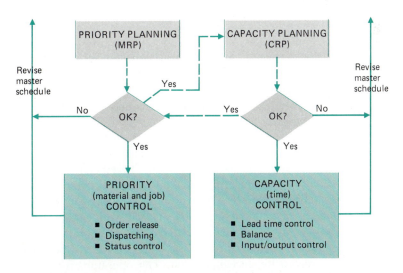

FIGURE 12-4   Priority and Capacity Control Activities

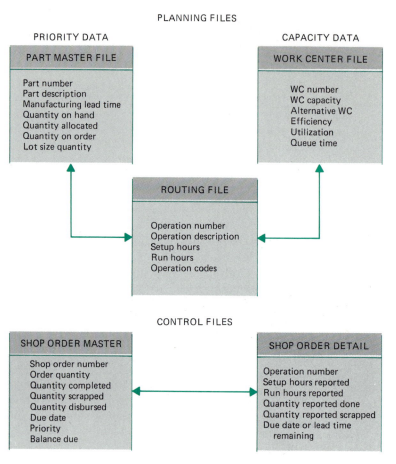

FIGURE 12-5   Planning and Control Files for PAC [8]

- The *part master file* contains all relevant component-part data, such as the description, standard cost, and inventory status. This file contains one record for each part number. Some companies have over 100,000 part numbers, so considerable computer storage space may be necessary.
- The *work center file* contains all relevant data associated with a work center, such as its capacity, load, and utilization history. For example, capacity data would include the number of shifts worked per week and the number of machine and labor hours per shift. The efficiency is expressed as the ratio of standard performance to actual performance (in number of hours). Utilization is the ratio of hours worked to hours available for work. The work center file contains one complete record for each work center.
- The *routing file* stores the data related to operations required to fabricate or asssemble an item. It contains a set of records for each manufactured part, with one record for each operation. The operation codes specify the number of

machines an operator may run simultaneously, whether an alternative operation is being used, if an outside supplier does an operation, etc.

- The *shop order master file* contains summary data on each active shop order. Along with the shop order detail file, it is especially useful for production activity controls. In addition to cost information and quantity data, this file contains the priority value assigned to the order. There is one record in this file for each active shop order.

- The *shop order detail file* stores all the scheduling, progress, and priority data relevant to each shop order. The due date or lead-time-remaining information is especially useful in recalculating priorities to keep them valid.

A satisfactory functioning PAC system is, of course, heavily dependent upon priority and capacity inputs, such as from an MRP system. The MRP system sets order release dates and lot sizes for products (and components) needed to satisfy the master schedule. If materials problems (for example, shortages) or capacity differences exist, the MRP system should be alerted. As planning and control files are updated with shop floor information, the MRP system should revise due dates (or signal revisions to the master schedule) as required.

Our discussion of the objectives and data requirements for production activity controls is now completed. Next we turn to scheduling strategy and methodologies, which are really techniques for effective dispatching (see Fig. 12-4). These methodologies are crucial to an operation and deserve extra attention.

SCHEDULING STRATEGY AND GUIDELINES

As the production quantities embodied in the aggregate plan and master production schedule are translated into specific job assignments, short-term or detailed scheduling comes into play. At this point individual jobs are assigned to specific work centers.

SYSTEM DIFFERENCES

All firms do not need the same level of scheduling, and indeed many firms do not use formal scheduling methods at all. Scheduling use is largely a function of the size and type of production system, as summarized in Fig. 12-6. Operational concerns (and scheduling needs) differ for continuous, intermittent and jobshop, and project-type systems.

- *Continuous systems* produce a limited class of products at fixed rates on assembly lines that usually follow fixed paths of manufacturing. The problems of order release, dispatching, and monitoring work status are not as complex here as in intermittent systems.

- *Intermittent and jobshop systems* typically produce batches or a wide variety of products on the same facilities. Each order may be individually routed to its

HIGH VOLUME	INTERMEDIATE VOLUME		LOW VOLUME
Continuous (flow operations) system	Intermittent (flow and batch operations) system	Job Shop (batch or single jobs)	Project (single jobs)
Key Characteristics			
• Specialized equipment • Same sequence of operations unless guided by microprocessors or robots	• Mixture of equipment • Similar sequence for each batch	• General purpose equipment • Unique sequence for each job	• Mixture of equipment • Unique sequence and location for each job
Design Concerns			
• Line balancing • Changeover time and cost	• Line and worker–machine balance • Changeover time and cost	• Worker–machine balance • Capacity utilization	• Allocating resources to minimize time and cost
Operational Concerns			
• Material shortages • Equipment breakdowns • Quality problems • Product mix and volume	• Material and equipment problems • Setup costs and run lengths • Inventory accumulations (run-out times)	• Job sequencing • Work center loading • Work flow and work in process	• Meeting time schedule • Meeting budgeted costs • Resource utilization

FIGURE 12-6 How Production System Concerns Affect Scheduling Strategy

unique combination of work centers. The variable quantities, work-flow paths, and processing times generate queues and work-in-process inventories which may require some rather complex production-activity controls.

▪ *Projects* typically have a unique sequence and location for each job. So special (project management) controls are frequently used for projects.

SCHEDULING STRATEGIES

Scheduling strategies differ widely among firms and may range from "no scheduling" to very sophisticated approaches. It is convenient to classify the strategies into four groups: (1) detailed, (2) cumulative, (3) cumulative-detailed, and (4) priority decision rules.

▪ *Detailed scheduling of specific jobs* as they arrive from customer orders is usually impractical in a manufacturing environment. Ordinary changes in orders, slippages, breakdowns, and unexpected events at other work centers soon invalidate earlier plans, leaving the production controller without a controllable schedule. Some service industries (such as doctors' offices and airlines) do make effective use of detailed scheduling far in advance of the service, however.

- *Cumulative scheduling of the total workload* is useful, especially for long-range planning of approximate capacity needs. However, this type of scheduling may result in the overloading of current periods and the underloading of future periods. It offers no guidance as to which jobs to do when, and there is no means of controlling which orders are being worked on.

- *Cumulative-detailed combination* is a feasible and practical approach, especially if the master schedule has "flexible" and "firm" portions, as was suggested earlier. Cumulative workload projections, made as jobs arrive, can be used to plan for approximate capacity needs. Capacities are planned on a *broad basis first* in terms of total labor and machine-hour requirements per week at key work centers. As changes occur during the weeks prior to manufacturing, the computer updates material and capacity requirements automatically. Capacity may then be allocated to *specific jobs later*, perhaps just a few days before the work is to be performed. (The actual time allowed at each work center is based on predetermined standard hour requirements for the job, but it usually does little good to try to specify which particular hour or minutes a worker shall work on a given job. Normally, one day is the shortest practical scheduling unit used in jobshops.)

- *Priority decision rules* are scheduling guides that have been used independently and in conjunction with one of the above strategies. Examples of such rules are "first come, first served" and "always work on jobs with the longest lead times." When used alone, priority rules essentially take the place of any other scheduling—but at some cost, such as high work-in-process inventory or reduced service to some customers. When used in conjunction with the combination of cumulative and detailed scheduling, priority rules can be very effective. We will elaborate on one widely used rule, the critical ratio, later in the chapter.

Two other strategy concerns relate to the scheduling time unit and the direction in which schedulers view the time, that is, forward or backward.

Scheduling Time Frame   We have seen that the master production schedule, as well as the material and capacity requirements plans, are typically expressed in weekly time buckets. As requirements are translated into shop orders, the weekly loadings are preserved, but more precision is sometimes needed for controlling the efficiency of operations. However, even though the jobs are given priorities on a daily basis and the precise times to do a job are measured (and recorded) in minutes, it is common practice to accept weekly precision for scheduling purposes in jobshops. This gives the shop flexibility to balance high- and low-priority work orders. Weekly time periods are also consistent with other production and inventory control activities.

Forward versus Backward Scheduling   Figure 12-7 illustrates two approaches to scheduling. Forward scheduling starts as soon as requirements are known and often results in the completion of the component before the required due date. The result is more work-in-process inventory and higher inventory carrying costs.

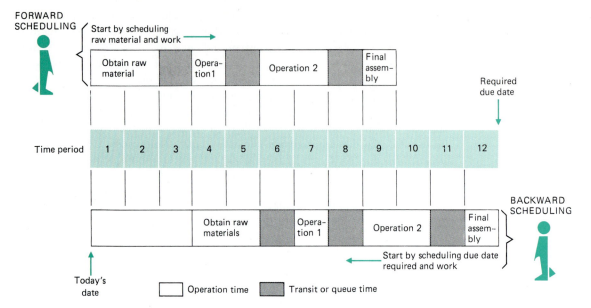

FIGURE 12-7   Forward and Backward Scheduling

Backward (or "set back") scheduling uses the same lead-time offset logic as MRP. Components are delivered "when needed" rather than "as soon as possible."

With finite capacity loading, some work centers may already be too loaded to accept more work in a given time period. For example, in Fig. 12-7 (backward scheduling) suppose the work center for operation 1 is unavailable during periods 6 and 7. Operation 1 could be moved ahead to period 5, with raw materials acquisition moved up to period 2.

Some firms combine both approaches by starting "today" with plans to finish "when due." Their rationale is to create some slack time in the intermediate weeks which will give them flexibility to handle changes and emergencies.

SCHEDULING AND LOADING GUIDELINES

Successful firms have developed some guidelines for scheduling jobs and loading work centers which are frequently useful—though not always applied [3,4,10]. Figure 12-8 summarizes some of them.

A realistic schedule is essential for getting the job done and maintaining credibility in the system. If planners call for twice as much work as is reasonable, the schedules will appear "stupid" and will be disregarded. Also, releasing all available jobs (number 4) as they are received is a common cause of increased manufacturing lead times and excess work-in-process. Good scheduling systems will release work at a reasonable rate that will keep unnecessary backlogs from the production floor. In service systems, the release of jobs can be more difficult

1   Provide a realistic schedule.
2   Allow adequate time *for* operations.
3   Allow adequate time *before, between,* and *after* operations.
4   Don't release all available jobs to the shop.
5   Don't schedule all available capacity in the shop.
6   Load only selected work centers.
7   Allow for necessary changes.
8   Gear shop responsibility to the schedule.

FIGURE 12-8   Scheduling and Loading Guidelines

because the incoming flow of orders (customers) and the service times may have more variability than in goods manufacturing.

SCHEDULING METHODOLOGY

The scheduling methodology depends upon the type of industry, organization, product, and level of sophistication required. We shall examine three general classes of methodology: (1) charts and boards, (2) priority decision rules, and (3) mathematical programming methods. The methods are not mutually exclusive, and many firms use a combination of scheduling techniques.

GANTT CHARTS, SCHEDULE BOARDS, AND COMPUTER GRAPHICS

Gantt charts and associated scheduling boards have been extensively used scheduling devices in the past, although many of the charts are now drawn by computer. Gantt charts are extremely easy to understand and can quickly reveal the current or planned situation to all concerned. They are used in several forms, including (a) *scheduling or progress charts*, which depict the sequential schedule, (b) *load charts*, which show the work assigned to a group of workers or machines, and (c) *record charts*, which are used to record the actual operating times and delays of workers or machines.

Figure 12-9 illustrates a simplified (a) scheduling chart and (b) load chart. The load chart depicts the specific customer orders (SO) to be worked on in work centers 2, 4, 5, and 7. The ⊠ signifies an unavoidable delay (for maintenance, and so on). Load charts can also be used to show the scheduled workload, maintenance, and idle time on key machines, and they can be used to show the accumulated backlog.

Another Gantt chart is shown in Fig. 12-10, where the "vee" indicates updating through July 7. This is a progress chart showing which activities must be done prior to other activities. It shows that the rod castings were delayed a day, probably due to extra maintenance on the casting furnace. The wires are half a day

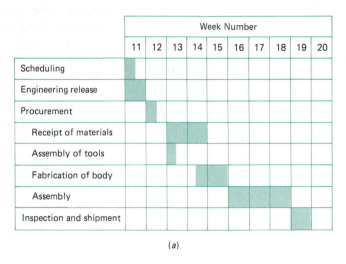
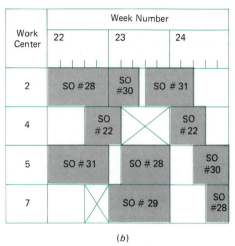

FIGURE 12-9   Two Forms of Gantt Charts: (a) Scheduling Chart. (b) Load Chart

behind schedule, and end-cap fabrication was 2 days late in getting started. With a planned 3-day schedule, it appears that the end caps will probably not be completed before the heater element assembly is begun on Monday, July 11, even though an extra day of slack was provided on July 8.

Keeping Gantt charts up to date has always been a major problem, especially as the number of jobs and work centers increases. Numerous mechanical and magnetic charts and boards are available to facilitate the revision process. A Boardmaster uses cards which snap into small grooves along the horizontal time scale. The Sched-U-Graph uses colored cards which are cut to a length corresponding to the scheduled time and inserted into a visible window. Produc-trol is another device which has a visible card window plus a tracking peg and cord to monitor the progress of the job. Other systems make use of magnetic card holders and revolving discs. In general, however, reliance on physical methods of control is diminishing in favor of the up-to-date reports that can be supplied by comput-

FIGURE 12-10   Progress Chart

ers. Computers can keep track of thousands of items of inventory and assist in generating revised schedules so quickly that the resultant schedules are nearly always an improvement over manual methods. Even if the firm has not advanced beyond a simple listing or charting technique, its computer can probably help.

PRIORITY DECISION RULES

Priority decision rules are simplified guidelines (heuristics) for determining the sequence in which jobs will be done. In some firms these rules take the place of priority planning systems such as MRP systems. In others, they are used in conjunction with some of these more advanced systems.

The search for "optimal" rules has identified numerous rules. A good deal of academic research having to do with assigning n jobs to m machines subject to various arrival patterns has been done. This includes extensive simulations to analyze the effects on processing time, labor utilization, inventory carrying, and other costs. No single rule is best for all situations.

Priority decision rules are extensively used, and a number of them are discussed below. We will begin with some single-criterion rules that are "static" in that they do not incorporate an updating feature. Next we will consider Johnson's rule. Following that, we will take up the critical ratio technique, a widely used priority system that permits regular updating and revision of priorities.

Single-Criterion Rules   The simplest but sometimes most effective priority rules assign jobs on the basis of a single criterion. Some of these rules are shown in Fig. 12-11.

One of the difficulties of selecting an appropriate rule lies in first deciding on the criterion. Rules which minimize flow time, or the average waiting time of orders, do not necessarily yield low in-process inventory costs or high labor or machine utilization. The rules listed in Fig. 12-11 use only one criterion as a determinant for decision. The first-come, first-served order, for example, may appear desirable from a "fairness" standpoint, but customers in urgent need of a particular product may desperately need faster service on some occasions. None of the single-criterion rules takes the "big picture" into account.

Symbol	Priority Rule
FCFS	First come, first served
EDD	Earliest due date
LS	Least slack (that is, time due less processing time)
SPT (SoT)	Shortest processing time
LPT (LoT)	Longest processing time
PCO	Preferred customer order
RS	Random selection

DUE DATE

FIGURE 12-11   Some Priority Decision Rules

SS - STATIC SLACK

Some priority rules are, however, generally better than others. Research has shown, for example, that the shortest-processing-time rule (SPT) has the lowest average flow time of numerous rules tested. This results in low in-process inventory costs. (On the other hand, consistently scheduling items with the shortest operation time will undoubtedly make some customers—those with long processing times—quite unhappy!) A rule of giving priority to those jobs that have the least slack time per remaining operations seems to be effective for focusing upon the lateness of jobs.

EXAMPLE 12-1

Shown here are the time remaining (number of days until due) and work remaining (number of days) for five jobs which were assigned a letter as they arrived. Sequence the jobs by priority rules: (a) FCFS, (b) EDD, (c) LS, (d) SPT, and (e) LPT.

Job	Number of Days until Due	Number of Days of Work Remaining
A	8	7
B	3	4
C	7	5
D	9	2
E	6	6

(The numerical amounts included in parentheses are for reference.)

	FCFS	EDD	LS	SPT	LPT
1st	A	B(3)	B(-1)	D(2)	A(7)
2d	B	E(6)	E(0)	B(4)	E(6)
3d	C	C(7)	A(1)	C(5)	C(5)
4th	D	A(8)	C(2)	E(6)	B(4)
5th	E	D(9)	D(7)	A(7)	D(2)

Combined-criteria rules sometimes yield better results than single rules. For example, the shortest-processing-time rule can be improved upon by establishing a limit on the maximum amount of waiting time for any job.

Johnson's Rule   A simple rule which yields a minimum processing time for sequencing n jobs through two machines or work centers (1 and 2) has been developed by S. M. Johnson [5]. Johnson's rule works well for situations in which the same processing sequence must be maintained on both machines and there are no in-process storage problems or overriding individual priorities. Later work has expanded the rule to sequencing n jobs through three machines. We shall examine the "two-machine" approach here.

Johnson's rule requires that all jobs be listed and that the amount of time each requires on a machine be shown. The jobs are then scanned for the shortest individual activity time. If the shortest time lies with machine 1, the job is placed as early in the schedule as possible, and if the shortest time lies with machine 2, the job is placed as late as possible. Once one job has been scheduled, it is eliminated from further consideration, and the decision rule is applied to the remaining jobs. The scheduling sequence that is derived then applies to both machines. By scheduling least-time jobs at the beginning and end of the schedule, the amount of concurrent operating time for machines 1 and 2 is maximized, and so the overall operating time to complete a specific number of jobs is minimized.

EXAMPLE 12-2

Wonderloaf Bakery has orders for five specialty jobs (A, B, C, D, and E) that must be processed sequentially through two work centers (baking and decoration). The amount of time (in hours) required for the jobs is shown below.

	Time Required (hours) for Job				
Work Centers	*A*	*B*	*C*	*D*	*E*
1 (Baking)	5	4	8	7	6
2 (Decoration)	3	9	2	4	10

Determine the schedule sequence that minimizes the total elapsed time for the five jobs, and present it in the form of a Gantt chart.

SOLUTION

Johnson's rule says to identify the shortest processing time. If it is at the first work center, place the (entire) job as early as possible. If it is at the second work center, place the job as late as possible. Eliminate that job from further consideration, and apply the decision rule to the remaining jobs. Break any ties between jobs by sequencing the job on the first work center earliest and that on the second work center latest. Jobs having the same time at both work centers can be assigned at either end of the available sequence.

(a) The shortest time is for job C in work center 2 (2 hours). Place job as late as possible.

				C

(b) The next shortest time is for job A in work center 2. Place job A as late as possible.

			A ⸍	C

(c) The next shortest time is a tie between jobs B and D. Sequence the job on the first work center (job B) as early as possible.

B			A	C

(d) The next shortest time is for job D in work center 2. Place the job as late as possible.

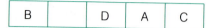

(e) Place job E in the remaining opening.

The sequential times are as follows:

Work Center 1	4	6	7	5	8
Work Center 2	9	10	4	3	2

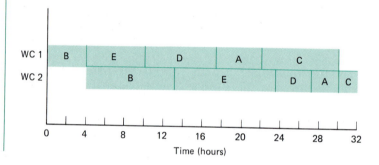

Critical Ratio

Critical ratio (CR) is a dispatching rule which yields a priority index number that expresses the ratio of time remaining to work remaining. In contrast to the "static" rules discussed earlier, critical ratio is dynamic. It is effective for advance scheduling, and it can be constantly updated weekly or even daily to provide close and timely control.

The critical ratio is designed to give priority to those jobs which most urgently need the work time so that orders can be shipped on schedule. As a job appears to be getting farther behind schedule, its critical ratio becomes lower. Jobs with a CR less than 1.0 are behind schedule. If the CR equals 1.0, the job is on schedule, and if the CR is greater than 1.0, the job has some slack.[1]

$$\text{Critical ratio} = \frac{\text{time remaining}}{\text{work remaining}} = \frac{\text{TR}}{\text{WR}} \qquad (12\text{-}1)$$

[1] Jobs that are already overdue have negative time-remaining values and yield negative ratios which require a modification to this analysis. Thus we are limiting our analysis to situations in which jobs are not already overdue.

Stated in terms of dates, the critical ratio is

$$CR = \frac{\text{date due} - \text{date now}}{\text{lead (work) time remaining}} = \frac{DD - DN}{LTR}$$

EXAMPLE 12-3

Today is day 22 on the production control calendar, and four jobs are on order as shown:

Job	Date Due	Workdays Remaining
A	28	8
B	26	2
C	24	2
D	30	12

Determine the critical ratio for each job, and assign priority ranks.

SOLUTION

Job	Time Remaining $(DD - DN)$	Work Remaining (LTR)	$CR = \dfrac{DD - DN}{LTR}$	Priority
A	$28 - 22 = 6$	8	.75	2
B	$26 - 22 = 4$	2	2.00	4
C	$24 - 22 = 2$	2	1.00	3
D	$30 - 22 = 8$	12	.67	1

With the critical ratio, jobs would be assigned in the order of D, A, C, and B. Job B is the only one with some slack. Jobs A and D have critical ratios of less than 1, meaning that the orders will not be shipped on time unless they are expedited. Job C, with an index of 1, is the only job "on schedule."

Priority decision rules are often simple heuristics, but they can be relatively effective if carefully chosen and evaluated. On the other hand, where more sophisticated mathematical methods can be used, those methods hold out a theoretical potential of optimization that priority rules can never claim. We turn now to some of the mathematical methods of scheduling.

MATHEMATICAL PROGRAMMING METHODS

Scheduling is, in many respects, a complex resource-allocation problem. Firms possess capacity, labor skills, materials, and so forth, and they seek to allocate their use so as to maximize a profit or service objective, or perhaps meet a demand while minimizing costs. The interdependencies, cost uncertainties, and assumptions that must be made, however, make a mathematical solution to the problem difficult. Nevertheless, as firms gain better productivity and cost data, the underlying assumptions become less restrictive. This, coupled with the availability of computers and advanced quantitative methods, has brought many of the scheduling problems closer to a logical, data-based solution than they were previously. A brief review of applications reveals that scheduling and production control are now very fertile areas for the use of standard simplex and distribution linear programming, assignment linear programming, and dynamic programming methods, all of which are mentioned below.

Linear Programming: Simplex and Transportation Methods   Many scheduling and production control problems fit well into the linear programming framework discussed earlier.

EXAMPLE 12-4

A firm can sell whatever quantities of three grades of steel it can produce. Each grade yields a different profit contribution and requires different times on common machines. The scheduling problem of designating which quantities to produce may be formulated as one of maximizing profit subject to machine-time availability constraints. The solution can proceed via the standard simplex method of linear programming.

EXAMPLE 12-5

A scheduler in a multiplant firm must direct the flow of raw materials from three peripheral supply points to five different mills in order to establish production quantities and operating times for each mill. The optimal allocation may be determined by setting up a transportation linear programming matrix covering supply and demand locations plus interconnecting transportation costs.

EXAMPLE 12-6

Eight shop orders calling for different quantities must be assigned to production on five machines. Each machine has a limited number of hours available, and so there may be a different cost per piece. The assignment of jobs to machines can be made using transportation linear programming methods after the hours of machine time and units of demand are converted into common units of equivalent standard hours (ESH).

Linear programming methods were described earlier, a discussion that will not be repeated here. Recall that they were used in product-mix and process selection situations to help select raw material amounts and product quantities to schedule on a profit maximization (or cost minimization) basis.

Linear Programming: Assignment Method   The assignment method of linear programming is a variation of the distribution method. It is useful for assigning jobs to machines or work centers, or workers to jobs, on the basis of some criterion such as cost, performance, quantity, time, or efficiency. Of course, only one criterion can apply at a time; in addition, the method requires that the number of items to be assigned equal the number of positions available. If the numbers are not equal, a dummy row or column is added and assigned a zero criterion coefficient (for example, to help identify which job to eliminate) or a high criterion coefficient (for example, to be sure the job never gets done). Similarly, if any worker-machine assignments are impractical or infeasible, the cell is blocked out or given an exorbitant cost that will prohibit any assignment.

The solution method for minimization problems involves forming a square matrix of criteria values and systematically developing zeros in the cells until a zero exists for each row-column combination. As soon as there is at least one zero in each row and each column, an optimal solution has been obtained. (See Solved Prob. 5.)

Maximization problems can also be solved by using the same assignment algorithm. The only change required is that all the values that appear in the initial maximization matrix (such as profits) must first be subtracted from the largest number in the matrix. This action essentially converts all the values into "relative costs," and from there on the procedure is the same.

The assignment method has been extensively used for assigning jobs in machine shops, for scheduling the use of heavy equipment, and in numerous other industrial settings where relatively accurate cost, profit, or time criteria have been available. As productive efforts in the economy gradually become more oriented toward services, we may expect to see expanded use of this method in the assigning of personnel to service-oriented tasks.

Dynamic Programming   Dynamic programming is another optimization technique that has some potential for scheduling applications. It is designed to solve problems that can be partitioned into time-dependent stages.

In production scheduling, it is often convenient to begin with output requirements for periods at the end of the planning horizon, as in backward scheduling, and then work backward in time to determine what goods or services must be produced in current periods in order to optimize (for example, minimize costs or maximize profits) over the total horizon. Dynamic programming methods are particularly suitable for this approach. The solution procedure is based upon enumeration of the possible solution values at a given stage, partial determination of the objective function, and systematically working toward an overall optimum by carrying potential optimum values sequentially back to preceding stages. The optimal production quantities, overtime arrangements, inventories, and so forth, are determined for the final period; then one works back to each preceding period to determine the optimal combination to produce the subsequent results. By the principle of optimality we know that once an optimal arrangement has been achieved in a later stage, the arrangement will remain optimal regardless of the route taken to enter the stage [9].

In dynamic programming, cost and other functions may be nonlinear, and the objective function can become somewhat complex and difficult to define. As a result, dynamic programming applications are still somewhat theoretical, and the

PRODUCTION WORK ORDER

ORDER NO.	PART NUMBER	ORDER QTY	SIGN NUMBER	DEPT.	ACCOUNT NO.	REQUESTOR	RJ
4830	113076	5		0000	11420300050581	DATE	5-5-81
CITY	STATE	REGION	REMOTE	S/C	W	APPROVAL	km

KIT DATE	ASSY. DATE	TEST DATE	RELEASE DATE	Q.C. DATE
5-6-81	6-2	6-16		6-16

DESCRIPTION: LAMPBANK CONTROL – 7 x 64 – M-220- DF 33W

E	DEPARTMENTS	W	Process Step	ISSUE DATE	DUE DATE	DATE COMP.	QTY. COMP.	BUDGET HRS.	ACTUAL HRS.
21	STOCKROOM	18		5-5	5-6				
22	ELEC. ASSY								
	PWB Assembly								
	Elect. Assy's								
24	ELEC./MECH. ASSY								
	Wiring	12	2	5-14	5-29			95	
	Mechanisms								
25	UNEX ASSEMBLY								
	Sub-Assembly								
	Final Assy								
27	MACHINE SHOP								
28	TEST & REPAIR		4	6-3	6-16			9	
29	INSPECTION (Q.C.)								
42	FABRICATION								
	Sheet Metal	10	1	5-8	5-13			27	
	Welding	11							
	Paint	14	3	6-1	6-2			10	
46	LAMINATION	14							
	PLASTICS	14							
	SILK SCREEN	14							
47	SHIPPING	15							

SERIAL NUMBERS: 4830-01   4830-05

NOTES:

ATTACHMENTS:
KIT LIST
DRAWING # 3506-27
DRAWING # 3506-28
DRAWING #
DRAWING #
BOM

FIGURE 12-12 Production Work Order (*Source:* American Sign and Indicator Company.)

technique is not widely used. In-depth coverage is beyond our scope here, but references are available [9].

PRIORITY CONTROL

A good priority control system should reflect true needs, rank the importance of those needs, and be capable of updating those rankings as quantities or due dates change. We turn now to the three major priority control activities necessary for a good priority control or "dispatching" system: order release, dispatching, and status control (see Fig. 12-4).

ORDER RELEASE

Order release is the crucial step that converts an order from a planned status to reality in the shop or on order with a vendor. When an open order is created, actual materials and labor may be charged against the job. Figure 12-12 illustrates a shop (work) order form used by a firm that produces electric signs to customer order. Purchase ordering procedures were discussed more fully in Chapter 9.

Figure 12-13 illustrates the order release function. Recall the "planned order release" and "scheduled receipt" entries on the MRP forms studied in Chapter 11. As the planned order release date moves into the current period, the release actually converts what was a "planned" receipt into a "scheduled" receipt. It makes the order "official."

Order release should not be automatic whenever an order arrives; it should be a conscious human (not computer) activity because it requires a judgmental assessment of several factors. Two key considerations identified in Fig. 12-13 are the *validity of the priority* and the *availability of the capacity.* Is the due date an accurate reflection of need? If so, will the necessary materials and components be

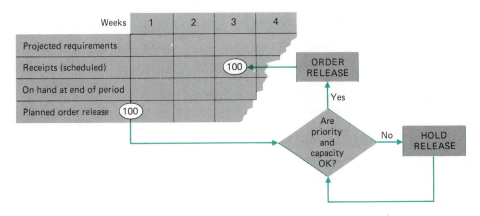

FIGURE 12-13   The Function of Order Release

available to support work on this shop order? Are routing and tooling data provided?

With respect to capacity, orders should be released to the shop at a planned (and steady) workload rate if possible. Using feedback from capacity records, the planner can schedule order release dates in conjunction with available capacity at specific work centers. If, for example, a check on the availability of a major machine or work center shows that a delay is anticipated, the planner may shift the release time slightly rather than begin an order only to have it held up.

The shop order file created by the release of a planned order becomes the vehicle for tracking manufacturing progress, collecting costs, and recording quantities produced for this order (see Fig. 12-5). The "start" and "due" dates developed from subsequent scheduling activities also become part of this file. The difference between the due date and the current date is a measure of lead time remaining and is useful in setting and revising priorities.

With the shop order goes a shop packet containing the necessary drawings, bills of material, and route sheets to produce the order. It may also contain paperwork (or computer terminal instructions) for issuing materials and tools, charging labor, moving the job between departments, and so on.

Special note should be made of the situation with firm planned orders. They are released to the shop even though the need date is not immediately apparent from the end-item requirements.

DISPATCHING

The dispatch list is probably the most widely used tool for priority control. It lists all jobs available to a work center and ranks them by a relative priority (or due date). When priorities have been assigned to specific jobs, the scheduling methodology (studied earlier in the chapter) becomes a reality. *Scheduling is implemented via the dispatch list.*

Figure 12-14 illustrates the relationship between the planned order releases and the dispatch list. Once orders are released (after appropriate material and capacity checks), scheduled receipt dates can be established. Much of the detail can be performed by computer.

Two of the most popular methods of ranking jobs for a dispatch list are (1) by *due date* and (2) by *critical ratio*. Figure 12-15 illustrates a dispatch list where the due date signals the job's priority. Note that this particular dispatch list separates the jobs currently running from the jobs available. Some firms add information on jobs that are coming, what work center they are coming from, and their current status.

Production control uses the dispatch list to assign work responsibility for jobs to the appropriate department supervisors. A good dispatching system will preserve the benefits of decentralized responsibility without sacrificing the advantages of close control. For example, a dispatch list which contains 2 or 3 days of work, such as the one in Fig. 12-15, will give the supervisor additional flexibility in

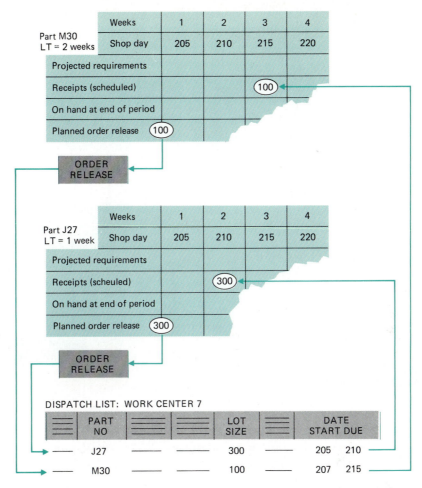

Part M30 LT = 2 weeks	Weeks	1	2	3	4
	Shop day	205	210	215	220
Projected requirements					
Receipts (scheduled)				(100)	
On hand at end of period					
Planned order release		(100)			

ORDER RELEASE

Part J27 LT = 1 week	Weeks	1	2	3	4
	Shop day	205	210	215	220
Projected requirements					
Receipts (scheuled)			(300)		
On hand at end of period					
Planned order release		(300)			

ORDER RELEASE

DISPATCH LIST: WORK CENTER 7

PART NO			LOT SIZE		DATE START DUE
J27			300		205 210
M30			100		207 215

FIGURE 12-14   Relationship between Planned Order Releases and Dispatch List

setting up and running jobs. Thus the supervisor has more decision-making responsibility, and the system can take better advantage of the supervisor's knowledge of set-up times, machine capabilities, and other operating complexities.

Some firms delete the due date column from the dispatch list. If the dispatch list contains only 1 day's work, this results in tighter control over the supervisor, for he or she now has little need for discretion. If the dispatch list contains 2 or 3 days' work, the supervisor (or someone else) must decide which jobs to work on next.

Suppose a firm uses a dispatch list with due dates but allows the work center to become overloaded. Then several jobs have the same relative priority (due

Date: 3/5   Shop date: 186

DAILY DISPATCH LIST: WORK CENTER 4 (LATHES)
Hours Available: 30

JOBS RUNNING

Shop Order Number	Part Number	Operation Number	Standard Hours Total	Standard Hours Remain	Date Start	Date Due	Next WC
432	M43	30	40	12	3/3	3/5	5
434	R33	45	14	6	3/4	3/6	3

Job standard hours remaining   18

JOBS AVAILABLE

Shop Order Number	Part Number	Operation Number	Operation Description	Lot Size	Std. Hours	Date Start	Date Date	Next WC
435	P27	40	Finish	100	10.0	3/5	3/6	7
437	M40	30	Rough	300	30.0	3/5	3/7	5
399	R23	50	Turn	20	18.5	3/6	3/8	3
442	M42	30	Rough	150	22.5	3/7	3/10	5

Job standard hours available   81.0

Priority by due date

FIGURE 12-15   Daily Dispatch List

date), but not all can be processed at once. At that point, an indexing method such as critical ratio has an advantage. With critical ratio each job has a relative priority—and the priorities can be readily updated.

The nature of demand and product-mix decisions makes overloads on some work centers a common occurrence. However, releasing too much load to the departments as a matter of policy is counterproductive.

Departmental supervisors then become burdened with the whole firm's scheduling and dispatching problems. Controlling the work flow is the responsibility of production control. Supervisors should not be forced to bargain with expediters over which customers' jobs are "hot." They should be able to direct their skills to the efficiency and quality of their operations and to the effective management of departmental personnel.

Dispatching in Continuous Production Systems   In continuous systems, the dispatching function is basically a release of authority to produce the next unit on the assembly line. If all items are the same, one release can suffice for a large production run. If each end product has different options, the choices must be delineated for each unit. But even that can be done with last-minute flexibility.

Figure 12-16 illustrates a dispatching form used by the production and

CAR BUILD SHEET

VAUXHALL MOTORS LTD., ELLESMERE PORT

PROD'N. & MATERIAL CONTROL DEPT.

DD6/19

VEHICLE SEQUENCE NUMBER	BODY TYPE	MODEL	DR.	DEST.	SALES ORDER NUMBER	COLOR	TRIM	MISC OPTION BLOCK	SEQUENCE SHEET NUMBER
0006293	011	9TB08	L	GER	506143	59L	60I		035

			HEAD LAMPS								SPECIAL REQUIREMENTS AND MAJOR CODES					MAJOR UNITS	
1—Mod. Inscript. Plate Large 2—Mod. Inscript. Plate Small 3—Vehicle Ident. Stamping 4—Fit 1 & 3 5—Fit 2 & 3	1—Cigar Lighter 2—Tailpipe Exhaust Emission 3—Fit 1 & 2	1—Heater 2—High Capacity Heater 3—Heater not required	1—Halogen Headlamps 2—Unified European H/Lamps Rd less France 3—Amber Headlamps 4—Fit 1 & 2 5—Fit 1 & 3	1—Laminated Windscreen 2—Heated Rear Window 3—Fit 1 & 2	1—R/D Kilo Speedo 2—L/D Miles Speedo 3—Repeater Lamps 4—Fit 1 & 3 5—Fit 2 & 3	1—Wash Wipe Rear Window 2—Rear Qtr. Opening Vent 3—Fit 1 & 2	1—Headlamp Beam Level Device 2—H/Lamp Wash Wipe System 3—Install Radio 4—Fit 1 & 2 5—Fit 1 & 3 6—Fit 2 & 3 7—Fit 1, 2 & 3	1—Colour Keyed Crash Pad 2—Tinted Glass all Windows 3—Fit 1 & 2	1—Reverse Lamps 2—4 Way Emergency Flashers 3—Fit 1 & 2	1—Rear Fogguard Lamp 2—Rear Fogguard Lamps Dual	J—XF6 · Greece K—XJ5 · Sweden L—XJ7 · Austria M—XK1 · Belgium N—XK2 · France O—XK3 · Finland P—XK4 · Italy Q—XK6 · Norway R—XL1 · Denmark S—XL2 · Switzerland T—XL6 · Portugal U—XO5 · Holland V—XG3 · Germany W—XE5 · New Zealand X—XJ3 · GM Holdens Y— Israel Z—Special Sales Package	1—4 Cyl. 1200 cc. 2—4 Cyl. 1300 cc. Low Comp. 3—4 Cyl. 1300 cc. Exh. Emiss. 4—4 Cyl. 1300 cc. 16 Valve 5—4 Cyl. 2300 cc. 6—4 Cyl. 2300 cc. 7—Special see ID Codes	1—4 Speed Manual 2—5 Speed Manual 3—Automatic Gearbox	1—Girling System 2—Opel System 3—GM France	1—H/Duty Front Suspension 2—H/Duty Rear Suspension 3—Fit 1 & 2	REAR AXLE AS PER I.D. CODES	FRONT AXLE AS PER I.D. CODES
3		1		2					3		V	3	1	1		LB	LJ

		FLOOR COVER		DECOR LEVEL	FRONT SEATS		SEAT BELTS				SUPPLIER	TYRES	WHEELS	Strg. Wheel	Mirrors	Battery		MAJOR UNIT
1—Alternator 28 Amp 2—Alternator H/D 45 Amp 3—Dust Excluder 4—Fit 1 & 3 5—Fit 2 & 3	1—Limited Power Output 2—H/Duty Starter 3—Fit 1 & 2	1—Fit Carpet Cut Pile 2—Fit Carpet Load Floor Cut Pile 3—Fit Mat Load Floor 4—Fit 1 & 2 5—Fit 1 & 3	1—Sunvisor Passenger with Mirror 2—Sunvisor Pocket Passenger 3—Console Front Floor 4—Fit 1 & 3 5—Fit 2 & 3	1—Kingston Seats 2—Bold Luton Plaid 3—Vinyl Seats	1—Fixed Front Seat with H/Rest 2—Fixed Folding Recliner with Headrest 3—Fixed Folding Recliner 4—Fixed Front Seat 5—Tipping Reclining	1—Luggage Compart. Lamp 2—Electric Clock 3—Fit 1 & 2	1—Fit Static Front 2—Fit Static Rear 3—Fit Inertia Front 4—Fit Inertia Rear 5—Fit 1 & 2 6—Fit 3 & 4 7—Fit 2 & 3	1—Front and Rear Bumper Guards 2—Anti-Freeze Protection 3—Fit 1& 2	1—Fit Wheel Trim Rings 2—Van Conversion 3—Fit 1 & 2	1—Exterior Body Mldgs. 2—Drip Rail Mldgs. 3—Fit 1 & 2	J—Fit Goodyear K—Fit Firestone L—Fit Michelin M—Fit Avon N—Fit Uniroyal O—Fit Pirelli P—Fit Free Issue Q—Fit Any Except J R—Fit Any Except K S—Fit Any Except L T—Fit Any Except M U—Fit Any Except N V—Fit Any Except O W—Fit L or M only X—Fit J, K or N only Y—Fit Dunlop Z—Fit Continental	1—155SR × 13 Radial 2—175/70SR × 13 3—175/70HR × 13 4—560 × 13 Crossply 5—205/60HR × 13 6—170/70SR × 13	1—5J × 13 × 9 Oblong Hole Std. 2—5½J × 13 Sports Road Wheel 3—6J × 13 Alloy	1—2 Spoke Standard 2—Soft Rim Simulated Leather 3—Sport Leather	1—Door Mtd. Mirror Pass. 2—Rr. View Tilt Mirror 3—Fit 1 & 2	1—Std. Wet 2—Large Capacity Wet 3—Std. Dry 4—Large Capacity Dry	1—Lining Luggage Compart. Cover 2—Grab Handle & Hook 3—Fit 1 & 2	POWER UNITS AS PER I.D. CODES
2		3	1	1	2		7	2		2	L	1	1	2	2	1	3	PD

IF THE RELEVANT OPTION BLOCK IS BLANK, FIT THE STANDARD UNIT AS SPECIFIED BY THE MODEL, DRIVE, DESTINATION, TRIM OR SPECIAL REQUIREMENTS CODE, MISC. OPTION BLOCK REFERS TO CODES RELEASED AFTER FORMAT PREPARATION OR TO SPECIAL CONVERSION ORDER NUMBERS.

Wilkes Business Forms

FIGURE 12-16 Car Build Sheet (*Source:* Vauxhall Motors Ltd.)

material control department of an automobile manufacturer. It is referred to as a *car build sheet.* Notice how simple yet complete it is. It permits customers to obtain a made-to-order car from a continuous production system. Each work station along the line simply responds with the option specified. No individual drawings, routings, priorities, or controls are required. Because all cars are rigidly sequenced along the same production process, the production control functions are greatly simplified, even though the end products have a significant number of options.

REPORTING AND STATUS CONTROL

Without a good reporting system, production control may not know about problems until an order is overdue to be shipped. The reporting and status control system gives information concerning orders that are being completed or reasons why they are not being completed.

Each company has its own unique production reporting requirements. Some are very detailed. Our concern will be limited to (1) reasons why feedback and corrective action are necessary, (2) how firms (generally) accomplish the reporting function, and (3) what types of status reports are in general use.

Why Feedback and Corrective Action Are Necessary   Those who have worked in a manufacturing environment can readily attest to the almost unbelievable morass of problems that can arise to sabotage an order. In many firms (too many!), changes are the order of the day. Engineering may make a change in material specifications or a design change to accommodate a new federal safety standard. Customers may change their specifications or quantities or may want earlier (never later) delivery dates—or they may cancel their order! Vendors supply substitute parts which don't quite fit. Components may be lost in transit or fail to pass receipt inspection.

Internal slippages and errors also exist. Incorrect routings may be specified or wrong lot sizes produced. Defects may run higher than expected, or they may go undetected until final assembly. In large shops it is not uncommon for components (or even whole orders) to be "temporarily set aside" and never found again.

For some companies, Murphy's Law (If anything can go wrong, it will.) seems to hold. Even if things are not that bad, there always seem to be deviations from the ideal quantities on a shop order. Reporting systems that summarize difficulties and deviations with respect to material and labor information are essential. They identify current problems and should reduce the magnitude of future problems.

Without accurate information on the current status of production, the master schedule would soon be invalid. Order releases would contain errors, and inventory records would be inaccurate. Production control has enough of these problems already.

The Reporting Function   Many firms still use numerous forms and paperwork to report on the status of jobs. However, with computers, bar coding, and remote terminal reporting, much of the paperwork can be reduced or eliminated. Nevertheless, some small firms may not warrant a computerized system.

Where justified, electronic reporting speeds the flow of data and permits faster updating of files. It is often tied to job progress (priority) and work center performance (capacity). Many companies have workers report directly to the computer via prepunched cards (or terminals in their area) as jobs are started and completed. Other control information is gleaned from CRTs at material control centers, inspection stations, and any other points where significant changes can occur in the status of orders. Some high-volume operations report only at specified checkpoints (milestones). Others report largely on an exception basis—that is, when deviations occur.

At a Westinghouse plant in Pennsylvania, job sheets and employee badges are bar coded in advance. Employee time and activities are then automatically bar coded into the shop floor control computer at points where the work is done. This system gives production controllers an online verification of what work is being done, what materials are being used, and what pieces must be reworked, or scrapped—and why [1:36].

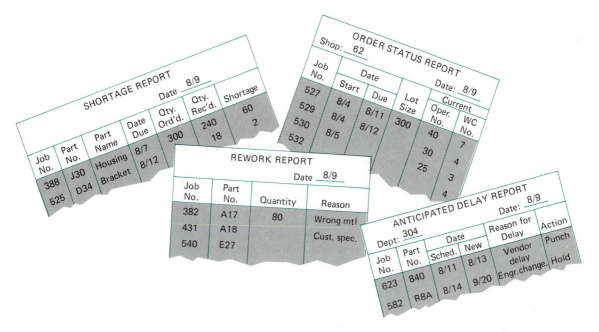

SHORTAGE REPORT Date 8/9

Job No.	Part No.	Part Name	Date Due	Qty. Ord'd.	Qty. Rec'd.	Shortage
388	J30	Housing	8/7	300	240	60
525	D34	Bracket	8/12		18	2

ORDER STATUS REPORT Shop: 62 Date: 8/9

Job No.	Date		Lot Size	Current	
	Start	Due		Oper. No.	WC No.
527	8/4	8/11	300	40	7
529	8/4	8/12		30	4
530	8/5			25	3
532					4

REWORK REPORT Date 8/9

Job No.	Part No.	Quantity	Reason
382	A17	80	Wrong mtl
431	A18		Cust. spec.
540	E27		

ANTICIPATED DELAY REPORT Dept: 304 Date: 8/9

Job No.	Part No.	Date		Reason for Delay	Action
		Sched.	New		
623	840	8/11	8/13	Vendor delay	Punch
582	R8A	8/14	9/20	Engr. change.	Hold

FIGURE 12-17   Commonly Used Status Reports

Status Reports   Figure 12-17 identifies a few of the commonly used status reports. Included is a shortage report, a rework report, a scrap report, an order status report, and an anticipated delay report. Other reports cover labor and material usage, production progress, downtime logs, completions, monthly activity, and so on. We will illustrate an input/output report in the section on capacity control.

Feedback, in the form of status reports, completes the link that makes production control activities a closed loop. It enables shop planners to be in close communication with everyone involved in an order, from purchasing and inventory control personnel to the supervisors on the shop floor. This way those involved with the entire production operation function as an integrated team.

CAPACITY CONTROL

We take up capacity control in this (new) section to emphasize the importance of separating priority and capacity problems. Many firms fail to correctly identify capacity problems. As a result, their "fix" is no solution at all. For example, assume that a shop is so loaded that some customers are getting upset with delays. Calling their orders "hot" or putting a red tag on them may placate some customers, but it won't do much to improve relations with others whose orders are displaced. Priority techniques do not solve capacity problems.

Capacity control ensures that the hours of labor and machine capacity actually delivered are in conformance with the capacity plans. This requires measurement of actual capacity output, feedback to a database, comparison with planned levels, and provision for corrective action.

As an essential element of capacity control, let us first recognize the role of lead time and other factors that affect capacity.

LEAD TIME AND OTHER RELEVANT VARIABLES

Lead time is the time interval between when an item is ordered and when it is available to be shipped. To a large extent, lead times reflect the amount of work in process. Uncontrolled lead times can result in an excessive number of jobs in process and a continuing shortage of space. Plants with poorly managed lead times are often behind schedule and unable to make accurate delivery promises. They tend to lose control over priorities and resort more to the use of expediters to make up for their lack of control.

Figure 12-18 illustrates the relationship between workload, capacity, and manufacturing lead time. Load is the *amount* of work, or backlog, on a work center. Capacity is the *rate* of work flow (in standard hours) through the work center (shown by arrows). For most work centers, capacity is relatively fixed. The pipe sizes governing the input and output rates in Fig. 12-18 suggest that the

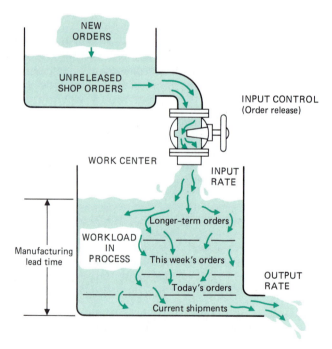

FIGURE 12-18   Lead-Time Control

input rate *could* be larger than the output rate. The input rate is limited only by how fast orders can be released. However, if work is released to a shop at a rate faster than its output rate, the work-in-process (and hence the manufacturing lead time) increases. Lead times are controlled by controlling the rate at which orders are released to the shop.

EXAMPLE 12-7

A farm machinery manufacturer has an output rate of 320 hours per week and has measured the load on his shop as follows:

Unreleased shop orders		640 hr
Work-in-process:		
Current requirements		960
Long-term orders		320
	Total	1,920 hr

(a) Find the manufacturing lead time.
(b) Comment on the inclusion of long-term orders in the lead time.

SOLUTION

(a) Lead time $= \dfrac{\text{work-in-process}}{\text{rate of output}}$

$= \dfrac{960 \text{ hr } + 320 \text{ hr}}{320 \text{ hr/week}} = 4 \text{ weeks}$

(b) Once the long-term orders are released to the shop, they become part of the work-in-process, and so they are included as "released backlog." If they contain only deferred requirements and are not required to keep the shop loaded, they should not have been released to the shop.

Production controllers are often pressured to quote manufacturing lead times (or less) to customers in order to accommodate an enthusiastic sales representative. This could be a mistake they later regret. The lead times quoted should accurately reflect not only the manufacturing lead time shown in Fig. 12-18 but also any unreleased order backlog. Unless marketing is willing to substitute the scheduled capacity of another released order in its place, the firm is promising what it cannot deliver. Overloading the capacity in this way causes a loss of credibility in the whole system.

Production analysts have found it convenient to classify lead time into the elements shown in Fig. 12-19. As suggested there, the dominant element of lead time is queue time, which is estimated to account for 70 to 90 percent of the total. Studies suggest that 10 percent or less of the lead time in an average company is actual run (working) time [10]. They strongly support the principle that a key to managing lead times is to control queue time. And queue time is, of course, a direct function of the number of orders released to the shop.

There are, however, other factors that affect capacity (and lead time). Ma-

- *Queue time* is the time a job spends in a backlog waiting for another job to be finished.
- *Setup* is the time required to adjust a machine with proper tooling for the job.
- *Run* is the time the job is actually worked on.
- *Wait* is the time a job spends waiting to be moved.
- *Move* is the actual time a job spends in transit.

FIGURE 12-19   Elements of Lead Time

chines break down and material shortages occur. Meetings, union activities, coffee breaks, and cleanup activities take time from the job. Some jobs have a high turnover or absenteeism index. All such factors require careful monitoring so that corrective action can be taken if necessary.

We turn now to two methods of measuring the capacity on a more quantitative basis: balance and input/output control.

BALANCE

Line of balance (LOB) is a control mechanism of slightly more complexity than Gantt charts; it is more suited to the monitoring of continuous systems. It is a charting and computational technique; the progress of component and subassembly parts is monitored and compared with delivery date requirements by charting the lead times ahead of final assembly. Capacity requirements planning techniques are now replacing LOB charts in many applications, so we will not cover them in detail here.

In brief, LOB control begins with a cumulative delivery schedule or objective. Purchased parts and subassembly components required to support the delivery schedule are then charted on a production plan which clearly identifies lead times required to meet the delivery schedule. The lead times in turn reflect what quantities of items should be on hand or in process at various stages, such as at weekly intervals, to meet the final shipment schedule.

The LOB chart depicts the physical number of components and subassembly parts on hand at any given time. An actual "line of balance" is then drawn as a solid line through the chart to designate the quantities of items that should be on hand at that time if the delivery schedule is to be met.

LOB is similar in concept to MRP systems with respect to time phasing subassembly and component requirements. Both approaches work backward to identify materials and capacities needed to meet delivery commitments. LOB provides a chart or graph which helps visualize the problem, but it does not offer the flexibility or responsiveness of an MRP system.

The need for balance extends beyond the specific LOB technique. This means that the workload assigned to a work center must be effectively balanced against the work center's capacity. It does not mean that assigned hours must exactly match the standard hours of capacity on a daily or weekly basis. But they should be roughly in balance over the planning period.

INPUT/OUTPUT CONTROL

A first step in controlling shop capacity is to compare the actual hours of work with the hours of work delivered by a work center. If insufficient hours are "produced," the firm may have a problem with the productivity (or perhaps the standard) of the work center. It may also signal a need for more capacity.

Output reports typically cover 12 or more weeks and are stated in standard hours. Example 12-8 illustrates a simple output control report. The planned hours of output are the average of past actual output adjusted for changes in capacity, such as overtime. Deviation is actual hours minus planned hours.

EXAMPLE 12-8 | Shop 62 has an average capacity requirement of 200 hours per week of work. Actual (standard) hours during weeks 9, 10, 11, and 12 were 180, 210, 170, and 160, respectively. Formulate an output control report showing cumulative deviation.

SOLUTION
Output Control Report: Shop 62

Hours	Week Number				
	9	10	11	12	13
Actual	180	210	170	160	
Planned	200	200	200	200	200
Cumulative deviation	−20	−10	−40	−80	

The simple output control report shown in Example 12-8 can satisfy the basic elements of control mentioned repeatedly throughout this text. *Measurement* of actual hours typically flows from labor hours and status reports. If labor data are logged into the computer via job number on a daily basis, the *feedback* process is greatly facilitated; otherwise, the data may have to be collected on cards or time forms. The *comparison* activity uses planned hours along with a maximum allowable cumulative deviation limit as a standard. The maximum deviation should be some prearranged cumulative amount, such as 1 week's average (200 hours in this case) or perhaps ½ week's average. When the cumulative deviation exceeds this limit, *corrective action* in the form of overtime, subcontracting, or perhaps revision of the master schedule is called for. (In Example 12-8, the cumulative deviation at the end of week 12 is 80 hours and does not yet exceed a week's average.)

Although the output control report is a useful measure of capacity, it does little to control lead times. In order to control lead times, the input to a shop must also be controlled, and combination input/output reports are more useful for this.

Solved Prob. 6 illustrates one such report (there are many others). In general, however, if the actual minus planned values are negative, there was less input (or output) than planned; if positive, there was more input (or output) than planned.

SUMMARY

Many U.S. firms are improving operations by automating their production systems or limiting the number of end-product options. Allen-Bradley can now produce 400 distinct products (without stopping) on an assembly line with four workers. And Chrysler has cut the number of permutations of Omni and Horizon cars from eight million to 42 [7:1]. But there are still thousands of inventory items to "track."

Production activity controls are the principles and techniques used to schedule and control production operations. Which ones are used depends on whether the system is continuous, intermittent, jobshop, or project-oriented. Key elements of priority control are order release, dispatching, and status control. Capacity control emphasizes lead-time control, balance of workload, and input/output control.

Every PAC system should be *r*ealistic, *u*nderstandable, and *n*ecessary (RUN). Loading principles suggest that not all jobs should (automatically) be released to the shop. Production control has the responsibility of releasing orders at a manageable rate so that manufacturing lead time (and work-in-process inventory) can be kept under control.

Gantt charts and schedule boards are still popular scheduling devices, but computerized methods now offer advantages for handling more data faster and more accurately.

Many firms rely largely upon priority decision rules. The critical ratio technique is becoming widely used because it provides a specific priority for each job, and updating is easy to do. For the specific assignment of jobs to machines and workers to jobs, the assignment method of linear programming has been available for some time.

Continuous processing activities require far less individual control, and reports of flow rates and efficiencies are useful. Some firms use a line-of-balance technique, but CRP systems are now eliminating the need for LOB charts. One of the best capacity control devices for intermittent systems is the input/output report.

SOLVED PROBLEMS

SCHEDULING METHODOLOGY

1 The following hours are required to complete six jobs which are routed through four work centers. The hours available at the work centers are 40 hours at W, 32 at X, 40 at Y, and 30 at Z.

	Hours Required at Work Center			
Job Number	W	X	Y	Z
A21	4	2	7	4
A22	7	—	—	8
A23	4	10	12	3
B14	—	5	6	5
B15	2	4	5	—
B16	8	1	6	7

Develop a load chart for assigning the jobs to the work centers.

Solution

Begin with the total time available at each work center, and subtract the time for each job to obtain a cumulative total of unused time. For example $40 - 4 = 36$, $36 - 7 = 29$, etc. See chart below.

Job Number	Work Center W Hours		Work Center X Hours		Work Center Y Hours		Work Center Z Hours	
	Required	Available	Required	Available	Required	Available	Required	Available
A21	4	40	2	32	7	40	4	30
A22	7	36	—	30	—	33	8	26
A23	4	29	10	30	12	33	3	18
B14	—	25	5	20	6	21	5	15
B15	2	25	4	15	5	15	—	10
B16	8	23	1	11	6	10	7	10
	Unused:	15	Unused:	10	Unused:	4	Unused:	3

A Gantt load chart could also be used to show the load on the various work centers.

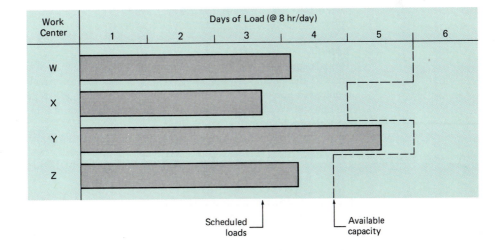

2 A firm that produces athletic supplies on an intermittent production system has the production and inventory characteristics shown below as of June 30th. Rank the items in terms of the urgency of scheduling replenishment inventories.

Item	Inventory on Hand	Released Orders (and WIP)	Demand Rate
A (soccer balls)	20 cases	30 cases	12 cases/wk
B (volleyballs)	110 cases	—	32 cases/wk
C (basketballs)	70 cases	30 cases	40 cases/wk

Solution

One method of scheduling the production of produce-to-stock inventory is to assign the highest priority to items with the lowest *runout time*.

$$\text{Runout time} = \frac{\text{inventory on hand} + \text{orders in process}}{\text{demand rate}} \tag{12-2}$$

A: $\dfrac{20 + 30}{12} = 4.2$ weeks   B: $\dfrac{110}{32} = 3.4$ weeks   C: $\dfrac{70 + 30}{40} = 2.5$ weeks

The scheduling sequence should be basketballs first, then volleyballs, then soccer balls.

3 A shop has eight shop orders that must be processed sequentially through three work centers. Each job must be finished in the same sequence in which it was started. Times (in hours) required at the various work centers are as shown below. Use Johnson's rule to develop the job sequence that will minimize the completion time over all shop orders.

Job No.	A	B	C	D	E	F	G	H
WC 1 Time	4	8	5	9	3	4	9	6
WC 2 Time	6	4	7	1	4	2	5	2
WC 3 Time	8	7	9	7	9	8	9	7

Solution

This is a special (3 WC) case of Johnson's rule, which may be used if the largest of the times at the middle work station (WC 2) is less than or equal to the smallest time required at one or both of the other two WCs. The (modified) procedure is to add the job times of WC 1 + WC 2 and of WC 2 + WC 3. Then use these combined times to solve the problem in the standard two-station approach.

Job No.	A	B	C	D	E	F	G	H
WC 1 + WC 2	10	12	12	10	7	6	14	8
WC 2 + WC 3	14	11	16	8	13	10	14	9

Now, the times are scanned, and the lowest value (6) is with the first combination (WC 1 + WC 2), so we place job F as early as possible. The next lowest (7) is also with the first combination, so job E goes second. Jobs D and H are tied for next, with D going as late as possible (last), and H going third. Continuing on, we have

1st	2d	3d	4th	5th	6th	7th	8th
F	E	H	A	C	G	B	D

4 A manufacturing coordinator has the following shop orders due to be shipped a week (5 working days) from now.

Shop Order Number	427	430	432	433	435	436
Number of Days of Work Remaining	2	4	7	6	5	3

Sequence the jobs according to priority as established by:
(a) Least slack
(b) Critical ratio

Solution

(a) The least-slack sequence is 432, 433, 435, 430, 436, 427.

(b) Critical ratio $= \dfrac{\text{time remaining}}{\text{work remaining}} = \dfrac{5 \text{ days}}{\text{work remaining}}$

SO Number	437	430	432	433	435	436
CR	$\frac{5}{2} = 2.50$	$\frac{5}{4} = 1.25$	$\frac{5}{7} = .71$	$\frac{5}{6} = .83$	$\frac{5}{5} = 1.00$	$\frac{5}{3} = 1.67$

∴ CR sequence is 432, 433, 435, 430, 436, 427.

Note: When the time remaining is constant across all jobs, the least slack and critical ratio result in the same priority.

5 Assignment linear programming A scheduler has four jobs that can be done on any of four machines with respective times as shown (minutes). Determine the allocation of jobs to machines that will result in minimum time.

		Machine		
Job	1	2	3	4
A	5	6	8	7
B	10	12	11	7
C	10	8	13	6
D	8	7	4	3

Solution

The solution methodology involves five steps.

Step 1. Subtract the smallest number in each row from all others in the row, and enter the results in the form of a new matrix.

Step 2. Using the new matrix, subtract the smallest number in each column from all others in the column, again forming a new matrix.

Step 3. Check to see if there is a zero for each row and column, and draw the minimum number of lines necessary to cover all zeros in the matrix.

Step 4. If the number of lines required is less than the number of rows, modify the matrix again by adding the smallest uncovered number to all values at line intersections and subtracting it from each uncovered number, including itself. Leave the other (lined-out) numbers unchanged.

Step 5. Check the matrix again via zero-covering lines, and continue with the modification (step 3) until the optimal assignment is obtained.

The five steps result in the following:

1. Row subtraction

	1	2	3	4
A	0	1	3	2
B	3	5	4	0
C	4	2	7	0
D	5	4	1	0

2. Column subtraction

	1	2	3	4
A	0	0	2	2
B	3	4	3	0
C	4	1	6	0
D	5	3	0	0

3. Cover all zeros

	1	2	3	4
A	0	0	2	2
B	3	4	3	0
C	4	1	6	0
D	5	3	0	0

4. Modify matrix

	1	2	3	4
A	0	0	2	3
B	2	3	2	0
C	3	0	5	0
D	5	3	0	1

5. Cover zeros again

	1	2	3	4
A	0	0	2	3
B	2	3	2	0
C	3	0	5	0
D	5	3	0	1

Optimum assignments

Job A to machine 1 at 5 min
Job B to machine 4 at 7 min
Job C to machine 2 at 8 min
Job D to machine 3 at 4 min

Note that the final allocation (circles in step 5 above) should begin with those jobs that are limited to one machine (B and D), for once they are assigned, this may constrain the assignment of the remaining jobs (A and C).

CAPACITY CONTROL

6 Work center 4, which has an average capacity of 260 hours a week, had a released backlog of 160 hours and an unreleased backlog of 180 hours as of the beginning of week 21. The planner scheduled to work off the backlog over the next 5 weeks by scheduling a 10 percent reduction in planned input, along with 6 hours of overtime each week. Actual input and output hours for the 5 weeks were as shown below. Depict this situation in an input/output report for WC 4, and determine the released backlog at the end of week 25.

Week Number	21	22	23	24	25	26
Actual Input	230	240	235	250	220	
Actual Output	265	260	270	280	280	

Solution

Planned reductions were to come from:

$$
\begin{array}{lll}
(1) & \text{Reduced input: 5 wk @ 26 hr/wk} & = \text{130 hr} \\
(2) & \text{Increased output: 5 wk @ 6 hr/wk} & = \underline{\ \ 30 \text{ hr}} \\
& & \quad\ 160 \text{ hr}
\end{array}
$$

Actual results were as shown in Fig. 12-20.

FIGURE 12-20   Input/Output Report WC 4

	Week Number	21	22	23	24	25	26
Input	Actual Hours	230	240	235	250	220	
	Planned Hours	234	234	234	234	234	260
	Cumulative Deviation, Σ (actual − planned)	−4	+2	+3	+19	+5*	
Output	Actual Hours	265	260	270	280	280	
	Planned Hours	266	266	266	266	266	260
	Cumulative Deviation, Σ (actual − planned)	−1	−7	−3	+11	+25	

* This means there were 5 hours more input than planned.

The initial released backlog (as of week 20) was 160 hours. Actual reductions came from:

$$
\begin{array}{lll}
(1) & \text{Reduced input:} & 130 - 5 = 125 \\
(2) & \text{Increased output:} & 30 + 25 = \underline{\ \ 55} \\
& & \text{Total reductions} = 180
\end{array}
$$

Net effect as of the end of week 25 was 160 hr − 180 hr = −20 hr. (*Analysis:* Five more hours of input than planned were released to the shop, so input was reduced by only 125 hours, but output was 30 more hours than planned. Therefore, all the released backlog was removed. In addition, 20 hours of the original 180 hours of unreleased backlog has been worked off.)

QUESTIONS

12-1   Describe the two major concerns of production activity control.

12-2   Identify some characteristics necessary to have a production activity control system run effectively.

12-3   What are the major activities associated with priority and capacity control?

12-4   Distinguish between forward and "set back" scheduling. Which results in a higher work-in-process inventory?

12-5   Assume that you wanted to set up some planning and control files for a shop floor control system. Your firm has 10,000 part numbers, 10 work centers, and 2 operations at each work center, and you wish to have computer capacity to handle 500 actual shop orders. Using Fig. 12-5 determine how many information fields you would need for the (a) part master file, (b) work center file, (c) routing file, (d) shop order master file, (e) shop order detail file.

12-6   Distinguish between a Gantt progress chart and a Gantt load chart.

12-7   What is a major restriction in applying Johnson's rule?

12-8   In what sense is the critical ratio technique a priority decision rule? What advantages does it hold over most other priority decision rules?

12-9   What single-criterion priority decision rule might you expect to find in use with regard to the following: (a) an airline ticket counter, (b) a hospital emergency room, (c) specification of security requirements for prison inmates, (d) delivering milk to rural areas, (e) repairing damaged missile-launching sites?

12-10   What is the major distinction between mathematical programming methods of scheduling and heuristic methods?

12-11   In assignment linear programming, how can one tell when an optimal solution has been reached?

12-12   Explain how a "planned release" in an MRP system becomes a "scheduled receipt."

12-13   How does assigning priorities by *due date* differ from assigning priorities by *critical ratio*? Identify some disadvantages of using due dates.

12-14   How does dispatching in continuous (flow) systems differ from dispatching in intermittent (order) systems?

12-15   Explain the composition of manufacturing lead time.

12-16   Why is it necessary to control lead times?

12-17   Why is input control important?

PROBLEMS

1   A piece of mining equipment requires the following times for manufacture:

	Activity	Weeks		Activity	Weeks
1	Engineering	3	5	Electrical	4
2	Purchasing	3	6	Control	1
3	Steel fabrication	1	7	Field test	2
4	Hydraulics	2	8	Packaging	1

Each of the activities must be done sequentially, except that the steel fabrication can begin 2 weeks after purchasing begins, and the hydraulics and electrical activities can be done concurrently. Construct a Gantt scheduling chart for this job.

2   A firm producing electronic signs has established the following times for the production of a sign from the receipt of a customer order. The plastic-cover work is done concurrently with other operations as shown. Use guidelines of rounding partial times off to (8-hour) days, allowing 1 day for movement between work centers and 5 days for order release.

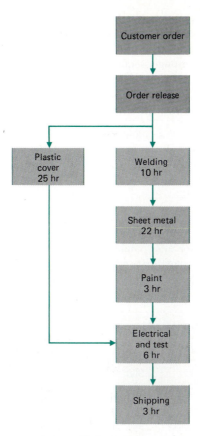

Assume that a customer order was received on day 1 and was due to be shipped on day 20. Construct a schedule, and graphically illustrate it using (a) forward scheduling and (b) backward scheduling.

3 A wood pattern shop has five shop orders that must be processed through six work centers during the coming week. The capacities of the work centers (in hours) are number 9 = 40, number 10 = 20, number 11 = 20, number 12 = 20, number 13 = 20, number 14 = 30.

Shop Order	Hours Required at Work Center					
	9	10	11	12	13	14
A	4	3	—	—	7	5
B	6	9	13	—	3	4
C	12	—	7	10	5	7
D	6	4	—	—	—	8
E	11	2	—	9	8	4

(a) Is the shop capacity sufficient to complete all jobs?
(b) Assume that the scheduling guidelines require 4 hours of move time *between* work centers (not included above). Rank the shop orders according to the longest processing (and transit) time.

4 The Ancient Maple Furniture Company has received five orders for chairs and tables that are estimated to require the production times shown. The plant is working two shifts per day. It can accommodate only one order in a given department at a given time and must follow a cutting-assembly-finishing sequence.

Order Number	Cutting (hours)	Assembly (hours)	Finishing (hours)	
75	40	32	24	96
76	16	24	8	48
77	24	24	40	88
78	8	32	24	64
79	24	32	16	72

(a) Prepare a daily Gantt chart schedule based upon the criterion of the shortest total processing time per order.
(b) How much sooner (or later) could the five orders be completed if they were scheduled on a first-come, first-served basis?

5 The following orders were received in a jobshop where scheduling is done by priority decision rules.

Job Number	Shop Calendar Date Received	Shop Calendar Date Due		Production Days Required
870	317	368	51	20
871	319	374	55	30
872	320	354	34	10
873	326	373	47	25
874	333	346	13	15

In what sequence would the jobs be ranked according to the following decision rules: (a) earliest due date, (b) shortest processing time, (c) least slack, (d) first come, first served?

6 UTEX Machinery has an automated plating shop in Houston where jobs are all sequenced first through a CM 1000 mill and then in a 600°F oven. Jobs require different times as follows:

Job	A	B	C	D	E	F	G
Mill (hr)	2	1	7	2	5	3	4
Oven (hr)	3	5	6	1	9	4	2

(a) Use Johnson's rule to develop a schedule sequence that will permit all work to be completed in the minimum amount of time.
(b) What is the total amount of time required to process the seven jobs?
(c) By how many hours would the overall time be increased if job A required 8 hours of mill time instead of 2? (Assume that the sequence could be revised before the jobs were started.)

7 Use Johnson's rule to determine the sequence that results in the minimum flow time

for the seven jobs listed below. All jobs must follow the same sequence of machine first, and then polish.

	Time Required to Do Job (min)						
	A	*B*	*C*	*D*	*E*	*F*	*G*
Machine	10	6	5	4	6	9	7
Polish	2	3	12	5	9	11	6

(a) What is the optimal sequence of jobs?

(b) What is the minimum time flow to finish these seven jobs?

8 An architectural firm schedules its work on a "continuous" calendar using priority decision rules. Today is day 103 on the calendar and the drafting department currently has eight jobs under contract with due dates and worktime remaining as follows.

TODAY'S DATE: 103

Job Designation	L14	M27	N31	O18	P38	Q21	R74	S14
Day Job Is Due	106	128	118	132	118	140	131	186
Workdays Left	1	12	15	4	11	8	20	41

(a) Use the critical ratio scheduling rule and compute the priority of each of the jobs.

(b) Which job has the highest priority?

9 A defense contractor in Chicago has six different jobs in process with the delivery requirements shown. Today is day 60, and the contractor uses a critical ratio scheduling technique. Rank the jobs according to priority, with number 1 = highest.

Job	A	B	C	D	E	F
Promised (Date Due)	60	72	67	72	65	70
Days of Work Remaining	2	2	5	4	5	6

10 A sports equipment company has a large demand for tents and sleeping bags and must now schedule production for next month. The time available and required times per unit are as shown. The sleeping bags yield a profit contribution of $10 per unit, whereas the tents provide $40 per unit. Use standard linear programming methods to determine (a) the number of bags and tents to produce and (b) the total profit contribution from the two items.

		Time Required per Unit (hr)	
	Time Available (hr)	Bags	Tents
Material preparation	800	1	2
Sewing	900	3	1

11 Collins Heating Company has four central heating installations to design within an 8-

week period (40 hours per week). It also has four capable designers, each of whom has been asked to estimate how long it would take to do each job. The work operations scheduler has compiled the estimates shown.

	Hours to Complete Job			
Designers	1	2	3	4
A	100	140	280	70
B	130	160	200	60
C	80	130	300	90
D	150	110	250	50

(a) Use assignment linear programming methods to determine how the jobs should be assigned so as to minimize the work time.
(b) Assuming that the estimates are correct, can the jobs be completed within the 8-week period without planning for overtime?
(c) Assuming that there is one designer per job and no overtime, could the work be completed in 5 weeks?
(d) In 3 weeks?

12 An electroplating shop scheduler has four jobs to schedule through a plating operation. Some jobs can be done in any one of five plating tanks, but some of the tanks are restricted to a specific use. The scheduling alternatives and variable costs of power, plating material, and labor are shown in the table. Which assignment of jobs to plating tanks will minimize the total cost?

	Plating Tank Cost ($)				
Job	1	2	3	4	5
A	120	n.a.	100	n.a.	200
B	80	70	50	130	300
C	40	70	90	n.a.	180
D	110	n.a.	150	n.a.	190

13 Indiana Equipment Company has a small shop with an output capacity of 280 hours per week. The production controller has been asked to provide a delivery estimate for a sales representative in Tampa. He generally allows 3 weeks for order release to obtain materials and tooling. The current lead-time situation is as follows:

Unreleased backlog	1,400 hr
Active orders (except current)	540 hr
Current orders	300 hr

Assuming that the controller follows a first-come, first-served policy, what is the best delivery time (in weeks) he can offer?

14 A work center at Zag Electric has a planned output capacity of 140 hours per week over the next 12 weeks. The actual hours of output for the past 6 weeks were 130, 150, 120, 110, 115, and 135. Zag Electric uses a control system which signals corrective action

when the cumulative deviation exceeds one-half of the planned average over the last three periods.

(a) Construct an output control report.

(b) When is corrective action required?

15 The Automated Billing Equipment Co. produces electric meter reading equipment which automatically transmits meter readings to a billing center at preset times. Production controllers in the factory have estimated the standard hours of capacity requirements at an assembly work station over the next quarter as shown below. The company uses an MRP system with output controls designed to signal corrective action when the cumulative deviation exceeds one-half the weekly average as computed from the forecast.

Week Number	1	2	3	4	5	6	7	8	9	10	11	12
Estimated Hours	370	340	290	350	360	410	320	350	330	340	380	360

Suppose the company plans to produce at a steady rate equal to the average estimated requirement.

(a) Formulate an estimated-requirements graph showing the average requirement as a dotted line.

(b) Assume that actual standard hours delivered over the first 8 weeks are 360, 310, 340, 280, 360, 300, 270, 370. Construct an output-control chart, and determine the cumulative deviation.

(c) Is corrective action warranted? If so, when?

16 A project team leader has four tasks that must be completed by personnel having different skill levels for each task. Times are as shown.

		Minutes to Complete Task		
Worker	1	2	3	4
A	2	7	3	11
B	5	9	12	4
C	8	10	6	7
D	4	6	5	8

(a) Use an assignment linear programming program to assign personnel to tasks so as to minimize the total time required.

(b) Assume the project leader has learned that materials for task 4 are not available. Reassign the workers so as to minimize the time required to complete tasks 1, 2, and 3 (only).

(c) Use the data from (a) and assume that materials are sufficient to complete all four tasks except worker A cannot be assigned to task 1 nor can worker B be assigned to task 4. In addition, a fifth worker (worker E) is available to work on either task 2 or task 3 with times of 3 minutes and 4 minutes, respectively. Now, what is the optimal assignment and optimal total time?

REFERENCES

[1] American Production and Inventory Control Society, *P&IM Review 1986 Reference Guide and Directory*, T.D.A. Publications, Hollywood, FL.

[2] Foxen, Richard: "Scheduling and Loading," in *Shop Floor Controls*, American Production and Inventory Control Society, Falls Church, VA, 1973.

[3] Griffin, K. R.: "Job Shop Scheduling," in *Shop Floor Controls*, American Production and Inventory Control Society, Falls Church, VA, 1973.

[4] Harty, James D.: "Controlling Production Capacity," in *Shop Floor Controls*, American Production and Inventory Control Society, Falls Church, VA, 1973.

[5] Johnson, S. M.: "Optimal Two and Three Stage Production Schedules with Set-up Time Included," *Naval Research Logistics Quarterly*, vol. 1, no. 1, March 1954.

[6] Koten, John: "Giving Buyers Wide Choices May Be Hurting Auto Makers," *The Wall Street Journal*, Dec. 15, 1983, p. 31.

[7] Sease, Douglas R.: "How U.S. Companies Devise Ways to Meet Challenge from Japan," *The Wall Street Journal*, Sept. 16, 1986, p. 1.

[8] *Shop Floor Controls*, An APICS Training Aid, Milwaukee APICS Chapter.

[9] Wagner, Harvey M.: *Principles of Management Science*, Prentice-Hall, Englewood Cliffs, NJ, 1970.

[10] Wight, Oliver: "Input/Output Control: A Real Handle on Lead Time," in *Shop Floor Controls*, American Production and Inventory Control Society, Falls Church, VA, 1973.

[11] Wight, Oliver: *Production and Inventory Management in the Computer Age*, Cahners Books, Boston, 1974.

SELF QUIZ: CHAPTER 12

Part I True/False [1 point each = 6]

1. __T__ One of the objectives of PAC systems is to ensure that the correct quantities of materials are in the right place at the right time.
2. __F__ Three of the most important capacity planning activities are order release, dispatching, and status control.
3. __T__ Detailed scheduling of manufacturing jobs as they arrive from customer orders is usually not a satisfactory method of scheduling.
4. __F__ Scheduling techniques that fail to take account of due dates are referred to as "backward scheduling" methods.
5. __F__ Input/output reports are among the most widely used (and most useful) tools for priority control.
6. __F__ If a firm's shops are overloaded and their customers are complaining about delays, they could probably solve their problems by red tagging "hot" jobs and using some priority control techniques.

Part II Problems [3 points each = 9. Calculate and select your answer.]

1. In a quality control activity each of seven jobs must be sequenced through inspection and repair before the next one is started. Using Johnson's rule, the minimum time to do all seven jobs is:
   (a) 38 hr
   (b) 44 hr
   (c) 46 hr
   (d) 52 hr
   (e) None of the above.

Job	A	B	C	D	E	F	G
Inspection (hr)	5	7	2	1	8	3	16
Repair (hr)	4	9	7	2	2	9	5

2. Today is day 68 on the shop calendar of a job shop that has the due dates and amount of work remaining as shown. If the jobs are ranked according to the critical ratio method, the jobs in order of highest priority are:
   (a) C B E F A D
   (b) B C A D F E
   (c) D A F E B C
   (d) E C B D A F
   (e) None of the above.

Job	A	B	C	D	E	F
Due on Day	73	75	70	78	88	83
Workdays Remaining	2	15	6	3	20	12

3. A prototype electronics shop has an average output capacity of 240 hours per week. However, it also has a (released) backlog of 80 hours of work. The supervisor is planning to keep the incoming work at 240 hours per week over the next 5 weeks, but work off the backlog by using equal amounts of overtime during the next 4 weeks. If actual input and output hours turned out to be those shown below, what is the backlog at the end of week 16?
   (a) 5 hr
   (b) 15 hr
   (c) 20 hr
   (d) 30 hr
   (e) None of the above.

Week No.	12	13	14	15	16
Input: Actual hours	280	230	200	235	260

Week No.	12	13	14	15	16
Output: Actual hours	250	270	265	250	230

PART THREE
MAINTAINING EFFECTIVE OPERATIONS

PREVIEW: CONTROLLING OPERATIONS

Quality goods and services at competitive prices do not automatically emerge from organizations. They result from operations that are carefully controlled. Part Three of the text completes our study of operations management by focusing upon the operations themselves, with emphasis upon quality control, maintenance, and cost-control activities.

ANALYSIS OF MANUFACTURING, SERVICE, AND PROJECT OPERATIONS (Chapter 13)

Chapter 13 reviews some methods of evaluating ongoing operations and includes three widely used techniques for analyzing manufacturing, service, and project activities. These are learning curves, queuing theory, and CPM/PERT (for project management).

QUALITY ASSURANCE (Chapter 14)

Nearly every manager has some quality control responsibilities. Chapter 14 emphasizes the meaning of quality and the techniques available to managers for ensuring that quality goods and services are produced.

MAINTENANCE AND COST CONTROL (Chapter 15)

Any viable organization must maintain both its facilities and its people. Maintenance and cost control are two key activities that affect the economic success of an organization. Chapter 15 first discusses underlying principles of maintenance and suggests some approaches to achieve maintenance objectives. The latter part of the chapter then explains the use of cost standards. Both are vital.

A STRATEGY FOR FUTURE OPERATIONS (Chapter 16)

The final chapter (Chapter 16) extracts some of the strategic variables we have discussed in the text and offers some brief thoughts about the role of those variables in the future. At this point you may wish to return to the schematic model of operations (from Chapter 1) that we have been building upon throughout the text.

CHAPTER 13
ANALYSIS OF MANUFACTURING, SERVICE, AND PROJECT OPERATIONS

OPERATIONS ANALYSIS AND CONTROL

Managerial responsibilities certainly do not end with the design or even the smooth operation of a production system. Business systems are dynamic—and even "established" and "secure" operations need constant analysis and monitoring. One need only look to the textile, steel, plastics, and electronic industries to see that competition can be brutal. Many operations fail.

Focus of This Chapter   This chapter focuses upon some variables that are strategically important for maintaining and improving operations. We begin by verifying the need for this type of analysis, and noting how the concepts of priority and capacity provide a useful framework for analyzing operations. Then we draw some comparisons among manufacturing, service, and project activities.

Although a wide range of quantitative methods can be useful for analyzing and controlling operations, we have already discussed many of them in previous chapters. Thus we shall limit our coverage here to a few techniques that have not been used previously, but still have widespread applicability. These are learning curves, queuing models, and CPM/PERT. *Learning curves* are useful for anticipating productivity improvements in both manufacturing and service systems. *Queuing models* are especially useful for studying delays and capacity effects, and they also have applications in manufacturing and service activities. Finally, *CPM* and *PERT* are well-known techniques for managing and controlling nearly all of the resources used in projects.

OPERATIONS ANALYSIS: WHAT IS IT?

Before considering some specific approaches to analyzing operations, let us first explore the meaning of the term in more detail.

> **Operations analysis** is the use of analytical methods to systematically study data relating to the productivity of operations over time.

As suggested in Fig. 13-1, the operations of concern here include the full range of manufacturing activities, service activities, and one-time projects.

The *analytical methods* used to study operations range from single algebra and cost analysis to more complex computer simulations of whole systems. Having an accurate and current database is, obviously, quite important.

The use of *data* sometimes involves abstracting a problem from an overall (macro) environment and breaking it down into its component (micro) parts in order to study them in isolation. The final solution must then be synthesized and implemented to complete the macro-micro-macro cycle. For example, if deliveries do not meet scheduled output, the waiting times at each work center may

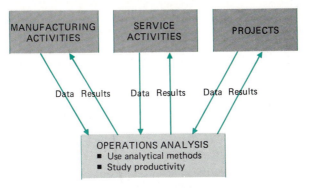

FIGURE 13-1   Operations Analysis Relies upon Data

have to be analyzed. Changes in releasing or routing work at individual work centers may be proposed. Then the total system may have to be reevaluated to ensure all the interaction effects are taken into account.

The concept of *productivity* is central to analyzing operations because it is a measure of the effectiveness of the production (or transformation) process. Recall that productivity relates the value of outputs to the cost of the inputs. Although benefits and costs are commonly measured in economic values, other measures of productivity such as units shipped per number of employees, or scheduled production compared to actual production, are also useful. We shall review some commonly used measures of performance for manufacturing organizations in a later section.

A unifying concept underlying the analysis of ongoing operations is the *focus on time.* Insofar as resources can be used to enhance the organization's economic value over time, much of operations analysis is concerned with making the most effective use of resources over time.

Operations control follows to ensure that the redesigned system (or solution) conforms to the original plan or goal. As with any control, the monitoring effort here involves the standard elements of measurement, feedback, comparison with a standard, and correction when necessary.

OPERATIONS ANALYSIS: WHY DO IT?

It is perhaps self-evident that all organizational operations (manufacturing, service, or projects) should be efficient and productive. But a careful look at the current state of the U.S. economy suggests that better analysis of ongoing operations is not only desirable, but vital to survival. A couple of examples will illustrate.

Manufacturing Activities   Alexander Graham Bell was one of many pioneering inventors whose work led to the industrialization of America. And his legacy, American Telephone and Telegraph Company, has taken its place along with other industrial giants founded by men like Edison, Westinghouse, DuPont, and Ford. So it was a shock to some when, in the mid 1980s, AT&T announced that it was transferring its main telephone production plant to Singapore. Writing in the *KKC Brief* of the Japan Institute for Social and Economic Affairs, Hajime Karatsu referred to the announcement as astonishing, saying it "signaled nothing less than the beginning of America's deindustrialization" [3].

Karatsu went on to point out that telephone manufacturing is following the same pattern as did automobiles, TV sets, computer parts, and VCRs. No sooner do new technologies start to create jobs in the United States than the work is shipped overseas. "Improvident American management has shot itself in the foot," concludes Karatsu. To substantiate that statement, he calls attention to the Japanese and Korean automobile and TV plants in the United States:

> Why then is there such a difference in productivity, quality, and cost? American executives should think about this. Japanese manufacturers are able to make a profit when they locate in the United States, but American manufacturers have to move abroad to beat the competition. The conclusion is inescapable: the problem lies in American management.

Manufacturing is of critical importance to American firms. It still delivers the bulk of our own goods and gives us exports that help offset trade imbalances. But if the manufacturing base of our economy is to survive and improve, *manufacturing management must be improved.*

Service Activities As a supplier of steel, electrical, and other manufactured products, the Pittsburgh area has, in the past, contributed significantly to the industrial base of the United States. But times are changing. Like many other "heavy industrial" cities, the employment base in Pittsburgh is shifting from a manufacturing to a service-based economy. Many of the high-paying (unionized) jobs in the mills and factories are either being phased out or are being taken over by mechanical robots. Over a recent 5-year period, more than 100,000 workers in steel and related industries have lost their jobs. This is the equivalent of 60 percent of Pittsburgh's manufacturing employment [1].

Industrial centers across the nation are facing a similar restructuring. About 73 percent of all U.S. workers are now employed in service industries, 24 percent in industrial, and 3 percent in agricultural [6]. And with the loss of 20,000–30,000 manufacturing jobs each month, some analysts figure manufacturing employment will drop to less than 20 percent before too long [3].

The structure of our economy is indeed changing. Services employ more people, but they don't create physical products that have asset values and can be exported in the same manner as goods. Thus they don't do as much to offset trade deficits. (In 1985, the United States became a net debtor nation for the first time in 71 years. The following year, the "net debt" of the United States became the largest of any country in the world.)

Service sector productivity is generally assumed to be lower than manufacturing productivity [3]. This effect, coupled with the decline of exports in the manufacturing sector, creates an even greater imbalance of trade, which in turn weakens the financial stability of the country. At the firm level, the inefficiencies also waste human resources and leave service firms vulnerable to more disruptive changes in their employment. So for many reasons, analyzing and *improving service activities is also important.*

Projects Projects comprise one-time production activities, anything from bringing a new product onto the market to the construction of a space platform. In the past, some major projects have been so far behind schedule and over budget that project managers (including the U.S. government) have insisted that contractors use established project management techniques. The two most widely used techniques are CPM and PERT, which will be taken up in the latter part of the chapter.

STRATEGIC VARIABLES IN ANALYZING OPERATIONS

A *strategy* is a plan for using an organization's capabilities to accomplish competitive objectives. For example, a strategy for a small manufacturer may be to improve customer service and enhance market share. *Tactics* are the means used to carry out the strategies. The manufacturer may achieve the strategy by taking advantage of the firm's more flexible manufacturing techniques to reduce lead times in order to secure orders that might otherwise go to competition.

The strategic variables to consider in analyzing operations are not significantly different from those we have been working with throughout the text. This section reviews those factors as they relate to maintaining effective manufacturing, service, and project activities.

PRIORITY AND CAPACITY FACTORS

Figure 13-2 depicts the strategic planning and analysis process in schematic form. Note that the major strategic variables arise from the *priorities* flowing from the competitive market (shown on the left) and the *capacities*, or organizational strengths of the individual firm (shown on the right). This is consistent with the framework we have been using all along. And, as we have seen earlier, the organizational entity must remain economically viable with respect to its industry characteristics as well as its own productivity and cost/volume relationships.

Strategic Focus Although strategic planning is important to all divisions of an organization, our emphasis here is on setting and implementing strategies for operations. Tailoring strategies to specific business segments and designated time frames is important [10]. Studies of numerous companies by Wickham Skinner

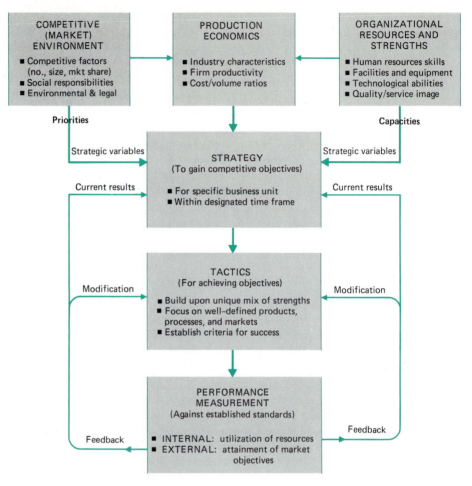

FIGURE 13-2 Operational Strategy and Tactics*

also suggest some useful guidelines for implementing strategies [8]. Skinner's work has given rise to the *focused factory* concept: The more successful operational strategies focus upon a limited range of products, processes, and markets. This concentration fosters a better knowledge of the particular market and enhances the organizational skills needed to compete in that market.

Much of operations analysis is concerned with measuring performance and suggesting modifications to the tactics being used to implement the strategies. Standards, such as cost and quality standards, are obviously essential for measuring performance toward operational goals.

* Portions of Figure 13-2 have been suggested and/or modified from [7, 8, and 9].

ANALYSIS OF GOODS VERSUS SERVICES SYSTEMS

Nature of Product   We have noted previously that value can be stored in goods whereas services are less tangible products and convey value directly to consumers as they are produced. Moreover, services frequently involve a social interaction with a psychological or emotional value extremely difficult to quantify [5:108]. This transitory and intangible nature of the product makes cost, productivity, quality, and other characteristics of services more difficult to measure than for goods.

Facility versus Personal Emphasis   With goods, once the quality is built into the product, it resides there as a measurable characteristic. But the quality of services can be less stable—especially if the services are strongly people-based. Figure 13-3 illustrates the range of people-based and facility-based services.

    Equipment-based services tend to be the most predictable and measurable— and the most subject to control. *People-based services* are more dependent upon the individual skill or knowledge levels of the provider, and are more variable in the quality of output. Thus we might expect more variability in the quality of service from an entertainer or stockbroker than from an electric utility.

Areas of Concern: Goods versus Services   We have noted that goods-producing facilities are concerned primarily with tangible *materials,* and with the quantities and qualities of the physical output. In services, consumers are more fully integrated as participants of the service delivery system itself. Services thus focus on

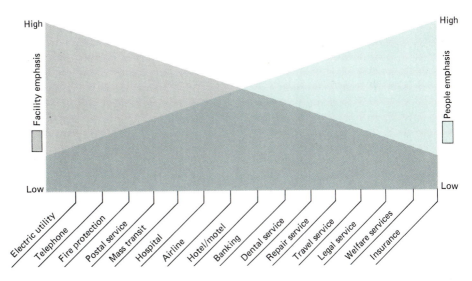

FIGURE 13-3   Facility Use and Personal Contact Emphasis in Services

GOODS	Primary Area of Concern	SERVICES
■ Influenced largely by *raw materials, labor* supply, and *inventory* considerations	Location and layout	■ Influenced strongly by location and convenience of *customers*
■ Interface *with machines* ■ May require technical skill ■ Motivation is important	Human resource inputs	■ Interface *with customers* ■ Requires more interpersonal skills ■ Training is important
■ Number of *units*	Forecasting	■ Number of *customers*
■ Availability and timing of *materials* that are built into the product	Inventory management	■ Availability and timing of *supplies consumed* by customer
■ Gross quantities and types of *products* produced ■ Specific *end items* to be produced	Aggregate planning and master scheduling	■ Gross quantities and types of *customers served* ■ Specific *types* of customers to be served
■ Flow of *materials* and scheduling of *facility* time	Material and capacity planning	■ Flow of *customers* and scheduling of *personnel* time
■ Priority rules applied to *materials* and *jobs* ■ Input-output control of *hours* (and *units*) *produced*	Production activity control	■ Priority rules applied to *customers* ■ Input-output control of *hours* (and *customers*) *served*
■ Quality inherent in stored product	Quality control	■ Quality in the service and process (e.g., time, environment)
■ Preventive and repair activities on equipment and product	Maintenance	■ Care and attention to individual performing the service

FIGURE 13-4   Operations Analysis and Control in Goods versus Services Systems

the flows and attention given to *customers*, so timing of delivery, procedures used to serve customers, and environmental conditions that prevail take on more importance. Figure 13-4 reviews some of the major areas of concern in analyzing production operations. Note the strong emphasis on measuring materials (also jobs and end items) in goods manufacturing versus the emphasis on customer interaction and flow time in service activities.

PERFORMANCE MEASURES

IN MANUFACTURING SYSTEMS

As suggested in Fig. 13-2, performance measurement is a vital step in planning and implementing an operational strategy. This includes measures of labor productivity, material costs, return on capital, inventory turnover, quality, maintenance effectiveness, and a host of other measures. While we cannot attempt to identify and discuss the myriad of possible measures, Fig. 13-5 does illustrate some measures relevant to production and inventory control. In general, the

	FUNC-TIONAL AREA	PERFORMANCE LEVEL FOR MONTH OF									
		Sept.	Oct.	Nov.	Dec.	Jan.	Feb.	Mar.	Apr.	May	June
TOP MANAGEMENT PLANNING	Sales plan	59	96	80	88	95	80	98	93	93	92
	Production plan	95	84	85	87	84	89	94	98	95	94
OPERATIONS MANAGEMENT PLANNING	Master schedule	95	84	80	83	87	92	93	90	92	98
	Materials plan	97	96	93	95	97	98	99	96	97	96
	Capacity plan				70	78	84	92	90	94	93
DATABASE	Bills of material	99	99	99	97	95	99	99	99	98	98
	Inventory control	97	87	92	91	84	95	92	95	96	96
	Routings	98	98	97	93	99	98	97	98	98	98
OPERATIONS MANAGEMENT EXECUTION	Purchasing	62	64	68	76	65	77	71	75	89	90
	Shop floor control	94	97	93	94	94	84	84	91	98	96
	Delivery performance	86	89	89	92	90	89	89	91	94	95
PERFORMANCE	Total	882	894	876	896	968	985	1008	1016	1043	1046
	Average	88	89	88	90	88	90	92	93	95	95
	Class	B	B	B	A	B	A	A	A	A	A

FIGURE 13-5   Performance History for Equipment Manufacturing Firm in Iowa*

numbers report the accuracy or percentage of achievement of various functional areas to a prearranged standard (such as, percentage accuracy of inventory records or BOM's).

The performance measures illustrated in Fig. 13-5 were suggested by an industrial consultant (David W. Buker, Inc.) who assisted the manufacturer in implementing an MRP II system. Work begins with a broad-based sales department forecast, from which a business plan, sales plan, and production plan are prepared.

A monthly sales forecast by product line is then developed using a worksheet that shows sales history for master-scheduled products for the past 3 years. This forecast covers a 13-month period. As each new month arrives, the thirteenth

* *Source*: "Class A MRP II at Ritchie Industries, Inc.," David W. Buker, Inc., Antioch, IL.

month is "rolled" into the plan and the system generates a summary giving the number of units and dollars expected by month. Then the business plan and sales forecast are matched and brought into agreement.

The master production schedule and material-requirements plan flow from the business plan, and the capacity plan is developed to show the standard hours of work required by each work center (by week). Daily work center schedules are developed in support of the master schedule. Performance reports are generated throughout the system to measure everything from master schedule accuracy to the labor hours used in various work centers.

Monthly meetings are held by the executive vice president with each functional area department head. If any performance is outside the predetermined criteria, the problems are discussed and action plans are developed to improve the performance. (When average performance equals or exceeds 90 percent, the firm qualifies for a class "A" rating.)

IN SERVICE SYSTEMS

Many performance measures in service activities are similar to those in manufacturing; however, less emphasis is placed on materials, and more emphasis is placed on customer satisfaction and on labor productivity.

The standards used at Cavanaugh's Motor Inns in Washington typify some of the more useful service industry standards. The company's main computer has preprogrammed standards for such items as number of housekeepers needed to accommodate various occupancy levels, restaurant supply costs, and utility costs. Data from all activities, such as guest registrations, meals served, and housekeepers on duty, is fed into the computer daily. The computer then compares the current levels of operations with preestablished standards and provides appropriate managers with comparative performance data on a daily basis. Then, for example, if the number of housekeepers is less than is warranted by the number of guests being housed, an adjustment is made immediately so that the quality of service is fully maintained.

The system at Cavanaugh's is so current that the company president normally has the previous day's occupancy, cost, and performance data on his desk at the beginning of each work day. (In fact, he can even get the data on his personal computer at home before he leaves for work if he wishes!) The system enables Cavanaugh's management to make useful comparisons among inns in different cities, as well as comparisons of current performance levels with those of previous months (or years).

We move on now to the three quantitative techniques mentioned at the start of the chapter—all of which relate closely to the effective use of time. Learning is a direct function of time, and queues form because of the imbalance between demand and service times. In addition, networks are time-oriented planning and control techniques. Time is indeed a key measure of performance, and a firm's ability to manage time reflects directly upon its costs, productivity, and quality.

LEARNING CURVE EFFECTS IN MANUFACTURING AND SERVICE SYSTEMS

Learning or *improvement curve effects* are the reductions in time per unit to perform specified activities. As the number of repetitions of doing a task increases, improvement results from the development of individual skills, plus other factors such as better organization of work, improved methods, and enhanced work environment. Learning-curve information is useful for planning and scheduling work, budgeting costs, negotiating price and delivery of purchased items, and pricing the firm's own products.

The improvement effect is normally expressed in terms of the percentage of time it takes to complete the unit which represents a *doubling* of output.[1] For example, if an activity followed an 80 percent learning curve and required 100 hours for the first unit, the second would take 80 hours, the fourth 64 hours, and the eighth 51.2 hours, as shown in Fig. 13-6.

Mathematically, the number of direct labor hours required to produce the Nth unit of a product Y_N, is exponentially related to the time to produce the first unit, Y_1, by the expression

[1] This approach to the learning curve effect is based on the Boeing formula, which states that each time the production quantity doubles, the number of *unit worker-hours* is reduced at a constant rate. Another commonly used approach states that each time the production quantity doubles, the *cumulative average number of unit worker-hours* is reduced at a constant rate. The two formulas yield similar but not identical results.

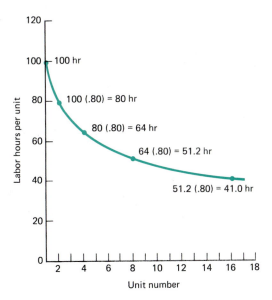

FIGURE 13-6 Eighty Percent Learning Curve

Natural Logs

LC = Learning Curve

$$Y_N = Y_1 N^X \tag{13-1}$$

where Y_N = time to produce Nth unit
Y_1 = time to produce first unit
N = unit number
$X = \dfrac{\text{log of learning } \% \; (lc)}{\log 2}$

$$LC = e^{\left[\left(\frac{Log\ 2}{Log\ N}\right)\left(Log\ Y_N - Log\ Y_1\right)\right]}$$

EXAMPLE 13-1

Production of a certain type of television series program follows an 80 percent learning curve and requires 100 hours to complete the first unit. Estimate the time required for the fourth unit of the series.

SOLUTION

$$Y_N = Y_1 N^X$$

where Y_1 = 100
N = 4
$X = \dfrac{\log .80}{\log 2} = -.322$ ← *natural logs*

$$Y_4 = 100(4)^{-.322} = \frac{100}{(4)^{.322}} = 64 \text{ hr}$$

The exponential nature of the function suggests that it would appear as a straight line on log-log paper, which it does. Calculations involving exponentials can become tedious, but fortunately coefficients of learning percentages in the common range of 70 percent to 98 percent have been developed which minimize the computational effort required. Selected values from such tables are provided in Appendix H. To use the tables, first express the desired unit number as a percentage of a base unit with known time:

$$\text{Percentage of base} = \frac{\text{desired unit number}}{\text{known base number}} \tag{13-2}$$

Then enter the table row corresponding to the percentage of base, go over to the column relevant to the specified learning percentage, and read off the learning coefficient L. The time to produce the desired unit, Y_N, is then

$$Y_N = Y_B(L) \tag{13-3}$$

where Y_B = base unit time
L = learning coefficient

EXAMPLE 13-2

The labor component of a ship construction activity required 12,000 worker days for the first project, and the firm has now received an order for three additional ships. Assuming that a 90 percent learning curve applies, how many worker days may be expected for the third unit?

SOLUTION

Express the unknown unit as a percentage of the base unit:

$$\text{Percentage of base} = \frac{\text{desired unit number}}{\text{known base number}} = \frac{\text{unit 3}}{\text{unit 1}} = \frac{3}{1} = 300\%$$

Determine the appropriate coefficient from Appendix H and multiply it by the base unit time.

$$Y_N = Y_B(L)$$

$$= (12,000)(.8462)$$

$$= 10,154 \text{ worker days}$$

The learning curve is applicable primarily in labor-intensive industries, for instance, those with assembly work. Continued improvement often extends over a long period of time (perhaps years), although the curve may level off in some cases. For example, highly routine activities may eventually be converted to robotic operations, which tend to operate at a constant pace.

When substantial changes are introduced to the routine work pattern, they may cause changes in the curve and temporarily increase the time (and costs). The expectation is that the changes will generate long-term savings that outweigh the temporary learning cost.

QUEUING MODELS FOR MANUFACTURING AND SERVICE SYSTEMS

Queuing theory is a quantitative (mathematical) approach to the analysis of systems that involve waiting lines, or queues. Examples range from supermarket checkout counters to banking activities and manufacturing jobs awaiting processing. The waiting lines may form even though the system (facility) has enough capacity, *on the average*, to handle the demand. This is because the arrival times and service times for the customers (jobs) are random and variable.

The *objective of queuing analysis* is to evaluate the service and the costs of a facility so as to maximize its usefulness. This often results in minimizing the total costs associated with the idle time of facilities or services versus the waiting time costs of employees or customers. Numerous computer software programs are available for queuing analysis. Calculations typically seek to estimate:

- System utilization ($\% U$) or average usage rate of capacity
- Mean number of customers in the queue N_q or in the system N_s
- Mean time customers spend in the queue T_q or in the system T_s
- Related idle facility and waiting time costs

	SINGLE PHASE			MULTIPLE PHASE				
	Input Source	Customers in Queue	Service Facility	Input Source	Customers in Queue	Service Facility	Customers in Queue	Service Facility
SINGLE CHANNEL	S →	• • • • •	A_1 →	S →	• • • •	A_1 →	• • • • •	A_2 →
MULTIPLE CHANNEL	S →	• • <	A_1 → B_1 → C_1 →	S →	• • • <	A_1 → B_1 → C_1 →	• • • • A_2 → • • B_2 → • • • C_2 →	

FIGURE 13-7   Types of Queuing Systems

Figure 13-7 illustrates the structure of four variations of queuing systems. The simplest of these is a single-channel, single-phase system. Multiple-channel, single-phase systems, such as those found at banks and toll-road pay stations, have more than one service facility. Multiple-phase systems incorporate two or more service activities and are more difficult to analyze mathematically. Simulation is often the most feasible technique for analysis of multiple-phase systems.

As depicted in Fig. 13-7, the most relevant characteristics of queuing systems are:

- *Input source.* This may be finite or infinite, and it generates customer arrivals, which are assumed to follow a Poisson distribution rate (λ units per period) unless specified otherwise.
- *Customers.* They form in a queue length that can theoretically vary from zero to infinity, unless the model used assumes a limited queue length. Customers are allocated to service facilities according to a dispatching rule called the *queue discipline.* A first-in, first-out discipline is assumed unless otherwise stated.
- *Service rate.* The service rate μ must be greater than the arrival rate λ or the queue can become infinite. *Service rate* (units serviced per period) is also Poisson-distributed, but analysis often concerns the reciprocal of service rate, which is service time (time per unit). Poisson service rates have negative exponential service times, which offer a strong probability of short service times, but allow for an occasional task that far exceeds the average time. Thus, a Poisson service rate of 5 units per hour has a negative exponential distribution time of 60 minutes per 5 units, or 12 minutes per unit.

SINGLE-CHANNEL, SINGLE-PHASE SYSTEMS

We will begin our inquiry of queuing systems with the simplest model, a single-phase, single-channel queuing model. Other assumptions are an infinite number of customers and unlimited waiting-line length, Poisson arrivals, and negative exponential service times. The queue discipline shall be first in, first out, with no defections from the waiting line allowed.

EXAMPLE 13-3

An equipment service facility has Poisson arrival and service rates and operates on a first-come, first-served queue discipline. Requests for service average λ = three per day. The facility can service an average of μ = six machines per day. Find the:
(a) Utilization factor (percentage U) of the service facility
(b) Mean time, T_s, in the system
(c) Mean number, N_s, in the system
(d) Mean waiting time, T_q, in the queue
(e) Probability, P, of finding n = 2 machines in the system
(f) Expected mean number, N_q, in the queue
(g) Percentage of time the service facility is idle (percentage I)

SOLUTION

(a) Utilization factor:

$$\% \ U = \frac{\text{mean arrival rate}}{\text{mean service rate}} = \frac{\lambda}{\mu} \tag{13-4}$$

$$= \frac{3}{6} = 50\%$$

(b) Mean time in the system:

$$T_s = \frac{1}{\text{mean service rate} - \text{mean arrival rate}} = \frac{1}{\mu - \lambda} \tag{13-5}$$

$$= \frac{1}{6 - 3} = \frac{1}{3} \text{ day}$$

(c) Mean number in the system:

$$N_s = (\text{mean time in system})(\text{mean arrival rate})$$

$$= \left(\frac{1}{\mu - \lambda}\right)\lambda = \frac{\lambda}{\mu - \lambda} \tag{13-6}$$

$$= \frac{3}{6 - 3} = 1 \text{ machine}$$

(d) Mean waiting time in the queue:

$$T_q = \text{mean time in system} - \text{service time}$$

$$= \frac{1}{\mu - \lambda} - \frac{1}{\mu} = \frac{\lambda}{\mu(\mu - \lambda)} \tag{13-7}$$

$$= \frac{1}{6 - 3} - \frac{1}{6} = \frac{1}{6} \text{ day}$$

(e) Probability of $n = 2$ machines in the system:

$$P_n = \text{(probability of no others)(probability of two)}$$

$$= \left(1 - \frac{\lambda}{\mu}\right)\left(\frac{\lambda}{\mu}\right)^n \tag{13-8}$$

$$= \left(1 - \frac{3}{6}\right)\left(\frac{3}{6}\right)^2 = .125$$

(f) Mean number in the queue:

$$N_q = \text{(mean number in system)} - \text{(mean number being served)}$$

$$= \frac{\lambda}{\mu - \lambda} - \frac{\lambda}{\mu} = \frac{\lambda^2}{\mu(\mu - \lambda)} \tag{13-9}$$

$$= \frac{3^2}{6(6 - 3)} = \frac{1}{2} \text{ machine}$$

(g) Percentage of idle time:

$$\%I = \text{total} - \text{percentage utilization} \tag{13-10}$$

$$= 100 - \%U$$

$$= 100\% - 50\% = 50\%$$

CONSTANT SERVICE RATES

When customers or pieces of equipment are processed according to a fixed or mechanically timed cycle, as in some machine-paced services, constant service times result. Automated services such as telephone stock-market reports and car washes often have constant service rates. Constant rates result in a certain, rather than uncertain, time requirement in the system and reduce the mean waiting time and number in the queue by half. When service rates are constant, Eq. (13-7) and Eq. (13-9) are modified as follows. [Constancy is designated by the subscript (c).] The mean waiting time is

$$T_{q(c)} = \frac{\lambda}{2\mu(\mu - \lambda)} \tag{13-11}$$

and the mean number in the queue is

$$N_{q(c)} = \frac{\lambda^2}{2\mu(\mu - \lambda)} \tag{13-12}$$

Under constant service rates, the mean time in the system, $T_{s(c)}$, is the mean waiting time in the queue plus the service time, or $T_{q(c)} + 1/\mu$. The mean number in the system, $N_{s(c)}$, is the mean number in the queue plus the mean number in the service facility, or $N_{q(c)} + \lambda/\mu$.

EXAMPLE 13-4

Metropolitan Collection Company (MCC) garbage trucks currently wait an average of 6 minutes each trip before being able to dump their load. MCC is considering hauling to a different collection center at an extra cost of $8 per trip for each truck. The new center can process the loads at a constant rate of 30 units per hour. Arrivals at the new center will be Poisson-distributed, with an average rate of 24 loads per hour. The system is a single-channel, single-phase system with unlimited queue length. If waiting time for the trucks is valued at $200 per hour, how much of a savings per hour would result?

SOLUTION

The mean waiting time at the new center is estimated as

$$T_{w(c)} = \frac{\lambda}{2\mu(\mu - \lambda)} = \frac{24}{2(30)(30 - 24)} = .067 \text{ hr}$$

Current waiting cost/trip: $\left(\frac{6 \text{ min}}{\text{trip}}\right) \left(\frac{\text{hr}}{60 \text{ min}}\right) \left(\frac{\$200}{\text{hr}}\right) = \$20.00$

Less: New waiting cost/trip: $\left(\frac{.067 \text{ hr}}{\text{trip}}\right) \left(\frac{\$200}{\text{hr}}\right) = -13.33$

$$\text{Savings} \qquad \$6.67/\text{trip}$$

The extra cost of $8 per trip exceeds the savings of $6.67 per trip in waiting time, so the change is not worthwhile.

MORE COMPLEX QUEUING MODELS

Thus far we have limited ourselves to an analysis of single-channel, single-phase queuing systems with Poisson arrivals and either Poisson or constant service rate distributions. We have also assumed that queue length is unlimited. However, waiting areas (for example, room sizes and storage space) do limit queue lengths. And having patronized supermarkets, airports, and banks, we know that multiple-channel systems are common. Unfortunately, the calculations for multiple-channel, multiple-phase queuing systems quickly become very complex. But (fortunately) easy-to-use computer software is readily available for all of the commonly used queuing models. So it is not necessary to go through the mathematics or use extensive reference tables for the more complex queuing models today. However, references are available [2,4].

Before leaving queuing models, it is worth noting that the models we have used assume that conditions are in a steady state, so the system is assumed to be in equilibrium. Managers typically attempt to "manage" the queues by varying the service capacity (for example, the number of checkout counters), using standby workers and machines, and opening special service channels (for example, express checkout lines). Other appointment and number-coded systems are also used.

Simulation   Simulation techniques are useful for analyzing complex problems that defy mathematical solution. Although they do not yield optimal results, they are relatively easy to use and offer a feasible approach to a wide range of problems. In addition, numerous computer simulation languages (such as GPSS, MODEL) and software packages are available.

Most computer simulations accommodate uncertainties by incorporating probability distributions into the simulation model. The distributions may be of a known statistical type if appropriate (such as normal, uniform, Poisson) or they may be derived from actual (empirical) data. Once the variable patterns of activity are structured into the model, random numbers are used to simulate activities and times. Then the system behavior is analyzed—much like the queue lengths and waiting times computed earlier. By utilizing computer simulations, analysts can compress years of hypothetical operations into minutes. This enables them to experiment with numerous decision alternatives at little or no risk.

PROJECT MANAGEMENT

Many production activities can capitalize on learning effects because they are performed repetitively over time. However, some tasks are unique or one-of-a-kind activities. Examples are mergers, installing a new computer system, launching a new product, completing a major plant overhaul, and constructing new facilities.

Special projects such as these may take months or even years to complete. They are not usually implemented through the normal productive system. Firms often use special project organizations for such tasks. Figure 13-8 summarizes some of the managerial concerns and approaches to handling special projects.

PROJECT PLANNING

A *project* is a set of unique activities that must be completed within a specified time by utilizing appropriate resources, frequently at a job site. The project organization often cuts across traditional boundaries. So the project team may be drawn from engineering, production, accounting, and whatever other departments can make a significant contribution to the success of the venture.

Planning begins with well-defined objectives, such as implementing a new management information system. This involves establishing project boundaries and identifying the controllable and uncontrollable variables that must be managed. For example, if the project is to install an information system, the project team must determine what needs the system will satisfy, what departments it will serve, and what it can and cannot be expected to do for the firm. Performance criteria should relate to the project objectives and are often stated in measures of time, cost, and quality (or operational) characteristics.

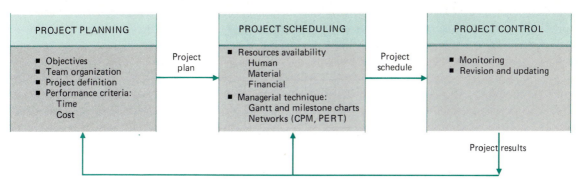

FIGURE 13-8   Project Planning and Control Flowchart

PROJECT SCHEDULING

Project scheduling involves charting the resource requirements or anticipated progress in completing component activities over the project's time horizon. Resource requirements are best managed by giving individual attention to the personnel, material, and financial needs of the project, as illustrated in Fig. 13-9. Each of the charts offers some means of comparing actual levels with planned levels. Computer graphics can provide these types of data on a real-time basis, at almost any level of detail that project managers deem appropriate.

Techniques for scheduling projects include traditional Gantt (load and progress) charts and network techniques. Gantt charts are easily understood and easily updated (if on computer), but they do not reflect the interrelationships among resources or the precedence relationships among project activities. Network techniques such as CPM and PERT overcome a shortcoming of Gantt charts by including a precedence relationship. This advantage, combined with the rapid updating capability stemming from computerization of the data, makes networks an extremely attractive tool for project management. Figure 13-10 identifies some advantages of network scheduling.

PROJECT CONTROL

Project controls are activities designed to measure the status of component activities, transmit that data to a control center where it is compared with the plan (the standard), and initiate corrective action when required. Computerized reporting systems often accumulate data online. Control reports can then be developed on a management-by-exception principle, which minimizes unnecessary paperwork. Managerial attention is then focused on critical or near-critical activities that are potentially troublesome.

NETWORK FUNDAMENTALS

A *network* diagram is a mathematical model that uses small circles (nodes) connected by links or branches (arcs) to represent precedence relationships. Net-

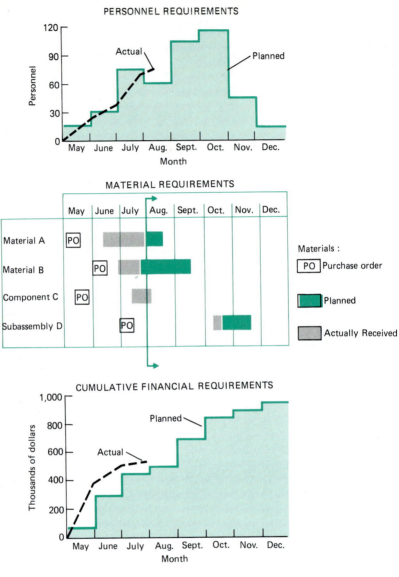

FIGURE 13-9   Project Resource Requirements Scheduling

works are frequently used to describe inventory or cash flows, shipping routes, and communication links. Network problems are also sometimes formulated as linear-programming problems.

The *critical path method* (CPM) and *program evaluation and review technique* (PERT) are network techniques for analyzing a system in terms of activities and events that must be completed in a specified sequence in order to achieve a

1 *Coordinates total project* and all interrelated activities. Shows relationship of each activity to whole project.
2 *Forces logical planning* of all activities. Facilitates work organization and assignment.
3 *Identifies precedence relationships* and activity sequences that are especially critical.
4 *Provides completion time (and/or cost) estimates* and a standard for comparing with actual values.
5 *Facilitates better use of resources* by identifying areas where human, material, or financial resources can be shifted.

FIGURE 13-10   Network Scheduling Advantages

goal. Some activities can be done concurrently, whereas others have precedence requirements. Although some formulations of CPM differ with this nomenclature, we shall consider *activities* as component tasks that take time and are designated by arrows (→).[2] *Events* are points in time that indicate that some activities have been completed and others may begin. They are sometimes called *nodes* and are designated by circles (○). A *network diagram* consists of the activities and events in their proper relationship, as depicted in Fig. 13-11.

The figure shows, in network form, the work activities necessary to construct an electrical power plant (the objective). Preference relationships are indicated by the arrows and circles. For example, the plant design (activity 1–2) must be completed before anything else can take place. Then the selection of the site,

[2] We use the activity-on-arrow (AOA) convention here. The activity-on-node (AON) approach uses circles (or rectangles) to represent project activities and arrows to show the required sequence. The AON method avoids the need for "dummy" activities.

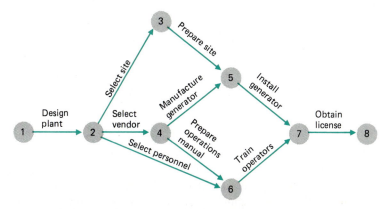

FIGURE 13-11   Network Diagram for Power Plant Construction

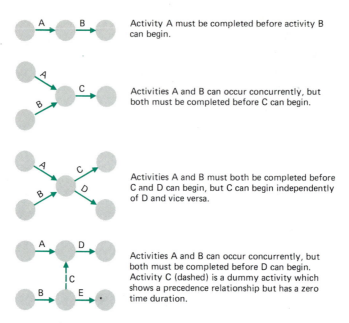

Activity A must be completed before activity B can begin.

Activities A and B can occur concurrently, but both must be completed before C can begin.

Activities A and B must both be completed before C and D can begin, but C can begin independently of D and vice versa.

Activities A and B can occur concurrently, but both must be completed before D can begin. Activity C (dashed) is a dummy activity which shows a precedence relationship but has a zero time duration.

FIGURE 13-12   Commonly Used Network Symbols

vendor, and personnel can take place concurrently. The generator installation (activity 5–7) cannot begin until the site has been prepared (3–5) and the generator has been manufactured (4–5). Note that there are really four paths through the network from event 1 to event 8. The site preparation (3–5) and generator manufacturing (4–5) are on different paths, but because they converge at event 5, either activity could delay the generator installation.

Sometimes precedence relationships are needed even though no time-consuming activities are involved. For example, in Fig. 13-11 suppose the site preparation activity (3–5) cannot begin until the vendor is notified. This means that the vendor selection activity (2–4) must be completed before activity 3–5 can begin. We can indicate this preference requirement by means of a "dummy activity," drawn as a dotted line from event 4 to event 3, which would be assigned a zero time. This dummy activity would then create another unique sequential path (1–2–4–3–5–7–8) through the network. Figure 13-12 summarizes the meaning of this and other commonly used network arrangements.

CRITICAL PATH METHOD

The critical path method (CPM) is extensively used for project management in construction, R&D, product planning, and numerous other areas. Briefly, the steps involved in implementing CPM are as follows:

1 Define the project in terms of activities and events.
2 Construct a network diagram showing the precedence relationships.
3 Develop a point estimate of each activity time.
4 Compute the time requirement for each path in the network.
5 Shift resources as warranted to optimize the attainment of objectives.

CRITICAL PATH

The path with the longest time sequence as computed in step 4 is called the *critical path*, for the activity times of all items on this path are critical to the project completion date. The summation of these activity times is the expected mean time of the critical path (T_E). Other paths will have excess (or slack) time, and the slack associated with any path is simply the difference between T_E and the time for the given path.

EXAMPLE 13-5

The time estimates for completing the plant construction project of Fig. 13-11 are as shown (in months) on the accompanying network diagram.
(a) Determine the critical path.
(b) How much slack time is available in the path containing the operations manual preparation activity?

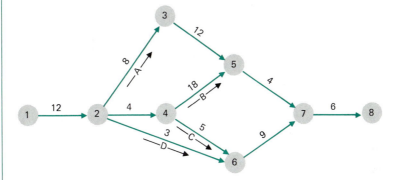

SOLUTION

Path		Times
A	1–2–3–5–7–8	12 + 8 + 12 + 4 + 6 = 42
B	1–2–4–5–7–8	12 + 4 + 18 + 4 + 6 = 44
C	1–2–4–6–7–8	12 + 4 + 5 + 9 + 6 = 36
D	1–2–6–7–8	12 + 3 + 9 + 6 = 30

(a) Path B is critical, with a time requirement of 44 months.
(b) The manual preparation activity is on path C:

$$\text{Slack} = \text{critical path B} - \text{path C} = 44 - 36 = 8 \text{ months}$$

The slack in path C suggests that, other things remaining the same, the manual writing (activity 4–6) could fall behind by 8 months before it would jeopardize the scheduled finish date for the project.

EARLIEST AND LATEST ACTIVITY TIMES[3]

In managing the activities of a project, it is sometimes useful to know how soon or how late an individual activity can be started or finished without affecting the scheduled completion date of the total project. Four symbols are commonly used to designate the earliest and latest activity times.

ES = the earliest start time for an activity. The assumption is that all predecessor activities are started at their earliest start time.

EF = the earliest finish time for an activity. The assumption is that the activity starts on its ES and takes its expected time t. Therefore, $EF = ES + t$.

LF = the latest finish time for an activity without delaying the project. The assumption is that successive activities take their expected time.

LS = the latest start time for an activity without delaying the project. $LS = LF - t$.

The process of calculating ES and EF times involves calculations in sequence from left to right (in the network) and is sometimes referred to as a *forward pass* of calculations. Thus, the ES of an activity can be determined by summing the times of all preceding activities. Where two paths converge at a node, the longest path (timewise) governs.

Latest times are computed in an opposite manner. We begin with the critical or ending time T_E and subtract each preceding activity up to the specified activity. If two or more paths converge on one event en route, the figure developed from the path with the shortest total time governs because that path has the least slack. We can illustrate this by using the network times developed in the previous example.

EXAMPLE 13-6

Compute the earliest start ES and latest start LS times for the activities in the network of Example 13-5. What are the earliest and latest times for the completion of event 6 such that the schedule will not be delayed?

SOLUTION

The ES time for each activity is shown on the left side of the tee at the beginning of the activity. Activity 1–2 begins at zero, and the other activity times are summed. For example, the ES for activity 6–7 is the maximum of the cumulative times leading to event 6. Thus:

[3] This material extends beyond that covered in some introductory texts.

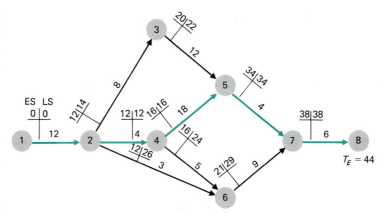

Via path 1–2–4–6, the time = 12 + 4 + 5 = 21.

Via path 1–2–6, the time = 12 + 3 = 15.

∴ ES = day 21 because the longest path governs.

The LS time for each activity is on the right side of the tee, and we begin with T_E and work backward. Thus the LS for activity 6–7 is

$$T_E - \text{preceding activity times} = 44 - 6 - 9 = 29$$

Other ES and LS times are shown in the accompanying table, along with slack times. Note that the ES and LS for all activities on the critical path are equal. For activities off the critical path the LS turns out to be the ES plus the amount of slack in the path (which seems like an easier way to compute it). The table also includes EF and LF times. They are also easily computed, for the EF is simply the ES plus the activity time, and LF is the LS plus the activity time.

Activity	Time	ES	LS	EF	LF	Slack
1–2	12	0	0	12	12	0
2–3	8	12	14	20	22	2
2–4	4	12	12	16	16	0
2–6	3	12	26	18	29	14
3–5	12	20	22	32	34	2
4–5	18	16	16	34	34	0
4–6	5	16	24	21	29	8
5–7	4	34	34	38	38	0
6–7	9	21	29	30	38	8
7–8	6	38	38	44	44	0

Slack   Example 13-6 shows the slack associated with each activity. The total slack for an activity is the difference between LS and ES (or between LF and EF).

Although we associate slack with each activity, it really belongs to the path, because once any activity uses up the slack in its path, all the activities along that path become critical. Activities along the critical path will always have zero slack if the target date, or planned completion date, for the project is the same as the earliest finish of the last activity.

The term "free slack" is used to denote the amount of time an activity can be delayed without delaying the earliest start of any succeeding activity. For example, activity 2–6 could be delayed until month 18 without affecting activity 6–7's ES on month 21. But if activity 4–6 is delayed any time at all, it will delay the ES of succeeding activity 6–7. Thus activity 2–6 is said to have 6 months of free slack, whereas activity 4–6 has no free slack. Both activities, however, have some total slack because neither is on the critical path.

The earliest and latest time data, along with the data on available slack, give project planners valuable information for shifting resources to better facilitate the attainment of objectives. For example, if some of the personnel scheduled for activity 4–6 could be allocated for expediting the generator manufacturing (activity 4–5), the critical path time might be reduced to less than 44 months. The manual preparation activity would undoubtedly take longer, but the increase would not have any effect on the overall project completion time until it reached the point where the activity's own path became critical.

EXAMPLE 13-7

The firm in Example 13-5 has determined that by shifting three engineers from manual writing (activity 4–6) to manufacturing assistance, activity 4–5 could be reduced to 15 months, whereas activity 4–6 would be increased to 10 months. What would be the net effect upon the schedule?

SOLUTION

Path A remains the same, at 42 months.

Path B = 12 + 4 + 15 + 4 + 6 = 41 months

Path C = 12 + 4 + 10 + 9 + 6 = 41 months

Path D remains the same, at 30 months.

Path A would become critical, and the new estimated completion time would be 42 months, a 2-month saving over the initial time.

PERT

PERT is, like CPM, a time-oriented planning and control device. However, whereas CPM develops only one central measure of completion time for a project, PERT develops both a measure of central tendency (a mean) and a measure of dispersion (a standard deviation). Given these two parameters of the completion time distribution for a project, probabilities of finishing the project in any specified lesser or greater time than the mean time can be readily determined. There are other subtle differences between CPM and PERT, but this incorporation of statistical probabilities into the network is the basic difference.

PERT ANALYSIS

PERT incorporates uncertainty (and probability) by including three time estimates for each activity rather than only one. These estimates are designated as

a = *optimistic time.* This is the best time that could be expected if everything went exceptionally well, and it would be achieved only about 1 percent of the time.

m = *most likely time.* This is the best estimate, or mode expectation.

b = *pessimistic time.* This is the worst time that could reasonably be expected if everything went wrong, and it would occur only about 1 percent of the time.

The expected mean time t_e and variance σ^2 of each activity can then be determined on the basis of the beta statistical distribution[4] as

$$t_e = \frac{a + 4m + b}{6} \tag{13-13}$$

$$\sigma^2 = \left(\frac{b - a}{6}\right)^2 \tag{13-14}$$

where a = optimistic time estimate
m = most likely time estimate
b = pessimistic time estimate

Individual activity times are then summed over the respective paths, and the path with the longest time is the critical path. Variances of the component activity times along this path may also be summed because individual variances are additive (whereas standard deviations are not). The (theoretical) assumptions here are that the time estimates along the critical path are independent and that the resulting variation of project completion times about the mean completion time is normally distributed. These assumptions normally pose no problems from an applications standpoint.

The ending (normal) distribution of completion times for a project can then be depicted as shown in Fig. 13-13 where the mean completion time T_E equals the summation of activity times along the critical path:

$$T_E = \Sigma t_e \tag{13-15}$$

---

[4] The beta distribution has been found to appropriately describe this type of data, has finite end points, and is relatively easy to calculate.

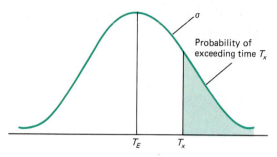

FIGURE 13-13 Ending Time Distribution

The ending distribution standard deviation σ is the square root of the sum of the variances of activity times along the critical path:

$$\sigma = \sqrt{\Sigma \sigma_{cp}{}^2} \qquad (13\text{-}16)$$

With this mean and standard deviation of the ending distribution, the probabilities of various completion times may be calculated using the normal distribution. For example, to determine the probability that a project would exceed time T_x in Fig. 13-13 we would compute

$$Z = \frac{T_x - T_E}{\sigma}$$

find the probability associated with that Z value from the normal distribution values listed in Appendix C (or with a hand calculator), and subtract the amount from .5000. The result would represent the shaded area under the curve in Fig. 13-13.

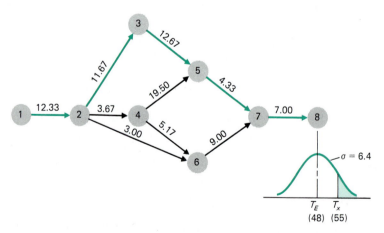

FIGURE 13-14 Network Diagram Showing Critical Path and Ending Time Distribution

EXAMPLE 13-8

Project planners have sought the experienced judgment of various knowledgeable engineers, supervisors, and vendors and have developed the time estimates shown below for the plant construction project depicted in Fig. 13-11.

(a) Determine the critical path.
(b) What is the probability that the project will be finished within 4 years?
(c) What is the probability that it will take more than 55 months?

Activity		Time Estimates			t_e $\dfrac{a + 4m + b}{6}$	σ^2 $\left(\dfrac{b - a}{6}\right)^2$
Description	Number	a	m	b		
Design plant	1–2	10	12	16	12.33	1.00
Select site	2–3	2	8	36	11.67	32.11
Select vendor	2–4	1	4	5	3.67	.44
Select personnel	2–6	2	3	4	3.00	.11
Prepare site	3–5	8	12	20	12.67	4.00
Manufacture generator	4–5	15	18	30	19.50	6.25
Prepare manual	4–6	3	5	8	5.17	.69
Install generator	5–7	2	4	8	4.33	1.00
Train operators	6–7	6	9	12	9.00	1.00
License plant	7–8	4	6	14	7.00	2.78

SOLUTION

(a) Values for t_e and σ^2 for the various activities have been calculated as shown in the example box. The t_e values are entered on the network diagram in Fig. 13-14. The critical path, as determined in the accompanying table, is now A and has been shown by a heavy solid line in the figure.

Path		Times
A:	1–2–3–5–7–8	12.33 + 11.67 + 12.67 + 4.33 + 7.00 = 48.00*
B:	1–2–4–5–7–8	12.33 + 3.67 + 19.50 + 4.33 + 7.00 = 46.83
C:	1–2–4–6–7–8	12.33 + 3.67 + 5.17 + 9.00 + 7.00 = 37.17
D:	1–2–6–7–8	12.33 + 3.00 + 9.00 + 7.00 = 31.33

* Critical path.

(b) The best estimate of completion time is $T_E = 48.0$ months, so there is a 50 percent chance that the project will be finished within the 4-year period.

(c) To determine any other completion time probabilities we must calculate the standard deviation of the distribution of completion times *along the critical path.*

$$\sigma = \sqrt{\Sigma \sigma_{cp}^{2}}$$

$$= \sqrt{1.00 + 32.11 + 4.00 + 1.00 + 2.78}$$

$$= 6.4 \text{ months}$$

$$Z = \frac{T_x - T_E}{\sigma} = \frac{55.0 - 48.0}{6.4} = 1.09$$

$$P(X > T_x) = .5000 - .3621 = .1379$$

$$\therefore \text{ Probability} \cong .14$$

Although the most likely times used in the PERT example were identical to those used in the earlier CPM example, the critical paths turned out to be different. This is, of course, due to the fact that PERT incorporates a measure of uncertainty, whereas CPM does not. A review of the individual activity variances in Example 13-8 reveals that although the site selection activity (2–3) has a most likely time estimate of 8 months, it has a pessimistic time estimate of 36 months, and $t_e = 11.67$, in contrast to the 8-month figure used in the CPM calculations. This estimate for the site selection probably reflects managerial awareness of public concern over the siting of power plants. A strong feature of PERT is that the effects of uncertainty are incorporated into the standard deviation of the completion time distribution. (See Fig. 13-14.) This is because all variances of activities along the critical path, whether they represent much uncertainty (such as the 32.11 value) or much precision (as a value of 0 would), are summed to get the ending distribution variance.

CRASHING: TIME-COST TRADEOFFS[5]

An extension of CPM and PERT referred to as *crashing* a project focuses attention on the tradeoff between time and cost objectives. The *normal* estimate of the time required for each activity (and its associated cost) has already been discussed. The *crash time* estimate is the shortest time that could be achieved if all effort (at any reasonable cost) were made to reduce the activity time. The use of more workers, better equipment, overtime, etc., would generate higher direct costs for individual activities as illustrated in Fig. 13-15. However, shortening the overall time of the project would also reduce certain fixed and overhead expenses of supervision, as well as indirect costs that vary with the length of the project.

Time-cost models search for the optimum reductions in time. We seek to shorten the length of a project to the point where the savings in indirect project costs is offset by the increased direct expenses incurred in the individual activities.

---

[5] This material extends beyond that covered in some introductory texts.

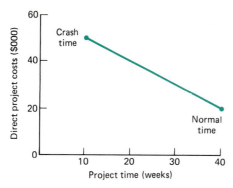

FIGURE 13-15   Crash Time and Crash Cost

EXAMPLE 13-9

A network has four activities with expected times as shown. The minimum feasible times and cost per day to gain reductions in the activity times are as follows:

Activity	Minimum Time	Time Reduction Direct Costs/Day
1-2	2	$40 (each day)
1-3	2	$35 (first), $80 (second)
2-4	4	None possible
3-4	3	$45 (first), $110 (others)

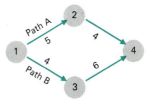

If fixed project costs are $90 per day, what is the lowest-cost time schedule?

SOLUTION

1   First we must determine the critical path(*) and critical-path time cost.

	Path Times	Total Project Cost
Path A	5 + 4 = 9	
Path B	4 + 6 = 10*	10 days × $90/day = $900

2   Next, we must select the activity that can reduce critical path time at the least cost.

Select activity 1–3 at $35 per day, which is less than the $90 per day fixed cost.

Reduce activity 1–3 to 3 days (as shown in the figure).

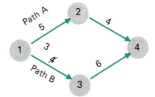

Revised Path Times	Total Fixed Cost	Savings over Previous Schedule
A: 5 + 4 = 9	9 × $90 = $810	$900 − ($810 + $35) = $55
B: 3 + 6 = 9		

3   Both paths are now critical, so we must select an activity on each path.

Select activity 1–2 at $40 per day and 3–4 at $45 per day, where $40 + $45 is less than $90.

Reduce activity 1–2 to 4 days and 3–4 to 5 days.

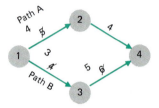

Revised Path Times	Total Fixed Cost	Savings over Previous Schedule
A: 4 + 4 = 8	8 × $90 = $720	$810 − ($720 + $40 + $45) = $5
B: 3 + 5 = 8		

4   Again we must reduce the time of both paths. Activity 1–2 is a good candidate on path A, for it is still at 4 days and can go to 3 for a $40 cost. But when this cost is combined with the $80 cost for reducing activity 1–3 another day, the sum is greater than $90, so further reduction is not economically justified. The lowest-cost schedule is as shown.

The final step in time-cost analysis is to compare the *crash times* and the costs associated with them (*crash costs*). A sufficient number of intermediate schedules are computed such that the total of the direct and indirect (fixed) project costs can be plotted.

EXAMPLE 13-10

Graph the total relevant costs for the previous example, and indicate the optimal time-cost tradeoff value.

SOLUTION

Project Length (Days)	Indirect Cost	Activity Reduced	Relevant Direct Cost		Relevant Total Cost
10	$900	None		$ 0	$900
9	810	1–3	$ 0 + $ 35 =	35	845
8	720	1–2 and 3–4	35 + 85 =	120	840
7	630	1–2 and 1–3	120 + 120 =	240	870
6	540	1–2 and 3–4	240 + 150 =	390	930

This is the time-cost diagram for completing the project in 6 to 10 days. The optimal time-cost tradeoff is to complete the project in 8 days at a cost of $840. However, extending it to 9 days adds only $5 to this cost.

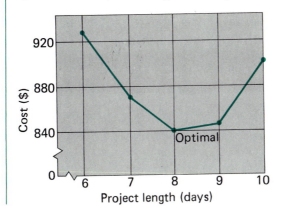

Numerous computer software programs are available for doing rather sophisticated time-cost analysis, and many are quite "user friendly." The analysis is frequently referred to as CPM-COST or PERT-COST. These methods give project managers more alternatives for meeting the often difficult time and cost constraints of a project. As the project progresses, actual costs are compared with budgeted costs to determine which activities are under, and which are over, budget.

SUMMARY

Operations analysis is the use of analytical methods to systematically study data relating to the productivity of operations over time. It is vital in (a) *manufacturing activities* because low productivity there has already led to the demise of many industries and now threatens some major high-tech industries as well. It is also vital to (b) *service industries* because nearly three-quarters of all U.S. workers are now employed in service activities, and productivity in services is already recognized as being lower than in manufacturing. Finally, it is important to (c) *projects* because without close control, projects frequently run over budget and take longer than expected—especially publicly financed projects.

This chapter identifies operations analysis most closely with the performance measurement component of the overall operational strategy and tactics pursued by an organization (Fig. 13-2). An organization's strategy is derived from key (strategic) priority and capacity variables. The *strategy* is a plan for using an organization's capabilities to accomplish competitive objectives, whereas *tactics* are the means used to carry out the strategy. *Performance measurement* follows to ensure, control, and possibly improve upon the results.

Measuring performance in manufacturing activities is perhaps somewhat easier than in services because it can relate to physical materials and units produced. Services are less tangible and frequently involve psychological and emotional values that are difficult to quantify. Equipment-dominated services (such as electrical service) do have more measurable outputs than people-dominated services, however.

Learning curve effects take place in repetitive goods and services production activities, so it is well to recognize and allow for them.

Queuing models readily accommodate the variability in arrival and service rates that we find in both manufacturing and service delivery systems. Single-channel, single-phase systems with Poisson arrivals and exponential service times are easily handled by mathematical models. But as the queuing systems become more complex, the mathematics becomes more difficult. Computer programs are available, however, and for very complex situations, empirical simulations may be the most feasible means of analysis.

Project management involves planning, scheduling, and control of one-time activities. Network techniques have proved to be a useful way of coordinating the interrelated activities of a project. They force the clear identification of precedence relationships and incorporate completion time (and/or cost) estimates which lead to better use of the available resources. Both CPM and PERT are extensively used; PERT offers the advantage of incorporating uncertainty by including optimistic, most likely, and pessimistic estimates of activity times. CPM-COST and PERT-COST are extensions that have increased the usefulness of these techniques.

SOLVED PROBLEMS

LEARNING CURVE EFFECTS

1 The operations manager of International Resort Hotels is preparing a budget for the labor cost required to handle several major conventions of the same type during the coming year. She estimates that the first one will take 300 labor hours at $12 per hour. Assuming that the work follows a 78 percent learning curve, what is the firm's estimated labor cost for the eighth convention?

Solution

$$\text{Percentage of base} = \frac{\text{desired unit number}}{\text{known base number}} = \frac{\text{8th}}{\text{1st}} = 800\%$$

Using the 78 percent column for 800 percent of base in Appendix H.

$$Y_n = Y_B(L) = 300(.4746) = 142.4 \text{ hr}$$

The estimated cost = (142.4 hr)($12/hr) = $1,708.

2 Emerald Electric has a new plant for producing home freezers. The firm has gone through a preliminary manufacturing period and believes it is experiencing an 88 percent learning curve. The 200th unit has required 1.40 labor hours for an assembly activity. Estimate the comparable time for (a) the 100th unit, (b) the 500th unit, (c) the 1,000th unit, and (d) the 5,000th unit.

Solution

(a) The 100th unit has already been completed, but we can estimate its time as a percentage of the base 200 as

$$\text{Percentage of base} = \frac{\text{desired unit number}}{\text{known base number}} = \frac{100\text{th}}{200\text{th}} = \frac{100}{200} = 50\%$$

$$Y_N = Y_B(L) = 1.40(1.1364) = 1.5910 \text{ hr}$$

(b) $\text{Percentage of base} = \dfrac{500\text{th}}{200\text{th}} = 250\%$

$$Y_N = 1.40(.8445) = 1.1823 \text{ hr}$$

(c) $\text{Percentage of base} = \dfrac{1,000\text{th}}{200\text{th}} = 500\%$

$$Y_N = 1.40(.7432) = 1.0405 \text{ hr}$$

(d) $\text{Percentage of base} = \dfrac{5,000\text{th}}{200\text{th}} = 2,500\%$

Note that our table of learning coefficients does not go to this high a percentage of the base, so we must establish a new (higher) base to operate from. The time for the 1,000th unit, developed in (c), will work satisfactorily, so we can designate 1.0405 hours for the 1,000th unit as the new base (100 percent) point.

$$\text{Percentage of base} = \frac{5,000\text{th}}{1,000\text{th}} = 500\%$$

$$Y_N = 1.0405(.7432) = .7733 \text{ hr}$$

QUEUING MODELS

3 Patients arrive at a medical clinic with an arrival rate that is Poisson-distributed with a mean of 6 per hour. Treatment (service) time averages 8 minutes and can be approximated by the negative exponential distribution. Find (a) the mean waiting time, (b) the mean number in the queue, and (c) the percentage of idle time.

Solution

$$\lambda = \text{arrival rate} = 6/\text{hr}$$

$$\mu = \text{service rate} = \left(\frac{\text{unit}}{8 \text{ min}}\right)\left(\frac{60 \text{ min}}{\text{hr}}\right) = 7.5/\text{hr}$$

(a) $T_w = \dfrac{\lambda}{\mu(\mu - \lambda)} = \dfrac{6}{7.5(7.5 - 6)} = .53$ hr $= 32$ min

(b) $N_q = \dfrac{\lambda^2}{\mu(\mu - \lambda)} = 3.20$ units

(c) $\%I = 100 - \%U = 100 - \dfrac{\lambda}{\mu} = 100 - \dfrac{6}{7.5} = 20\%$

4   Rent-A-Dent Ltd. receives an average of 15 requests per day for older-model cars. It can fill 20 such requests per day. However, if fewer than 3 cars are rented, the company loses money as follows: If only 2 cars are rented the loss equals $220 per day, if only 1 car is rented the loss equals $260 per day, if no cars are rented the loss equals $290 per day. The losses are, of course, offset by gains from renting 3 or more cars. Considering the *losses only*, what is the expected value of the loss per day? Assume that there are Poisson arrivals and service rates, and that there is unlimited line length with no defects from the queue.

Solution

$$P(n = 2) = \left(1 - \dfrac{\lambda}{\mu}\right)\left(\dfrac{\lambda}{\mu}\right)^2 = \left(1 - \dfrac{15}{20}\right)\left(\dfrac{15}{20}\right)^2 = .141$$

$$P(n = 1) = \left(1 - \dfrac{15}{20}\right)(.75)^1 = \qquad\qquad .188$$

$$P(n = 0) = \left(1 - \dfrac{15}{20}\right)(.75)^0 = (.25)(1) = \qquad \dfrac{.250}{.579}$$

Expected loss $= \Sigma[XP(X)] = \$220(.141) + \$260(.188) + \$290(.250) = \$152.40/\text{day}$

CPM AND PERT

5   Study the data shown in the accompanying table for a PERT network.

Preceding Event	Event	Activity Time (Days)		
		a	m	b
1	2	5	6	13
1	3	2	7	12
2	4	1.5	2	2.5
2	5	1	3	5
3	5	4	5	6
3	6	1	1	1
4	7	2	3	10
5	7	4	5	6
6	7	3	5	7

(a) Draw the network, and find the critical path.
(b) What are the parameters of the ending time distribution?
(c) Which activity has the most precise time estimate?
(d) Determine the earliest start, latest start, and slack time for all activities.
(e) Each day the project can be shortened is worth $5,000. Should the firm pay $12,500 to reduce activity 3–5 to 2 days?

Solution

(a)

Activity	$\dfrac{a + 4m + b}{6}$	$\left(\dfrac{b - a}{6}\right)^2$
1–2	7	1.78
1–3	7	2.77
2–4	2	.02
2–5	3	.44
3–5	5	.11
3–6	1	.00
4–7	4	1.78
5–7	5	.11
6–7	5	.44

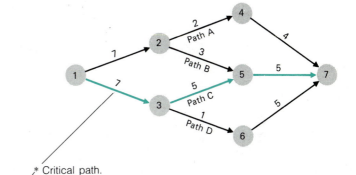

* Critical path.

Path		Times
A	1–2–4–7	7 + 2 + 4 = 13
B	1–2–5–7	7 + 3 + 5 = 15
C	1–3–5–7	7 + 5 + 5 = 17*
D	1–3–6–7	7 + 1 + 5 = 13

(b) $T_E = 17$

$$\sigma_{cp} = \sqrt{\Sigma \sigma_{cp}^2} = \sqrt{2.77 + .11 + .11} = 1.73$$

(c) The most precise time is for activity 3–6, with a variance of zero.
(d) The ES and LS times for activities on the critical path (path C) are both the same and are simply cumulative totals of the activity times. They are dominating values, for they are maximums in terms of computing ES times (in the forward direction) and minimums in terms of computing LS times (in the reverse direction).

Values for all activities in the network are shown below.

Activity	Time	ES	LS	Slack
1–2	7	0	2	2
1–3	7	0	0	0
2–4	2	7	11	4
2–5	3	7	9	2
3–5	5	7	7	0
3–6	1	7	11	4
4–7	4	9	13	4
5–7	5	12	12	0
6–7	5	8	12	4

For example, the ES for activity 5–7 is the maximum of

$$\text{Via path B} = 7 + 3 = 10$$
$$\text{Via path C} = 7 + 5 = 12$$
$$\therefore \text{ES} = \text{day 12.}$$

For example, the LS for activity 1–2 is the minimum of

$$\text{Via path A} = 17 - 4 - 2 - 7 = 4$$
$$\text{Via path B} = 17 - 5 - 3 - 7 = 2$$
$$\therefore \text{LS} = \text{day 2.}$$

(e) Activity 3–5 is on the critical path, and the reduction from 5 to 2 days would reduce the path C time to $17 - 3 = 14$ days. However, path B would become critical at 15 days, so the net reduction would be 2 days at $5,000 per day $= \$10,000$ savings versus the $12,500 cost. The firm should not pay the $12,500.

6 Worldwide Constructors, Inc. uses PERT and expected value techniques to prepare bids and manage construction jobs. Its bid price is set to give it a 30 percent gross profit over expected costs. In calculating the PERT network for a bridge construction job, T_E was found to be equal to 60 days, and total variance along the critical path was $\sigma_{cp}^2 = 36$. Total expenses for the project are estimated at $335,000, but if the bridge is not completed within 70 days, there is a penalty of $50,000. Determine the appropriate bid price.

Solution

$$\text{Bid price} = \text{expected costs} + \text{penalty allowance} + \text{profit}$$

where expected costs $= \$335,000$
  penalty allowance $= (\text{amount of penalty})(\text{probability of penalty})$

$$Z = \frac{T_x - T_E}{\sigma} = \frac{70 - 60}{6} = 1.67$$

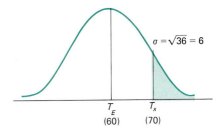

$$\sigma = \sqrt{36} = 6$$

$P(Z) = .4525$

$\therefore P(X > T_x) = .5000 - .4525 = .0475$

Penalty allowance $= (\$50,000)(.0475) = \$2,375$

Profit $= .30(\$335,000 + \$2,375) = \$101,212$

Bid price $= \$335,000 + \$2,375 + \$101,212 = \$438,587.$

T_E (60) T_x (70)

7   An electrical firm has developed a PERT plan for the electrical wiring activity of power plant control panels. It expects that assembly operations will follow a 90 percent learning curve. The project team, composed of workers, electricians, and supervisors, feels the first assembly will most likely be completed in 14 days but could take as long as 24 days, or if everything went exceptionally well, it would be finished in 10 days. What is the expected assembly time of the fourth unit?

Solution

$$t_e = \frac{a + 4m + b}{6} = \frac{10 + 4(4) + 24}{6} = 15$$

Fourth unit % base $= \dfrac{4}{1} = 400\%$

Then, from Appendix H we have

$$Y_N = Y_B(L) = 15(.81) = 12.15 \text{ days}$$

QUESTIONS

13-1   What is operations analysis and how does it relate to a firm's strategy?

13-2   Explain what is meant by the focused factory concept.

13-3   How does the emphasis upon facility use versus personal contact influence the quality level of services?

13-4   The chapter suggests that goods-producing facilities and service delivery systems do not have the same central focus of concern. In general terms, how does the main focus of flow and attention in goods manufacturing systems differ from that in service systems?

13-5   Suppose you were starting up a small manufacturing firm. Identify three or four measures of performance in the production and inventory control area that you feel would be especially worthwhile.

13-6   How is the improvement effect from a learning curve normally expressed, and what is the meaning of that expression?

13-7   As an operations manager, would you prefer to see your activities on a 70 percent or 90 percent learning curve? Why?

13-8   What assumptions underlie the most basic queuing model discussed in the chapter?

13-9   Give an example of a single-channel, multiple-phase queuing situation, and illustrate the structure of such a queuing situation with a simple diagram.

13-10   What is the effect upon the mean waiting time and mean number in the queue when service rates are constant rather than Poisson-distributed?

13-11   What approach can be taken to solve queuing problems which are too complex (mathematically) to handle with standard queuing equations?

13-12   Identify the following terms pertaining to network diagrams and analysis:
     (a) A task that "takes time" and is done as part of a total project
     (b) The name given to the sequence of events that has the longest (controlling) time
     (c) The chance that one of the optimistic or pessimistic times will occur
     (d) The symbol for Σt_e along the longest path
     (e) The kind of statistical distribution that is used to estimate mean times and variances of individual tasks within a network
     (f) The name given to the difference between total time for jobs on the longest path and jobs on another path

PROBLEMS

1   A manufacturer of radar assemblies has received a contract for 32 units and has produced the first one in 100 hours. If the activity follows a 90 percent learning curve, how long will it take to produce (a) the 2d unit, (b) the 4th unit, (c) the last unit?

2   Management is considering installing $20,000 worth of new equipment on a servicing operation that has been following a 90 percent learning curve. The firm has just completed the fourth unit, which took 30 days, at direct labor costs of $1,000 per day, and the contract calls for a total of eight units. The new equipment is expected to increase the time of the fifth unit to 31 days but would facilitate other improvements that would put the operation on a 70 percent learning curve. Show calculations to determine whether the new installation is economically justified.

3   Rocket Control Inc., a Long Beach firm, does control panel wiring for solid-fueled rocket engines. The firm is currently preparing delivery estimates for a government contract for 80 panels. The first unit is expected to take 200 worker-hours, and the firm usually experiences an 84 percent learning curve for this type of work.
     (a) What average time per unit can be expected for the first three units?
     (b) How many worker-hours should be scheduled for the 40th unit?

4   Given Poisson arrivals at 20 per hour, a Poisson service rate of 24 per hour, and a single-channel, single-phase queue with unlimited line, find (a) T_s, (b) N_s, (c) T_q, and (d) N_q.

5   A car rental agency at a large airport receives an average of 12 requests per day for a certain model W car. It can fill 15 such requests per day. However, if fewer than 3 cars are rented, the agency loses money according to the following schedule:

$$\text{Only 2 cars rented} = \$200 \text{ loss/day}$$
$$\text{Only 1 car rented} = \$240 \text{ loss/day}$$
$$\text{No W cars rented} = \$280 \text{ loss/day}$$

The losses are, of course, offset by gains from renting 3 or more cars.
     (a) Considering the losses *only*, what is the expected value of the loss per day? Assume

that there are Poisson arrivals and service rates and unlimited line length with no defects from the queue.

(b) Discuss the validity of the basic queuing model assumptions for this problem.

6 Freeway Auto Service Technicians Inc. (FAST) advertises a (constant) standard time of 6 minutes to wash and lubricate passengers cars. Requests for service arrive according to a Poisson distribution with a mean of λ = four per hour.

(a) Express the standard time as a service rate.

(b) What is the mean waiting time (minutes) for service?

7 A large appliance service firm has Poisson arrival rates and negative exponential service times and is open 24 hours per day on a first-come, first-served basis. If the firm receives service orders at a mean rate of 30 per day and has the personnel and facilities to handle up to 35 per day,

(a) How many orders, on the average, will it have in its shop at any one time?

(b) How many hours, on the average, will a customer's appliance have to wait *before the service firm starts work* on it?

(c) How many hours, on the average, would the customer's appliance have to wait before the firm started work on it if the firm had a *constant* service rate of 35 per day?

8 A medical research information center in San Antonio is linked to hospitals nationwide via an electric mail (computer) system. Requests for information arrive at an average rate of three per hour and queue up on the research center's computer. A research librarian requires 15 minutes (on average) to search out and convey the information, and all requests are handled on a first-come, first-served basis. Assume that arrivals are Poisson-distributed and service times are exponential.

(a) How long does it take, including waiting and individual service time, to satisfy an individual request?

(b) How many requests, on average, are waiting to be fulfilled?

(c) *Requires computer program* Estimate the number of requests waiting to be fulfilled if the time to search out and convey each request followed a normal distribution with a mean time of 15 minutes and standard deviation of 1.5 minutes.

9 (*Requires computer program for single-channel, single-phase, Poisson arrival rate, exponential service time, with limited queue length*) Use the data from Prob. 8 [parts (a) and (b)], except assume the number of requests in the system (waiting and being worked on) is limited to five. Then:

(a) Find the time in the system.

(b) Find the number in the queue.

10 In calculating the PERT network for a freeway construction job, the supervisor optimistically felt a welding activity could conceivably be completed in 12 days, whereas the welder, after citing all the possible delays, said it might take as long as 24 days. Both agreed that the most likely time was 15 days.

(a) What is the expected activity time t_e?

(b) What is the estimate of activity variance σ^2?

11 The expected completion time of a PERT project is T_E = 15 days, and σ_{cp}^2 = 4 days. What is the probability that the project will take 18 or more days to complete?

12 A PERT network has expected times t_e in days as shown in the diagram. The time estimates for activity 6–7 are a = 1, m = 4, and b = 7. For the network, what is the

(a) Expected completion time T_E?

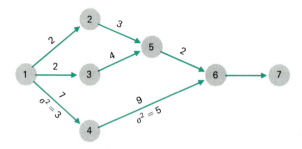

(b) Completion time standard deviation σ?

(c) Probability the project will take more than 21.5 days to complete?

13 A microwave relay station construction project is being planned on a PERT basis with the data shown given in days.

Activity	a	m	b
1–2	2	3	10
1–3	8	12	20
1–4	10	14	16
2–5	6	10	12
3–5	14	20	26
3–7	3	5	7
4–6	8	12	20
5–7	1	1	1
6–8	6	10	12
7–8	1	3	7

(a) Construct a PERT network showing the expected mean time t_e for each activity.

(b) What is the critical path?

(c) What is the expected completion time T_E?

(d) How much slack exists in the path containing event 2?

(e) What is the latest day event 2 can be completed without delaying the project?

(f) Find σ_{cp}.

(g) What is the probability the project will take longer than 41 days to complete?

14 Given the data in the previous problem, assume that each day of improvement in the completion schedule results in a $1,000 savings (or bonus). For a cost of $1,500 the firm could do any one of the following:

(a) Reduce the t_e of activity 3–7 by 4 days

(b) Reduce the t_e of activity 7–8 by 2 days

(c) Reduce the t_e of activities 3–5 and 6–8 by 2 days each

Evaluate the alternative choices, and indicate which, if any, is preferable.

15 A building contractor company has bid on a job for a water reservoir that must be completed within 34 days ($T_L = 34$), or else the company must pay a $2,000 penalty. If the project is finished within 28 days, the company will get a $1,000 bonus. Expenses associated with the project are estimated to be $30,000. The company has developed a PERT chart of the project and found that $T_E = 31$ days. The variance estimates of the five activities along the critical path are 1.3, 2.2, 2.1, .9, and 2.5 days, respectively.

(a) What is the probability of obtaining the bonus (accurate to two digits)?

(b) Assuming that the company wishes to adjust its bid price to allow for the expected bonus or penalty and come out with only a long-run expected profit of $5,000, for what contract price should it be willing to accept the job?

16 A PERT chart is to be used to estimate the assembly time for a new component which is later to be manufactured. Subsequent production is expected to follow an 80 percent learning curve. The optimistic, most likely, and pessimistic assembly times for the first assembly are estimated at 2, 4, and 12 hours, respectively. What is the expected assembly time of the fourth unit?

17 The earliest start (ES) and latest start (LS) times for activity 6–7 of a network are as shown. Determine appropriate values for all other activities of the network, and show them in a similar manner.

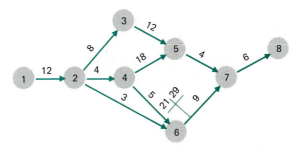

18 *PERT-COST* The minimum feasible times and costs per day to gain reductions in the activity times shown in the network are given in the following table:

Activity	Minimum Times (Days)	Times Reduction Direct Costs/Day
1–2	3	$20 (first), $45 (second)
1–3	4	$35 (first), $60 (others)
2–3	2	$90
3–4	3	$10 (first), $90 (second), $130 (third)

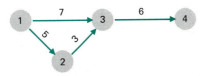

Assume that indirect project costs are $100 per day, and develop a graph showing (a) the normal-time cost, (b) the crash-time cost, and (c) the optimal-time cost.

REFERENCES

[1] Hymowitz, Carol, and Thomas F. O'Boyle: "Pittsburgh's Evolution from Steel to Services Sparks a Culture Clash," *The Wall Street Journal*, Aug. 21, 1984, p. 1.

[2] Dervitsiotis, Kostas N., *Operations Management*, McGraw-Hill, New York, 1981, pp. 244–245.

[3] Karatsu, Hajime: "The Deindustrialization of America: A Tragedy for the World," *KKC Brief,* Japan Institute for Social and Economic Affairs, no. 31, Oct. 1985.

[4] Monks, Joseph G.: *Schaums Outline Series: Theory and Problems of Operations Management*, McGraw-Hill, New York, 1985, pp. 310–315.

[5] Norman, Richard: *Service Management: Strategy and Leadership in Service Businesses*, Wiley & Sons, Ltd, England, 1984.

[6] "Service Industries," *The Wall Street Journal*, Aug. 7, 1985, p. 1.

[7] Skinner, Wickham: "Manufacturing—Missing Link in Corporate Strategy," *Harvard Business Review*, vol. 47, no. 3 (May–June 1969), pp. 136–145.

[8] Skinner, Wickham: "The Focused Factory," *Harvard Business Review*, May–June 1974, pp. 113–121.

[9] Wheelwright, Steven C.: "Reflecting Corporate Strategy in Manufacturing Decisions," *Business Horizons*, Feb. 1978, pp. 57–66.

[10] Zeithaml, Valarie, A. Parasuraman, and Leonard L. Berry: "Problems and Strategies in Services Marketing," *Journal of Marketing*, vol. 49 (Spring 1985), pp. 33–46.

SELF QUIZ: CHAPTER 13

POINTS: 15

Part I True/False [1 point each = 6]

1. __F__ Manufacturing employment is increasing in the United States because firms are capitalizing on foreign technology to create more domestic jobs.
2. __F__ An example of a corporate strategy would be achieving 99 percent accuracy on all bills of material.
3. __T__ Equipment-based services tend to be more controllable than people-based services.
4. __F__ An employee operating on a 95 percent learning curve is improving at a faster rate than one operating on an 80 percent curve.
5. __T__ A Poisson service *rate* of 10 units per hour has a negative exponential distribution service *time* of 6 minutes per unit.
6. __F__ The CPM scheduling technique yields an ending time distribution that reflects the uncertainty of items on the critical path.

Part II Problems [3 points each = 9. Calculate and select your answer.]

1. Analysts at a medical center have found that the time to do a certain type of complicated surgery follows a 94 percent learning curve. The fourth operation has just been completed and took 212 minutes. If this same trend continues, what time should analysts expect for the 36th operation?
   - (a) 174 min
   - (b) 187 min
   - (c) 199 min
   - (d) 208 min
   - (e) None of the above.

2. A computer manufacturing firm has a troubleshooting station that can replace a computer component in an average time of 3 minutes. Service is provided on a first-come, first-served basis and the service rate is Poisson-distributed. Arrival rates are also Poisson-distributed with a mean of 18 per hour. Assuming this is a single-channel, single-phase system, what is the average waiting time before a component is repaired?
   - (a) 2 min
   - (b) 8 min
   - (c) 18 min
   - (d) 27 min
   - (e) None of the above.

3. A PERT network has expected times (days) as shown. The three estimates for activity 6–7 are 1, 4, and 7. For the network, what is the probability that the completion time will exceed 21.5 days?
   - (a) .27
   - (b) .31
   - (c) .38
   - (d) .55
   - (e) None of the above.

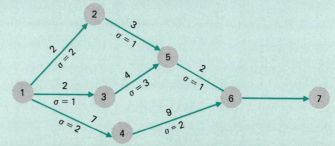

577

CHAPTER 14

QUALITY ASSURANCE

INTRODUCTION

Those sleek, dark-windowed buses should have been a tribute to Yankee know-how. They were designed with the presumed benefits of the newest government wisdom, built by a major company that has decades of manufacturing experience, and put through their paces in trials on New York's scarred streets.

But, instead of bringing glory and profit to their makers, the buses are being denounced as high-tech lemons by customers from Connecticut to Hawaii. Their frames crack, their doors stick and their air conditioners balk. [11]

Fortunately, not all products face the stigma of these hapless flexible buses. But numerous industrial, office, and home products—from generators to copying machines to television sets—seem to be deluged with quality problems. Long after products reach the market, problems still arise. Recall costs of correcting deficiencies in automobiles alone run into millions of dollars a year. What is the basis for such problems? Is the quality of a product such an elusive thing that producers and consumers must resort to courts of law to distinguish between good and poor quality? And what of the quality of services which now consume more productive effort than goods? Can their quality level really be controlled—and if so, how?

Figure 14-1 illustrates the quality question we begin with in this chapter. We look first at the meaning of the word "quality," and some measures of quality in goods and services. And we examine the relevant costs of quality control, and the role of quality "circles" and inspection. The two major methodologies used for controlling quality are then discussed: acceptance sampling and process control. Both methods make extensive use of statistical techniques, and we shall see how sampling plans and control charts are established and where they are best applied.

OBJECTIVES OF QUALITY ASSURANCE

Suppose you know the operations supervisor of the firm producing air conditioners for buses. Bidding was close, but your friend's firm was able to secure the contract for 245 units by cutting out some frills and concentrating on the job to be done. Air conditioners for buses don't need 8 or 10 push buttons, with lighted adjustments for five different speeds and bells to ring when they go on and off. The contract called for air conditioners that would cool buses from outdoor temperatures of 95 degrees. Control was to be from a simple on-off switch.

Like quality control in many other companies, the quality control in your friend's company could have been better in the past. Being very customer-conscious, however, he resolved to do better in the future—there would be no skimping on this job. He knew the buses would be going to Houston and Tucson, where temperatures often exceed 95 degrees. So in an effort to "ensure quality" he had his workers use a slightly larger compressor than was required. Next

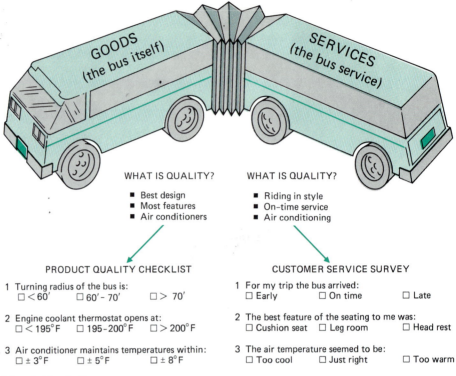

FIGURE 14-1 What Is Quality?

summer, when the buses were performing so well in the hot southwest, he could expect compliments from the divisional vice president.

Come July and your friend is called into the vice president's office. Air-conditioning units in the new Houston and Tucson buses are being recalled, and it is costing the company dearly. He is in trouble! It seems that passengers are all complaining that the buses are too hot when the air conditioner is off and too cold when it is on. The original compressor would have worked fine because designers had anticipated the effect of very high outside temperatures. They purposely planned to allow the inside temperature to rise slightly so as to reduce the shock from the temperature differential for riders entering the bus. The oversize compressors kept the buses too cool, and there was no way to adjust them. So all 245 units now had to be recalled and fitted with an expensive auxiliary temperature control device.

Your unemployed friend now comes to you explaining that in all his efforts to improve quality, his boss had always encouraged him to "keep at it—things could be worse." So he had kept at it—and sure enough! Now he hopes you can explain where he went wrong.

Unlike the understanding of quality held by the operations supervisor described above, high quality is not necessarily represented by the most cooling, extra features, the longest life, or even the best design of a product. These attributes may or may not be indicative of quality. For example, a fuse that provides a long life of service by carrying a current overload is not as satisfactory as one that fails at a specified amperage level. Similarly, the added features (and gasoline consumption) of a larger V-8 engine would not represent higher quality to a self-employed taxi driver who ordered an economical 4-cylinder compact. A businesswoman flying from Seattle to a meeting in Denver would probably not appreciate receiving the added "service" of a stopover in Poughkeepsie, New York.

Although "quality" is often equated with having the best or most costly features, that definition affords a very limited perspective of the elusive nature of the property "quality." We shall try to be more specific, recognizing that quality has both (1) a perceived (qualitative) facet and (2) a specific (quantitative) meaning.

APPROACHES TO QUALITY

Shewhart and Deming   Two individuals associated most closely with quality control work are Walter Shewhart and Edwards Deming. Shewhart pioneered the early use of statistical control methods. Deming carried those techniques to Japan after World War II and is recognized as the world's major authority on the subject of quality [7]. His work helped transform Japan into a quality producer and an economic power.

Japan's reputation for quality could not have been much worse at the time Deming was invited to give a series of lectures on quality control to Japanese engineers in 1950 [7]. Deming insisted that the heads of the companies attend the lectures, so 45 Japanese industrialists were invited—and all showed up! Deming promised that if they listened to him and learned the statistical quality control techniques he was to teach them, they would be able to compete with the West in 5 years. His listeners were desperate for every word and followed his advice meticulously. The rest is history!

Deming is now obsessed with America's lack of response to the Asian challenge. He points out that although many U.S. companies have good intentions, they have rewarded those who have maximized production and minimized costs but have rarely rewarded efforts to improve quality. If we are to become more competitive, Deming says, "then we have to begin with our quality" [7]. This means using statistical sampling, histograms, control charts, and probability distributions to analyze defective rates.

Japanese Concept   But the Japanese approach to quality control encompasses more than just statistical techniques. Quality in Japanese firms is a holistic concept, a way of thinking that pervades the entire organization and affects everyone. Employees assume quality objectives as an inherent or even primary work goal. And workers at all levels cooperate in groups to identify any quality problems, solve them, and strive for defect-free production. High quality is an accepted philosophy of the organization.

Dimensions of Quality   Quality is a multidimensional measure of a product that is not easily defined. In discussing quality as a strategic weapon, David Garvin has identified three approaches to quality [6]. He suggests it may be perceived as:

- Conformance of products to their requirements
- A measure of the fitness of a product for its intended use
- An innate excellence in the product

Synthesizing these approaches, Garvin has derived eight dimensions of product quality: (1) performance, (2) features, (3) reliability, (4) conformance, (5) durability, (6) serviceability, (7) aesthetics, and (8) perceived quality. He suggests that firms define the quality dimensions on which they hope to compete, and then use those measures. Insofar as these dimensions can be measured (or specified), the association of quality with the conformance of products to their requirements seems to be a very useful (and encompassing) approach. However, the manifestation of quality differs between goods and services.

Quality in Goods and Services   With goods, quality is a constant, tangible characteristic, because it resides in a physical product. Services are consumed as they are produced, and they frequently rely upon social interactions. With services, quality is a fleeting and less tangible characteristic than with goods. Nevertheless, quality standards are widely used in services. We find them everywhere from hospitals and hotels to banks and post offices. And some organizations, such as McDonald's, have developed fairly precise and sophisticated measures. Even some countries (such as Ireland) have national guides to quality management in service industries [8].

DEFINITION OF QUALITY

Given the above background, let us acknowledge the qualitative dimension of quality and then go on to define quality more quantitatively as we will use it in this chapter.

In a broad sense, quality is a holistic concept that gives direction to an organization and links its members. The acceptance and pursuit of common goals of product excellence tend to unite employees in a team spirit that extends beyond quality specifics to productivity and other effects. So the concept of "quality" can have a penetrating meaning. Nevertheless, for purposes of controlling quality, we must remain fairly specific.

> **Quality** is a measure of how closely a good or service conforms to specified standards.

Quality standards may relate to time, materials, performance, reliability, appearance, or any quantifiable characteristic of the product. The objective of quality control efforts is to ensure that specified standards are adhered to in the production of a firm's products and, where required, in their application.

Although we sometimes tend to associate quality with cost, the quality level for an inexpensive product may be "high" or "low," just as it may be "high" or "low" for an expensive product. It depends upon the extent to which the product meets specified or advertised characteristics. Unfortunately, we are not always careful to define the product line and specify the relevant standards of comparison. As a result, we sometimes use the word "quality" very loosely.

For example, if we speak of the quality of "automobiles" without being any more specific than that, our individual standards could be almost anything that happens to come to mind, such as appearance and performance. Since human preferences tend to be for "more" rather than "less," many persons would unconsciously associate high quality with the most expensive models in the product line. However, if our criteria related to specific variables such as surface finish, fuel consumption, maneuverability, and cost per mile, we could measure the extent to which a given automobile (such as a Volkswagen) met its standards. Volkswagens can be of high or low quality, just as BMWs can, for both are produced to different specifications for different market segments.

Some customers prefer one product to another of equal quality on the basis of a subjective preference which varies with the individual. Subjective feelings are difficult to identify with quality, for they reflect the utility value of a good or service to a specific consumer. The quality of a good or service per se is not changed by the preference of the individual who owns or uses it (for example, by the owner of a car or user of a phone service). Quality is more specific and definite than that.

Services do, however, present more of a problem because they have no existence apart from the consumer. And they may involve a social interaction that disposes the consumer to like or dislike the service. Moreover, the success of a service may be influenced by the perceptions of the consumer. In this situation, management may be more concerned with the *perceived quality of the service* than with quantitative specifications per se. (Fortunately, the measures of perceived quality are also useful measures of service quality.)

QUALITY ASSURANCE SYSTEMS

Organizations ensure the quality of their products through quality assurance activities. *Quality assurance* is the system of policies, procedures, and guidelines that establishes and maintains specified standards of product quality. It encompasses both external and internal elements that significantly affect quality.

Figure 14-2 describes some key elements of a quality assurance system. It begins with the formulation of quality management objectives which reflect both customer priorities and the firm's own organizational capabilities or capacity. Product quality specifications are then formulated as part of the overall product specifications. These standards can pertain to goods or services, or both.

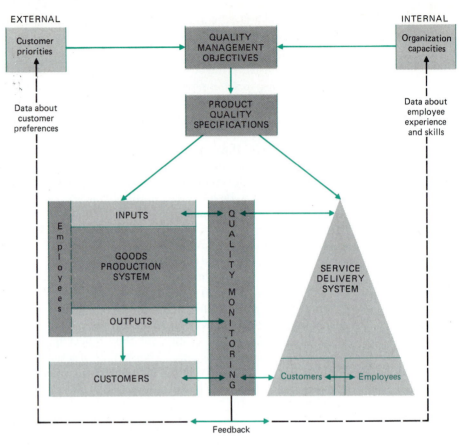

FIGURE 14-2   Elements of a Quality Assurance System

The product specifications constitute standards against which the goods and services are measured (frequently by statistical sampling). The standards for *goods* are used to control the quality of incoming raw materials from suppliers, the production process itself, and the outputs, or goods destined for customers. With *services*, the standards typically apply to the process wherein employees interact with customers.

Absence of Defined Standards   Where quantifiable standards are absent, quality becomes a matter of opinion and is not really controllable from a scientific standpoint. An abstract painting, for example, may appear exquisite to one person and detestable to another, depending upon their subjective impressions. Such a painting would be of questionable quality until such time as some recognized standard were established. In many cases interest groups within a culture develop surrogate standards, such as simply the name of an artist, composer, or performer. They then attempt to equate this substitute characteristic with quality. But cultural value systems differ widely, and the value attached to such a work is usually more a matter of *subjective preference* than it is of measurable characteristics. *It properly belongs in the realm of art rather than science*. When measurable characteristics can be developed and compared with quantified standards, then some logical basis for evaluation can be established. Only then can consistent decisions be made with respect to acceptance, rejection, or correction of a product. Only then can a product's quality be scientifically controlled.

Like any other control activity the control of quality involves measurement, feedback, comparison with standards, and correction when necessary. The feedback of monitoring information from both employee and customer reactions is very important in a quality assurance system. This data "closes the loop" by suggesting and supporting changes to the system, which then enable it to survive and improve within the competitive environment. We focus now upon the purpose of, responsibility for, and methods of controlling quality.

PURPOSE AND METHODS OF CONTROLLING QUALITY

Purpose   The purpose of quality control activities is to provide assurance that goods and services conform to specified standards. The responsibility for controlling quality rests with everyone who is in a position to affect quality. However, a quality assurance group frequently has the responsibility for coordinating quality control activities. In the United States these activities are generally staff rather than line functions. However, even though quality control inspectors report to their own line management, they often work informally with operating personnel. This method of operation preserves the autonomy of an inspector and yet expedites action on quality deficiencies.

Nevertheless, many firms have achieved considerable success in shifting the inspection (and control) responsibility to the workers themselves. Self-inspection fosters a pride in workmanship that can be highly motivating.

Statistical Methods   The two major approaches to controlling quality are *acceptance sampling* of incoming or outgoing products, and *process control* of the actual transformation activities. See Fig. 14-3. Both methods involve statistical sampling techniques. However, acceptance sampling methods rely upon estimating the levels of defective items before or after a process has been completed. Process control is more useful during a process to ensure that production is not outside acceptable limits. The primary means of process control is via the use of control charts.

The quality characteristic being observed is classified as either an attributes or variables characteristic. *Attributes characteristics* are either present or not, such as defective or nondefective, or passing a test or failing it. There is no measure of the degree of conformance. For attributes data, a discrete distribution, such as the binomial or Poisson, is used to make inferences about the population characteristic being controlled. *Variables characteristics* are present in varying degrees and are measurable. Examples are dimensions, weights, and times. For variables data, continuous distributions such as the normal are used.

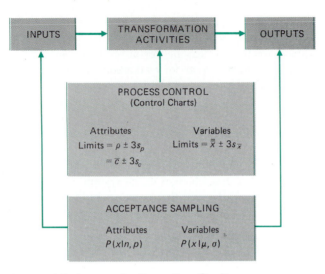

FIGURE 14-3 Statistical Techniques for Controlling Quality

QUALITY MEASURES IN GOODS AND SERVICES

Measures of quality typically relate to a product's specifications, properties, market characteristics, and performance. Figure 14-4 reveals the striking difference in these characteristics as applied to goods and services.

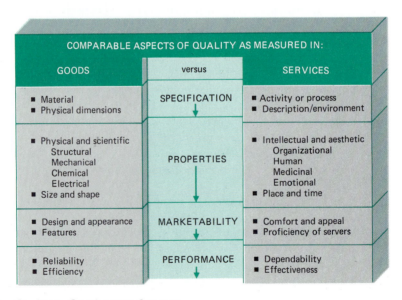

FIGURE 14-4 Quality in Goods versus Services

Goods Quality control in the production of goods rests heavily upon the measurement of material characteristics. Physical dimensions and properties, design, and product reliability are key elements. In addition, as mentioned earlier, characteristics such as durability, serviceability, and aesthetics can be useful if they are measurable.

But the quality information concerning goods need not always flow from measurements of the product itself. For example, the director of product assurance for Ford Motor Company has cited studies which show that satisfied customers tell 8 other people about their cars, whereas dissatisfied customers complain to 22 people [4]. Customer impressions are obviously important to manufacturers.

Services As recognized earlier, services can be difficult to measure—especially ones that convey intellectual and aesthetic benefits. Examples are medical services that endeavor to make their customers "feel" good, restaurants and airlines that try to show "hospitality," universities that "educate," and television that "informs and entertains." But even these intangibles can be measured to some extent.

Managers use a variety of dimensions to measure service quality, such as the facilities used, the "efficiency" of the service, the expectations of customers, and a comparison to the performance of competitors. For purposes of our study, we shall relate service quality to three measures: proficiency of the service, timeliness of the service, and service environment.

- *Proficiency* is a measure of the degree of skill with which the service is carried out. Examples of "defective services" are misspelled words by a typist, incorrect entries by a bank teller, lost (or delayed) goods by a transport service, dirty tables in a restaurant, and erroneous legal or tax advice. Ratings and comparisons to the performance of competition are common measures for television programs, restaurants, universities, and so on.
- *Service timeliness* refers to the point in time when the service is to be performed and the length of time required to carry it out. For example, Wendy's, the Bank of America, and United Airlines are all anxious to process customers with a minimum amount of waiting time. Late reports, late starting times (for conferences, entertainment), delays in service, and services at wrong times (such as hospital medications) are all examples of time-related quality problems. Queue lengths and service times are common ways of assessing the quality of services.
- The *service environment* includes such things as the facilities used and the space and expectations of customers. Convenient access, pleasant surroundings, and friendly people help convey the impression of a courteous, quality environment. In hospitals, cleanliness standards serve as one measure of the quality of health care. Universities feel their campus environment reflects on the quality of their education. City and state governments use air and water pollutants as measures of environmental quality.

Absolute measures of service proficiency, timeliness, and environment are, of course, not always easy to get. Relative (or comparative) measures may also be useful, however, because quality can also be measured by the "change in state" of a process [8]. For example, assessing the quality of a laundering operation might include checking the number, type, and size of stains removed. This approach might then be supplemented by measures of the time required to do the job, the packaging of the item, courtesy of the receptionist, and so on.

Variation in performance is also a useful measure of quality in services. And, as we shall see later, control charts are one of the best ways of tracking the variability in performance. Numerous applications exist in medical, hospitality, professional service, and public service areas.

QUALITY COSTS AND ZERO-DEFECT PROGRAMS

Quality costs have traditionally been classified into two major categories: (1) *inspection and control costs* and (2) *defective product costs.* As expenditures for inspection and control increase, the costs attributable to defective products decrease. The optimal level of expenditure on quality control activities can be graphically portrayed as the lowest point on the total quality control cost curve, as shown in Fig. 14-5a.

Inspection and Control Costs Inspection and control costs include costs for training, administration, and operation of the quality control program as well as costs for the labor and materials used in inspection and testing activities. In service activities, the training of employees is especially critical. This is because servers cannot store their work in a physical product that can be corrected later (if it has a defect). They must respond "online" to their customers. They may even have to help shape their customers' expectations if the quality of a service depends upon a customer's disposition or frame of mind when the service is rendered [10:108]. Hence the soft music in dentists' offices and pleasant flight attendants to

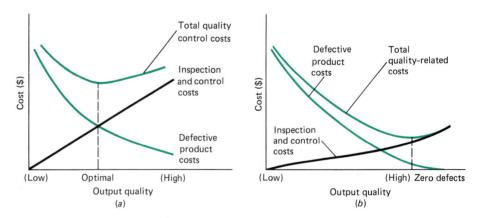

FIGURE 14-5   Quality Costs under (*a*) Traditional and (*b*) Zero-Defect Programs

greet airline passengers. (One measure of airline quality is also the *number* of personal contacts between a passenger and the flight attendants.)

Defective Product Costs Defective product costs include the scrap, machine downtime, and rework costs within the plant or service facility. Also included are any repair and replacement costs (and loss of goodwill) after the product gets into the hands of the consumer. These costs are, of course, difficult to assess, but avoiding consideration of them does not eliminate their impact.

Zero-Defect Approach The *zero-defect approach* is a program arising from the aerospace industry in the 1960s that aims at building defect-free products in the first place rather than having to deal with defectives. It is a relatively holistic quality concept that incorporates the necessary training, advertisement (such as banners), and motivation needed to gain a quality commitment from the entire firm. The zero-defect philosophy blends well with the Japanese approach to quality assurance and has been assimilated by many Japanese firms.

Figure 14-5*b* illustrates the cost relationships assumed in a zero-defect approach. Note that the total costs extend to *any quality-related* costs. Although it is not always practical to achieve "absolute zero defects," the goal of problem-free production can be very useful. An example from the semiconductor industry will illustrate.

Chip manufacturing is a high-tech operation, and a variety of problems can render the glasslike silicon chips defective (for example, static electricity, temperature extremes, abrasion, dust).[1] It is not uncommon to have only 70 to 80 percent of the chips meet specifications, and for some new designs the yield rate may be as low as only 20 to 30 percent. No more than about 100 particles of dust per 30 cubic centimeters of air can be tolerated [9].

In the early years of the personal computer market, American firms were able to sort out a sufficient number of satisfactory chips to support their manufacturing activities. But Japanese competition has aimed for fewer defectives. Moreover, Japanese manufacturers look upon human beings as "walking dust clouds" compared to robots (which are not only clean but can work 24 hours per day at a constant pace.) Thus American firms were startled when Japanese chip makers obtained 40 percent of the market for 16K random access memory (RAM) chips. When the 64K chips came out, the Japanese won 70 percent of the market and increased that to 90 percent for 256K chips. As explained by a Japanese engineer, who was a Deming prize winner for his work in quality control [9],

> The reason for their [American] failure was simple: With only a few exceptions, American manufacturers had yields of usable chips so low that they could not meet orders, and the failure rates of their products could not begin to compete with that of

---

[1] Electronic chips are used in a wide range of products, and defects might affect anything from a compact disk player or automobile braking system to a 747 jet or a space shuttle. A defective computer chip is even thought, by some to have been responsible for alerting the U.S. Strategic Air Command to a (nonexistent) Soviet missile attack in 1980. Fortunately that alert was called off when radar observers reported no sign of incoming missiles.

Japanese RAMs, which was on the order of one ten-millionth per hour, or to put it another way, one failure in a thousand years. This high level of reliability is exceptional, even in requirements for supply to the U.S. military. . . . The next stage is megabit RAMs, samples of which Japanese companies are now shipping. According to some sources, the American industry may not even be able to take part in this upcoming contest.

Not all American industry is willing to fall behind, however. Extensive quality assurance programs are under way in countless firms such as Xerox, IBM, and Ford. Several major companies such as General Electric have already reported savings on the order of millions of dollars as a result of zero-defect programs. At Armco, Inc. (a steel supplier) inspecting, scrapping, and reworking products previously accounted for 10 to 20 percent of their manufacturing costs. Management decided to change its culture by developing "corrective action teams" and inviting employee suggestions on how to promote a quality attitude [14]. The savings from "building products right the first time" is estimated to be in the millions of employee-hours.

The zero-defect approach has indeed been effective in motivating U.S. workers to participate more actively in setting and achieving high quality standards, and it is enhancing the awareness of quality in industry.

INSPECTION AND QUALITY CIRCLES

Quality must be embodied in a good or service. Two commonly used approaches to enhancing quality are by (1) inspecting for specific requirements and (2) motivating workers to strive for improved quality by programs such as quality circles.

Inspection: When, Where, and How Much Measurement and inspection activities are designed to detect unacceptable quality levels before a product gets additional investment or is put into service. They cannot convert a defective item into an acceptable product, nor do they add any noticeable value to the product.

In an operational sense, the timing, location, and amount of inspection are a function of the type of process and the value added at each stage. A general guideline is to inspect when the cost of inspection at any given stage is less than

---

- Upon receipt of raw materials
- Before costly and irreversible operations
- Before work that could hide defects
- Upon completion of the product
- Before stocking high-value items
- Before shipment to customers

FIGURE 14-6 When to Perform Quality Control Inspections

the probable loss from not inspecting. The times and/or places suggested in Fig. 14-6 are often appropriate.

Inspections are frequently performed by quality control inspectors who are independent of the production supervisor. This separation in the chain of command lends objectivity to the control efforts. Many firms have, however, integrated the inspection tasks into an enlarged job of the production worker. This requires more skills of the employee, but it also evidences a trust and responsibility that can be positively motivating. Inspections are not always clear-cut, nor are they necessarily easy.[2] Inspectors must exercise careful judgment in interpreting the results of measurements and tests. Job pressures from the work environment (heat, noise, fatigue, delivery schedules, and so on) can cause them to err.

The effects of undetected inspection errors can be detrimental and long-lasting. This is why firms like General Motors simply drop suppliers if they fail to measure up to their quality requirements. Undetected inspection errors can result in anything from scrapping a few parts to losing customer goodwill and incurring future product recall costs—problems that can cause losses of millions of dollars. When product failures endanger human life, such as in the space shuttle disaster in 1986 (the O-rings in a solid rocket engine failed to seal), the ramifications are even greater. Products such as solid propellant engines present significant testing problems because they are destroyed in the testing process. In these situations statistical samples may provide the most useful basis for quality control decisions.

Quality Circles Quality circles are small groups of employees (for example, 8 to 10 in a group) who meet voluntarily for about an hour a week to share ideas in an attempt to solve job-related quality and productivity problems. The group includes foremen as well as employees who perform similar jobs. Members are sometimes taught how to collect data and do the statistical analysis necessary to analyze the cause of quality problems. In other cases (perhaps up to 50 percent of the time), they simply discuss common problems. Their recommendations are recognized and acted upon by management.

The quality circles reflect a philosophy that the responsibility for quality production rests with the many workers rather than with a few inspectors or supervisors. They have become so successful in Japan that in most major manufacturing companies about 85 percent of the workers are active in the quality circle movement. Joji Arai, manager of the Japan Productivity Center, has stated that "the QC Circle program is the largest contributing factor that has enabled Japan to win the worldwide reputation as the producer of high-quality and durable goods" [1:3].

Thousands of U.S. companies have also joined the quality circle bandwagon. Firms such as Westinghouse and Honeywell have hundreds of quality circles

---

[2] This was vividly brought out to me when, as a young engineer, I had a very large shipload of material sampled and tested, and it failed the test. I was forced to have the material returned from Seattle to the supplier in Los Angeles. It was a very costly move for the supplier, for the shipment consisted entirely of lead—tons of it! The supplier was most unhappy, but the next shipment was fully within specifications.

operating. Proponents claim that defects are often reduced (perhaps by two-thirds) and productivity is increased. In addition, job satisfaction is improved, with a resulting reduction in turnover and absenteeism. This improvement in the quality of worklife, stemming from worker participation in decision-making activities, is acknowledged as the most important benefit for some firms.

ACCEPTANCE SAMPLING OF INCOMING AND OUTGOING QUALITY

When 100 percent inspection is not practical, taking samples is usually the next best way of estimating the incoming or outgoing quality of a good or service. Random samples provide each element with an equal chance of being selected and permit logical inferences to be made about the population quality on the basis of sample evidence. The parameters of most interest are usually the mean μ and the standard deviation σ of the population, which are estimated from the sample mean $\bar{x}$ and sample standard deviation s.

STANDARD ERRORS

We have noted previously that in a sampling situation any one sample mean may be expected to differ somewhat from the population mean simply because of variation among samples. Nevertheless, the deviation of the sample means or standard error of the mean $s_{\bar{x}}$ can be estimated and controlled, for it is a function of the sample size, n.

$$\text{Standard error of mean:} \qquad s_{\bar{x}} = \frac{s}{\sqrt{n}} \qquad (2\text{-}12)$$

As the sample size approaches the population size, N, the standard error gets smaller; it is reduced to zero when the sample size is as large as the population.

**EXAMPLE 14-1
(Standard
Error)**

A quality control sample of $n = 100$ items is taken, and the standard deviation is calculated to be .250 inch.
(a) Estimate the standard error of the mean.
(b) What would be the standard error if the sample size were 1,000 instead of 100?

SOLUTION

(a) $s_{\bar{x}} = \dfrac{s}{\sqrt{n}} = \dfrac{.250}{\sqrt{100}} = .025$ inch

(b) $s_{\bar{x}} = \dfrac{.250}{\sqrt{1,000}} = .008$ inch

The determination of the standard error of the mean is particularly important in quality control work, for it facilitates statistical estimation and tests of hypothesis (H_0). Much of the inference made about the quality of large lots is based upon statistical theory, which holds that regardless of the shape of the population distribution, the distribution of sample means (that is, the sampling distribution of the means) is approximately normal if the sample size is sufficiently large (greater than 30). Of course, the same theory holds when we are making an inference based upon sample proportions, except, as we saw earlier, proportions require a larger sample size (such as 50 or 100), and the standard error of proportion is

$$\text{Standard error of proportion:} \qquad s_p = \frac{\sqrt{pq}}{\sqrt{n}} \qquad\qquad (2\text{-}11)$$

In practice we find that a good deal of acceptance sampling activities rely upon the comparison of actual sample means, or proportions, with what might theoretically be expected on the assumption of a normal distribution of means or proportions.

There are other situations in quality control work in which the characteristics of the population are fairly well documented, and we wish to make deductive statements about specific items rather than inductive statements about the population as a whole. For example, we know that individual machined parts often have dimensions that follow a normal distribution, and failures of a machine often follow a Poisson distribution. If the variable of interest in a population is known to follow a normal, Poisson, or other statistical distribution, the probabilities of individual events can be deduced from our prior knowledge of the population itself. This use of probability theory represents an application of *deductive logic*, whereas the inference about the population on the basis of sample evidence is an application of *inductive logic*. In this section we shall look first at some deductive situations, then at the inductive applications involving the use of operating characteristic curves, and finally at the economics of sampling.

STATISTICAL DISTRIBUTIONS FOR DEFECTIVES

We saw earlier that a frequency distribution describes a random variable. Very often the actual frequency distributions we encounter in quality control activities conform closely to theoretical probability distributions which have been mathematically defined. Some of the more common distributions are shown in Fig. 14-7. A review of all these distributions is beyond our scope here, but let us illustrate two applications of deductive inference—one involving attributes (using the binomial distribution) and one involving variables (using the normal distribution). Recall that attributes are countable, or discrete, whereas variables are measurable, or continuous.

EXAMPLE 14-2
(Binomial
Distribution)

Fifteen percent of the accounts audited by a CPA firm turn out to have errors that necessitate the payment of additional taxes. What is the chance that exactly 2 accounts taken from a random sample of 10 will owe additional taxes?

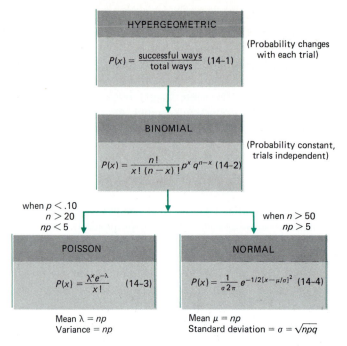

FIGURE 14-7   Probability Distributions Useful in Quality Control

SOLUTION

The error rate is given as a percentage and can be taken as constant. If we can assume that each account is independent of others, then the binomial distribution applies.

$$P(x = 2 \mid n = 10, p = .15) = \frac{n!}{x! \, (n - x)!} \, p^x q^{n-x}$$

$$= \frac{10!}{2! \; 8!} \, (.15)^2 \, (.85)^8 = .2759$$

Note that the solution value could also be obtained more directly from the table of binomial probabilities given in Appendix D.

EXAMPLE 14-3
(Normal
Distribution)

Cans of corn at the Crescent Valley Cannery are filled by a machine which can be set for any desired average weight. The fill weights are normally distributed with a standard deviation of .4 ounce. If quality standards specify that 98 percent of the cans should contain 16 ounces or more, where (that is, on the ounce scale) should the quality control supervisor recommend the machine be set?

SOLUTION

The machine average, μ, must be set high enough so that 48 percent of the cans containing less than the mean still contain 16.0 ounces. Knowing that the fill is normally distributed, we can use the expression for the standard normal deviate.

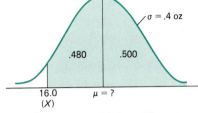

$$-Z = \frac{X - \mu}{\sigma}$$

where X = specified fill = 16.0 oz

        μ = unknown mean setting

        σ = .4 oz

        Z = number of standard deviations from μ to X (*Note:* This corresponds to an area of 48 percent. We must enter the body of the normal distribution table—Appendix C—as close as possible to the value of .48 and read off the number of standard deviations from the margin.)

For $P(Z)$ = .480, $Z = -2.05$.

$$\therefore \mu = X - (-Z)\sigma = X + Z\sigma$$
$$= 16.0 + 2.05\,(.4) = 16.8 \text{ oz}$$

Both of the preceding examples assumed that there was prior statistical knowledge of the population or production process. We used that knowledge to deduce something about a specific event (that is, the number of accounts in error) or to set limits for a specific process (that is, fill levels for cans of corn). We will proceed now to the use of individual or sample information to make statistical inferences about the parent population.

SAMPLING PLANS FOR ATTRIBUTES AND VARIABLES

Quality control inspectors are often charged with the responsibility of making a decision as to whether an incoming or outgoing shipment is of acceptable quality or not. They are usually forced to decide on the basis of a limited sample because the inspection cost, or perhaps the destructive nature of testing activities, makes 100 percent inspection uneconomical or infeasible.

Since the decision to accept or reject a lot must be made on the basis of sample evidence, the firm's managers must be willing to accept some risks of rejecting good lots or accepting bad lots. Fortunately, the amount of risk can be specified in terms of a sampling plan so that its consequences can be evaluated. Then if the expected costs of making a wrong decision are too great, perhaps the risks of error can be shifted by mutual agreement between the producer and consumer, or even reduced in total by taking a larger sample.

Sampling Plan   A *sampling plan* is simply a decision rule which specifies how large a sample (n) should be taken and the allowable measurement, number, or percentage (c) of defectives in the sample. If the items to be inspected are classified *qualitatively* according to an attribute, such as good or bad, acceptable or not acceptable, and so on, then the sampling plan is referred to as an *attributes plan,* and the probabilities of defectives in the parent population are estimated from discrete distributions such as the binomial and Poisson. An attributes sampling plan might read as follows: "Select a random sample of size $n = 40$, and count the number of defectives c. If $c \leqslant 3$, accept the lot; otherwise reject it."

If the items to be inspected are classified *quantitatively* according to some measurable characteristic, they will require a *variables sampling plan.* Since variables plans necessitate the recording of actual measurements instead of simply a dichotomous classification (such as of good or bad), they provide more information and require fewer inspections for the same degree of assurance than do comparable attributes plans. Variables plans typically use the normal distribution and might be stated as follows: "Select a random sample of size $n = 40$, and determine the mean tensile strength $\bar{x}$. If $\bar{x} > 12,000$ psi, accept the lot; otherwise reject it."

Operating Characteristic Curve   The acceptance and rejection characteristics of both attributes and variables sampling plans can be described by *operating characteristic* (OC) curves. These curves always pertain to a specific plan, an n and c combination. They show the probability that the given plan will accept lots of various (unknown) quality levels. Thus, the OC curve for a given sampling plan will indicate what percentage of lots of any (hypothesized or actual) quality may be expected to be accepted. We shall illustrate the determination of n and c values and the construction of OC curves in the forthcoming discussion on sampling plans for attributes.

Sampling Plans and OC Curves for Attributes   Suppose that an electronics producer supplies a consumer with miniaturized logic units that the consumer in turn uses in his own production process. The two have agreed on the price, delivery schedule, and quality level required for a proposed shipment of $N = 100$ units. If the quantity of defective units in the shipment is less than or equal to $2\frac{1}{2}$ percent, the shipment is to be accepted, and if the quantity is greater than $2\frac{1}{2}$ percent the shipment is to be rejected and returned at the producer's expense. Now suppose further that an independent laboratory (that never makes mistakes) inspects all 100 items and accurately determines the percentage of defectives. Figure 14-8 shows that if the lot contains either 1 percent or 2 percent defectives, the probability of acceptance by the consumer is 1.0—that is, there is no chance of rejecting the lot. Similarly, if the lot contains 3 percent or more defectives, there is no chance that it will be accepted. As shown on the operating characteristic curve for this plan, for a p value $\geqslant 2\frac{1}{2}$ percent, the $P(\text{accept}) = 0$.

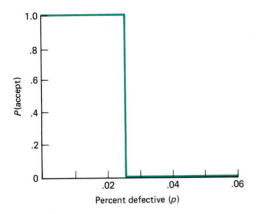

FIGURE 14-8   OC Curve for 100 Percent Inspection

Producer and Consumer Risk   The above plan called for 100 percent inspection of the population, and assuming that it was accurately done, the plan entailed no risk of error to either the producer or the consumer. Let us assume now that the next shipment is much larger ($N = 1,000$), and the producer and consumer are forced to adopt a sampling plan in order to reduce inspection costs. As with any decision based upon sample evidence, each now incurs some risk of error:

- *Producer's risk.*   This is the risk of getting a sample which has a higher proportion of defectives than the lot as a whole, and rejecting a good lot. It is designated as the alpha (α) risk. Producers hope to keep this risk low, say at 1 to 5 percent. If a good lot is rejected, we refer to this as a *type I error.*
- *Consumer's risk.*   This is the risk of getting a sample which has a lower proportion of defectives than the lot as a whole, and accepting a bad lot. It is designated as the beta (β) risk. Consumers want to keep this risk low. If a bad lot is accepted, we refer to this as a *type II error.*

AQL and LTPD Levels   To derive a sampling plan, the producer and consumer must specify not only the level of the α and β risk but also the lot quality level to which these risks pertain. Thus we must further define "good lot" and "bad lot" in terms of the percentage defective in the population.

- *AQL.*   The *acceptable quality level* (AQL) is the quality level of a good lot. It is the percentage defective that can be considered satisfactory as a process average and represents a level of quality which the producer wants accepted with a high probability of acceptance.
- *LTPD.*   The *lot tolerance percent defective* (LTPD) is the quality level of a bad lot. It represents a level of quality which the consumer wants accepted with a low probability of acceptance.

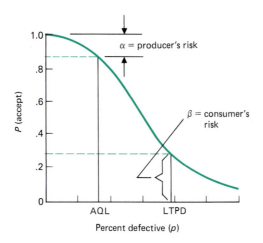

FIGURE 14-9   OC Curve for Less Than 100 Percent Inspection

Lots which have a quality level between the AQL and LTPD are in an "indifferent" zone.

The relationship between α, β, AQL, and LTPD is shown in Fig. 14-9. The α risk at the AQL level and the β risk at the LTPD level establish two points from which the sample size, n, and acceptance number, c, are determined. Given these two points, the OC curve can then be drawn to describe the risk characteristics of the specific sampling plan.

Designing the Sampling Plan   The methodology of arriving at a sampling plan (given the α and AQL and the β and LTPD values) involves a trial-and-error process whereby different values of n and c are tried in order to find the combination that most closely passes through the two points. For a small sample, the OC curve is likely to be rather flat, resulting in high risks to both the producer and the consumer. Increasing the sample size makes the OC curve more discriminating between good and bad lots to the point where a 100 percent sample results in the curve shown in Fig. 14-8, where the respective risks have been reduced to zero.

Figure 14-10 illustrates the effect of changing the value of the acceptance number, c. When c is very low (for example, zero), the OC curve is concave to the origin with relatively high α risk and relatively low β risk. Note the two sampling plans of size $n = 100$. For the acceptance number $c \leq 1$, the α risk is about 25 percent and the β risk only 2 percent. Changing to a plan of $c \leq 4$ shifts the risk from producer to consumer, so the α risk is nil, and β is nearly 30 percent. As c is increased, the curve first takes on more of an S shape and then moves away from the origin in convex fashion, becoming less discriminating. At high values of c, the risk is shifted largely to the consumer.

The sampling plan shown in the dashed line in Fig. 14-10 is more discriminating between good (AQL) and bad (LTPD) lots. Notice that the α risk is only about

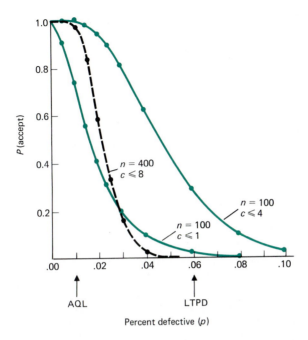

P(accept)

n = 400
c ⩽ 8

n = 100
c ⩽ 4

n = 100
c ⩽ 1

AQL   LTPD

Percent defective (p)

FIGURE 14-10   Effect on the OC Curve of Changing the Sample Size and the Acceptance Number

2 percent and the β risk virtually nil. This reduced risk has, of course, come about at the expense of increasing the sample size.

Let us see how an OC curve is constructed for a given sampling plan. Our purpose here is to understand the underlying theory of sampling plans. It is not necessary for quality control analysts to repeat these calculations every time they wish to set up a sampling plan. Several tables of standard plans have been determined and printed, including the Dodge and Romig tables [5] and the U.S. Military Standard MIL-STD-105 [12].

EXAMPLE 14-4

A shipment of 1,000 semiconductors is to be inspected on a sampling basis. The producer and consumer have agreed to adopt a plan whereby the α risk is limited to 5 percent at AQL = 1 percent defective and the β risk is limited to 10 percent at LTPD = 5 percent defective. Construct the OC curve for the sampling plan $n = 100$ and $c \le 2$, and indicate whether this plan satisfies the requirements.

SOLUTION

To construct the OC curve we must determine the probabilities of acceptance of the shipment for various possible values of the true percentage of defectives in the population. Since the shipment is accepted when there are ≤ 2 defectives in the sample, the probabilities we seek are $P(c \le 2)$, given the alternative values of the population. If we were working with a binomial distribution, we could write this probability as

$$P(c \leqslant 2 \mid n,p) \tag{14-5}$$

and obtain the values from a calculator or Appendix D. However, from Fig. 14-7 we note that the binomial probabilities of defectives can be approximated by a Poisson distribution here because the sample size (100) is > 20, we appear to be working with a small percent defective of $p < .10$, and np looks to be in the neighborhood of 5. Using Appendix E we can obtain the Poisson probabilities as

$$P(c \leq 2 \mid \lambda) \tag{14-6}$$

where c = number of defectives in sample
λ = mean of Poisson distribution = np
p = (alternative) percentage of defectives in population

Thus, for the AQL percentage of $p = .01$, we can find the probability of acceptance of the lot as

$$P(c \leq 2 \mid \lambda)$$

where $\lambda = np = (100)(.01) = 1.$

$$\therefore P(c \leq 2 \mid \lambda = 1) = .92 \qquad \text{(from Appendix E)}$$

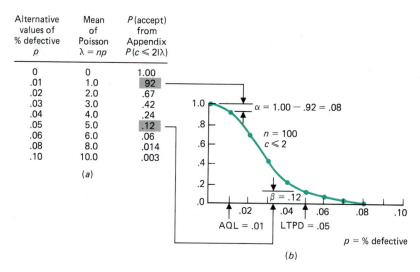

Alternative values of % defective p	Mean of Poisson $\lambda = np$	P(accept) from Appendix $P(c \leqslant 2 \mid \lambda)$
0	0	1.00
.01	1.0	92
.02	2.0	.67
.03	3.0	.42
.04	4.0	.24
.05	5.0	.12
.06	6.0	.06
.08	8.0	.014
.10	10.0	.003

(a)

$\alpha = 1.00 - .92 = .08$

$n = 100$
$c \leqslant 2$

$\beta = .12$

AQL = .01   LTPD = .05

p = % defective

(b)

FIGURE 14-11   OC Curve Values and Operating Characteristic Curve for Sampling Plan $n = 100$, $c \leqslant 2$

Probabilities for other possible values of the true mean are given in Fig. 14-11a, and these values are plotted as an OC curve in Fig. 14-11b.

Note that this plan ($n = 100$, $c \leq 2$) yields an α risk of .08 and a β risk of .12. Both exceed the respective limits of .05 and .10. Since both risks are exceeded, a larger sample size will be required, and the calculations will have to be repeated.

In the above example we assumed a sampling plan and then calculated the α and β risks to see if the plan satisfied them. In practice, an improved procedure calls for first establishing an OC curve which satisfies the α and AQL requirements and then substituting various values of n and c until the plan also satisfies β at the LTPD. The widely used MIL-STD-105 follows a different technique in that it identifies a sample size and the various levels of protection available to the producer and consumer depending upon the AQL level specified. Since the AQL does not describe the β risk to the consumer, the MIL-STD-105 makes it necessary to refer to the operating characteristic curves of the various plans to determine what protection the consumer will have. Booklets of MIL-STD-105 plans are available from the U.S. Government Printing Office.

Double and Multiple Sampling   Double or multiple sampling plans are sometimes used to reduce inspection costs. Figure 14-12 illustrates the underlying concepts. With double sampling, a smaller sample is drawn first, in hopes that if the lot is either very good or very bad a decision can be made on the basis of the smaller sample at a lower cost. If the first sample is not decisive, a second is drawn, and the lot is either accepted or rejected on the basis of the total of the two samples. Figure 14-12a illustrates the preliminary situation in terms of two OC curves.

A *multiple*, or *sequential*, *sampling plan* would involve a number of OC curves. Multiple sampling plans use even smaller sample sizes than double sampling plans, for they allow for the drawing of whatever number of samples are necessary to reach a decision.

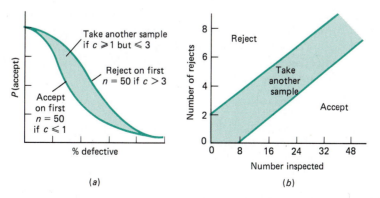

(a)   (b)

FIGURE 14-12   Other Sampling Plans. (a) OC Curves for Double Sampling; (b) Sequential Sampling

Figure 14-12*b* depicts a multiple sampling plan in terms closely related to a decision rule. Using this plan, if inspectors found no rejects out of the first dozen items inspected, they would accept the lot. If, however, they found two rejects by that time, they would continue sampling until the sample results placed the lot in either an "accept" or "reject" classification.

Sampling Plans for Variables   Variables plans entail measurements, on a continuous scale, of how closely a given variable conforms to a specified characteristic. It is often reasonable to assume that these measurements follow a normal distribution, but even if they do not, the distribution of the means of samples of the measurements does approach normality, especially if they contain 30 or more observations.

The objectives and risks involved in variables sampling are similar to those in attributes sampling. However, in constructing the variables sampling plan we must determine sample size and some maximum or minimum measurement (reject limit, c) or both, rather than simply an acceptable percentage of defectives. In this case, the reject limit, c, controls the producer's α risk or consumer's β risk, or it controls both α and β. The problem is to determine a reject limit that is an appropriate number of standard errors above or below a specified mean value such that the probabilities of rejecting good lots (if concerned with α only) or accepting bad lots (if concerned with β only) or both are limited. In our first example, below, we shall specify a single quality level and determine the reject limit that is required to control the α risk, given a preassigned sample size. (We could alternatively have specified the reject limit and solved for the sample size, for the two are intimately related.) This will be followed by an example specifying two quality levels that results in control of both the α risk and the β risk. In this latter example, the specification of both risks will fully determine the reject limit, c, and the sample size, n.

EXAMPLE 14-5
(Given only α risk and n: Solving for c)

A metals firm produces titanium castings whose weights are normally distributed, with a standard deviation of $\sigma = 8$ pounds. Casting shipments averaging less than 200 pounds are considered of poor quality, and the firm would like to minimize such shipments.

Design a sampling plan for a sample of $n = 25$ that will limit the risk of rejecting lots that average 200 pounds to 5 percent. (Assume that sample means are normally distributed.)

SOLUTION
The problem situation is described schematically below. We assume that the distribution of sample means is approximately normal, with mean $\mu = 200$. Since σ is known, we can compute $\sigma_{\bar{x}}$ directly instead of estimating it by $S_{\bar{x}}$:

$$\sigma_{\bar{x}} = \frac{\sigma}{\sqrt{n}} = \frac{8}{\sqrt{25}} = 1.6 \text{ lb}$$

The limit, c, is then

$$c = \mu - Z\sigma_{\bar{x}}$$

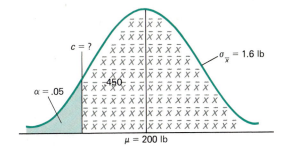

where Z = value corresponding to area of .450
  = 1.64   (from Appendix C)

$$\therefore c = 200 - 1.64(1.6) = 197.4 \text{ lb}$$

Plan: Take a random sample of $n = 25$ ingots, and determine the mean weight. If $\bar{x} > 197.4$ pounds, accept the shipment; otherwise reject it.

In the preceding example, with the limit set at 197.4 pounds, the risk of rejecting a lot that really averages 200 pounds (a good lot) is limited to 5 percent. The plan was established wholly on the basis of the α risk and a given sample size. A larger sample size would, of course, be more discriminating. For example, with a sample of $n = 100$ the reject limit could be raised to 198.7 pounds.

EXAMPLE 14-6
(Given α and
β Risks:
Solving for
n and c)

A metals firm produces titanium castings whose weights are normally distributed, with a standard deviation of $\sigma = 8.0$ pounds. Casting shipments averaging 200.0 pounds are of good quality, and those averaging 196.0 pounds are of poor quality. Design a sampling plan that satisfies the following requirements:
(a) The probability of rejecting a lot with an average weight of 200 pounds is .05.
(b) The probability of accepting a lot with an average weight of 196 pounds is .10.

SOLUTION
The problem situation is described schematically in Fig. 14-13. The solution procedure is to first set up simultaneous equations defining the reject limit, c, in terms of Z standard errors. Then solve for n, and substitute it back into either one of the equations to find c. The two equations locating c are

(a) From above: $$c = \mu_1 - Z_\alpha \frac{\sigma}{\sqrt{n}} = 200.0 - 1.645 \frac{(8)}{\sqrt{n}}$$

(b) From below: $$c = \mu_2 + Z_\beta \frac{\sigma}{\sqrt{n}} = 196.0 + 1.28 \frac{(8)}{\sqrt{n}}$$

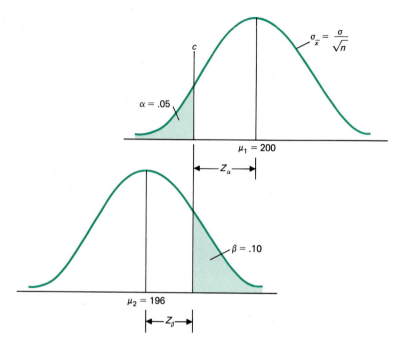

FIGURE 14-13 Sampling Distributions Where α and β Are Specified

Setting the two equations for c equal to each other:

$$200.0 - 1.645\frac{(8)}{\sqrt{n}} = 196.0 + 1.28\frac{(8)}{\sqrt{n}}$$

$$n = \left(\frac{23.40}{4}\right)^2 = 34$$

$$\therefore c = 200.0 - 1.645\frac{(8)}{\sqrt{34}} = 197.7 \text{ lb}$$

Plan: Take a random sample of $n = 34$ ingots, and determine the mean weight. If $\bar{x} > 197.7$ pounds, accept the shipment; otherwise reject it.

The above examples assumed that the shipment standard deviation, σ, was known. When σ is unknown, the sample standard deviation, s, is usually an acceptable substitute. However, some authorities recommend that a larger sample size be used to compensate for the inherent uncertainty.

While MIL-STD-105 and other standard plans are available for attributes sampling, there are a number of standard plans available for variables. MIL-STD-414 is a widely disseminated standard for variables plans that contains plans for situations where σ is known and for situations where it is unknown [13; 3:746].

In the former case the sampling plan is based upon the sample mean, and in the latter it is based upon the sample standard deviation. MIL-STD-414 also contains plans based upon the sample range. Like the attributes standard, MIL-STD-414 includes an option of several levels of inspection and yields an upper and lower specification limit for the measurement being controlled.

ECONOMICS OF SAMPLING: AOQ, ASN, AND ATI

The sample size n and acceptance limit c are not the only characteristics of interest in a sampling plan. Often, when inspection activities reveal defects, the defects are then removed. What then is the quality level of the resultant lot after the "purified" sample is returned? This and other questions can be answered by constructing other curves describing a sampling plan. Three such curves, the AOQ, ASN, and ATI, are described briefly below [3:740]. A more detailed discussion of these curves may be found in Burr [2].

The *average outgoing quality* (AOQ) curve shows the expected quality in all outgoing lots after the rejected lots from the sample have been 100 percent inspected and all defectives have been removed. The AOQ curve reflects the fact that incoming lots with a small percentage of defects will be passed with a resultant high outgoing quality. Those with a slightly larger proportion of defects will result in the worst level of outgoing quality because lots that have a large proportion of defects will end up undergoing 100 percent inspection, with only the acceptable items being passed.

The shape of a typical AOQ curve is illustrated in Fig. 14-14. Values for the ordinate of the curve represent the percentage of defectives (P_D) in lots of size N after inspection. They can be computed from the equation.

$$AOQ = \frac{P_D P_A (N - n)}{N} \qquad (14\text{-}7)$$

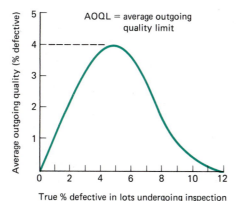

FIGURE 14-14   Typical AOQ Curve

where P_A is the probability of accepting the lot for various values of the percent defective (from the OC curve) and n is the sample size.

EXAMPLE 14-7

An OC curve reveals that lots with a true percentage of defectives of 2 percent have a probability of being accepted if $P_A = .67$. If the sampling plan for lots of $N = 1,000$ called for samples of size $n = 100$, what would be the average outgoing quality (AOQ) level?

SOLUTION

$$AOQ = \frac{P_D P_A (N - n)}{N}$$

$$= \frac{(.02)(.67)(1,000 - 100)}{1,000}$$

$$= .012 = 1.2\%$$

In this example, since the sample size is $n = 100$ and 2 percent of the items in the sample are defective (on the average), then the 2 defective items would be removed from the sample and replaced before the lot was allowed to continue on its way. For lots of $N = 1,000$ items, the number of defects would then be reduced to 2 percent of the 900 uninspected items. This amounts to 18 in 1,000, or 1.8 percent of the items. Since the probability of acceptance of a lot of 2 percent defectives is (from the OC curve) only .67, then the expected value or average outgoing quality level for lots (of 2 percent defectives) is (.67)(1.8 percent) or 1.2 percent defective.

In a similar manner, numbers could be computed for other possible values of the true percentage of defectives. Upon plotting, these values would take a shape similar to that shown in Fig. 14-14. The highest (worst) percentage of defectives for outgoing quality is known as the *average outgoing quality limit* (AOQL).

The *average sample number* (ASN) curve applies to double and multiple sampling plans and also depends upon the quality of the incoming lot. This curve reveals the average number of items that must be inspected before a decision can be made to accept or reject the lot.

The *average total inspection* (ATI) curve shows the average total amount of inspection in a given lot, including both the original sample and the follow-up 100 percent inspection required.

We have used statistical techniques to find the optimal sample size required to limit risks to a given level, but we have not related the risk to a production or marketing cost of passing defectives or the sample size to a cost of sampling. In this sense, we have taken a classical approach of assuming a given risk (for example, $\alpha = .05$) and solving the problem from there, rather than asking how one might originally establish the risk level. In the past, many managers have set risk levels on an intuitive or judgmental basis. This has supposedly incorporated knowledge of the production process requirements, knowledge of costs, experience with suppliers and customers, and so on. Bayesian and other techniques of analysis are now lending greater insight into such decisions by introducing sampling costs into the analysis in a much more explicit manner. The Bayesian material is beyond the scope of this text, but references and computer programs are available that explore this further [3].

CONTROL OF PROCESS QUALITY

Control charts were introduced to industry by Walter Shewhart in the middle 1920s. They are statistically designed devices used to record selected quality characteristics of a production process over time. In contrast to acceptance sampling, control charts measure variation of the process *during operation* rather than the acceptability of materials or products before or after operations.

Control charts help to ensure that only acceptable goods or services are produced by monitoring the process average, which is expected to stay within the bounds of upper and lower statistical limits. If the process average falls outside the limits, this indicates that the process is out of control and suggests that some identifiable cause is responsible. In effect, control charts are standards upon which measurements are recorded so that corrective action may be taken when necessary.

In this section we will consider the problem of process variability and how control charts for variables and attributes can be designed and used to control quality.

TOLERANCE LIMITS OF A PROCESS

Almost any human or machine activity has some inherent variation. Consider anything around you—your own weight, the accuracy of your watch, even the exact dimensions of the pages in this book. We tend to accept minor variations as inherent and consider them random, for although they obviously have a cause, we are not interested in or perhaps are not capable of assigning a cause to them. Variations in product quality that arise from random factors or so-called unassignable causes are usually not of major concern to quality control managers. Their interest lies primarily in identifying and correcting assignable causes, such as excessive tool wear and improper materials.

Many production processes have empirically been found to exhibit a "natural" variability that is normally distributed. For example, the diameters of ½-inch rods, when measured to an accuracy of .001 inch, can be expected to vary in a normal manner about the mean dimension of .500 inch. When this is the case, we say the process has natural tolerance limits such that 99.7 percent of the individual items will lie within 3σ of their mean. The upper natural tolerance limit (T_{UN}) and lower natural tolerance limit (T_{LN}) are then

$$T_{UN} = \mu + 3\sigma \tag{14-8}$$

$$T_{LN} = \mu - 3\sigma \tag{14-9}$$

Knowledge of the natural tolerance limits of a process can be useful to design engineers, production analysts, and marketing personnel for ensuring the proper application of a product. But natural tolerance limits are *not* the control limits used in a production process. *Control limits* do not rely upon the underlying normality of the production process, for they are based upon the *distribution of sample means—and sample proportions—*not individual values. Figure 14-15 illustrates the difference. The population has an unknown mean μ, standard deviation σ, and natural tolerance limits which are 3σ away from μ. Samples are drawn from the population, and the sample statistic belongs to the theoretical sampling distribution of the statistic. For sample means, this distribution is normally distributed (via the central limit theorem),with a mean $\bar{\bar{x}}$, and a standard deviation, $\sigma_{\bar{x}}$. Because it is normally distributed, we expect that if the process is in control, 99.7 percent of the sample means will be within $3\sigma_{\bar{x}}$ of the center line, $\bar{\bar{x}}$.

We fully expect that some individual X values might be outside the control limits (as is point m in Fig. 14-15). However, when these individual points are averaged with others, it is highly unlikely that the mean of a random sample will lie outside the control limits unless the process has shifted because of some identifiable cause.

We will now turn to an examination of the construction and use of control charts. We look first at charts for variables and then at charts for attributes.

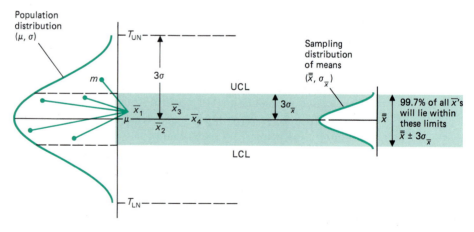

FIGURE 14-15   Relationships between Natural Tolerance Limits and Control Limits for Sample Means

CONTROL CHARTS FOR VARIABLES

Control charts for variables are used to monitor processes by recording measurements of the central tendency (mean) and dispersion of the variable of interest. A control chart of means is called an $\bar{x}$ chart, and the most common (and simplest) chart for dispersion is a range, or R, chart. Many processes use both charts.

The $\bar{x}$ chart reveals variation *among* samples, while the R chart reveals variation *within* samples. Both charts base their limits upon the presumed normal distribution of the mean and range statistics. Figure 14-16 illustrates a variables chart for both, where the means and ranges of four hypothetical samples have been recorded. Note that the control limits for the sample means are

$$\text{UCL}_{\bar{x}} = \bar{\bar{x}} + 3\sigma_{\bar{x}} \tag{14-10}$$

$$\text{LCL}_{\bar{x}} = \bar{\bar{x}} - 3\sigma_{\bar{x}} \tag{14-11}$$

where $\bar{\bar{x}}$ is the mean of the sample means ($\bar{x}$'s). Since $\sigma_{\bar{x}}$ is often unknown, $s_{\bar{x}}$ serves as an estimator of $\sigma_{\bar{x}}$.

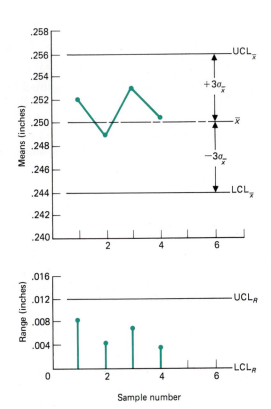

FIGURE 14-16   Control Chart (Variables)

FIGURE 14-17 Factors for Computing Control Limits

Sample Size n	Mean Factor A	Upper Range B	Lower Range C
2	1.880	3.268	0
3	1.023	2.574	0
4	.729	2.282	0
5	.577	2.114	0
6	.483	2.004	0
7	.419	1.924	.076
8	.373	1.864	.136
9	.337	1.816	.184
10	.308	1.777	.223
12	.266	1.716	.284
14	.235	1.671	.329
16	.212	1.636	.364
18	.194	1.608	.392
20	.180	1.586	.414
25	.153	1.541	.459

Source: Adapted from "Quality Control Materials," Special Technical Publication 15-C, pp. 63, 72, American Society for Testing Materials, Philadelphia, 1951. Used with permission.

In practice, the calculation of control limits is simplified by the use of tables based upon range values rather than standard deviations. As illustrated in Fig. 14-17, three factors are used—a factor A for calculating the control limits for means, and factors B and C for calculating the range limits.

On the basis of Fig. 14-17, the control limits for means and ranges are

$$\text{Mean:} \qquad \text{UCL}_{\bar{x}} = \bar{\bar{x}} + A\bar{R} \qquad (14\text{-}12)$$

$$\text{LCL}_{\bar{x}} = \bar{\bar{x}} - A\bar{R} \qquad (14\text{-}13)$$

$$\text{Range:} \qquad \text{UCL}_R = B\bar{R} \qquad (14\text{-}14)$$

$$\text{LCL}_R = C\bar{R} \qquad (14\text{-}15)$$

The procedure for establishing and using control limits is much like setting any other standard from empirical data:

1 Select the job to be controlled; identify the relevant characteristics and method of measurement.
2 Take approximately 20 samples of size n, and compute the sample means ($\bar{x}$'s) and ranges (R). Plot $\bar{x}$ and R points on a chart.[3]

---

[3] Sample sizes of $n = 4$ or 5 are frequently used. Note, however, that if the equation $\bar{\bar{x}} \pm 3\sigma_{\bar{x}}$ is used, the n used to compute $\sigma_{\bar{x}} = \sigma/\sqrt{n}$ should be the same size as that used later when taking the samples.

3 Compute the mean and range control limits—per Eq. (14-12) through Eq. (14-15)—and plot them on the same chart.

4 Discard any samples with means or ranges outside the control limits, and recalculate the mean and range control limits.

5 Evaluate the economic feasibility of the limits. If satisfactory, place them on standard forms for the job, and begin regular sampling activities.

6 Investigate for assignable causes when the process is out of control, as evidenced by:

(a) An $\bar{x}$ or R point outside the control limits

(b) A predominance of $\bar{x}$ points on one side of the center $\bar{\bar{x}}$ line

(c) Any two points in a row at a location of $> \frac{2}{3}$ of the distance to a control limit

EXAMPLE 14-8
(Variables Chart)

A precision casting process is designed to produce blades having a diameter of 10.000 ± .025 centimeters. To establish control limits, 20 samples of $n = 5$ blades are randomly selected from the first 500 blades produced as follows:

Sample 1	Sample 2	$\cdots$ Sample 20
10.010	10.018	10.004
9.989	9.992	9.988
10.019	9.996	9.990
9.978	10.014	10.019
10.008	10.005	9.983
50.004	50.025	49.984
$\bar{x}$ = 10.0008	10.0050 $\cdots$	9.9968
R = .041	.026 $\cdots$	.036

The grand mean, $\bar{\bar{x}}$, of the sample means and the mean $\bar{R}$ of the sample ranges were found to be

$$\bar{\bar{x}} = \frac{\Sigma \bar{x}}{\text{no. samples}} = \frac{10.0008 + 10.0050 + \cdots + 9.9968}{20} = 10.002 \text{ cm}$$

$$\bar{R} = \frac{\Sigma R}{\text{no. samples}} = \frac{.041 + .026 + \cdots + .036}{20} = .032 \text{ cm}$$

(a) Find the control limits for the sample means.
(b) Find the control limits for the sample ranges.

SOLUTION

(a) Mean:
$$\text{UCL}_{\bar{x}} = \bar{\bar{x}} + A\bar{R} = 10.002 + .577(.032) = 10.020 \text{ cm}$$
$$\text{Center} = \bar{\bar{x}} = 10.002 \text{ cm}$$
$$\text{LCL}_{\bar{x}} = \bar{\bar{x}} - A\bar{R} = 10.002 - .577(.032) = 9.984 \text{ cm}$$

(b) Range:
$$\text{UCL}_R = B\bar{R} = (2.114)(.032) = .068 \text{ cm}$$
$$\text{Center} = \bar{R} = .032 \text{ cm}$$
$$\text{LCL}_R = C\bar{R} = (.000)(.032) = .000 \text{ cm}$$

FIGURE 14-18   Control Limits for Attributes Data

Proportions (p charts)*		Numbers (c charts)	
$\text{UCL}_p = p + 3s_p$	(14-16)	$\text{UCL}_c = \bar{c} + 3s_c$	(14-18)
$\text{LCL}_p = p - 3s_p$	(14-17)	$\text{LCL}_c = \bar{c} - 3s_c$	(14-19)
where p = proportion of defectives in sample		where $\bar{c}$ = average number of defects per unit	
$= \dfrac{\text{number of defectives}}{\text{total number of items}}$		$= \dfrac{\Sigma c}{N} = \dfrac{\text{total no. of defects/unit in samples}}{\text{no. of samples}}$	
$s_p = \sqrt{\dfrac{pq}{n}}$		$s_c = \sqrt{\bar{c}}$	(14-20)
where n = sample size to be used for monitoring			

* Because p is often the mean value of the proportions from several samples, it is sometimes denoted as $\bar{p}$. However, it can simply be considered a proportion in its own right (but based upon more observations), and maintaining the symbol as p preserves the consistency with earlier portions of the text.

CONTROL CHARTS FOR ATTRIBUTES

Control charts for attributes typically rest upon the classification of an item as defective or nondefective. The classification can result either from data on the percentage of defectives (p) or from the number of defects per unit of output (c). As a result, attributes charts are referred to as either *p charts for the fraction of defectives* or *c charts for the number of defects*. Both convey a similar type of information, but the *p* charts are based upon a normal approximation to a binomial distribution, and the *c* charts are based upon the Poisson distribution.

Because the dichotomous classification of attributes does not include any measurement of variation, attributes charts do not include anything comparable to the *R* charts derived from the range in variables sampling. In other respects, however, the attributes chart is similar to the chart for variables, for the control limits are set at three standard errors away from the average number or percentage of defectives. As with the chart for variables, too, because the population values of number and proportion are unknown, we use estimators derived from the sample data. Figure 14-18 summarizes the expressions involved.

EXAMPLE 14-9
(Attributes
p Chart)

A sportswear firm has set up for automated production of a line of sweaters. Twenty samples of size $n = 50$ are to be withdrawn randomly during the first week of production in order to establish control limits for the process. Defects remain in the shipment but bring less revenue, for they eventually sell as "seconds." The defectives detected in the 20 samples are shown below. Compute the control limits for this process.

Defective Items in 20 Samples of $n = 50$ Sweaters

Sample Number	Number of Defective Items	Percentage of Defective Items
1	2	.04
2	3	.06
3	4	.08
4	1	.02
5	0	.00
6	2	.04
7	4	.08
8	1	.02
9	1	.02
10	3	.06
11	0	.00
12	1	.02
13	2	.04
14	1	.02
15	0	.00
16	3	.06
17	7	.14
18	2	.04
19	1	.02
20	2	.04
Total	40	

SOLUTION

$$\mathrm{UCL}_p = p + 3s_p$$

where $p = \dfrac{\text{number of defectives}}{\text{total number of items}} = \dfrac{40}{50 \times 20} = .040$

$$s_p = \sqrt{\frac{pq}{n}} = \sqrt{\frac{(.040)(.960)}{50}} = .028$$

$$\therefore \mathrm{UCL}_p = p + 3s_p = .040 + 3(.028) = .124$$

$$\mathrm{LCL}_p = p - 3s_p = .040 - 3(.028) = .000$$

Using these limits, a preliminary chart is constructed, and the data points are plotted as shown in Fig. 14-19.

Note that the fraction defective in sample 17 is outside the upper control limit. Suppose the reason for this is investigated and the cause is found to be that a new machine was phased in at that point before receiving final adjustments from a mechanic. This data point is then discarded, and a new value for p and new control limits are calculated.

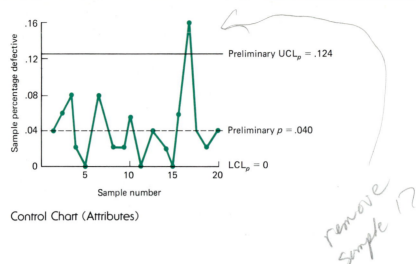

FIGURE 14-19   Control Chart (Attributes)

$$p = \frac{33}{50 \times 19} \doteq .0347$$

$$s_p = \sqrt{\frac{(.0347)(.9653)}{50}} = .0259$$

$$\text{UCL}_p = .0347 + 3(.0259) = .112$$

$$\text{LCL}_p = .0347 - 3(.0259) = .000$$

None of the remaining sample values fall outside the new limits, so these limits become the standard for controlling the process in the future.

Note that although the total number of items ($50 \times 20 = 1,000$) is used to estimate p, the control limits are set using an n equal to the sample size that will be used for the monitoring process. This assures that the control limits are properly positioned for the expected sample size.

Control charts for the number of defects per unit (that is, c charts) are useful for numerous applications where a large (perhaps even uncountable) number of imperfections, blemishes, missing parts, and so on, could occur. But the number which does occur is relatively small. Defects may be air bubbles on a painted surface, poor connections on a circuit board, or keypunch errors. The commonality is that the number of potential occurrences is large. The actual average is small, and the probability of defect follows a Poisson distribution. The standard error for a Poisson distribution is $\bar{c}$, where $\bar{c}$ is the mean number of defects per unit.

EXAMPLE 14-10
(Attributes
c Chart)

The Metropolitan Transit System uses the number of written passenger complaints per day as a measure of its service quality. For 10 days, the number of complaints received was as follows:

Day (sample) No.	1	2	3	4	5	6	7	8	9	10	Total
No. of Complaints/Day	4	8	2	0	3	9	10	0	6	4	46

Compute the $3s_c$ control limits.

SOLUTION

We seek limits for the number of defects per unit, where defects are written customer complaints and the unit is 1 day. Thus the Poisson distribution applies:

$$\bar{c} = \text{average number of defects per unit} = \frac{46 \text{ complaints}}{10 \text{ days}} = 4.6 \text{ complaints/day}$$

$$s_c = \sqrt{\bar{c}} = \sqrt{4.6} = 2.14$$

$$\text{UCL}_c = \bar{c} + 3s_c = 4.6 + 3(2.14) = 11.0$$

$$\text{LCL}_c = \bar{c} - 3s_c = 4.6 - 3(2.14) = 0 \qquad \text{(negative values are assigned zero)}$$

The (process) average is 4.6 complaints per day, and control limits are from zero to 11 complaints per day.

Suppose a chart is set up with the limits developed in Example 14-10, and the observed number of complaints is plotted over a 2-week period. A pattern such as that shown in Fig. 14-20 would signal a situation that is out of control for at least two reasons: (1) the data are evidencing a trend and are not randomly distributed about the control average (of 4.6 complaints), and (2) an observation (in this case two observations) lies outside the upper control limit of 11 complaints per day. Depending upon the significance (and cost) of analysis, management may wish to begin an investigation into the causes of the increased number of complaints.

One final note on control charts. The normal, Poisson, and other distributions

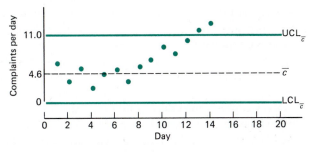

FIGURE 14-20   Process That Is Out of Control

have proved to be valuable guidelines for quality control in the past where data were expensive to gather and decisions had to be based upon limited data. Today, electronics and microprocessors are removing much of the uncertainty from production processing. Computers continuously monitor tool wear, tolerances, and electrical and chemical properties and provide signals which automatically adjust controls so that defectives are not produced. For example, FMC, a food machinery manufacturer, markets food processing equipment that individually weighs and sorts apples—at a rate of up to 25 bushels a minute. The apples are in six to eight rows or lanes in individual cups. A microcomputer keeps track of the moving location of each cup and unloads it at a predetermined location onto one of 14 secondary belts, each of which is for apples of a specific size. This accurate process control eliminates much of the inspection effort required in the past. The abundance of accurate data today has also lessened the need to rely upon statistical distributions that are *assumed* to fit a particular situation. Instead, the product characteristics can often be accurately measured and stored in a process computer. The computer can then use empirical data to continuously model the process, establishing its own control limits if desirable. Then control decisions are based upon current, realistic data rather than on an assumed distribution of data.

SUMMARY

Quality is a measure of how closely a good or service conforms to specified standards. The quality of goods is a relatively constant, tangible characteristic—not changed by the location or the subjective preference of the consumer. But services are less tangible; they have no existence apart from the consumer, and their "success" is influenced by the disposition of the consumer. Fortunately, however, the measures of *perceived quality* (proficiency, timeliness, and environment) are also useful measures of service quality.

Quality assurance is the system of policies, procedures, and guidelines that establishes and maintains specified standards of product quality. An increasing number of firms are finding that goals of defect-free production are improving employee motivation as well as giving the firm lower overall quality-related costs. A popular quality assurance tool, *quality circles,* has been cited as a major contributing factor in Japan's economic success. Quality circles are currently being used to improve quality (and productivity) in countless American firms as well.

Acceptance sampling activities rely upon knowledge of the statistical properties of the population. Quality characteristics of individual items can often be deduced from a knowledge that the parent population is distributed as a hypergeometric, binomial, Poisson, or normal distribution.

Acceptance sampling procedures often take the form of a sampling plan (or decision rule) which specifies both how large a sample (n) to take and what the allowable measurement or percentage of defectives (c) in the sample is to be. Sampling plans for attributes are based upon the classification of an item as defective or nondefective, whereas variables plans require a measurement of the characteristic in question. Both types of plans can be expressed as operating characteristic (OC) curves, which show the probability that the given plan will accept a lot as a function of the actual (unknown) quality level.

To completely specify a sampling plan, the producer and consumer should agree on the producer's risk α at the acceptable quality level (AQL) and the consumer's risk β at the lot tolerance percent defective (LTPD) level. Varying the acceptance number c will change the shape of the OC curve and shift the risk, but the only way to reduce both α and β risks simultaneously is to increase the sample size. MIL-STD-105 is a widely used standard for selecting attributes plans.

Variables plans also offer the opportunity to control α and β risks by establishing a sample size n and reject limit c based upon the known normality of the distribution of sample means. The n and c values are determined by solving a pair of equations locating c from both the AQL point and the LTPD point.

Control charts are used to make inferences about the current process quality on the basis of an ongoing series of random samples. Variables charts monitor processes by recording mean ($\bar{x}$) and range (R) values, whereas attributes charts are set up to control the percent defective ($\bar{p}$) or the number of defects (c). In most cases, the upper (UCL) and lower (LCL) control limits are set at a distance of three standard errors away from the mean of the sample means, $\bar{\bar{x}}$, or the expected sample proportions, p, or the mean number of defects, $\bar{c}$. A sample value outside the control limits suggests that some assignable cause of the variation exists and constitutes a call for identification and corrective action.

SOLVED PROBLEMS

QUALITY ASSURANCE SYSTEMS

1   The marketing manager of Roller Bearings International (RBI) estimates that "defective bearings that get into the hands of industrial users cost RBI an average of $20 each" in replacement costs and lost business. The production manager counters that "the bearings are only about 2 percent defective now, and the best a sampling plan could do would be to reduce that to 1 percent defective—but not much better (unless we go to 100 percent inspection)." Should RBI adopt a sampling plan if it costs (a) \$.10/bearing? (b) \$.25/bearing? (c) How much per bearing can RBI afford to spend on inspection costs before it begins to lose money on inspections?

Solution
For purposes of illustration, assume that all comparisons are based upon a lot of 100 bearings.
(a) *Without inspection:*

Defect cost $= 100(.02)(\$20/\text{bearing}) =$ $40

   With inspection:

Inspection cost $= 100(\$.10/\text{bearing}) =$ \$10
Defect cost $= 100(.01)(\$20/\text{bearing}) =$ \$20
$30 $\longrightarrow$ 30

Advantage from inspection $\dfrac{}{\$10} = \$.10/\text{bearing}$

(b) *Without inspection:*
Defect cost = $40

With inspection:
Inspection cost = 100($.25/bearing) = $25
Defect cost = $20
Disadvantage from inspection $45 $5 = $.05/bearing

(c) Let X = the inspection cost per bearing. Then the minimum cost is where
Defect cost without inspect = inspect cost + defect cost with inspect
$$100(.02)(\$20/\text{bearing}) = X(100) + (100)(.01)(\$20/\text{bearing})$$
$$X = \frac{40 - 20}{100} = \$.20/\text{bearing}$$

ACCEPTANCE SAMPLING OF INCOMING AND OUTGOING QUALITY

*2   Laser Magic Inc. wishes to make performance tests on some finished compact disk players. The quality control inspector has randomly selected five disk players. In how many ways can disk players be selected for three tests if
(a) Any disk player can be used for any or all of the tests, so both duplication and different order of selection count as a different way (*multiple choices*)?
(b) No disk player can be used for more than one test, but the order of selection makes a difference (*permutations*)?
(c) No disk player can be used for more than one test, and the order of selection does not count (*combinations*)?

Solution
Let x = 3 disk players chosen from n = 5 disk players.
(a) Multiple choices:

$$N^x = 5^3 = 5 \cdot 5 \cdot 5 = 125 \text{ ways}$$

(b) Permutations:

$$P^n_x = \frac{n!}{(n - x)!} = \frac{5!}{(5 - 3)!} = \frac{5 \cdot 4 \cdot 3 \cdot 2 \cdot 1}{2 \cdot 1} = 60 \text{ ways}$$

(c) Combinations:

$$C^n_x = \frac{n!}{x!(n - x)!} = \frac{5!}{3!(5 - 3)!} = \frac{5 \cdot 4 \cdot 3 \cdot 2 \cdot 1}{3 \cdot 2 \cdot 1 \cdot 2 \cdot 1} = 10 \text{ ways}$$

3   In an industrial plant in Portugal, the mean weight of a certain packaged chemical is μ = 82.0 kilograms, and the standard deviation is σ = 4.0 kilograms. If a sample of n = 64 packages is drawn from the population for inspection, find the probability that
(a) An *individual package* in the sample will exceed 82.5 kilograms. (Assume that the population is normally distributed for this part.)
(b) The *sample mean* will exceed 82.5 kilograms.

Solution

(a)
$$Z = \frac{X - \mu}{\sigma} = \frac{82.5 - 82.0}{4} = .125$$

$P(Z) = .050$ (Appendix C)

$P(X > 82.5) = .500 - .050 = .450$

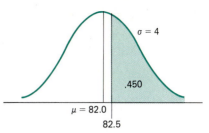

(b) $Z = \dfrac{\bar{x} - \mu}{\sigma_{\bar{x}}}$ where $\sigma_x = \dfrac{\sigma}{\sqrt{n}} = \dfrac{4}{\sqrt{64}} = .5$

$$Z = \frac{82.5 - 82.0}{.5} = 1.0 \qquad \therefore P(Z) = .34$$

$P(\bar{x} > 82.5) = .50 - .34 = .16$

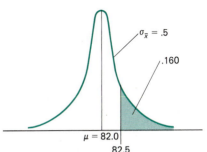

Note that this example illustrates the concept of a *sampling distribution* as used in quality control work. The probability of getting a sample mean $\bar{x}$ more than ½ kilogram away from the true mean is substantially less than the chance of getting an individual value X (a 16 percent versus a 45 percent chance).[4]

4 *Poisson approximation* A very large shipment of textbooks comes from a publisher who usually supplies about 1 percent with imperfect bindings. What is the probability that among 400 textbooks taken from this shipment, exactly 3 will have imperfect bindings?

Solution

This problem could be solved by using the binomial expression for $P(x = 3 \mid n = 400, p = .01)$. However, unless one has a calculator that handles exponents, the solution would be tedious. It can be closely approximated by the Poisson distribution since $p < .10$, $n > 20$, and $np > 5$.

$$P(X) = \frac{\lambda^x e^{-\lambda}}{x!}$$

where $\lambda = np = 400(.01) = 4.0$
$\qquad X = 3$
$\qquad e = 2.718 \text{(constant)}$

$$P(X = 3 \mid \lambda = 4.0) = \frac{\lambda^x e^{-\lambda}}{x!} = \frac{4^3 e^{-4}}{3!} = \frac{(64)(.018)}{3 \cdot 2} = .195$$

---

[4] For means, the standard error $(\sigma_{\bar{x}})$ is obtained by dividing the standard deviation (σ) by $\sqrt{n}$. Thus $\sigma_{\bar{x}} = \sigma/\sqrt{n}$. For proportions, the standard error (σ_p) is obtained by dividing the standard deviation $(\sqrt{npq})$ by n. Thus $\sigma_p = \sqrt{npq/n^2} = \sqrt{pq/n}$. Multiplying the standard error $(\sqrt{pq/n})$ by n yields a standard deviation in terms of number $(\sqrt{npq})$.

The solution could also be obtained more directly from the table of summed Poisson probabilities given in Appendix E. Go down the λ column to $\lambda = 4$ and then right to the columns where the events are designated as values of c. Since we need $c = 3$, we must find the difference between $c \leq 3$ and $c \leq 2$, which is $.433 - .238 = .195$.

5 Which probability distribution will yield an appropriate answer in a reasonable amount of time if we wish to know the probability of getting 10 or fewer defects in a sample of 400 from a population that is 1 percent defective?
   (a) Hypergeometric
   (b) Binomial
   (c) Normal
   (d) Poisson
   (e) Student's t

Solution

$$n = 400 = > 20$$

$$np = (400)(.01) = 4 = < 5$$

$$p = .01 = < .10$$

∴ Poisson distribution is appropriate (d).

$$P(X \leq 10 \mid \lambda = 4) = .997 \qquad \text{(from Appendix E)}$$

SAMPLING PLAN FOR ATTRIBUTES

6 An orange grower (producer) and packing plant (consumer) have agreed on a sampling plan that calls for a random sample of 150 oranges from a shipment, and acceptance if 3 or fewer are spoiled.
   (a) Does this plan meet the specifications of limiting the grower's risk of rejecting lots that are as good as 2 percent spoiled to less than or equal to 20 percent, and does it limit the packing plant's risk of accepting shipments that are as bad as 4 percent spoiled to less than or equal to 25 percent?
   (b) What would be the effect of changing the acceptance value to $c \leq 4$?

Solution
   (a) This is an attributes plan calling for $\alpha \leq .20$ at AQL $= .02$ and $\beta \leq .25$ at LTPD $= .04$. Though we could construct an entire OC curve, it is necessary to check only two points: AQL and LTPD.

p	$\lambda = np$	$P(c \leq 3 \mid \lambda)$	Risk
.02	$(150)(.02) = 3.0$	$P(c \leq 3 \mid \lambda = 3.0) = .647$	$\alpha = 1.000 - .647 = .353$
.04	$(150)(.04) = 6.0$	$P(c \leq 3 \mid \lambda = 6.0) = .151$	$\beta = .151$

The grower's risk (α) of .35 is larger than .20 and so is unsatisfactory (too high). The packaging plant's risk (β) of .15 is less than .25 and so is satisfactory.

(b) With $c \leqslant 4$: $P(c \leqslant 4 | \lambda = 3.0) = .815$, so $\alpha = 1.000 - .815 = .185$
$P(c \leqslant 4 | \lambda = 6.0) = .285$, so $\beta = .285$

The grower's risk (α) is less than .20 and is satisfactory, but the packing plant's risk (β) is greater than .25 and so is unsatisfactory.

CONTROL OF PROCESS QUALITY

7 A control chart is established, with limits of ± 2 standard errors, for use in monitoring samples of size $n = 20$. Assume the process is in control.
  (a) Would you expect many *individual values* to lie outside these limits?
  (b) How likely would a *sample mean* fall outside the control limits?
  (c) What kind of error would be committed in erroneously concluding that the process is out of control?

Solution
  (a) Yes, the limits are set to control mean values, not individual values.
  (b) Assuming normality, 95.5 percent of the sample means are within ± 2 standard errors, so about 4.5 percent of the means would lie outside.
  (c) Type I. This is concluding the process is out of control when it is not.

8 Nuclear Fuel Company manufactures uranium pellets to a specified diameter of .500 ± .005 centimeter. In 25 random samples of 9 pellets each, the overall mean of the means ($\bar{\bar{x}}$) and the range ($\bar{R}$) were found to be .501 centimeter and .003 centimeter, respectively. Construct an $\bar{x}$ and R chart which includes the specified tolerances.

Solution
$$\text{UCL}_{\bar{x}} = \bar{\bar{x}} + A\bar{R} = .501 + (.337)(.003) = .502$$

$$\text{LCL}_{\bar{x}} = \bar{\bar{x}} - A\bar{R} = .501 - (.337)(.003) = .500$$

$$\text{UCL}_R = B\bar{R} = (1.816)(.003) = .0054$$

$$\text{LCL}_R = C\bar{R} = (.184)(.003) = .0006$$

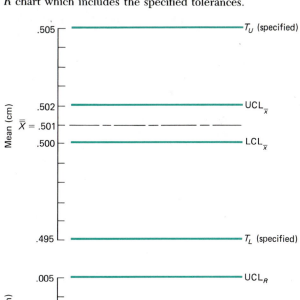

9 A daily sample of 30 items was taken over a period of 14 days in order to establish attributes control limits. If 21 defectives were found, what should be the LCL_p and UCL_p?

Solution

$$p = \frac{\text{no. of defectives}}{\text{total observations}} = \frac{21}{420} = .05$$

$$s_p = \sqrt{\frac{pq}{n}} = \sqrt{\frac{(.05)(.95)}{30}} = .04$$

$$UCL_p = p + 3s_p = .05 + 3(.04) = .17$$

$$LCL_p = p - 3s_p = .05 - 3(.04) = 0$$

QUESTIONS

14-1 What was the role of Edwards Deming in quality control work?

14-2 Define "quality." What is the purpose of quality control activities?

14-3 What constitutes a quality painting?

14-4 Services are intangible products. Can the quality of services be measured? Explain.

14-5 What two types of costs make up the total quality control costs? What is the optimal output quality under the zero-defect approach?

14-6 How does the quality circle approach to quality control differ from the traditional approach of inspection by a quality control inspector?

14-7 From an acceptance sampling standpoint, how do the hypergeometric, binomial, Poisson, and normal distributions differ? (Do not answer the question by simply expressing an equation for the distribution.)

14-8 A box containing 18 electronic parts is stored on a spaceship before a voyage. Three are defective, but the crew does not know which three. After the spaceship gets under way, pairs of $n = 2$ are withdrawn and installed periodically. If only one defective is found in the first two pairs, which probability distribution would be suitable for calculating the probability of a defective part in the next pair? Why? Suppose the variable of interest was the number of flaws in the weld of a seam on the inside of the vehicle (which is normally very low but could range from zero to a hundred). Which probability distribution would apply for predicting the number of flaws in the seam weld?

14-9 How do sampling plans for attributes differ from those for variables?

14-10 What does an operating characteristic curve show, and what determines the shape of the curve?

14-11 The sampling distribution of means for a variables sampling plan is shown in Fig. 14-13. Copy the figure, and then superimpose another plan with a substantially larger sample size using a dotted line. What is the effect upon the α and β risks?

14-12 A newly promoted supervisor recently issued a directive calling for fraction defective (p) and range (R) charts on "every process in the plant where the percentage of defectives can be determined." Comment.

14-13   Briefly outline the steps involved in constructing an attributes control chart.

14-14   When is a process "out of control"?

PROBLEMS

QUALITY ASSURANCE SYSTEMS

1   A firm producing robotic machines is considering adopting a reduced-defects policy. They are currently producing 1,000 robots per year, but about 3 percent of them are defective and, once a defective robot is produced, it costs them an average of $800 in service and repair time to fix it. Management estimates that the new policy would increase the production cost by $10 per robot, but the defective rate would be reduced to only one-third of what it is now (in other words, to 1 percent defective).

  (a) How much could be saved per year by going to the reduced-defects policy?

  (b) How much could the production cost per robot increase before the reduced-defects policy would no longer be economical?

ACCEPTANCE SAMPLING OF INCOMING AND OUTGOING QUALITY

2   A sample of 60 camera lenses is taken to verify the quality of a large shipment from Korea. Three of the lenses are found to be defective. What is the estimated standard error (s_p) in terms of proportions and the standard deviation in terms of numbers? (*Hint:* See the footnote of Solved Prob. 3.)

3   A random sample of 400 items is drawn from a production process in order to test the hypothesis that the process has 10 percent defectives. Eighty defectives are found.

  (a) What is the theoretical (hypothesized) standard error of proportion (σ_p)?

  (b) What is the estimated standard error of proportion based upon the sample evidence only (s_p)?

STATISTICAL DISTRIBUTIONS FOR DEFECTIVES: BINOMIAL

4   Thirty percent of the bricks delivered by an out-of-state contractor are defective in some way. What is the probability that exactly three bricks will be defective in a random sample of six?

5   In a crystal manufacturing plant, 15 percent of the glasses are defective. Suppose 10 glasses are selected at random without inspection. What is the probability that 2 or more of the glasses will be defective?

6   A city transit company has data to show that 40 percent of their customers favor a no-smoking rule on all buses. If two customers are selected at random for a TV interview about smoking on buses, what is the probability both would favor the no-smoking rule?

STATISTICAL DISTRIBUTIONS FOR DEFECTIVES: POISSON

7   A welding robot used on a rocket engine assembly project typically welds 10 feet of steel seam with only 3 minor defects. What is the (Poisson) probability of having no defects in 10 feet of weld?

8 A manufacturer of fiber optics has developed a process that produces an average of only .40 defect per standard length of tube. Assuming the probability of defects is independent on each tube length, what is the chance that an inspection of three tubes will show them to be defect-free?

9 The operations department of a city-owned gas company has a quality service performance standard of no more than four complaints per hour. If the company averages four complaints per hour, what is the probability of 30 minutes passing with no complaints?

10 If defective components are coming off an assembly line at an average rate of 3.5 per minute, what is the probability that more than 6 defects will arrive in 1 minute?

STATISTICAL DISTRIBUTIONS FOR DEFECTIVES: NORMAL

11 The time required for a license examiner to give an applicant a driving test is known to be normally distributed with a mean of 17 minutes and standard deviation of 4 minutes. Suppose an examiner begins a test at 4:40 p.m. What is the probability the test will be finished by 5:00 p.m.?

12 If $n = 60$ and $p = .3$, what are the mean and standard deviation of the normal distribution which approximates this binomial distribution? (*Hint:* See Fig. 14-7 for μ and σ equations.)

13 The weight of boxes of laundry soap is known to be normally distributed, with a mean of 20 pounds and a standard deviation of .4 pound. Approximately what percentage of the boxes in a carload shipment could be expected to weigh less than 19.5 pounds if an incoming receipt inspection is made?

SAMPLING PLANS FOR ATTRIBUTES AND VARIABLES

14 A producer and a consumer agree that they want a sampling plan where $\alpha \leq .10$ at $p = .003$ and $\beta \leq .30$ at $p = .006$. The producer's QC "old-timer" says the sampling plan ($n = 300$, $c \leq 2$) will be "just fine for both of us."
(a) What is the specified AQL level?
(b) What is the specified LTPD level?
(c) What is the actual level of producer risk offered by this plan?
(d) What is the actual level of consumer risk offered by this plan?
(e) Should the plan be acceptable to both producer and consumer?

15 Northeast Paper Company packages a large volume of tissue under a brand name for a national chain of food stores. Occasionally the packages are defective because they are from end cuts, the color is bleached, or they are not properly sealed. The paper company and food chain have agreed to adopt a sampling plan so that the risk to Northeast Paper Company of rejecting lots that are as good as .5 percent defective ($p = .005$) is limited to 2 percent and the risk of the food chain accepting lots as bad as 4 percent defective is no more than 5 percent.
(a) Construct an OC curve for the sampling plan ($n = 200$, $c \leq 3$).
(b) Does this plan satisfy the agreed-upon paper company risk?
(c) Does this plan satisfy the food chain risk?

16 (a) Construct an OC curve for the attributes sampling plan $n = 50$, $c \leq 4$.
(b) What is the value of α at AQL $= .04$?
(c) What is the value of β at LTPD $= .16$?

17 A national bank has established quality standards for its branch banks and allocates a portion of its salary budget on this basis. One measure of service level is the time

required to complete all arrangements for opening a checking account. A time of more than 12 minutes is considered "poor service," and times have a known standard deviation of 4.2 minutes.

Design a variables sampling plan, for a sample of $n = 36$ observations, that will allow the headquarters to sample branch banks so that the risk of rejecting a branch's claim (that it averages $\leq$ 12 minutes) is limited to 1 percent (when the true mean time is really 12 minutes).

18 A machine is supposed to produce only a small proportion of defectives. The quality control supervisor proposes to take a random sample of 100 units and recommend adjustment of the machine if the sample contains too many defects. If the machine is actually producing as much as 20 percent defectives, the supervisor wants the probability of adjustment to be .95. Design a decision rule for this quality control situation.

19 The QC supervisor at National Bakery has been asked to direct the receipt inspection of a carload shipment of flour. Each bag is supposed to weigh at least 50 kilograms, and the Chicago mill has said that the standard deviation is 4 kilograms. Management wishes to limit the risk of rejecting a good lot to 2 percent. On the other hand, if the true mean weight of the bags is only 48 kilograms, management wants to limit the chance of accepting the shipment to 5 percent.

(a) Diagram the situation in terms of a sampling distribution showing the α and β risks.

(b) How large a sample size is required?

(c) What is the critical value, c, of the sample mean that will satisfy the given conditions?

20 A carload of lead sheets has been received by a shipyard for use in shielding work. Each sheet is supposed to weigh *at least* 250 pounds (H_0: $\mu \geq 250$), and it is known that the process producing them has a standard deviation of 20 pounds. An inspection agreement is reached whereby the supplier's risk of type I error is limited to .05. On the other hand, if the true mean weight of the sheets is as low as 240 pounds, the shipyard wants only a 10 percent chance of accepting the shipment. It seeks to determine the critical value (borderline weight) of the sample mean that will satisfy these conditions.

(a) What are the respective values of α, Z_α, β, and Z_β?

(b) How large a sample is required?

(c) What is the critical value c of the sample mean?

CONTROL CHARTS

21 In an effort to set up a control chart of a process, samples of size $n = 25$ are taken, and it is determined that $\bar{\bar{x}} = .98$ centimeter and the standard deviation $s = .020$ centimeter. Find the control limits for the process.

22 In an aluminum production facility, a casting operation was sampled to establish variables control limits for a critical length. If 50 samples of $n = 5$ yielded an $\bar{x}$ of 20 inches with an average range $(\bar{R})$ of .3 inch, what are the (a) $UCL_{\bar{x}}$, (b) $LCL_{\bar{x}}$, (c) UCL_R, and (d) LCL_R?

23 The U.S. Department of Testing (USDT) requires that the 100-pound-bag shipments of the Prairie Seed Company do in fact average 100 pounds or over. Sample data from $N = 10$ samples of $n = 6$ bags each showed the following weight deviations from 100 pounds (positive deviation, over; negative, under).

						Sample Number				
	1	2	3	4	5	6	7	8	9	10
	2	3	4	1	6	0	2	−1	1	5
	−1	0	5	2	4	−2	3	−1	2	4
	4	3	6	2	3	2	2	2	0	5
	1	1	2	0	4	−1	2	0	0	2
	0	2	4	4	1	3	4	1	4	3
	2	1	2	2	4	0	6	−1	3	0
Σ	8	10	23	11	22	2	19	0	10	19
Mean ($\bar{x}$)	1.33	1.67	3.83	1.83	3.67	.33	3.17	0	1.67	3.17
Range (R)	5	3	4	4	5	5	4	3	4	5

(a) What are the center line ($\bar{\bar{x}}$) and the upper and lower control limits for $\bar{x}$?

(b) What are the upper and lower control limits for the range? (Round your calculations to two significant digits beyond the decimal.)

24 In a rare-metals production facility, a casting operation was sampled to establish attributes control limits. If one sample of size $n = 100$ revealed that 10 percent were defective, what should be the lower and upper control limits?

25 A quality control policy requires setting up control limits on the basis of data from random samples of $n = 100$ per day taken from a 10-day pilot run of a plastics molding activity. A total of 200 defectives were found.

(a) What are the UCL_p and LCL_p for the process (in percentage of defectives)?

(b) If samples of $n = 100$ continue to be taken, what would be the control limits in numbers of defectives (rather than in percentage)? (*Hint:* This is not c. See the footnote for Solved Prob. 3; $\mu = np$ and $\sigma = \sqrt{npq}$.)

REFERENCES

[1] Arai, Joji: Japanese Productivity and its Prospect," *NC/CAM Journal*, November/December 1979, pp. 1–4.

[2] Burr, Irving W.: *Engineering Statistics and Quality Control*, McGraw-Hill, New York, 1953.

[3] Daniel, Wayne M., and James C. Terrell: *Business Statistics*, 4th ed., Houghton Mifflin, Boston, 1986.

[4] Darlin, Damon: "Although U.S. Cars Are Improved, Imports Still Win Quality Survey," *The Wall Street Journal*, Dec. 16, 1985, p. 29.

[5] Dodge, Harold F., and H. G. Romig: *Sampling Inspection Tables, Single and Double Sampling*, 2d ed., Wiley, New York, 1959.

[6] Garvin, David A.: "Product Quality: An Important Strategic Weapon," *Business Horizons*, May/June 1984, pp. 40–43.

[7] Halberstam, David: "Quality: What We Can Learn From the American Who Taught Japan," *The Spokesman-Review Parade*, July 8, 1984.

[8] Institute for Industrial Research and Standards, *Draft Irish Standard "Guide to Quality Management in the Service Industries,"* Dublin, Ireland, 1985.

[9] Karatsu, Hajime: "The Deindustrialization of America: A Tragedy for the World," *KKC Brief*, Japan Institute for Social and Economic Affairs, no. 31, October 1985.

[10] Normann, Richard: *Service Management: Strategy and Leadership in Service Businesses*, Wiley, New York, 1984.

[11] "Out of Order: Repair People Struggle to Keep Up with the Glut of Breaking Products," *The Wall Street Journal*, Jan. 5, 1981, p. 1.

[12] U.S. Department of Defense: MIL-STD-105, *Sampling Procedures and Tables for Inspection of Attributes*, U.S. Government Printing Office, Washington, DC, 1963.

[13] U.S. Department of Defense: MIL-STD-414, *Sampling Procedures and Tables for Inspection by Variables for Percent Defective*, U.S. Government Printing Office, Washington, DC, 1957.

[14] Winter, Ralph E.: "Concerns' Push to Improve Quality of Products Puts Heat on Suppliers," *The Wall Street Journal*, Sept. 20, 1983, p. 29.

SELF QUIZ: CHAPTER 14

POINTS: 15

Part I True/False [1 point each = 6]

1. __F__ Quality is the inherent worth or features of a product, as assessed by the individual who owns or uses it.
2. __T__ Japanese industry was introduced to statistical quality control by an American named Edwards Deming.
3. __F__ Because services are intangible processes, there are really no satisfactory ways to measure their quality level.
4. __T__ Attributes characteristics might properly be described by a discrete distribution, such as the binomial or the Poisson.
5. __T__ If a variables sampling plan has specified a 15 percent producer risk and a 5 percent consumer risk when the AQL and LTPD are 16 ounces and 20 ounces, respectively, the reject limit c will be closer to 16 ounces than to 20 ounces.
6. __F__ Control limits for a process are typically set at two or three standard deviations from the process mean.

Part II Problems [3 points each = 9. Calculate and select your answer.]

1. Kyoto Camera has arranged to purchase film rewind motors from a Belgian supplier under a plan that is to limit α to .20 at AQL = 2 percent defective and β to .10 at LTPD = 6 percent. Using the Poisson distribution, to what extent does the plan [n = 120, $c \leqslant 3$] satisfy the specification?
   (a) Both α and β are okay.
   (b) α is okay, β is not.
   — (c) α is not, β is okay.
   (d) Neither is okay.
   (e) Cannot be determined.

2. A supplier of nylon cord has negotiated a contract in which the risk of type I error is limited to $\leqslant$ .08 if the cord has a mean strength of 200 pounds. Also, the probability of accepting a mean strength of 170 pounds is to be limited to $\leqslant$ .04. If σ = 60 pounds, approximately how large a sample is required?
   (a) 30
   (b) 40
   (c) 50
   (d) 60
   (e) None of the above.

3. In an effort to establish control limits on the proportion of city buses that travel late, samples of size n = 8 buses were monitored on randomly selected routes on 30 different days. The total number of late schedules was 18. What control limits should be used for this service for samples of n = 8?
   (a) .08 and .32
   (b) .03 and .12
   (c) .00 and .22
   (d) .00 and .35
   (e) None of the above.

CHAPTER 15
MAINTENANCE AND COST CONTROL

INTRODUCTION

Shortly after midnight on October 9 an electrical short sent a huge arc crackling across the rotor of a big motor at Jones & Laughlin Steel Corporation's Cleveland plant. A direct-current generator driven by the motor failed, knocking out a critical finishing mill.

The breakdown could hardly have been more frustrating. Not only did it threaten to leave the plant in the red while other companies in the long-depressed steel industry were beginning to break into the black, but J & L had just completed an extensive $4.3 million maintenance program in the plant aimed at preventing such failures.

Herculean effort to cut the loss followed. . . . In 14 hours workers strung more than eight miles of garden-hose-sized cable through the plant while others hooked up a makeshift control panel on a piece of fiberboard. The effort saved nearly $30 million of orders and avoided an incalculable loss of customer confidence, but at a price that included $270,000 for the cable, $130,000 in overtime pay and plenty of agony.

The biggest problem in running an industrial plant today is just that—keeping it running. [6]

The Wall Street Journal goes on to quote a plant consultant who says that from today's productivity and bottom-line points of view, downtime may be the "most significant problem" of plant management. Not only is the loss of capacity costly from a customer standpoint, but repair costs can be overwhelming. Today's complex machines require computers and oscilloscopes to mend their ills, not wrenches and oil cans. Advanced technology along with the high cost of capital equipment has pushed maintenance into an area of key importance to operations managers.

In this chapter, the objectives of maintenance are defined, and some approaches to managing maintenance are explored. We will investigate the methods of determining the reliability against failure and the service rates and costs of handling breakdown situations.

Insofar as maintenance efforts (like other operating activities) are heavily dependent upon an analysis of relevant costs, we take the opportunity to summarize some essential cost-control concepts in the second part of the chapter. These include the use of budgets, standard costs, and the concept of cost variance. Upon completing the chapter, you should be conscious of the costs and benefits of maintenance and be able to explain the basic concepts of cost control.

MAINTENANCE OBJECTIVES

Maintenance is any activity designed to keep resources in working condition or restore them to operating status. This does not necessarily mean that everything should be in the absolute best operating condition with all new parts so that breakdowns never occur—that is infeasible from a practical standpoint. It does, however, mean that maintenance activities should be evaluated in light of the goals (and costs) of the total system of facilities, equipment, and people. In many cases, the system goals are best satisfied by minimizing long-run maintenance costs. At other times employment stability, safety considerations, reliability, or short-term economic conditions may be overriding criteria.

FACILITIES AND PERSONNEL MAINTENANCE

Figure 15-1 depicts the two major categories of organizational maintenance activities: facilities and personnel. Within each category there are two main types of activities (preventive and breakdown maintenance), which we shall take up momentarily. But first, let us recognize the resource-based distinction.

Facilities and Equipment We typically associate maintenance activities with building upkeep, servicing equipment, replacing worn-out parts, or doing emergency repairs. These are central concerns to any organization, for poorly maintained facilities can be unsafe to operate and can create high costs in the form of delays and idle (lost) time.

Many firms encourage their operating personnel to do much of their own maintenance as a means of both (1) reducing costs and (2) motivating employees by broadening the scope of their jobs. However, today's machinery is often sophisticated, with humanlike qualities that enable it to maneuver, detect light and sound, and store information in memory. So specialists may be required.

The facilities maintenance staff normally includes craftspeople with sufficient skills to do routine service and repair work of a frequently occurring nature. In breakdown situations, equipment suppliers sometimes augment a firm's staff by supplying factory-trained engineers. Centralization of maintenance activities usually results in better utilization of individual craftspeople, but decentralization of

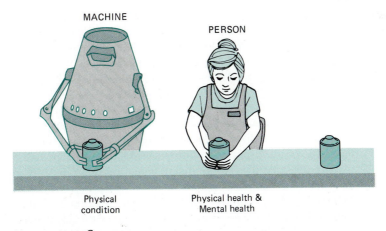

MACHINE

PERSON

Physical
condition

Physical health &
Mental health

FIGURE 15-1 Maintenance Concerns

maintenance crews into different areas of the plant may yield faster service (at a slightly higher cost).

Personnel Human resources become exhausted and break down too, so they also need care and repair—only with people we usually refer to *repair* as *healing*. Hence the emergence of health maintenance organization (HMOs). Company medical facilities, gymnasiums, training programs, and vacations are all personnel-oriented maintenance activities.

As recognized in Fig. 15-1, personnel maintenance is more complex than machine maintenance because people have both a physical and mental dimension. *Physically,* the digestive, circulatory, respiratory, and other systems must function satisfactorily. But problems can often be corrected by operations or medicine, and the body also has natural recovery capabilities of its own. *Mental* illness is more complex because it rests in the brain and can be related to physical anomalies or to emotional disturbances, or both. Psychological or spiritual healing, such as that conveyed through love, care, and/or reconciliation, may be effective here.

Personnel (health) maintenance facilities are often centrally located because clients can more easily go to the service facility (which might be a recreational, medical, or counseling center). Large firms sometimes have departments that maintain ongoing programs to limit alcohol and drug abuse or discourage smoking on the job. These programs have become more important in recent years as firms have recognized the lost-time impact of drug and alcohol abuse, and gained access to statistical data verifying the reduction in productivity due to smoking-related activities. In some countries, alcohol-related absences are believed to approach 4 workweeks per year.

Much of our analysis here will follow the traditional focus upon equipment maintenance. Nevertheless, a close look will reveal many parallels in the area of personnel maintenance.

PREVENTIVE VERSUS BREAKDOWN MAINTENANCE

Maintenance activities are of two general types. *Preventive maintenance* (PM) is the routine inspection and service activities designed to detect potential failure conditions and make minor adjustments or repairs that will help prevent major operating problems. *Breakdown maintenance* is the repair, often of an emergency nature and at a cost premium, of facilities and equipment that have been used until they fail to operate. For personnel, preventive maintenance may be anything from a proper diet to regular exercise. Breakdown maintenance is likely to be a sick leave, hospitalization, or other healing period during which the employee is incapable of performing at a normal level.

An effective preventive maintenance program for equipment requires properly trained personnel, regular inspections and service, and an accurate records system [5]. By planning maintenance activities on a scheduled basis (annually, monthly, or daily—perhaps during a second or third shift), management can make good use of skilled maintenance technicians, and the lost production time is often less than if breakdowns are simply allowed to occur. The inspection records system should include equipment specifications and an inspection checklist, plus information on repair frequency, cost, and spare parts inventory availability. With computerized data files these records can be complete and readily accessible.

MAINTENANCE COSTS

Equipment breakdowns idle workers and machines, resulting in lost production time, delayed schedules, and expensive emergency repairs. These downtime costs usually exceed the preventive maintenance costs for inspections, service, and scheduled repairs up to a point, M, as shown in Fig. 15-2. Beyond this optimal point an increasingly higher level of preventive maintenance is not economically justified, and the firm would be better off waiting for breakdowns to occur.

Whereas the optimal level of maintenance activity, M, is easily identified on a theoretical basis, in practice this necessitates knowing a good deal about the various costs associated with both the preventive and breakdown maintenance activities. This includes knowledge of both the probability of breakdowns and the amount of repair time required. Although these data are not always easily obtained, good maintenance records will provide substantial help in estimating the probability distributions of breakdown and repair times.

Deciding on the size of the maintenance crew is a specific application of the concept of minimizing the total of preventive and breakdown maintenance costs. As illustrated in Fig. 15-3, when the crew size is increased the downtime costs tend to be decreased. And crew sizes are increasing. At General Motors, for example, one skilled maintenance or service technician is required for every 5.6 assembly line workers. With the increasing use of robots and other electronic units in car production, some GM officials expect that the need will rise to one skilled worker for each unskilled worker by the year 2000. Unfortunately, industry already has a shortage of electronic manufacturing equipment service employees

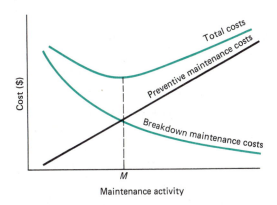

FIGURE 15-2   Maintenance Costs

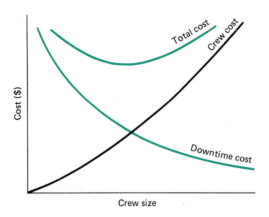

FIGURE 15-3   Crew-Size Costs

estimated at 20,000 to 50,000, so costs for this element of maintenance are not likely to ease in the foreseeable future [**6**].

The crew costs and downtime costs are, in effect, components of the more generalized situation depicted in Fig. 15-2, wherein crew costs are incorporated into overall preventive maintenance costs, and downtime costs constitute a part of the breakdown maintenance costs. The maintenance models in the next section illustrate how the preventive and breakdown maintenance costs can be estimated and compared in order to help minimize total maintenance costs.

MODELS FOR MAINTENANCE MANAGEMENT

Space does not permit us to examine the numerous sophisticated models for maintenance management that abound in the literature. However, it is useful to review some expected value and simulation techniques for estimating breakdown cost and mention a relatively standardized probability model for selecting an appropriate preventive maintenance policy. We shall finish this section with some discussion of queuing models, because maintenance activities are often best analyzed from the standpoint of parts or equipment waiting for service or repair.

EXPECTED VALUE MODEL FOR ESTIMATING BREAKDOWN COST

Preventive maintenance is most effective when service requirements are well known or failures can be predicted with some degree of reliability. The following example assumes that the firm has maintained good records of the frequency and cost of breakdowns in the past. By using the simple concept of expected value, the current breakdown policy can be compared with a given preventive maintenance policy.

EXAMPLE 15-1

Worldwide Travel Services (WTS) has experienced the indicated number of breakdowns per month in its automated reservations processing system over the past 2 years.

Number of Breakdowns	0	1	2	3	4
Number of Months This Occurred	2	8	10	3	1

Each breakdown costs the firm an average of $280. For a cost of $150 per month WTS could have engaged a data processing firm to perform preventive maintenance which is guaranteed to limit the breakdowns to an *average* of one per month. (If the breakdowns exceed this limit, the firm will process WTS data free of charge.) Which maintenance arrangement is preferable from a cost standpoint, the current breakdown policy or a preventive maintenance contract arrangement?

SOLUTION

By converting the frequencies into a probability distribution and determining the expected cost per month of breakdowns, we have the information shown in the accompanying table.

Number of Breakdowns X	Frequency, in Months $f(X)$	Frequency, in Percentages $P(X)$	Expected Value $X \cdot P(X)$
0	2	.083	0
1	8	.333	.333
2	10	.417	.834
3	3	.125	.375
4	1	.042	.168
	24		Total 1.710

Breakdown cost per month:

$$\text{Expected cost} = \left(\frac{1.71 \text{ breakdowns}}{\text{month}}\right)\left(\frac{\$280}{\text{breakdown}}\right) = \$479/\text{month}$$

Preventive maintenance cost per month. Since the data processing firm guarantees to limit the cost to an "average" of one breakdown per month and the expected number (1.710) is greater than 1, we may assume that WTS will, in the long run, always incur the cost of one breakdown per month.

Average cost of one breakdown/month	$280
Maintenance contract cost/month	150
Total	$430

Preventive maintenance advantage = $479 − $430 = $49/month

SIMULATION MODEL FOR ESTIMATING BREAKDOWN COST

Simulation techniques enable maintenance managers to "try out" numerous maintenance policies on a computer before actually implementing them. Many large firms simulate maintenance activities before shutting down a plant so that uncertainties can be carefully analyzed and downtime minimized.

The following example illustrates how simulated breakdown and repair time values could be used to estimate breakdown cost and help reach a decision on the appropriate crew size. Whereas only five breakdowns are simulated here to illustrate the methodology, in actual practice many thousands of trials would be analyzed via computer.

EXAMPLE 15-2

A management analyst is attempting to study the total cost of the present maintenance policy for machinery in a decentralized section of a shoe manufacturing plant in Boston. The analyst has collected some historical data and simulated breakdowns of machinery over a 16-hour period as shown in the accompanying table. (Clock times are measured on a 24-hour basis.)

Request for Repair (Arrival clock time)	Total Repair Time Required (worker-hours)
0100	1.0
0730	3.0
0800	.5
1150	2.0
1220	.5
Total	7.0

The firm has two maintenance technicians and charges their time (working or idle) at $34 per hour each. The downtime cost of the machines, from lost production, is estimated at $360 per hour.

(a) Determine the simulated service maintenance cost.
(b) Determine the simulated breakdown maintenance cost.
(c) Determine the simulated total maintenance cost.
(d) Would another technician be justified?

SOLUTION

(a) Simulated service maintenance cost:

$$\text{Service cost} = (2 \text{ technicians})(\$34/\text{hr})(16 \text{ hr}) = \$1,088$$

(b) Simulated breakdown maintenance cost (note that we assume that two technicians are twice as effective as one and reduce the downtime accordingly):

(1)	(2) Repair Time Required (2 technicians)		(3)	(4)	(5)	(6)
Request Arrival Time	hr	min	Repair Time Begins	Repair Time Ends	Machine Downtime hr (2 technicians)	Machine Downtime hr (3 technicians)
0100	.50	30	0100	0130	.50	.33
0730	1.50	90	0730	0900	1.50	1.00
0800	.25	15	0900	0915	1.25	.67
1150	1.00	60	1150	1250	1.00	.67
1220	.25	15	1250	1350	.75	.33
	3.50				5.00	3.00

The machine downtime is shown in the accompanying table, in hours, in column 5, as the decimal difference between the request arrival time (1) and the ending repair time (4). Note that on the 0800 breakdown the technicians were not available until 0900, when they finished the earlier job.

$$\text{Breakdown cost} = (\$360/hr)(5\ hr) = \$1{,}800$$

(c) Simulated total maintenance cost:

$$\text{Total cost} = \text{service} + \text{breakdown}$$

$$= \$1{,}088 + \$1{,}800$$

$$= \$2{,}888/\text{period}$$

(d) The machine downtime hours for three technicians would have to be calculated in the same way as was done for two. The calculations are not included, but the final result is shown in column 6.

Service maintenance cost = (3)($34)(16)	= $1,632
Breakdown maintenance cost = ($360)(3 hr) =	1,080
Total	$2,712

There appears to be an advantage to adding a third technician.

Figure 15-4 summarizes the two examples we have just studied and extends the comparison to the probability and queuing models we will study next. The queuing analysis rests upon concepts presented in Chapter 13, so you may want to review them if you have any questions about using the queuing equations. The discussion of probability and queuing models in this chapter is condensed, but both are more fully illustrated in the Solved Problems.

FIGURE 15-4 Four Models for Maintenance Analysis

Model Type	Preventive Maintenance (or Crew Size) Cost	Breakdown Maintenance (or Downtime) Cost	Model Solution
Expected value (Example 15-1)	Given PM ($150) and unavoidable breakdown costs ($280), compute total TC = $150 + $280 = 430 ←	Given BD cost ($280) and frequency distribution of BD. Convert to probability distribution. Use expected value (1.71) to compute costs = $479.	Compare PM with BD: $430 (*best*) versus $479.
Simulation (Example 15-2)	Given crew cost per person ($34/hr and 16 hr). Compute service costs, assuming 2 technicians: $1,088 3 technicians: $1,632	Given simulated BDs and BD cost ($360/hr). Compute downtime cost: + $1,800 + $1,080	Compare total costs, and select optimal crew size. = $2,888 = $2,717 (*best*) ←
Probability (Solved Prob. 3)	Given PM service cost per unit ($100). Use failure probabilities and breakdown costs to compute costs for service based upon PM intervals of: 1 month = $8,000 2 months = $5,400 ← 3 months = $5,920 4 months = $7,158	Given conditional probabilities of failure after 1, 2, 3, and 4 periods and BD cost ($500), compute expected BD cost = $6,897.	Compare best PM with BD: $5,400 (*best*) versus $6,897.
Queuing (Solved Prob. 2)	Given crew cost per worker ($30/hour). Compute costs with: 1 worker = $30 2 workers = $60 3 workers = $90 4 workers = $120	Given downtime costs ($150/hr per machine) and statistical arrivals (Poisson) and service (exponential) of breakdowns. Use queuing equations to estimate number of units in repair and compute total downtime costs. + $300 + $ 75 + $ 38 + $ 30	Compare total costs, and select optimal crew size. = $330 = $135 = $128 (*best*)← = $150

The two examples discussed above use expected value and simulation concepts to help analyze the cost structure underlying Fig. 15-2. In Example 15-1 we simply converted the frequency distribution of breakdowns into a probability distribution and used it to compute a breakdown cost per month that was then compared with a preventive maintenance policy cost per month. Both policies were assumed to be fairly well fixed, so the decision problem involved a choice between a preventive (PM) policy and a breakdown (BD) policy.

In Example 15-2 the firm again had established (simulated) breakdown and repair time distributions which determined the plant downtime, or breakdown, cost. In this example, however, the downtime cost could be reduced by providing additional service maintenance technicians. These service technicians are effectively a preventive maintenance cost which is incurred even if the technicians are idle, and the cost increases as the crew size increases. The decision problem in this example was concerned with adjusting the crew size to where total maintenance costs were minimal. With three technicians the expected total cost per period was $176 less than with two technicians over a 16-hour period. Other less tangible considerations might also be important factors in this situation, but the cost calculation at least establishes the economic preference for three technicians.

PROBABILITY MODEL FOR SELECTING PREVENTIVE MAINTENANCE POLICY

A more sophisticated cost tradeoff situation exists when the decision must be made as to not only whether a breakdown or preventive maintenance policy should be followed but also if a preventive maintenance policy is followed, how often service should be performed. The analysis proceeds as follows.

Data are collected on (1) the preventive maintenance servicing cost, (2) the breakdown cost, and (3) the probability of breakdown. The probability of breakdown reflects the fact that breakdowns will occur even if preventive maintenance is performed, but the chance of breakdown usually increases with time after a maintenance activity.

The cumulative expected number of breakdowns B in M months is:

$$B_n = N \sum_1^n P_n + B_{n-1}P_1 + B_{n-2}P_2 + \cdots + B_1P_{n-1} \tag{15-1}$$

where N = number of units
P = probability of breakdown during a given month after maintenance
n = maintenance period

EXAMPLE 15-3

A computer service center has established the following probabilities of failure after maintenance for a line of printers that have been in service for several years. If they have 75 such printers, what is the expected number of breakdowns in the second year?

Years after Maintenance	1	2	3	4	5
Probability of Breakdown	.2	.4	.2	.1	.1

SOLUTION

$$B_n = N \sum_1^n P_n + B_{n-1}P_1$$
$$= N(P_1 + P_2) + B_{2-1}P_1 = N(P_1 + P_2) + B_1P_1$$

where $N = 75$ units
$$P_1 = .2$$
$$P_2 = .4$$
$$B_1 = N(P_1) = 75(.2) = 15$$

$$B_2 = 75(.2 + .4) + 15(.2) = 45 + 3 = 48 \text{ printers}$$

Analysis The preventive maintenance cost for various policies, such as preventive maintenance every month, every 2 months, and so on, can be calculated by summing the servicing cost and the breakdown cost. Servicing cost is simply the number of units serviced multiplied by the service cost per unit. Breakdown cost is based on the expected number of breakdowns between services times the breakdown cost per unit. After these costs have been calculated for alternative policies and the lowest-cost policy determined, its cost is compared with the cost of a simple breakdown policy which is based on an average time between breakdowns. The best policy is then the one with the lower cost.

This approach fully accounts for the uncertainties of breakdown by incorporating them probabilistically into each appropriate period and then determining expected costs. The computation process is tedious and a good candidate for help from the firm's computer. However, with a conscientious effort to obtain realistic data and a willingness to apply an appropriate methodology, the analysis can suggest a preferable maintenance policy. True, there may be uncertainties in the data, but it is hoped that the model-building activities will bring them out into the open so they can be realistically evaluated. They should also help to identify deficiencies—which may be corrected with time. This is better than arbitrarily selecting some preventive maintenance policy, say a 6-month policy, and blindly incurring unnecessarily high costs—perhaps much higher than necessary. Solved Prob. 3 illustrates this probability model.

QUEUING MODEL FOR ANALYZING MAINTENANCE SERVICE FACILITIES

Maintenance is a service activity and, as we saw in Chapter 13, queuing models are useful for analyzing service activities. This is because attention must be given to the rates of arrival of service requests, the service times required, and other considerations such as the length of the line waiting for service. The following example illustrates the application of queuing expressions to find the average length of the waiting line, N_q, and the average waiting time, T_q, for a maintenance activity that has a constant service time. Recall from Chapter 13 that when service times are constant, the standard equations for N_q and T_q are modified by inserting a 2 in the denominator and adding a subscript (c).

EXAMPLE 15-4

The time required to replace a filter on any of 500 industrial mixers can be considered a constant at 15 minutes per filter. Maintenance records show that the failure rate of filters is distributed according to a Poisson distribution, with a mean of 2 per hour.

(a) Find the average number of mixers waiting for a filter replacement.
(b) Find the average waiting time of a mixer for repair.

SOLUTION

(a) $\quad N_{q(c)} = \dfrac{\lambda^2}{2\mu(\mu - \lambda)}$

$$\text{where } \lambda = \text{arrival rate} = 2/\text{hr}$$
$$\mu = \text{service rate}$$
$$= \left(\frac{\text{filter}}{15 \text{ min}}\right)\left(\frac{60 \text{ min}}{\text{hr}}\right) = 4/\text{hr}$$

$$N_q(c) = \frac{2^2}{2(4)(4 - 2)} = .25 \text{ mixer}$$

(b) $\quad T_{q(c)} = \dfrac{\lambda}{2\mu(\mu - \lambda)} = \dfrac{2}{2(4)(4 - 2)} = 1.25 \text{ hr} = 7.50 \text{ min}$

RELIABILITY AGAINST FAILURE

Preventive maintenance is worthwhile when it can increase the operating time of the asset by reducing the frequency or severity of breakdowns. It is often the unexpected and untimely nature of a breakdown that causes the greatest damage, disrupting operations when they seem to be most critical. Thus power plant managers strive to plan their maintenance for off-peak seasons rather than mid-winter, when demand is high, and astronauts hope that their system reliability is adequately restored when their spaceship is on earth so that they don't have to deal with a failure while in space.

> **Product reliability** is the mathematical probability of a product performing a specific function in a given environment for a specific length of time or number of cycles.

Product reliability is a characteristic of a product that is measurable on a probabilistic basis. The following excerpt, headlined "Cardiac Pacemakers Inc. Advises Some Doctors of Problem Parts," illustrates:

St. Paul—Cardiac Pacemakers Inc. said it has advised certain physicians to monitor more closely about 750 microlith-P programmable pacemakers that don't appear to meet the company's reliability standards because of a parts problem.

The company said the probability that there will be any difficulty with a given unit in the group is less than 3%. . . .

The device is placed in a patient's body and regulates the heart. [2]

Goods   Reliability measures of goods are calculated more often than many of us realize. The reliability of such things as washing machine timers, automobile tires, electronic calculator components, and entire space systems is routinely determined. The Boeing Company, for example, makes thousands of reliability calculations in the form of a "fault-tree analysis" in order to combine the component reliabilities of thousands of items to determine the ultimate reliability of a total missile system for defense purposes. NASA scientists knew there was a probability of failure during the tragic launch of the space shuttle *Challenger*, in which six astronauts and school teacher Christa McAuliffe died in 1986.[1] Airline companies are faced with the realities of continually transporting passengers in airplanes that have limited reliabilities. Each critical component is tested and evaluated quantitatively by the manufacturers to minimize the chance of some component, (perhaps even a $2 item) causing the loss of several hundred lives and millions of dollars' worth of equipment.

Services   The reliability of services can be difficult to assess because of their intangibility and the absence of a physical product. Some equipment-based services (such as electrical, phone, and transportation services) can be measured on a time-available, or frequency-of-downtime, basis. People-based services such as child care, police protection, and household services require more creative measures. Where quantitative measures are not established, consumers frequently apply their own (subjective) criteria of "ongoing dependability," such as reliance, honesty, and trust.

Failure Pattern   Product breakdowns often tend to follow a Poisson distribution; that is, failures occur infrequently during the normal life of a product. Equipment manufacturers have found that the failure rate during the very early and late stages of product life often differs from that experienced during the normal operating life. This difference in failure rates is depicted in the form of the "bathtub" curve shown in Fig. 15-5. Early failures (perhaps due to improper assembly or damage in shipment) may tend to follow a negative exponential pattern. During the typical operating lifetime, failures occur on a *rare-event* basis, often described by a Poisson distribution. As components wear out and fail, the products may follow a pattern described by a normal distribution.

   We might view the composite of Fig. 15-5 by tracing the life expectancy pattern of a simple product such as an installation of a group of fluorescent light tubes in a large plant. One would hope that factory testing had removed manufacturing defectives, although some early failures may result from such things as rough handling during transportation. During normal operation some failures could be expected, but probably not enough to warrant the time of a worker to replace tubes on an individual basis. Toward the end of the average life of the

---

[1] NASA had estimated one chance in 500 of a booster engine failure, but an Air Force study using bayesian analysis found the probability was one booster failure in 35 flights. This was to have been the 25th flight (see *Discover*, April 1986, p. 56).

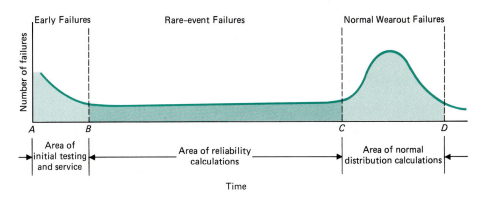

FIGURE 15-5   Product Failure Rates

tubes, failures would probably begin to occur on a normally distributed basis. Group replacement could best be scheduled by taking this statistical wear-out failure rate into account.

Questions sometimes arise as to how many lights, bearings, transistors, and the like to replace at one time, or what other items to replace when one component fails, causing an entire machine or system to break down. This decision should be analyzed on a cost basis, taking labor and material costs plus downtime costs into account. Solved Problem 4 illustrates a situation like this. A major unknown here is the length of service that can be expected after repair, depending upon what worn parts are replaced. Because subsequent failures involve statistical probabilities of failure, stochastic simulation models have been found to be useful for evaluating various alternatives in this type of maintenance decision situation.

DETERMINING FAILURE RATES

A *failure* is simply an event that changes a product from an operational condition to a nonoperational condition. Manufacturers sometimes provide failure-rate data on their equipment, especially in critical applications such as those involving nuclear and space vehicles. Of primary interest to users are usually the failure rates and mean time between failures. The failure rate (FR) represents (1) a percentage of failures among the total number of products tested or (2) a number of failures per given operating time.

$$\mathrm{FR}_{\%} = \frac{\text{number of failures}}{\text{number tested}} \tag{15-2}$$

$$\mathrm{FR}_{n} = \frac{\text{number of failures}}{\text{operating time}} = \frac{F}{\mathrm{TT} - \mathrm{NOT}} \tag{15-3}$$

where F = number of failures
TT = total time
NOT = nonoperating time

EXAMPLE 15-5

Fifty artificial heart valves were tested for 10,000 hours at a medical research center, and three valves failed during the test. What was the failure rate in terms of
(a) Percentage of failures?
(b) Number of failures per unit-year?
(c) On the basis of this data, how many failures could be expected during a year from the installation of these valves in 100 patients?

SOLUTION

(a) $FR_\% = \dfrac{\text{number of failures}}{\text{number tested}} = \dfrac{3}{50} = 6.0\%$

(b) $FR_n = \dfrac{\text{number of failures during period}}{\text{operating time}} = \dfrac{F}{TT - NOT}$

Note that the operating time is reduced by those units that failed. In the absence of actual data we assume that failures are averaged throughout the test period.

$\therefore$ Total time = (10,000 hr)(50 units) =   500,000 unit-hr
     Less: Nonoperating time of 3 failed units for
     average of $\dfrac{10,000}{2}$ hr, or 3(5,000) =   − 15,000 unit-hr
     Operating time =   485,000 unit-hr

$FR_n = \dfrac{3 \text{ failures}}{485,000 \text{ unit-hr}} = .0000062 \text{ failure/unit-hr}$

$= (.0000062) \left(\dfrac{24 \text{ hr}}{\text{day}} \right) \left(\dfrac{365 \text{ days}}{\text{yr}} \right) = .0542 \text{ failure/unit-yr}$

(c) From 100 units,

$\left(\dfrac{.0542 \text{ failure}}{\text{unit-yr}} \right) (100 \text{ units}) = 5.42 \text{ failures/yr}$

Mean Time between Failures   When a (relatively small) Asian company decided it was time to take on IBM in the U.S. personal computer market, they brought out their strategy in *The Wall Street Journal* [4]. After claiming that their personal computer was "just plain better" than the IBM PC (at just about half the price), they presented some of their argument:

The Leading Edge PC is faster (by more than 50%), more powerful, more flexible and more dependable (for example, our disk drives have a "mean time between failures" of 20,000 hours, versus an 8,000-hour MTBF for theirs). It's compatible with just about all the software and peripherals that the IBM is.

Mean time between failures (MTBF) is a useful and widely used term in maintenance and reliability analysis. The MTBF is simply the reciprocal of FR_n:

$$\text{MTBF} = \frac{\text{operating time}}{\text{number of failures}} = \frac{\text{TT} - \text{NOT}}{F} \tag{15-4}$$

EXAMPLE 15-6

Find the MTBF for the heart valves described in the previous example.

SOLUTION

$$\text{MTBF} = \frac{\text{TT} - \text{NOT}}{F} = \frac{500,000 - 15,000}{3} = 161,667 \text{ unit-hr/failure}$$

$$= \frac{161,667}{(24)(365)} = 18.46 \text{ unit-yr/failure}$$

The figure of 18.46 unit-years per failure represents the mean service time between failures that might be expected from a group of units during their several years of service. It is not necessarily indicative of the expected life of an individual unit. Recall from Fig. 15-5 that we are dealing here with reliability calculations and rare-event failures as opposed to normal wear-out failures. The 10,000-hour test time in the examples represented only slightly over 1 year of actual operating time and was not adequate to obtain data on normal wear-out failures.

RELIABILITY MEASUREMENT AND IMPROVEMENT

We indicated earlier that the reliability of individual components and systems is routinely measured and analyzed for many products. Factory and independent laboratory tests, such as illustrated by the heart valve example above, are used to establish mathematical reliability figures, which in turn enable engineers and systems designers to improve total system reliability. Some ways to improve reliability are listed in Fig. 15-6.

Many of the suggested methods of improving reliability seem obvious, once they are delineated. Several of the ways mentioned will undoubtedly tend to

- Improve the design of components.
- Simplify the design of the system.
- Improve production techniques.
- Improve quality control.
- Test components and the system.
- Install parallel systems.
- Perform periodic preventive maintenance.
- Derate components and/or the system.

FIGURE 15-6   Ways to Improve Reliability

increase production costs, but of course these are preventive maintenance expenses that can often be justified by the alternative breakdown and downtime expense. There is also the possibility that design simplification and improvement in component design and production techniques could reduce production costs. Derating the system so that it does not operate at full design capacity could also lessen product warranty costs.

The installation of parallel systems is a standard design procedure in many hazardous and capital-intensive applications. Rapid transit systems, space vehicles, nuclear reactors, and other critical installations commonly have parallel or back-up systems that improve the overall system reliability at some cost of duplication. We can illustrate the improvement effect by taking an elementary example of series and parallel circuits in an electrical network. The reliability of components in series, R_s, is simply the multiplicative sum of the individual component reliabilities:

$$\text{(Series)} \quad R_s = R_1 \cdot R_2 \cdots R_n \tag{15-5}$$

For parallel circuits the reliability, R_p, of the system is determined by

$$\text{(Parallel)} \quad R_p = 1 - (1 - R_{s1})(1 - R_{s2}) \tag{15-6}$$

EXAMPLE 15-7

An acid control system has three components in series with individual reliabilities (R_1, R_2, and R_3) as shown in the diagram.
(a) Find the reliability of the system.

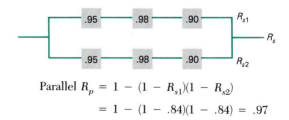

(b) What would be the reliability of the system if a parallel circuit were added?

SOLUTION
(a) Series $R_s = R_1 \cdot R_2 \cdot R_3 = (.95)(.98)(.90) = .84$
(b) The parallel system design would be as shown, where R_{s1} and R_{s2} are the computed reliabilities of the respective series circuits.

Parallel $R_p = 1 - (1 - R_{s1})(1 - R_{s2})$

$= 1 - (1 - .84)(1 - .84) = .97$

As can be seen, the installation of a parallel circuit renders a substantial improvement in the probability of the system functioning as planned without failure. Although parallel systems can be costly, when hundreds of items are series-dependent, as in some control circuits, the rapid deterioration in system reliability often necessitates the use of parallel systems. Verbal communications in people-based systems share some of these same characteristics. Messages often lose their credibility if there are too many persons in the chain of communications.

NORMAL STATISTICAL FAILURE

As a product moves along the time continuum of Fig. 15-5 from rare-event failures to the area of normal wear-out failures, standard techniques of analysis using the normal statistical distribution often become appropriate. We will illustrate this with an example concerning the fluorescent light tubes used to discuss Fig. 15-5.

EXAMPLE 15-8

The manufacturing area in the plant of a New Jersey drug manufacturer requires 5,000 fluorescent light tubes. The lights have a normally distributed lifetime, with a mean of 4,000 hours and a standard deviation of 120 hours. The plant manager has found that after 10 percent of the lights burn out, the quality of output and the productivity of workers in the plant are affected. He would like to schedule maintenance activities so that all lights are replaced when 10 percent fail. After how many hours of operation should the replacement activities be scheduled?

SOLUTION

At the mean lifetime μ, 50 percent of the lights are still operating. We wish to find the earlier time, X, such that 40 percent more (or 90 percent total) are operating. Because the distribution is normal, we know (from Appendix C) that the number of standard deviations required to include an area of .40 is $Z = 1.28$.

$$-Z = \frac{X - \mu}{\sigma}$$

then $X = \mu - Z\sigma$

$\qquad = 4,000 - 1.28(120)$

$\qquad = 3,846 \text{ hr}$

This concludes the material on maintenance. Having discussed objectives, some illustrative models for maintenance management, and the concept of reliability, we now move on to the topic of cost control.

COST-CONTROL CONCEPTS

At a time when a number of airlines were "struggling to stay aloft," *The Wall Street Journal* reported that Northwest Airlines was "beginning to soar" [1].

Northwest is at or near the top by the important measures of cost, profit and debt ratio. [They are] in the best shape of any major carrier to get through today's turbulence [of competition brought on by deregulation and recession]. . . . For years, Northwest has been run as if competition were fierce . . . has fought labor-union demands, and hammered away to increase productivity.

Northwest's overhead costs are only about 2% of total costs, compared with about 5% for major competitors. The lean operation is nowhere more evident than in the starkly plain windowless headquarters here. . . . Northwest's labor costs were the lowest of any of the 11 major airlines, at 24.2% of operating revenue. . . . Operating revenue per employee was 27% higher.

Costs are, of course, one of the most critical determinants of success—and of survival! Whether an organization is profit- or nonprofit-oriented, and whether it concentrates on the production of goods or of services, costs form the basis for an immense number of managerial decisions. They are one of the most important manageable aspects of an operation. So their control warrants special concern.

COST COMPONENTS

In nonprofit organizations, costs have to be kept within budgeted amounts. Thus, welfare programs, public school operations, and even police and fire protection services all operate on limited budgets. In competitive profit-making organizations, unless the costs are kept below the revenues, no profit will result, and in the long run, the organization will fail. Figure 15-7 shows the cost composition of a typical manufacturing firm. Control of the total system costs clearly depends upon control of the individual component costs. For the operations manager, this usually means responsibility for control of the labor, materials, and overhead that make up the cost of goods sold.

COST TYPES

The collection of costs and their allocation into various accounts is basically a cost-accounting function. The method of collecting costs depends heavily upon the type of production system involved and is broadly classified into process and job costing.

- *Process costing.* Continuous systems charge costs directly to the responsible department or process and allocate costs to products by dividing them up into the units produced according to some logical apportionment procedure. Process costs nearly always represent some form of average costs.
- *Job costing.* Intermittent systems often use a job-order costing arrangement whereby costs are collected according to the job or customer. Project costs are also handled on this basis.

Elements of both process costing and job costing are often found in the same organization. In addition, the cost elements are typically broken down into subele-

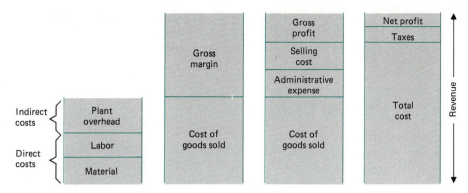

FIGURE 15-7   Cost Components

ments or collected on a time-sequenced basis. Whatever the cost unit is, it should be chosen with a view toward providing information useful for management decision making. The cost units should also facilitate control by relating the costs to specific positions which are filled by individuals who can exercise control over the costs. Nothing (but frustration) is accomplished by holding people responsible for costs that they are not in a position to control.

A common classification of costs relates to their ability to be traced to a specific product. *Direct costs* are items such as labor and materials which can be directly identified with a given good or service. Since these costs vary directly with the volume of production, they are also termed *variable costs*, and we have previously referred to them as such.

Indirect costs are legitimate costs of supporting activities which are not directly identifiable with specific products. They include overhead items such as depreciation, office supplies, and insurance which (at least in theory) do not vary with production volume. We have referred to these as *fixed costs*, recognizing that in the long term many so-called fixed costs are at least semivariable. Total indirect costs are often two or three times as much as direct costs.

COST CONTROL

Effective control of costs requires all the elements common to any control system—only in this case they pertain to costs:

- *Measurement* and *allocation* of actual labor, material, and overhead costs
- *Feedback* of actual cost data via cost summary and cost variance information system reports
- *Comparison* with standard (planned or budgeted) cost levels and standard costs
- *Correction* when costs differ from standards

If any control elements are missing or defective, the whole cost-control system will suffer. Thus, faulty measurement, slow feedback, inaccurate standards, or an inability to take corrective action will invalidate any cost-control system. Whereas all these elements are important, the detailed operation of the cost-accounting system is outside the scope of this text. We shall, however, call attention to the vital area of budgets and cost standards, for they are very important to operations managers.

BUDGETS: FIXED AND FLEXIBLE

A **budget** is an operating plan which coordinates and summarizes individual estimates and plans for future periods. An organization may develop several types of budgets, including capital expenditures budgets, cash budgets, and operations budgets.

The operations budget is an important tool for cost control of production activities. It typically shows fixed, semivariable, and variable costs projected for the expected volume of production in a future period. The budgeted costs are derived from labor, material, and overhead standard costs. Subsequent performance reports may include room for both projected costs and actual costs, plus explanations as to why costs were greater than or less than budgeted values.

Advantages In addition to facilitating production cost control, budgets serve several other purposes. They facilitate setting objectives, help guide future activities, provide measures of performance toward meeting objectives, establish centers of responsibility for production activities and cost control, and provide cost information for decision making with respect to financing, marketing, and other functional activities.

Types Budgets are generally classified as either fixed (static) or flexible (variable), depending upon whether they vary with the volume of production. The distinction is very important, and Fig. 15-8 illustrates the two types. *Fixed budgets* are prepared for one chosen level of activity (such as 5,000 units), and comparisons of actual performance are always made against this initial plan. Thus, even if production turned out to be 6,000 units, basic comparisons would be made

FIGURE 15-8   Fixed and Flexible Budgets for Shop 62 for the Month Ending May 31, 19XX

Fixed Budget		Flexible Budget			
Elements	5,000 Units	Elements	4,000 Units	5,000 Units	6,000 Units
Direct labor	$ 75,000	Direct labor	$ 60,000	$ 75,000	$ 90,000
Direct materials	30,000	Direct materials	24,000	30,000	36,000
Variable overhead	20,000	Variable overhead	16,000	20,000	24,000
Fixed overhead	160,000	Fixed overhead	160,000	160,000	160,000
Total	$285,000	Total	$260,000	$285,000	$310,000

against the costs projected for a 5,000-unit budget. Fixed budgets are frequently used in association with long-range planning.

Flexible budgets project costs for a range of volume. Thus a firm may set up budgets for several possible levels of production and wait until after the time period is over to designate which budget applied. Since it is the variable costs and not the fixed costs which change with volume, flexible budgets are often referred to as *variable budgets* and are sometimes based on variable costs only. However, they can and often do contain the fixed-cost elements as well, as illustrated by the fixed overhead in the flexible budget of Fig. 15-8. By providing standards for what costs should be for various levels of output, flexible budgets provide reasonable and often more meaningful guides for cost control. This is because the underlying basis of comparison (the activity level) is common to both the budget and the actual cost figures.

COST STANDARDS

A *cost standard* is a declaration of what a component or activity *should cost* under specified operating conditions. Standard costs are usually based upon attainable levels of performance rather than upon ideal levels (that may appear unreasonable to operating employees). Whereas the *budgeted costs typically refer to total amounts*, such as a budget for 50,000 units, *standard costs usually refer to unit costs*, such as material cost per unit and labor cost per unit or per hour. In the case of overhead costs, the individual unit costs are not always the most relevant for many decisions. Overhead costs, being composed of numerous items (many of which are not directly identifiable with the product), are often handled on a total (budget) basis rather than on a unit (standard cost) basis.

Standard costs are used to establish budgets and production schedules. Thus it is important that all factors affecting the costs be properly weighted in the standards. The standards may be derived in different ways, such as from historical costs, from estimates of experienced estimators, or from more analytical approaches that stem from the buildup of costs based upon specifically defined materials and work methods. One method of determining cost standards for labor, material, and overhead is discussed next.

LABOR COSTS

Standard times, developed by time studies, predetermined time standards, or work sampling, often form the basis for labor-cost standards. The most commonly used standards are set at a level where about 95 percent of the workers can meet the standard if they work at a normal pace (that is, a 100 percent rating factor). The standard labor cost for a particular unit of activity (C_l) is then the summation of the standard times (ST) multiplied by the base labor rate (LR).

$$C_l = \Sigma(ST)(LR) = \Sigma(hr/unit)(\$/hr) \tag{15-7}$$

MATERIAL COSTS

The efficient use of material is the concern of much design and value engineering effort, as well as production control effort. Material requirements for a given product are typically specified on engineering drawings or production control documents. Using the bills of material on the drawings (or the production control data files), purchasing and engineering personnel can determine standard material unit costs, C_m.

OVERHEAD COSTS

Some elements of overhead cost, such as building depreciation, are fixed costs (FC), whereas other components, such as supervision, maintenance, and factory supplies, are often classified as variable, V, or perhaps semivariable, SV.

Under flexible budgeting the overhead variable budget varies depending upon the projected volume. For example, in Fig. 15-8, if shop 62 produces 4,000 units during May, the variable overhead cost standard will be $16,000 (or $16,000 ÷ 4,000 units = $4/unit). For volumes of 5,000 and 6,000 units, the budget increases to $20,000 and $24,000, respectively (but of course the *per-unit* standard amount remains at $4), and intermediate amounts would be adjusted accordingly.

A convenient and popular method of expressing variable overhead standards is in terms of a cost per direct labor hour. Thus, for example, if the direct labor standard (the $60,000 in Fig. 15-8) represents 10,000 direct labor hours, the variable overhead cost would be expressed as $16,000 ÷ 10,000 direct labor hours, or $1.60 per direct labor hour. Fixed overhead costs are usually retained as a total cost (such as $160,000) rather than converting them to per-unit costs because they are typically analyzed on a total basis anyway.

With fixed budgets, the overhead standard cost, C_{OH}, does not differ depending upon the actual volume, so a single standard must be developed that is (it is hoped) representative of all the overhead costs. This is often derived from an estimate of the overhead cost per unit at the midpoint of a likely volume range. One method of determining an overhead standard cost is by summing the FC + the mean of the V or SV overhead costs and dividing by the midpoint or expected volume. This overhead allocation is referred to as the *overhead liquidation* (or *absorption*) *rate* and is denoted by A in Fig. 15-9 [3:92].

$$C_{OH} = \frac{FC + (\text{mean of } V_{OH} \text{ or } SV_{OH})}{\text{midpoint volume}} \qquad (15\text{-}8)$$

EXAMPLE 15-9 | A West Coast firm uses a fixed budget and produces legend plates for the instrument panels of aircraft. The legend plate operation has fixed costs of $50,000 per year and other overhead costs for administration, supervision, maintenance, and utilities of from $20,000 to $40,000, depending upon the volume, which may range from 35,000 to 45,000 units. Material costs for the Micarta average $.26 per unit, with painting and sanding supplies and

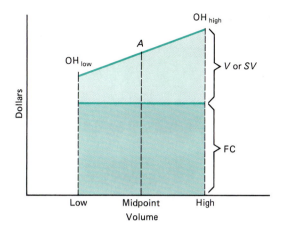

FIGURE 15-9   Overhead Costs

packaging materials at $.03 per unit and $.01 per unit, respectively. A work-sampling study revealed the accompanying standard times (ST) with the respective labor rates (LR).

Activity	ST (min)	LR ($/hr)
Cutting	1.2	13.20
Engraving	9.0	13.20
Sanding	1.8	13.00
Inspection	.6	13.00
Packaging	.6	13.00

Find the:
(a) Labor standard cost, C_l
(b) Material standard cost, C_m
(c) Overhead standard cost, C_{OH}

SOLUTION
(a) Labor standard cost, C_l:

$$C_l = \Sigma(ST)(LR)$$

Activity	ST (min)	ST (hr)	LR ($/hr)	(ST)(LR)
Cutting	1.2	.02	13.20	$ .264
Engraving	9.0	.15	13.20	1.980
Sanding	1.8	.03	13.00	.390
Inspection	.6	.01	13.00	.130
Packaging	.6	.01	13.00	.130
			Total = C_l	$2.894 unit

(b) Material standard cost, C_m.

$$C_m = \Sigma \text{ material unit costs}$$
$$= \text{Micarta} + \text{supplies} + \text{packaging materials}$$
$$= \$.26 + \$.03 + \$.01 = \$.30/\text{unit}$$

(c) Overhead standard cost, C_{OH}:

$$C_{OH} = \frac{FC + (\text{mean of } V_{OH} \text{ or } SV_{OH})}{\text{midpoint volume}}$$
$$= \frac{\$50,000 + \$30,000}{40,000 \text{ units}} = \$2/\text{unit}$$

ANALYSIS OF COST VARIANCE

The purpose of analyzing the deviation of actual costs from budgeted or standard costs is to identify causes of the variance and then make use of this information to capitalize on favorable variances or try to prevent unfavorable variances from occurring in future planning. Variance can usually be classified into one or more of three categories:

1 *Variance in volume*, V_v, where the actual is less than or greater than the forecast
2 *Variance in rate*, V_r, or price, V_p, where the purchase cost per unit differs from standards
3 *Variance in efficiency*, V_e, where the actual time or usage differs from standards

If flexible budgeting procedures are used, the budget is adjusted to suit the volume produced, and the volume variance may be eliminated. Information from fixed budgets tends to be more useful for planning, while reports from flexible budgeting systems are more useful for control, but both are used. Regardless of the type of system used, the prime requirement of any cost-reporting system is that the cost information be timely and relevant to decision making.

SUMMARY

Maintenance is any activity designed to keep resources in working condition or restore them to operating status. Facilities maintenance is concerned with a physical condition only, whereas personnel maintenance must deal with both physical and mental health.

Preventive maintenance consists of prior inspections and servicing, whereas breakdown maintenance is often concerned with emergency repairs following some type of failure. From a cost standpoint, the optimal level of maintenance activity is attained when the total cost of preventive and breakdown maintenance is minimized.

Among the numerous models available for analyzing maintenance activities, four were discussed in this chapter.

1 The *expected value model* was used to compare the cost of a given preventive maintenance policy with the expected cost of breakdowns over the same time period, where the breakdowns occur on an empirical probabilistic basis.

2 A *simulation model* was used to illustrate how simulated breakdown and repair time values can be used to estimate both the preventive (service crew) cost and the breakdown (downtime) cost so that the most economical crew size can be determined.

3 The *probability model* uses historical data on servicing costs as well as breakdown probabilities (and costs) to help select the appropriate preventive maintenance policy to minimize maintenance costs. This model extends somewhat beyond the earlier models not only to choose between a breakdown maintenance policy and a given preventive maintenance policy but also to evaluate various preventive maintenance policies and discriminate between them on the basis of expected cost.

4 The *queuing model* has some applications potential for analyzing the workload and utilization characteristics of maintenance facilities by accounting for the statistical patterns of arrival and service rates.

Failures of components during what might be classified as a normal operating lifetime occur on a rare-event (Poisson) basis, whereas those in the late stages of product life often occur on a normally distributed basis. The rare-event failures present reliability problems, and a number of ways exist to measure, analyze, and improve reliability, including such things as parallel systems. The wear-out distributions also lend themselves to statistical analysis.

Cost control is one of the most universal responsibilities of managers, and like other control activities it necessitates the development of reasonable standards. Cost standards specify what a component or activity *should* cost under normal operating conditions. Standards are typically established for labor, materials, and overhead costs. The analysis of cost variance is concerned with how much and why the actual costs differ from standards in terms of volume, rate (or price), and efficiency.

SOLVED PROBLEMS

QUEUING MODELS

1 Breakdowns of conveyor belt drives in a canning plant occur according to a Poisson distribution on an average of $\lambda = 2$ per day. Repair service times follow a negative

exponential distribution with a mean time of one-third of a day. All breakdowns are handled on a first-come, first-served basis by the one available maintenance crew.
(a) What is the average number of conveyors down at any time?
(b) What is the average waiting time before the maintenance crew can begin service?

Solution

First compute the service *rate*, which is

$$\mu = \left(\frac{\text{conveyor}}{.33 \text{ day}}\right) = 3 \text{ conveyors/day}$$

(a) The mean number in the system (both in breakdown awaiting service and in repair) is:

$$N_s = \frac{\lambda}{\mu - \lambda} = \frac{2}{3 - 2} = 2 \text{ conveyors}$$

(b) The mean waiting time in the queue is

$$T_q = \frac{\lambda}{\mu(\mu - \lambda)} = \frac{2}{3(3 - 2)} = \frac{2}{3} \text{ day}$$

2 A textile firm uses a cost of $30 per hour for direct and indirect labor maintenance and estimates downtime costs on any of a large group of spinning machines at $150 per hour per machine. If breakdowns are distributed according to a Poisson distribution with a mean of four per hour and the mean number of units a worker can service is six breakdowns per hour (distributed exponentially), what is the optimal maintenance crew size?

Solution

In the absence of other information, estimate the total maintenance costs (crew + downtime) per hour, beginning with one worker, and increase the crew size until total costs are minimized. The number of units in breakdown is the mean number in the system, N_s:

$$N_s = \frac{\lambda}{\mu - \lambda}$$

where λ = mean arrival rate = 4/hr
μ = mean service rate (varies depending upon crew size)

For crew size of 1:

$$\text{Crew cost} = 1 \text{ worker at } \$30/\text{hr} = \$\ 30$$

$$\text{Breakdown cost} = (N_s)(\text{cost/hr})$$

$$= \left(\frac{4}{6 - 4}\right)(\$150/\text{hr}) = \frac{300}{\$330/\text{hr}}$$

For crew size of 2:

$$\text{Crew cost} = 2 \text{ workers at } \$30/\text{hr} = \$60$$

$$\text{Breakdown cost} = \left(\frac{4}{12 - 4}\right) (\$150/\text{hr}) = \underline{\quad 75 \quad}$$
$$\$135/\text{hr}$$

For crew size of 3:

$$\text{Crew cost} = 3 \text{ workers at } \$30/\text{hr} = \$90$$

$$\text{Breakdown cost} = \left(\frac{4}{18 - 4}\right) (\$150/\text{hr}) = \underline{\quad 43 \quad}$$
$$\$133/\text{hr}$$

For crew size of 4:

$$\text{Crew cost} = 4 \text{ workers at } \$30/\text{hr} = \$120$$

$$\text{Breakdown cost} = \left(\frac{4}{24 - 4}\right) (\$150/\text{hr}) = \underline{\quad 30 \quad}$$
$$\$150/\text{hr}$$

The total costs for crew sizes of two and three are so close that other, noneconomic factors should probably be deciding criteria.

PROBABILITY MODEL

* 3 *Probability model* A copper refinery in Arizona has 40 flotation cells which can be serviced on a preventive maintenance schedule at $100 each. If the cells break down, it costs $500 to get them back into service (including unscheduled clean-out time and all breakdown costs). Records show that the probabilities of breakdown after maintenance are as shown in the accompanying table.

Months After Maintenance	Probability of Breakdown
1	.2
2	.1
3	.3
4	.4

Should a preventive maintenance (PM) policy be followed? If so, how often should the cells be serviced?

Solution
Determine the costs of the alternative preventive maintenance policies, and compare them with the cost of a breakdown policy.

(a) *Preventive maintenance*

$$\text{Cost} = \text{servicing cost} + \text{breakdown cost}$$

$$= \begin{pmatrix} \text{number of} \\ \text{units} \\ \text{serviced} \end{pmatrix} \begin{pmatrix} \text{service} \\ \text{cost/} \\ \text{unit} \end{pmatrix} + \begin{pmatrix} \text{expected number} \\ \text{of breakdowns} \\ \text{between services} \end{pmatrix} \begin{pmatrix} \text{breakdown} \\ \text{cost/} \\ \text{unit} \end{pmatrix}$$

The cumulative expected number of breakdowns, B, in M months may be expressed by means of the equation

$$B_n = N \sum_1^n P_n + B_{n-1}P_1 + B_{n-2}P_2 + \cdots + B_1P_{n-1}$$

where N = number of cells
P = probability of breakdown during a given month after maintenance
n = maintenance period

Thus:
$$B_1 = N(p_1) = (40)(.2) = 8.0$$

$$B_2 = N(p_1 + p_2) + B_1p_1 = 40(.2 + .1) + 8(.2) = 13.6$$

$$B_3 = N(p_1 + p_2 + p_3) + B_2p_1 + B_1p_2$$

$$= 40(.2 + .1 + .3) + 13.6(.2) + 8(.1) = 27.52$$

$$B_4 = N(p_1 + p_2 + p_3 + p_4) + B_3p_1 + B_2p_2 + B_1p_3$$

$$= 40(1.0) + 27.52 (.2) + 13.6(.1) + 8(.3) = 49.26$$

The differences between the monthly cumulative totals then represent the individual period breakdowns. Thus the expected number of breakdowns during period 2 is $13.6 - 8.0 = 5.6$. The following (preventive maintenance cost analysis) table carries forward the cost analysis to the determination of an expected total cost for the various preventive maintenance policies.

Preventive Maintenance Cost Analysis—PM Policy

	1 month	2 months	3 months	4 months
Cumulative breakdowns during PM period	8.00	13.60	27.52	49.26
Cost at $500 each	$4,000	$6,800	$13,760	$24,630
Add: PM cost at $100/cell	+4,000	+4,000	+4,000	+4,000
Total cost for	$8,000	$10,800	$17,760	$28,630
M-month PM policy	(1*M*)	(2*M*)	(3*M*)	(4*M*)
Monthly cost				

(b) *Breakdown maintenance* The cost of following any PM policy (for example, $5,400 for a 2-month policy) must then be compared with the cost of a breakdown policy. The expected cost of following a breakdown policy, C_p, is simply the cost, C_r, of repairing the cells, N, divided by the expected number of periods between breakdowns, $\Sigma T_n(p_n)$:

$$C_p = \frac{NC_r}{\Sigma T_n(p_n)} \qquad (15\text{-}9)$$

where T_n = number of time periods after repair
$\quad\quad\;\; p_n$ = probability of breakdown during given time period, n

Thus: $\qquad\qquad \Sigma T_n(p_n) = 1(.2) + 2(.1) + 3(.3) + 4(.4)$

$$= 2.9 \text{ months between breakdowns}$$

$$C_p = \frac{NC_r}{\Sigma T_n(p_n)}$$

$$= \frac{(40 \text{ cells})(\$500/\text{breakdown-cell})}{2.9 \text{ months/breakdown}}$$

$$= \$6,897/\text{month}$$

Conclusion: Both the 2-month and 3-month preventive maintenance policies (at expected costs of \$5,400 and \$5,920, respectively) are preferred to the breakdown policy (\$6,897), with the 2-month policy being most preferable.

RELIABILITY AGAINST FAILURE

4 *Replacement decision where operating life is known and constant* An automatic machine at an underground mine in Wyoming has two clutches that must be replaced periodically. Clutch A costs \$40, can be installed for \$50, and will operate satisfactorily for 300 hours. Clutch B costs only \$30, can be installed for \$35, and will operate for 400 hours. Both parts can be installed on one shutdown for \$45. Compare the costs of replacing the clutches individually and replacing them together (use a cycle time of 3,600 hours).

	Hours	
	Clutch A	Clutch B
Replace A Cost: \$90	300	
		400 — Replace B Cost: \$65
Replace A Cost: \$90	600	
		800 — Replace B Cost: \$65
Replace A Cost: \$90	900	
Replace both Cost: \$115	1,200	1,200
Replace A Cost: \$90	1,500	
		1,600 — Replace B Cost: \$65
Replace A Cost: \$90	1,800	
		2,000 — Replace B Cost: \$65
Replace A Cost: \$90	2,100	
Replace both Cost: \$115	2,400	2,400
Replace A Cost: \$90	2,700	
		2,800 — Replace B Cost: \$65
Replace A Cost: \$90	3,000	
		3,200 — Replace B Cost: \$65
Replace A Cost: \$90	3,300	
Replace both Cost: \$115	3,600	3,600

Solution
Individual replacement:

$$
\begin{array}{rlr}
\text{A:} & 9 \text{ times at } \$90 = & \$810 \\
\text{B:} & 6 \text{ times at } 65 = & 390 \\
\text{A + B:} & 3 \text{ times at } 115 = & \underline{345} \\
& \text{Total} & \$1,545
\end{array}
$$

All joint replacement (every 300 hr):

$$\text{A + B:} \quad 12 \text{ times at } \$115 = \$1,380$$

Conclusion: Costs of individual replacement are $1,545 - $1,380 = $165 less per 3,600 hours.

5 Records show that employees of a large city bus system make an average of 4.6 visits per day to the city's medical service center due to illness or injury. Work schedulers have found that if 10 or more employees must leave their work stations on any given day, the operations must be curtailed. Using the Poisson distribution, what is the probability that operations must be curtailed tomorrow?

Solution
The Poisson table in Appendix E gives $P(X \le c|\lambda)$. Therefore we can find $P(X \le 9)$ and subtract it from 1.00 to get $P(X \ge 10)$.

$$P(X \le 9|\lambda = 4.6) = .980 \qquad \therefore P(X \ge 10) = 1.00 - .980 = .020$$

QUESTIONS

15-1 In what major respect are facilities and personnel maintenance different?

15-2 Identify the major components of preventive and breakdown maintenance costs. Which do you feel are most significant?

15-3 Briefly summarize (in two or three sentences for each model) the purpose and methodology of the four models for maintenance management discussed in the chapter. In what respects are the models similar?

15-4 How would a breakdown probability distribution be obtained, what would it show, and how might it be useful to a maintenance manager?

15-5 Would preventive maintenance generally be more applicable to machines that have a high or a low variability in their breakdown time distribution? Why? (*Note:* You may want to make a sketch similar to Fig. 15-5 to illustrate your answer.)

15-6 A maintenance manager remarked to the plant manager, "The most important thing I've got to do in this plant, as I see it, is to do everything I can to minimize the total of all downtime costs. I work at that eight hours a day, and you're still on my back! What more do you want?" Discuss.

15-7 Give an example of a maintenance queuing situation, and illustrate the structure of such a queuing situation with a simple diagram.

15-8 Define product reliability. How is the reliability of a complex system determined?

15-9   Distinguish between failures distributed as Poisson and failures distributed normally. Which type of distribution is most closely associated with (a) maintenance activities and (b) reliability concerns?

15-10 Define (a) cost standard, (b) job costing, (c) direct costs, and (d) budget.

15-11 Explain what is meant by the overhead liquidation rate.

15-12 Many very small firms make no cost variance analysis and still get by satisfactorily. Why is it done in larger firms?

15-13 Suppose you were asked to set up a cost-control program for an established glass manufacturing firm. Briefly, what steps would you feel were absolutely vital to such a program?

PROBLEMS

1   Manchester (England) Woolen Mills has kept records of breakdowns on its carding machines for a 300-day workyear as shown.

Number of Breakdowns	Frequency (in days)
0	40
1	150
2	70
3	30
4	10
	300

The firm estimates that each breakdown costs $65, and it is considering adopting a preventive maintenance program that would cost $20 per day and limit the number of breakdowns to an average of one per day. What is the expected annual savings from the preventive maintenance program?

2   The following data were derived from a simulation of maintenance activities in the plant of a multinational book publisher in New Jersey. The firm has several machines but only one crew, and occasionally (20 minutes per day—see accompanying table) there are two machines out of service at the same time.

Average number of service calls/day	5 calls/day
Average idle time/day of service crew	5 hr/day
Total delay time/day of machines awaiting service	20 min/day

The service call (repair) materials cost is essentially fixed at $25 per call, and the operations manager uses a cost of $120 per hour per machine for each machine out of service. (Note that this applies to 3 hours per day when a machine is being worked on plus the 20-minute-per-day delay time when a second machine is also out of service and waiting to be worked on.) In addition to the cost of $120 per hour per machine, the service crew cost is $50 per hour. For an 8-hour day,

(a) What is the simulated crew idle-time cost?

(b) What is the simulated total maintenance cost?

(c) Considering the crew cost of $50 per hour × 8 hours = $400 as a preventive maintenance expense, comment upon the suitability of the crew size.

3 Cascade Plastics has a group of molding machines that require breakdown maintenance at a (Poisson-distributed) mean rate of six per day. Each maintenance technician can service an (exponentially distributed) average of eight per day. If downtime costs are $400 per 8-hour workday, what size maintenance crew will be the least costly? Maintenance labor costs are $15 per hour.

4 Machine breakdowns average 10 per day and follow a Poisson distribution. Service rates are exponentially distributed and average 11 per day with one maintenance worker, 15 per day with two, 18 per day with three, and 20 with four. If labor costs are $150 per day per worker and downtime costs are $400 per day per machine, what is the optimum crew size?

5 In a simulated operation, a firm's maintenance worker received requests for service and provided service during an 8-hour period, as shown.

Request Arrival (Clock) Time	Service Time (hours)
0:00	1.5
1:00	.5
3:30	2.0
4:00	.5
7:00	1.0

The maintenance labor cost is $14 per hour, and delay time (when machines are not being operated or repaired but instead are simply waiting for service) is $45 per hour.
(a) Find the idle-time cost for the maintenance worker.
(b) Find the delay-time cost for the machinery.

6 Requests for maintenance service made upon a centralized facility have been simulated for a typical 8-hour day, with arrival and service time patterns as shown in the accompanying table.

Request Arrival (Clock) Time	Repair Service Time
1:30	60 min
2:00	18 min
4:15	45 min
4:30	120 min
5:30	30 min
7:00	9 min

Labor attached to the maintenance center is charged at a rate of $40 per hour, whether working or idle. The delay (waiting) time of operators and machinery that is broken down is costed at $70 per hour.
(a) Find the idle-time cost of the maintenance facility.
(b) Find the delay-time cost of the operators and machinery—the waiting-time cost only, not including actual repair.
(c) Find the total facility idle-time and machinery delay-time cost.

(d) Assume that for an additional cost of $10 per hour the maintenance center could add another worker and decrease the repair times by one-third. Would the additional cost be justified?

(e) Show the effect of (d) by sketching Fig. 15-2 and locating two additional vertical dotted lines: line A should depict the $40-per-hour maintenance center rate and line B the $50 rate.

*7 *Probability model* Worldwide Construction Company has received a large contract for a highway construction project wherein it will be penalized $2,500 per day for each day the project falls behind schedule. Each breakdown of a carryall during the day shift costs an average of $50 in repair and service maintenance costs plus the lost of $\frac{1}{10}$ day in completion time. The carryalls can be serviced on an overtime basis during an evening shift (with no loss of production time) at a cost of $80 each. Assume 10 carryalls.

Weeks After Maintenance	Probability of Breakdowns
1	.1
2	.1
3	.3
4	.5

(a) What would be the expected cost of following a policy of simply waiting until carryalls break down to service them?

(b) How often should the carryalls be serviced?

8 A tool crib attendant receives requests for tools at a mean Poisson rate of 18 per hour and can service an average of 20 requests per hour on an exponential basis. If requests are handled on a first-come, first-served basis, what are (a) the mean number in the waiting line and (b) the mean waiting time?

9 A vegetable processing plant in the Sacramento Valley has one maintenance crew to service breakdowns in any one of several buildings on a first-call priority basis. Breakdowns occur at an average of $\lambda = 5$ per week (Poisson distribution), but the crew could service an average of $\mu = 8$ breakdowns per week (Poisson distribution). Find (a) % U, (b) T_s, (c) N_s, (d) T_q, (e) N_q, and (f) probability of finding the crew with three breakdowns to worry about at one time.

*10 Green River Mills has 12 automatic machines that each do the work of several laborers for a net savings of $200 per machine per day. The machines break down randomly at times corresponding to a Poisson distribution with a mean of $\lambda = 2$ per day.

(a) What is the probability of more than one machine breaking down on any given day?

(b) Assume that manual labor can be substituted for machines that are down. On the basis of the average failure rate of two machines per day, what is the expected incremental (added) cost of the labor?

(c) The firm can maintain standby machines for an extra cost of $130 per machine per day. How many standby machines are justified on an expected value basis?

11 Quick Freeze Foods has a corn line with two stripper saws operating in sequence to cut kernels from corn cobs. Blades on both the primary, P, and secondary, S, saws get dull and must be replaced periodically, as shown in the accompanying table.

Saw	Blade Cost ($)	Installation Cost ($)	Operating Life (hr)
Primary	60	70	80
Secondary	40	60	100
Both	100	90	

Should the blades be replaced individually at the end of their operating lives, or should both be replaced every 80 hours? Make your comparison over an 800-hour period.

12 International Leasing Company has 15 Orange-plus computers leased to Auto Imports, Inc. for $100 per machine per month. The machines fail according to a Poisson distribution with an average of 2.2 machines down each month. If any computer fails during the month, no rent is received for that machine that month.
(a) How much revenue is lost each month because of the failure rate of 2.2 machines per month?
(b) What is the chance of having exactly three machines down in a given month?

13 In response to a customer request for failure-rate data, an instrument manufacturer tested a group of 30 instruments over a 2,000-hour test period and found that four failed. Find (a) $FR_\%$ and (b) FR_n (in failures per unit per year).

14 A firm producing automobile exhaust filters was required to provide the Environmental Protection Agency with failure-rate data based upon a 10-hour test. If 200 units were tested and 8 failed, what are (a) the failure rate in failures per unit per year and (b) the mean time between failures?

15 The purification system in a water treatment plant has three components in series (R_1, R_2, and R_3). The component reliabilities for a 3-month period *remain constant* and are as shown in the diagram. At the end of each 3-month period all components are replaced regardless of the length of service. In the meantime, each time any component breaks down, the cost of downtime and repair is $300. What is the annual expected cost of downtime and repair?

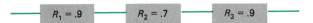

$$R_1 = .9 \qquad R_2 = .7 \qquad R_3 = .9$$

16 A firm with a processing system using machines X and Y in sequence has now installed another machine, Z, which performs an equivalent job. If the respective reliabilities of X, Y, and Z are .9, .8, and .7, what is the total reliability of the system?

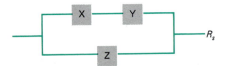

17 The maintenance manager for a nationwide trucking firm has found that a substantial savings in tire cost can be gained by contracting with a tire manufacturer to replace tires on the entire fleet of trucks at one time. For safety purposes, the manager feels this should be done at the time 15 percent of the tires are worn out. If tire life is normally distributed with a mean of 30 months and a standard deviation of 3 months, when should the replacement take place?

18 A maintenance superintendent has determined that in a certain application, bearing life follows a normal distribution with a mean of 620 hours and a standard deviation of

20 hours. What percentage of the bearings should have lives between 600 and 660 hours?

19 The XRON Company has fixed costs of $180,000 and other, variable overhead costs which range from $30,000 at a volume of 20,000 units to $50,000 at 60,000 units. It uses a nylon material which costs $.30 per foot, and each unit requires 4 feet of material. A work-sampling study revealed the following standard times for the manufacturing activity.

Activity	Standard Time (hr/unit)	Standard Labor Rate ($/hr)
Cutting	.06	6.50
Stamping	.01	4.00
Cleaning	.03	4.00
Inspection	.01	5.00
Packaging	.01	4.00

Find (a) the labor standard cost, (b) the material standard cost, and (c) the overhead standard cost. Use the overhead absorption rate method.

REFERENCES

[1] Byrne, Harlan S.: "At Northwest Airlines, Emphasis on Keeping Costs Low Pays Off," *The Wall Street Journal*, Oct. 31, 1984, p. 1.

[2] "Cardiac Pacemakers Inc. Advises Some Doctors of Problem Parts," *The Wall Street Journal*, Aug. 28, 1978, p. 5.

[3] Horngren, Charles T.: *Cost Accounting: A Managerial Emphasis*, 5th ed., Prentice-Hall, Englewood Cliffs, NJ, 1982.

[4] Leading Edge Products, personal computer advertisement, *The Wall Street Journal*, Dec. 29, 1983, p. 14.

[5] *Maintenance Hints*, HB-6001-MM, Westinghouse Electric Corporation, Pittsburgh.

[6] "Out of Order: Avoiding Plant Failures Grows More Difficult for Many Industries," *The Wall Street Journal*, Jan. 8, 1981, p. 1.

SELF QUIZ: CHAPTER 15

Part I True/False [1 point each = 6]

1 _____ One might properly associate the word "healing" with breakdown maintenance activities.
2 _____ The goal of maintenance activities is to do enough servicing and upkeep to prevent any breakdowns from occurring.
3 _____ The probability model for selecting a preventive maintenance policy assumes that breakdowns will continue to occur after preventive maintenance is performed.
4 _____ The normal wearout and failure of products (such as lightbulbs) after an operating lifetime tend to follow a Poisson distribution pattern.
5 _____ If a system has two components in parallel, each with .90 reliability, the system reliability of that section would be .99.
6 _____ Fixed budgets incorporate both variable costs and fixed costs for a given level of activity.

Part II Problems [3 points each = 9. Calculate and select your answer.]

1 A truck manufacturing firm with 200 robots has been relying upon breakdown maintenance (only), and has experienced the following monthly breakdown pattern.

Number of Breakdowns	0	1	2	3
Number of Months This Occurred	6	3	6	3

If each breakdown costs the firm $8,000 in lost time and repairs, how much could they afford to pay for a preventive maintenance program that would limit the average breakdowns to one per month?
(a) $ 4,000
(b) $ 8,000
(c) $12,000
(d) $24,000
(e) None of the above.

2 A maker of computer disk drives has tested 20 units continuously for 4,000 hours and found that four units stopped working during the test. What is the MTBF for the disk drives?
(a) 18,000 hours
(b) 20,000 hours
(c) 64,000 hours
(d) 72,000 hours
(e) None of the above.

3 A small publisher of a magazine has known fixed costs of $45,000 per year, plus some overhead costs for supervision and maintenance that vary from $50,000 to $70,000 depending upon the volume of business, which ranges from 400,000 to 475,000 units. They have established a labor standard of $.048 per unit and material standard cost of $.144 per unit. Including the overhead liquidation rate, what is the total standard cost per unit?
(a) $.200 per unit
(b) $.284 per unit
(c) $.432 per unit
(d) $.665 per unit
(e) None of the above.

CHAPTER 16
A STRATEGY FOR FUTURE OPERATIONS

WHERE WE HAVE BEEN

American business has fared well under the democratic free enterprise system of government set up by the framers of our Constitution. The constitutional freedoms we enjoy, coupled with the natural and human resources we possess, have released a creativity and enterprise that were never imagined. And this has propelled us through an industrial and scientific revolution to the age of computers and robotics—and now on to factories in space. We have become one of the more dominant nations of technology, affluence, and power.

But the fruits of success can weigh heavily upon the human spirit. Affluence weakens one's resolve and willingness to work. And it dulls the sense of urgency and concern about the future.[1] Moreover, the productivity growth we once took for granted in the United States is no longer assured [8, 11]. Thus our efforts in this text have been to study production operations and to emphasize methods and approaches to revitalizing them.

Production Systems   In Part One of the text, we focused upon some systems design concepts that hold promise for improving the operation of firms producing goods and services. We saw that decision making is a skill that can be learned and applied to facilities, layouts, products, and processes. We also noted that people are the key resource of an organization and that successful operations are ones that encourage employees to use their knowledge, values, and skills at the highest level possible.

Production and Inventory Control   The increasing availability of computers and programmable machines since the 1960s has brought about a data- and materials-processing revolution unparalleled in history. Our inquiry showed that better forecasting, planning, inventory management, and production control are now "really feasible" in a practical sense. Materials can be automatically tracked from suppliers through the various processes and onto distribution shelves. And both machine and human capacity can be better utilized—down to the available minutes.

Maintaining Operations   Analytical developments ranging from linear programming and learning curves to queuing and PERT now have widespread applications in both manufacturing and service operations. Statistical quality control measures have received a high priority in manufacturing, due in part to competitive pressures from Japan. But everyday maintenance and cost control activities are also critical to any well-run operation.

---

[1] Unless that future appears threatened (for example, by military or other economic forces). So we might, paradoxically, give credit to the Soviet Union, Japan, and other countries that have challenged our position and the status quo.

WHERE WE STAND NOW

Figure 16-1 draws upon the factors mentioned in Chapter 1, which, you will recall, are the dimensions used by anthropologists to define a culture. Our purpose here is to gain an appreciation of the influence of cultural factors upon productivity in order to better understand the current status of our productive activities here in the United States. This understanding will be useful for making some judgments about future directions later on in the chapter.

THE CULTURAL AND RESOURCE ENVIRONMENT

As suggested in Fig. 16-1, our cultural environment affects how resources are used for productive purposes. Production systems draw priorities and capacities from the cultural environment, along with physical resources from the natural environment. Productive efforts then add value to create wealth that flows back into society.

Wealth (if distributed) raises the living standards of the people and enables

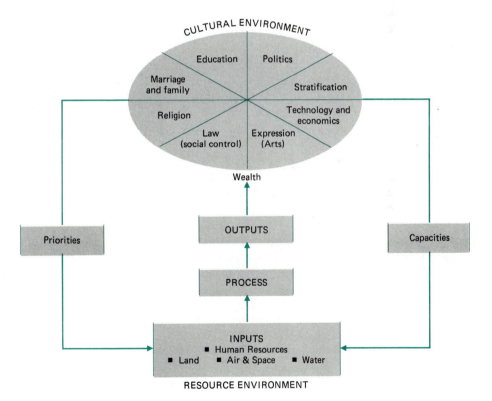

FIGURE 16-1   Cultural and Resource Environment

them to invest and create more wealth. However, the wealth remains concentrated in some cultures and is subject to heavy tax and social controls in others. So the impact of productive activities differs from one culture to another.

SHIFTS IN CULTURAL FACTORS

Within the United States, shifts over the past 50 years have significantly affected both (a) our ability to produce and (b) the allocation of benefits from production. Let us briefly note how some of the selected cultural factors affect our productive activities.

Politics   Political forces exert some of the most profound impacts upon a nation's productive capability. For example, political and legal forces restrict free enterprise endeavors in some cultures and promote them in others. Our political system, in general, encourages free enterprise.

But the political impacts upon production are many and varied. Monetary policies and tax laws influence the amount of business investment, labor policies (for example, minimum wage laws) affect employment, social programs have an impact upon welfare and security, and foreign policies affect our balance of trade. The continuing threat of inflation, growth of trade deficits, and problems of dealing with the national debt are additional examples of political concerns that affect the productive capability of our country. These latter factors all tend to undermine the financial stability of our currency, which affects the cost of funds (as lenders incorporate some compensation for risk).

Social Stratification and Education   Although our Constitution (along with subsequent amendments) grants equal rights to all citizens, all members of our society do not really enjoy equal opportunities to be productive. The best (economic) opportunities seem to be afforded the rich and well-educated. And while about $\frac{1}{2}$% of our population now control 35% of our nation's wealth, over 10% of our citizens remain classified as "poor."

This does not preclude any individual in our country from achieving "economic success." And the United States is not unique in its rich–poor stratification. On the contrary, our civil rights and equal opportunity legislation has made some historic inroads toward social equality. But our inheritance, tax, and other policies suggest that we will probably have to contend with effects of economic stratification for some time into the future.

What are the impacts on national productivity? Educational opportunities among the poor are extremely limited. Little or no job training is available, and unemployment runs high among minority groups. Thus the talent and human energy of a significant portion of our population are not being realized. Nor are the unemployed accorded the dignity of doing something worthwhile to provide for their own families.[2] Instead of realizing their potential skills and abilities in a

---

[2] This is akin to the sense of "task importance" mentioned previously in the Job Diagnostic Survey (Ch. 6), but on a larger scale.

productive manner, the unemployed are more likely to become a burden on the welfare roles and rehabilitation centers of the society.

Technology Technological advancements (in the chemical, medical, electronic, space, and other fields) have been the "shining star" of the American economy. And high-tech products such as computers have done much to counter our sagging productivity growth rate. Unfortunately, we have not been able to capitalize on all our inventions, because our wage levels are not always competitive with those of less-developed countries. But the world has truly benefited from American creativity, and we have the type of free and enterprising economy that will continue to foster new ideas in the future.

Economics and the Law By and large, U.S. managers work within our economic and legal system in the fair practice of their business. But we must also recognize that some corporate managers have interpreted the traditional economic model as a license to pursue profits at the expense of anything that is legal. A congressional study (in 1986) revealing grossly inadequate (but profitable) care by operators of nursing homes exemplifies this attitude. Other examples abound, such as over-charging on government contracts.

Unacceptable business behavior such as this has given rise to volumes of laws designed to control all manner of economic behavior—from monopolies to environmental protection to individual safety. The result has been an exponential increase in the paperwork necessary to ensure that federal and state regulations are satisfied. These bureaucratic regulations, in turn, cause a significant drain on productivity (although they do create employment for some professionals) [1].

Marriage and Family Patterns The most basic economic and social unit of society is the family. Families are the training centers where personal values are handed down to future members of society in an environment of sharing and concern for one another. They are the living cells that make up the body politic.

Nevertheless, family life in the United States is changing; it is not the steadfast unit it was in the past. Lifestyles are different. Affordable cars and shifting employment opportunities have made family members more mobile. Retirement programs and social security have lessened the dependence upon the traditional "family." And although few would deny the emotional and psychological benefits of stable family relationships, today nearly everyone must deal with some emotional disturbance and stress arising from the home environment at one time or another.

Stress carried to the workplace is, of course, only one of the ways family patterns affect productivity. The work errors and quality problems posed by alcohol and drug abuse are more visible problems. (They have also prompted firms like General Motors to undertake extensive counseling programs.) And, as in some other countries, there is increasing acceptance in the United States of the "right" to maternity leave. So numerous family considerations affect productivity—even though they are not all easily quantified.

Religion and Ethics   Ethical standards of conduct stem primarily from religious beliefs or training—often handed down by parents [6:7]. These beliefs recognize a dependence of people on a creator, and emerge as standards of behavior with much in common across various religions (Christian, Muslim, Jewish, Buddhist, etc.). People seem to rely most heavily upon religious support at critical times in life (for example, when facing sickness, tragedy, or death). This is because religious values extend beyond immediate material existence to more enduring and higher-level (intangible or spiritual) concerns that are uniquely human.

In general, the religions of our country foster such virtues as honesty, fairness, and justice. One of the more universal tenets is the *golden rule*, which encourages us to "Do unto others as you would have them do unto you." Insofar as virtues and guidelines such as these influence the creation and distribution of wealth, religious values also play a key role in *ordering priorities* or establishing relative levels of importance. Moreover, this ordering complements (or extends) the use of human knowledge, values, and skills brought out earlier in connection with Maslow's hierarchy (Chapter 6).

Ethical standards are important in a productive sense because they set the behavioral expectations for the conduct of business activities. Personal standards surface in the interaction of employees within the workplace, as well as in relationships with suppliers, stockholders, consumers, and society in general. One need only scan the daily paper to find an exposé of persons (or companies) who the public feels are "out of line."

According to a Gallup survey commissioned by *The Wall Street Journal*, "65% of Americans think the overall level of ethics in American society has declined in the past decade" [12]. The unethical business practices cited as more common in recent years include bribes, falsifying documents, improper financial statements, bid rigging, and price collusion. Most business executives admitted taking home work supplies (74 percent) and using company phones for personal long-distance calls (78 percent) while lesser percentages overstated deductions on tax forms (35 percent) or called in sick when they were not ill (14 percent). The survey also showed that younger Americans consistently indicated they were "more likely to take the unethical path" than their elders.

This does not necessarily mean that most businesspersons perceive themselves as unethical, or that they are unethical. What may seem unethical to one person is not necessarily unethical to another. The more important point is, perhaps, that the perceived level of ethical activity is declining. This may not be surprising for, according to Gardner:

> Values always decay over time. Societies that keep their values alive do so *not* by escaping the process of decay but by powerful processes of regeneration. There must be a perpetual rebuilding. . . . Leaders of organizations and groups must concern themselves with the affirmation of values. [6:8–9]

Expression and the Arts   As societies become more affluent, people can afford to devote more time to the arts (for example, music, literature, movies, and museums) and less to obtaining the essentials of life. The arts are important vehicles for expressing any culture—rich or poor, free or controlled. They also play an important role in transmitting the history and traditions of a culture from one generation to the next.

If fundamental segments of the expressive activities shift inordinately to self-centered entertainment, however, the culture may suffer some decay from within. For example, some businesses seek protection for pornographic and illicit ventures under the guise of the freedom of expression guaranteed by our Constitution.[3] The effect of protection here would be analogous to that of protecting a single firm spewing heavy pollution to the surrounding city, except that the damage is debasing to the cultural traditions and moral standards of the community instead of to its air or water. Activities that degrade a culture are counterproductive to those activities designed to "enhance the level of existence of members of society," which is the purpose we assigned to productive activities in Chapter 1 (see Fig. 1-1).

PRODUCTIVITY PROGRESS: FALLING SHORT

FROM AGRICULTURE TO MANUFACTURING TO SERVICES

The United States has witnessed many changes since colonial times, when over 90 percent of our workers were needed for *agricultural* or related activities. Now the figures are reversed. But even with only 3 percent of U.S. workers engaged in farming, production is so high that we must either pile wheat on the ground or pay farmers not to produce—a problem of priorities or capacity?

In the meantime we have gone through an industrial revolution to become an economy wherein nearly three-quarters of our work force is now engaged in *service* activities. Service jobs do frequently pay less than manufacturing work. But service opportunities are more numerous, and most service jobs involve a social interaction (with the customer). This makes them seem more satisfying and "human" than assembly line work. Moreover, the server, as well as the customer, can benefit (psychologically) from this interaction.

Within *manufacturing*, robots are being used in increasing numbers to do the repetitive and boring work that can be done by machines. Humans must therefore move up to more challenging design, programming, and control positions. This shift of workers away from mindless manufacturing (and office) tasks to more intellectually challenging positions can enhance the quality of work life—but such changes won't come easily or cheaply.

Employment Effects Should the introduction of "smart" robots and other new technology cause us concern about future employment? Yes, people will continue to be replaced by machines, and maybe even at an alarming rate. However,

---

[3] The 1986 report by the U.S. Attorney General's Commission on Pornography cited detrimental social effects from pornographic materials.

history shows that technological advances ultimately create more jobs than they abolish. The automobile diminished the need for blacksmiths and buggywhips but generated a far greater demand for steel, rubber, highways, and auto mechanics. Isaac Asimov suggests that the challenge of the next 25 years will be reeducation and retraining to expand our level of creativity:

> Clearly, if we are going to revolutionize our notion of work into two classes: "non-creative" for robots to do, and "creative" for human beings to do, then we must revolutionize our notion of education to accent creativity [2].

He goes on to forecast that with computer outlets in every home, mass education will become outmoded. People will be able to "indulge in learning" on their own initiative, rather than be forced to study a fixed curriculum en masse.

WHY DEINDUSTRIALIZATION CONTINUES

In earlier chapters, we expressed a concern over the decline of the textile, shoe, steel, electronic, and other U.S. industries. Continued declines could export financial problems to much of the free world. And although some American firms can point with pride to successful countermeasures, the overall problem of "deindustrialization" and U.S. trade deficits remains [8:10].

By now it is probably apparent that there is no quick fix to our industrial situation—many small causes combine to create "a big problem." The most convenient label for it seems to be "productivity," which has become a catch-all term that embodies everything from high wages and quality problems to the short-term perspective of some American managers. But, in essence, our productivity problems stem from a myriad of causes that lie embedded in our culture. Nevertheless, many hold that we also have the potential of correcting those problems [4, 5].

Not surprisingly, many of the components of the "productivity problem" have two dimensions that, if abstracted, might provide a clearer picture of the problem and suggest a strategy for the solution. These two dimensions are the familiar concepts of *priority* and *capacity* that we have dealt with throughout the text. Let us take a moment to reassess some of the productivity factors in light of what we have learned.

REASSESSMENT OF PRODUCTIVITY FACTORS

Figure 16-2 relates some priority and capacity aspects to the productivity factors introduced in Chapter 1, by posing one or two related questions. In summary, Fig. 16-2 suggests that a priority and capacity approach may be useful for analyzing productivity problems, much as we have seen with more detailed production and inventory control problems. This approach elevates considerations to two prime issues: (1) *priority*: what is the relative importance of the factors involved,

FIGURE 16-2   Priority and Capacity Aspects of Productivity Factors

Productivity Factor	Priority Dimension	Capacity Dimension
1 Capital/labor ratio	Is investment in equipment or people most essential?	Should we invest for the long term or the short term?
2 Resource scarcity	What resources are most vital to us?	How much resources do we have and how long will they last?
3 Workforce changes	What training is important now and for the future?	Do we have the skills needed now and for the future?
4 Innovation and technology	Where should R&D efforts be directed; what is important?	What level of creativity do we have?
5 Regulatory effects	What environmental conditions are most critical?	What amount of regulation is appropriate?
6 Bargaining effects	Who deserve the most rewards from a firm's production?	How much return is available to distribute?
7 Managerial factors	Rank the importance of various managerial responsibilities.	How capable are managers of carrying out their duties?
8 Quality of work life	What factors need most concern in the work environment?	How well equipped is the firm to meet its work objectives?

and (2) *capacity*: what resources do we have to satisfy the rankings we have assigned?

SOME LESSONS FROM SUCCESSFUL FIRMS

Business Objectives   Paul Thayer, chairman of the board and CEO for LTV has said, "The first and foremost responsibility of business remains its function as employer, supplier of goods, and profit maker. This must be uppermost in the minds of business decision-makers as they set policies and make strategic decisions" [10]. Like many other firms, LTV management sees a joint responsibility to communities, stockholders, employees, and society in general. As Thayer points out, they must all remain healthy for business to be healthy.

A review of healthy, successful organizations reveals some interesting observations, many of which have been brought out in earlier chapters. Let us summarize a few key points, and then draw some conclusions about the adequacy of our view of priorities and capacities.

LESSONS FROM ASIAN FIRMS

Employee Relations An extensive study of productivity policy in five Asian countries by the Committee for Economic Development (CED) has noted the special relationship between management and labor in Japan. In particular they observed [4:97]:

> The widespread practice of granting workers tenure in their jobs, the use of quality circles, the smaller disparities in wages between workers and management, the greater loyalty of employees to their companies, and the far greater care typically exercised in the selection of the Japanese work force have all been widely noted.

Nevertheless, the report goes on to downplay these characteristics in relation to the fact that workers in Japan are given a direct stake in the future of the firm and that management has a direct stake in the morale of the workers. Both groups are aware of this "reciprocal relationship," and considerable emphasis is placed on the spirit in which the job security is administered.

Taiwan has no employment security system, but job security has been available de facto because of the rapid growth of its firms. In Singapore and Hong Kong, many of the businesses are family enterprises, so a paternalistic relationship exists among the employees.

Taxation, Savings, and Investment Of many factors investigated, however, the strongest lesson the CED drew from the study of the Asian successes was the importance of having incentives for saving and investment (that is, a political factor). All countries had either a low income tax rate or some means of encouraging savings which ultimately flowed into business investment. The Japanese save about 22 percent of their disposable income, which is in sharp contrast to Americans, who save only 5 percent [4:101]. These figures are consistent with an estimate published in the *Journal of the American Production and Inventory Control Society* that the Japanese invest 20 percent of their GNP on new plants and equipment whereas the United States spends less than 4 percent in this area [5:86].

LESSONS FROM AMERICAN FIRMS

With higher wage costs, American success stories fall into two categories. One area of emphasis is employees, participation, and a desirable quality of work life. A second is state-of-the-art equipment that is highly automated and requires very little labor [9]. We have discussed both categories already, so we will simply note a few brief examples here.

Westinghouse and General Motors Many management groups, like those of Westinghouse and General Motors, are taking convincing steps to revitalize their firms [4:77; 13]. Westinghouse has established a corporate productivity and quality center that is showing results in terms of improved job satisfaction, reduced absenteeism, improved product quality, and increased efficiency. The firm's 1500 quality circles (in over 200 locations) have identified problems and developed solutions that have generated savings estimated at between $500,000 and $1 million per year. At General Motors, an employee suggestion plan is estimated to have already saved the firm over $1.34 billion [4:84].

Mazak Corporation This builder of parts for Ford Motor Company engines and General Electric Company appliances has one of the world's largest automated factories [7]. Mazak's plant in Kentucky is so totally automated that from midnight to 8 a.m. the plant runs without a single person in attendance. If a problem arises, the machines try to solve it, and if they cannot, they simply shut themselves down. The frequency of serious injury has dropped to zero, because automation now handles the dangerous jobs. The vice president of operations, Fenton Kohler, has remarked:

> If we didn't automate, we wouldn't be able to compete in the world market. We're the world innovator in unmanned systems. We're showing that American industry can be competitive again. If American industry doesn't automate, the trade deficit is just going to grow.

Batesville Casket Company This highly automated firm uses a staff of robots to weld, sand, finish, and paint caskets. Robots even sew the interior materials in the caskets [7]. According to a company vice president, the demand for technicians is great, but they are used to rewire or reprogram robots—not to assemble caskets. The robots do a more cost-efficient and high quality job.

General Electric General Electric invested $60 million to automate an appliance factory [7]. The automation boosted production, and the division was able to retain the same level of employment (about 1,500), although some workers had to be retrained to service automated equipment. In the words of a local union official, "I don't think anybody likes to see a robot take jobs that could have been a human's. But I think man understands there have to be changes in order to stay competitive." The president of a statewide industry group observed:

> You could build an argument that, without robots, people would have those jobs. But if you don't automate, the products will be priced out of the market. So the plant will close and nobody will have a job. . . . The net result of automation is positive for the workers as well as the companies. The companies get better production, and the workers get more interesting jobs.

WHAT'S NEEDED: REALIGNMENT AND COMMITMENT

A review of the orientation and operations of successful firms suggests that the concepts of priority and capacity have considerable bearing on the current status of U.S. productivity. This is especially true as we address the *real importance* (priority) of factors affecting productivity and the *actual use* (capacity) that is being made of our resources.

REALIGNMENT OF PRIORITY PRINCIPLES

We have seen that priorities arise from the value system of the culture. Both material progress and spiritual goals are important. For example, the industrial base of U.S. productivity was instrumental in bringing both World War I and World War II to an end. On the other hand, in those same conflicts, thousands of Americans gave up their lives for the (spiritual) ideals of freedom and concern (love) for others. The high-level priority of freedom pulled industries and individuals together in a cooperative effort to "win the battle."

But with affluence can come independence and self-sufficiency. And the cooperative, trust, and loyalty values that have fostered success in Japanese and other cultures appear to be waning in our own. Instead, each group tends to look out for its own self-interest. Lobbyism has become a growth industry in the United States, and the law is often invoked. Strikes frequently occur when self-interests are threatened. Consumers seek protection from unsafe products, while firms repeatedly fight against paying the costs of damages. Meanwhile, some managers are fighting to save their jobs against hostile takeovers by financiers who may be interested only in quick profits for themselves and not the welfare of the workers.

Figure 16-3 illustrates the dichotomy we face—the fundamental question of the purpose and orientation of cultural (including productive) activities. It suggests the need for reassessment, and perhaps reorientation, of some of our priorities, from a tendency toward self-orientation to a culturally higher level value of *other* orientation.

A self-orientation that overemphasizes our own wants is a *priority dimension* of our productivity problem. This has natural roots, of course. The desire to do

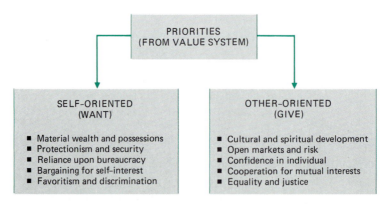

FIGURE 16-3   Priorities: Self-Oriented or Other-Oriented?

well and be successful is both healthy and productive. However, living in a society as we do, a concern for others constitutes an equal if not higher level of orientation, and the development of respect and trust among members of the society not only is consistent with our human nature, but also leads to more enduring (personal and business) relationships.

COMMITMENT TO BETTER USE OF CAPACITIES

The failure to use our resources in a manner that benefits society as a whole is a capacity dimension of our productivity problem. As illustrated in Fig. 16-4, we are again faced with a *self* versus *other* situation.

We have a natural tendency to consume resources to satisfy our own (sometimes selfish) desires—to be served rather than to serve. But organizational production is per se a cooperative effort wherein all must serve together for the achievement of common goals. In the words of Harold Davis, "loyalty and motivation reduce antagonism and increase productivity" [5]. Some firms, like Hewlett-Packard, feel so strongly about the perceptions of equality and cooperation that they have gone so far as to remove the (physical) office walls that typically isolate managers from their subordinates.

As we have seen earlier, innovation, automation, and robotics are helping to enhance productive capacity in many firms. Continuing research into technologies that promise more efficient production is important. Are organizations doing enough to encourage the research and development of goods and services that will enhance society? Or are our talents misdirected into unpromising, debasing, or self-destructing goods or services that will slow the progress (or speed the decay) of our culture?

Some equally fundamental questions relate to the long-term management of human resources. Will organizations assume the responsibility for retraining personnel and providing an atmosphere in which human talents and capabilities can be developed? Will workers be encouraged to enhance both their own level of

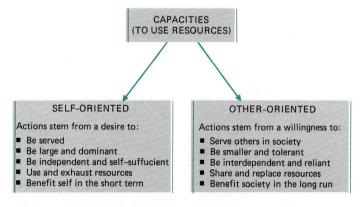

FIGURE 16-4   Capacities: Self-Oriented or Other-Oriented?

existence and that of others? Will firms make effective use of the higher level capabilities of their people? Or will firms act myopically to benefit themselves at the expense of society and the environment—and anyone else who blocks their path to "success"?

These priority and capacity choices will have an important bearing on our nation's organizational productivity in the future. They will strongly influence the direction of our entire culture. Will it be toward a *self (want)*- or *other (give)*-oriented society?

A STRATEGY FOR THE FUTURE

In this final section, we state some strengths we have, some choices we must make, and some tactics that will enhance progress toward a more productive and enduring business environment.

NATIONAL STRENGTHS

Our individual and economic freedoms and rights of private ownership are constitutionally based strengths of the United States. Added to that are a relative abundance of natural resources and a creative and energetic population that has transformed the country into an industrial giant among nations. We have a large capital base, well-developed industries, and extensive transportation and communications systems. We also enjoy the benefits of a high level of education, advanced technology, and an affluence that is shifting us into more knowledge- and service-type activities.

American firms have introduced many of the technical, analytical, and managerial innovations that now guide the world's production activities. Advances in quantitative techniques, along with computers and automated systems, have vastly improved forecasting, inventory, and other production scheduling and control functions. MRP systems are setting higher standards for performance throughout the world. And we have also learned from other countries. Our renewed emphasis on product quality and the quality of work life is traceable to lessons from Asian and European firms.

NATIONAL CHOICES

Strategic plans usually attempt to build upon an organization's strengths, while correcting any inherent weakness. Our nation's businesses have a noteworthy tradition of strengths referred to above. And it is logical to continue to build within the context of the successful, free-enterprise, creative environment that has emerged—but in a more responsible manner. In particular, we have identified two weaknesses that have arisen from shifts in our culture and threaten our future productivity. Simply put, they are:

- An overemphasis of *self* versus *other* orientation in our priorities.
- A tendency to misuse capacities to *satisfy self* rather than to *benefit society*.

It is important for us to recognize and critically assess these trends, because the self-versus-other orientation is closely linked to our national productivity. That is, the natural end of individually selfish actions can be destructive and debasing, whereas the natural end of self-giving actions is constructive and elevating. To proceed on the road of self-satisfaction may erode the moral and ethical values upon which our culture is built, whereas to foster values such as respect and participation in the workplace and justice to all interests in a business will have upgrading and positive effects upon the culture. Moreover, these are the values successfully promoted by our nation's largest international competitor (Japan).

Figure 16-5 illustrates some of the choices involved; it is not intended to be comprehensive, nor are the choices always clear-cut. For example, our society would flounder without some regulations, directives, and security measures.

TACTICS THAT WILL ENHANCE PROGRESS

How can we enhance future progress? It may take some realignment of priority principles as well as a commitment to better use of capacities. Fortunately, as mentioned earlier, substantial programs are already under way in many firms, and the efforts are bearing results. Old concepts like responsibility, trust, and company loyalty are taking on new meaning. But a more universal effort is needed if the tide is to be turned. Three areas that constitute challenging objectives are (1) social responsibility, (2) participation and cooperation, and (3) justice.

Social Responsibility An organization's "mission" or "statement of goals" should be consistent with its orientation to serve not only the immediate short-run

FIGURE 16-5 Strategic Choices Affecting Future Productivity

Toward Individual (Self) Interests	← or →	Toward Common (Societal) Interests
Pollution of environment		Preservation of environment
More regulations		Fewer regulations
Independence		Interdependence
Confrontation		Cooperation
Directives		Participation
Bureaucratic rules		Individual initiative
Importance of position		Importance of individual
Security to protect possessions		Sharing and trust of others
Discrimination		Equality and justice

interests of the shareholders but also the long-run interests of employees, consumers, and society. A written mission statement is desirable because it forces a clarity of thought and establishes a commitment. Many leading firms, such as General Motors, have well-defined codes of social conduct. Others could benefit from developing and following them.

Participation and Cooperation   One analyst has observed that "the participative management techniques recommended by such writers [as McGregor, Argyris, Likert, and Drucker] are used by managers in most large Japanese companies, while still widely resisted here" [5]. Participative activities (such as quality circles) benefit both the individual and the organization. *Individuals* gain the opportunity to contribute on a level where the use of their knowledge, skills, and decision-making abilities helps confirm their individual worth. *Organizations* benefit from the participation by having more satisfied workers and by capitalizing on the resulting suggestions and improvements.

Having a stake in the success of a business is also a form of greater participation. Many firms have had successful experiences with stock ownership, profit sharing, and cooperative ownership agreements [3].

Justice for All   Justice demands (1) that all business transactions be conducted with honor and dignity and (2) that the benefits of the work activities be properly shared among the participants. These values thus incorporate the obligation of fair wages and humane working conditions as well as nondiscrimination. Further, the principles of distributive justice hold that extreme benefits to some should not be allowed to go so far as to restrict the basic necessities of others.

Of course, publicly funded social programs are deemed necessary to alleviate unemployment. However, organizations that use societal resources also have an obligation, under distributive justice, to help fund charitable activities in accordance with their ability to pay.

SUMMARY

Our culture has done much to promote free enterprise and advance technology to the age of computers and robotics. In our drive toward affluent materialism, however, we may have drifted from the social and ethical values that helped build our nation. Position, possessions, and pleasures may well have assumed too great an importance in our culture, and we may be focusing too much inwardly on *self* rather than outwardly on *others*.

Our wages have long been bargained up to levels that make it difficult to compete with those of less-developed countries. Some basic industries have collapsed; others are in decline; and we are attempting to salvage others by automation. But productivity in both manufacturing and service industries remains a problem. As a nation, we're having difficulty capitalizing on human values of trust and cooperation as some of our international competitors do. Instead, we have a tendency to rely more on laws and regulations, burglar alarms, and bureaucracies.

The chapter suggests a need for (1) a realignment of our personal and business *priorities* and (2) a commitment to the better use of our *capacities*. Priorities based on respect, trust, and justice will lead to more enduring relationships among all those involved (that is, employees, suppliers, customers, and society in general). And using capacities in a way that benefits both individuals and society will help maintain a "healthy" social environment that is essential if business is to be healthy.

The United States is a nation of vast resources and great constitutional, economic, and technological strengths. A major challenge for the future lies in revitalizing the integrity and value dimensions of our culture and enhancing the concepts of social responsibility, participation, and justice for all.

QUESTIONS

16-1 Why is the cultural environment of special importance in our concerns about productivity?

16-2 What are some (national and personal) effects of not granting equal opportunities to all members of a society?

16-3 Are religious and ethical standards important in a productive sense? Why or why not?

16-4 Do robots cause unemployment? Discuss.

16-5 Is there one cause of our "productivity problem," or many? What two dimensions does the text suggest we review to assess the problem?

16-6 How important do you consider company loyalty in Japanese firms compared to American firms? What effect do you think this has on productivity?

16-7 In what respect does automation have a positive effect on workers?

16-8 What kind of "realignment" does the text suggest is needed with respect to priority principles?

16-9 What are some of the major productive strengths of the United States?

16-10 What three challenges does the text suggest as avenues for enhancing progress in the future?

REFERENCES

[1] American Bar Association: "Need a Lawyer?" *The Wall Street Journal*, Sept. 27, 1985, p. 31.

[2] Asimov, Isaac: "The Robot Task Force," *The Herald*, Seattle, WA, April 14, 1985, p. 1E.

[3] Carrica, J. L.: "Cooperation in Capitalism: A Socio-Economic Phenomenon to Help the Indigent," Gonzaga University Working Paper, Spokane, WA, 1986.

[4] Committee for Economic Development: *Productivity Policy: Key to the Nation's Economic Future*, CED, New York, 1983.

[5] Davis, Harold S.: "Management—What We can Learn from the Japanese," *Produc-*

tion and Inventory Management, American Production and Inventory Control Society, vol. 27, no. 1, 1986, pp. 85–89.

[6]   Gardner, John W.: "The Task of Leadership," Independent Sector, Washington, DC, March 1986.

[7]   Gibson, Jane: "Experience Demonstrates Displacement by Robots Can Save Jobs for Humans," *The Spokesman-Review and Spokane Chronicle*, Spokane, WA, Dec. 22, 1985, p. 3C.

[8]   Karatsu, Jajime: "The Deindustrialization of America: A Tragedy for the World," *Keizai Koho Center Brief*, no. 31, October 1985.

[9]   Lotenschtein, Sergio: "Just-In-Time in The MRP II Environment," *Production & Inventory Management Review*, February 1986, pp. 26–29, 52–54.

[10] LTV Corporation: "Corporate Social Responsibility: Where Does it Begin? Where Does it End?" *The Wall Street Journal*, Sept. 7, 1982, p. 11.

[11] Myers, Henry F.: "U.S. Productivity Gains Still Fall Short," *The Wall Street Journal*, Feb. 10, 1986, p. 1.

[12] Ricklefs, Roger: "Executives and General Public Say Ethical Behavior Is Declining in U.S.," *The Wall Street Journal*, Oct. 31, 1983, p. 27.

[13] Smith, Roger B.: "Creating the General Motors of the 21st Century," Address to 76th Annual Meeting of GM Stockholders, Detroit, May 25, 1984.

SELF QUIZ: CHAPTER 16

Part I True/False [1 point each = 6]

1. __T__ Political factors can significantly affect a nation's productivity.
2. __F__ All citizens in the United States enjoy equal economic opportunities.
3. __F__ The firm, or corporation, is the most basic economic and social unit of our society.
4. __F__ The cultural element most closely associated with the ordering of priorities is technology.
5. __F__ Priority realignment refers to shifting from an emphasis on producing services to an emphasis on producing more exportable goods.
6. __F__ Among the tactics recommended to enhance progress are greater independence, more self-reliance, and better security.

Part II Multiple Choice [3 points each = 9. Circle the correct answer.]

7. Which element of the cultural environment would be most closely associated with new tax laws designed to encourage small business activities?
   (a) Technology.
   (b) Expression and arts.
   (c) Religion.
   (d) Politics.
   (e) None of the above.

8. The two dimensions of our productivity problem receiving most attention in the chapter are:
   (a) Labor cost and material cost.
   (b) Regulatory and bargaining effects.
   (c) Priority and capacity factors.
   (d) Budget deficits and balance of trade problems.
   (e) None of the above.

9. The major problem with implementing new technologies like robotic assembly lines is that:
   (a) They are not cost efficient.
   (b) The quality level of robotic activities is not high enough.
   (c) They always end up creating unemployment.
   (d) Robots may initiate a hostile takeover if they become the majority.
   (e) None of the above.

	TRUE/FALSE QUESTION NO.						PROBLEM NUMBER		
	1	2	3	4	5	6	1	2	3
Ch. 1	F	T	F	F	F	T	b	d	a
Ch. 2	T	F	T	T	T	F	d	b	b
Ch. 3	T	F	F	F	F	T	b	c	a
Ch. 4	T	T	F	T	F	F	c	b	c
Ch. 5	T	F	F	T	F	T	c	b	d
Ch. 6	T	F	F	F	T	F	b	d	b
Ch. 7	F	T	T	F	T	F	c	c	a
Ch. 8	F	T	F	F	T	F	a	d	b
Ch. 9	F	T	T	F	T	T	e	d	c
Ch. 10	T	T	F	F	F	T	c	a	c
Ch. 11	T	T	F	F	F	T	d	b	d
Ch. 12	T	F	T	F	F	F	b	a	c
Ch. 13	F	F	T	F	T	F	a	d	b
Ch. 14	F	T	F	T	T	F	c	b	d
Ch. 15	T	F	T	F	T	T	a	a	c
Ch. 16	T	F	F	F	F	F	d	c	e

APPENDIX B
ANSWERS TO ODD-NUMBERED PROBLEMS

CHAPTER 2

1   14,000 seats/game
3   (a) $265;   (b) .76
5   (a) 2,000 passengers;   (b) 1,389 passengers
7   (a) Profit = $11,000;   (b) There are two BEPs; one at volume A, and the other at C;   (c) To produce more than 200 units per year, additional FC of $10,000 must be incurred. These costs are not reflected in the VC but do cause an incremental increase in the FC.
9   1,500 units
11   (a) $80/unit;   (b) $32,000
13   (a) .10;   (b) .50;   (c) .04;   (d) .56
15   (a) .53;   (b) .63
17   (a) continuous;   (b) .02 oz;   (c) .023
19   (a) 34.2 lb;   (b) 8.7 lb;   (c) 2.76
21   E(solar) = $234.6 million and E(coal) = $225.0 million, so the coal is less costly by $9.6 million.

CHAPTER 3

1   (a) 108,000 chips;   (b) 162,000 chips
3   67%
5   (a) 200,000 parts/yr;   (b) 18 parts/hr;   (c) 5.6 (say 6 machines)
7   $209,790
9   2.7 yr
11   4 yr
13   $235,076
15   $2,574/yr
17   From PV_a table for n = 5 yr, $i \cong 20\%$
19   16%
21   (a) $106,552;   (b) $25,168/yr;   (c) Machine B has the lower equivalent annual cost by $2,230/yr.

CHAPTER 4

1   (a) Volume range 0 to 10,000; dollar range $0 to $800,000; TC at 10,000 units are A = $600,000, B = $650,000, C = $800,000.   (b) $\Sigma[XP(X)]$ = 6,000 so select city B.   (c) 1,600 units

3

	Boulder	Claremont	Kent	
Pomona	5	2	7	350
Red Bluff	11	5	3	500
Sacramento	10	8	5	280
	400	400	330	1,130

5 More than one solution may be optimal at transportation cost = \$7,400.

7 More than one solution may be optional at production and distribution cost = \$10,000.

9 Manila (with 79 points)

11 Cost of alternative 1 = \$600; cost of alternative 2 = \$470; alternative 2 is less costly.

13 (a)   (b) One arrangement is

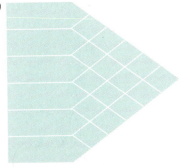

3	4	1
2	6	5

15 80%

17 (a) 8 min/unit;   (b) 3.8 employees;   (c) 94.5%

19 (a) One solution is: (b) 76%

Work Station	A	B	C	D	E
Tasks	1,2	3,6	4,5	7,8	9
Actual Times	.8	.9	1.0	.7	.4

CHAPTER 5

1 Objective: Max $Z = 40X_1 + 50X_2$
Programming constraint: $X_1 \leq 50$
Total time constraint: $X_1 + 2X_2 \leq 80$

3

$C \rightarrow$		40	50	0	0	
		Decision Variables				Solution Values
	Variables in Solution	X_1	X_2	S_1	S_2	(RHS)
0	S_1	1	0	1	0	50
0	S_2	1	2	0	1	80
	Z	0	0	0	0	0
	$C - Z$	40	50	0	0	

5 (a) Max $Z = 5X_1 + 7X_2$
   Constraints: $.8X_1 + .4X_2 \leq 20{,}000$
                  $.2X_1 + .6X_2 \leq 8{,}000$
   (b) Slope $= -\frac{5}{7}$ or $-\frac{7}{5}$ (depending upon choice of variables)

7 (a) Slope $= -2$; optimum is at corner where $A = 60$, $B = 80$.
   (b) Profit $= 1(60) + 2(80) = \$220$

9 Standard $= 2$, deluxe $= 4$

11 Standard $= 2$, deluxe $= 4$, and $Z = 260$

13 (a) Max $Z = 187X_1 + 45X_2 + 95X_3$
   (b) $200X_1 + 180X_2 + 80X_3 \leq 600$
       $500X_1 + 0X_2 + 90X_3 \leq 500$
       $40X_1 + 40X_2 + 0X_3 \leq 120$

15 (a) *Objective function:*
   Max $Z = (.40)(280)X_1 + (.15)(210)X_2 - (.05)(150)X_3 + (.30)(230)X_4 + (.25)(180)X_5$

   Constraints:
   (1) $280X_1 + 210X_2 + 150X_3 + 230X_4 + 180X_5 \leq 800$
   (2) $1X_1 + 0X_2 + 0X_3 + 0X_4 + 0X_5 \leq 1$
   (3) $0X_1 + 1X_2 + 0X_3 + 0X_4 + 0X_5 \leq 1$
   (4) $0X_1 + 0X_2 + 1X_3 + 0X_4 + 0X_5 \leq 1$
   (5) $0X_1 + 0X_2 + 0X_3 + 1X_4 + 0X_5 \leq 1$
   (6) $0X_1 + 0X_2 + 0X_3 + 0X_4 + 1X_5 \leq 1$
   (7) $0X_1 + 210X_2 + 150X_3 + 0X_4 + 0X_5 \leq 250$
   (8) $0X_1 + 0X_2 + 0X_3 + 230X_4 + 180X_5 \leq 300$
   (9)* $-140X_1 + 0X_2 + 150X_3 + 10X_4 + 0X_5 = 0$
   * This constraint satisfies requirement that cost on project 3
   must equal 50% of the cost on project 1.
   Cost of project 3 $= .50$(cost of project 1)
   $150X_3 = .50(280X_1) = 140X_1$
   $-140X_1 + 150X_3 = 0$

CHAPTER 6

1 $n \cong 200$ observations
3 10.0 min
5 (a) 116%; (b) 5.16 min/cycle
7 39.93 sec
9 39 observations
11 9.60 min/cycle
13 (a) .005; (b) .0245
15 .45

CHAPTER 7

1 .87, .93, and .99 (all in millions)
3 (a) Graph should show time on X axis, tons on Y. (b) Curves will differ, but forecasts will be around 1,200,000 tons. (c) 200, 167, 400, 567, 600, 467, 533, 667
5 (a) $a = 478$, $b = 78.3$, $Y_c = 478 + 78.3X$ (1979 $= 0$, $X =$ years, $Y =$ tons); (b) 1,182,700 tons

7 (a) 720 units/yr, 864 units/yr; (b) $Y_c = 720 + 12X$ (July 1, 1988 = 0, X units = 1 month, Y = annual sales rate in units); 720 units/yr; 864 units/yr; (c) $Y_c = 60 + 1X$ (July 1, 1988 = 0, X units = 1 month, Y = monthly sales rate in units); 60 units/month; 72 units/month

9 (a) and (b) Graph should show time on X axis, units on Y axis. (c) Longer average yields more smoothing; (d) 1.2

11 (a) $Y_c = 20 + 4X$ (1984 = 0, X = yr, Y = number of accidents); (b) 56 accidents

13 (a) 20,800; (b) Each forecast would reflect last period's demand—i.e., no smoothing.

15 (a) 444; (b) 456

17 (a) 525 units; (b) 554 units

19 (a) 24; (b) 10

21 (a) 8.3 accidents; (b) 42%; (c) .65; (d) $r < .754$, so not significant

23 (a) 33; (b) 30 to 36; (c) .5; (d) 50% of the variation in the number of vacuums sold is explained by the magazine advertisements.

25 (a) .64; (b) It tells the percentage of variation in campsites demanded that is explained by (or associated with) automobile traffic at the selected site; (c) .80

27 (a) 6.67; (b) .85

29 (a) 570; (b) .53; (c) Tracking signal is < 4. Yes.

CHAPTER 8

1 (a) Chart should show January through December demands of 200, 250, 300, 300, 200, 100, 100, 150, 250, 400, 400, 350. (b) Histogram should show cumulative production days on X axis, production rate (units/day) on Y axis. Cumulative requirement should show cumulative production days on X axis and cumulative demand (units) on Y axis. (c) 255.4 units

3 (a) $\bar{x} = 50$ persons/day; $s = 19.65$ persons/day; (b) 5 counselors; (c) 7.5 counselors (say 8)

5 (a) Histogram should show quarters on X axis and production rate (units/quarter) on Y axis. (b) 10; (c) Variable rate is $50/year less costly.

7 Graph shows period on X axis and demand level on Y axis. Plan costs are 1 = $90,000; 2 = $140,000; 3 = $160,000; 4 = $220,000; and 5 = $160,000.

9 5,620 units

11 (a) One optimal solution is as follows:

Initial inventory	Use in first quarter.
First RT	Use in first quarter.
Second RT	Use 500 in second quarter, 200 in fourth.
Third RT	Use 200 in third quarter, 500 in fourth.
Third OT	Use 200 in fourth quarter.
Fourth RT	Use 700 in fourth quarter.
Fourth OT	Use 300 in fourth quarter.

(b) $208,500

13 The solution should have the following entries in the row-column (r, c) matrix location:

(Initial inv., 1) = 100
(1 RT, 1) = 640
(2 RT, 1) = 60, (2RT, 2) = 500, (2 RT, 3) = 60, (2 RT, 4) = 20

```
( 3 RT,  3) = 640
( 4 RT,  4) = 640
( 5 RT,  4) = 240, (5 RT, 5) = 400
( 6 RT,  6) = 300, (6 RT, 9) = 80, (6 RT, 10) = 60, (6 RT, 11) = 200
( 7 RT,  7) = 400, (7 RT, 9) = 240
( 8 RT,  8) = 600, (8 RT, 9) = 40
( 9 RT,  9) = 640
(10 RT, 10) = 640
(11 RT, 11) = 640
(11 OT, 11) = 60, (11 OT, 12) = 240
(12 RT, 12) = 640
(12 OT, 12) = 320
```

The unused capacity column should show the remainder values from 640 RT and 320 OT.

15 Production required is 50 units in periods 2, 4, and 8. Ending inventories in periods 1 through 10 are 30, 60, 35, 65, 50, 40, 30, 60, 45, and 35.

17 (a) Master Schedule for Castings

		Period and Units/Period					
Product		1	2	3	4	5	Standard hr/unit
A		8	10	10	8	10	10
B		4	8	2	—	2	60
C		10	6	—	30	20	30
Standard hrs of load		620	760	220	980	820	Cumulative: 3,400
Standard hrs of capacity @ 620 hr/period		620	620	620	620	620	Cumulative: 3,100

(b) See if sales can get some customers scheduled for shipments in period 2 to accept delay until period 3, and reschedule work from periods 2, 4, and 5 into period 3. In total the plant is approximately 10% overloaded, so it may want to plan on some overtime in periods 2, 4, or 5. In any event, the master schedule should be revised to reflect a better balance of load versus capacity.

CHAPTER 9

1 Highest expected score is Food Fair with 8.9.
3 (a) Cost to produce is $18,900 − $18,480 = $420 less.   (b) 4,200 units
5 1.82 hr
7 245 tapes/yr
9 (a) 400 units/order;   (b) 10;   (c) $20,600
11 (a) 8,000 cans;   (b) 10,000 with a total cost of $2,433.60
13 5,000 units
15 (a) 90 items/day;   (b) Computer solution: $X_1 = 1.00$, $X_2 = .52$, $X_3 = .93$, $X_4 = 1.00$, $X_5 = .22$;   (c) Optimal dollar value return on investment

$$Z = (.40)(280)(1.00) + (.15)(210)(.52) - .05(150)(.93) + (.30)(230)(1.00)$$
$$+ (.25)(180)(.22)$$

$$= 112.0 + 16.4 - 7.0 + 69.0 + 9.9 = \$200.3 \text{ million}$$

Note: This represents an ROI of $200.3 million/$800 million $= .25$ or 25%.

17 Produce 750 units/day of Early American for profit of $18,750.

19 (a) 2.5 trucks (say 3 trucks); (b) Use 2 trucks @ $16/hr vs. 3 @ $17/hr.

21 (a) Breakpoints are (1) from A to B at 75 units and (2) from B to C at 200 units; (b) Use A; (c) $750; (d) Use B; (e) $1,300; (f) $550; (g) 20 units

23 Assuming a uniform distribution where $a = 1$ and $b = 10$, the simulated values (rounded) are 9, 8, 7, 2, and 3.

25 (a) Use the frequencies to form a cumulative probability distribution (i.e., with values of 0, .013, .073, etc., for frequencies 0, 4, 18, etc.). Then the corresponding three-digit random number groups are 000–000, 000–012, 013–072, etc., and simulated demands, D_s, are:

RN	697	667	248	063	887	432	732	970	449	425
D_s	27	27	24	22	28	26	27	29	26	26

(b) Mean $= 26$ trucks; (c) Standard deviation $= 2$ trucks

CHAPTER 10

1   120 units

3   (a) 6 tons; (b) 4 tons; (c) $720/yr; (d) 4 tons

5   67 units

7   (a) 10 days; (b) 700 sheets; (c) $.18/sheet

9   Stock 20, where maximum EMV $=$ EMV* $= \$760$

11 (a) $P(D) = .38$; (b) Stock the quantity closest to the cumulative probability of .38 (which is .40), or 800 cases.

13 (a) $P(D) = .20$, $I_{opt} = 208.4$ lb

15 (a) EOQ $= 173$ units; (b) 108 units; (c) 408 units

17 (a) and (b) should be of sufficient size and accuracy to yield reasonably accurate values for the 50% and 10% demand levels. Values may vary but should be around 130 to 150 steers for (c) and from $39,650 to $45,750 for (d).

19 $SF_{MAD} = 2.5$, SL $= 97.72\%$

21 For the same level of service, the safety stock will be the same, because SS $= SF_{MAD}$ (MAD) and neither MAD nor SF_{MAD} will change.

23 (a) 10 days; (b) 240 bags; (c) 99.38%; (d) 26 or 27 bags

CHAPTER 11

1   $480/yr

3   A $= 10$, B $= 20$, C $= 260$, D $= 80$, E $= 80$, F $= 240$

5   C $= 400$, D $= 200$, G $= 400$, J $= 400$, H $= 800$

7   (a)

(b) A = 100, B = 100, C = 100, D = 200, E = 200, F = 200, G = 100, H = 300, J = 600, K = 200

9   Motors = 8, controllers = 23

11   Switches = 25, microprocessors = 0, keyboards = 11

13   (a) Level 0 is skateboard; level 1 is baseplate (1) and wheel assembly (2); level 2 is mounting bracket (1), axle (1) and wheels (2); and level 3 is bearing (1) and shell (1);   (b) 270 bearings

15   PPA C_o = 200 part periods. Order 330 units in period 1,250 in period 3, 625 in period 4, and 410 in period 7

17   MRP should have planned order releases of 200 in weeks 1, 3, and 5. There are 85 units on hand at end of period 8.

19   Release orders for the following: 400 B in period 5, 1,600 C in period 4, and 400 C in period 6, 400 D in period 1, 1,600 E in period 2 and 400 E in period 4, 1,600 F in period 3 and 400 F in period 5.

21   (a)

BILL OF MATERIAL					
Part No. C099: Cart				Level 0	
Part No.		Description	Quantity/Assembly	Units	Level
1001		Bed	1	each	1
1002		Frame assembly	1	each	1
	2001	Ring	1	each	2
	2002	Handle	1	each	2
	2003	Grips	2	each	2
	2004	Support	2	each	2
1003		Wheel and axle assembly	2	each	1
	2005	Axle	1	each	2
	2006	Wheel assembly	2	each	2
	3001	Tire	2	each	3
	3002	Wheel	2	each	3
	3003	Bearing	2	each	3
	3004	Cap	2	each	3

(b)   Your MRP charts should show the following:

	Projected Requirements	Scheduled Receipts	On Hand at End of Period	Planned Release
Cart (C099)	3 in wk 10	3 in wk 10	—	3 in wk 8
Bed (1001)	3 in wk 8	3 in wk 8	—	3 in wk 7
Frame (1002)	3 in wk 8	3 in wk 8	—	3 in wk 6
Wheel and axle assembly (1003)	6 in wk 8	6 in wk 8	—	6 in wk 6
Ring (2001)	3 in wk 6	3 in wk 6	—	3 in wk 5
Handle (2002)	3 in wk 6	3 in wk 6	—	3 in wk 5
Grip (2003)	6 in wk 6	6 in wk 6	—	6 in wk 4
Support (2004)	6 in wk 6	6 in wk 6	—	6 in wk 5
Axle (2005)	6 in wk 6	4 in wk 6	2 until wk 6	4 in wk 5
Wheel assembly (2006)	12 in wk 6	11 in wk 6	1 until wk 6	11 in wk 3
Tire (3001)	11 in wk 3	11 in wk 3	—	11 in wk 1
Wheel (3002)	11 in wk 3	11 in wk 3	—	11 in wk 1
Bearing (3003)	11 in wk 3	11 in wk 3	—	11 in wk 1
Cap (3004)	11 in wk 3	11 in wk 3	—	11 in wk 1

23 308 units

CHAPTER 12

1

	1	2	3	4	5	6	7	8	9	10	11	12	13	14	15	16
Engineering																
Purchasing																
Steel fabrication																
Hydraulics																
Electrical																
Control																
Field test																
Package																

3 (a) Total shop load is 147 hours versus a capacity of 150 hours. However, work center 13 is overloaded, so it may restrict shop capacity. The balance is reasonably close, however.
(b) With 4 hours of move time, the processing time per shop order is A = 31, B = 51, C = 57, D = 26, E = 50. Therefore, the rank according to LPT is C, B, E, A, D.

5 (a) 874, 872, 870, 873, 871;   (b) 872, 874, 870, 873, 871;   (c) 874, 873, 872, 871, 870;   (d) 870, 871, 872, 873, 874

7 (a) Sequence is D, C, E, F, G, B, A   (b) 52 min

9 Priority 1 = A, 2 = E, 3 = C, 4 = F, 5 = D, 6 = B

11 (a) Assign A to 4, B to 3, C to 1, D to 2;   (b) yes;   (c) yes;   (d) no

13 With forward scheduling there are 8 weeks of load. Order release can be accomplished while the unreleased backlog is being worked on. There are already 8 weeks of work, so the shop could not ship until the ninth week.

15 (a) Average = 350;   (b) Cumulative deviation in weeks 1 through 8 is 10, −30, −40,

$-110, -100, -150, -230, -210$; (c) Yes, during (or at end of) week 7. Cumulative deviation of -230 exceeds one-half the average, or $350 \div 2 = 175$.

CHAPTER 13

1 (a) 90 hours; (b) 81 hours; (c) 59 hours
3 (a) 173; (b) 79.1 hours
5 (a) $120/day
 (b) (1) The (infinite) number of customers is probably satisfactory. (2) Poisson arrivals are probably correct. (3) Poisson service rates could be satisfactory, but many customers may end their rental period at the end of a day. (4) First in, first out is probably a correct queue discipline. (5) The average service rate is greater than the average arrival rate. Probably the weakest assumption is (6) that of unlimited waiting line length. Customers would probably take a different car rather than wait for a W car.
7 (a) 6 sets; (b) 4.11 hours; (c) 2.06 hours
9 (a) $T_s = .64$; (b) $N_q = 1.1$ requests
11 .07
13 (a) The network should show activities as arrows and events as circles, beginning with event 1 and ending with 8; (b) 1–3–5–7–8; (c) 37 days; (d) 19 days; (e) day 23; (f) 3 days; (g) .0918
15 (a) .1587; (b) $35,160
17 The chart should show the following:

	Activity									
	1–2	2–3	2–4	2–6	3–5	4–5	4–6	5–7	6–7	7–8
ES	0	12	12	12	20	16	16	34	21	38
LS	0	14	12	26	22	16	24	34	29	38

CHAPTER 14

1 (a) $6,000; (b) $16/robot
3 (a) .015; (b) .02
5 .4557
7 .018
9 .135
11 .2266
13 10.6%
15 (a) Use Poisson; (b) yes, risk of .019 okay; (c) Yes, risk of .042 okay
17 If $x \leq 13.63$ min, accept
19 (a) Alpha risk, .02; beta, .05; (b) 55 bags; (c) 48.88 kg
21 UCL = .992 centimeters, LCL = .968 centimeters
23 (a) $\bar{x} = 102.30$ lb, 104.39 lb, 100.21 lb; (b) 8.68 lb, 0 lb
25 (a) UCL = .32, LCL = .08; (b) 32 and 8

CHAPTER 15

1 $1,800/yr
3 Two technicians
5 (a) $35; (b) $90
7 (a) $938; (b) Every 3 weeks
9 (a) 62.5 percent; (b) .33 weeks; (c) 1.67 breakdowns; (d) .20 weeks; (e) 104; (f) .09
11 Replace both at 80 hours.
13 (a) 13.3 percent; (b) .625 failures/unit-yr
15 $519.60
17 26.9 months
19 (a) $.64; (b) $1.20/unit; (c) $5.50/unit

APPENDIX C
AREAS UNDER THE NORMAL
PROBABILITY DISTRIBUTION

Values in the table represent the proportion
of area under the normal curve between
the mean ($\mu = 0$) and a positive value of Z.

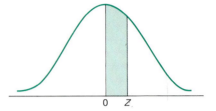

Z	.00	.01	.02	.03	.04	.05	.06	.07	.08	.09
.0	.0000	.0040	.0080	.0120	.0160	.0199	.0239	.0279	.0319	.0359
.1	.0398	.0438	.0478	.0517	.0557	.0596	.0636	.0675	.0714	.0753
.2	.0793	.0832	.0871	.0910	.0948	.0987	.1026	.1064	.1103	.1141
.3	.1179	.1217	.1255	.1293	.1331	.1368	.1406	.1443	.1480	.1517
.4	.1554	.1591	.1628	.1664	.1700	.1736	.1772	.1808	.1844	.1879
.5	.1915	.1950	.1985	.2019	.2054	.2088	.2123	.2157	.2190	.2224
.6	.2257	.2291	.2324	.2357	.2389	.2422	.2454	.2486	.2517	.2549
.7	.2580	.2611	.2642	.2673	.2703	.2734	.2764	.2794	.2823	.2852
.8	.2881	.2910	.2939	.2967	.2995	.3023	.3051	.3078	.3106	.3133
.9	.3159	.3186	.3212	.3238	.3264	.3289	.3315	.3340	.3365	.3389
1.0	.3413	.3438	.3461	.3485	.3508	.3531	.3554	.3577	.3599	.3621
1.1	.3643	.3665	.3686	.3708	.3729	.3749	.3770	.3790	.3810	.3830
1.2	.3849	.3869	.3888	.3907	.3925	.3944	.3962	.3980	.3997	.4015
1.3	.4032	.4049	.4066	.4082	.4099	.4115	.4131	.4147	.4162	.4177
1.4	.4192	.4207	.4222	.4236	.4251	.4265	.4279	.4292	.4306	.4319
1.5	.4332	.4345	.4357	.4370	.4382	.4394	.4406	.4418	.4429	.4441
1.6	.4452	.4463	.4474	.4484	.4495	.4505	.4515	.4525	.4535	.4545
1.7	.4554	.4564	.4573	.4582	.4591	.4599	.4608	.4616	.4625	.4633
1.8	.4641	.4649	.4656	.4664	.4671	.4678	.4686	.4693	.4699	.4706
1.9	.4713	.4719	.4726	.4732	.4738	.4744	.4750	.4756	.4761	.4767
2.0	.4772	.4778	.4783	.4788	.4793	.4798	.4803	.4808	.4812	.4817
2.1	.4821	.4826	.4830	.4834	.4838	.4842	.4846	.4850	.4854	.4857
2.2	.4861	.4864	.4868	.4871	.4875	.4878	.4881	.4884	.4887	.4890
2.3	.4893	.4896	.4898	.4901	.4904	.4906	.4909	.4911	.4913	.4916
2.4	.4918	.4920	.4922	.4925	.4927	.4929	.4931	.4932	.4934	.4936
2.5	.4938	.4940	.4941	.4943	.4945	.4946	.4948	.4949	.4951	.4952
2.6	.4953	.4955	.4956	.4957	.4959	.4960	.4961	.4962	.4963	.4964
2.7	.4965	.4966	.4967	.4968	.4969	.4970	.4971	.4972	.4973	.4974
2.8	.4974	.4975	.4976	.4977	.4977	.4978	.4979	.4979	.4980	.4981
2.9	.4981	.4982	.4982	.4983	.4984	.4984	.4985	.4985	.4986	.4986
3.0	.4987	.4987	.4987	.4988	.4988	.4989	.4989	.4989	.4990	.4990

Source: From Paul G. Hoel, *Elementary Statistics,* 2d ed., John Wiley & Sons, Inc., New York, 1966. Reproduced by permission of the publisher.

APPENDIX D
BINOMIAL DISTRIBUTION VALUES

$$P(X|n,p) = \frac{n!}{x!\,(n-x)!}\,p^x q^{n-x}$$

n	X	.05	.10	.15	.20	.25	.30	.35	.40	.45	.50
1	0	.9500	.9000	.8500	.8000	.7500	.7000	.6500	.6000	.5500	.5000
	1	.0500	.1000	.1500	.2000	.2500	.3000	.3500	.4000	.4500	.5000
2	0	.9025	.8100	.7225	.6400	.5625	.4900	.4225	.3600	.3025	.2500
	1	.0950	.1800	.2550	.3200	.3750	.4200	.4550	.4800	.4950	.5000
	2	.0025	.0100	.0225	.0400	.0625	.0900	.1225	.1600	.2025	.2500
3	0	.8574	.7290	.6141	.5120	.4219	.3430	.2746	.2160	.1664	.1250
	1	.1354	.2430	.3251	.3840	.4219	.4410	.4436	.4320	.4084	.3750
	2	.0071	.0270	.0574	.0960	.1406	.1890	.2389	.2880	.3341	.3750
	3	.0001	.0010	.0034	.0080	.0156	.0270	.0429	.0640	.0911	.1250
4	0	.8145	.6561	.5220	.4096	.3164	.2401	.1785	.1296	.0915	.0625
	1	.1715	.2916	.3685	.4096	.4219	.4116	.3845	.3456	.2995	.2500
	2	.0135	.0486	.0975	.1536	.2109	.2646	.3105	.3456	.3675	.3750
	3	.0005	.0036	.0115	.0256	.0469	.0756	.1115	.1536	.2005	.2500
	4	.0000	.0001	.0005	.0016	.0039	.0081	.0150	.0256	.0410	.0625
5	0	.7738	.5905	.4437	.3277	.2373	.1681	.1160	.0778	.0503	.0312
	1	.2036	.3280	.3915	.4096	.3955	.3602	.3124	.2592	.2059	.1562
	2	.0214	.0729	.1382	.2048	.2637	.3087	.3364	.3456	.3369	.3125
	3	.0011	.0081	.0244	.0512	.0879	.1323	.1811	.2304	.2757	.3125
	4	.0000	.0004	.0022	.0064	.0146	.0284	.0488	.0768	.1128	.1562
	5	.0000	.0000	.0001	.0003	.0010	.0024	.0053	.0102	.0185	.0312
6	0	.7351	.5314	.3771	.2621	.1780	.1176	.0754	.0467	.0277	.0156
	1	.2321	.3543	.3993	.3932	.3560	.3025	.2437	.1866	.1359	.0938
	2	.0305	.0984	.1762	.2458	.2966	.3241	.3280	.3110	.2780	.2344
	3	.0021	.0146	.0415	.0819	.1318	.1852	.2355	.2765	.3032	.3125
	4	.0001	.0012	.0055	.0154	.0330	.0595	.0951	.1382	.1861	.2344
	5	.0000	.0001	.0004	.0015	.0044	.0102	.0205	.0369	.0609	.0938
	6	.0000	.0000	.0000	.0001	.0002	.0007	.0018	.0041	.0083	.0156

(Cont. on Next Page)

n	X	.05	.10	.15	.20	.25	.30	.35	.40	.45	.50
7	0	.6983	.4783	.3206	.2097	.1335	.0824	.0490	.0280	.0152	.0078
	1	.2573	.3720	.3960	.3670	.3115	.2471	.1848	.1306	.0872	.0547
	2	.0406	.1240	.2097	.2753	.3115	.3177	.2985	.2613	.2140	.1641
	3	.0036	.0230	.0617	.1147	.1730	.2269	.2679	.2903	.2918	.2734
	4	.0002	.0026	.0109	.0287	.0577	.0972	.1442	.1935	.2388	.2734
	5	.0000	.0002	.0012	.0043	.0115	.0250	.0466	.0774	.1172	.1641
	6	.0000	.0000	.0001	.0004	.0013	.0036	.0084	.0172	.0320	.0547
	7	.0000	.0000	.0000	.0000	.0001	.0002	.0006	.0016	.0037	.0078
8	0	.6634	.4305	.2725	.1678	.1002	.0576	.0319	.0168	.0084	.0039
	1	.2793	.3826	.3847	.3355	.2670	.1977	.1373	.0896	.0548	.0312
	2	.0515	.1488	.2376	.2936	.3115	.2965	.2587	.2090	.1569	.1094
	3	.0054	.0331	.0839	.1468	.2076	.2541	.2786	.2787	.2568	.2188
	4	.0004	.0046	.0185	.0459	.0865	.1361	.1875	.2322	.2627	.2734
	5	.0000	.0004	.0026	.0092	.0231	.0467	.0808	.1239	.1719	.2188
	6	.0000	.0000	.0002	.0011	.0038	.0100	.0217	.0413	.0403	.1094
	7	.0000	.0000	.0000	.0001	.0004	.0012	.0033	.0079	.0164	.0312
	8	.0000	.0000	.0000	.0000	.0000	.0001	.0002	.0007	.0017	.0039
9	0	.6302	.3874	.2316	.1342	.0751	.0404	.0207	.0101	.0046	.0020
	1	.2985	.3874	.3679	.3020	.2253	.1556	.1004	.0605	.0339	.0176
	2	.0629	.1722	.2597	.3020	.3003	.2668	.2162	.1612	.1110	.0703
	3	.0077	.0446	.1069	.1762	.2336	.2668	.2716	.2508	.2119	.1641
	4	.0006	.0074	.0283	.0661	.1168	.1715	.2194	.2508	.2600	.2461
	5	.0000	.0008	.0050	.0165	.0389	.0735	.1181	.1672	.2128	.2461
	6	.0000	.0001	.0006	.0028	.0087	.0210	.0424	.0743	.1160	.1641
	7	.0000	.0000	.0000	.0003	.0012	.0039	.0098	.0212	.0407	.0703
	8	.0000	.0000	.0000	.0000	.0001	.0004	.0013	.0035	.0083	.0176
	9	.0000	.0000	.0000	.0000	.0000	.0000	.0001	.0003	.0008	.0020
10	0	.5987	.3487	.1969	.1074	.0563	.0282	.0135	.0060	.0025	.0010
	1	.3151	.3874	.3474	.2684	.1877	.1211	.0725	.0403	.0207	.0098
	2	.0746	.1937	.2759	.3020	.2816	.2335	.1757	.1209	.0763	.0439
	3	.0105	.0574	.1298	.2013	.2503	.2668	.2522	.2150	.1665	.1172
	4	.0010	.0112	.0401	.0881	.1460	.2001	.2377	.2508	.2384	.2051
	5	.0001	.0015	.0085	.0264	.0584	.1029	.1536	.2007	.2340	.2461
	6	.0000	.0001	.0012	.0055	.0162	.0368	.0689	.1115	.1596	.2051
	7	.0000	.0000	.0001	.0008	.0031	.0090	.0212	.0425	.0746	.1172
	8	.0000	.0000	.0000	.0001	.0004	.0014	.0043	.0106	.0229	.0439
	9	.0000	.0000	.0000	.0000	.0000	.0001	.0005	.0016	.0042	.0098
	10	.0000	.0000	.0000	.0000	.0000	.0000	.0000	.0001	.0003	.0010

Source: Adapted from R. S. Burington and D. C. May, Handbook of Probability and Statistics with Tables, 2d ed., McGraw-Hill Book Company, New York, 1970. Reproduced by permission of the publisher.

APPENDIX E
POISSON DISTRIBUTION VALUES

Values of c

$$P(X \le c|\lambda) = \sum_{o}^{c} \frac{\lambda^x e^{-\lambda}}{x!}$$

Note: The table shows 1,000 times the probability of c or fewer occurrences of an event that has an average number of occurrences of λ.

λ	0	1	2	3	4	5	6	7	8	9	10
0.02	980	1000									
0.04	961	999	1000								
0.06	942	998	1000								
0.08	923	997	1000								
0.10	905	995	1000								
0.15	861	990	999	1000							
0.20	819	982	999	1000							
0.25	779	974	998	1000							
0.30	741	963	996	1000							
0.35	705	951	994	1000							
0.40	670	938	992	999	1000						
0.45	638	925	989	999	1000						
0.50	607	910	986	998	1000						
0.55	577	894	982	998	1000						
0.60	549	878	977	997	1000						
0.65	522	861	972	996	999	1000					
0.70	497	844	966	994	999	1000					
0.75	472	827	959	993	999	1000					
0.80	449	809	953	991	999	1000					
0.85	427	791	945	989	998	1000					
0.90	407	772	937	987	998	1000					
0.95	387	754	929	984	997	1000					
1.00	368	736	920	981	996	999	1000				
1.1	333	699	900	974	995	999	1000				
1.2	301	663	879	966	992	998	1000				
1.3	273	627	857	957	989	998	1000				
1.4	247	592	833	946	986	997	999	1000			
1.5	223	558	809	934	981	996	999	1000			
1.6	202	525	783	921	976	994	999	1000			
1.7	183	493	757	907	970	992	998	1000			
1.8	165	463	731	891	964	990	997	999	1000		
1.9	150	434	704	875	956	987	997	999	1000		
2.0	135	406	677	857	947	983	995	999	1000		

λ	0	1	2	3	4	5	6	7	8	9	10	11	12	13	14	15	16	17	18	19	20	21	22
2.2	111	359	623	819	928	975	993	998	1000														
2.4	091	308	570	779	904	964	988	997	999	1000													
2.6	074	267	518	736	877	951	983	995	999	1000													
2.8	061	231	469	692	848	935	976	992	998	999	1000												
3.0	050	199	423	647	815	916	966	988	996	999	1000												
3.2	041	171	380	603	781	895	955	983	994	998	1000												
3.4	033	147	340	558	744	871	942	977	992	997	999	1000											
3.6	027	126	303	515	706	844	927	969	988	996	999	1000											
3.8	022	107	269	473	668	816	909	960	984	994	998	999	1000										
4.0	018	092	238	433	629	785	889	949	979	992	997	999	1000										
4.2	015	078	210	395	590	753	867	936	972	989	996	999	1000										
4.4	012	066	185	359	551	720	844	921	964	985	994	998	999	1000									
4.6	010	056	163	326	513	686	818	905	955	980	992	997	999	1000									
4.8	008	048	143	294	476	651	791	887	944	975	990	996	999	1000									
5.0	007	040	125	265	440	616	762	867	932	968	986	995	998	999	1000								
5.2	006	034	109	238	406	581	732	845	918	960	982	993	997	999	1000								
5.4	005	029	095	213	373	546	702	822	903	951	977	990	996	999	1000								
5.6	004	024	082	191	342	512	670	797	886	941	972	988	995	998	999	1000							
5.8	003	021	072	170	313	478	638	771	867	929	965	984	993	997	999	1000							
6.0	002	017	062	151	285	446	606	744	847	916	957	980	991	996	999	1000							
6.2	002	015	054	134	259	414	574	716	826	902	949	975	989	995	998	999	1000						
6.4	002	012	046	119	235	384	542	687	803	886	939	969	986	994	997	999	1000						
6.6	001	010	040	105	213	355	511	658	780	869	927	963	982	992	997	999	1000						
6.8	001	009	034	093	192	327	480	628	755	850	915	955	978	990	996	998	999	1000					
7.0	001	007	030	082	173	301	450	599	729	830	901	947	973	987	994	998	999	1000					
7.2	001	006	025	072	156	276	420	569	703	810	887	937	967	984	993	997	999	1000					
7.4	001	005	022	063	140	253	392	539	676	788	871	926	961	980	991	996	998	999	1000				
7.6	001	004	019	055	125	231	365	510	648	765	854	915	954	976	989	995	998	999	1000				
7.8	000	004	016	048	112	210	338	481	620	741	835	902	945	971	986	993	997	999	1000				
8.0	000	003	014	042	100	191	313	453	593	717	816	888	936	966	983	992	996	998	999	1000			
8.5	000	002	009	030	074	150	256	386	523	653	763	849	909	949	973	986	993	997	999	999	1000		
9.0	000	001	006	021	055	116	207	324	456	587	706	803	876	926	959	978	989	995	998	999	1000		
9.5	000	001	004	015	040	089	165	269	392	522	645	752	836	898	940	967	982	991	996	998	999	1000	
10.0	000	000	003	010	029	067	130	220	333	458	583	697	792	864	917	951	973	986	993	997	998	999	1000

Source: Adapted from E. L. Grant, *Statistical Quality Control*, McGraw-Hill Book Company, New York, 1964. Reprinted by permission of the publisher.

APPENDIX F PRESENT VALUE FACTORS FOR FUTURE SINGLE PAYMENTS

Periods until Payment	1%	2%	4%	6%	8%	10%	12%	14%	15%	16%	18%	20%	22%	24%	25%	26%	28%	30%	35%	40%
1	.990	.980	.962	.943	.926	.909	.893	.877	.870	.862	.847	.833	.820	.806	.800	.794	.781	.769	.741	.714
2	.980	.961	.925	.890	.857	.826	.797	.769	.756	.743	.718	.694	.672	.650	.640	.630	.610	.592	.549	.510
3	.971	.942	.889	.840	.794	.751	.712	.675	.658	.641	.609	.579	.551	.524	.512	.500	.477	.455	.406	.364
4	.961	.924	.855	.792	.735	.683	.636	.592	.572	.552	.516	.482	.451	.423	.410	.397	.373	.350	.301	.260
5	.951	.906	.822	.747	.681	.621	.567	.519	.497	.476	.437	.402	.370	.341	.328	.315	.291	.269	.223	.186
6	.942	.888	.790	.705	.630	.564	.507	.456	.432	.410	.370	.335	.303	.275	.262	.250	.227	.207	.165	.133
7	.933	.871	.760	.665	.583	.513	.452	.400	.376	.354	.314	.279	.249	.222	.210	.198	.178	.159	.122	.095
8	.923	.853	.731	.627	.540	.467	.404	.351	.327	.305	.266	.233	.204	.179	.168	.157	.139	.123	.091	.068
9	.914	.837	.703	.592	.500	.424	.361	.308	.284	.263	.225	.194	.167	.144	.134	.125	.108	.094	.067	.048
10	.905	.820	.676	.558	.463	.386	.322	.270	.247	.227	.191	.162	.137	.116	.107	.099	.085	.073	.050	.035
11	.896	.804	.650	.527	.429	.350	.287	.237	.215	.195	.162	.135	.112	.094	.086	.079	.066	.056	.037	.025
12	.887	.788	.625	.497	.397	.319	.257	.208	.187	.168	.137	.112	.092	.076	.069	.062	.052	.043	.027	.018
13	.879	.773	.601	.469	.368	.290	.229	.182	.163	.145	.116	.093	.075	.061	.055	.050	.040	.033	.020	.013
14	.870	.758	.577	.442	.340	.263	.205	.160	.141	.125	.099	.078	.062	.049	.044	.039	.032	.025	.015	.009
15	.861	.743	.555	.417	.315	.239	.183	.140	.123	.108	.084	.065	.051	.040	.035	.031	.025	.020	.011	.006
16	.853	.728	.534	.394	.292	.218	.163	.123	.107	.093	.071	.054	.042	.032	.028	.025	.019	.015	.008	.005
17	.844	.714	.513	.371	.270	.198	.146	.108	.093	.080	.060	.045	.034	.026	.023	.020	.015	.012	.006	.003
18	.836	.700	.494	.350	.250	.180	.130	.095	.081	.069	.051	.038	.028	.021	.018	.016	.012	.009	.005	.002
19	.828	.686	.475	.331	.232	.164	.116	.083	.070	.060	.043	.031	.023	.017	.014	.012	.009	.007	.003	.002
20	.820	.673	.456	.312	.215	.149	.104	.073	.061	.051	.037	.026	.019	.014	.012	.010	.007	.005	.002	.001
21	.811	.660	.439	.294	.199	.135	.093	.064	.053	.044	.031	.022	.015	.011	.009	.008	.006	.004	.002	.001
22	.803	.647	.422	.278	.184	.123	.083	.056	.046	.038	.026	.018	.013	.009	.007	.006	.004	.003	.001	.001
23	.795	.634	.406	.262	.170	.112	.074	.049	.040	.033	.022	.015	.010	.007	.006	.005	.003	.002	.001	
24	.788	.622	.390	.247	.158	.102	.066	.043	.035	.028	.019	.013	.008	.006	.005	.004	.003	.002	.001	
25	.780	.610	.375	.233	.146	.092	.059	.038	.030	.024	.016	.010	.007	.005	.004	.003	.002	.001	.001	
26	.772	.598	.361	.220	.135	.084	.053	.033	.026	.021	.014	.009	.006	.004	.003	.002	.002	.001		
27	.764	.586	.347	.207	.125	.076	.047	.029	.023	.018	.011	.007	.005	.003	.002	.002	.001	.001		
28	.757	.574	.333	.196	.116	.069	.042	.026	.020	.016	.010	.006	.004	.002	.002	.002	.001	.001		
29	.749	.563	.321	.185	.107	.063	.037	.022	.017	.014	.008	.005	.003	.002	.002	.001	.001			
30	.742	.552	.308	.174	.099	.057	.033	.020	.015	.012	.007	.004	.003	.002	.001	.001	.001			

APPENDIX G PRESENT VALUE FACTORS FOR ANNUITIES

Years (N)	1%	2%	4%	6%	8%	10%	12%	14%	15%	16%	18%	20%	22%	24%	25%	26%	28%	30%	35%	40%
1	.990	.980	.962	.943	.926	.909	.893	.877	.870	.862	.847	.833	.820	.806	.800	.794	.781	.769	.741	.714
2	1.970	1.942	1.886	1.833	1.783	1.736	1.690	1.647	1.626	1.605	1.566	1.528	1.492	1.457	1.440	1.424	1.392	1.361	1.289	1.224
3	2.941	2.884	2.775	2.673	2.577	2.487	2.402	2.322	2.283	2.246	2.174	2.106	2.042	1.981	1.952	1.923	1.868	1.816	1.696	1.580
4	3.902	3.808	3.630	3.465	3.312	3.170	3.037	2.914	2.855	2.798	2.690	2.589	2.494	2.404	2.362	2.320	2.241	2.166	1.997	1.849
5	4.853	4.713	4.452	4.212	3.993	3.791	3.605	3.433	3.352	3.274	3.127	2.991	2.864	2.745	2.689	2.635	2.532	2.436	2.220	2.035
6	5.795	5.601	5.242	4.917	4.623	4.355	4.111	3.889	3.784	3.685	3.498	3.326	3.167	3.020	2.951	2.885	2.759	2.643	2.385	2.168
7	6.728	6.472	6.002	5.582	5.206	4.868	4.564	4.288	4.160	4.039	3.812	3.605	3.416	3.242	3.161	3.083	2.937	2.802	2.508	2.263
8	7.652	7.325	6.733	6.210	5.747	5.335	4.968	4.639	4.487	4.344	4.078	3.837	3.619	3.421	3.329	3.241	3.076	2.925	2.598	2.331
9	8.566	8.162	7.435	6.802	6.247	5.759	5.328	4.946	4.772	4.607	4.303	4.031	3.786	3.566	3.463	3.366	3.184	3.019	2.665	2.379
10	9.471	8.983	8.111	7.360	6.710	6.145	5.650	5.216	5.019	4.833	4.494	4.192	3.923	3.682	3.571	3.465	3.269	3.092	2.715	2.414
11	10.368	9.787	8.760	7.887	7.139	6.495	5.937	5.453	5.234	5.029	4.656	4.327	4.035	3.776	3.656	3.544	3.335	3.147	2.752	2.438
12	11.255	10.575	9.385	8.384	7.536	6.814	6.194	5.660	5.421	5.197	4.793	4.439	4.127	3.851	3.725	3.606	3.387	3.190	2.779	2.456
13	12.134	11.343	9.986	8.853	7.904	7.103	6.424	5.842	5.583	5.342	4.910	4.533	4.203	3.912	3.780	3.656	3.427	3.223	2.799	2.468
14	13.004	12.106	10.563	9.295	8.244	7.367	6.628	6.002	5.724	5.468	5.008	4.611	4.265	3.962	3.824	3.695	3.459	3.249	2.814	2.477
15	13.865	12.849	11.118	9.712	8.559	7.606	6.811	6.142	5.847	5.575	5.092	4.675	4.315	4.001	3.859	3.726	3.483	3.268	2.825	2.484
16	14.718	13.578	11.652	10.106	8.851	7.824	6.974	6.265	5.954	5.669	5.162	4.730	4.357	4.033	3.887	3.751	3.503	3.283	2.834	2.489
17	15.562	14.292	12.166	10.477	9.122	8.022	7.120	6.373	6.047	5.749	5.222	4.775	4.391	4.059	3.910	3.771	3.518	3.295	2.840	2.492
18	16.398	14.992	12.659	10.828	9.372	8.201	7.250	6.467	6.128	5.818	5.273	4.812	4.419	4.080	3.928	3.786	3.529	3.304	2.844	2.494
19	17.226	15.678	13.134	11.158	9.604	8.365	7.366	6.550	6.198	5.877	5.316	4.844	4.442	4.097	3.942	3.799	3.539	3.311	2.846	2.496
20	18.046	16.351	13.590	11.470	9.818	8.514	7.469	6.623	6.259	5.929	5.353	4.870	4.460	4.110	3.954	3.808	3.546	3.316	2.850	2.497
21	18.857	17.011	14.029	11.764	10.017	8.649	7.562	6.687	6.312	5.973	5.384	4.891	4.476	4.121	3.963	3.816	3.551	3.320	2.852	2.498
22	19.660	17.658	14.451	12.042	10.201	8.772	7.645	6.743	6.359	6.011	5.410	4.909	4.488	4.130	3.970	3.822	3.556	3.323	2.853	2.498
23	20.456	18.292	14.857	12.303	10.371	8.883	7.718	6.792	6.399	6.044	5.432	4.925	4.499	4.137	3.976	3.827	3.559	3.325	2.854	2.499
24	21.243	18.914	15.247	12.550	10.529	8.985	7.784	6.835	6.434	6.073	5.451	4.937	4.507	4.143	3.981	3.831	3.562	3.327	2.855	2.499
25	22.023	19.523	15.622	12.783	10.675	9.077	7.843	6.873	6.464	6.097	5.467	4.948	4.514	4.147	3.985	3.834	3.564	3.329	2.856	2.499
26	22.795	20.121	15.983	13.003	10.810	9.161	7.896	6.906	6.491	6.118	5.480	4.956	4.520	4.151	3.988	3.837	3.566	3.330	2.856	2.500
27	23.560	20.707	16.330	13.211	10.935	9.237	7.943	6.935	6.514	6.136	5.492	4.964	4.524	4.154	3.990	3.839	3.567	3.331	2.856	2.500
28	24.316	21.281	16.663	13.406	11.051	9.307	7.984	6.961	6.534	6.152	5.502	4.970	4.528	4.157	3.992	3.840	3.568	3.331	2.857	2.500
29	25.066	21.844	16.984	13.591	11.158	9.370	8.022	6.983	6.551	6.166	5.510	4.975	4.531	4.159	3.994	3.841	3.569	3.332	2.857	2.500
30	25.808	22.396	17.292	13.765	11.258	9.427	8.055	7.003	6.566	6.177	5.517	4.979	4.534	4.160	3.995	3.842	3.569	3.332	2.857	2.500

APPENDIX H
LEARNING CURVE COEFFICIENTS

% base	70%	74%	78%	80%	82%	84%	86%	88%	90%	94%	98%
2	7.486	5.469	4.065	3.523	3.065	2.675	2.343	2.058	1.812	1.418	1.121
5	4.672	3.674	2.927	2.623	2.358	2.125	1.919	1.738	1.577	1.307	1.091
10	3.270	2.718	2.283	2.098	1.933	1.785	1.651	1.529	1.419	1.228	1.069
20	2.290	2.012	1.781	1.674	1.585	1.499	1.420	1.346	1.277	1.155	1.048
30	1.858	1.687	1.540	1.473	1.412	1.354	1.300	1.249	1.201	1.113	1.036
40	1.602	1.489	1.389	1.343	1.300	1.259	1.221	1.184	1.149	1.085	1.027
50	1.429	1.351	1.282	1.250	1.220	1.190	1.163	1.136	1.111	1.064	1.020
60	1.300	1.248	1.201	1.178	1.158	1.137	1.118	1.099	1.081	1.047	1.015
70	1.201	1.167	1.137	1.121	1.108	1.094	1.081	1.088	1.056	1.032	1.010
80	1.122	1.101	1.083	1.074	1.066	1.058	1.050	1.042	1.034	1.020	1.007
90	1.056	1.047	1.039	1.034	1.031	1.027	1.023	1.020	1.016	1.010	1.003
100	1.000	1.000	1.000	1.000	1.000	1.000	1.000	1.000	1.000	1.000	1.000
110	.9521	.9593	.9665	.9696	.9731	.9764	.9796	.9827	.9855	.9916	.9973
120	.9105	.9239	.9369	.9428	.9492	.9551	.9610	.9670	.9726	.9839	.9947
125	.8915	.9076	.9321	.9307	.9381	.9454	.9526	.9552	.9667	.9803	.9935
130	.8737	.8921	.9104	.9200	.9279	.9359	.9447	.9528	.9609	.9769	.9923
140	.8410	.8640	.8864	.8974	.9084	.9188	.9294	.9399	.9501	.9704	.9903
150	.8117	.8381	.8645	.8776	.8905	.9029	.9156	.9280	.9402	.9645	.9882
160	.7852	.8152	.8452	.8595	.8744	.8885	.9028	.9170	.9309	.9590	.9864
170	.7611	.7938	.8270	.8428	.8591	.8752	.8910	.9067	.9225	.9538	.9847
175	.7498	.7842	.8183	.8352	.8520	.8687	.8854	.9020	.9185	.9513	.9838
180	.7390	.7746	.8103	.8274	.8452	.8624	.8798	.8974	.9144	.9489	.9830
190	.7187	.7568	.7947	.8133	.8322	.8510	.8698	.9885	.9070	.9443	.9815
200	.7000	.7400	.7800	.8000	.8200	.8400	.8600	.8800	.9000	.9400	.9800
220	.6665	.7098	.7540	.7759	.7981	.8201	.8423	.8646	.8870	.9321	.9772
240	.6373	.6835	.7306	.7543	.7783	.8022	.8265	.8508	.8754	.9249	.9748
260	.6116	.6602	.7103	.7349	.7607	.7863	.8123	.8384	.8649	.9182	.9726
280	.5887	.6392	.6915	.7177	.7447	.7717	.7992	.8270	.8550	.9122	.9704
300	.5682	.6203	.6743	.7019	.7301	.7586	.7875	.8161	.8462	.9066	.9684
400	.4900	.5476	.6084	.6400	.6724	.7056	.7396	.7744	.8100	.8836	.9604
500	.4368	.4970	.5616	.5956	.6308	.6671	.7045	.7432	.7830	.8662	.9542
600	.3977	.4592	.5261	.5617	.5987	.6372	.6771	.7187	.7616	.8522	.9491
700	.3674	.4294	.4978	.5345	.5729	.6129	.6548	.6985	.7440	.8406	.9449
800	.3430	.4052	.4746	.5120	.5514	.5927	.6361	.6815	.7290	.8306	.9412
900	.3228	.3850	.4549	.4929	.5331	.5754	.6200	.6668	.7161	.8219	.9380
1000	.3058	.3678	.4381	.4765	.5172	.5604	.6059	.6540	.7047	.8142	.9351

Source: R. W. Conway and Andrew Schultz, Jr., "The Manufacturing Progress Function," *Journal of Industrial Engineering,* vol. 10, no. 1, January/February 1959, pp. 39–54; and Thomas E. Vollman, *Operations Management,* Addison-Wesley, Reading, MA, 1973, pp. 381–384. Reproduced by permission of the AIIE and Addison-Wesley.

APPENDIX I
TABLE OF UNIFORMLY DISTRIBUTED RANDOM NUMBERS

Row \ Col	1	2	3	4	5	6	7	8	9	10
1	27767	43584	85301	88977	29490	69714	94015	64874	32444	48277
2	13025	14338	54066	15243	47724	66733	74108	88222	88570	74015
3	80217	36292	98525	24335	24432	24896	62880	87873	95160	59221
4	10875	62004	90391	61105	57411	06368	11748	12102	80580	41867
5	54127	57326	26629	19087	24472	88779	17944	05600	60478	03343
6	60311	42824	37301	42678	45990	43242	66067	42792	95043	52680
7	49739	71484	92003	98086	76668	73209	54244	91030	45547	70818
8	'8626	51594	16453	94614	39014	97066	30945	57589	31732	57260
9	66692	13986	99837	00582	81232	44987	69170	37403	86995	90307
10	44071	28091	07362	97703	76447	42537	08345	88975	35841	85771
11	59820	96163	78851	16499	87064	13075	73035	41207	74699	09310
12	25704	91035	26313	77463	55387	72681	47431	43905	31048	56699
13	22304	90314	78438	66276	18396	73538	43277	58874	11466	16082
14	17710	59621	15292	76139	59526	52113	53856	30743	08670	84741
15	25852	58905	55018	56374	35824	71708	30540	27886	61732	75454
16	46780	56487	75211	10271	36633	68424	17374	52003	70707	70214
17	59849	96169	87195	46092	26787	60939	59202	11973	02902	33250
18	47670	07654	30342	40277	11049	72049	83012	09832	25571	77628
19	94304	71803	73465	09819	58869	35220	09504	96412	90193	79568
20	08105	59987	21437	36786	49226	77837	98524	97831	65704	09514
21	64281	61826	18555	64937	64654	25843	41145	42820	14924	39650
22	66847	70495	32350	02985	01755	14750	48968	38603	70312	05682
23	72461	33230	21529	53424	72877	17334	39283	04149	90850	64618
24	21032	91050	13058	16218	06554	07850	73950	79552	24781	89683
25	95362	67011	06651	16136	57216	39618	49856	99326	40902	05069
26	49712	97380	10404	55452	09971	59481	37006	22186	72682	07385
27	58275	61764	97586	54716	61459	21647	87417	17198	21443	41808
28	89514	11788	68224	23417	46376	25366	94746	49580	01176	28838
29	15472	50669	48139	36732	26825	05511	12459	91314	80582	71944
30	12120	86124	51247	44302	87712	21476	14713	71181	13177	55292
31	95294	00556	70481	06905	21785	41101	49386	54480	23604	23544
32	66986	34099	74474	20740	47458	64809	06312	88940	15995	69321
33	80620	51790	11436	38072	40405	68032	60942	00307	11897	92674
34	55411	85667	77535	99892	71209	92061	92329	98932	78284	46347
35	95083	06783	28102	57816	85561	29671	77936	63574	31384	51924

Source: Paul G. Hoel, *Elementary Statistics*, 2d ed., Wiley, New York, 1966. Reproduced by permission of the publisher.

APPENDIX J
TABLE OF NORMALLY DISTRIBUTED
RANDOM NUMBERS

Row \ Col	1	2	3	4	5	6	7	8
1	.34	−.25	−.97	−.62	.37	−1.89	−.79	−.87
2	−1.09	1.13	.99	.72	−.82	.46	−.41	.35
3	−1.87	.35	−.56	−.53	.91	−.48	1.31	.95
4	1.57	.75	1.20	2.29	.02	.67	−.41	.35
5	2.09	−1.54	1.02	−1.06	.65	−2.05	.73	−1.06
6	.37	.64	1.26	−.39	−.25	.53	.29	−.14
7	.03	−.71	1.08	.53	.28	.37	.27	−1.06
8	1.42	−.41	−.60	.75	−1.02	.91	2.11	.35
9	−.26	.99	−1.09	3.29	−.62	1.23	−1.36	.79
10	.93	.29	−.46	.63	1.84	−.36	.46	−1.00

APPENDIX K
SAFETY STOCK LEVEL FACTORS FOR NORMALLY DISTRIBUTED VARIABLES

$$SS = SF_\sigma(\sigma) \quad or \quad SS = SF_{MAD}(MAD)$$
$$OP = D_{LT} + SS$$

| | Safety Factor Using | |
Service Level (percentage of order cycles without stockout)	Standard Deviation SF_σ	Mean Absolute Deviation SF_{MAD}
50.00	.00	.00
75.00	.67	.84
80.00	.84	1.05
84.13	1.00	1.25
85.00	1.04	1.30
89.44	1.25	1.56
90.00	1.28	1.60
93.32	1.50	1.88
94.00	1.56	1.95
94.52	1.60	2.00
95.00	1.65	2.06
96.00	1.75	2.19
97.00	1.88	2.35
97.72	2.00	2.50
98.00	2.05	2.56
98.61	2.20	2.75
99.00	2.33	2.91
99.18	2.40	3.00
99.38	2.50	3.13
99.50	2.57	3.20
99.60	2.65	3.31
99.70	2.75	3.44
99.80	2.88	3.60
99.86	3.00	3.75
99.90	3.09	3.85
99.93	3.20	4.00
99.99	4.00	5.00

Source: Adapted from G. W. Plossl and O. W. Wight, *Production and Inventory Control: Principles and Techniques*, 1967, p. 108. Reprinted by permission of Prentice-Hall, Englewood Cliffs, NJ.

INDEX